S0-BZV-690

Chicago Architecture and Design

1923-1993

Chicago Architecture and Design

1923-1993

Reconfiguration
of an American Metropolis

Edited by John Zukowsky

With essays by

Mark J. Bouman, David Brodherson, Robert Bruegmann,
Dennis P. Doordan, Neil Harris, Victor Margolin,
Ross Miller, Deborah Fulton Rau, Sidney K. Robinson, Pauline Saliga,
Franz Schulze, R. Stephen Sennott, Stanley Tigerman, Carol Willis,
Wim de Wit, and John Zukowsky

Prestel

This book was published in conjunction with the exhibition
"Chicago Architecture and Design, 1923-1993: Reconfiguration of an
American Metropolis," organized by The Art Institute of Chicago
and presented June 12-August 29, 1993.

© 1993 The Art Institute of Chicago and Prestel-Verlag, Munich
© of works illustrated: see Photography Credits, page 478

A companion volume, *Chicago Architecture, 1872-1922: Birth of a Metropolis*,
was published in 1987. ISBN 3-7913-0837-8 (hardcover edition)

Front cover: View looking west along the Chicago River, 1992.
Back cover: Night view of the Gold Coast of Chicago, 1992.
Spine: View looking east from Wabash Avenue along South Water Street, 1992.
Frontispiece: View looking north over downtown Chicago, 1992.
Endpapers: Aerial view of Chicago, c. 1935.

Prestel-Verlag, Mandlstrasse 26, D-8000 Munich 40, Germany
Tel. (89) 38 17 090; Fax (89) 38 17 09 35

Distributed in Continental Europe by Prestel-Verlag
Verlegerdienst München GmbH & Co. KG
Gutenbergstrasse 1, D-8031 Gilching, Germany
Tel. (8105) 38 81 17; Fax (8105) 38 81 00

Distributed in the USA and Canada on behalf of Prestel by te Neues Publishing Company,
15 East 76th Street, New York, NY 10021, USA
Tel. (212) 288 02 65; Fax (212) 570 23 73

Distributed in Japan on behalf of Prestel by YOHAN-Western Publications
Distribution Agency, 14-9 Okubo 3-chome, Shinjuku-ku, J-Tokyo 169
Tel. (3) 32 08 01 81; Fax (3) 32 09 02 88

Distributed in the United Kingdom, Ireland and all remaining countries on behalf of Prestel by
Thames & Hudson Ltd., 30-34 Bloomsbury Street, London WC1B 3QP, England
Tel. (71) 636 54 88; Fax (71) 636 16 59

The exhibition and book were made possible by the support of:

The National Endowment for the Humanities
Continental Bank, Sharing Chicago's History
The Seymour H. Persky Fund for Architecture at The Art Institute of Chicago
The National Endowment for the Arts—Design Arts Program
The Graham Foundation for Advanced Studies in the Fine Arts
The Benefactors of Architecture at The Art Institute of Chicago
Commonwealth Edison Company

This book is a publication of the Ernest R. Graham Study Center
for Architectural Drawings at The Art Institute of Chicago

Edited by Robert V. Sharp and Carol Jentsch
Designed by Dietmar Rautner, Munich

Paper: BVS* matt, Papierfabrik Scheufelen, Lenningen
Composition: OK Satz GmbH, Unterschleissheim
Offset lithography: Gewa-Repro GmbH, Munich (color and duotone);
Karl Dörfel Repro GmbH, Munich (black and white)
Printing: Aprinta GmbH & Co. KG, Wemding
Binding: Conzella GmbH & Co. KG, Aschheim-Dornach
Printed in Germany

ISBN 3-7913-1251-0

Contents

7   FOREWORD *by James N. Wood*

9   ACKNOWLEDGMENTS *by John Zukowsky*

INTRODUCTION

John Zukowsky   15   The Burden of History: Chicago Architecture before and after the Great Depression and World War II

ARCHITECTURE AND INFRASTRUCTURE

Mark J. Bouman   33   "The Best Lighted City in the World": The Construction of a Nocturnal Landscape in Chicago

R. Stephen Sennott   53   "Forever Inadequate to the Rising Stream": Dream Cities, Automobiles, and Urban Street Mobility in Central Chicago

David Brodherson   75   "All Airplanes Lead to Chicago": Airport Planning and Design in a Midwest Metropolis

THE COMMERCIAL CITY

Deborah Fulton Rau   99   The Making of the Merchandise Mart, 1927-1931: Air Rights and the Plan of Chicago

Carol Willis   119   Light, Height, and Site: The Skyscraper in Chicago

Franz Schulze   141   Mies van der Rohe in America

THE CITY AND THE SUBURB

Robert Bruegmann   159   Schaumburg, Oak Brook, Rosemont, and the Recentering of the Chicago Metropolitan Area

Neil Harris   179   The City That Shops: Chicago's Retailing Landscape

Sidney K. Robinson   201   The Postwar Modern House in Chicago

ARCHITECTURE AND POLITICS

Dennis P. Doordan   219   Exhibiting Progress: Italy's Contribution to the Century of Progress Exposition

Wim de Wit   233   The Rise of Public Housing in Chicago, 1930-1960

Ross Miller   247   City Hall and the Architecture of Power: The Rise and Fall of the Dearborn Corridor

DESIGN IN CHICAGO

Pauline Saliga   265   "To Build a Better Mousetrap": Design in Chicago, 1920-1970

Victor Margolin   283   Graphic Design in Chicago

THE LEGACY OF CHICAGO ARCHITECTURE

Ross Miller   303   Helmut Jahn and the Line of Succession

Stanley Tigerman   311   Chicago Architects: Genealogy and Exegesis

327 PLATES

    Urban Images 329
    Transportation 332
    Institutions and Government 342
    Commerce and Business 349
    Industry 368
    Shopping 376
    Houses and Housing 387
    Recreation 401

409 CATALOGUE *by John Zukowsky*

458 BIOGRAPHICAL GLOSSARY *by Maurice Blanks*

475 INDEX OF ARCHITECTS AND DESIGNERS

Foreword

The past seventy years have witnessed momentous events for all American cities: the major reorganization of society and the economy brought about by the Great Depression and World War II; the extraordinary rise of American political and industrial supremacy, which prompted sweeping population shifts from south to north and from cities to suburbs; the build-up of urban centers, their subsequent deterioration, and the current struggle to reinvigorate them. The war brought us out of the Depression, but it also confronted us with critical concerns: increasingly strained race relations, the need for decent and affordable housing caused by the postwar population boom, the emerging differences between urban and suburban life, the changing patterns of transportation and shopping, new definitions of work and play, the effectiveness of social services and public amenities, and so on. Developments in these areas continued throughout the broad economic expansion and national prosperity of the 1950s, but their lack of satisfactory resolution prompted the social and political unrest and idealism of the late 1960s and 1970s, with similar swings characterizing the 1980s and 1990s.

Throughout these years, Chicago has played a crucial role. We should not forget that the first controlled atomic reaction was staged by Enrico Fermi beneath the University of Chicago in Hyde Park, or that the massive political protests during the 1968 Democratic Convention occurred in Grant Park. The city has also been at the center of interchange between social life and architectural expression: from the rise of postwar American modernism under Moholy-Nagy at the New Bauhaus (Institute of Design) and under Ludwig Mies van der Rohe at the Illinois Institute of Technology, to the design of the great American fast-food icon—the McDonald's restaurant—and the rise of corporate office towers that now form Chicago's distinctive skyline, Chicago and its architecture have figured in the forefront of modern American urban life.

Chicago Architecture and Design, 1923-1993: Reconfiguration of an American Metropolis am-bitiously attempts to take full measure of this great metropolitan center by focusing on the impact that world events have had on its development. This book and the exhibition it accompanies demonstrate the ways in which Chicago has remained a vibrant and richly engaging city, and certainly its architecture has contributed to the excitement that Chicagoans and visitors alike feel in this metropolis. The project is a sequel to the very successful exhibition and book, *Chicago Architecture, 1872-1922: Birth of a Metropolis*, which the Art Institute sponsored in 1987-88.

That project and this one were intelligently and efficiently organized by John Zukowsky, Curator of Architecture at the Art Institute. Under his energetic leadership, the museum's Department of Architecture has been recognized by architects, scholars, and lay enthusiasts as a leading force in the study and appreciation of American architecture. The department's recently opened Ernest R. Graham Study Center for Architectural Drawings, and the many exhibitions organized by Mr. Zukowsky and Associate Curator Pauline Saliga focusing on contemporary European trends have given it importance well beyond Chicago, as have the critically acclaimed series of books published over the last decade.

Chicago Architecture and Design, 1923-1993 has been made possible by generous funding from the National Endowment for the Humanities and Continental Bank, as well as additional support from the National Endowment for the Arts—Design Arts Program, the Graham Foundation for Advanced Studies in the Fine Arts, and the Seymour H. Persky Fund for Architecture. Their financial support has enabled the Art Institute's Department of Architecture to add this important exhibition and publication to its already distinguished program, and we are extremely grateful to each of them.

James N. Wood
Director
The Art Institute of Chicago

Lenders to the Exhibition

Arquitectonica Chicago Inc.

The Austin Company

Banks/Eakin Architects

Belli & Belli Architects & Engineers

Mr. and Mrs. Edward H. Bennett, Jr.

Bethlehem Steel Corporation

Booth/Hansen & Associates, Ltd.

The John Buck Company

Ralph Burke Associates

Capital Planning & Construction, Chicago Transit Authority

Chicago Bridge & Iron Company—CBI Industries, Inc.

The Chicago Dock and Canal Trust

Chicago Historical Society, Architectural Collection and Decorative and Industrial Arts Collection, Prints and Photographs Department

Chicago Housing Authority

Chicago Park District Special Collections

The Chicago Public Library, Special Collections Department

Chicago White Sox

City of Chicago Department of Public Works: Bureau of Bridges

City of Chicago Department of Transportation

Cordogan, Clark & Associates

Mr. George E. Danforth

Decker and Kemp Architecture and Urban Design

Decorators Supply Corporation

Deborah Doyle and Associates, Architects

Arthur Dubin Collection

Elvehjem Museum of Art, University of Wisconsin—Madison

A. Epstein and Sons International, Inc.

Florian-Wierzbowski Architecture, P.C.

Gelick Foran Associates, Ltd.

Bertrand Goldberg Associates, Inc.

Great Lakes Dredge & Dock Company

HTI/Space Design International

Hasbrouck Peterson Associates

Ms. Amy R. Hecker

Hedrich-Blessing, Ltd.

Himmel-Bonner Architects

Holabird & Root

Albert Kahn Associates, Inc.

Kohn Pedersen Fox Associates, P. C.

Ronald Krueck, Krueck & Sexton Architects

Dr. Kisho Kurokawa, Kisho Kurokawa Architect and Associates

Gregory Landahl, FAIA/The Landahl Group, Inc.

Peter Landon Architects Ltd.

Ms. Tannys Langdon

Mr. Jim Y. Law

Daniel Levin and The Habitat Company as Receiver for the CHA Scattered Site Program

The Linpro Company and Subsidiaries of Shell Pension Fund Foundation (The Netherlands)

Loebl, Schlossman and Hackl, Inc.

Lohan Associates

McDonald's Corporation Archives

Mr. John Macsai

Eva L. Maddox, Eva Maddox Associates, Inc.

Lewis and Susan Manilow

Marshall Field's, The Department Store Division of Dayton Hudson Corporation

Mastro and Skylar Architects

The Merchandise Mart Properties, Inc.

The Metropolitan Pier and Exposition Authority and Mc3D

Mr. Andrew Metter for A. Epstein & Sons International, Inc.

Meyer Glass Design

Miglin Beitler, Inc.

Motorola Museum of Electronics

Mr. Jordon Mozer, Jordon Mozer Associates Ltd.

Murphy/Jahn Architects

Nagle, Hartray & Associates Ltd.

O'Donnell, Wicklund, Pigozzi and Peterson

Pappageorge/Haymes Ltd.

Pei Cobb Freed & Partners Architects

Perkins & Will

Mr. Seymour H. Persky

Frederick Phillips & Associates

Playboy Enterprises, Inc.

Powell/Kleinschmidt, Inc.

Kathryn Quinn Architects

Radio Flyer, Inc.

Mr. Christopher H. Rudolph, Rudolph & Associates, P. C.

St. Benedict the African Church

Ms. Pauline A. Saliga through Ms. Penny McCue

Schmidt, Garden & Erikson

Mr. Ken Schroeder, Schroeder Murchie Laya Associates

Mr. Milton M. Schwartz

Shelby Williams Industries

SITE

Skidmore, Owings & Merrill

Rael D. Slutsky, Rael D. Slutsky & Associates, Inc.

Solomon Cordwell Buenz & Associates, Inc.

State Historical Society of Wisconsin

Stein & Company

Robert A. M. Stern Architects

Mr. John M. Syvertsen

Terp/Meyers Architects

Mr. Stanley Tigerman, Tigerman McCurry Architects

U. S. General Services Administration

Special Collections, The University Library, University of Illinois at Chicago

Mr. John Vinci, The Office of John Vinci, Inc.

Weese Langley Weese

Wheeler Kearns Architects

Mr. David Woodhouse

Acknowledgments

After the success of the 1987-88 exhibition and book *Chicago Architecture, 1872-1922: Birth of a Metropolis*, it was only natural that The Art Institute of Chicago organize a sequel. Director James N. Wood encouraged us to begin planning this project, and the Committee on Architecture offered equal support and encouragement throughout the process: Chairman David C. Hilliard, James N. Alexander, J. Paul Beitler, Thomas Boodell, Jr., Edwin J. DeCosta, Stanley Freehling, Graham C. Grady, Neil Harris, Lynn Maddox, Carter H. Manny, Jr., Peter Palumbo, Seymour H. Persky, Mrs. J. A. Pritzker, Harold Schiff, Patrick Shaw, Thomas Theobald, and Stanley Tigerman. A team of local scholars and Art Institute staff members met almost monthly for a three-year period, from 1989 to 1992, to shape what became much more than a sequel. Some of the more active participants on this team deserve special mention: Mark J. Bouman, Robert Bruegmann, Dennis P. Doordan, and Neil Harris.

Chicago Architecture, 1872-1922 explored the international, particularly European, roots of Chicago's early architecture; the current project examines Chicago's designed environment before and after the two most significant historic periods of our century — the Great Depression of the 1930s and World War II.

Two planning grants helped formulate the concept of the exhibition, the book, and the exhibition installation. The first came in 1990 from the Graham Foundation for Advanced Studies in the Fine Arts. We especially thank that foundation and its director, Carter H. Manny, Jr., for helping to get our project off the ground. The second planning grant came from the National Endowment for the Arts — Design Arts Program. This allowed us to hire eight young Chicago architects to work with the intellectual concepts developed by the local scholars. We are especially grateful to Wendy Clark of that division, and Mina Berryman, the former Director, for their assistance. As planning continued, we received a major grant from the National Endowment for the Humanities to implement this project. Marsha Semmel, the NEH's Director of the Museums Program, was particularly helpful, and we are very grateful for her advice and critique of our ideas. Continental Bank provided us with the corporate support necessary to make our ambitious project a reality; we thank Thomas Theobald, the bank's Chairman, Kurt P. Stocker, Chief Corporate Relations Officer, and Elizabeth W. Bruce, Manager of Corporate Events, who were consistently enthusiastic about our endeavor. At the Art Institute, Larry R. Ter Molen, Executive Vice President for Development and Public Affairs, and his staff were instrumental in assisting us in establishing the project's financing. Particular expressions of gratitude go to: Amy R. Rule, formerly Assistant Director of Government and Foundation Relations; Karin Victoria, Assistant Director of Government and Foundation Relations; Mary Jane Keitel, Director of Government and Foundation Relations; and Linda J. Noyle, Director of Corporate Relations. The project received further reinforcement from Department of Architecture funds, the Seymour H. Persky Fund for Architecture, and the Benefactors of Architecture: J. Paul Beitler, John Buck, Charles Gardner, Lee Miglin, Sandi Miller, Stuart Nathan, Harold Schiff, and Richard Stein. Additional funds for building materials used in the exhibition were supplied by Commonwealth Edison Company, and Steve Solomon, Energy Education Administrator of the Power House.

A number of people assisted in helping to realize our project as conceived by the historians and architects. Crucial to the success of the exhibition were the loans. We are very grateful to all of the lenders (listed on p. 8) and would like here to thank staff members of the corporations, museums, and architectural firms that generously lent objects, helped answer a multitude of questions, and secured photography. They are: Donald J. Stolpa of the Austin Company; J. Michael Heagy of Bethlehem Steel Corporation; Lauren Westreich and Jacqueline Davidson of Booth/Hansen and Associates; Donna A. Wright of the John Buck Company; Larry Donoghue of Ralph

Burke Associates; G. Graham Harper of CBI Industries; Amy Hecker and Chris Thomas, formerly of Chicago Dock and Canal Trust, and current employees Mary Lou Smokowicz and Jim Staller; Daniel Barron, Eileen Flanagan, Scott La France, Larry Viskochil, and Wim de Wit, all of the Chicago Historical Society; Andrew Rodriguez and Andre Garner of the Chicago Housing Authority; Bart Ryckbosch of the Special Collections of the Chicago Park District; Kathy Hussey-Arntson and Gaylen Wilson of the Special Collections in the Chicago Public Library; Yeongfu Chen, Thomas Kato, and John Stubitsch of the Chicago Transit Authority; Howard Pizer and Jeffrey Szynal of the Chicago White Sox; Richard Hankett and John LaPlante of the Department of Transportation, City of Chicago; Louis Chrzasc and Glenn Hanck of the Department of Public Works, City of Chicago; Mary Beth Carroll of Decker and Kemp; Stephen Grage of Decorators Supply Corporation; Arthur D. Dubin of Dubin, Dubin and Moutoussamy; Patricia Junker of the Elvehjem Museum of Art; Edward W. Gjertsen of Fujikawa Johnson and Associates; Lesa Rizzolo of Gelick Foran Associates, Ltd.; Richard Adams of the Great Lakes Dredge and Dock Company; Philip A. Hickman and Mark Braun of Habitat; Mike Houlahan and Jack Hedrich of Hedrich-Blessing, Ltd.; Dana Collins of Hellmuth, Obata and Kassabaum; Diane Richard of Holabird and Root; Geoffrey McNally with HTI/Space Design International; Patricia Blenkle of Albert Kahn Associates, and Joseph Bedway, formerly with that firm; Nancy Cheung and Ilona Rider of Kohn Pedersen Fox; Sawako Takeuchi of Kisho Kurokawa Architect and Associates; Dennis Kluge of the Landahl Group; Clara Lopez of Peter Landon Architects; Edward M. Polich and Michael Pepper of the Linpro Company; Constance B. Day of Loebl, Schlossman and Hackl; Jane Powell of Lohan Associates; Helen Farrell and Lois Dougherty of McDonalds Corporation Archives; Mary Willmorth of Eva Maddox Associates; Alan Adamec of Marshall Field's; Gloria Zylowski, formerly with the Merchandise Mart, and current employee Jennifer Fontanals; Burton Meyer of Meyer Glass Design; Mark Jarasek of Miglin-Beitler Development; Terri Sinnott and Kim Griffith of the Motorola Museum of Electronics; Keith Palmer of Murphy/Jahn Architects; Anne Royston of Nagle, Hartray and Associates; Mark J. Sullivan with Pappageorge/Haymes; Janet Adams Strong with Pei Cobb Freed and Partners; Mary Sue Kranstover of Perkins and Will; Marcia Terrones, Tim Hawkins, and Barbara Hoffman of

Playboy Enterprises; Mark Pasin of Radio Flyer; Robert Dahl of Schmidt, Garden and Erikson; Catherine L. Kasper of Schroeder Murchie Laya Associates; Paul Steinfeld of Shelby Williams Industries; Mark Sokol and Melode Ferguson with SITE Projects; Brett Kedzior and Diane McCormick of Skidmore, Owings and Merrill, and Gary Van Zante, formerly with SOM and now with Hammond, Beeby and Babka; Christine Momich of Solomon Cordwell Buenz and Associates; Christine Schelshorn of the State Historical Society of Wisconsin; Constance K. Dickinson and Donna Goethals of Stein and Company; George Young of Robert A. M. Stern Architects, and Adrianne Hachmeister, formerly with that firm; Lisa Andrykowski, Claire Theobald, Melany Telleen, Janet Barry, and Linda Cox, all of Tigerman McCurry Architects; Gretchen Lagana and Mary Ann Bamberger, both of the Special Collections in the University of Illinois at Chicago; Ward A. Miller of the Office of John Vinci; and Arne Weingart of Weingart Associates.

Others who assisted in the massive effort to obtain photographs for the publication include John Gronkowski, who patiently worked to get the perfect photograph for our distinctive front cover; Lawrence Okrent, who generously permitted access to his extensive collection of aerial photographs; and photographers such as Brandt and Associates, Judith Bromley, Chester Brummel, Orlando Cabanban, Wayne Cable, Evanston Photographic Studios, Timothy Hursley, Howard N. Kaplan, Balthazar Korab, Gregory Murphey, James Steinkamp, and Ezra Stoller, all of whom allowed access to their materials. Others who graciously supplied us with additional material or sent us photographs from their archives are: Dennis McClendon of the American Planning Association; Ralph Stowe of AMOCO; Barbara Lach of Fermilab; Carol Kelm of the Historical Society of Oak Park and River Forest; Sari Mintz of the Illinois Toll Highway Authority; Harry Gann of McDonnell Douglas; Fath Davis Ruffins of the National Museum of American History; Vicki Cwiok of Sears, Roebuck and Co.; and Warren Platner of Warren Platner Associates.

In addition, a number of staff of local firms and organizations exerted great effort to coordinate various programs with our project; we are particularly grateful to Sally Hess of the Chicago Architecture Foundation in this regard. The design architects for our installation in Chicago provided invaluable advice as well as striking designs for their theme spaces: Darcy Bonner, Howard Decker, Ronald Krueck, Kathryn Quinn,

Christopher Rudolph, Daniel Wheeler, Maria Whiteman, and Stephen Wierzbowski. Their designs were coordinated by Stanley Tigerman of Tigerman McCurry Architects; he, Melany Telleen, and Claire Theobald of his Office deserve our warmest thanks for making the installation an exciting experience for visitors. Craig Jackson and Alan Perelgut of Chicago Scenic Studios carefully constructed the architects' designs for the installation.

We wish to thank Timothy J. Grace; Cathy Tully and Josephine Lincoln of Frameway Studio; and Robert Weinberg and his staff of the Chicago Conservation Center for conserving works and preparing frames for the installation. The staff of Gene Young Effects are to be thanked for creating a spectacular scale model of the "Chicago Skymaster," a C54 transport plane, for the exhibition. The staff at Prestel-Verlag, Munich, created, as they did with the previous project, another superbly produced book on Chicago's architectural environment in this volume. We also wish to acknowledge the design expertise of Dietmar Rautner, who produced this fine sequel to Chicago Architecture, 1872-1922.

Last, but not least, we want to thank a number of staff members of the Art Institute for their efforts on behalf of this project. The Department of Architecture staff devoted long hours and conscientious labor to make this complex project a reality. Research Assistants Sarah Mollman Underhill and Amy Gold shaped the checklist; Ms. Gold also assumed the arduous task of compiling the loan forms and gathered relevant data from lenders. In addition to contributing an essay, Associate Curator of Architecture Pauline Saliga assisted in locating design artifacts for the checklist, as did Victor Margolin of the University of Illinois. Luigi Mumford, the department's Technical Specialist, supervised the preparation of the hundreds of works in the exhibition, with the assistance of interns and volunteers Kate Blumgren, Phil Kennedy, Linda Lazowski, Amanda Mullin, Leslie Pitner, Pamela Samuels, Elin Tuason, and Jane Yates; and Elizabeth Alexander filed the countless photographs accumulated for the project. Betty Blum, our Oral History Specialist, coordinated information from her materials with data for the book and exhibition. With Jane Clarke, Associate Director of Museum Education, and Celia Marriott, Associate Director of Media Programs, she helped document electronically the works of some prominent Chicago architects. Research Assistant Maurice Blanks assisted Ms. Saliga in design-history research, and he coordinated and compiled the extensive biographies in this book. Secretary Linda Adelman typed the checklist and related materials published here.

Over the past twelve years, the museum's Publications Department, especially its Associate Director, Robert V. Sharp, has collaborated closely with the Department of Architecture to produce a number of titles that, I hope, have contributed to the field of American architectural history, especially that of Chicago and the Midwest. This book is no exception: Robert Sharp and his co-editor Carol Jentsch worked ceaselessly and devotedly to bring the book into existence, helping to shape its contents, interacting with authors, gathering illustrations, and coordinating the project with our copublisher, Prestel-Verlag. Andrew Huckman also generously assisted with picture editing. I am very grateful to Robert and his staff for their continuing support in what has become an invaluable partnership. Their efforts in research, fact-checking, and the endless search for high-quality photographs were aided on an almost daily basis by the knowledgeable staff of the Ryerson and Burnham Libraries, under Executive Director Jack P. Brown, most notably by Architectural Archivist Mary Woolever, along with Susan Perry and Maureen Lasko. Alan Newman, Executive Director of Imaging and Technical Services, and members of his staff—Chris Gallagher, Anne Morse, Pam Stuedemann, and Leslie Umberger—readily supplied photographs of objects from the permanent collection for the book and exhibition and prepared numerous other photographs to serve as illustrations to this volume's many essays. We are also extremely grateful to the authors of these essays: they have contributed substantially to this volume and to our understanding and appreciation of Chicago.

Advice and assistance regarding the financial operations for the show were provided by: Robert E. Mars, Executive Vice President for Administrative Affairs; Calvert W. Audrain, Assistant Vice President for Administrative Affairs—Operations; Dorothy M. Schroeder, Assistant Director for Exhibitions and Budget; and Mayno Burke, Assistant Director of Grants in the Financial Planning Office. The objects within the exhibition itself received the best of care and handling thanks to the late William R. Leisher, Executive Director of Conservation, and his staff. Executive Director of Registration Mary Solt, with the assistance of Mary S. Mulhern, Associate Registrar for Loans and Exhibitions, insured that the pieces were appropriately recorded. Reynold V. Bailey, Manager of Art Handling, and his staff

carefully installed the objects, working closely with George T. Preston, Executive Director of Physical Plant, and his staff. The Public Affairs Department, under Executive Director Eileen Harakal, promoted the exhibition to a wide audience; and Alice Sabl, President of the Architecture Society, and her board organized the opening celebration befitting this large-scale project.

In all, then, the collaboration and ready cooperation of many people within the museum and outside its walls helped turn this large and extremely complex project into a substantial exhibition and book. The success of this endeavor is, essentially, a tribute to their creative spirit and heroic efforts.

John Zukowsky
Curator of Architecture
The Art Institute of Chicago

Chicago Architecture
and Design, 1923-1993

Essays

The Burden of History: Chicago Architecture before and after the Great Depression and World War II

John Zukowsky

Like all America, Chicago inhabited very different worlds before and after the two most traumatic events of the twentieth century: the Great Depression of the early 1930s and the global war of the 1940s (fig. 1). Before these historic events, the architectural and social environments of Chicago and other American cities were essentially developments of turn-of-the-century tendencies. In contrast to the dramatic, and often extreme, situations within Central European society after World War I, postwar changes in America's urban condition were more evolutionary than revolutionary. Many of the essays in this volume deal with Chicago's architectural condition, before and after those critical decades of the thirties and forties. Likewise, this introduction will survey some aspects of Chicago's architectural scene during these years, with observations on the nature of Chicago's urban and suburban environment, past and present. This essence is often a dualistic and contradictory one, and the city has been alternately perceived as conservative and avant-garde in its architectural and cultural activities. And, surprisingly enough, an overriding concern for the city's prominent architectural heritage has conditioned all Chicago's architects in the twentieth century.

The Twenties and Thirties: Beyond Gangsters and Speakeasies

The period after World War I witnessed America's coming of age as a worldwide industrial and commercial power. Chicago itself was already an established commercial city in the late nineteenth and early twentieth centuries, with a population of about two and a half million people before World War I. (Today that population still numbers only about 2,780,000 people.) Unlike their European counterparts from Vienna to Berlin, Munich to Cologne, or Lille to Rheims, American cities and towns were untouched by the ravages of war and postwar revolutions. The physical, commercial, and industrial bases of American urban environments

remained intact and ripe for further development.

Chicago's centerpiece of postwar development, for example, was the upgrading of Michigan Avenue into a boulevard with classically inspired commercial buildings intended to rival those of European cities like Paris. The widening of Michigan Avenue and construction of the Michigan Avenue Bridge (1918-20; see Sennott, fig. 4) prompted the rise of various skyscrapers at this famous urban intersection throughout the next decade. The size and shape of these buildings were influenced by a change in zoning in 1923—enabling the occupied space to be higher than 264 feet, as in the Tribune Tower—but even this urban renewal program had its roots in the 1909 *Plan of Chicago* by Daniel H. Burnham and Edward H. Bennett.[1] Classical sources and Beaux-Arts planning principles, both via France, greatly influenced American buildings of the early twentieth century before and after World War I. Americans continued to study in Paris at the Ecole des Beaux-Arts, and the cultural and social connections to France became even stronger after America entered the Great War. In Chicago the School of Architecture at the Armour Institute of Technology and the School of the Art Institute maintained an essentially Beaux-Arts curriculum. Skyscrapers in New York, Chicago, and other American metropolises affected variants of masonry modernism popularized after the 1925 Art Deco exhibition in Paris. These variants often combined French Beaux-Arts classical planning with local details in an eclectic combination of traditional and avant-garde elements, characterized as being part of a conservative approach to modernism throughout America. This was especially true in comparison with the more radical solutions that issued from Central European countries, particularly Germany, as they tried to establish a new democratic social identity that was distinct from a classical imperial past.[2]

Although Chicago's commercial architecture of the late nineteenth century is represented in even the most basic books on architectural his-

Fig. 1 Douglas Aircraft Company C54 transports, the type of airplane constructed after 1943 at a factory on the present site of Chicago's O'Hare International Airport.

Fig. 2 Holabird and
Root, 333 North
Michigan Avenue, 1928.

Fig. 3 Burnham
Brothers, Perspective
study of the Carbide and
Carbon Building, 230
North Michigan Avenue,
1927-29 (cat. no. 199).

Fig. 4 William F.
Deknatel, Perspective
rendering of the Lambert
H. Ennis House,
200 Dempster Street,
Evanston, 1941
(cat. no. 447).

Fig. 5   Abel Faidy,
Dining room of Ernst
Byfield's Penthouse at
the Sherman Hotel, 1939
(now demolished).

Holabird and Root. Buildings by them and their colleagues (figs. 2, 3; pls. 41, 42) filled the cityscape, rivaling those in New York, Los Angeles, and San Francisco.

Because of its strong design traditions and the international reputation of buildings and architects of the so-called Chicago School of commercial architecture and the Prairie School of residential design, Chicago attracted design professionals from abroad. Those who emigrated from Central Europe and Germany included Abel Faidy and Henry Harringer. Faidy (fig. 5; see also Saliga, fig. 3), a Swiss-born interior architect and furniture designer, came to Chicago, via San Francisco and Omaha, in 1918; Harringer brought his expertise in architecture and interior design from his native Hamburg in 1927 and developed a successful career here in marketing and advertising (see Bouman, fig. 16; pl. 93). But designers and architects also came from as far away as Tokyo; Richard Yoshijiro Mine immigrated in 1919 to study at the University of Illinois at Champaign/Urbana. He entered the Chicago Tribune tower competition in 1922 and remained in the Midwest to work as an architect for General Motors, Kraft, and Sears.[3]

The Prairie School tradition continued to influence American approaches to modern residential architecture, as best seen in works by architects such as William Deknatel (fig. 4; see Robinson, figs. 15-17) and Paul Schweikher (see Robinson, figs. 4-7), among others. Thus, a hybridized modernism, albeit one with a French accent, prevailed throughout American and Chicago architecture of the twenties and thirties, and this hybridization is, in many ways, emblematic of the eclectic origins of those design ideas and personnel. It was, in the end, a very American situation, melding different design philosophies and tastes.

The Great Depression

The Stock Market crash of October 29, 1929, and its aftermath brought far-reaching changes to American society and, naturally, to the way architecture was done throughout this country. The crash, at first, had no immediate effect on architectural offices; things went on much as they had before. The office of McNally and Quinn, for example, partnered by structural engineer Frank McNally and architect James Edwin Quinn, built numerous high-rise apartment houses in the 1920s: 399 Fullerton Parkway and 1366 North Dearborn Street, both 1926; 73 East Elm Street and 415 Fullerton

tory, its buildings of the 1920s and 1930s, though published soon after construction, have received recognition by historians only within the past decade or so. The public's imagination is still captured by the image of Chicago as a town of gangsters and gun molls, filled with speakeasies selling bootlegged liquor, despite the fact that numerous tangible contributions to the city were made in these decades by such noted firms as Graham, Anderson, Probst and White and

Fig. 6   McNally and
Quinn, Exterior view of
the Woodruff Penthouse,
1500 North Lake Shore
Drive, 1928.

Parkway, both 1928; 2000 Lincoln Park West and 1100 North Dearborn, both 1929; and, undoubtedly their most famous and most opulent, the luxury apartments and penthouse villa at 1500 North Lake Shore Drive from 1928 (fig. 6; cat. nos. 422-25). In these good times they had some twenty employees. After the crash, they maintained a similarly scaled office staff to complete unfinished jobs and compete for new speculative ventures (fig. 7). As the nation, and the world, drifted deeper into the Depression, McNally and Quinn received fewer commissions, and in 1932-33, their office staff dwindled to only two or three designers working on a handful of small jobs and remodelings. Finally, they dissolved their practice in 1939. Quinn continued in private practice, doing homes such as the Vincent J. Sheridan House in the Beverly Hills neighborhood in 1940 (fig. 8) and, after the war, he was an architect for numerous highways and overpasses in Cook County related to the interstate highway system (cat. nos. 63-73).[4]

The story of McNally and Quinn in the early 1930s is just one example in thousands of how the Depression affected careers, and how people had to reconfigure their lives during these years of financial and social crisis. Architectural associations were hit by the Depression as well. The Chicago Architectural Club—founded in 1895 as the Chicago Architectural Sketch Club—counted as members designers and architects who were publishing and exhibiting their works before the Depression. In 1929 and 1930 they published elaborately illustrated catalogues to complement their exhibitions at the Arts Club of Chicago, but after their 1931 show and an exhibit within the General Exhibits Building of the 1933-34 Century of Progress Exposition, the club's publishing and exhibiting activities virtually ceased. The Chicago Architectural Club and related organizations like the Chicago Chapter of the American Institute of Architects (founded in 1869) and the Illinois Society of Architects (founded in 1897) continued to downscale their operations during the thirties. The Architectural Club itself was gone by 1940, another victim of the Depression.[5]

In all of this there were some positive outcomes related to architecture in Chicago. First, the architectural consortium began to replace the individual architect. As is well known, Daniel H. Burnham was the first architect to organize his architectural firm on the corporate model, with several vice-presidents of design reporting to Burnham himself as chief executive officer. He applied the same principle to his organization of architects for the World's Columbian Exposition of 1893.[6] The success of this organizational structure inspired other architects to emulate Burnham. In some ways, consortia of various associated firms working together on large projects, but coordinated by one firm, are a natural outgrowth of the corporate model. These conglomerates of various partners with design, engineering, and client contact specialties flourished after the Great Depression and World War II. But they had a head start during the Depression, working on large public housing developments among other big projects (see de Wit, figs. 5-8; cat. nos. 439-41, 452). For better or worse, then, the practice of having several large architectural firms work together on their respective specialties of design, engineering, and the preparation of working drawings, along with

Fig. 7 McNally and Quinn, Perspective view of the Hearthstone Hotel Apartment Building project, Chicago River and Michigan Avenue, delineated by George A. Hossack, 1931 (cat. no. 428).

Fig. 8 James Edwin Quinn, Perspective rendering of the Vincent J. Sheridan House, 9323 South Bell Avenue, delineated by George A. Hossack, 1940 (cat. no. 446).

checking or correcting designs and supervising construction, became commonplace in large governmental projects of the 1950s and 1960s, such as the Federal and Civic centers (see Miller, "City Hall," figs. 1, 14, 15).

A second positive and very tangible outcome of the Great Depression was an improvement of the infrastructure as part of various governmental programs, such as the Public Works Administration (PWA) and the Works Progress Administration (WPA). Among the great federal and state architectural and engineering projects undertaken during Franklin Delano Roosevelt's administration, numerous post offices were constructed or redecorated throughout the country, and there were other marvels of engineering, such as the Golden Gate Bridge of 1933-37 and the Oakland Bay Bridge of 1933-36, along with the Hoover Dam of 1936 and a number of dams designed for the Tennessee Valley Authority. Although Chicago can boast of no great monuments like these, important improvements completed here range from the 1931-32 remodeling of Ogden Avenue by Great Lakes Dredge and Dock Company to the same company's construction of the Outer Drive Bridge between 1931 and 1937 (fig. 9; see Sennott, fig. 17). Then the largest bascule bridge in the world, the Outer Drive Bridge was officially opened on October 5, 1937, by President Roosevelt.[7] In addition to these public initiatives, a number of individual corporations with local and national clients continued to operate during the Depression and afterward, and today they still provide high quality products for the public. These range from small family-owned companies like Radio Flyer Wagons (see pls. 75-77) to large national and international companies like Kraft-General Foods (see cat. nos. 291, 292) and Motorola (see cat. nos. 329-31, 356-57, 480-81).

A third and, for our purposes here, final benefit of the worldwide Depression of the 1930s was the emigration of a number of talented architects and designers from Central Europe, and particularly from National Socialist Germany. The most famous and influential of these was Ludwig Mies van der Rohe, who came to Chicago in 1938. He, along with his émigré colleagues Ludwig Hilberseimer and Walter Peterhans, changed the curriculum at the Architecture School of the Armour Institute of Technology and influenced generations of architects to come who trained under them. This long-term association with younger architects, in one sense, made Mies much more influential than his postwar buildings.[8] Similar observations might also be made about designers such as Serge Chermayeff and Gyorgy Kepes and artists like László Moholy-Nagy, who, along with others, created the New Bauhaus in Chicago in 1937 and influenced designers and artists here afterward.[9]

Fig. 9   The Outer Drive Bridge, 1937.

What Did You Do in the War, Daddy?

If the question of what one did in the war were asked of Chicago and its architects, the answer would be "plenty!" In the early years of World War II, before America joined its Allies in combat, Chicago and the Midwest were centers of isolationist movements whose supporters ranged from respected *Chicago Tribune* publisher Colonel Robert R. McCormick and renowned aviator Charles A. Lindbergh, to the anti-semitic Michigan priest Father Charles Coughlin, the publisher of *Social Justice*.[10] Architect Philip Johnson was one of the war correspondents who wrote for *Social Justice*, reporting favorably on Germany's successes in Poland after the September 1939 invasion. Even a Chicago architect like Paul Schweikher, and others of German descent in this city, which had a large German minority, supported Germany's quick victories in the first years of the war.[11] All support faded, however, with the Japanese attack on Pearl Harbor on December 7, 1941, and Germany's subsequent declaration of war on America. Ironically, World War II provided Mies and his associates a certain amount of time to reshape the architecture curriculum at the Armour Institute and to train their first generation of designers to reshape the American cityscape. The hiatus in nonessential building during the war also gave Mies a chance to phase in his designs for the new campus and buildings for the School of Architecture and other facilities at the newly renamed Illinois Institute of Technology.

Most important, however, America's entry into World War II provided an enormous catalyst to revitalize industries that were just beginning to make their way out of the decade-long Depression. New defense plants were constructed in Chicago, a number of them designed by an industrial specialist, architect Albert Kahn (see pls. 80-85). In 1943 Douglas Aircraft Company built a factory that produced C54 transports (fig. 1); the plant and its airfield served as the beginnings of O'Hare International Airport (see Brodherson, figs. 17-19; pls. 86-87). In conjunction with industrial facilities such as this, wartime housing, like the 1943 apartments in Oriole Park Village, accommodated workers then and now (fig. 11). Large construction concerns also supported the war effort. Chicago Bridge and Iron Company, a firm specializing in the development of steel construction for bridges and later for oil and water storage facilities (see pls. 88-89), opened a massive shipyard in nearby Seneca, Illinois, one of four it operated on the inland waterways of the United States for the production of flat-bottomed boats used in the war effort. The Seneca Yard, operating from 1942 through 1945, produced 157 LSTs (Landing Ship Tanks) that were used to transport troops, armor, and equipment (fig. 10) in the invasions of Iwo Jima, Dutch New Guinea, Normandy, and southern Italy.[12]

Finally, desperate times encourage desperate measures. The urgency of the war acted as a catalyst for both Axis and Allied citizens to experiment with various materials and techniques that would contribute to the war effort. In Chicago the most famous of these great experiments was physicist Enrico Fermi's controlled atomic reaction on December 2, 1942, which, within three years, would lead to the age of nuclear warfare in the devastation of Hiroshima and Nagasaki in August 1945. Other less dramatic expressions of experimentation can be found from architects as disparate as John R. Fugard and Bertrand Goldberg. Fugard, an engineer by training who specialized in high-rise buildings, proposed a standardized rural cheese plant in 1944 for the Kraft Cheese Company to be constructed of stainless armorply (cat. no. 328). Standardized, industrialized, yet decentralized, cheese plants would be vital to the continued war effort, because companies like Kraft supplied food to soldiers and citizens alike, and shipped cheese products to the Allies.[13] Fugard's experimentation with new industrial materials

Fig. 10   A Sherman Tank unloads from LST (Landing Ship Tank) 202, the Alice Kirby Birchard, *commissioned March 16, 1943, at the Seneca Shipyard in Seneca, Illinois, operated by the Chicago Bridge and Iron Company.*

is consistent with the innovative work of other designers during the war. For instance, R. Buckminster Fuller's 1943 Dymaxion Car for Henry Kaiser, though it was an extension of his earlier Dymaxion autos, made extensive use of aircraft aluminum in its structural members (pls. 11-12; see Saliga, fig. 5). Bauhaus-trained Bertrand Goldberg served with the Office of Strategic Services (OSS) during the war. Like his Axis counterpart, fellow "Bauhausler" Ernst Neufert, Goldberg experimented with prefabricated forms in wartime housing, such as that at Suitland, Maryland, in 1941.[14] He also experimented with other movable and industrialized forms that even included a mobile delousing unit.

From large-scale factories, then, to small experimental projects, Chicago and its architects actively participated in the war effort. With the end of the war, a number of civic memorials were dedicated. These include the 1949 renaming of Chicago's Municipal Airport to Midway Airport in honor of the famed 1942 aerial battle over the Pacific, and concurrently, the renaming of Orchard Field (the airfield on the site of the Douglas Aircraft Company plant) in honor of America's first ace in World War II, Lt. "Butch" O'Hare. Other structures that were left incomplete during the war were finished afterward, the most notable being the Bataan-Corregidor Memorial Bridge over the Chicago River at State Street (1942-49), completed only after the State Street subway tunnel had been finished below.[15]

The war's end, however, brought more than memorialization, including a few important architectural conditions that followed soon after the cessation of hostilities. First, once war production was no longer needed and factories began to close, a number of properties became available for future development. Some factories were converted relatively quickly to other uses, such as the recycling of Albert Kahn's famous Amertorp Naval Ordinance Plant of 1942 into Forest Park Mall (see pls. 80-81). Next, architects' experiments in prefabrication and industrialization with new materials, particularly plastics and aluminum, continued after the war. Ideas such as Bertrand Goldberg's prefabricated modular bathroom of 1945-47 became reality (see Saliga, fig. 11). R. Buckminster Fuller's Airbarac Dymaxion House, originally developed for the Army, was meant to serve as inexpensive housing produced by the Beech Aircraft Company once the war's end slowed the production of aircraft (see Robinson, figs. 23, 24). Although this house did not go into production (the sole example was recently donated to the Henry Ford Museum in Greenfield Village, Dearborn, Michigan), other more popular designs were published throughout the war in magazines such as *Small Homes Guide* and entered in competitions such as the *Chicago Tribune*'s Chicagoland Prize Homes Competition of 1945 (pls. 107-12). These homes bear some relationship to the tradition of homes constructed for European housing exhibits, particularly in Germany, in the 1920s and early 1930s, and to the model homes exhibited at the 1933-34 Century of Progress Exposition in Chicago (see Robinson, figs. 2, 3) and the 1939 World's Fair in New York.[16] But their relationship with many of these modernist precedents is dwarfed when one considers the impact of Frank Lloyd Wright's early Prairie and later Usonian homes on the development of postwar American ranch homes. Most of these postwar ranch homes are eclectic hybrids of traditional, vernacular, and modernist forms, and they covered the suburban landscape in the 1950s and 1960s.[17]

Countless examples can be seen throughout Chicago's suburbs and at the fringes of the city limits. It is clear, then, that a building such as Mies van der Rohe's famed Farnsworth House (see Schulze, fig. 8) was the exception rather than the rule when it came to immediate postwar homes, even for the affluent. With the war's end, we can also observe that some architectural firms were well positioned to profit from the boom in the decades that followed.

Fig. 11 Wartime housing, 5300 North Harlem Avenue and 7200 Balmoral Avenue, Harwood Heights, 1943.

A New World Order

While Mies van der Rohe trained a generation of students at the Illinois Institute of Technology, and built more and larger constructions in America after World War II than he did in Germany before it (see essay by Schulze), the new world order for architecture in Chicago meant even more than Mies and his followers. It meant the chance to rebuild America as well as a war-torn Europe. One Chicago firm was particularly well prepared to participate. The partnership of Skidmore, Owings and Merrill (SOM) was begun by Louis Skidmore and Nathaniel Alexander Owings after both had participated in the planning and construction of the 1933-34 Century of Progress Exposition. Although they often received small commissions during the Depression, the firm, with offices in both New York and Chicago, was catapulted to the forefront with its work on facilities in Oak Ridge, Tennessee, during World War II in conjunction with the government's efforts to refine uranium for production of the first atomic bomb. Gordon Bunshaft, one of the firm's leading designers of the fifties and sixties, had his start with SOM designing the Hostess Pavilion of the Great Lakes Naval Training Center in late 1941 and early 1942.[18] After the war Bunshaft was one of the partners who led the firm in spreading its form of Americanized corporate modernism around the world, from corporate headquarters in New York for Lever Brothers in 1952, Union Carbide in 1960, and Chase Manhattan Bank in 1961, to the American consulates in Düsseldorf and Bremen in 1954, the Hilton Hotel of 1955 in Istanbul, and Banque Lambert in Brussels in 1965. SOM's Chicago partners, such as Walter A. Netsch and Bruce J. Graham, were equally influential in shaping the firm's destiny.

But Skidmore, Owings and Merrill was not the only partnership to capitalize on postwar reconstruction. Loebl, Schlossman and Bennett, a firm begun by Jerrold Loebl and Norman Schlossman after they too had worked together on 1933 fair projects, acted as both architects and partial investors in Park Forest. This suburban community south of Chicago, built from 1947 to 1952, included what was one of the first suburban shopping malls in the nation (see Harris, fig. 9). Future suburban developments were spurred on by loans from the Veterans Administration and the Federal Housing Authority, as well as by Cold War policies that promoted "defense through decentralization" in 1951 and the subsequent construction of the Interstate Highway

System (approved by Congress and President Dwight D. Eisenhower in 1956) for evacuation before potential nuclear attack. The factors that assisted in the success of Park Forest itself led to similar jobs for Loebl, Schlossman and Bennett, particularly in regard to developing suburban shopping centers in the region.[19]

Another prospering older firm, whose specialty included hospital design, was Schmidt, Garden and Erikson. German-born Richard Schmidt was its founder and the architect of Michael Reese Hospital in 1906.[20] The firm continued to receive health care projects, as well as the commission for the Veterans Administration Hospital in the Streeterville section of Chicago from 1955 (fig. 12). Still others who survived included the great architectural firms of the 1920s—Holabird and Root and Graham, Anderson, Probst and White. Although Holabird and Root had a strong institutional and governmental base that got the firm through the Depression and war, Graham, Anderson, Probst and White was weakened, after Ernest Graham's death in 1936, by the departure of some of the firm's leading lights, including Charles F. Murphy and Alfred Shaw. In fact, the development of Murphy's various firms was one of the great post-

Fig. 12 Schmidt, Garden and Erikson, Veterans Administration Hospital, 333 East Huron Street, 1955.

war success stories in Chicago, due, in part, to the personal relationship between Murphy and Mayor Richard J. Daley (see essays by Tigerman and Miller, "City Hall").

Postwar Modern Chicago

It took a little while for Chicago to adapt to the new world order, but not too long. Although the city's revised zoning ordinance of 1957 encouraged the modern slab-in-the-plaza development, the buildings constructed soon after World War II were similar to those done in the late 1920s and 1930s, that is, masonry modernist or moderne. One need only read the comments on Naess and Murphy's Prudential Building (1952-55; see Rau, fig. 12): *Architectural Forum* said that it "was no design experiment, no Lever House, no Alcoa, no U.N. Secretariat," its limestone facade being comparable to Rockefeller Center of the early 1930s and used, in part, because "in Chicago, more conservatism exists."[21] This was certainly true of Prudential and of Schmidt, Garden and Erikson's Veterans Hospital, as well as of 1960s buildings by Perkins and Will (cat. no. 214) and Shaw, Metz and Associates. In this regard, Alfred Shaw stated in 1965 that "the stereotyped rectangular building we've seen so much of has begun to be a little dreary. Forms are changing. There's a little more imagination coming. People are fed up with [glass houses]. I've been fed up with them a long time."[22] The limestone skyscraper of the 1930s continued well beyond Miesian expressions of the type and well beyond the steel-clad contemporaries by C. F. Murphy Associates and Skidmore, Owings and Merrill. Varied approaches to high-rise design in this period in Chicago ranged from the concrete expressionism of Bertrand Goldberg (fig. 13) and Walter Netsch (fig. 14) through the individualistic approaches to materials and design forms promoted by Harry Weese (pls. 43-44).[23] Thus, when one thinks of corporate or international modernism after World War II, one must realize that there was a wide range of design expressions that could fit within that overall framework, and not a simple monolithic viewpoint.

Related to the explosion of these various approaches to modern design in the 1950s and 1960s in Chicago are the less well known stories of architectural organizations in these decades. The foremost among them was the Chicago Chapter of the American Institute of Architects (AIA). In conjunction with the Chicago Association of Commerce and Industry, the local chap-

Fig. 13 Bertrand Goldberg and Associates, Marina City, north bank of the Chicago River between State and Dearborn streets, 1964-67.

Fig. 14 Walter Netsch of Skidmore, Owings and Merrill, Administration Building, University of Illinois at Chicago, 1960-65.

Fig. 15 Belli and Belli,
St. Patrick's High
School, northeast corner
of Austin Boulevard
and Belmont Avenue,
1952-55 (cat. no. 137).

foundation organized a think-tank session with, among others, architects Pietro Belluschi, Rudolph Arnheim, Eero Saarinen, and William and Catherine Wurster, it established a program to award fellowships in architecture and the visual arts. John Entenza, the noted publisher of *Arts and Architecture* and promoter of the avant-garde case-study houses in Southern California during and after the war, became the foundation's next director in 1960.[24] He was followed in 1971 by its current director, architect Carter H. Manny, Jr. In the last two decades, the Graham Foundation has been the most active private foundation in the field of architecture and design, supporting a variety of publications and exhibitions throughout the world. Its own building, the historic Madlener House of 1902 designed by Richard Schmidt, was remodeled in 1963-64 by Brenner Danforth Rockwell with C. F. Murphy Associates, and it received an AIA Citation of Merit in 1965.

In some ways, the renovation of the Madlener House and the almost concurrent renovation of the historic Newberry Library by Harry Weese and Associates—awarded an AIA Citation of Merit in 1963—represent some of the best in design attitudes that respected older historic structures in Chicago. But historic preservations per se were not given AIA awards until the American Bicentennial of 1976 redirected national attention. The restoration of Navy Pier by the City of Chicago was one of the first historic buildings to receive the Distinguished Building Award recognition by the local chapter in 1976. In the 1960s, early preservation efforts were, ironically, against the widespread rebuilding of the city that building awards actually tended to encourage. With the demolition of such internationally renowned landmarks as the 1891 Schiller Building of Adler and Sullivan in 1961, the City of Chicago eventually formed the Commission on Chicago Historical and Architectural Landmarks. Local awareness of Chicago's great design heritage was also increased by organizations like the Chicago Architecture Foundation, which acquired H. H. Richardson's famous 1885-87 Glessner House in 1966.[25] Periodicals such as the *Prairie School Review* (1964-76), a journal of the Prairie School Press of Wilbert and Marilyn Hasbrouck, also published reprints of important volumes on Louis H. Sullivan, Daniel H. Burnham, and Walter Burley Griffin. Their combined efforts in the 1960s were truly remarkable in a city where the whims of developer, investor, and land speculator alike have often held sway since its founding in 1833.

ter of the AIA launched a program of architectural awards that continues today. The first year of its awards in 1955 honored sixteen new buildings built between 1950 and 1955, some of which no one has heard about since; among them are the Sawyer Biscuit Company by Skidmore, Owings and Merrill; Village Market by Mittelbusher and Tourtelot; the Alexander Hamilton Monument by Marx, Flint and Schonne; St. Patrick's High School by Belli and Belli (fig. 15; cat. no. 137); the Veterans Administration Hospital by Schmidt, Garden and Erikson (fig. 12); Lake Meadows Apartments by Skidmore, Owings and Merrill; and the American Bar Center and Evergreen Plaza shopping center, both by Holabird and Root and Burgee.

Concurrent with the establishment of this program to increase the public's awareness of contemporary architecture was another effort established by private means. The Graham Foundation for Advanced Studies in the Fine Arts was founded in the mid-1950s from the estate of architect Ernest R. Graham. Charles F. Murphy, the executor of Graham's estate, was the foundation's first president and William E. Hartmann, an architect with Skidmore, Owings and Merrill, became its first director. After the

Postmodern Chicago: Classicism, Conservatism, and Consumerism

Ever since 1978, when Stanley Tigerman created his well known photomontage of Mies van der Rohe's Crown Hall sinking into Lake Michigan (fig. 16), people have associated the development of postmodernism in Chicago with the demise of modernism after the death of Mies in 1969.[26] The Museum of Contemporary Art's hosting of the 1976 exhibition "100 Years of Architecture in Chicago" reinforced the view that modernism was at the core of Chicago's architecture. But the image of Miesian modernism in Chicago was always much stronger than the reality of architecture built here, as was brought to the forefront in a competing exhibition, "Chicago Architects," also in 1976.[27] The importance of this revisionist look at Chicago's architectural past is that it spawned further similar efforts, ranging from the 1981 exhibition catalogue *New Chicago Architecture* through the 1979 revival of the Chicago Architectural Club and subsequent publication of the *Chicago Architectural Journal* from 1981 through 1989.[28] In fact, the promotion of pluralism, contextualism, and historicism by the club relates closely to the popularized acceptance of postmodernism in Chicago's architectural circles in that decade. But what happened in the early to mid-seventies, following the death of Mies and the demise of his interpretation of modernism, to encourage this movement?

The late 1960s was a period of social unrest in America and the world. The character of the era in the United States was epitomized by protests against the Vietnam War and the rising Civil Rights Movement, especially after the assassina-tion of Martin Luther King in 1968. Incidents in Chicago included the riots at the Democratic Convention of 1968. This period of social change and the rise of the "cult of the individual" during the sixties and early seventies found architectural expression in more individualized approaches to modernist design, as we have already seen in works by Bertrand Goldberg, Walter Netsch, and Harry Weese. This was also the time when the recession of 1974 found unemployed architects exhibiting their drawings in gallery shows. One such show, organized by the Richard Gray Gallery in 1976-77, was entitled "Seven Chicago Architects" and it featured the work of the so-called "Chicago Seven" (named after the unorthodox political group from the turbulent 1968 convention): Thomas Beeby, Laurence Booth, Stuart Cohen, James Ingo Freed (who later moved to New York), James Nagle, Stanley Tigerman, and Ben Weese; Helmut Jahn was next to join this group in further exhibitions.[29] Public interest in these gallery exhibitions of architecture in the mid-1970s may account for the increased acceptance of architectural archives and the establishment of personnel for their care at both the Chicago Historical Society (1976) and The Art Institute of Chicago (1978). But the most likely explanation for the increased architectural awareness by professionals and public alike was probably the Bicentennial.

The Bicentennial fostered an awareness of America's history all across the country. One Bicentennial project was the exhibition "200 Years of American Architectural Drawing," organized by the Architectural League of New York and the American Federation of the Arts, which toured the country, including a stop in

Fig. 16 Stanley Tigerman, The Titanic, 1978 (cat. no. 343).

Chicago at the Art Institute in 1977. Another very important project was a history of public works in America, sponsored by the Chicago-based American Public Works Association.[30] Although local industry and the stockyards were in decline in the early seventies (the latter closed in 1971), the Chicago Historical Society celebrated the city's past in a Bicentennial exhibition, "Chicago: Creating New Traditions." The Chicago Architecture Foundation founded its Archicenter, its base for tours with a bookshop and exhibition space, as a Bicentennial project. The foundation also acquired the historic Widow Clark House—Chicago's earliest surviving home, from 1843—and moved it to its present Prairie Avenue location in 1976. In addition to this and other historic preservation efforts, a major initiative was organized to save Frank Lloyd Wright's home and studio in Oak Park. The National Trust for Historic Preservation and the Frank Lloyd Wright Home and Studio Foundation purchased this renowned building in 1974-75 and, soon afterward, established a plan for restoring the structure to its 1909 appearance—the last year that Wright lived there. The plan was published in 1978 and the architectural restoration was completed in 1987. Architec-

tural exhibitions, club activity, and publications in Chicago during the mid- to late seventies must, then, be seen in this broader context of renewed interest in our local and national heritage.[31]

In the building boom of the 1980s, architects freely incorporated design references to the city's architectural heritage within their new buildings, almost to the point of being historicist. Examples include Hammond, Beeby and Babka's classicism in their addition to the North Shore Congregation Israel (pls. 25-27); Burgee and Johnson's 190 South LaSalle Street (pls. 61-64), with its overt references to John Wellborn Root's Masonic Temple of 1891; Tannys Langdon's painted furniture (pls. 126-28); and Laurence Booth's classical House of Light (pls. 123-25). Architects became even more attuned to history because of the Economic Recovery Tax Act of 1981, which, until its reform in 1986, gave substantial tax credits to building owners for restoration, and prompted renovations of major buildings such as the Monadnock, the Rookery, and the Chicago Theater (fig. 17).[32]

This taste for history in the late 1980s often found expression in the extreme, with an enlargement and distortion of scale and form, making both major and minor monuments that were baroque or imperial in feeling. But this essentially eclectic mixture of classical and romanesque regional form associated with the Chicago School, as in 190 South LaSalle Street (pls. 61-64) and, especially, the Harold Washington Library Center (pls. 28-30), is part of the very tradition of architecture in Chicago and, by extension, America.[33] So, it will come as no surprise that historicist, or postmodernist, architects evoked another tradition in their high-rise buildings—

Fig. 17 Rapp and Rapp, Chicago Theater, 175 North State Street, 1920-22 (photo c. 1986).

Fig. 18 Daniel Wheeler of Wheeler Kearns Architects, Lapoint House, Camp Madron in Buchanan Township, Michigan, 1990-91 (see cat. no. 572).

Fig. 19 Adrian Smith
of Skidmore, Owings
and Merrill, AT&T
Building, 227 West
Monroe Street, 1985-89.

Fig. 20 Cesar Pelli,
Model of the proposed
Miglin-Beitler Tower,
201 West Madison
Street, c. 1990
(cat. no. 287). The AT&T
Building and the Sears
Tower are immediately
to the right of Pelli's
proposed tower.

the tradition of masonry modernism as the form that characterizes the vitality of American cities.

Helmut Jahn, first in glass and then in masonry and metal, has consciously evoked this era (see pl. 38). Other recent additions to the skyline that hark back to this heyday of the American skyscraper include: the addition to the Prudential Building designed by Steven Wright of Loebl, Schlossman and Hackl (cat. no. 276); Cesar Pelli's 181 West Madison Street (pls. 65-67); the AT&T (fig. 19) and NBC buildings (pls. 71-72) by Adrian Smith of Skidmore, Owings and Merrill; and One North Franklin Street (pl. 73) by Joseph Gonzalez of Skidmore, Owings and Merrill. It is undoubtedly the image of set-back supremacy from the twenties that underlies Cesar Pelli's design for the proposed Miglin-Beitler Tower (fig. 20). Its 1,999-foot-high termination would top the record currently held by the Sears Tower (pl. 50) at 1,454 feet. Additional sites of varying scale, such as the Morton International Building (pls. 69-70) by Ralph Johnson of Perkins and Will and the shops Communicate and Oililly (pls. 98-100) by Florian-Wierzbowski at 900 North Michigan Avenue, demonstrate an interest in non-Miesian

modernism of the 1920s that has its roots in the Dutch De Stijl movement. Still others, such as a recent house by Daniel Wheeler (fig. 18), provide an almost historicist approach to 1950s modernism.

Thus, the 1980s were overtly historicist, whether classical or modern in their sources. But what seemed as a progressive reaction to the severity of corporate or Miesian modernism sometimes turned out to be a more conservative, even shallow, continuation of attitudes from previous eras.[34] The economic opportunism that characterized much of the consumer-oriented 1980s gave architects the chance to blanket the cityscape with their eclectic creations for corporate and individual clients alike.

The Nervous, Neo-Modern Nineties

Chicago architects have much to be nervous about these days. Newspapers and television programs are filled with stories about the recession, and Chicago's building community has been experiencing it firsthand since 1990. Offices are being reorganized, with giants like Skidmore, Owings and Merrill downsizing their operations. Vacancy rates for both downtown

and suburban office buildings rose from 13.8 percent in 1989 to 16.7 percent in 1990. With a 14 percent rate predicted through the mid-1990s and a number of empty urban and suburban blocks remaining to be developed, the picture for the immediate future does not look promising. This is especially so for approximately nineteen projected office buildings of the late 1980s that have yet to be begun.[35] Moreover, the hegemony that Chicago architects had in both the pre- and post-World War II eras has been slipping away dramatically.

In the 1950s and 1960s, buildings by Chicago architects could be found all over the country, from Milton Schwartz's Dunes Hotel in Las Vegas to C. F. Murphy Associates' FBI Building in Washington, D.C. Later decades witnessed the continued export of Chicago's buildings, and the work of Murphy/Jahn is particularly important in this regard, since the firm continues to be active throughout the recession-plagued early 1990s (fig. 21).

But, much to the chagrin of many local designers, out-of-town architects increasingly received jobs in Chicago during the 1980s, with many of the larger commercial buildings commissioned from Kohn Pedersen Fox of New York, or from such firms as Roche and Dinkeloo, or John Burgee with Philip Johnson. Chicago has also witnessed the completion of work by some foreign architects, such as the American Medical Association Building by Kenzo Tange from 1990; 77 West Wacker Drive by Ricardo Bofill in 1992; the Sporting Club by Kisho Kurokawa in 1990 (fig. 24); and the Manilow House by Max Gordon, completed by John Vinci in 1992 after Gordon's death (figs. 22, 23). The loss of local commissions to foreign architects continued with the Museum of Contemporary Art's controversial 1991 selection of Josef Paul Kleihues of Berlin to design its new building.

Although we see no new speculative office buildings being developed, other types of work continue, in housing, particularly low-cost housing (see pls. 131-32), in health care facilities, and in larger public works like the new International Terminal at O'Hare Airport (see Brodherson, fig. 23). New corporate buildings projected for the suburbs by Perkins and Will, Holabird and Root, and Skidmore, Owings and Merrill have something in common with their 1980s predecessors in that they are drawing upon the imagery of a previous era, but this time their source is 1950s modernism (pl. 74). While other projects may be viewed as incorporating aspects of deconstruction, as is now popular in a sort of "Chaos

Fig. 21 Helmut Jahn of Murphy/Jahn Architects, Messeturm, Frankfurt, 1984-91.

Fig. 22 Max Gordon, with John Vinci, Associate Architect, Exterior view of the Manilow House, 1900 North Howe Street, 1992.

Fig. 23 Living room of the Manilow House.

Theory" of design, these buildings in their reliance on earlier prototypes, are all more conservative than other well-published deconstructivist designs (see pls. 101-02). This conservatism is distinct from the more individualist exponents of realized, yet dematerialized, architectural forms in the 1980s and 1990s such as Coop Himmelblau, SITE, or Peter Eisenman. As with the architecture of Chicago's previous decades, which seems more eclectic and conservative than avant-garde, Chicago's architects in the nineties also draw on historic precedent. If

Fig. 24 Kisho Kurokawa, Architect and Associates; Fujikawa Johnson, Associate Architects, the Sporting Club, 211 North Stetson Avenue, 1990.

the ubiquitous pedimented and arched entrance represents the architecture of the postmodern eighties, it looks as if the angled and curvilinear form and flat-arched roof will somehow become the symbols of neo-modern buildings in the deconstructivist nineties.

The Burden of History

Why are Chicago's architects drawn to history and historic forms? In one way, Chicago is really no different from New York, Los Angeles, or any other American city in that regional eclecticism has been one of the hallmarks of American culture since the beginnings of our nation. But Chicago is different because it has a greater responsibility to architectural history than most other American cities. In this way, it is more like Glasgow, Vienna, and Hamburg—cities with strong and individualistic commercial design traditions from the early twentieth century. It is this burden of history that makes being an architect in Chicago difficult indeed. It is not, however, the burden of history suffered by architects and developers in the older cities of Philadelphia, Boston, and New York—cities with landmark buildings more than a century older than Chicago's nineteenth-century landmarks. If anything, Chicago's traditions encourage rather than discourage land development, thereby continually challenging architects to respond or react to the city's past.

Thus, a dualistic, contradictory nature has existed throughout the history of Chicago and its architecture. Architects may be intimidated by their predecessors (and who would not be intimidated by the likes of Louis Sullivan, John Wellborn Root, Daniel H. Burnham, Mies van der Rohe, and Frank Lloyd Wright?), yet they have always been encouraged to produce, and produce often, for their clients. Since the turn of the century, the image of Chicago has been that of a town on the cutting edge of architecture. But the record shows that it was always slightly less pioneering than that, and more a part of America than a unique case. Even the famed Chicago School of commercial building and the Prairie School of residential design were, in the end, more eclectic in taking their sources from Europe and Asia and less individualistic and pioneering than was first assumed.[36] Historians and writers have observed that this dualism of the contradictions between the forces of history and the avant-garde is an almost schizophrenic characteristic that runs throughout Chicago's cultural condition.[37] But, in many ways, this grand debate between conservative and radical encapsulates the history of American society as a whole.

Chicago's architects and their architecture over the past seventy years have characteristics, then, of pragmatism, eclecticism, and historicism, much as any architecture built in America. But Chicago's burden of architectural history helps to make its architectural environment stronger and, one would hope, better able to meet the design demands of American society in the next century.

Facing the Future: The Next Millennium

As Chicago approaches both the end of the century and the beginning of the next millennium, what fate awaits its architects? More important, what fate awaits its citizens at the hands of these architects? Since the end of World War II people have become increasingly vocal about their own personal economic and social situations. Electronic communications have increased tremendously over the past forty years and have been partly responsible for shaping our world today, playing a major role in pulling down the Iron Curtain and toppling the Berlin Wall in 1989. But, as the world has become smaller, living conditions and societal pressures have become much more intense and complex than they were several decades ago. The crisis of confidence in authority that has continued to develop from the 1970s and 1980s to the recession-plagued early 1990s has something of the pessimism of millennial fears of the future, in addition to the mistrust of the present. Today, people have become less trusting than they once were, questioning all our society's historic values and putting standards to sociocultural situations that may well be impossible to achieve.[38]

The essays that follow, as well as the exhibition that this book accompanies, offer no definitive answers for the future. Rather, they provide information on a variety of architectural and urban developments to show how dramatically our world has changed since the Great Depression and World War II. In so doing, the essays examine the reconfiguration of these tangible expressions of American culture, using Chicago as a case study for the postwar American city. Chicago is ideal for this examination because of its prewar strength and its dynamic postwar growth. And, after all, what better American city is there to study for its architectural growth than one whose architects have such a strong sense of the past?

NOTES

1. Before 1923 Chicago's zoning law stipulated that a building could be no more than 264 feet high, with a taller tower atop that was not to be occupied. After 1923 existing towers taller than that height could be occupied, and taller new towers could not exceed one-sixth of the entire building's volume and had to conform to set-back requirements. See Carol Herselle Krinsky, "Sister Cities: Architecture and Planning in the Twentieth Century," in John Zukowsky, David Van Zanten, and Carol Herselle Krinsky, *Chicago and New York: Architectural Interactions* (Chicago, 1984), pp. 58-64, for a discussion of New York (1916) and Chicago (1923) zoning laws in relation to buildings in each city; see also Robert Bruegmann, "When Worlds Collided: European and American Entries to the Chicago Tribune Competition of 1922," in John Zukowsky, ed., *Chicago Architecture, 1872-1922: Birth of a Metropolis* (Munich and Chicago, 1987), pp. 305-06, for zoning issues related to the competition. For the *Plan of Chicago*, see the Art Institute's exhibition catalogues, *The Plan of Chicago: 1909-1979* (Chicago, 1979) and Joan Draper, *Edward H. Bennett: Architect and City Planner, 1874-1954* (Chicago, 1982).

2. For the eclectic, yet French-oriented modernism of America in the 1920s, see Rosemarie Haag Bletter and Cervin Robinson, *Skyscraper Style: Art Deco New York* (New York, 1975), and Richard Guy Wilson, *The AIA Gold Medal* (New York, 1984), especially chaps. 3, 4, and 5.

3. For the international, particularly Central and Northern European, connections to Chicago's architecture, see essays in *Chicago Architecture* (note 1), especially pp. 18-21, 39-53, 91-134, 157-205. For the work of Abel Faidy, see *Villa Dionysos and Estate by Abel Faidy* (Chicago, 1980). For Faidy and Richard Yoshijiro Mine, see John Zukowsky, Pauline Saliga, and Rebecca Rubin, *Chicago Architects Design: A Century of Architectural Drawings from The Art Institute of Chicago* (Chicago, 1982), pp. 82-83, 100.

4. A slightly fuller description of the twenties work of McNally and Quinn is in John Zukowsky, "Chicago in the Twenties: More than Speakeasies and Skyscrapers," *Chicago Architectural Journal* 4 (1984), pp. 25-27.

5. Wilbert R. Hasbrouck, "The Early Years of the Chicago Architectural Club," *Chicago Architectural Journal* 1 (1981), pp. 7-14; John Zukowsky, "The Chicago Architectural Club, 1895-1940," *Chicago Architectural Journal* 2 (1982), pp. 170-74.

6. David Van Zanten, "The Nineteenth Century: The Projecting of Chicago as a Commercial City and the Rationalization of Design and Construction," in *Chicago and New York* (note 1), pp. 42-47.

7. *The WPA Guide to Illinois*, with a new introduction by Neil Harris and Michael Conzen (New York, 1983), p. 243.

8. For Mies's coming to America, see the somewhat controversial book by Elaine S. Hochman, *Architects of Fortune: Mies van der Rohe and the Third Reich* (New York, 1989). For Mies and the curriculum at Armour Institute of Technology (later Illinois Institute of Technology), see Rolf Achilles, Kevin Harrington, and Charlotte Myhrum, eds., *Mies van der Rohe: Architect as Educator* (Chicago, 1986). For Mies and his followers, see John Zukowsky, ed., *Mies Reconsidered: His Career, Legacy, and Disciples* (Chicago, 1986).

9. Peter Hahn et al., *50 Jahre New Bauhaus: Bauhausnachfolge in Chicago* (Berlin, 1987).

10. James C. Schneider, "The Battle of the Two Colonels," *Chicago History* 28, no. 3 (Fall 1989), pp. 4-33; Stan Cohen, *V for Victory: America's Home Front during World War II* (Missoula, Mont., 1991), pp. 4-5.

11. See, for example, Philip Johnson, "Poland's Choice between War and Bolshevism Is a Deal with Germany," *Social Justice* (Sept. 11, 1939), p. 4, and idem, "War and the Press," *Social Justice* (Nov. 6, 1939), p. 12. See also William L. Shirer, *Berlin Diary 1934-1941* (New York, 1941), p. 213. For Paul Schweikher's early support of Germany and America's entry into the European war, see Betty Blum, *Paul Schweikher: Oral History* (Chicago, 1984), pp. 72-73, a transcript of which is available in the Art Institute's Ryerson and Burnham Libraries.

12. *The Bridge Works: A History of Chicago Bridge and Iron Company* (Chicago, 1987), pp. 99-113, and *Our Prairie Shipyard: Historical Edition, 1942-1945* 4 (June 1945), both published by the Chicago Bridge and Iron Company, now CBI Industries.

13. Cohen (note 10), pp. 140-42; and Perry Duis and Scott La France, *We've Got a Job to Do: Chicagoans and World War II* (Chicago, 1993), pp. 70-71.

14. For Ernst Neufert's work in prefabrication during the Third Reich, see Tilman Harlander and Gerhard Fehl, eds., *Hitlers Sozialer Wohnungsbau, 1940-45* (Hamburg, 1986), p. 481, and Werner Durth, *Deutsche Architekten: Biographische Verflechtungen, 1900-1970*, 3rd ed. (Braunschweig and Wiesbaden, 1988), especially pp. 152-56, 210-12, 264-71.

15. *In Commemoration of the Opening to Traffic of the Bataan-Corregidor Memorial Bridge and North Approach Viaduct at State Street, Saturday, May 28, 1949 at 12:30 PM* (dedication booklet, Ryerson and Burnham Libraries).

16. Brian Horrigan, "The Home of Tomorrow, 1927-1945," in Joseph J. Corn, ed., *Imagining Tomorrow* (Cambridge, Mass., 1986), pp. 137-63; Krinsky (note 1), pp. 68-71; Helen Searing, "Case Study Houses in the Grand Modern Tradition," in Elizabeth A. T. Smith, ed., *Blueprints for Modern Living: History and Legacy of the Case Study Houses* (Cambridge, Mass., 1990), pp. 106, 130.

17. Stanley Tigerman, *The Postwar American Dream*, exhibition catalogue in the Art Institute's *Architecture in Context* series (Chicago, 1985).

18. Carol H. Krinsky, *Gordon Bunshaft of Skidmore, Owings and Merrill* (Cambridge, Mass., 1988).

19. Rita Caviglia, *Design for Better Living: The Architecture of Richard Marsh Bennett, 1937-1973* (Cambridge, Mass., 1984), pp. 28-31, 42-52. For Cold War politics and suburbia, see Elaine Tyler May, *Homeward Bound: American Families in the Cold War Era* (New York, 1988), chap. 7, esp. pp. 168-74.

20. Richard E. Schmidt and John Allan Hornsby, *The Modern Hospital* (Philadelphia and London, 1913); *Chicago Architects Design* (note 3), pp. 62-63.

21. *Architectural Forum* 97 (Aug. 1952), pp. 90-99.

22. Quoted in *Chicago* (Spring 1965), p. 49.

23. Ross Miller, "Chicago Architecture after Mies," *Critical Inquiry* 6, no. 2 (Winter 1979), pp. 271-89.

24. *Blueprints for Modern Living* (note 16), especially pp. 14-16, 83-84, 145-47.

25. Marian A. Despres, *Chicago Architecture Foundation: The First Twenty Years, 1966-1986* (Chicago, 1990), pp. 12-29.

26. The collage was prepared with a "Letter to Mies 1978," the text of which was published in Stanley Tigerman, *Versus: An American Architect's Alternatives*, with essays by Ross Miller and Dorothy Metzger Habel (New York, 1982), pp. 29-30.

27. See Oswald Grube, Peter Pran, and Franz Schulze, *100 Years of Architecture in Chicago* (Chicago, 1976); and Stuart Cohen, *Chicago Architects*, with an introduction by Stanley Tigerman (Chicago, 1976).

28. Maurizio Casari and Vincenzo Pavan, eds., *New Chicago Architecture: Beyond the International Style* (New York, 1981).

29. Stanley Tigerman, "Significant Events Leading to the Revival of the Chicago Architectural Club," *Chicago Architectural Journal* 2 (1982), pp. 175-77.

30. David Gebhard and Deborah Nevins, *200 Years of American Architectural Drawing* (New York, 1977); Ellis L. Armstrong, Michael C. Robinson, and Suellen M. Hoy, eds., *History of Public Works in the United States, 1776-1976* (Chicago, 1976).

31. The fight to save Adler and Sullivan's Chicago Stock Exchange Building and the building's demolition in 1971 served as the impetus behind the founding of the private, nonprofit organization Landmarks Preservation Council of Illinois; see Pauline Saliga, ed., *Fragments of Chicago's Past: The Collection of Architectural Fragments in The Art Institute of Chicago* (Chicago, 1990), pp. 64-65.

32. Ibid. See also Donovan Rypkema and Ian D. Spatz, "Rehab Takes a Fall: The 1986 Tax-Reform Law Severed the Link between Historic Buildings and Investment Dollars, and America's Committees Are the Losers," *Historic Preservation* 42, no. 2 (Sept./Oct. 1990), pp. 51-58.

33. For observations by Mark Alden Branch and Catherine Ingraham on the rampant eclecticism of the new public library, see *Progressive Architecture* (Feb. 1992), pp. 60-71. On eclecticism, which even throughout the nineteenth and early twentieth centuries was considered one of the national styles characteristic of American architecture, see Richard Guy Wilson, "American Architecture and the Search for a National Style in the 1870s," *Nineteenth Century* 3, no. 3 (Autumn 1977), pp. 74-80; and Walter C. Kidney, *The Architecture of Choice: Eclecticism in America, 1880-1930* (New York, 1974).

34. Intentional continuity with earlier eras is found in the famed postmodern classicist Michael Graves, who has said that his work on the 1982 Humana Building in Louisville strives to connect to the traditions of humanistic classicism that continued from the Renaissance through pre-Depression American skyscrapers and that was replaced after the war by a technically oriented modernism. See Christian Norberg-Schulz, "Michael Graves and the Language of Architecture," in Karen Vogel Nichols, Patrick J. Burke, and Caroline Hancock, eds., *Michael Graves: Buildings and Projects, 1982-1989* (New York, 1990), pp. 13-14; and Peter Arnell and Ted Bickford, eds., *A Tower for Louisville: The Humana Competition* (New York, 1982), pp. 89-96. For classical conservatism as the mainstream of Chicago's architecture in relation to similar values in American society, see John Zukowsky, "The Chicago School, Classicism, and Conservatism: Observations on Chicago's Architecture," in Stanley Tigerman, ed., *Chicago Architecture: The New Zeitgeist, In Search of Closure* (Lisbon, 1989), pp. 14-33. A very perceptive observation on the superficial nature of numerous postmodern classicist buildings of the late 1980s can be found in Paul Goldberger, "After Opulence, a New 'Lite' Architecture," *New York Times* (May 20, 1990), sec. 2, pp. 1, 38.

35. Of the numerous articles on the plight of development in Chicago during recent years, some better ones are M. W. Newman and Jerry C. Davis, "Cash Crunch Stalling New Skyscrapers," *Chicago Sun-Times* (July 9, 1990), pp. 1, 12-13; Steven R. Strahler, "Downtown Vacancy Rates Continue to Climb," *Crain's Chicago Business* (Feb. 4, 1991), pp. 24-25; idem, "Downtown Glut: When Will It End?," *Crain's Chicago Business* (Feb. 3, 1992), Real Estate Section, pp. 19-22; and Janet Neiman, "Block 37: It Isn't Just on State Street. Even Suburbs Have Fair Share of Big Craters," *Crain's Chicago Business* (Feb. 17, 1992), pp. 1, 34.

36. This is the premise of much of the revisionist writing about the Chicago School in the past decade, including many of the essays in *Chicago Architecture* (note 1).

37. Nelson Algren, *Chicago: City on the Make* (Chicago, 1951), and Ross Miller, *American Apocalypse: The Great Fire and the Myth of Chicago* (Chicago, 1990), are two books that explore the polarities of Chicago. See also M. W. Newman, "Contradictions Are the Key," *Portfolio* (April/May 1979), pp. 111-12, and Zukowsky (note 34), pp. 23-29.

38. See Robert Hughes, "The Fraying of America," *Time* 139 (Feb. 3, 1992), pp. 44-49.

"The Best Lighted City in the World":
The Construction of a Nocturnal Landscape in Chicago

Mark J. Bouman

Down State Street in October 1926, marching bands paraded and floats rolled through two huge decorative arches, accompanied by a throng of 250,000 people reveling in the "Splendors that Out Babylon Ancient Babylon." Was this event a rehearsal for Lindbergh or the celebration of a pennant for the Cubs? No, those events would be celebrated *in* this place; but this ceremony was a celebration *of* this place. For in the White House, President Coolidge tapped a golden telegraph key and 140 new street lamps in Chicago flickered and grew bright—brighter, it is claimed, than on any other street in the world.[1]

It is difficult to imagine such a scene being played on the day that relatively clean water first began to flow into the city from the intake cribs out in Lake Michigan. Of all the elements of any city's infrastructure, exterior lighting most conspicuously captures the public's attention. As State Street businessmen erected the lights that they hoped would ensure trade, they also found a way to symbolize their city's emphatic grip on its own future, its clear command of the economic life of its hinterland, and its volition to stop at nothing to control nature.[2]

Chicago, like all modern cities, has obliterated darkness. But the insistent zeal to be "the best lighted city in the world"—long a favorite incantation of Chicago's City Beautiful civic movement—distinguishes the city from its urban competitors and raises questions not only about the quality of its light, but about the tenebrous conditions to be left behind. Darkness has long had many connotations: among them, sleep and death, crime, disorientation, accident, economic stagnation, and social disparity. Indeed, at the very same time as the State Street celebration, University of Chicago sociologist Harvey Zorbaugh was exploring the brightly lighted Gold Coast community and its less fortunate near neighbors who lived in the "shadow of the skyscrapers." Zorbaugh's *The Gold Coast and the Slum* of 1929 captured the essence of a metropolis so socially and economically bifurcated that nineteenth-century metaphors of social "light and darkness" still carried power, even

though gas and electric lighting were found all over town.[3]

As much as one might take the lighting of a metropolis for granted, it is not as natural as it may seem. As city environments become ever more "distant from nature," a richly textured path emerges from local aspirations, social arrangements, and economic necessities. Eventually, these paths on the landscape come to seem like "second nature," as William Cronon put it—as utterly natural as "first nature" itself.[4] So, while Chicago's path toward a luminous night is very similar to other cities, there is, nonetheless, a discernible "Chicago style" to the night.

What Chicago shares with most Western industrial cities is a lighting style that emerges from three types of demand: security, urbanity, and utility.[5] Security may be understood from Ralph Waldo Emerson's phrase that, as light "is the best nocturnal police, so the universe protects itself by pitiless publicity." Crime and public order are frequently given as reasons to light the streets, and the order represented in the lighted landscape is one imposed by a central authority on an often eagerly accepting public. Social hierarchy is also implied in much "urbane" lighting; its highly aestheticized forms result from a desire to provide attractive public spaces for social intercourse, or to convey messages about the highest aspirations of the metropolis. The tallest or most central buildings are often singled out for special lighting attention (fig. 1). Utility follows logically from the increased pace of nocturnal activity in an industrialized society. The modern model of lighting provision is, of course, for large central power plants to generate the gas and electricity; for major industrial firms to manufacture the fixtures; and for city governments to contract for or to manage directly the operation of the system, to provide the locations for the fixtures, to settle on their design, and to raise the funds necessary for their emplacement.

As a center of electrical manufacturing, as a source of innovation in power supply, as a fount of inspiration in urban design, as a city with a loud and long tradition of civic boosterism, and

Fig. 1   Night view of Palmolive Building, Water Tower, and North Michigan Avenue, 1931.

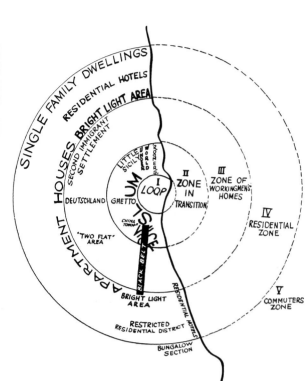

as a distinctly politicized social environment, Chicago has witnessed a gradually shifting set of priorities relative to the three sources of demand. Where at one time being the "best lighted city" meant drawing heavily on the city's distinguished, urbane local planning tradition, by the end of World War II it had shifted to imply maximum "utility" for automobile traffic with a strong element of "security" to inhibit crime. In most cases, the forces that compose the "urban growth machine" worked to foster the changes.[6]

Undergirding this shift in focus have been changes in the spatio-temporal structure of the metropolis. Though Chicago has long been seen in a regional context, the daily flows and rhythms are less centered on the core than they once were.[7] The skeins of commuter rail, streetcar, and rapid transit lines were once so tightly knotted in the Loop that prior to World War II, Chicago epitomized the monocentric American metropolis (see fig. 2). Newly arriving immigrants moved outward in concentric waves and along transportation lines from the post-fire business center (see fig. 3). The downtown population was, of course, much lower by night than by day.[8] Radial streetcar lines slashing through those lines that replicated the regularity of the Chicago grid created highly accessible outlying locations. Commercial districts blossomed here, with movie theaters, stores, and specially lighted streets that became the "bright lights" areas of fig. 3 (see figs. 4, 5; pl. 94).[9] At Rapp and Rapp's Tivoli Theater (1921), for example, "the entrance [gave] an alluring view of the lofty colonnade and beautiful light fixtures of the

grand lobby through a large arched window and being brilliantly lighted contrast[ed] splendidly with the severe lined commercial buildings in the neighborhood."[10] Throughout the city, the fundamental difference between the business district and residential areas was reflected in functionally distinct lighting styles, a pattern

Fig. 2   View of State Street, looking north from Madison Street, c. 1926.

Fig. 3   Map showing the zonal social geography of the city; from Ernest W. Burgess, "The Growth of the City: An Introduction to a Research Project," in Robert E. Park et al., eds., The City (Chicago, 1925), p. 55.

Fig. 4   Alexander L. Levy and William J. Klein, Granada Theater, 6427 North Sheridan Road, 1926.

*Fig. 5   Intersection of
Cicero Avenue,
Milwaukee Avenue, and
Irving Park Road,
c. 1939.*

still easily viewed from above the city at night. After World War II, the metropolis took on more of a polycentric form, less tied to the city's original radial transportation corridors. Though highway upgrading had gone on since the 1920s, expressway construction (with related developments in highway lighting techniques) was the dominant public works activity in the 1950s and 1960s. As the Chicago region's population and wealth grew, more people owned and drove cars. Yet many commuter trips remained centered on the metropolitan core. Railroad commutation remained at high levels, though streetcars were converted to bus lines after 1954. But in the 1960s and 1970s the core lost its position of absolute dominance. Widely scattered outlying office and industrial centers now generate as many trips as the Central Business District. The Loop itself, having lost much of its major shopping function to suburban shopping centers, was abandoned by most of its theaters and movie houses. Many more shopping trips are now dependent upon the automobile, with landscapes featuring in-front parking and attention-grabbing signage (see pls. 95-96).[11]

Recent events, however, indicate a reversal of these fortunes: the core of the city has been reinvigorated by new office, hotel, and residential construction. The residential population of the Loop has grown substantially since the 1980s, generating a significant nighttime population for the first time in decades.[12] And all the salesmanship that the "growth machine" can muster has been used to maintain the center as a recreational and tourist destination.

The Production of Light

Regardless of the use or display of light at night, it has been characteristic of modern lighting supply since the first gas lighting systems in early nineteenth-century London to separate the consumption of light from the point of production.[13] So to look at the lighted landscape itself is to see only one part of a whole system, and Chicago was one of the first places where this basic insight was made. Both the landscape of gas production and consumption harked back to the nineteenth century, to what Lewis Mumford called the paleotechnic period of industry. Chicago's gas industry, in existence since 1850, relied heavily on coal; retorts, coke ovens, and huge gasometers were prominent features not only of the landscape, but of the city's smellscape.[14] Gas lamps flickered from cast-iron poles not far above the heads of pedestrians.

By the 1920s, gaslight had already acquired the patina of quaintness and was generally considered to be obsolete. Even the gas industry's own survey of its achievements in 1925 did not touch on lighting. Chicago committed itself to a program of replacing gas street lights with electric ones, but the Depression and World War II held up the process for many years. In 1954, the last eighteen gas lamps in the city were removed.[15] But gas lighting lingered in suburban pockets. When, in the late 1970s, Congress prepared to ban outdoor gas lights in the wake of rising energy costs, communities like Riverside, with gas lights of "traditional... cultural or architectural style," were exempted. In any case, with their low crime rates such communities did not have high demand for the crime-fighting potential of electric lights and did not care to be associated with anything like the bright lights image of Chicago.

The comment by Riverside's village manager that the gas lamps gave the town "that rustic, bucolic, country-like atmosphere" not only reasserts the old rural ideal operative in suburbia, but it is the perfect argument by negation for the urbanity of electric lighting.[16]

But Chicago has had many positive arguments as well. As a center of innovation in electrical production and distribution techniques and in the manufacturing of electrical equipment, Chicago has as much claim as Menlo Park, New Jersey, or Schenectedy, New York, to the title of "Electric City." A large local community of talent included such electrical industry luminaries as Elisha Gray, Elmer Sperry, Augustus Curtis, and, not least of all, Samuel Insull, who con-

structed the first and most famous American regional utility.[17]

In order to compete with gas lighting, Insull found that the cheapest way to produce electricity was to take advantage of economies of scale. Massive central generating stations were constructed in Chicago to house the larger steam turbines that replaced reciprocating steam engines; the great prototype was the D. H. Burnham-designed Fisk Street Station in 1903. To make the most efficient use of such a large capital investment, the power plants had to run as close to capacity as possible. But daily demand for electricity varied, with nocturnal valleys and strong industrially based midday peaks. In order to raise the load factor of his generating facilities (i.e., the average proportion of capacity actually used), Insull needed smoother daily demand curves. A more diverse demand could be realized by extending service to the broadest possible area through long-distance high-voltage transmission lines and a growing stable of affiliated power companies. Nocturnal demand could also be raised through increased consumption of domestic electrical appliances, the lighting of buildings, and contracts for street lighting (although Chicago's street lighting demands were serviced by the Metropolitan Sanitary District's hydro-electricity into the 1950s). In short, demand had to be created for the supplier's benefit and the use of advertising to create this demand has always played an exceptionally important role for local utilities.[18]

Chicago's nocturnal landscape thus comes to rest on an integrated regional network of large-scale power plants, transmission lines (often running on wide rights-of-way), and substations. The high stacks and huge proportions of Commonwealth Edison's coal-fired plants such as Fisk Street, Quarry Street, Northwest, Crawford Avenue, and State Line clearly show the building's function, though facades of red brick, terracotta inlays, arched windows, and some small details such as keystones and quoins are occasionally added for "architectural dignity" (see figs. 6-7). Easily the most impressive of the power stations was Graham, Anderson, Probst and White's State Line Generating Company (1921-29; fig. 8), conceived as a "citadel of electricity."[19] The utility has tried to harmonize its substations with their surroundings, as in the classically detailed Rush Street Substation (Holabird and Roche, 1923-24; now demolished); the modern Dearborn Street Substation (Holabird and Root, 1929-31; see Miller, "City Hall," fig. 2), which now stands in lonely contempla-

6

7

Figs. 6, 7 Graham,
Anderson, Probst and
White, Commonwealth
Edison Co., Crawford
Avenue Generating
Station, 1924-25; from
The Architectural Work
of Graham, Anderson,
Probst and White
(London, 1933).

Fig. 9 Tigerman,
Fugman and McCurry,
Commonwealth Edison
Substation, 51 West
Ontario Street, 1986-89.

tion of the Daley Center; and the Ontario Street Substation (Holabird and Roche, 1923-24; now demolished).[20] Tigerman, Fugman and McCurry's Hard Rock Cafe was designed to play off the Neo-Georgian design of the neighboring Ontario Street Substation. When the utility decided to replace the substation, it selected Tigerman's firm to design a new building in the same vocabulary as the Hard Rock Cafe, and, therefore, of the older substation (see fig. 9).

The Urbanely Lighted Growth Machine

Chicago's urbane nocturnal landscape was based not only on the pioneering work of Samuel Insull, but also on that of other civic leaders who insisted on the city's leadership in commerce and culture. Light played a major role at both of Chicago's World's Fairs; it figured as a key image in the local physical planning tradition; it was used as a tool to establish and maintain the dominance of the retail core; and it figured heavily as an aesthetic and advertising tool in the city's burgeoning skyline. The result was a highly localized urbane landscape: a Central Business District aglow with White Ways, lighted skyscrapers, monumental bridges and plazas; light beribboned boulevards linking the city center to elegant public parks; and scattered outposts of

Fig. 8 Graham,
Anderson, Probst and
White, Chicago District
Electric Generating Co.,
State Line Generating
Station, Hammond,
Indiana, 1921-29; from
The Architectural Work
of Graham, Anderson,
Probst and White
(London, 1933).

urbanity in the outlying "bright lights" districts. World's Fairs had been closely associated with electricity at least since the display of the Corliss Engine at the 1876 Centennial Exhibition in Philadelphia. A rising tide of illumination peaked at the 1893 World's Columbian Exposition, where the formal spaces and grandiose buildings of the "White City" used more lamps than any city in the country then had.[21]

The "official face" of the night, as eventually codified in the 1909 Plan of Chicago, was derived from this classical, formalist, intensely illuminated tradition. The ideal Beaux-Arts nocturne is depicted in several of Jules Guérin's renderings in the Plan. Plate 127, for example, entitled "Bird's-Eye View at Night of Grant Park, the Facade of the City, the Proposed Harbor, and the Lagoons of the Proposed Park on the South Side," depicts a skyline twinkling grandly, and a harbor full of boats enjoying a nocturnal sail (fig. 10). The harbor design includes lighted obelisks, beacons, or lighthouses at the corners (on the site of the Adler Planetarium). Another Guérin drawing, "View Looking West, of the Proposed Civic Center Plaza and Buildings" (plate 132), shows how City Beautiful lamp standards envelop and define the formal space at night, with ribbons of light extending into the darkening countryside.

Fig. 10   Jules Guérin, Bird's-Eye View of Grant Park at Night; from Daniel H. Burnham and Edward H. Bennett, Plan of Chicago (Chicago, 1909), pl. 127.

The *Plan of Chicago* therefore formalized one of the great conventions of American urban form: that the American downtown is as much a "central illuminating district" as a Central Business District. Hierarchy is written in lumens as well as in land values, and at the very apex of both is the Great White Way.[22] New York's Broadway, the American prototype, had its Chicago counterpart in the theater district centered on Randolph Street, but Chicago's White Way was really State Street, its pulsating retail heart. State Street had been the site of some of the earliest uses of arc lights and the Edison incandescent system in Chicago in the 1880s. By the turn of the century, according to Harold Platt, "the bright lights shining from the palaces of consumption along State Street would have been difficult to miss."[23]

In 1926, with lighting provided by the State Street Lighting Association to provide "facilities for evening promenade," State Street was to become, as we have seen, the "World's Greatest White Way." The light poles themselves, designed by Graham, Anderson, Probst and White, were formally approved by the Chicago Plan Commission. Each block had four poles on a side directly opposite each other. Atop the poles were two 2,100-watt, 9,000-candle-power (c.p.) lamps (fig. 11). At the time, the brightest street lights

anywhere else in the city had 1,000 c.p.[24] As if to confirm the notion voiced by a lighting advocate fourteen years earlier that "the number of persons passing a point in the evening is in direct proportion to the illumination at that point," within a week of the announcement of the new lighting scheme came the results of a survey finding State and Madison to be Chicago's busiest corner.[25]

Thirty-two years later, however, State Street was in trouble. Declining sales volume at the

Fig. 11   View of State Street at Monroe Street, 1955, showing street lights installed in 1926.

Fig. 12 View of State Street, looking north from Van Buren Street, 1959, showing street lights installed in 1958.

Fig. 13 View of State Street at night, looking south from Lake Street, 1958, showing new street lights.

major department stores and at other retail outlets reflected the growing competition from suburban shopping malls and the suburbanization of the labor force (see essays by Bruegmann and Harris). In 1958, a year in which office construction began to boom, the State Street merchants again made the decision to try to lure more customers with the "world's brightest lights."[26]

In this case, the designer, Robert Burton, set out in true modernist fashion "to design a standard of pure and artistic form, free from ornateness, yet a creation of simplicity and lasting beauty." Each pole had three luminaires that splayed obliquely out of the top of the pole thirty-four to thirty-six feet up; at twenty-four feet, another luminaire branched out over and parallel to the sidewalk (see fig. 12). Each luminaire contained six fluorescent tubes, with special color properties. According to the special newspaper published for the occasion, "when the General Electric wizards were busy dreaming up these newfangled lights for State Street one of their priority targets was to eliminate the annoying quirk of most fluorescent street lights that tended to change women's rosy complexions to a ghastly green or pasty yellow ... these new lights actually tend to flatter complexions!"[27] Once again, bands played and speeches were made, one hundred actors performed the pageant "Light Through the Ages," and President Eisenhower flipped the switch (see fig. 13).

Were these lights successful in drawing trade back to State Street? Probably not: both the number of shoppers and retail volume continued to decline. In the late 1960s, those generators of night traffic—restaurants and entertainment places—continued to disappear. So State Street was remade again in the 1970s. The twenty-year-old lighting fixtures gave way to a new urban design scheme: this time, the lighting plan fea-

tured the now-familiar high-pressure sodium lamps on forty-foot-high standards, two to a block front. Proposed low-level accent lighting on twelve-foot-high poles was never built. Today, while several Graham, Anderson, Probst and White fixtures have been reinstalled north of the historic White Way between Wacker Drive and Lake Street and in certain other parts of the Loop in and around LaSalle Street, plans are afoot for yet another redesign for State Street.[28]

Outlying commercial districts followed the State Street example, with local business associations purchasing smaller versions of the White Way or ornamental lighting systems (see fig. 14). Clark Street in the Near North area, one of the first to do so, was known as the "little white way."[29] Paralleling the efforts of State Street merchants in an era of decline, the South Chicago Chamber of Commerce also improved its lighting in the 1970s, earning the claim from the city's commissioner of streets and sanitation that South Chicago was "the best lit business community in the country." Other districts chose deliberately antiquarian looks. Old Town, for example, strove for an "Old Chicago" look, and so installed 125 globe lamps somewhat redolent of the City Beautiful White Way lighting.[30]

The *Plan of Chicago* yielded other corridors of urbanity: wide boulevards edged by trees and buildings of uniform cornice line. By night, these corridors were to be accentuated by numerous globe-topped white lights; the poles, such as those designed by Daniel Burnham for the South Park Commissioners, were to be exercises in street furniture classicism (see fig. 15). The boulevards were clearly intended for evening promenade, as the Guérin drawings show, and, as such, they represent extensions of the central illuminating district into the region beyond. But the boulevards were also intended for vehicular traffic, and it is the genius of the Michigan Avenue Bridge and Wacker Drive that they somehow combine both functions. Wacker Drive itself is a brilliant example of Beaux-Arts city planning (see essay by Sennott), and its ornamental lighting contributes in no small measure (see Sennott, fig. 1). Given how they function, however, most of the bridges over the Chicago River were designed without lighting because of the jarring effects of traffic. Ornamental lamp posts were removed from the Jackson (1916) and Michigan Avenue (1918-20) bridges because vibration destroyed the incandescent fixtures.[31]

Of course, the Chicago Plan envisioned other places for pedestrian promenade, especially Grant Park, with its grand entrance and lighting

fixtures by Edward Bennett. The grand centerpiece is Buckingham Fountain (Bennett, Parsons, and Frost; 1927). Now operated by computer, the fountain's changing array of colored lights was originally controlled by Curtis Lighting's "Lumitone" system. It used a paper roll much like a player piano to produce an ever-changing pattern of forty-five-million-c.p. lights.[32]

What the Plan and its executors did for grandiose horizontal spaces, the skyscraper tower did for the vertical. Few more visually exciting changes have swept across the landscape of the American city than the building of the skyline, especially as punctuated by high-rise towers. From the start, tower construction went hand in hand with illumination; from the start, the romantic landscape thus created became richly symbolic, evocative of America's progressiveness, modernity, and technical precocity, as well as simply being interesting new additions to the scene.[33] They almost invariably drew comment from or directed to visitors, as in this from a 1930s guidebook:

Fortunate is the visitor whose first view of Chicago is from the deck of a steamer. Approaching the city by water, one obtains a breathtaking idea of Chicago's greatness from its far-famed skyline. Michigan Avenue and Grant Park are seen against a backdrop of lofty towers, symbols of Chicago's energy and achievement. To the North and South stretch mile after mile of shining boulevards and parks. At night, the twinkling lights, the great Lindbergh beacon, the harbor signals, and the great glow of the gigantic city against the sky form a picture of unequalled beauty.[34]

What were the roots of this tradition? After the Columbian Exposition, illuminating engineers

Fig. 14   Dubin and Dubin, Hollands Jewelry, 6335 South Halsted Street, 1935.

Fig. 15 View of Michigan Avenue, looking north from Randolph Street, c. 1933.

Fig. 16 Graham, Anderson, Probst and White, Perspective rendering of the entrance to the Field Building (now LaSalle National Bank Building), 135 South LaSalle Street, delineated by Henry Harringer, c. 1930-31 (cat. no. 202).

began to concentrate more on the use of light for artistic effect than on maximum output. Lighting designer Luther Stieringer pioneered a method he called the "luminous sketch," in which only the outline of the structure was lighted. Some early examples include the Eiffel Tower (1900), the Electricity Tower at the Pan-American Exposition in Buffalo (1901), and the Singer Building in New York City (1908). The lighting of the diamond-shaped top of the Associates Center (A. Epstein and Sons; 150 North Michigan Avenue; 1983-84) is descended from this approach.[35]

Floodlighting was pioneered by Walter D'Arcy Ryan at the 1915 Panama Pacific Exhibition. His technique was to shine lights on the buildings from a distance, to use reds in corners and, perhaps, green on St. Patrick's Day. Ryan's work would not have been possible without a device that could direct the light's rays on to the subject instead of diffusing it uselessly into the night sky. Chicago happened to be the home of the man known as the "archenemy of glare" and the "pioneer of indirect illumination," as Curtis Lighting (formerly the National X-Ray Reflector company) referred to its founder, Augustus Curtis. The company was "devoted to the de-

sign, manufacture, and installation of engineered lighting equipment which provides the correct amount of illumination for proper architectural and lighting effect." Two basic methods were employed: one set the projectors far from the building and attempted to project as much white light as possible upon the building slab; and the other placed the projectors directly on the building, accentuating through careful placement, and, perhaps, color, the building's silhouette, its ornamentation, setbacks, and accents.[36]

Publicists for Curtis Lighting described floodlighting as "one of the most emphatic advertising mediums. It establishes the location of a structure much more convincingly than the street designation."[37] Building lighting did indeed play an increasingly important advertising role in the great wave of skyscraper construction that followed on the end of World War I. In 1922, the *Chicago Central Business and Office Building Directory* made only one reference to exterior lighting: the New World Building (109 North Dearborn Street; 1914) was a structure "worthy of Dearborn: The Best Lighted Street in Chicago." But in 1932, three buildings (Carbide and Carbon, Chicago Temple, and

Palmolive) called attention to their lighting schemes, and three others (Board of Trade, One North LaSalle Street, and the Buckingham at 59-67 East Van Buren Street) were depicted in nocturnal photographs or artistic renderings; by 1942, the number had risen to four.[38] As Chicago architects experimented with new forms and new uses of light, the perspective renderings for publicity materials by the likes of Gilbert Hall of Holabird and Root, Henry Harringer, and Hugh Ferriss more frequently took a nocturnal turn. Harringer's charcoal and pencil drawing of the Field Building, for example, designed by Graham, Anderson, Probst and White, shows the building entry by night, illuminated by searchlights and automobile headlights, crowds thronging the sidewalks and streets (fig. 16).[39]

The earliest major nocturnal landmark in Chicago was the Wrigley Building (Graham, Anderson, Probst and White; 1919-24), whose location, brilliant floodlighting, and white-enameled terra-cotta cladding made the building an instant favorite.[40] The combination of light and materials had a precedent in New York's Woolworth Building (Cass Gilbert; 1911-13), the first commercial building to be evenly flood-lighted, with lights made by National X-Ray Reflector. No doubt the other most recognizable landmark in the interwar years was the two-billion-c.p., 150-foot-high beacon atop the Palmolive Building (Holabird and Root; 1927-29; fig. 1).

The building itself cut a prominent figure, towering as it did at the north end of Michigan Avenue. The beacon, originally named for Charles Lindbergh and donated by Elmer Sperry, was renamed the Palmolive Beacon in 1931 when Lindbergh did not publicly accept the honor.[41]

The beacon was an important navigational tool for many years. Some airline passengers claimed to be able to read newspapers by it twenty-seven miles away. Beneath it an 11-million-c.p. lamp pointed the way to the Chicago Municipal Airport. One ironic commentator likened the "great light, sweeping calmly and majestically in its circle" to "an angel guarding the city, which so needs true guidance from the skies." But that light, rotating twice a minute, became an annoyance when high-rise apartments, especially at the John Hancock Center, were built to its level in the 1960s. The beacon was partially shielded from its neighbors in 1968 and permanently retired in 1981; a glowing light replaced it in 1990.[42]

Another well-known aviation beacon in the 1930s sat atop Holabird and Root's LaSalle-Wacker Building (221 North LaSalle Street; 1929-30). As in the case of the Palmolive Building, LaSalle-Wacker's location, at the intersection of two important axes from the Chicago Plan, drew attention to an important node in the grid of the downtown area. The building was also flood-

Fig. 17 Graham,
Anderson, Probst and
White, Merchandise
Mart, 1931.

Fig. 18 Night view of
the Electrical Building,
Century of Progress
Exposition, 1933-34.

lighted so that the recessed bays were illuminated, creating a vertical rhythm of light and
dark at the top of the structure.[43]

Beacons were not the only method of calling
attention to the top of a building. Four searchlights pointed in the cardinal directions from the
beehive atop the Straus Building (today replaced
by a blue light).[44] The Trustee System Service
Building at 201 North Wells (Thielbar and
Fugard; 1929-30; see pl. 42) was topped by a zig-
gurat and lantern.[45] The Jewelers Building by
Giaver and Dinkelberg with Thielbar and Fugard
(1926; 35 East Wacker Drive) wore a distinctive
crown in the Stieringer manner, while Holabird
and Root's 333 North Michigan Building of 1928
wore a lighted crown rather more like the 1960s
John Hancock Center.[46]

The Union Carbide company sought a "distinctive and perpetual advertisement" for the occu-
pants of its new regional headquarters building
at 230 North Michigan Avenue. Advertisements
for the Carbide and Carbon Building (Burnham
Brothers; 1929; see Willis, fig. 14) called attention to its illuminated gold-leaf tower and cam-
panile, and the building was called a "landmark
on the Chicago skyline, an imposing symbol of
power and success."[47]

The even floodlighting method was wonder-
fully suited to skyscrapers built after zoning
changes encouraged the use of telescoping
forms. As architects began to abandon elabo-

rate ornamentation in the late 1920s, the building mass itself and floodlights mounted on the
setbacks provided the architectural interest.
For example, while the Palmolive Building's
elongated fenestration gave a daytime impression of elegant verticality, by night the floodlighting of each of the setbacks emphasized
the horizontality of the breaks between them
(see fig. 1).[48]

Few buildings could claim as much surface
area to be lighted as the Merchandise Mart
(Graham, Anderson, Probst and White; 1927-31;
fig. 17; see essay by Rau). Massive facades were
relieved by a composition of vertically banded
windows set between cornice lines near the base
and two slight setbacks near the top. Here the
lighting took advantage of cornice lines near the
top of the eighteen-story structure, the turrets at
the corners, and the massive central tower that
rises seven floors higher than the rest of the building. The vertical window bands were lighted
from lamps placed above the fourth-floor cornice. The setbacks were brilliantly illuminated.
The tops of the corner turrets and the top three
floors of the tower and its pyramidal tower were
also lighted. The effect was surprisingly graceful
for so large a structure, with the rhythm of the
top of the building emphasized at night, rather
than the massive limestone walls. Guidebooks
made certain to point out the building to visitors
by night. A guide for visitors to the Century of

Figs. 19, 20 Night views of the Electrical Building and the Hall of Science, Century of Progress Exposition, 1933-34.

Progress Exposition of 1933-34 found the Mart's nocturnal aspect to be "thrillingly beautiful." The authors of the *WPA Guide* were no less enthusiastic: "concealed lighting of the massive symmetrical structure form[ed] a beautiful composition of light and shadow in the Chicago night scene."[49]

By the time of the Century of Progress Exposition, then, illuminating engineering was in full maturity and prepared to use light to "amaze and delight even the most blasé city dwellers," as Hubert Burnham put it.[50] Ironically, Walter D'Arcy Ryan, the fair's director of illumination, succeeded in that goal because he "leaned more toward the utilitarian than the aesthetic" and sought to maximize foot candles per dollar because of the fair's tight finances. In fact, the largest monument to illumination, Ralph Walker's Tower of Water and Light, would not be built for monetary reasons (see pl. 133). Ryan would employ virtually all the techniques already in use in the downtown streets and skyline (see figs. 18-20). He would bring the judicious use of neon to the public's attention, and he would play off the highly sculptured architectural forms that were painted in Joseph Urban's vivid palette. Windowless walls were floodlighted in white and outlined in neon; fountains were bathed in changing beams of light; searchlights beamed brightly into the night. Street lights were a mixture of lanterns, mercury-neon pylons, opal glass pylons, tubular incandescent standards, and the unique indirect "mushroom lights." In 1934, cables of the Sky Ride across the lagoon were festooned with small incandescent lamps in the Stieringer manner. From the rocket cars of the Sky Ride one could look down over the whole fairground, and back across Monroe Harbor and Grant Park to the Loop, which from a distance truly became an illuminated landscape.[51]

Compositions of Chicago's night scene were so common by mid-century that they threatened to become cliché.[52] But spectacular illuminations soon threatened to become extinct. Older fixtures were often not repaired after breakage, and maintenance was frequently deferred. Bands of lighted office windows shining through glass curtain walls sufficed for nocturnal display in most of the modernist buildings (see fig. 21), with the major exception of the John Hancock "crown."[53] And rising energy prices in the 1970s seemed about to end all such skyline display forever.

Fig. 21 Shaw, Metz and Associates, Florsheim Shoe Company, Canal, Adams, Clinton streets, 1947-49.

Daley Night: Security and Utility in the Best Lighted City

The State Street celebrations showed a city willing to use light to boost its main shopping street and to promote a bold image of itself to the world at large. But according to city engineers in 1925, the continual demand for better street lighting arose "on account of the automobile problem and public safety protection and the rapid continuous growth of the city." Exactly what was needed was spelled out: "At least twenty more square miles of residential street lighting; the adequate lighting of all street car line streets; the adequate lighting of the downtown loop; the rehabilitation of the underground facilities in many parts of the city; the rehabilitation of much of the steel pole equipment of the city; the adequate lighting of the through streets and reinforcement of lighting in many sections of the city."[54]

Since 1910, the city had bought its electrical power for street lighting from the Sanitary District of Chicago, which produced hydroelectricity at its dam in Lockport.[55] By 1925, 89 percent of the city's 70,873 lamps were electric; the rest were gas or gasoline. The two most commonly used electric lamps were tungsten incandescents: 600 c.p. for commercial districts and 100 c.p. for residential areas. In 1924, the city began a program of adding 1,000-c.p. lamps to widened thoroughfares and upgrading the residential lights to 250 c.p.[56] The 250-c.p. lamps installed between 1924 and 1931 were mounted on posts fourteen feet high, three feet from the curb on alternate sides of the street. The pillar form cast light on street and on sidewalk—and also into the sky.[57]

By the end of World War II, however, the system was in major need of repair, in spite of Mayor Edward Kelly's rather self-congratulatory report in 1947 that "practically the entire area of Burnham and Grant Parks has been rebuilt since 1934, embellished, lighted, improved and made one of the finest lakefront parks in the world."[58] The mayor's report did not say that most of the work took place under the aegis of the Chicago Park District, using federal New Deal funds.[59] Nor did it admit that the 1920s vintage electric lighting was inadequate to modern needs, and that newer sections of town were still unlighted, while older sections showed the effects of a decline in maintenance. All this was a major loss of civic face. On several occasions the *Chicago*

Tribune even reported that Chicago was "one of the poorest lighted major cities in the United States."[60]

Thus began a campaign to upgrade the system that seemed to have no end. From the outset of the rebuilding program, the city's priorities were clearly articulated: to enhance lighting for vehicular traffic and to use lighting to reduce crime. City officials were fond of quoting traffic safety statistics, emphasizing function over aesthetics, and they asserted that "modern street lighting is designed to provide convenience to the public, to safeguard motorists and pedestrians from accidents and molestation at night."[61]

Between 1944 and 1952, $13 million was spent to replace the older lamps.[62] The new lamps were now twenty feet high and were attached to an arm that projected ten feet beyond the curb line in an arc that reminded everyone of a "cobra head." Reflectors ensured that the light was directed on to the street itself, so posts needed to be placed on only one side of the street. And all this lifted lighting far beyond the sphere of the pedestrian sidewalk (see fig. 22).[63]

By 1954, the gas lamps were gone and the electrical program had intensified. In some places their passing was wistfully noted, in others, more bitterly. In a period of rapid technological progress in lighting, the continued existence of gas lighting stirred the ashes of nostalgia for the old landscape.[64] On North Dearborn Street in the Gold Coast, for example, one gentleman recalled that

the gas lamps are part of the atmosphere of our neighborhood. Perhaps they may not be so bright as the electric light concerning which we have been learning so much of late. But they are mellower and, perhaps because we have been used to them for so long, they seem friendlier. They have a warmth about them — particularly as they guide the traveler home on a snowy night in winter — that is peculiarly their own. They make this neighborhood something different from the rest of Chicago — something peculiarly our own.[65]

By the time the fifteen-year upgrade program was over in 1959, Richard J. Daley had been mayor for four years. All lamps had been replaced with mercury vapor, and some city officials were saying that the new system would last the city satisfactorily for at least fifty years.[66] But new rounds of street lighting upgrades were to commence as soon as the old were finished. Again, each new program was sold to the public on the basis of traffic safety, crime reduction, and the appeal to being the "best lighted city in the United States." Daley and street lights became entwined in the popular imagi-

nation, as in this resonant passage from Mike Royko's *Boss*:

Across Halsted Street, then a turn down Lowe Avenue, into the glow of the brightest street lights of any city in the country. The streets were so dark before, a person couldn't see who was there. Now all the streets have lights so bright that some people have to lower their shades at night. He turned on all those lights, he built them.[67]

Under Daley, the city also assumed responsibility in 1959 for lighting the 200 miles of Chicago Park District boulevards, 40 percent of which had already received mercury-vapor lamps by that time.[68] The Park District itself got into the act with a "security lighting program" for Grant Park that placed modernistic lamps on walkways previously reliant on street lighting for illumination. Having covered its parks, the city turned its attention to the alleys in the 1960s. Designed to "end crime-breeding darkness and promote greater use of alleys," 51,000 mercury-vapor lamps were installed at the ends and in the center of the alleys.[69]

Mayor Daley announced another major upgrade in 1973: $7.5 million would be spent to replace the fourteen-year-old bluish white mercury-vapor lamps with yellowish high-pressure sodium-vapor ones.[70] Some of the first efforts centered on high-crime areas like Lawndale,

while sodium-vapor advocates cited their higher energy efficiency and greater illumination. In spite of objections, the program moved forward and was completed in 1981 with the installation of high-pressure sodium in all the alleys.[71]

For several years, the debate over the lights sizzled. But it was clear that being the "best lighted city" now meant being the "most lighted city." Even areas that were traditionally treated with great attention to design felt the change. Lake Shore Drive, for example, had been lined for many years with globe-encased Mazda lamps on decorative concrete poles. Yet, Lake Shore Drive was clearly becoming a high-speed throughway, not a park drive. Today, high-pressure sodium-vapor lamps and cobra heads proliferate. Their presence represents the final abandonment of the pretense that Lake Shore Drive is not an expressway. The urbane ranks of globe-topped standards have been replaced by what Harry Weese has called "a marching column of rickety double bracketed orange-tipped fruit gibbets," whose "orange pools of late night light [are] wasted on empty stages waiting for crime."[72]

Did all this brightening of the night sky succeed in driving away crime? The Chicago Police Department did report a decline in the incidences of some night crime, but such statistics must be handled with extreme caution. There is little conclusive evidence that street lighting lowers the level of crime; the best that can be said is that street lighting can lessen the *fear* of crime.[73]

The sodium-vapor controversy also reached into the suburbs, especially those with architecturally or historically significant street lighting systems. An explicit rejection of the Chicago aesthetic was heard from Wilmette environmentalists who said that "new light[s] would make Wilmette look like State and Madison."[74] But the controversy raged most fiercely in Oak Park and Evanston. Both cities boast lighting designs by architect Thomas Eddy Tallmadge. In Evanston, the fluted columns are ornamented with oak leaves and waves, and a distinctive octagonal luminaire that has become one of the city's architectural symbols (see fig. 23). The city council's efforts to scrap all 6,800 lights in 1976 were met with immediate and widespread protest. Several years later, the city decided to keep the Tallmadge luminaires or replicas on residential streets, to reject crime as a reason for bright, high-pressure sodium-vapor lights, and to allow neighbors to decide on the wattage of bulb to be used. Nonetheless, it proposed cobra-head light standards for major arterial streets for the very reason Chicago did in 1948: to direct the light directly onto the thoroughfare.[75]

Fig. 22   View of the intersection of 73rd Street and Coles Avenue, showing popular harp-shaped lighting fixture of the 1920s and later cobra-head style, c. 1950.

Fig. 23   View of Evanston, showing lamps by Thomas E. Tallmadge, 1958.

Urbanity Rekindled

As if to signal a general downtown revitalization and the growing dissatisfaction with the overwhelming emphasis placed on security and utility, old buildings began to be relighted or newly lighted in the 1980s, and new buildings shook off the dark modernist aesthetic for brightly illuminated tops, as a way of drawing attention to the virtues of a particular address.[76] Lighting programs also received a boost from the recommendations of the "Light Up Chicago" committee, formed in 1983 by the Woman's Board of The Art Institute of Chicago to advise Mayor Jane Byrne on the priority and feasibility of lighting various landscape elements, public art, and architecture for Chicago's sesquicentennial.[77]

Some notable structures, of course, had never really lost their lights, such as the Kemper Insurance, Wrigley, Chicago Tribune, and Chicago Temple buildings. For others, the "Light Up Chicago" committee recommended that "an overall priority would be to focus on buildings of the twenties and thirties whose dramatic lighting was an integral part of the urban environment." Relighted structures included the Art Institute's garden facades; the Chicago Board of Trade (in conjunction with the construction of the Annex); the Merchandise Mart; the Hotel Intercontinental; the Chicago Hilton and Towers; 75 East Wacker Drive; 680 North Lake Shore Drive (formerly the American Furniture Mart); 188 West Randolph Street; and 310 South Michigan Avenue.

Since many of the newest buildings with illuminated tops have been postmodernist structures drawing on classical or moderne forms, they have adopted the lighting vocabulary of the 1920s and 1930s as well. Outlining characterizes the pediment of Ricardo Bofill's new tower at Wacker and Clark. Full-scale floodlighting has also been used at 900 North Michigan Avenue, the AT&T Building, NBC Tower, the Sheraton Hotel, and 181 West Madison Street (see pls. 65-67). Perhaps the most famous, or notorious, example of all is the very brightly illuminated "castle" atop 311 South Wacker Drive (fig. 24), which has managed to draw attention away from its neighbor, the Sears Tower, at night.

The dark lake to the east therefore shimmers again with the reflected urbanity of the metropolis. Overhead the orange-bottomed clouds blanket the city with the hue of security. But beneath, real life goes on, as often as not oblivious to the obliteration of darkness in the Chicago-style night.

Fig. 24   Kohn Pedersen Fox Associates, 311 South Wacker Drive, 1986-90.

NOTES

1. See "The Shopper's Paradise," *Greater Chicago Magazine* (Nov. 1926), pp. 20-21.

2. One of the maxims of the City Beautiful street lighting scheme that commenced around 1905 was that "trade follows the light"; Harry Miles, "Installing Ornamental Lighting in Michigan City, Indiana," *American City* 10 (1914), pp. 476-77.

3. For a religious/phenomenological view on darkness, see Ernst Thomas Reimbold, *Die Nacht im Mythos, Kultus, Volksglauben, und in der transpersonalen Erfahrung: Eine religionsphaenomenologische Untersuchung* (Cologne, 1970). For images of darkness in the industrial city, see the chapter "Cities of Darkness and Light," in Raymond Williams, *The Country and the City* (New York, 1973); Asa Briggs, *Victorian Cities* (Harmondsworth, 1968), p. 62; Stuart Blumin, "Explaining the New Metropolis: Perception, Depiction, and Analysis in Mid-Nineteenth Century New York City," *Journal of Urban History* 11 (1984), pp. 9-38; Mark J. Bouman, "The 'Good Lamp is the Best Police' Metaphor and Ideologies of the Nineteenth Century Urban Landscape," *American Studies* 32, no. 1 (Fall 1991), pp. 63-78; and Yi-Fu Tuan, *Landscapes of Fear* (New York, 1979), pp. 145-74. Zorbaugh wrote that "the Near North Side is an area of high light and shadow, of vivid contrasts — contrasts not only between the old and the new, between the native and the foreign, but between wealth and poverty, vice and respectability, the conventional and the bohemian, luxury and toil"; it "shades from light to shadow, from shadow to dark"; Harvey Warren Zorbaugh, *The Gold Coast and the Slum: A Sociological Study of Chicago's Near North Side* (Chicago, 1929), pp. 3-9.

4. William Cronon, *Nature's Metropolis: Chicago and the Great West* (New York, 1991), p. xix. For geographer Yi-Fu Tuan, urban lighting is one example of "The City: Its Distance From Nature," *Geographical Review* 68 (Jan. 1978), pp. 1-12. Many older histories of lighting took for granted that street lighting has always been demanded (or should have been demanded); Arthur H. Hayward, *Colonial Lighting*, 3rd ed. (New York, 1962), p. 5; F. W. Robins, *The Story of the Lamp (And the Candle)* (London, 1939); William T. Dea, *The Social History of Lighting* (New York, 1958); Matthew Luckiesh, *Torch of Civilization: The Story of Man's Conquest of Darkness* (New York, 1940); and Kate Bolton, "The Great Awakening of the Night: Lighting America's Streets," *Landscape* 23 (1979), pp. 41-47. Such uncontextual histories pave the way for a progressive frontier reading of nocturnal history; Murray Melbin, *Night as Frontier: Colonizing the World After Dark* (New York and London, 1987); Nigel Thrift, "The Frontier is Alive and Well in the City at Night," *Comparative Frontier Studies* 8 (Summer 1977); David Livingstone and Brian Harrison, "Meaning Through Metaphor: Analogy as Epistemology," *Annals of the Association of American Geographers* 71, no. 1 (March 1981), pp. 95-107; and Mark J. Bouman, "Time's Wilderness? A Critique of the *Night as Frontier* Hypothesis," paper delivered at the Annual Meeting of the Association of American Geographers, 1991. But just as Western history now has staunch revisionists who eschew Turnerian "frontier" language, a growing nocturnal environmentalist movement has emerged, speaking of the "right to night" and light pollution; see "Light Pollution Foes Plead for Right to Night," *Chicago Tribune* (Aug. 27, 1978). Lorus J. Milne and Margery J. Milne's *The World of Night* (New York, 1948; rpt. New York, 1981) remains an environmental classic.

5. What follows is necessarily schematic; for more on demand, see Bouman (note 3); idem, "Luxury and Control: The Urbanity of Street Lighting in Three Nineteenth Century Cities," *Journal of Urban History* 14, no. 1 (Nov. 1987), pp. 7-37; idem, "Urban Geography and the History of Technology: A Demand-Based Approach," paper delivered at the Annual Meeting of the Association of American Geographers, 1989; Harold L. Platt, *The Electric City: Energy and the Growth of the Chicago Area, 1880-1930* (Chicago, 1991), pp. 10-15; Wolfgang Schivelbusch, *Disenchanted Night: The Industrialization of Light in the Nineteenth Century* (Berkeley, Los Angeles, and London, 1988); David Nye, *Electrifying America: Social Meanings of a New Technology* (Cambridge, Mass., 1990); James M. Tien, Vincent F. O'Donnell, Arnold Barrett, and Pitu B. Mirchandani, *Street Lighting Projects*, National Evaluation Program Phase I Report (U.S. Department of Justice, Law Enforcement Assistance Administration, National Institute of Law Enforcement and Criminal Justice, 1979), p 3. For Tien et al., the three major categories of demand are "security and safety," "community character and vitality," and "traffic orientation and identification." All this suggests that technologies such as lighting may be studied not only as agents of impact on urban life (as in Bolton [note 4]), but also as results of it.

6. Chicago was perhaps the most spectacular case of what Harvey Molotch calls the "urban growth machine"; see "The City as a Growth Machine," *American Journal of Sociology* 82, no. 2 (1976), pp. 309-30; see also John R. Logan and Harvey L. Molotch, *Urban Fortunes: The Political Economy of Place* (Berkeley, 1983), pp. 54-55. In a sense, the "urban ethos," a coalition of growth oriented politicians, capitalists, and pundits, was operative much earlier in Chicago than in the cities that Blaine Brownell describes in *The Urban Ethos in the South, 1920-1930* (Baton Rouge, 1975).

7. Early regional sensibilities were present in Dwight Perkins's proposal for a Metropolitan Park System (1904) and more explicitly in Burnham and Bennett's 1909 *Plan of Chicago*, with its scheme of regional traffic arteries connecting semi-independent satellite cities; Chicago, Special Park Commission, *Report of the Special Park Commission to the City Council...of Chicago on the Subject of a Metropolitan Park System*, compiled by Dwight Heald Perkins (Chicago, 1904); Daniel H. Burnham and Edward H. Bennett, *Plan of Chicago*, ed. Charles Moore (Chicago, 1909). On the regional nature of the *Plan of Chicago*, see Carl W. Condit, *Chicago, 1910-29: Building, Planning, and Urban Technology* (Chicago, 1973), p. 65; Sally Chappell, "Chicago Issues: The Enduring Power of the Plan," in Robert Bruegmann, Sally Chappell, and John Zukowsky, *The Plan of Chicago: 1909-1979* (Chicago, 1979), pp. 7-15; Joan E. Draper, "Paris by the Lake: Sources of Burnham's Plan of Chicago," in John Zukowsky, ed., *Chicago Architecture, 1872-1922: Birth of a Metropolis* (Munich and Chicago, 1987), pp. 107-19. The Chicago Plan's circulation system rested more in a vision of Chicago's regional imperialism than in a sophisticated understanding of traffic movements. Scholars at the University of Chicago enhanced the understanding of metropolitan interdependence, by which, generally, was meant a pattern of commuting from suburb to city; see, for example, Roderick D. McKenzie, *The Metropolitan Community* (New York, 1933). The notion of a suburban "commuter shed" reached its apex in the 1960s in geographer Brian Berry's notion of a "daily urban system"; Brian J. L. Berry, *Metropolitan Area Re-evaluation Study* (Chicago, 1967); Brian J. L. Berry, Irving Cutler, Edwin H. Draine, Ying-cheng Kiang, Thomas R. Tocalis, and Pierre de Vise, *Chicago: Transformations of an Urban System* (Cambridge, Mass., 1976), pp. 13-28.

8. On the monocentric metropolis, see Ernest W. Burgess, "The Growth of the City: An Introduction to a Research Project," in Robert E. Park, Ernest W. Burgess, and Roderick McKenzie, *The City* (Chicago, 1967); Homer Hoyt, *The Structure and Growth of Residential Neighborhoods in American Cities* (Washington, D.C., 1939); Chauncy D. Harris and Edward L. Ullman, "The Nature of Cities," *Annals of the American Academy of Political and Social Sciences* 242 (Nov. 1945). For a later view, based on land economics, see William Alonso, *Location and Land Use* (Cambridge, Mass., 1964). For the population in the Loop, see Gerald W. Breese, *The Daytime Population of the Central Business District of Chicago* (Chicago, 1949).

9. On the not necessarily deterministic role of streetcars in creating this pattern, see Michael P. Conzen and Kathleen Neils Conzen, "Geographical Structure in Nineteenth-Century Urban Retailing: Milwaukee, 1836-90," *Journal of Historical Geography* 5 (1979), pp. 45-66; for Chicago, see Brian J. L. Berry, *Commercial Structure and Commercial Blight: Retail Patterns and Processes in the City of Chicago*, University of Chicago, Department of Geography Research Paper No. 85 (Chicago, 1963). Lighting companies recognized the hierarchical nature of shopping districts as early as 1930. Curtis Lighting, for example, prescribed wattages for store windows in the Central Business District (300-500 watt with lamps 15" apart); community centers (200 watt, 12" apart); outlying districts (100-150 watt, 12-18" apart); and business districts in small towns (100-150 watt, 24" apart); J. L. Stair, *The Lighting Book* (Chicago: Curtis Lighting, 1930), p. 251.

10. George L. Rapp, "History of Cinema Theater Architecture," in Arthur Woltersdorf, ed., *Living Architecture* (Chicago, 1930), p. 62.

11. This paragraph is, of course, a deeply compressed portrait of a nationwide trend; for an overview, see Kenneth T. Jackson, *Crabgrass Frontier: The Suburbanization of the United States* (New York, 1985). The magnitude of the change as it affects Chicago is seen in these summary statistics: in 1972, the city had nearly 56 percent of the jobs in the six-county region; by 1990, its share had dipped to less than 40 percent; Illinois Department of Employment Security, *Where Workers Work* (Springfield, Illinois, 1991). In 1920, Chicago contained nearly 80 percent of the region's 3,394,966 people; by 1970, it accounted for 48.3 percent of 6,974, 755; in 1990, only 38.3 percent of the region's 7,261,176 people lived in the city; *U.S. Census of Population*. Finally, more Fortune 500 firms (ranked by 1990 sales) are now headquartered in the suburbs (22) than in the city (20).

12. The Loop's population has grown from 6,462 in 1980 to 11,954 in 1990, an 85 percent increase.

13. This follows for the consumption of power in general; electricity, in particular, has been a liberating locational force for industry, and in this respect it, too, has fostered suburbanization.

14. It was often the lot of residents of slum areas such as "Little Hell" to live near the sources of production. Zorbaugh (note 3) reported that the neighborhood's name came from "the smell of gas from the huge 'gas house' by the river, whose belching flames make the sky lurid at night" (pp. 159-60). In 1931, the first high-pressure gas pipeline from the Texas and Oklahoma gas fields was completed to Chicago, and by 1950, the coal gas share of the city's gas supply had dropped to 15 percent, a decline that helped to clear the air; "100 Years Ago Today City Got First Gas Light," *Chicago Tribune* (Sept. 4, 1950).

15. "Survey of Public Service," in Chicago Association of Commerce, *A Survey of Chicago* (1925), pp. 9-11; "Gas Light Era of City Blinks Out — For Good," *Chicago Tribune* (June 2, 1954).

16. "Riverside Lamps Stay as Most Gaslights Go," *Chicago Daily News* (Jan. 5, 1978).

17. On "electric city" and the "community of talent," see Platt (note 5), pp. 19-20. Elisha Gray was a competitor of Alexander Graham Bell's and a founder of Western Electric; Perry R. Duis, "Yesterday's City," *Chicago History* 16 (Spring 1987), pp. 66-72. Elmer Sperry was an arc light pioneer and the inventor of the gyroscope; Thomas Parke Hughes, *Elmer Sperry: Inventor and Engineer* (Baltimore, 1971). Augustus Curtis was the entrepreneur who developed the first reflectors used in floodlighting; F. Romer, *Reflection: Being the Buyography of a Torchbearer and His House* (Chicago: Curtis Lighting, 1928).

18. Platt (note 6), passim; idem, "Samuel Insull and the Electric City," *Chicago History* 15 (Spring 1986), pp. 20-35; Thomas P. Hughes, *Networks of Power: Electrification in Western Society, 1880-1930* (Baltimore, 1983), pp. 201-26; idem, *American Genesis: A Century of Invention and Technological Enthusiasm, 1870-1970* (New York, 1989), pp. 226-43; Forrest McDonald, *Insull* (Chicago, 1962). Commonwealth Edison still advertises aggressively and creatively; for example, it sponsors Sky Nights (formerly Venetian Night), which features popular light sculptures by John David Mooney.

19. Sally A. Kitt Chappell, *Architecture and Planning of Graham, Anderson, Probst and White, 1912-1936: Transforming Tradition* (Chicago, 1992), pp. 73-77; 253-55. Donald Des Granges wrote in 1929 that large power

stations "are being looked upon as institutions of public service" needing "a certain architectural dignity"; "The Designing of Power Stations," *Architectural Forum* 51 (Sept. 1929), pp. 361-72, quoted in John Stilgoe, *Metropolitan Corridor: Railroads and the American Scene* (New Haven, 1983), p. 122. However, Martin Roche, writing in *American Architect* in 1920 of the Commonwealth Edison Company Northwest Station (1910-15), said that "when we consider [that] the development of steam and electric power is a modern enterprise the temple or French Renaissance palace, in whole or in part, cannot express properly the modern power house"; Robert Bruegmann, *Holabird and Roche and Holabird and Root: An Illustrated Catalog of Works, 1880-1940* (New York and London, 1991), vol. 1, pp. 372-75.

20. Bruegmann (note 19), vol. 2, p. 264; vol. 3, pp. 87-90; vol. 2, p. 265.

21. Nye (note 5), pp. 37-38.

22. Bouman, "Luxury and Control" (note 5), p. 28.

23. Platt (note 5), pp. 28-39; 91. See also Neil Harris, "Shopping — Chicago Style," in Zukowsky (note 7), pp. 137-55.

24. "Shopper's Paradise" (note 1); "State Street Lights to be World's Best," *Chicago Commerce* 22 (Sept. 9, 1926), p. 13; "Survey of Public Improvements" in *Survey of Chicago* (note 15), p. 18.

25. "Shopper's Paradise" (note 1); John Corcoran, "The City Light and Beautiful," *American City* 7 (1912), pp. 46-47; "Congestion Peak Found on Chicago Corner," *Chicago Commerce* 22 (Oct. 2, 1926), p. 11. See also Miles (note 2).

26. See Berry et al. (note 7), pp. 71-79, for changes in the CBD retail environment.

27. *State Street Special* (Nov. 13, 1958), a special four-page newspaper printed for the occasion, now in the collection of the Chicago Historical Society.

28. Berry et al. (note 7), pp. 71-79; Chicago Department of Planning, City and Community Development, *State Street Transit Mall Before/After Study Phase One Final Report* (Chicago, 1978); William Gruber, "State Street Plans Due Soon," *Chicago Tribune* (June 5, 1992).

29. Zorbaugh (note 3), pp. 105, 115. The North Clark Street Business Men's Association had contracted with Insull in 1895 to supply the lights, rather than with the city; Platt (note 6), pp. 100-01. The success of the effort led to other commercial streets being so lighted: North Avenue, Wells and Division streets, and Cottage Grove Avenue and 31st Street.

30. "McDonough 'Turns On' South Chicago With New Lighting," *Daily Calumet* (April 21, 1973); "Lights Up," *Daily Calumet* (April 18, 1973); "Wells Street to be Great White Way," *North Loop News* (July 29, 1971); "Old Town Chamber Reveals Lighting Plans for Area," *North Loop News* (Aug. 12, 1971).

31. City of Chicago, Department of Public Works, *Chicago Bridges* (Chicago, 1984), p. 63. Ornamental lamps shown on drawings for the Lake Street Bridge were never installed (p. 66). In the case of the Oakwood Boulevard Viaduct (Bennett; 1931) over the Illinois Central Railroad, cobra-head poles have replaced the original fixtures (pp. 85-86). See the same fixures on the State Street Bridge (p. 122).

32. Stair (note 9), pp. 56-57.

33 Christopher Tunnard and Henry Hope Reed, *American Skyline: The Growth and Form of Our Cities and Towns* (New York, 1956), pp. 154-55; Robert Bruegmann, "Relighting the Skyline," *Inland Architect* 26 (March/April 1982), pp. 51-57.

34. Quoted in Bruegmann (note 33), p. 51. See also Jane O'Kane, "The Wonders of Chicagoland," *The City Beautiful* (Sept. 1931), p. 5.

35. Nye (note 5), pp. 57-73.

36. Stair (note 9), pp. 25, 235; Glenn A. Bishop and Paul T. Gilbert, *Chicago's Progress: A Review of the Fair City* (Chicago, 1933), p. 83. Stair's *Lighting Book* was written in the year of Light's Golden Jubilee, 1929, which commemorated Edison's invention of the incandescent light bulb. The "Curtis Creed" was "to bring brighter blessings and bigger benefactions into all lives through light; to make the hum of industry throat a happier song; to make the wheels of commerce roll more happily along; to create hallowed harmony in such sacred precincts as church and home; to take glare from the rays and to comfort the gaze, opening the eyes of the world to greater joy in seeing, through lighting that is correct, be it direct or indirect." Curtis had its own exhibit at the Century of Progress Exposition.

37. Stair (note 9), p. 234.

38. Various editions of the *Chicago Central Business and Office Building Directory* are available at the Harold Washington Library Center.

39. Chappell (note 19), p. 62, likens the Harringer drawing to a Hollywood premiere. Hall's perspectives use the same motifs and are found throughout Bruegmann (note 22), beginning about 1925. See the Ferriss rendering of the Chicago Temple in Bruegmann, vol. 2, p. 225.

40. Chappell (note 19), pp. 52-55; idem, "As if the Lights Were Always Shining: Graham, Anderson, Probst and White's Wrigley Building at the Boulevard Link," in Zukowsky (note 7), pp. 290-301.

41. Pauline A. Saliga, ed., *The Sky's the Limit: A Century of Chicago Skyscrapers* (New York, 1990), pp. 139-41.

42. Bruegmann (note 19), vol. 2, pp. 414-24; Alfred Granger, *Chicago Welcomes You* (Chicago, 1933), p. 144; Federal Writer's Project, *The WPA Guide to Illinois,* with a new Introduction by Neil Harris and Michael Conzen (New York, 1983), pp. 242-43.

43. The proposed 75-story Crane Tower, one of the first contemplated structures on the Illinois Central Railroad air rights at Randolph Street, was also supposed to have had a beacon. See the drawing in Paul Gilbert and Charles Lee Bryson, *Chicago and Its Makers* (Chicago, 1929), p. 594. A beacon was also found atop the Wrigley Building; Chappell, "As if the Lights" (note 40), p. 300. The Chicago Temple was also to have had a beacon; Bruegmann (note 19), vol. 2, pp. 224-31.

44. Chappell (note 19), pp. 158-62.

45. John Zukowsky, Pauline Saliga, and Rebecca Rubin, *Chicago Architects Design: A Century of Architectural Drawings from The Art Institute of Chicago* (New York and Chicago, 1982), p. 98.

46. Initial plans for 333 North Michigan called for a 92-foot lighted pylon; Bruegmann (note 19), vol. 2, pp. 400-06.

47. Saliga (note 41), pp. 144-45; *Chicago Central Business and Office Building Directory* (1932).

48. Saliga (note 41), p. 139.

49. Granger (note 42), p. 50; *WPA Guide* (note 42), p. 249.

50. Hubert Burnham, "Architectural Expression for Chicago's 1933 World's Fair," in Woltersdorf (note 10), p. 130.

51. For "illumination's dramatic role," see Lenox R. Lohr, *Fair Management: The Story of A Century of Progress Exposition* (Chicago, 1952), pp. 101-10; *Official Guide, Book of the Fair, 1933, with 1934 Supplement* (Chicago, 1933), pp. 25-29. Among the articles on the fair in the collections of the Chicago Historical Society can be found the following: C. W. Farrier, "Illumination Features of the Century of Progress Exposition," *The Armour Engineer* 23 (Nov. 1931), pp. 3-5; Walter D'Arcy Ryan, "Lighting an Exposition," *Electrical World* 101 (May 27, 1933), pp. 687-88; idem, "Lighting 'A Century of Progress,'" *Electrical Engineering* (May 1934); J. L. McConnell, "Lighting Heads the List of Special Facilities," *Engineering News-Record* 110 (March 2, 1933), pp. 283-85.

52. An excellent example is the work of Fred Korth. Not only do the photographs in his 1949 collection show the standard postcard images of Chicago, but his captions also drive home the point. Of the Oak Street Beach at night, he wrote, "Incandescent jewels against the velvet backdrop of the night sky. Lights gleam from thousands of windows in the Gold Coast Towertown while below street lights of the Outer Drive resemble a line of fairy lanterns"; Fred G. Korth, *The Chicago Book: Photographs by Korth* (Chicago, 1949), pp. 10-11.

53. For an appreciation of the modernist approach to nocturnal architecture, see Yoshinobu Ashihara, *The Aesthetic Townscape,* trans. Lynne E. Riggs (Cambridge, Mass., 1983), pp. 80-97.

54. "Survey of Public Improvements," in *Survey of Chicago* (note 15), p. 19; "Proper Street Lighting Saves Lives and Reduces Traffic Accidents," in Chicago Plan Commission, *Chicago Looks Ahead: Design for Public Improvements* (Chicago, 1945).

55. "Survey of Public Improvements," in *Survey of Chicago* (note 15), pp. 18-19; see also Sanitary District of Chicago, *Report on Contracts for Street Lighting System Installed By the Sanitary District of Chicago for the City of Chicago* (Chicago, 1916), available from the Municipal Reference Library.

56. See Chicago Bureau of Public Efficiency, *The City Bond Issues to Be Voted Upon November 4, 1924,* a document in the collections of the Chicago Historical Society. The bureau, chaired by Julius Rosenwald, urged passage of a bond issue that would finance the addition of six square miles of the new lighting to eight already approved in 1922. (Twenty-eight square miles of unlighted or underlighted areas were to be improved by the whole program.)

57. "Tackle Problem of Lighting City Instead of Sky," *Chicago Tribune* (April 3, 1948). By 1932, Chicago had 93,374 electric street lights, which made it, in the words of a 1973 city publication, "the largest municipal electric street lighting system in the world"; Chicago, Department of Public Works, *Chicago Public Works: A History,* ed. Daphne Chritenson (Chicago, 1973), p. 62.

58. City of Chicago, *Chicago's Report to the People, 1933-1946* (1947), p. 9.

59. Roger Biles, *Big City Boss in Depression and War: Mayor Edward J. Kelly of Chicago* (DeKalb, Illinois , 1984), pp. 79-80.

60. "City is Leader in Developing Street Lighting," *Chicago Tribune* (April 4, 1948). The same article calls Chicago at the time "one of the poorest lighted of the nation's major cities." In an article later in the year, *Tribune* reporter Clayton Kirkpatrick, noting the decline of the existing system due to deferred maintenance, repeated the charge; "City's Street Lighting Plant Held Obsolete," *Chicago Tribune* (December 6, 1948). In general, newspaper reports were highly favorable to the whole project.

61. Commissioner of Streets and Electricity Lloyd M. Johnson asserted that 65 percent of all traffic accidents and 75 percent of fatalities occur at night, and that "good street lighting and adequate traffic control signals are imperative in reducing night accidents"; "City Sets 250-mile Street Lights Goal," *Chicago Times* (May 14, 1947).

62. The voters had approved a $3 million bond issue in 1944, though the work did not begin until 1946; $5 million bond issues were passed in 1948 and 1950; the work proceeded almost immediately thereafter. See City of Chicago Engineering Board of Review, *Report on Street Lighting,* nos. 141, 154, and 159, in the Municipal Reference Library.

63. *Chicago's Report* (note 58), pp. 212-15.

64. When the last lamps were removed from Devon Avenue in the 41st Ward, Alderman Immel wrote, "All of us who have lived in the ward since when we were youngsters cannot help but experience a feeling of nostalgia as we mark the passing of an era"; "Remaining Gas Lamps in Ward to be Removed," *Edison-Norwood Review* (Jan. 23, 1953).

65. The comments of Matthew Blackton were reported in the *Herald-American* (April 16, 1949).

66. More bond issues were to be passed in order to finance the program. By 1958, $63 million had been raised in seven bond issues; another $15 million was raised in the issue of that year. Again, major newspapers editorialized in favor of passage, though the *Tribune* complained about the practice of submitting bond questions on the low-turnout judicial ballots rather than at general elections; "For Street Lighting," *Chicago Sun-Times* (May 29, 1958); "Vote 'Yes' on Bonds," *Chicago Tribune* (June 2, 1958). By that year, city officials were stating that the overall cost of upgrading the system would be $119 million; "City to Vote Tomorrow on Lighting Bonds," *Chicago Tribune* (June 1, 1958). Mercury vapor replacements came as early as 1956; "9 Miles of Chicago Streets Get New Lights," *Chicago Sun-Times* (July 30, 1956); "City Replacing Lamps on 50,000 Street Lights," *Chicago Daily News* (Sept. 14, 1959). By the end of the ten-year round of upgrades, the *Tribune* proclaimed boosterishly that "Chicago is the

first major city to modernize itself out of the gas street light era"; "Chicago Ends Era of Old Gas Street Lights," *Chicago Tribune* (Aug. 7, 1956); "City's Bright Street Lights Cheat Death," *Chicago Tribune* (Oct. 11, 1959). The fifty years prediction was repeated in 1962; "City Updates Street Lights: 40,000 New Ones Going Up," *Chicago Daily News* (Jan. 18, 1962). At the time, the city was replacing all its postwar incandescent lamps with mercury vapor. For some perceived and real drawbacks to mercury vapor, see "Irate Citizens Taking a Dim View of New Street Lighting," *Chicago Sun-Times* (June 5, 1960).

67. Mike Royko, *Boss: Richard J. Daley of Chicago* (New York, 1971), p. 29.

68. The Park District had adopted cobra-head designs in 1945: "Install Lights in Boulevard Work Program," *Chicago Tribune* (June 16, 1958); "Park Light Project Completed," *Chicago American* (June 16, 1958).

69. "Alley Light Bids Out; City to Do Work Itself," *Chicago Daily News* (Oct. 6, 1966); "First Alley Lights Turned On," *Chicago Tribune* (Oct. 18, 1966); "Alley Lights Go Up Despite Snow, Ice and Bad Guesses," *Chicago Tribune* (Nov. 10, 1966). In announcing the program, Mayor Daley said, "Chicago will be the first major city in the United States to provide lighting in all of its alleys. In fact, it will be the only city in the United States where all of its public ways are illuminated. The lighting of alleys will result in a reduction of crime, the saving of lives, and a decrease in accidents caused by vehicles, and a general convenience to every family in every neighborhood in Chicago"; "Bright Idea: North Side Alley Lighting Continues," *North Town* (Dec. 21, 1966). And, of course, "Alley Lights Will Be Up by Election Day," *Chicago Tribune* (March 11, 1967). This brought charges from Alderman Scholl: "Charges City Spends to Aid Daley's Image," *Chicago Tribune* (March 17, 1967). Virtually every effort to upgrade the system was met with boosterish sentiment; "City of Light: It's not Paris, but Chicago," *Chicago Daily News* (Dec. 9, 1967). Five years later, an official city publication claimed that the number of lights installed "has never been equaled before or since anywhere," and that "a greater volume of favorable public reaction was evoked over this alley lighting program than any other program in the history of City government"; *Chicago Public Works* (note 57), p. 62.

70. "Lights On! City Turning Yellow After Dark," *Chicago Daily News* (Nov. 28, 1973). Reporter Jay McMullen referred to "Chicago, the Yellow City," and quoted the Commissioner's response to objections about the color: "You'll get used to it. It isn't yellow. Golden is the word." Stanley Ziemba of the *Tribune* wrote that "harsh metallic-blue mercury vapor street lights" would be replaced "with more cheerful, brighter, gold-colored sodium vapor lamps"; "Lights of the City Soon May be Brighter," *Chicago Tribune* (Dec. 5, 1973).

71. "Better Street Lights Urged to Fight Crime in Lawndale," *Chicago Tribune* (April 9, 1972); "A Sodium-Vapor Attack on Street Crime," *Business Week* (May 12, 1973); "New Lights to Brighten Alleys, Cut Energy Costs," in *Chicago '81*, a document in the Municipal Reference Library.

72. Harry Weese, "Our Sodium Vapor-swept Shore," *Inland Architect* 26 (Jan./Feb. 1982).

73. Tien et al. (note 5), p. i. This report, which contains a number of trenchant criticisms of existing street lighting practice, also notes that existing Illuminating Engineering Society design standards place a far greater emphasis on vehicular roadways than pedestrian walkways, and that to claim that lighting systems will improve both traffic safety and fight crime is misleading (p. 25).

74. "Environment Units Dim Suburban Lighting Plans," *Chicago Tribune* (Aug. 20, 1972).

75. Paul Gapp, "How to Fight City Hall: Round 1," *Chicago Tribune* (Dec. 25, 1976); "Long Study Leads Evanston to the Light," *Chicago Tribune* (Dec. 7, 1978); "Evanston Residents Fight Plan to Darken Historic Streetlights," *Chicago Tribune* (Dec. 4, 1980).

76. For an overview of the economic geographic underpinnings of revitalization, see H. Briavel Holcomb and Robert A. Beauregard, *Revitalizing Cities*, Resource Publications in Geography (Washington, D. C., 1981).

77. The "Light Up Chicago" Committee, *Light Up Chicago*, A Report to Mayor Jane Byrne, 1982. The committee recommended that forty-three sculptures be given the highest lighting priority. While the committee did provide a useful inventory of sculpture and building lighting possibilities, it was not as comprehensive as the Milwaukee lighting plan established in 1990; Judith Davidson, "The Light that Makes Milwaukee Famous," *Architectural Record Lighting* (Nov. 1991), pp. 30-35.

The Construction of a Nocturnal Landscape   51

"Forever Inadequate to the Rising Stream": Dream Cities, Automobiles, and Urban Street Mobility in Central Chicago

R. Stephen Sennott

The image of private automobiles speeding along an open highway confirmed America's post-World War II faith in the improved technological landscape. Without fanfare on the evening of August 28, 1958, suburban Chicago motorists lined up along the North Tri-State Tollway to participate in an inaugural drive along one of the nation's most modern and efficient limited-access highways.[1] To mark the occasion, tollway authorities awarded Tri-State Pioneer window stickers to the first fifty thousand motorists, many of whom would eventually visit one of the Oasis restaurant and service areas. Promoted in magazine advertisements as "service plazas of the future,"[2] the five original over-the-tollway restaurants and service areas were designed not simply to provide food and fuel along the side of the highway. Integrated into an enormous metropolitan highway landscape, these transparent, air-conditioned structures also constructed a view toward a distant horizon, a panorama tailored from a tradition of twentieth-century urban visions representing high-speed, orderly automobile travel.

The Oasis and Illinois Tollway scheme descends from an urban planning and architectural tradition of American dream cities. Made of concrete, glass, and steel, these highway restaurants conformed to the modernist aesthetic, and represented postwar America's highest expectations associated with technology, urbanism, efficiency, and most especially, the automobile. Combined with Chicago's postwar expressway system, the Illinois Tollway represented advanced highway engineering and regional planning concepts that were intended to control large volumes of traffic generated by suburban commuters and commercial vehicles entering and

Fig. 1 View looking east on Wacker Drive, 1935.

Fig. 2 View looking south on State Street from the intersection with Madison Street, c. 1917.

exiting the city, or traveling through the region. At once idealistic and practical, ambitious Chicago architects and planners had conceptualized their city as a "dream city" ever since it had hosted the World's Columbian Exposition in 1893.[3] Wishing to apply similar standards of urban beauty and order to the comprehensively planned city of the motor age, the Commercial Club powerfully embodied these conceptions of utility and mobility in Daniel H. Burnham and Edward H. Bennett's now famous 1909 *Plan of Chicago*. As the dream city ideals of this plan were articulated by the Chicago Plan Commission, later architects and planners were challenged to design improved streets, raised sidewalks, elevated urban superhighways, regional highway networks, tall office buildings, and parking garages in order to redefine the city street and the uses of urban space to accommodate masses of pedestrians and automobiles (fig. 2).

At street level the Chicago Plan Commission's task was defined by traffic surveys, all indicating a dire need for improved urban street systems and related transportation architecture. In 1909, when the *Plan of Chicago* was completed, only 7,110 automobiles were registered in Chicago, and the population per automobile was approximately 300 to 1. When the Plan Commission reached its fifteenth anniversary in 1924, nearly 261,000 automobiles were registered, and the population per automobile had dropped sharply to just 11 to 1.[4] These figures mirrored similarly overwhelming national growth trends. In 1909 the country produced 127,731 automobiles and 3,255 motor trucks. In 1922 those numbers had risen to 2,406,396 automobiles and 252,668 motor trucks.[5] The U.S. Bureau of Public Roads provided city planners with national motor vehicle (auto and truck) registration figures showing an increase from 2,445,666 registered vehicles in 1915 to 15,092,177 in 1923, an alarming 23 percent increase over the previous year for 1923 alone.[6] Writing to a national audience in 1924, Eugene S. Taylor, the manager of the Chicago Plan Commission, calculated that every Saturday night another 1,150 more automobiles were added to the city's street space.[7] From the beginning of the motor age, the narrow streets that crossed the Central Business District of Chicago, New York, Detroit, and other expanding cities were so jammed by growing numbers of pedestrians, private automobiles, delivery trucks, motor buses, surface-rail trolley cars, and horse-drawn wagons that business leaders, planners,

and city officials feared that they were losing any ability to plan efficiently for future urban transportation requirements. Despite two decades of urgent planning efforts to redefine the street, New York architect Harvey W. Corbett echoed in 1927 the anxiety of most city planners: "This movement of traffic is just as essential to the life of the city as the movement of the blood is to the life of the body. Thin traffic like thin blood represents an anemic condition. Congested traffic, like excessive blood pressure, threatens the health of the body, that is to say, the normal and proper growth of the city."[8] For Corbett in New York or Taylor in Chicago, the gigantic numbers of automobiles gave new meaning to the city street, and traffic congestion could only be reduced when architects and planners successfully redesigned the urban street structure to facilitate easy and fast movement within the city.

A new demand for unprecedented urban highway systems and modern automobile buildings defined a particularly important role for architects, planners, and engineers during the automobile age. Corbett and his colleagues in Chicago investigated two interrelated planning and architectural issues: efficient street systems and highways for easy mobility within the metropolitan area, and convenient automobile parking facilities. Manipulating horizontal and vertical space, the generation of planners associated with Burnham and Bennett introduced significant proposals for adapting streets and buildings to the high-speed automobile.[9] Yet no one, not the Commercial Club of Chicago, nor Daniel

Fig. 3   Edward H. Bennett, Perspective study of a proposed multi-level street system, separating pedestrian and vehicular traffic; from The Chicago Business Center and the Subway Question *(Chicago, 1926).*

Fig. 4 View of the Michigan Avenue Bridge and Wacker Drive, 1929.

Burnham and Edward H. Bennett, had accurately predicted how rapidly urban transportation and planning would be overwhelmed and then redefined by the automobile. Nonetheless, a small group of important architects, planners, and engineers recognized very early on how the relationship between buildings, streets, and automobiles would alter their conception of urban mobility, efficiency, and spatial capacity.

After composing the Chicago Plan, Edward Bennett directed much of his professional efforts to projects that addressed the problem of the automobile and urban traffic congestion. In a paper presented in 1913 to the Fifth National Conference on City Planning, Bennett declared that "the most important consideration of the city plan, and one to which everything practically leads in the end, is the street system .... And on the disposition, width and treatment of the streets depends the livable character of the city."[10] A longstanding consulting architect and planner to the Chicago Plan Commission, Bennett investigated designs for wider streets, elevated streets and sidewalks, rapid transit, and early superhighway engineering. For his vision of "all streets and every street in the Loop [developed] into channels of easily flowing wheel and pedestrian movement," Bennett incorporated four transportation systems: rapid transit, surface traction, bus lines and vehicular traffic, and pedestrians. To improve "traffic stagnation and pedestrian congestion," due to blocked intersections, narrow and outdated road spaces, and the constant disorder at street corners where pedestrians competed with street traffic, Bennett proposed ramping cross-streets below major through roadways and elevating pedestrians on sidewalks over the traffic lanes and beneath the elevated tracks. For streets with retail and department stores, additional sidewalk space would be provided by arcades cut within building lines (fig. 3). Bennett argued that without improved circulation, the city should not develop a subway, believing that subway use would not reduce automobile use.[11]

If one looked down upon the spacious urban boulevards rendered by idealistic planners of the City Beautiful movement, the future of the American city might have appeared to be under control, especially when those comprehensive plans were designed by members of the emerging city planning profession.[12] They gained some sense of control from a belief in their scientific traffic surveys used to predict population growth

and future automobile use. Confident that they could manage the automobile's impact on the city, architects and engineers often proposed multi-level street systems and double-deck super-highways leading out from the city center. In theory, the planners sought movement and distribution of congested traffic, and so they recommended widened, uninterrupted streets. For Chicago, Bennett and members of the Plan Commission identified four wide thoroughfares—called quadrangle streets—to circulate congested traffic around the Loop: Roosevelt Road (south), South Water Street (north), Canal Street (west), and Michigan Avenue (east).[13] Completed in 1920, the Michigan Avenue improvements, with a bi-level separation of commercial and auto traffic, and the bi-level Michigan Avenue bridge—recommended in Burnham and Bennett's Chicago Plan to relieve traffic congestion along the city's most important north-south thoroughfare—demonstrated that double-deck streets could improve traffic mobility and reduce congestion.[14] In 1924 Taylor boasted that Bennett's modern bridge carried 73,000 vehicles per day, a dramatic increase over the 9,725 vehicles per day carried previously by the Rush Street bridge (fig. 4).[15]

Four years after the completion of the Michigan Avenue bridge, the Chicago Plan Commission initiated construction of the adjacent Wacker Drive (formerly South Water Street), the only double-deck street completed in accordance with the *Plan of Chicago* (figs. 5-7).[16] While promoting the project in 1923, Plan Commission chairman Charles Wacker had argued that a widened and improved Wacker Drive, connected

to and extending west from Michigan Avenue to Lake and Market streets and thereby to the new Canal Street and its nearby railroad terminals, would bring significantly greater rewards than Michigan Avenue because its separated levels would improve the riverfront's freight facilities, increase traffic circulation and street capacity in the vicinity of the business district, and greatly reduce traffic congestion in the Loop.[17] When commercial streets like South Water Street were clogged with slow-moving trucks, produce stands, and horse-drawn wagons, automobiles were often unable to circulate along the city streets. Indeed, South Water Street characterized an outdated market street type, a nearly motionless street space made obsolete in the city center by the arrival of the automobile. Bennett and Chicago Plan Commission engineer Hugh E. Young proposed double-deck streets to segregate freight traffic from automobile traffic.[18] Originally 80 feet wide, the upper level of Wacker Drive was widened to 100 feet for automobile traffic, and the lower, freight level to 135 feet. Lower Wacker Drive linked riverfront freight facilities with nearby railroad terminals and other manufacturing districts, thus removing heavy freight traffic from the Loop streets.[19] Demonstrating the close alliance between architects and engineers in the early planning profession, Bennett and Young collaborated in planning efforts to join Wacker Drive to the lakefront and to connect the Central Business District's encircling quadrangle streets to roads radiating from the city center and to outlying regional highways of the metropolitan region, as proposed originally in Burnham and Bennett's *Plan*

Fig. 5 View looking southeast of the riverfront docks and warehouses along South Water and Market streets, c. 1920.

Fig. 6 Edward H. Bennett, Cutaway perspective view of South Water Street Improvement (now Wacker Drive), c. 1924.

South Water Street Improvement
Typical Cross-section
City of Chicago Board of Local Improvements

Fig. 7 View of South Water Street Improvement (now Wacker Drive), under construction, July 18, 1925.

So.Water St. Imp't.
Sec. 4.
Column Forms Sec. 4.
7-18-25
Cont.10-25

of Chicago.[20] Wacker Drive gained national prominence because it demonstrated very quickly the benefits of reduced traffic congestion along a major central city thoroughfare.

While the Wacker Drive improvement may have been motivated by practical necessities, Bennett and the Chicago Plan Commission incorporated sculptural features and monumental architectural elements to provide the riverfront vista with civic beauty. Adhering to the standards of the Chicago Plan, the riverfront facade of the Wacker Drive improvements represented Bennett's commitment to the City Beautiful movement (fig. 8).[21] Andrew Rebori was one of

the few commentators to echo Charles Wacker's and Edward Bennett's calls for improved standards of civic beauty. Describing the entire Wacker Drive project as "Napoleonic in conception," Rebori praised the upper-level plaza with its wide pedestrian promenades, monumental fountain, arched lower-deck openings, and spacious automobile boulevards, all completed in 1926.[22]

Because of Wacker Drive's location along the river at the northern edge of the business district, Bennett's designs provided the upper and lower levels of Wacker Drive with important features for handling freight, providing space for

Fig. 8 Bennett, Parsons and Frost for the Chicago Plan Commission, Bird's-eye view of proposed Wacker Drive and riverfront improvements, Jan. 1926.

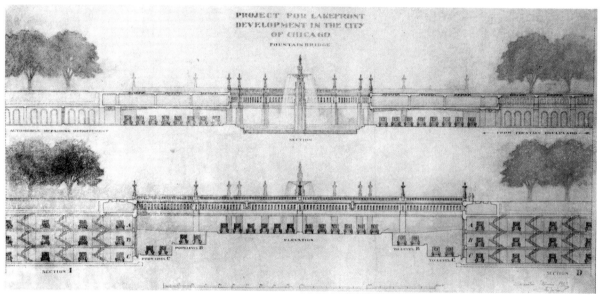

Fig. 9 Eliel Saarinen, Elevation and sections of an automobile terminal for a proposed Grant Park lakefront development project; from American Architect 124 (Dec. 5, 1923), p. 499.

automobile parking and storage, and establishing links to gateway bridges and roads leading out of the city.[23] Accessible only from the ends and one central ramp, the lower level provided four bays, two for traffic and two for parking or wharfage. At the east end, near Michigan Avenue, three decks were proposed. Beneath the uppermost Michigan Avenue level, a middle deck provided automobile parking, and a third level provided for a freight station connected to the 62-mile-long underground tunnel system operated by the Chicago Tunnel Company.[24] Combined with the new street, this electric rail freight tunnel reduced street congestion by eliminating the need for hundreds of motor truck transfers across the Loop between riverfront docks, freight and passenger rail stations, department stores, office buildings, and warehouses. Finally, since municipal transportation across

the central business streets worsened whenever motorists parked their cars in the street, Bennett incorporated parking space in the lower decks for automobile storage at the edge of the business district (fig. 1). Together, Wacker Drive and the Michigan Avenue bridge transformed the image of the Chicago River and the city itself, removing vestiges of the city's nineteenth-century congested public market. Adjacent to the site of the city's earliest waterfront settlement, they offered, instead, a potent iconic image of Chicago, now with endless lines of automobiles traveling over wide, elevated streets lined by skyscrapers that represented the modern city.

Wacker Drive and the activities of the Chicago Plan Commission attracted wide attention from the planning profession. In Chicago, an ambitious proposal for Grant Park and the lakefront east of Michigan Avenue was envisioned by Eliel

Fig. 10 Hugh Ferriss for Harvey Wiley Corbett, Perspective study of a proposed multi-level street system, separating pedestrian and vehicular traffic; from Architectural Forum 46 *(March 1927), p. 207.*

neath Grant Park (fig. 9). While it resembles in scale and imagery the large urban plazas designed by City Beautiful planners, Saarinen's proposal was significant for its monumental scale and its total deference to the needs of the automobile in the skyscraper city.

Throughout the 1920s architects and planners devised buildings and street systems that could increase street capacity. In New York the Committee on the Regional Plan of New York and Its Environs invited delineator Hugh Ferriss and architect Harvey W. Corbett to join its Advisory Committee of Architects. In 1923 Ferriss and Corbett produced some of the most visually imaginative and monumental projects for the separation of pedestrian and vehicular traffic in the city of the future.[26] In a 1924 article for *American City* and in a nearly identical one in 1927 for *Architectural Forum*, Corbett accepted the idea that efficient street mobility in New York and other metropolises depended on segregation of pedestrian and motor traffic.[27] Corbett argued (with Ferriss's drawings) for double-deck surfaces to separate pedestrian traffic from automobile and truck traffic (fig. 10). Supporting the skyscraper city, Corbett believed that automobiles should simply be given more and more street space horizontally across the urban grid, spreading in traffic lanes laid out beneath buildings that formerly faced the roadway. Expressing his generation's belief that the automobile problem was indeed controllable, Corbett claimed that "the New York of the future will be an adaptation of the metropolis to the needs of traffic, freeing the city from the unsightly congestion and turmoil of the present." He believed planners and architects could provide over time "a system of traffic division so perfected that the city can continue to grow and the streets can still take care of the increasing traffic."[28]

In graphic visions of the dream city Hugh Ferriss celebrated the prosperous urban setting of the 1920s. He expressed his belief in technology in his famous illustrated 1929 book, *Metropolis of Tomorrow*, in which he depicted tall skyscrapers surrounded by multi-level highways carrying high-speed automobiles and elevated sidewalks carrying masses of pedestrians.[29] In the accompanying text Ferriss rejected two-dimensional widened streets as "forever inadequate to the rising stream," arguing that only three-dimensional elevated streets could relieve traffic congestion. The metropolis envisioned by Ferriss and Corbett depicted buildings that were inseparable from the surrounding multiple levels of streets and superhighways. Despite this faith,

Saarinen, the Finnish architect who had won second prize in the Chicago Tribune tower competition of 1922.[25] Praising Burnham and the Chicago Plan, he created for Grant Park and its surroundings a project of wide boulevards, an automobile terminal, symmetrical pedestrian plazas with fountains and arcades, a centralized railroad terminal, and a large hotel tower—all laid out along a north-south axis parallel to the lake. A city planner, Saarinen described how the automobile was redefining city planning practices, and he arranged the park, plazas, buildings, and boulevards in an effort to remedy Chicago's traffic problem by providing sufficiently wide, high-speed roadways, a north-south supplementary boulevard parallel to Michigan Avenue, as well as ample, efficiently designed, parking space for 47,000 automobiles in a vast triple-deck automobile parking terminal located be-

many architects and regional planners realized that the automobile problem was unending. Predicting that the superhighway would become the "major traffic artery of the future city," Daniel L. Turner, consulting engineer for the Detroit Transit Commission, noted in 1924 that "within a decade the automobile has revolutionized street traffic conditions and has created one of the most difficult problems now confronting cities."[30]

In this context, the Chicago Plan Commission published in 1929 a substantial report, *West Side Superhighways*, in which Bennett, Young, and Joshua d'Esposito suggested various proposals for high-speed, limited-access, double-deck superhighways connecting the central city with the outlying region.[31] The committee's aim was to identify the east-west street or streets stretching west from Canal Street between Chicago Avenue to the north and Roosevelt Road to the south, namely the most efficient route by way of an elevated or sunken highway. Although the proposal for a Congress Street expressway eventually prevailed, the committee had asked Bennett and Young to submit proposals for a Monroe Street Superhighway, located slightly north and more serviceable to downtown traffic for its link to the Outer Drive. In his Monroe Street Superhighway proposal Hugh Young eliminated cross-traffic intersections and left-hand turns along an uninterrupted, elevated roadway, while in theory maintaining use of commercial property at the lower level (fig. 11). Storefronts were located on the upper level, and commercial facilities were accessible below at street level. Access ramps to the upper level were located midway along

the block. Seeking to unify transportation systems, Young proposed a four-track "open-cut transit subway" line beneath the normal street level. Prior to the automobile's dominance of the urban street, Henry A. Blair sought to consolidate urban transportation networks and increase the downtown's capacity, while simultaneously adapting segregated levels for transit lines, pedestrians, and automobiles (fig. 13).[32] The removal of trains to subway tunnels increased street capacity, and Blair's scheme provides an enclosed and spacious pedestrian street

Fig. 12 Aerial view of Grant Park, looking northeast, showing Chicago Park District parking lot on Monroe Street, c. 1938.

Fig. 11   Hugh E. Young,
Cutaway perspective
view of a proposed
Monroe Street
Superhighway; from
Chicago Plan
Commission, West Side
Superhighways
(Chicago, 1929), p. 218.

Fig. 13   Henry A. Blair,
Cutaway perspective
view of a proposed
multi-level street and
subway system; from A
Plan for a Unified
Transportation System
for the City of Chicago
(Chicago, 1927), p. 8.

protected from weather and unthreatened by automobiles.

Architects across the country were developing a variety of new building types for the sale, servicing, and storage of automobiles. Yet, it can be argued that few early motor age building types other than the urban automobile garage depended upon so many important urban planning and siting decisions. In 1929 engineer Ernest P. Goodrich underscored the problem of automobile storage when he wrote that "the place of the garage in City Planning is one of the most troublesome of all planning problems."[33] Depending on the size of the lot, architects designed either a ramp garage or one with a mechanical elevator, the latter designed specifically for narrow or compact lots. Ramp garages, because they required more space, had to accommodate a sufficiently large number of parking spaces to realize a profitable return. According to Goodrich, two kinds of garage were particularly important for the urban district: parking garages built within an office building used by the building's tenants, and public garages for motorists who used nearby buildings, such as hotels, department stores, or office buildings.[34] As a tool for the city planner, the city garage was often located as an element of a larger, comprehensive parking program that resulted from a study of surrounding street types, traffic patterns, commercial interests, and existing buildings. For Miller McClintock, a widely respected traffic

planning consultant from Harvard University, the street had to accommodate vehicles moving along the street as well as those parked on it.[35] The automobile required architects to integrate individual garage building programs with the necessities of adjacent streets and traffic needs.[36] Among important early efforts to design efficient and profitable urban garages, a group of Detroit automobile manufacturers and garage architects collaborated in 1924 to build three experimental multi-story garages in downtown Detroit.[37] Garage architect Robert O. Derrick emphasized location over all other factors, and he advised architects to build garages on a corner site bounded by principal streets.

Planners recognized that concentration meant congestion. In Chicago, where hundreds of motorists parked their cars on lakefront Park District property adjacent to the Michigan Avenue business blocks (fig. 12), the Plan Commission recommended that ramp or mechanical garages be located along the Loop's perimeter—Canal Street, Wacker Drive, Michigan Avenue, and Roosevelt Road—in order to reduce Loop congestion. Automobiles stored off the street in garages or open lots would open up more street space and theoretically permit street traffic to move more efficiently.

With the skyscraper building boom of the 1920s, some architects included interior mechanical garage space so that tenants and clients could conveniently park at their work place. The

boundary between the street and architecture was theoretically eroding, as the private skyscraper garage provided interior space to accommodate spatial needs previously relinquished to the public street. Nowhere in Chicago was the crossing between the public street and architecture more revealed than along Wacker Drive, by 1930 an icon of the modern city and the automobile. Built at the same time as Wacker Drive, the Jewelers Building was situated at the corner of Wacker Drive and Wabash Avenue (fig. 15). Dominating the riverfront, this office building contained at its center a twenty-five-story garage, open day and night, capable of storing six hundred cars. For security purposes, jewelers could safely enter the building through a private doorway located on lower Wacker Drive.[38] These motorists thus lost no time walking from a distant garage, and easy access to Wacker Drive and adjacent roads shortened commuting time otherwise lost in congested city streets. In a similar venture about this time, Andrew Rebori, with Holabird and Root, initiated designs in 1928 for the forty-one-story LaSalle-Wacker Building (see Willis, fig. 1), located on a similarly prestigious riverfront intersection of two principal thoroughfares, "the Gateway to Finance," and approached by motorists traveling over the Chicago River bridges.[39] The plans initially called for an adjacent thirteen-story ramp garage at the back of the site with an entrance open to lower Wacker Drive, although ultimately only two basement levels of parking were built.[40] Further east, with an electrically lighted sign facing motorists on the Outer Drive and Michigan Avenue, the fifteen-story Chicago Motor Club provided travel services to its members in an elegant, art moderne elevator lobby decorated with a mural of America's nineteen transcontinental highways and national parks painted by Chicago muralist John Norton.[41]

Whether using automatic elevators or inclined ramps, the architects of parking garages had devised convenient floor plans to fit different building sites and still arrange efficient, multiple parking rows. One widely published mechanical garage, the Kent Automatic Parking Garage in New York by Jardine, Hill and Murdock, adapted the mechanical system to a relatively small and narrow city lot (fig. 14).[42] Although the skyscraper garage was acclaimed in American and French publications because its mechanical hoisting system could maneuver 1,050 cars, many garage architects criticized this arrangement, noting the long time required to retrieve cars located in outer-edge parking spaces on the

Fig. 14 Jardine, Hill and Murdock, Cutaway perspective view of the Kent Automatic Parking Garage, New York; from American Architect 133 (June 20, 1928), p. 837.

Fig. 15 Giaver and Dinkelberg with Thielbar and Fugard, Jewelers Building, 35 East Wacker Drive, 1924-26, shown under construction with Wacker Drive.

Fig. 16   Lewis M. Kroman, 55th Ritz Garage and Auto Showroom (now University National Bank), southwest corner of Lake Park Boulevard at 55th Street, 1929 (photo 1992).

upper decks. Automobile dimensions determined the number of parking rows that a convenient site could contain. Architects then had to determine economical ceiling heights, ramp design, column widths and distances, and the layout of optional service areas, public lobbies, show rooms, offices, chauffeur recreational rooms, stairwells, and elevators.[43]

From the city planner's perspective, the aim of any well-situated garage was to provide off-street parking day or night so that traffic could move easily through more spacious streets. In 1923 Chicago Plan Commission engineer Hugh Young examined the parking problem in relation to street parking, street layout, increased population, and increased use of automobiles.[44] Noting that the city's narrow streets were too frequently blocked by freight traffic or parked cars, he discouraged street parking in the business districts. Ban downtown street parking, he argued, and a street's capacity could be doubled with no added expense. To provide ample automobile storage and parking in business and other crowded urban districts near apartment buildings, hotels, or theaters, Young strongly recommended multi-floor ramp garages. Architects and developers sought to locate their garages in proximity to every transportation system, such as railroad terminals, elevated and surface line stations, and bus routes. Concurrent in 1926 with the increased use of motor buses for urban transit, Young and Taylor proposed a system of automobile garages located strategically along motor

coach routes and along the edge of the congested Loop. Motorists would park their cars in the double-spiral ramp garages, board buses driving through the garage, and ride to their final destination. Young and Taylor's garages would be built in two stages, producing a multi-level ramp garage with foundations capable of supporting a tall office tower that might later be built atop it and be serviced by the garage beneath.[45]

The increasing demand for parking facilities stimulated private investment in mortgage real estate bonds for modern parking garages. Architect for the Harrison Hotel (1930), Alfred Alschuler was commissioned by Motoramp Garages of Illinois to design a multiple-floor reinforced-concrete garage on Federal Street in the city's club district. Within walking distance of eighty Loop office buildings, ten major retail stores, and thirteen hotels, the garage could hold at least five hundred automobiles, and it would be utilized by a diverse group of motorists traveling to this retail district from many parts of the city. In Hyde Park, a prosperous residential and commercial neighborhood, Lewis M. Kroman designed the 55th Ritz Garage in 1929, still distinctive for its terra-cotta ornament cast in the shape of automobiles, wheels, stoplights, and automobile motors (fig. 16). This reinforced-concrete garage, occupying a large corner lot, contained three floors for garage space and a basement recreation room for chauffeurs. To store a greater number of automobiles in future years, the garage's foundations were designed to accept

an additional two floors.[46] With a capacity for four hundred cars, the Ritz Garage was carefully located in proximity to the Illinois Central railroad and surface trolley lines and within walking distance of ten nearby residential hotels and the University of Chicago.

The garage's location gave motorists direct access to the Outer Drive (then called Leif Eriksen Drive), an early urban concrete parkway laid along reclaimed lakefront land south of the city between Jackson Park and Grant Park. Chicago Plan Commission chairman James Simpson appointed the Outer Drive Committee in 1926, the same year that the modern double-deck Wacker Drive was completed along the Chicago River. Their purpose was to complete the more than twenty-mile lakefront development envisioned in the *Plan of Chicago* between Lincoln, Grant, and Jackson parks, and to connect over the river the two lakefront boulevards, North Lake Shore Drive and the Outer Drive (fig. 17).[47] Once again, Young and Bennett were asked to design an efficient street network consisting of viaducts and a monumental bridge to cross railroad freight yards, the Chicago River, and the Michigan Canal at the lakefront to connect North Lake Shore Drive with the Outer Drive. Local and through traffic could be separated to reduce congestion in the Loop. Despite the dramatically improved traffic circulation and standards of civic beauty that defined the Michigan Avenue, Wacker Drive, and other major quadrangle street improvements, Michigan Avenue was increasingly clogged by north-south traffic because motorists wishing to drive from one end of the city to the other were required to use Michigan Avenue, the most direct street connecting North Lake Shore Drive with the Outer Drive. According to the Plan Commission, the Outer Drive improvement would not only provide an essential link in the continuous lakefront park and boulevard system, but it would also direct increasing volumes of through traffic away from an already congested Michigan Avenue.

Considering costs, construction time, and the impact on the existing transportation systems, Young and Bennett, in concert with park commissioners and railroad officials, examined the strengths and weaknesses of three different methods for spanning the river: a moveable, low-level bascule bridge; a tunnel; or a fixed, high-level suspension bridge.[48] For aesthetic and economic reasons, the architects chose the low-level bascule bridge and accompanying viaducts, providing for future Outer Drive connections to East Wacker Drive and other important east-west streets. The viaducts were also designed to accommodate a future mezzanine level for storage or commercial motor truck traffic for the harbor and existing railroads in a manner similar to Wacker Drive. In keeping with the Plan Commission's standards for civic beauty, the viaducts were to be ornamented with balustrades and pylons similar to those decorating Wacker Drive. At the point where the lake joined the river, Young wanted a double-bascule bridge to provide "a pleasing and harmonious appearance, a fitting gateway to the city" (see Zukowsky, fig. 9).[49] Contracts for the project were finalized in 1929, but the Depression delayed completion until October 5, 1937, when the Outer Drive was opened by President Franklin D. Roosevelt in an inaugural ceremony on the bridge.

As Young had predicted, the Outer Drive became the city's most important north-south traffic route and a principal distributor highway for regional through traffic. Recognizing the highway's advantages, Young and the Chicago Plan Commission initiated plans to extend the Outer Drive farther north.[50] By 1942 North Lake Shore Drive had been extended or improved with innovative features, including grade separations and bridges at Belmont Avenue, LaSalle Street, and North Avenue. As part of the improvement and extension of Lake Shore Drive north of North Avenue, engineers installed an electric "movable traffic separator."[51] For about two miles, three remote-controlled, concrete-and-steel movable barriers were installed in trenches parallel to the eight traffic lanes in order to regulate heavy traffic flowing north or south during peak hours. Resembling a modern highway more than a traditional boulevard with numerous intersections, Chicago's Lake Shore Drive accommodated ever-faster automobiles with updated designs for entrance and exit ramps aligned along wide, sweeping curves that allowed for uninterrupted motion. The 1933-34 Century of Progress Exposition celebrated motion, and the lakefront site was planned by a commission of nationally famous architects, including Harvey Corbett, Edward Bennett, John Holabird, Raymond Hood, and others who conceived of elevated decks with moving sidewalks and escalators to shuttle crowds through the multi-story exhibition halls.[52] South of Grant Park, the Outer (Leif Eriksen) Drive, a modern limited-access, high-speed roadway, suited the fair's theme of motion, and its celebration of transportation and the automobile.[53] Among the exhibits by automobile manufacturers and their consulting industrial de-

signers, R. Buckminster Fuller displayed his Dymaxion automobile, a streamlined machine designed to race along superhighways high over the urban landscape of the future (see pls. 11-12; see Saliga, fig. 5).[54]

Norman Bel Geddes, a contemporary industrial designer and a rival of Fuller, also designed automobiles, consulted with automobile companies, and wrote about modern highways and the automobile. In *Magic Motorways* (1940) Bel Geddes contrasted existing traffic problems with his famous General Motors "Futurama" display designed for the 1939 World's Fair, "The World of Tomorrow," his vision of how the American metropolis would appear in 1960.[55] He cited the interior garage of the Jewelers Building and the Outer Drive, which partially conformed to his ideal motorway, but Bel Geddes recommended that motorways of the future should not transport automobiles directly to the center of densely built cities.[56] *Magic Motorways* was published when efforts were underway by the Bureau of Public Roads, in carrying out the Federal Highway Act of 1938, to explore a national system of highways. Bel Geddes's own "National Motorway Plan" of 1939 showed a gridlike pattern of motorways and feeder highways laid out to provide direct travel between cities.

In 1939, ten years after *West Side Superhighways*, Chicago's Department of Superhighways published *A Comprehensive Superhighway Plan for the City of Chicago*, motivated in part by the 27 percent increase in the number of registered automobiles in Chicago between 1929 and 1939. Regional, county, and state highway planning issues overlapped with Loop planning issues between 1920 and 1930, a decade when city population increased by 25 percent but when that of the metropolitan region increased by nearly 59 percent.[57] Seeking to accommodate one third of the state's total traffic then concentrated in the streets of Chicago, Hugh Young continued to develop several regional highway plans that had been considered in past years by the Chicago Plan Commission, including a 1933 comprehensive system of "limited ways."[58] Planners compiled origin and destination traffic surveys that proved how the Outer Drive, Michigan Avenue, Roosevelt Road, and Wacker Drive were inadequate to the rising numbers of automobiles entering the Loop.[59] And the parking problem remained critical.[60] In 1939 state, county, and city agencies recommended a redesigned radial system of depressed multi-lane, limited-access superhighways to deal with rush hour traffic surges and to separate through and local metropolitan traffic. The report recommended a West Side route along Congress Street with both elevated and depressed, or "parkway" highways. Aerial photographs show how the existing neighborhoods would be divided by large-scale superhighways and embankments cut through vast stretches of the urban environment. But World War II delayed any large-scale commitment to a regional and national network of

Fig. 17   Aerial view of the Outer Drive, 1929-37 (photo 1956).

high-speed motorways until the 1956 Federal Interstate Highway Act.

Immediately following the end of wartime restrictions on the use of gasoline and the production of automobile equipment, American motorists shifted back to the private automobile as the primary means of transportation. The metropolitan area was now much larger geographically, and the city's projected system of urban expressways radiating outward from the city's center would encourage even more automobile use and thereby dramatically strain the close relationship between architecture, the existing street system, and available parking facilities. When the Parking Committee of the Chicago Association of Commerce and Industry published its *Parking Plan for the Central Area of Chicago* in 1949, their proposals were significantly determined by the estimated 75 percent increase in the number of automobiles entering the Loop and the 65 percent increase in the number of passengers brought in by automobile since 1926.[61] How and where urban expressways connected to the Central Business District determined how effectively the peak traffic could be distributed to parking facilities. Ideally, numerous ramps would carry traffic to distributor streets, and adequately scaled parking garages would be built along peripheral business district streets to keep automobiles out of the congested core.[62]

Parking lots had been operated by the Chicago Park District at Monroe Street beginning in 1921 (fig. 12), behind the Art Institute and the Goodman Theater in 1937, and adjacent to Soldier Field in 1946. Planners believed that garages located at the edge of the business district would relieve congestion in the business center, but they discovered that there was relatively less open space available for new garage structures along the city's major thoroughfares.[63] The 1949 *Parking Plan for the Central Area of Chicago* recommended the immediate construction of seven new multi-level parking facilities located along the edges of the Central Business District, and within three blocks of major destinations in order to best serve those who worked and shopped in the city.[64] Connected to the Outer Drive and first envisioned in Young's *West Side Superhighways* as a major east-west thoroughfare, Monroe Street received four of these projects. With a projected capacity of 1,500 spaces, the largest of these 1949 proposals, however, was located in Grant Park adjacent to Michigan Avenue between Monroe and Randolph streets. With ties to Saarinen's 1923 project for a large

underground automobile terminal at the lakefront, the two-level Grant Park underground lot would be connected with both Michigan Avenue and Monroe Street, the latter to provide easy access to motorists from the Outer Drive.

In 1952 the City of Chicago embarked upon a comprehensive off-street parking program that included ten Loop facilities and thirty-four nearby facilities, all designed to satisfy increased demand for parking following the projected completion of the expressways.[65] To supplement this project, the Chicago Park District initiated plans for an enormous and costly underground parking garage in Grant Park. Completed in September

Fig. 18   Mayor Martin Kennelly officially opening the Grant Park North Underground Garage on Michigan Avenue at Monroe Street in September 1954.

Fig. 19   Shaw, Metz and Dolio, City of Chicago Parking Facility Number One, southwest corner of Wacker Drive and State Street, 1954-55 (now demolished).

Fig. 20   Skidmore, Owings and Merrill, Loop Transportation Center, 203 North LaSalle Street, 1982-85.

Fig. 21   Skidmore, Owings and Merrill, Loop Transportation Center, section.

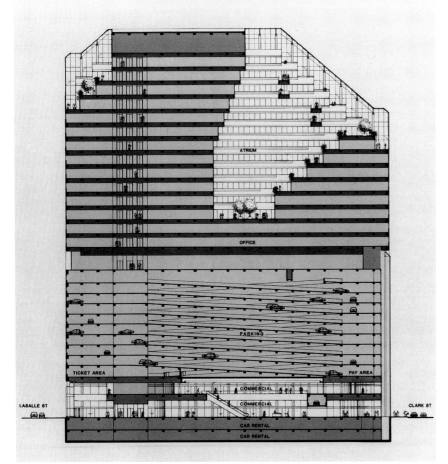

1954 after designs by Chicago consulting engineers Ralph H. Burke, Inc., the Grant Park North Underground Garage was hailed as the world's largest underground parking facility with capacity for 2,359 cars, when Mayor Martin Kennelly ceremoniously drove a Cadillac through a paper gateway (fig. 18).[66] Two basement levels and a mezzanine provided short-term self- or attendant-parking for Loop customers, who entered from Michigan Avenue ramps.[67] From inside the garage, underground passageways linked pedestrians to the Illinois Central's Randolph Street Station and the new Prudential Building on Randolph Street.[68]

As part of the 1952 parking program, the City of Chicago commissioned local architectural firms to design several new garages.[69] Parking Facility Number One opened in 1955, providing space for 718 cars that were hoisted mechanically to one of fourteen floors by five elevators designed by the Bowser Parking System, a mechanical elevator system used nationally in urban centers where confined sites made ramps unworkable (fig. 19).[70] The garage consisted of two storage towers with the Bowser elevator placed in between. Brick walls masked the elevators and linked the pair of open, cantilevered concrete-slab structures. Shaw, Metz and Dolio used an unusual screen of vertical steel cables, and situated the garage on Wacker Drive at State Street because Wacker Drive continued to serve as a primary distributor street for motorists who entered the city on the new expressways.

For the more than thirty intercity regional and national bus lines entering Chicago twenty-four hours a day, Skidmore, Owings and Merrill located their multi-level 1953 Greyhound Bus Terminal on an urban block in the congested Central Business District (see pl. 15). By 1956 approximately 1,650 out-of-town buses were entering and exiting the business district during a twelve-hour workday period, carrying nearly 25,500 passengers in and out of the city.[71] To preserve the block's retail character, buses were carried below street level in a tunnel connecting nearby Wacker Drive to the basement-level bus concourse. Above, a central waiting room and restaurant were joined by escalators to street-level retail shops. Similar to Hugh Young's earlier garage and office towers sited along motor coach routes, the terminal included a two-level auto parking garage on top, with provision for future office tower development. Now demolished, this terminal building serviced two principal forms of urban transportation, the bus and the car. The same firm designed the Loop Trans-

portation Center (1982-85; 203 North LaSalle Street), a twenty-six-story building next to the State of Illinois Building, combining retail and office space with facilities to meet the modern transportation needs of travelers using the subway, private automobile, or rental cars (figs. 20, 21). Suggesting images of contemporary airport design, a two-story atrium, over a pedestrian arcade joining the surrounding streets, contains offices for airlines, commercial chains, and car rental companies. Fulfilling 1920s visions of multi-level planes separating traffic types, one level below the street holds 150 rental cars, and the second level below grade joins the subway station and a pedestrian arcade with commercial space. In the tradition of the Jewelers Building and recent mixed-use skyscrapers erected along Wacker Drive, this combined garage and office building contains ten parking levels beneath the top thirteen office floors, all connected by separate elevator banks.[72]

Responding to the 1980s building boom and ever-increasing demand for Loop parking, contemporary Chicago architects have rejected the prototypical modernist slab garage structure, showing in several new garages a postmodern sensitivity to local materials, historic architectural traditions, and above all, to the pedestrian on the sidewalk. Anticipating the centennial of Marshall Field's and its restored department store, Lucien LaGrange and Associates was commissioned to design a twelve-story, mixed-use, self-park garage with space for 1,100 cars (fig. 22). The character of this pedestrian shopping district is retained by the ornamented and appropriately scaled street-level retail storefronts. Above, piers are paralleled by applied metal columns that unite with articulated concrete decks to represent the historic Chicago window.[73]

When the Oasis restaurants opened in 1959, they overlooked a metropolitan traffic reality that showed little in common either with the dream city promised in Bel Geddes's "Futurama" exhibit at the 1939 World's Fair or with the fantastic urban images from Ferriss's *The Metropolis of Tomorrow*. In 1953 a more practically minded Illinois State Toll Highway Commission was authorized by the State of Illinois to design and operate a system of toll highways "for the purpose of promoting the public welfare, and to facilitate vehicular traffic by providing convenient, safe and modern highways designed for the accommodation of the needs of the traveling public within and through the state of Illinois."[74] Having considered existing rural highway routes,

Chicago's expressway system, and a range of modern engineering problems, the planners outlined a beltway linking the expressways radiating from Chicago with existing state or county highways. The 187-mile tollway was under construction by September 1956 and completed in December 1958.[75]

In its early years the Illinois State Toll Highway Commission was chaired by economist Charles L. Dearing, for many years a staff member of the Brookings Institution and a prolific and influential writer on transportation. Dearing's commission hired consulting architect and planner Charles Genther and Pace Associates of Chicago to design its toll plazas, administration buildings, and restaurant service areas.[76] In Pace's contract, Genther stipulated that engineers would inspect the nation's existing turnpikes during 1956, including those in New Jersey, Massachusetts, Pennsylvania, Ohio, New York, and Oklahoma, with an aim to design the most up-to-date tollway system.[77] They discovered that most architects designed two separate

Fig. 22 Lucien LaGrange and Associates, Randolph-Wabash Self Park Garage and Retail Center, 1990-91.

and identical service areas, one on each side of the highway, accessible from the right lane, yet frequently located miles apart. But as part of their proposal submitted in December 1956, Genther and Pace put forward a prototype design for a group of identical over-the-highway restaurants, each of a type they cleverly called an Oasis, to be strategically sited along the Illinois Tollway around the perimeter of metropolitan Chicago (fig. 23). The simple glass-walled Oasis restaurants, which opened throughout 1959, provided diners with a sensational elevated view of the highway below.[78]

In the early expressway era Chicago had become a center for professional materials associations, including the American Concrete Institute and the Portland Cement Association. The Oasis structures relied on advanced engineering, concrete slab research, and the technology of prestressed concrete bridge girders.[79] The tollway's advanced engineering was symbolized by a construction and assembly system for bridge girders that were cast and pretensioned in nearby fields, and then transported by special tractors to bridge sites.[80] Stretched by engineers to new limits, prestressed, precast concrete helped the

commission meet tollway opening dates, while also saving fifty percent in construction time and millions of dollars in costs. In recognition of the tollway's modern design and short construction period, the prestigious Chicago Building Congress presented its annual award for highest achievement to the Illinois State Toll Highway Commission in 1959.

Charles Genther and the other three original partners of Pace Associates had worked or studied with Mies van der Rohe, and they displayed the training he had given them in economy and minimal design based upon the structural characteristics of the building materials.[81] Pace Associates designed a low, horizontal restaurant structure from concrete, glass, steel, and aluminum, economic in form and tied visually and materially to the flat ribbon of concrete highway. Similarly, the gridded concrete ceiling emulated the endless grid of the artificially sectioned landscape. Representing the relationship between the automobile and modern transportation architecture, the Oasis building conformed to theoretical design issues important to Charles Genther. Only a few years after the completion of his Oasis restaurant buildings, while address-

Fig. 23 Pace Associates; Charles Genther, principal architect, Des Plaines Oasis on the Northwest Tollway (now I-90), 1956-59 (aerial photo August 21, 1959).

Fig. 24 Hudgins, Thompson, Ball and Associates, Restaurant and service area on the Oklahoma Turnpike, near Vinita, 1956-58 (photo July 27, 1958).

ing a 1963 symposium celebrating modern architecture, Charles Genther delivered a paper entitled "Habitats for American Cosmopolites."[82] Genther examined two of his projects with Mies, Promontory Apartments and 860-880 North Lake Shore Drive, yet his opening comments reveal much of his own ideas about the relationship between architecture and technology, between "cosmopolites" and their built environments. According to Genther, the "cosmopolite American" possessed a "desire for the long view," one amply provided by the lakefront horizon visible through the glass walls of 860-880 North Lake Shore Drive. Similarly, in Genther's imagination motorists traveling in air-conditioned comfort along new interstate highways pursued open vistas, and they were presented with a "long view" from inside an Oasis overlooking the highway (fig. 25). Genther wrote that the cosmopolite "wants to view the horizon, to comprehend what is beyond, and to know that there is a beyond." This quest seems particularly expressive of the independence and mobility offered by the automobile. Here seems to be where Genther isolated a personal, guiding design principle that elucidates the "desire for the vast view," which he provided for motoring cosmopolites seated along window walls inside the Oasis restaurants. When first operated as a Fred Harvey Restaurant, the Oasis was decorated in an elegant modernist aesthetic, and visitors were accustomed to taking leisurely meals while traveling along the tollway.[83]

A principal link in the national highway network ran between Chicago and Oklahoma City,

where the Oklahoma Turnpike Authority had planned a four-lane divided turnpike system. The plans included modern restaurant and service areas.[84] Hired by the Oklahoma Turnpike Authority, planners at Continental Oil Company proposed an over-the-highway restaurant with dual service stations to serve motorists traveling in both directions along the Will Rogers Turnpike. In 1956 Continental Oil collaborated with the Oklahoma City architectural firm of Hudgins, Thompson, Ball and Associates to complete architectural drawings for an over-the-highway restaurant located near Vinita.[85] On the Turner Turnpike the soaring parabolic arch exploited the expressive and structural potential of prestressed and reinforced concrete (fig. 24).[86] Advanced methods of concrete shell construction permitted architects at Vinita to open up a vast and flexible interior space. Rising directly in view of motorists, the sweeping curve of the 52-foot-tall arch and the 100-foot, wide-span concrete beams stretched unimpeded over four lanes of traffic. Ironically, the Oklahoma Turnpike Authority subsequently permitted McDonald's to operate one of their restaurants at this site, and the soaring parabolic arch was promptly painted the same color as the chain's famous golden arch (see pls. 13-14).[87]

These inventive over-the-highway structures were emblematic of this country's infatuation with modernism, technology, and especially with the automobile and high-speed turnpike travel. A tradition of visionary plans and dreamlike cities, resplendent with soaring towers and endless avenues of carefully managed vehicles, com-

Fig. 25 *View looking out from an Illinois Tollway Oasis, c. 1959.*

plemented the desires and dreams captured in the automobile's capacity for independence and mobility. But throughout the motor age in Chicago, the noisy and congested streets and sidewalks obliterated the promising images of urban planners from the minds of most pedestrians and motorists. The inhabitant of the Jazz Age skyscraper city envisioned in Saarinen's 1923 lakefront plan might seem exhilarated by the auto-

mobile landscape: "He looks down and sees the dark endless chain of automobiles rush on ....He can follow it as far as the eye reaches." Seventy years later, during the centennial of the World's Columbian Exposition, Chicago's lingering dream city images seem removed in time and space when the highway landscape is viewed from an Oasis restaurant, an earlier world of tomorrow.

NOTES

This essay originated in a paper, "Oasis Ahead: Elevated Restaurants and Service Stations Across the Midwest's Interstate Highways," presented in 1990 to a conference, sponsored by the Society for Commercial Archeology, entitled "Highways to History: The Automobile Age." Two of my colleagues from the Society of Commercial Archeology, Jan Jennings (Cornell University) and Tyko Kihlstedt (Franklin and Marshall College), read early drafts of the essay, and their clarifying insights and suggestions are greatly appreciated.

1. Horton Trautman, "'Average Motorist' to Open Section of Tri-State Tollway," *Chicago Daily News* (Aug. 28, 1958), pp. 5, 56 (illus.). The North Tri-State Tollway connected Chicago's Edens Expressway with US Route 41 near the Wisconsin border. The Northwest Tollway connecting Chicago with South Beloit had opened on August 20, 1958, and the occasion was marked with automobile caravans and speeches by Illinois Governor Stratton and other officials.
2. *Architectural Forum* 109 (Sept. 1958), pp. 208-09. Accompanied by a color rendering, this advertisement for the American Steel and Wire Division of United States Steel boasts of speed and efficiency in the construction of these prestressed concrete structures.
3. As Plan Commission chairman James Simpson was supervising the design and initial construction of the Outer Drive, his editors in 1929 linked Chicago's comprehensive city planning efforts in architecture and landscape with the "dream city" built by the architects

of the World's Columbian Exposition; see James Simpson, "Chicago Is Pushing Out into Lake Michigan," *American Civic Annual* 2 (1929), p. 168.
4. Population and automobile figures (1906-70) from the Public Information Department of the Chicago Transit Authority are reproduced in Carl Condit, *Chicago, 1910-29: Building, Planning, and Urban Technology* (Chicago, 1973), pp. 320-21.
5. Roy D. Chapin, "The Motor's Part in Transportation," in Clyde L. King, ed., *The Automobile: Its Province and Problems, The Annals of the American Academy of Political and Social Science* 116 (Nov. 1924), p. 2.
6 Ibid., p. 5.
7. Eugene S. Taylor, "The Plan of Chicago in 1924, With Special Reference to Traffic Problems and How They Are Being Met," in King (note 5), p. 225.
8. Harvey Wiley Corbett, "The Problem of Traffic Congestion, and a Solution," *Architectural Forum* 46 (March 1927), p. 201.
9. The diverse responses of Chicago architects, urban planners, city boosters, and motorists to the automobile in the city is the subject of this author's dissertation at the University of Chicago. For a history of American roadside buildings such as the service station, automobile showroom, motel, and restaurant, see Philip Langdon, *Orange Roofs, Golden Arches: The Architecture of American Chain Restaurants* (New York, 1986), or Chester H. Liebs, *Main Street to Miracle Mile: American Roadside Architecture* (Boston, 1985). For an examination of Chicago's early automobile culture, see R. Stephen Sennott, "Chicago Architects and the

Automobile, 1906-26: Adaptations in Horizontal and Vertical Space," in Jan Jennings, ed., *Roadside America: The Automobile in Design and Culture* (Ames, Iowa, 1990), pp. 157-69. Described in *Rand-McNally's Souvenir Guide to Chicago* (Chicago, 1921), Automobile Row was the name given to Michigan Avenue south from 12th Street to 28th Street, where tourists could watch "the parade of motor cars" in the vicinity of showrooms and service garages.
10. Edward H. Bennett, "Some Aspects of City Planning With Reference to the Chicago Plan," in *Proceedings of the Fifth National Conference on City Planning* (Cambridge, Mass., 1913), p. 94.
11. Raised sidewalks had been previously imagined for Chicago, and Bennett's raised or arcaded sidewalk scheme resembles designs by Corbett. An arcaded sidewalk within the building line was eventually executed along a widened Congress Street in the Auditorium Building and Congress Hotel. Edward H. Bennett, *The Chicago Business Center and the Subway Question* (Chicago, 1926), p. 6; portions of this booklet were reprinted in "Raised Sidewalks and Traffic Separation Urged for Chicago," *American City* 35 (Sept. 1926), pp. 334-36. Objections to elevated sidewalk or street plans included poor light and air quality and detriment to existing architecture at street level. Some extreme proposals in New York for multi-decked structures of six to twelve stories carrying various transportation and pedestrian systems for miles along existing street corridors were rejected by some planners as gargantuan; see "Must We Come to This? And How About This?" *American City* 36 (June 1926), pp. 801-05.

12. The history of this urban planning movement is under revision; see William H. Wilson, *The City Beautiful Movement* (Baltimore, 1989). For an examination of Chicago and the City Beautiful Movement, see Daniel Bluestone, *Constructing Chicago* (New Haven, 1991); and Joan E. Draper, "Paris by the Lake: Sources of Burnham's Plan of Chicago," in John Zukowksy, ed., *Chicago Architecture, 1872-1922: Birth of a Metropolis* (Munich and Chicago, 1987), pp. 107-20; see also Mario Manieri-Elia, "Toward an 'Imperial City': Daniel H. Burnham and the City Beautiful Movement," in Giorgio Ciucci et al., *The American City: From the Civil War to the New Deal* (Cambridge, Mass., 1979). The history of urban planning in America has been explored in Blaine A. Brownell, "Urban Planning, the Planning Profession, and the Motor Vehicle in Early Twentieth-Century America," in Gordon E. Cherry, ed., *Shaping an Urban World* (New York, 1980); Peter Hall, *Cities of Tomorrow* (Oxford, 1988); John W. Reps, *The Making of Urban America: A History of City Planning in the United States* (Princeton, 1965); Daniel Schaffer, ed., *Two Centuries of American Planning* (Baltimore, 1988); Stanley K. Schultz, *Constructing Urban Culture: American Cities and City Planning, 1800-1920* (Philadelphia, 1989); and Mel Scott, *American City Planning since 1890* (Berkeley, 1969).

13. Taylor (note 7), pp. 226-27.

14. The history of Michigan Avenue, its bridge, and its architecture is examined in John W. Stamper, *Chicago's North Michigan Avenue* (Chicago, 1991). Prior to the bridge's completion, traffic entered Chicago from the north over the Rush Street bridge, which allegedly was burdened with 16 percent more traffic than the London Bridge; see Robert H. Moulton, "The Plan of Chicago," *Architectural Record* 46 (Nov. 1919), p. 462.

15. Taylor (note 7), p. 227.

16. Conceived as part of the Chicago Plan, the Wacker Drive improvement was initiated by the Chicago Plan Commission in 1917. Following the 1922 passage of a city ordinance, construction was begun by the Board of Local Improvements in late 1924. See Hugh E. Young, "New Wacker Drive Supplants Run-down Water-Front Street," *American City* 34 (April 1926), pp. 381-85.

17. On May 28, 1923, Charles Wacker delivered a lengthy address to the Chicago Plan Commission, the City Council, and the Mayor's cabinet, in which he stressed the need to continue to develop the city's architecture and streets in compliance with the Chicago Plan. His comments provide a vivid profile of the determination and civic pride that informed the planning efforts during the prosperous 1920s in Chicago. See "Proceedings of the Twenty-third Meeting of the Chicago Plan Commission," in *Thirteenth Annual Report of the Chicago Plan Commission* (Chicago, 1923), p. 1177.

18. When the Michigan Avenue improvement began, Robert H. Moulton published an article that described Michigan Avenue, Wacker Drive, and related lakefront improvements as a planning group, as well as park and railroad improvements; see Moulton (note 14), pp. 457-70.

19. Wacker Drive and all ongoing Plan Commission work was summarized annually; for Wacker Drive, see Chicago Plan Commission, *Chicago Plan Progress* (Chicago, 1927), pp. 35-36.

20. Young (note 16), pp. 381-82. One writer analyzed the role of Burnham's Plan in solving Chicago's street congestion; see Anne Lee, "Chicago's Traffic Problems Solved by Burnham Plan," *Architectural Record* 62 (Oct. 1927), pp. 262-72.

21. See Joan E. Draper, *Edward H. Bennett: Architect and City Planner, 1874-1954* (Chicago, 1982), pp. 16-17. In 1920 Hugh E. Young was asked to establish a separate engineering office. He lectured and published articles about Wacker Drive and other city planning projects.

22. See Andrew S. Rebori, "South Water Street Improvement, Chicago," *Architectural Record* 58 (Sept. 1925), pp. 217-22. Rebori details the demolition process and emphasizes the civic beauty of the project.

23. See "Chicago Double Deck Street for Congested District," *Engineering News Record* 85 (July 1920), pp. 173-75.

24. William Hudson Harper, ed., *Chicago: A History and Forecast* (Chicago, 1921), p. 249.

25. See Eliel Saarinen, "Project for Lake Front Development of the City of Chicago," *American Architect* 124 (Dec. 5, 1923), pp. 487-514. For discussion of this project in the context of the Chicago Tribune tower competition, see Robert Bruegmann, "When Worlds Collided: European and American Entries to the Chicago Tribune Competition of 1922," in Zukowsky (note 12), pp. 313-16.

26. Carol Willis, "Drawings Towards Metropolis," in Hugh Ferriss, *Metropolis of Tomorrow* (1929; rpt. Princeton, 1986), p. 160.

27. Harvey Wiley Corbett, "Different Levels for Foot, Wheel and Rail," *American City* 31 (July 1924), pp. 2-6, and idem, "The Problem of Traffic Congestion, and a Solution," *Architectural Forum* 46 (March 1927), pp. 201-08. In this article Corbett mentions double-deck boulevards in Chicago, referring to Wacker Drive and Michigan Avenue. The entire March 1927 number of *Architectural Forum* was devoted to articles about architecture for the automobile.

28. Corbett, "The Problem of Traffic Congestion" (note 27), p. 204.

29. In particular, see "Pedestrians Over Wheel Traffic," in Ferriss (note 26), pp. 66-67, in which he represents a raised pedestrian passage much like the sketches of multi-level streets he prepared for Corbett.

30. Daniel L. Turner, "The Detroit Super-Highway Project," *American City* 32 (April 1925), p. 373. Turner believed that the rail problem was just as important as the automobile problem. Not surprisingly, the concept for superhighways was developed in conjunction with planning for urban rapid-transit rail lines.

31. The Committee on West Side Improvements was formed in February 1928 by the Chicago Plan Commission, and the group issued their report in September 1929. The committee studied four superhighway proposals for transporting high-speed automobile traffic to and from the city along the following thoroughfares: Monroe, Austin-Kinzie, Polk, and Congress; see Chicago Plan Commission, *West Side Superhighways* (Chicago, 1929). Working with the Committee on West Side Streets, Edward Bennett examined elevated highways and the conflicting proposals regarding the Monroe and Polk Street Superhighways or his own Congress Street Superhighway, in his *Axis of Chicago* (Chicago, 1929), pp. 35-43.

32. Henry A. Blair, *A Plan for a Unified Transportation System for the City of Chicago* (Chicago, 1927), p. 7. In 1911 financier Henry Blair (1852-1932) had helped to consolidate the city's elevated roads under the Chicago Elevated Railways Collateral Trust, where he was a trustee until 1916.

33. Ernest P. Goodrich, "The Place of the Garage in City Planning," *Architectural Record* 65 (Feb. 1929), p. 198.

34. Urban garages were designed to suit a wide range of urban sites; see "Technical News and Research, Featuring Garages," *Architectural Record* 65 (Feb. 1929), pp. 177-97.

35. Miller McClintock, *Street Traffic Control* (New York, 1925), and McClintock and the Street Traffic Committee of the Chicago Association of Commerce, *Report and Recommendations of the Metropolitan Street Traffic Survey* (Chicago, 1926). For his discussion of traffic congestion, street parking, and street efficiency, see McClintock's "The Better Use of the City Street with Special Reference to Parking on and off the Street," *Bulletin of the Planning Foundation of America* (Oct. 1930).

36. Hawley S. Simpson, "Downtown Parking Garages," in Austin Macdonald, ed., *Planning for City Traffic. Annals of the American Academy of Political and Social Science* 133 (Sept. 1927), pp. 82-89.

37. Robert O. Derrick, "The City Parking Garage," *Architectural Forum* 46 (March 1927), pp. 233-40. For information about Albert Kahn's automobile and garage buildings, see Albert Kahn, "Sales and Service Buildings, Garages and Assembly Plants," *Architectural Forum* 46 (March 1927), pp. 209-14. For discussion of the city garage in relation to modern skyscrapers, see Albert Kahn, "Fisher Building Garage," *American Architect* 135 (Feb. 1929), pp. 265-68.

38. Equipped with a completely mechanized Ruth Safety Garage, the building contained four automobile elevators that automatically raised or lowered cars. The building was later known as the Pure Oil Building; see Sennott (note 9), pp. 166-67. Once used in Chicago, an inventive electric parking machine, something like a Ferris wheel, was developed by Westinghouse Electric and Manufacturing Company for use inside office buildings, theaters, hotels, or in vacant lots. See "Parking by Slot Machine," *American Architect* 136 (Nov. 1929), p. 74.

39. *The Gateway to Finance* was the title of a promotional brochure lent to the author by Robert A. Sideman.

40. Robert Bruegmann, *Holabird and Roche and Holabird and Root: An Illustrated Catalog of Works, 1880-1940* (New York, 1991), vol. 2, pp. 364-68. The architects designed several impressive garages during the early motor age, including the five-story concrete LaSalle Garage (1916-18, 1923 addition) on West Washington Street, and two projects for multi-story garages in 1926 for A. K. Foss; see Bruegmann, vol. 2, p. 362.

41. Ibid., vol. 2, pp. 387-91. Demolished for the Chicago Bar Association's new building, Marshall and Fox's Chicago Automobile Club was located in the city's elegant club district; see Sennott (note 9), pp. 160-61. A clubhouse for the Illinois Automobile Club (once the Motorists' Association of Illinois), designed by Philip Maher, was erected at the corner of 24th Street and South Michigan Avenue; see "Illinois Auto Club to Build on South Side," *Chicago Tribune* (Dec. 8, 1934). The Chicago Motor Club was described in "Architects Achieve Rare Beauty on Lobby Floor," *Motor News* (Jan. 1929), pp. 10-12. The author is grateful to Robert A. Sideman for providing these sources.

42. This important garage was frequently reproduced in American architectural journals; see *American Architect* 133 (June 20, 1928), pp. 835-37, and *Architectural Record* 65 (Feb. 1929), p. 191. Thanks to Isabelle Gournay for providing this reference for the Kent Garage, one of several American buildings that was reproduced in French popular culture magazines.

43. See Harold Blanchford, "The Layout of Automotive Buildings," *Architectural Forum* 46 (March 1927), pp. 281-87.

44. Hugh Young, "Day and Night Storage and Parking of Motor Vehicles," *Proceedings of the Fifteenth National Conference on City Planning* (Cambridge, Mass., 1923), pp. 176-211.

45. Hugh E. Young and Eugene S. Taylor, *Solving the Traffic Problem* (Chicago, 1926). This efficient building type sought to link motor coach and automobile transportation needs at six sites along major bus routes outside the quadrangle.

46. "Garage Resembling Bank Is Rising in Hyde Park," *Chicago Tribune* (May 19, 1929), part 3, p. 1. Ironically, the garage building now contains a bank and other retail outlets. See also "Loop, North Side Get Two New Garages," *Chicago Tribune* (June 23, 1929), part 3, p. 1. On West Lake Street, Nimmons, Carr and Wright designed an "Elizabethan style" multi-story garage, with rooftop wash racks, to hold over three hundred cars. On North Clark Street, Fox and Fox designed a multi-story garage — notable for carved limestone ornaments of winged tires — to hold over five hundred cars opposite a new tall apartment building. Each garage was erected on foundations that would be capable of holding additional garage levels at some future date, assuming the original buildings were financially viable. Thanks to Robert A. Sideman, who provided citations and additional information for these 1920s garages.

47. North Lake Shore Drive ended north of the river at Ohio Street, and the Outer Drive ended in Grant Park south of the river at Monroe Street. Each lakefront boulevard was developed at different times by the separate efforts of the Lincoln Park Commissioners and the South Park Commissioners. With the Chicago Plan Commission, these two groups collaborated to finance and design this important Outer Drive improvement. For an informative summary of the events preceding the formation of this committee, see Simpson (note 3), pp. 163-68. For a report on this improvement that includes drawings and maps for several different proposals, see Eugene Taylor, *The Outer Drive* (Chicago, 1929).

48.   Ibid., pp. 36-45. D. H. Burnham and Company proposed a monumental skyscraper bridge of twenty-five or more stories, one of several examples of this novel skyscraper type envisioned for American cities situated on waterfronts; see "A Skyscraper Bridge Proposed for Chicago," *Architectural Record* 64 (April 1928), p. 383. See also one for San Francisco in the same volume (July 1928), pp. 162-64.

49.   The features of the recommended Plan Number 2 for the Outer Drive improvement were described in a resolution presented to the park commissioners by the Chicago Plan Commission in June 1927; see Taylor (note 47), pp. 49-51.

50.   Hugh E. Young, "Lakefront Boulevard Link Forms Milestone in Chicago Plan," *Engineering News Record* 118 (April 15, 1937), pp. 546-48.

51.   Many of these improvements were completed with the assistance of the Works Administration Program; see Earl Minderman, "Chicago's New Lake-Front Highway," *American City* 57 (June 1942), pp. 41-42.

52.   "Preliminary Studies for the Chicago World's Fair," *Pencil Points* 10 (April 1929), pp. 217-28. Numerous site plans showed multi-level buildings joined by raised, moving sidewalks.

53.   Entry for the Chrysler Building in *Chicago, A Century of Progress, 1833-1933* (Chicago, 1933), p. 58.

54.   For more about Fuller's automobile and industrial design for the Century of Progress Exposition, see Richard Guy Wilson, "Transportation Machine Design," in *The Machine Age in America, 1918-1941* (New York, 1986), pp. 131-32.

55.   See Roland Marchand, "Part II — The Designers Go to the Fair: Norman Bel Geddes, General Motors 'Futurama,' and the Visit-To-the-Factory Transformed," *Design Issues* 8 (Spring 1992), pp. 23-40.

56.   Norman Bel Geddes, *Magic Motorways* (New York, 1940), pp. 69, 211, 230, 245.

57.   Philip Harrington, Department of Superhighways, *A Comprehensive Superhighway Plan for the City of Chicago* (Chicago, 1939), p. 23. Initial construction plans included five superhighways extending from the city totaling 32.5 miles.

58.   Committee on Traffic and Public Safety, *A Limited Way Plan for the Greater Chicago Traffic Area* (Chicago, 1933). Active from 1927 to 1931, the committee hired Miller McClintock, director of the Albert Russel Erskine Bureau at Harvard University, to assist with physical and fiscal matters.

59.   To educate the motoring public, the Chicago Plan Commission sponsored a series of ten WJJD radio broadcasts entitled "SOS Chicago!" the third of which featured a round-table discussion on Chicago's Superhighways. On the evening of July 24, 1939, an announcer led a discussion between newspaper journalists, Hugh Young, consulting engineer Charles DeLeuw, and realtor William McLennan concerning the financing, employment, and superhighway design features. Prewar planners believed that "breathing spaces," landscaped parkways between the highways and surrounding buildings, would benefit property abutting the system. See "SOS Chicago!" (Broadcast #3) "Superhighways for Chicago," typescript in the Chicago Historical Society.

60.   Planners discussed both private and municipal garages. Orin Nolting and Paul Oppermann, *The Parking Problem in Central Business Districts, With Special Reference to Off-Street Parking* (Chicago, 1938).

61.   Chicago Association of Commerce and Industry, *Parking Plan for the Central Area of Chicago* (Chicago, 1949), p. 9.

62.   George Emory, "Urban Expressways," *American Planning and Civic Annual* (1947), p. 128.

63.   With the increased number of cars, architects enlarged the scale and capacity of urban garages. See "Garages Grow Up," *Architectural Forum* 98 (Feb. 1953), pp. 121-41; Geoffrey H. Baker and Bruno Funaro, *Parking* (New York, 1958); and Dietrich Klose, *Metropolitan Parking Structures* (New York, 1965).

64.   *Parking Plan* (note 61), pp. 27-37.

65.   Baker and Funaro (note 63), p. 67.

66.   "A Gate Crasher Opens the World's Biggest Underground Garage," *Clay Pipe News* 20 (Nov./Dec. 1954), cover and pp. 6-7, 11. New suburban shopping centers threatened the viability of downtown shopping districts, so parking rates were kept low to attract shoppers back to the city.

67.   Henry Kramer, "Parking 5,000 Cars a Day," *American City* 70 (June 1955), pp. 166-71. During construction, traffic was diverted to a parallel temporary avenue east of Michigan Avenue as ramps and portions of the garage were completed beneath Michigan Avenue and a replanted Grant Park. A similar parking facility with a capacity for approximately 1,500 cars, the Grant Park South Underground Garage, also designed by Ralph H. Burke, Inc., opened March 4, 1965.

68.   Klose (note 63), pp. 32-33 and 184-87. At the time, the owners of the Prudential Building boasted that their structure had the biggest built-in garage serving a single office building in the country; see "Chicago's Prudential Building," *Architectural Forum* 97 (Aug. 1952), pp. 90-99.

69.   "Nine Garages for City of Chicago Make a Frontal Attack on Parking Problem," *Architectural Record* 115 (March 1954), pp. 153-58.

70.   Louis Farina, "Chicago's Comprehensive Parking System," *American City* 74 (May 1959), pp. 110-11.

71.   "Greyhound's New Chicago Terminal," *Architectural Record* 115 (April 1954), pp. 167-73. For related transportation statistics on regional highway development, see the report prepared for the Chicago Regional Planning Association by Daniel H. Burnham, Jr., and Robert Kingery, *Planning the Region of Chicago* (Chicago, 1956), p. 169.

72.   Information on this building was provided by Greg Beard of Skidmore, Owings and Merrill.

73.   As an indication of the improved design status of this formerly unpopular building type, the Randolph-Wabash Retail Center and Self Park Garage, along with the North Michigan Avenue Crate and Barrel Store, was awarded "Best New Building of 1991" by the Friends of Downtown; see Eric Joss, "Parking + Retail + Equity = Quality Long Term Investment," *Realty and Building* (Feb. 1, 1992).

74.   See Joseph K. Knoerle and Associates, *Toll Road Program for the State of Illinois* (May 1954), p. 1.

75.   Following the first full year of operation in 1959, additional extensions and routes have been completed; see *Illinois Tollway, Concise History* (Chicago, 1989), a brief booklet published for the tollway's thirtieth anniversary.

76.   The consulting engineering firm Joseph K. Knoerle and Associates of Chicago and Baltimore was contracted to supervise the entirety of the tollway project, including soil testing and traffic analysis. This firm designated Pace Associates to design the special facilities for the tollway, including plazas, lighting, safety barriers and other modern safety and engineering features. In February 1957 Charles Dearing discussed the Illinois Tollway in two radio broadcasts for the NBC program "New World."

77.   The author wishes here to express his appreciation to Sari Mintz, Shirley Hazelton, and Susan Rader of the Illinois Tollway Authority who provided months of generous assistance as well as access to their document and photo archives.

78.   Following a competitive bidding period, leases were arranged in 1957 with Standard Oil Company of Indiana to pay for construction, and with Fred Harvey Company to operate the restaurants and gift shops.

Opening between May and November 1959, the five original Oasis restaurants were located near Lake Forest (Tri-State), Des Plaines (Northwest), Hinsdale (Tri-State), Belvidere (Northwest), and O'Hare (Tri-State).

79.   In part motivated by the perceived urgency of Department of Defense needs, the federal highway program generated large-scale research projects to determine maximum loads for concrete structures and pavements. Between La Salle and Ottawa, Illinois test loops were designed for testing pavements. See "King-Size Test Road Holds Future Answers," *Engineering News-Record* 160 (June 19, 1958), pp. 52-55. The Illinois Tollway in Charles Dearing's era was cited for its engineering and material expertise. See "AASHO Bridge Studies Will Start Soon," *Engineering News Record* 161 (July 10, 1958), pp. 49-51; Paul Gordon, "Cutting Forming Time for Bridge Piers," *Engineering News-Record* 162 (May 28, 1959), pp. 37-38; and Edward Abdun-Nur and Joseph Waddell, "Control of Concrete Mixes," *Journal of the American Concrete Institute* 30 (March 1959), pp. 947-61.

80.   See "$441 Million Tollways to Open," *Engineering News-Record* 161 (Aug. 7, 1958), pp. 37-42.

81.   Many thanks to Shirley Genther for access to her late husband's files, and for a memorable and fascinating conversation about Charles ("Skipper") Genther and Pace Associates. See "The Fast Pace," *Newsweek* (Sept. 8, 1952), p. 55. Pace Associates was begun in January 1946 by Charles Genther, with John Kausal, William B. Cobb, and W.H. Binford. Thanks to John Kausal and John Black, two former Pace architects, for informative interviews.

82.   See Charles Genther, "Habitats for American Cosmopolites," *Four Great Makers of Modern Architecture* (New York, 1963), pp. 124-28.

83.   Following the original five Oasis restaurants, the Illinois Tollway later opened additional over-the-highway restaurants, including one by David Haid. Near South Holland, Illinois on the Tri-State Tollway, Haid's single-span steel structure, noted for its unadorned character and its aesthetic refinement, was given an award in 1968 by the American Institute of Steel Construction; see Donald David Logan, "Rest Stop 1000 Feet Ahead — In Quality," *Architectural Forum* 129 (Sept. 1968), pp. 76-79.

84.   See H. E. Bailey, "A Turnpike-Expressway System for Oklahoma: A Plan," *Traffic Quarterly* 10 (Jan. 1956), pp. 45-66.

85.   The firm Hudgins, Thompson, Ball and Associates was formed in 1942. Employed as an engineering draftsman during the 1930s by the Oklahoma State Highway Commission, architect Ed Hudgins designed this turnpike structure, which opened in February 1958. It was the country's first over-the-highway restaurant to open for business; see Robert Paul Jordan, "Our Growing Interstate Highway System," *National Geographic Magazine* 133 (Feb. 1968), pp. 195-218; and "Red Carpet in the Sky," *Red Triangle Magazine* (Jan./Feb. 1958), cover and pp. 2-5.

86.   The National Restaurant Association's annual conventions regularly included sessions on restaurant architecture and design directed by a nationally important restaurant architect. For two examples of parabolic arched restaurants, see "Eye-Catching in Design, Efficient in Layout," *American Restaurant Magazine* 42 (Feb. 1958), pp. 50-51. For drive-in restaurants catering to transient customers, see "Drive-In Restaurants and Luncheonettes," *Architectural Record* 100 (Sept. 1946), pp. 99-113.

87.   Thanks to Vinita, Okla., librarian Annabelle Southern, who managed the Glass House Restaurant for many years, for her generous assistance in arranging a tour of the building in 1990 and for access to her collection of photographs and clippings related to this structure.

"All Airplanes Lead to Chicago": Airport Planning and Design in a Midwest Metropolis

David Brodherson

Even before World War I proved the dependability and safety of airplanes for commercial transportation, Chicagoans had begun to make the city a national and international aviation hub. Approximately fifteen years before the passage of the Federal Air Commerce Act of 1926, which delegated responsibility to local governments for the development of airports, private- and public-sector groups in the Chicago metropolitan area were laying the foundation for the construction of ground facilities for regularly scheduled passenger air transportation.[1] Although the Air Commerce Act did not prohibit further private-sector airport investment, municipalities assumed greater powers and had bigger treasuries to make long-term commitments to the construction and constant improvement of these costly infrastructural complexes. Just as ancient Rome became a node in a network of roads and traffic, the claim was made in 1927 that "all airplanes lead to Chicago."[2]

Between December 1903, when the Wright Brothers made the first powered airplane flight, and the mid-1920s, Chicago had only rudimentary and temporary airfields that were generally little more than open fields with storage buildings or tents used by barnstormers.[3] By 1931, however, twenty-five airports or airfields, including Chicago Municipal Airport (now Midway Airport), were operating in the region. In the postwar years Chicago added Meigs Field and O'Hare International Airport. Without a doubt, Midway and O'Hare have contributed most to the development of the Chicago metropolitan area as an air hub. But the city has lately undertaken planning a new airport for a site near Lake Calumet on the Southeast Side. Any decision related to a third airport will be equally important to the city and the region.

From the early 1920s the airport, much like the skyscraper, became important to Chicago, as an expression of progressive government and commerce, urban pride and competition. In 1922 Lieutenant Bert Shoemaker, an employee of the Chicago Aeronautical Bureau and the supervisor of the city's first municipal airfield, boastfully predicted its aerial hegemony: "Chicago is destined to be the air center of the world."[4] Two years later Charles H. Wacker, chairman of the Chicago Plan Commission, declared that the development of satisfactory airfields was "one of the first necessities toward the development of this city as a center of the aircraft industry."[5] Wacker believed that the airplane would be to Chicago what the automobile was to Detroit. In 1944 Ralph H. Burke, a civil engineer, devoted civil servant, and the director of the Postwar Economic Advisory Council of Chicago, completed the *Report of Commercial Airport Requirements for Chicago*. Outlining the plans for a new Municipal Airport, Burke reminded his political and professional colleagues that "the industrial leadership of Chicago depends upon its ability to remain a great center of travel."[6]

In the post-World War II decades the air transportation industry matured, and sophisticated airport plans and designs became tantamount to mass-transit facilities serving millions of passengers annually. In 1988, for example, 26,596,800 people boarded planes at O'Hare International Airport, while 3,174,057 enplaned at Midway Airport.[7] As a result of the ever-increasing volume of air travelers, these facilities grew to be cities within cities instead of static monuments of architecture. Chicagoans have shouldered aside other cities in the competition to develop the best and busiest airports benefiting the city and the region. In the summer of 1961 Commissioner of Aviation William E. Downes, Jr., with the construction of O'Hare International Airport underway, boasted, "Once the crossroads of America, Chicago is now the crossroads of the world."[8] More recently, Mayor Richard M. Daley, unveiling plans for the new International Terminal at O'Hare Airport, announced that "if Chicago is to retain its position as a world-class city, then nothing is as important to this goal as building a world-class international terminal."[9] Not surprisingly, civic officials, led by Mayor Daley, invoked the same sort of rhetoric as they pushed their plans for a new regional airport at Lake Calumet.[10]

Fig. 1   Paul Gerhardt, Jr., Chicago Municipal Airport (now Midway Airport), 5700 South Cicero Avenue, 1945-47.

Chicago's First Airports

In 1926 contractors completed construction of one of the first airport passenger terminals in the United States. Architect Albert Kahn designed the facility on a 1,440-acre tract in Lansing, Illinois, for Henry and Edsel Ford. Unlike the divided responsibility for our air transportation system today, private enterprises that linked airport development with other aspects of commercial development were commonplace in the 1920s and early 1930s. Kahn's building, a "depot-hangar," combining an office, passenger waiting room, and a hangar, was sited on the Ford Airport and housed Ford Tri-motor airplanes flown by a Ford airline primarily serving Ford Motor Company business in nearby Hegewisch. This simple, factorylike but attractive depot-hangar still stands.[11]

Meanwhile, on the opposite side of the city in the northern suburbs, private-sector groups were developing three airports all clustered within a radius of three miles of each other. These facilities, the Curtiss-Reynolds, Sky Harbor, and Palwaukee airports, were almost due west of the suburb of Winnetka. In the late 1920s the Curtiss-Wright Corporation, an aircraft manufacturing company, developed a "chain of strate-

Fig. 2 Andrew N. Rebori of Rebori, Wentworth, Dewey and McCormick, Perspective rendering of the entrance to the Curtiss-Reynolds Airport, 1930; from Western Architect 39 (March 1930), opp. p. 39.

Fig. 3 Andrew N. Rebori of Rebori, Wentworth, Dewey and McCormick, Ground-floor plan of the Curtiss-Reynolds Airport; from Western Architect 39 (March 1930), pl. 35.

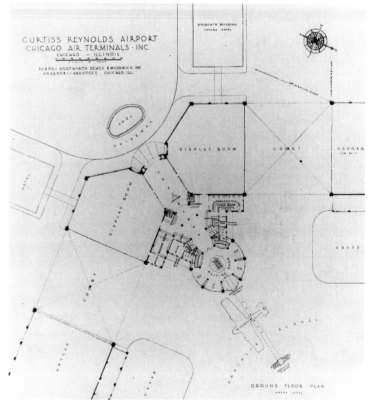

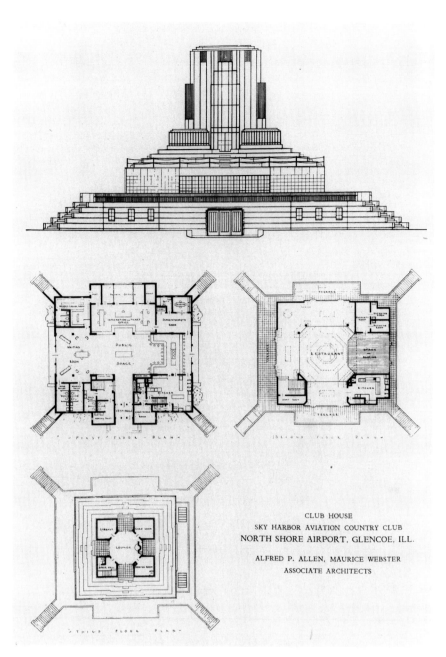

CLUB HOUSE
SKY HARBOR AVIATION COUNTRY CLUB
NORTH SHORE AIRPORT, GLENCOE, ILL.

ALFRED P. ALLEN, MAURICE WEBSTER
ASSOCIATE ARCHITECTS

Fig. 5 Alfred P. Allen and Maurice Webster, Elevation and plans of Sky Harbor Aviation Country Club, North Shore Airport, Glencoe, c. 1929; from American Architect *136 (July 1929), p. 88.*

Fig. 4 Andrew N. Rebori of Rebori, Wentworth, Dewey and McCormick, Perspective rendering of the waiting room and restaurant of the Curtiss-Reynolds Airport; from Western Architect *39 (March 1930), pl. 33.*

gically located airports" stretching across the country. Curtiss-Wright airports, some of which were built or operated with local financial assistance, were located in or near such cities as New York and Baltimore in the East, Chicago, Milwaukee, and St. Louis in the Midwest, and Los Angeles and San Francisco in the West. By 1930 the Curtiss-Wright network had grown to include twelve airports and thirty-five "flying service bases."

In 1929 architect Andrew N. Rebori of Rebori, Wentworth, Dewey and McCormick developed the master plan of and designed individual buildings for the Curtiss-Reynolds Airport, located near Glenview, approximately twelve miles northwest of the Loop. The architects planned a passenger terminal complex and a private aviation club. Both were to be situated at the end

of a major diagonal axis extending from the intersections of two roadways. A row of symmetrically arrayed and connected outbuildings extended from each side of the club and the passenger terminal.[12]

Rebori's passenger terminal, which was never erected, was an unusual mélange (fig. 2).[13] It included automobile parking lots, offices, service spaces, and an array of amenities to serve waiting travelers, as well as outbuildings including a hotel and hangars; but the terminal also had two display rooms, where aircraft were exhibited. Divided into two distinct but connecting buildings with partially separated paths for incoming and outgoing people, the terminal was a precursor of ones erected after World War II (fig. 3). The "landside" building housed preliminary passenger processing such as ticketing, in addition to a waiting room, rest rooms, information desk, concessions, lunch room, and restaurant on the ground floor. The second story contained offices; the third floor had a restaurant with a dance floor and a stage for a band, as well as a promenade leading to an outdoor observation deck (fig. 4). The Curtiss-Reynolds Airport, however, operated only briefly as part of a private-enterprise transportation network. The owners never finished the passenger terminal, and this site never became a substantial hub of commercial air transportation. The United States Navy took over the ground facility in 1937 along with an adjacent golf course, and then combined the two facilities into what is now the Glenview Naval Air Station.[14]

The Sky Harbor Airport, variously named the North Shore Airport and the Sky Harbor Aviation Country Club, was located approximately five miles west of Glencoe. Sky Harbor, which began operating in 1929, was the patrician aviator's answer to the plebeian automobilist's roadhouse. Alfred P. Allen and Maurice Webster created a "modernistic" building, the exterior of which was almost a literal stone-for-stone interpretation of a Mayan temple (fig. 5). Facilities for travelers, such as a lunch counter, information and ticket office, waiting room and rest rooms occupied the first floor. A restaurant, stage, dance floor, and terrace were on the second floor. A lounge was located in the middle of the third floor surrounded by a library, card room, and a sleeping room.[15] The building also accommodated commercial and general aviation passengers. The Grey Goose Air Lines utilized space on the first floor of the terminal as part of its service linking the North Shore to Chicago's Municipal Airport.[16]

Airport Planning and Design   77

Of the three airports originally developed in the northern suburbs of the Chicago metropolitan area, only the Palwaukee Airport remains available for public use. What was a privately owned facility constructed around 1929 is now a modestly sized, modern municipal airport serving local general aviation. The original Palwaukee terminal is notable because it combined facilities to fuel automobiles and to house passengers briefly.

The Airports Today

In 1993 Meigs Field, Midway Airport, and O'Hare International Airport together assure that Chicago remains a major hub in a national and international transportation network. Recently, the city and state have been debating the site of a proposed new airport to perpetuate this aerial hegemony. But in 1920, in response to the widely recognized *Plan of Chicago* of 1909 prepared by Daniel H. Burnham and Edward H. Bennett, the City of Chicago began a landfill creating Northerly Island in Lake Michigan. This island was one of several suggested lakefront sites for an airport, which eventually resulted in the development of Meigs Field. Waterfront locations both raised and solved certain urban, environmental, and aeronautical problems. The lake, for example, could serve a wide variety of water-based craft such as seaplanes and flying boats in addition to land-based craft operating from the adjacent shore. But stormy, lake-effect weather could make operations hazardous. While an airport in or at the edge of the lake would be conveniently close to Chicago's Loop, it would be an environmentalist's and park planner's nightmare—a hazard to park users, a noisy nuisance, and a potential source of water pollution. It would also be more difficult to engineer and more costly to build and maintain. Consequently, despite the benefits of a waterfront airport near the Central Business District, the decision to build such an airport was delayed from 1924 until approximately 1945, even though dozens of schemes had been proposed.[17]

Before Chicago employed Northerly Island as the site for an airport, the city used and considered the island for other purposes. The city also contemplated other sites for such an offshore airport, from suburban Evanston to "points well south of the Loop."[18] Harold F. McCormick was one of the earliest proponents of an airport on the lake.[19] A year after observing the enthusiasm for an air show held in Grant Park in 1911, the industrial magnate envisaged an airport on this

site as a "threshold" for "guests" winging their way to the city. In 1924, under the leadership of Charles H. Wacker, the Chicago Plan Commission suggested the construction of two lakefront airports, one of which would be on an island slightly further east from the shore than Northerly Island.[20] Wacker and his successors to the Plan Commission in the 1920s and 1930s, James Simpson and Colonel A. A. Sprague, all believed that a waterfront airport would beautify the park lining the lake. In December 1934 the famed American World War I aviator Captain Eddie Rickenbacker complained that air traffic clogged the Municipal Airport.[21] He thought that a lakefront airport at 16th Street—considered by the Chicago Plan Commission, backed by Mayor Edward J. Kelly, and supported by the Aeronautics Branch of the United States Department of Commerce—was an ideal solution. Rickenbacker believed that an additional ground facility would lessen congestion at the Municipal Airport at Cicero Avenue and 63rd Street and add a convenient airlink between it and the Central Business District. Although the Chicago Plan Commissioners and other civic leaders realized the importance of an airport as an integral component of urban access systems, they were unable to implement their idea.

In 1930 the New York architectural firm of Voorhees, Gmelin and Walker had advised that an airport be located on the east side of Northerly Island as part of their proposed multi-island site plan for the 1933-34 Century of Progress Exposition (fig. 6). The airport would have two symmetrically arranged passenger terminals strategically located to serve both airplanes and seaplanes, and eight runways to permit more craft to operate simultaneously, as well as to avoid landing or takeoff in cross winds, to which airplanes of the period were particularly sensitive. The airport was never built as anticipated, but Northerly Island still served as the home of the Century of Progress Exposition (see Doordan, fig. 3).

In 1945 the engineering firm De Leuw, Cather and Company and consulting architect Andrew N. Rebori proposed several designs for an airport in the lake near the eastern tip of Navy Pier.[22] In one version a causeway in shallow water would extend northeast from the pier across an existing breakwater to the island airport. The facility would have three runways, the longest of which would be 10,000 feet, and a completely protected harbor for seaplane anchorage and partially protected water for landing and takeoff. The airport would have a single passenger terminal stra-

Fig. 6   Voorhees,
Gmelin and Walker,
Site plan study for the
Century of Progress
Exposition, c. 1930
(cat. no. 15).

Fig. 7   Andrew N.
Rebori, Bird's-eye view
of proposed Chicago
Harbor Airport, 1945
(cat. no. 100).

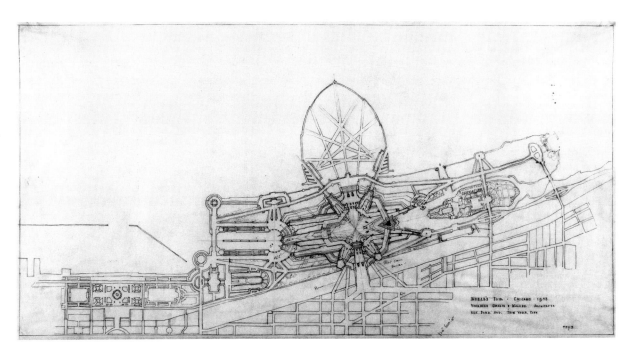

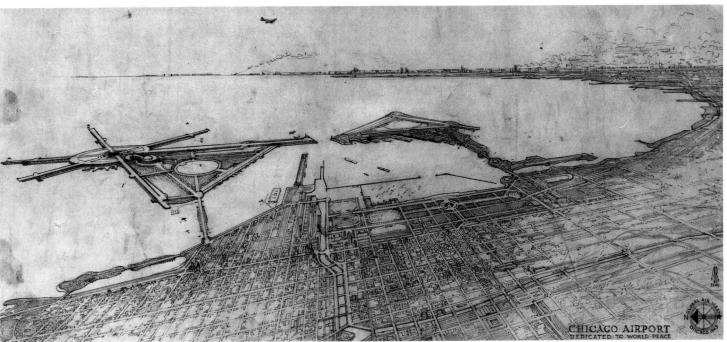

tegically located to serve both airplanes and sea-planes. Instead of buildings for repair and storage of airplanes above ground, the airfield would have three lifts, which, much like a naval aircraft carrier, would move vehicles between an underground hangar and the flight deck. In a more elaborate scheme the airport would be closer to shore but slightly further north (fig. 7). The airport itself was to have been part of a multi-modal transportation complex at the mouth of the Chicago River, with another land-scaped island and maritime facilities to the south. A causeway from Northerly Island, where a short runway was planned, would have con-nected the additional island to the city.

After the Chicago Citizens Committee, chaired by Mayor Kelly, had failed in its 1945 attempt to persuade the recently founded United Nations to locate its headquarters on Northerly Island,[23] the city itself, guided by consulting engineer Ralph Burke, began to construct a small airport, which opened in December 1948 at a cost of $2 million with the provisional name of Northerly Island Air Strip (fig. 8).[24] Six months later the City Council renamed the airport Meigs Field, in honor of Merrill C. Meigs, a local civic leader and aviator. Even before the city erected a per-manent passenger terminal on the island, the field was the "busiest single runway airport in [the] world" for many years.[25] In 1951 the

Airport Planning and Design   79

Department of Aviation erected a modest, wood-frame passenger terminal, and a year later it added an air traffic control tower operated by the Federal Aviation Administration.[26] By 1959 the Department of Aviation had made plans to replace the old passenger terminal, criticized as a dirty and inadequate "shack," and the department employed the Chicago architectural firm Consoer and Morgan to design a new, larger terminal, finished in the fall of 1961.[27] The boxy but well-proportioned cruciform-plan building measures 182 by 60 feet. The glass-walled center pavilion rises three stories, while the two symmetrical, precast masonry wings are two stories. A second-floor observation balcony bridges the lobby in the center section connecting the wings and forms an interior observation deck.

In the late 1960s Chicagoans began to search for a location for an additional major airport. Civic leaders and designers revived the idea of an airport in the lake. After conferring with Commissioner of Aviation William Downes and William McKee, the local administrator of the Federal Aviation Administration, Congressman Roman C. Pucinski suggested that an airport be built on stilts in Lake Michigan.[28] Pucinski thought that the runways could be electrically heated using atomic power to keep them clear of ice and snow in the severe winters. A causeway could connect the airport to the shore. At the request of Mayor Richard J. Daley, the architectural firm of C. F. Murphy Associates prepared a design for a major jetport a few miles out in the lake, but, again, citizens resisted the proposal, and the idea went no further.[29]

At the same time that Chicago civic leaders, aviators, architects, engineers, and planners were promoting or actually constructing waterfront airports, they were also planning inland airports to make the city an aerial hub. Their efforts resulted in the construction of Midway and O'Hare airports and have boosted current plans for a new third airport. While these prewar and postwar airports share many features, their terminals differ. Passenger terminals in the prewar period were beautiful but static works of architecture, similar to railroad stations. After World War II, particularly with the introduction of jet aircraft such as the Boeing 707 in 1957, such depots were no longer adequate. The capacity of aircraft grew so large and the disparity in size between surface vehicles and airplanes became so great that architects, engineers, and planners were forced to rethink airport design. Especially in the 1950s, as designers began to approach air transportation as "mass transit," these special-ists devised terminals such as the ones at O'Hare International, which, in addition to being beautiful buildings, were mechanical conveyances to move and process people as a form of delicate freight. Designers prior to World War II had advocated the incorporation of mechanical features such as retractable loading gangways or "jetways," moving walkways, and light rail systems linking the airport to the Central Business District, but architects, engineers, and planners did not begin building these mechanical systems for airports and their passengers until the 1950s, when large numbers of air travelers were attracted by lower fares, and bigger and faster aircraft made these mechanical improvements financially feasible.[30] Since that time, major airports like O'Hare have become semi-autonomous cities within cities covering thousands of acres with independent newspapers, medical facilities, security staffs, restaurants, hotels, entertainment and conference centers, chapels, internal surface transit systems, electrical or heating and cooling plants, all operated by distinct and specialized administrative structures and staffs.

The city's first municipal facility was established in 1922 by the Chicago Aeronautical Bureau on the Southwest Side at the intersection of 63rd Street and Cicero Avenue (fig. 9).[31] On December 13, 1927, the City of Chicago dedicated its new airport, a facility that served seven airlines making sixteen departures daily. A newly expanded subdivision of the Department of Public Works, the Bureau of Parks, Recreation and Aviation, managed the airport. Here passengers en route to New York, the Twin Cities, Dallas, San Francisco, and intermediate points boarded from factorylike buildings attached to hangars constructed for such companies as National Air Transport, Boeing Air Transport, Grey Goose Air Lines, and Universal Air Line.

The following year the City of Chicago began planning an "enormous administration building," approving a bond of approximately $150,000 in 1931 for a terminal and other airport improvements.[32] After conferring with airport managers, studying other terminals, and examining the results of the Lehigh Airport Competition, City Architect Paul Gerhardt, Jr., designed a building based upon the concept of a union railroad depot that combined spaces and services for several air transportation companies while acting as a single impressive urban gateway (figs. 10, 11).[33] Monumentally sited and internally divided like a railroad depot, Gerhardt's terminal was on the eastern edge of the airport at the intersection of Cicero Avenue and 62nd

Fig. 8 Aerial view of Northerly Island and Meigs Field, c. 1958.

Fig. 9 Aerial view of Chicago Municipal Airport, Cicero Avenue at 63rd Street, 1929.

Street. Gerhardt incorporated motifs from civil and military aviation such as waiting room light fixtures that were modeled after aerial bombs, pilasters capped by flying corps insignia, and a stainless steel ornament over the main entrance that combined a flying corps insignia with the seal of the City of Chicago. Bentwood furniture occupied the marble-floored waiting room; otherwise, the city architect created an attractive but austere and relatively inexpensive building, a pleasing mix of Art Deco and modernist architecture. Mayor Anton Cermak and other local dignitaries dedicated the building on November 15, 1931.

Within eight years, however, airport traffic had increased so quickly despite the Depression that the terminal, outbuildings, and the access roads from the Loop had all become inadequate. Between 1931 and 1943 passenger traffic alone increased more than 600 percent.[34] Despite the demands of commercial air transportation upon Chicago Municipal Airport, the Depression and World War II stalled city plans to build a new higher-capacity passenger terminal. At the same time, the Illinois National Guard, which had operated from a hangar on the south side of the airport since the early 1920s, expanded its airport headquarters.[35] The resulting building complex by Klekamp and Whitmore comprised two hangars, space for personnel to live, and room to prepare for operations. These included a machine shop, garage, officers' club and quarters, enlisted men's quarters, offices, lunch room, conference room, and a parachute packing room.

In 1939 the architectural firm of Burnham and Hammond was employed by one of the major airlines to plan and design a new terminal at

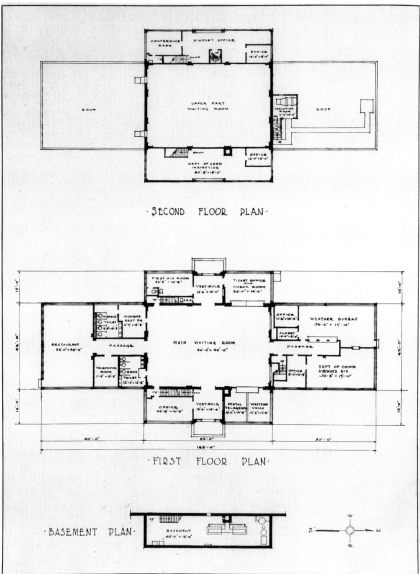

Municipal Airport, as well as to help persuade competing lines and city officials of its need. Although the city recognized the need to in-

Fig. 10 Paul Gerhardt,
Jr., Chicago Municipal
Airport, Cicero Avenue
at 62nd Street, 1929-31
(now demolished).

Fig. 12 Paul Gerhardt,
Jr., Chicago Municipal
Airport (now Midway
Airport), 5700 South
Cicero Avenue, 1945-47
(now greatly altered).

Fig. 11 Paul Gerhardt,
Jr., Plan of the
Administration
Building, Chicago
Municipal Airport,
1929-31; from
Architectural Record 71
(Feb. 1932), p. 18.

crease passenger terminal capacity, it lacked the funds for any new construction because it had committed all available money to other airport projects. Instead of the immediate erection of a terminal, the local government negotiated an agreement with the airlines for financing terminal improvements, which became an enabling act on January 29, 1942. This law, which has continued to be the foundation for the financing of terminal design and construction, required that the airlines loan the city money for these projects. The city would own and operate the airports, and it would repay the loan from the income derived from the operation of the airport. Although the enabling act resolved financial problems, the subsequent restrictions upon the use of strategic materials designated for World War II precluded construction.[36]

Once the war was over, the Department of Public Works erected a new terminal designed by Paul Gerhardt in 1945, and completed in 1947 on the west side of Cicero Avenue at the north-

Fig. 13 Albert Kahn,
United Airlines
Administration
Building, 5959 South
Cicero, 1938.

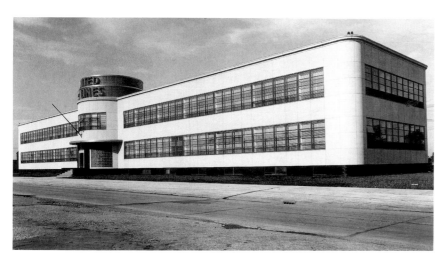

ern edge of the airport approximately a mile closer to the Loop. Expecting rapid but unpredictable change in the airline industry, Gerhardt created a low-cost building to be amortized in less than ten years of operation (figs. 1, 12). The terminal could serve only fifteen aircraft simultaneously. Gerhardt's design was one of several concepts architects began to utilize in order to decentralize passenger processing and to increase the orderly flow of travelers in the postwar period. Each airline independently operated a similar portion or "unit" of the terminal preparing passengers for arrival and departure. These units or modules were strung together in a long narrow building, which was the predecessor of the now common "linear" or "gate arrival" terminal. The terminal's depth minimized walking distances between the curb and gate. In December 1950 the Chicago City Council unanimously voted to rename the airport in commemoration of the heroes of the battle of Midway Island.[37]

Over the years, at or near Midway Airport the city and individual airlines continued to make improvements (fig. 13), although the additions to the terminal itself have still left most of Gerhardt's design obvious (fig. 14). But hemmed in by residential, commercial, and industrial neighborhoods prohibiting major runway extension to serve the first jet aircraft such as the Boeing 707, Chicago Midway Airport has languished. New plans prepared by the airport planning firm of Landrum and Brown; the development of smaller jets such as the Douglas DC-9 and the Sud "Caravelle"; the formation of new air transportation companies such as Midway Airlines; and even the efforts of the city's power-

Fig. 14 Aerial view of
Midway Airport, c. 1956.

ful mayor, Richard J. Daley, have all failed to remake the airport a hub.[38] What was once the busiest airport in the world is now almost a "ghost airport." Instead, most airplanes now lead to O'Hare International Airport.

In response to the American entry into World War II, the Army Air Force in April 1942 sought to find a suitable site for an additional assembly plant needed for the Douglas Aircraft Company. Immediately, the search committee focused upon Chicago, which was safely inland, had a capable labor force and an array of available raw materials, and was already a surface transportation hub. The Chicago district of the Army Corps of Engineers and the regional office of the Civil Aeronautics Authority, as well as representatives of the Chicago Regional Planning Association, the Chicago Association of Commerce, and the Douglas Aircraft Company assisted the Army's search committee. After the war, the site selected for Douglas Aircraft's production line was to become the location of Chicago's new inland air hub, O'Hare International Airport. The Corps of Engineers employed the Austin Company, an experienced architectural and engineering firm, to design and erect the assembly plant (see pls. 86-87). In an effort to conserve strategic war materials—particularly steel—the Austin

Company architects, engineers, and builders created a timber-frame factory and auxiliary buildings. Albert S. Low, vice-president and chief engineer of the company, supervised the project, while Harold A. Anderson was chief designer and project engineer. The Pratt trusses they used for the roof gave the structure almost 150-foot clear spans, while column designs facilitated clear heights ranging from twenty-five to thirty-five feet. The engineers clad the building with a cement-and-asbestos siding. Praised as the "Steel Saver," the Douglas Aircraft Company assembly plant and airport played a brief but important role assembling airplanes for World War II. The main building, which was both the biggest aircraft plant and the biggest wood-frame building in the world, housed the assembly line of the four-engine piston-driven Douglas C-54 Skymaster, used by the Army Air Force's Air Transport Command. Soon after the factory opened, Jennie Giangreco, "Miss C-54," an aircraft riveter, christened the "Chicago," the first plane off the line on July 30, 1943.[39]

At the same time that the Army Air Force, the Corps of Engineers, Douglas Aircraft, and the Austin Company were developing their huge assembly plant and runways, a consortium of public- and private-sector planning, aviation and

O'HARE MASTER PLAN · 1952
RALPH BURKE ASSOCIATES

Fig. 15 Ralph Burke Associates, Bird's-eye view of proposed master plan for an airport at Orchard Field (now the site of O'Hare International Airport), 1952 (cat. no. 102).

business groups, and airlines—including the Chicago Plan Commission, the Chicago Regional Planning Association, the Chicago Aero Commission, Eastern Air Lines, the Airline Pilots Association, the Committee on Plan of Chicago of the Commercial Club, and the Civil Aeronautics Authority—was already planning a new inland airport for the postwar period. A special committee composed of George T. Horton and T. T. McCrosky of the Chicago Plan Commission, Daniel H. Burnham, Jr., and Robert Kingery of the Chicago Regional Planning Association, and Jack Vilas and E. P. Querl of the Chicago Association of Commerce began planning a regional system.

The most important part of the plan, which would provide the bulk of service to metropolitan-area commercial carrier aviation, called for three major publicly owned air terminals within ten miles of the Loop: first, the expansion of Chicago Municipal Airport; second, the creation of a new airport that would be sited in or near the Central Business District as either an island or lakefront airport, or as a replacement for the Illinois Central Railroad yards or on air rights above the yard, or as part of a proposed West Side slum clearance project; and third, in a rural area northwest of the city.[40]

Although World War II dragged on, the issue continued to be an important one for Chicago civic leaders and urban planners, who were concerned with the reemployment of troops returning to civilian life, the reinvigoration of the local economy, and the importance of remaining a leading transportation hub. In 1944 City Engineer Ralph Burke, the director of the Postwar Economic Advisory Council of Chicago, suggested five possible locations for a new facility: expansion of Municipal Airport; the Clearing Industrial District southwest of the Municipal Airport; Lake Calumet on the far south end; Lake Michigan; and the Douglas Aircraft Company assembly plant and airport northwest of the city.[41] Burke believed that the Lake Calumet and Douglas sites were the best choices, but he deferred the final decision to the local, regional, and federal aviation and planning agencies. The Chicago Plan Commission, a joint airline technical committee, and Alderman William J. Cowley, whose 41st Ward would benefit most, also favored the Douglas plant location, but development could not begin at this location until the end of the war.[42] Despite the wartime limits upon commercial air transportation in the region, Burke prepared designs for each of the five prospective locations. In contrast with the

earlier studies, Burke favored a single, massive, high-capacity commercial facility. He argued that a single hub eliminated inconvenient air-port-to-airport transfers, centralized operations and maintenance, avoided scheduling confusion, and lessened the hazard of air route crossings. Despite differences in location and in the number and orientation of runways, Burke's proposed airport master plans placed the terminal in an island at the center of the airport accessible by automobiles and mass transit traveling through an underground passageway beneath the taxi-ways and runways.

Throughout the summer of 1945 the City of Chicago rehashed the plan for an airport at the Douglas site. Although the municipality had not yet chosen one of the five prospective sites, citizens approved a bond in June 1945 to finance a postwar airport. Two months later Mayor Kelly appointed yet another site selection board. Merrill C. Meigs led the board, which included Burke, William Patterson, president of United Airlines, Commissioner of Public Works Oscar E. Hewitt, and other leaders from labor, business, and politics. On October 30, 1945, the board finally selected the Douglas assembly plant and airport at the behest of Burke and air-lines representatives. With the conclusion of World War II, the Douglas plant became surplus. In view of Chicago's desire to construct an air-port there, the War Assets Corporation granted the city approximately 1,000 acres in March 1946, retaining approximately 300 acres for mili-tary use. Burke, a friend of Mayor Kelly and previously Kelly's colleague as a civil engineer in the offices of the Chicago Sanitary District, re-tired from government service in 1946 to form the private-sector engineering firm chiefly re-sponsible for the design of the new airport.[43]

What stands today—what has grown to be al-most a semi-autonomous city, a component of both air and surface transportation systems, and as much efficient machinery as beautiful archi-tecture—is based upon the final version of the original concept developed by Burke, his staff, and an airlines committee (fig. 15). These experts completed the first master plan in January 1948. After considering several configurations, they rec-ommended a variation of the "finger terminal," with fingerlike extensions and mechanical, tele-scoping gangways for deplaning and enplaning, projecting from the main building. This configu-ration minimized walking distances to an aver-age of 735 feet, a distance shorter and more con-venient than railroad depots and comparable airport terminals of the period. The main con-course on the upper level of the terminal, from which passengers would deplane and enplane, straddled surface transportation, both light rail and automobile, on the lower level. Each finger split near the distal end forming a Y-shaped ter-minal. Eventually five such "split fingers" were to project from each angle of an irregular penta-gonal terminal. A circular approach road and a light rail station would bisect one of the longer sides of the irregular pentagon. The first stage of construction for the foundation of the terminal and its fingers began in 1949. Although financial difficulties and airlines dissension slowed com-pletion, part of the building was in a position to begin serving travelers using non-scheduled air-lines in 1953.[44]

The city officials who selected the Douglas site to be Chicago's second air hub also agreed that construction of an express highway was a necessary part of the urban transportation sys-tem linking air travel to the Central Business District. Although city, county, and state govern-ments approved the creation of a Northwest Expressway in 1947, financial problems pre-cluded the start of construction for approxi-mately a decade (fig. 16).[45] In 1955 newly elected Mayor Richard J. Daley was largely responsible for settling the problems that delayed comple-tion of the new metropolitan air hub. First, the mayor successfully pressured the reluctant air-lines to transfer their operations to the unfin-ished O'Hare in 1957, in exchange for his as-surances that financing would be available and that construction would be completed. Then, when the Illinois State Toll Highway Com-mission designed a seven-mile portion of the Northwest Expressway to the airport without space in the median for rapid transit tracks, Daley pressured the Highway Commission to reverse its decision, and the commission trans-ferred this portion of the proposed freeway back to city, county, and state governments. Road builders completed the highway in November 1960, but a decade more elapsed before construc-tion crews finished the mass-transit rail link to the Jefferson Park station, where a bus connected to the airport. Workers finished the last leg of the system to the airport in the fall of 1984 (see pls. 8-9).[46] Finally, before airport construction was completed, the mayor had appointed a new con-sultant. Ralph Burke, in whom Daley did not have full confidence, died in 1956. The following year the mayor brought in the architectural firm of Naess and Murphy, which was shortly re-formed as C. F. Murphy Associates, upon the re-tirement of Sigurd E. Naess.[47]

During the spring and summer of 1957 when Carter Manny, Jr., the partner in charge, and Stanislaw Gladych, the chief designer, and a team of senior designers, Otto Stark, Gertrude Kerbis, Harvey Stubsjoen and Botho Schneider, began the project, they first reviewed completed construction and existing plans. With the assistance of the airport consulting firm of Landrum and Brown of Cincinnati, who made traffic projections and helped prepare the master plans, the architects found three problems: insufficient space for people, cars, and airplanes. The airlines were about to begin using Boeing 707 jets, which could carry approximately 130 passengers or about double the capacity of most earlier aircraft. Suddenly a huge disparity between the capacity of surface and air transportation vehicles required a complete rethinking of all concepts of terminal design: air transportation capacity grew so sharply that airport design became mass-transit design. Insufficient room existed for these craft to manuever and park between the split fingers. The terminal was too small, the curbs were too short to permit enough automobiles and buses to load or unload travelers, and too little vehicular parking space existed. In response, the design team suggested several terminal configurations: first, three connecting terminals with fingers and split fingers in a circle in the middle of taxiways and runways; second, a "mobile lounge terminal" much like Washington's Dulles International Airport; and third, five symmetrically and rectilinearly arrayed terminals,

akin to Los Angeles's International Airport. The architects preferred the mobile lounge concept because it enabled more aircraft to load or unload simultaneously. They also liked the simpler, more compact design of such a terminal. But the airlines rejected these ideas, claiming, for example, that a method of loading and unloading that required two bus or lounge rides to transfer from one craft to another would be inefficient, time consuming, and costly in a hub like Chicago and, moreover, was unproven in the United States.[48]

In a compromise plan of February 1958 the airlines, the city, and the architects involved decided to modify crucial components of Burke's original scheme and retain an existing building as an international terminal. Instead of Burke's original pentagonal building, the architects employed a more decentralized horseshoe-shaped array of interconnected terminals with a two-level approach road (figs. 17, 18). Engineers Nick Le Bar and Alfred Benesch Associates consulted about the concept of the dual-level roadway, which has distinctive supporting columns. Enplaning passengers arrive at the airport on the upper roadway; deplaning passengers depart on the lower one. Several reasons for this arrangement exist.[49] First, deplaning passengers require more time to get into surface transportation than enplaning passengers require to unload from surface transportation. Therefore, more curb space is required for waiting vehicles. Engineers can more readily design a larger curb-

Fig. 16   James Edwin Quinn, Bird's-eye view of superhighways at the proposed Orchard Field airport, 1948 (cat. no. 101).

Fig. 17 C. F. Murphy
Associates, O'Hare
International Airport,
1957-63 (photo 1969).

Fig. 18 C. F. Murphy
Associates, O'Hare
International Airport,
1963, arrival and
departure levels and
entrance to terminal.

side at grade at a lower cost of construction for deplaning travelers. Second, location of this roadway coordinates with the restriction that passengers boarding a plane must do so at the same level as the aircraft cabin door sill to facilitate loading. If enplaning passengers arrive on the lower level of a dual roadway system, some sort of supplementary machinery and additional time would be necessary to bring them up to the aircraft door sill. Third, the design and construction of luggage delivery systems to the deplaning passenger departing on the lower level is likewise easier and more economical.

Travelers embarking on domestic flights walked into either of two almost identical International Style buildings with gray, heat absorbing glass and black metal mullions. The buildings have terrazzo floors, while the structural support system is primarily reinforced concrete.[50] Designers considered the incorporation of moving walkways to shorten a traveler's walk down the 1,000- to 1,200-foot-long fingers, but the initial $5,000,000 capital investment and the annual maintenance cost of approximately $300,000 discouraged the architects. Eventually architects and engineers would install moving walkways linking the terminal to the parking areas.[51]

These two domestic terminals were part of a series of four semi-autonomous buildings closely connected by walkways on the upper level. A circular restaurant building is attached to these two, flanking, rectangular plan buildings (fig. 19). Gertrude Kerbis, who had just finished the design of a major food-service facility for the Air Force Academy, was responsible for the design of this building. It turned the corner of the complex and contrasted with the other grid-patterned facades. The most distinctive, but hidden, feature

Fig. 19   C. F. Murphy Associates, O'Hare International Airport, 1963.

of the 190-foot-diameter restaurant building is its cable-suspended roof, which creates an interior of free spans and huge windows through which diners can observe the action on the airfield.[52]

The now ubiquitous mechanical loading gangways were a modestly sized but crucial device for the efficient operation of the terminal. These devices extend, retract, and swing from the immobile building to aircraft doors. These architectural machines protect passengers and ease loading by eliminating the need to ascend or descend stairs into the waiting aircraft. While such gangways had been proposed decades earlier, the volume of air travelers, the designs of aircraft, and the construction of terminals with ground-level loading and unloading never required the construction of these costly devices. New jets and terminals suddenly made them feasible. Before C. F. Murphy Associates began work on the terminals, Ralph Burke had successfully pressed for the incorporation of these machines at O'Hare.

In 1962 Landrum and Brown advised the construction of a new air traffic control tower at O'Hare for the Federal Aviation Agency. That same year the FAA employed I. M. Pei and Associates to begin design of a standardized air traffic control tower. In 1966 the designers

adapted the reinforced-concrete tower capped by a glass and metal cab, where controllers worked, to O'Hare International Airport. Builders completed construction of the tower in 1971 (see pls. 17-18).[53]

On March 23, 1963, while standing at the monument to World War II hero Lieutenant Commander Edward O'Hare, Mayor Daley and President John F. Kennedy dedicated the completed airport. Within as little as five years, however, O'Hare was suffering from its success. The airport was already overcrowded. The growth in popularity of air transportation continued to exceed greatly all expectations. Jumbo and widebody jets became standard. The Boeing Corporation introduced the 747, while Lockheed placed the L-1011 in service and Douglas made available the DC-10, all at approximately the same time. The largest of these aircraft, the Boeing 747, which began flight in 1970, could hold as many as 490 passengers, but airlines normally configured seating in the craft to carry 366 travelers, almost triple the capacity of the Boeing 707. In order to accommodate these newest biggest aircraft and to assure that "all airplanes lead to Chicago," the Midwest metropolis and its consultants began a new phase of planning, design, and construction.

The success of O'Hare formed an ever expanding airport city sprawling over thousands of acres with many of the same urban design problems found elsewhere. Yet, Landrum and Brown and C. F. Murphy Associates saw potential for expansion at O'Hare. They and the city wished to ensure that the airport remained an important economic stimulus in the immediate environs and the further reaches of the metropolis.[54] Two of the numerous changes or additions are most obvious to air travelers: in 1973 the airport opened a hotel and parking lot, both designed by Carter Manny, Jr., and John M. Novack of C. F. Murphy Associates. The hotel, like the terminals, was an International Style building of gray glass and black anodized aluminum trim.[55] The parking lot, which accommodated 9,300 automobiles, was claimed to be the "largest in the world, and the fourth largest building of any type!" Although it and the hotel enhanced the use of the airport, these two buildings obscured much of approaching motorists' view of the air traffic control tower, destroying the most important component of the architectural image of the airport and safe air transportation.[56]

At the same time that the airport was opening such substantial buildings, C. F. Murphy Associates was already reevaluating another program of airport construction. In response to the use of the airport by thirty-three million travelers, the master planners considered several modifications to the terminals: extending the existing fingers; widening the existing fingers; removing the three split fingers and replacing them with three chevron-shaped satellites located as islands in the apron accessible by underground passages with a rail transit system (fig. 21). They also weighed a second light rail transit system to carry passengers between the existing domestic terminals and a proposed International Terminal.[57] During an almost ten-year hiatus in construction, the Department of Aviation and its consultants continued changing several key elements of the masterplan before money was available to finance the projects. During this period traffic rose to almost forty-nine million air travelers in 1979, despite a lengthy fifty-two-day strike halting operations of United Airlines.[58]

Finally, in 1981 O'Hare Associates, a consortium of the renamed firm of Murphy/Jahn, Envirodyne Engineers, Schal Associates, and Landrum and Brown, began finalizing several key components of the new plan. Of the many changes to the passenger terminal complex, three are substantial modifications with great aesthetic and functional impact on travelers: the United Airlines Terminal, the International Terminal, and the internal transit system, a "people mover" linking the airport city together. Although maintenance hangars are less apparent to travelers, these too are indispensable to the safe and dependable operation of the numerous aircraft at O'Hare.

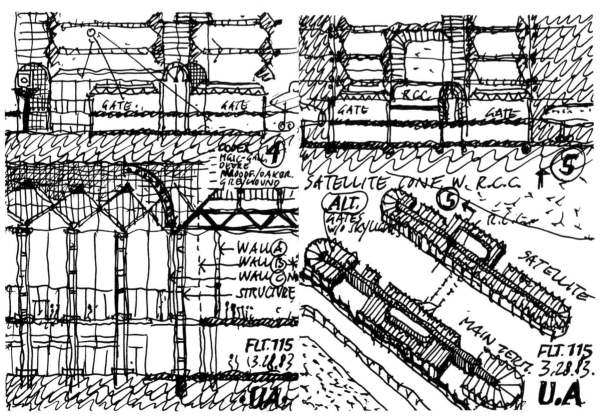

Fig. 20 Helmut Jahn of Murphy/Jahn, Preliminary sketches for the United Airlines Terminal at O'Hare International Airport, March 1983 (cat. no. 105)

Fig. 21 Aerial view of O'Hare International Airport, 1976.

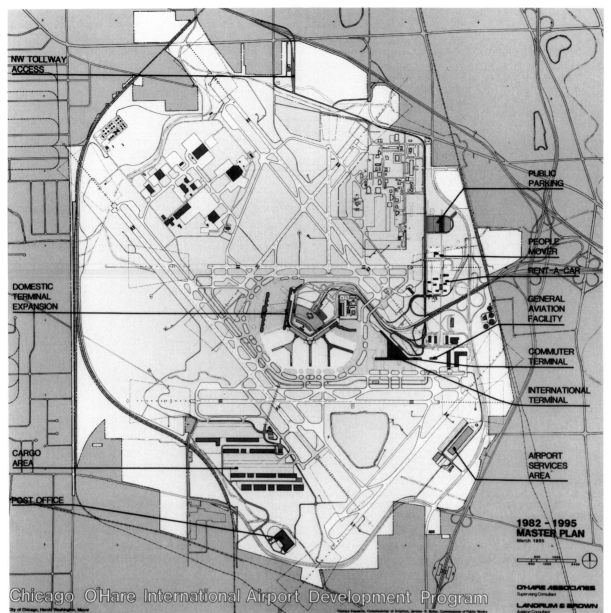

Fig. 22 O'Hare Associates with Landrum and Brown, Master plan of Chicago O'Hare International Airport Development Program, March 1985.

Within image:
NW TOLLWAY ACCESS

PUBLIC PARKING

PEOPLE MOVER

RENT-A-CAR

GENERAL AVIATION FACILITY

DOMESTIC TERMINAL EXPANSION

COMMUTER TERMINAL

INTERNATIONAL TERMINAL

CARGO AREA

AIRPORT SERVICES AREA

POST OFFICE

1982 – 1995 MASTER PLAN
March 1985

Chicago O'Hare International Airport Development Program

City of Chicago, Harold Washington, Mayor

Thomas Kapsalis, Commissioner of Aviation, Jerome R. Butler, Commissioner of Public Works

O'HARE ASSOCIATES
Supervising Consultant

LANDRUM & BROWN
Aviation Consultant

After difficult negotiations with the other airlines and the Department of Aviation to move the international facility to an interim location in the basement of the recently constructed parking garage,[59] United Airlines was free to reconsider plans to erect a new terminal on the site of the old international facility in September 1980. In the middle of the 1970s United and the Department of Aviation had tentatively selected a plan calling for two parallel linear terminals, one of which would be a remote satellite in the middle of an apron and accessible to travelers via an underground passage.[60] Soon after determining the location of the new international terminal, the Department of Aviation with the agreement of United Airlines employed Murphy/Jahn as primary architects for United's new terminal. In 1983 Helmut Jahn completed preliminary conceptual sketches of the building (see fig. 20).

The concept incorporated the basic features of the earlier plan separating the parallel linear buildings sufficiently to permit two elephantine Boeing 747s to taxi past each other safely. Although contractors did not finish the terminal until 1988, the airline began using it in 1987 (see pls. 19-21). On August 3 of that year, Chicago Mayor Harold Washington and United Airlines CEO Richard Ferriss dedicated the terminal, which was designed to serve an average of 70,000 travelers daily.[61] The terminal's two concourses have forty-two gates at United Airlines' biggest hub. Although moving pedestrian walkways in the concourse in the remote satellite and between the concourses represent some of the latest mechanical equipment for funneling passengers toward their destinations, the wide halls and the grand steel-and-glass vaults are reminiscent of cavernous nineteenth-century iron-and-

Fig. 23   Perkins and
Will, International
Terminal, O'Hare
International Airport,
1989-93, shown under
construction, December
1992.

Fig. 24   Austin
Company, Elevation and
section of United
Airlines Hangar, O'Hare
International Airport,
1987 (cat. no. 109).

glass train sheds. Likewise, the ticketing areas link and even contrast the image of two eras or modes of transportation; the informational video display screens and supermarket-style check-in counters equipped with computers, all in an airy steel-and-glass version of a railroad head house, rush travelers toward their flights.[62]

The city, the airlines, and the planning consultants had earmarked the site of the old international facility for use by United Airlines, but they had not yet agreed on a permanent location for a new international terminal.[63] Several sites were considered before O'Hare Associates in conjunction with the newly formed government agency, the O'Hare Development Program Management Office, in late 1982 located the international terminal, southwest of the intersection of the Kennedy Expressway and Mannheim Road closer to existing surface transportation networks (fig. 22). Perkins and Will designed the building, with the assistance of Heard and

Associates, and Consoer, Townsend and Associates (fig. 23). Contractors began work in the fall of 1990 and expect to finish the terminal by the summer of 1993.[64] Primarily of steel and glass on the upper levels and concrete on the lower level, the terminal will be huge by any measure: 150 ticketing positions; a gross building area of slightly more than one million square feet, equal to almost half the area of the Empire State Building; eighteen gates for wide-body jets plus two more gates for smaller jets; and a peak hour capacity of about 6,550 people, making the terminal a grand mass-transit facility.

In 1982, as part of the airport master plan locating the international terminal southwest of the junction of the Kennedy Expressway and Mannheim Road, O'Hare Associates established the route over which the MATRA-designed airport transit system will operate. Before construction, planned to begin in late 1985, occurred, O'Hare Associates, the airlines, and the Department of Aviation further simplified the system and reduced its cost.[65] MATRA, a French high-technology heavy industrial conglomerate, created a system based on cars previously used in the Paris Métro. O'Hare airport planners believe that the installation of this transportation network will both lessen congestion in the central area of the airport and stimulate the development of businesses on the periphery.[66] To help achieve these goals, MATRA designed the trains to run fast and frequently twenty-four hours a day. Instead of trains controlled by an engineer in the cab of the forward car, a crew in a central office with the aid of a computer and video monitors will control the whole system. Each car in the system is self-propelled by high voltage elec-

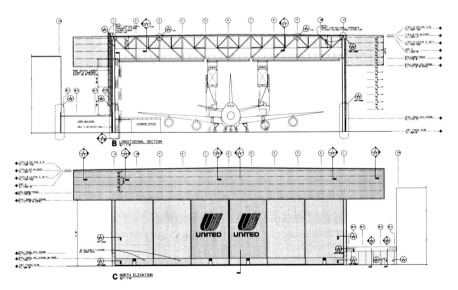

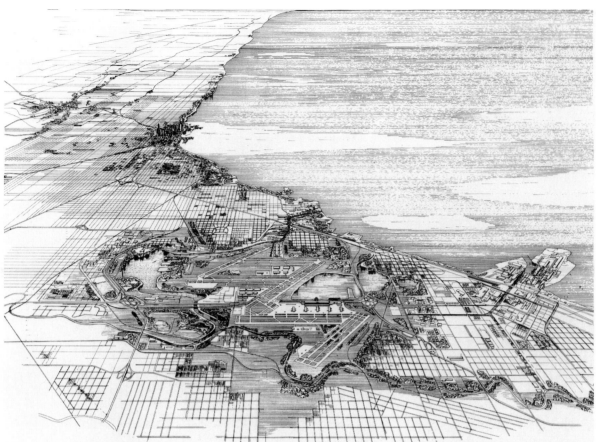

Fig. 25 City of Chicago and various consultants, Bird's-eye view of proposed Lake Calumet Airport, 1991; from Lake Calumet Airport: Crossroads of the Nation . . . Future of the Region *(Chicago, 1991), frontispiece.*

tric motors; consequently, either a single unit can run independently or trains of up to three cars can operate. Engineers formulated the people-mover system to operate initially with a train every two minutes traveling at a maximum speed of fifty miles per hour and carrying 2,400 passengers in each direction during periods of peak demand. Eventually, a six-mile network operated by a staff of sixty will have a capacity of 6,400 passengers per hour in each direction.

Recently, United Airlines employed the Austin Company to design and build an additional hangar at the O'Hare hub (fig. 24). The team of engineers led by Ranjit Roy created a steel column and truss roof hangar with a clear span of 250 feet. The corrugated-metal-clad building, which was largely completed and used for aircraft repair by November 1987, is big enough to house one Boeing 747, or one DC-10 and two Boeing 737 aircraft. The Structural Engineers Association of Illinois granted the Austin Company an award for the hangar, noting it one of the year's six best structural engineering projects.[67]

Long before Chicago began to implement the current master plan for O'Hare International Airport, the city considered the need for a third air hub. Although Chicago has not yet constructed three major airports, the city did develop

O'Hare, the busiest airport in the United States and perhaps even the world. Recently, officials of the states of Illinois and Indiana and of the City of Chicago, in particular Mayor Richard M. Daley, have revived proposals for a third airport. Moreover, the latest plan for a new regional air hub has once again suggested a location adjacent to Lake Calumet. Since the 1940s, when planners first proposed this location, industry—especially the steel industry—has abandoned the area, leaving it polluted and in economic decay. In 1990 city planners working with Mayor Daley proposed a controversial scheme, now apparently withdrawn, to reconfigure and revive a major portion of the metropolitan area on the Southeast Side of the city (figs. 25, 26). They advised the construction of a 5,200-acre airport park with seven runways and a terminal with 160 gates, projected to handle over forty-four million enplanements and deplanements in 2020 as part of a grand public works project, akin to a New Deal Depression-era construction effort. The city expected such a project to remedy a host of environmental problems, stem urban sprawl, restimulate a depressed economy by creating 235,800 jobs, and rechannel the Calumet River, while developing a new urban gateway. Although the Department of Aviation has suggested that Midway Airport might be

closed by 2005, the city expects to remain an important node in a mass air transportation system handling 106 million enplanements and deplanements at O'Hare Airport and the new Lake Calumet facility (or a revived Midway Airport, if Lake Calumet fails to get state approval). Planners anticipate that this figure might grow to 131 million airport users in 2020, assuring that "all airplanes lead to Chicago" well into the next century.[68] City planners and politicians have proudly replaced housing projects and highways with airports as the latest form of urban renewal. Despite this New Deal-like impetus of the Calumet project, airports proposed and completed after World War II differ from their predecessors. Although aviation grew during the Depression and World War II, afterward commercial air transportation became tantamount to mass transit. Air transportation ground facilities equipped with supplementary mechanical conveyances began handling huge crowds and began sprawling across thousands of acres. Airports became places *through* which people go rather than places *to* which people go.

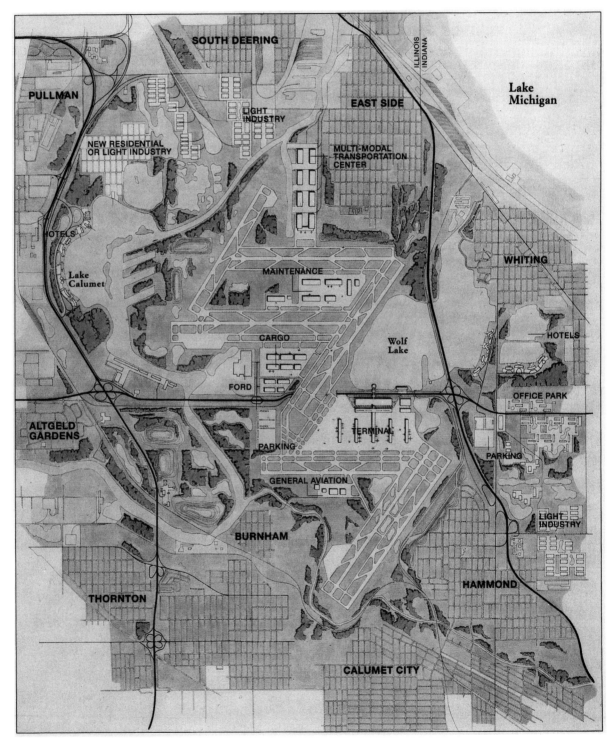

Fig. 26   City of Chicago and various consultants, Regional plan of proposed Lake Calumet Airport, 1991; from Lake Calumet Airport: Crossroads of the Nation . . . Future of the Region *(Chicago, 1991), fig. 5.9.*

NOTES

I wish to thank John Reps, Professor Emeritus of City and Regional Planning, Cornell University, who encouraged my interest in the history of transportation planning, and John Zukowsky, Curator of Architecture at The Art Institute of Chicago, who encouraged my study of the history of airports.

1. For a more thorough history of the legal foundation for airport planning and design, see David Brodherson, "What Can't Go Up Can't Come Down: The History of American Airport Policy, Planning and Design" (Ph.D. diss., Cornell University, 1993).

2. D. B. Coyler, "The Air Mail Service," *Journal of the Western Society of Engineers, Technical Papers* 32 (June 1927), p. 162. Coyler was general superintendent of the United States Air Mail Service.

3. Eugene C. Kirchherr, "Aviation and Airport Land Use in the Chicago Region, 1910-1941," *Bulletin of the Illinois Geographical Society* 17 (Dec. 1974), pp. 32-47; idem, "The Changing Pattern of Airport Land Use in the Chicago Region, 1941-1975," *Bulletin of the Illinois Geographical Society* 25 (Spring 1983), pp. 2-22. I am indebted to Professor Kirchherr of Western Michigan University for generously sharing his articles with me.

4. "Municipal Air Field to Open this Week," *Chicago Daily News* (Oct. 3, 1922).

5. Milton S. Mayer, "Wings Over the Lake Front," *Fashions of the Hour* (Autumn 1935), p. 20.

6. Ralph H. Burke, *Report of Commercial Airport Requirements for Chicago* (Chicago, 1944), p. 1; see also Arthur Evans, "Act to Assure City Place as Aviation Hub," *Chicago Tribune* (Dec. 17, 1944). Evans noted how "Idlewood," actually New York's Idlewild, now named John F. Kennedy International Airport, was "getting a head start as Chicago's competitor No. 1 port of entry on the great circle world routes."

7. United States Department of Transportation, Federal Aviation Administration, *FAA Statistical Handbook of Aviation: Calendar Year 1988* (Washington, D.C., [1989]), p. 82. Normally enplanements equal deplanements; therefore to compute the total number of travelers using each of these airports, double the number of enplanements stated in this Department of Transportation publication.

8. William E. Downes, "Downes Tells Why Our City Is Air's Giant," *Chicago Daily Tribune* (Aug. 11, 1961).

9. See the press release issued by the Department of Aviation, City of Chicago, "Mayor Daley Showcases Plans for New International Terminal, Meets with Airline Executives" (Oct. 31, 1989).

10. See, for example, City of Chicago, *Lake Calumet Airport: Crossroads of the Nation... Future of the Region* (Chicago, 1991); Rob Karwath, "South Suburbs Trying to Land 3d Area Airport," *Chicago Tribune* (July 7, 1987), pp. 1, 4; Michael Gillis, "Fasten Your Seat Belts: Airport Debate to Start," *Chicago Sun-Times* (Dec. 16, 1991), p. 13; Gary Washburn, "Daley Downsizes Lake Calumet Airport Plan," *Chicago Tribune* (Dec. 3, 1991), pp. 1, 14; Joe Cappo, "Like Father, Like Son: An Airport in a Lake," *Crain's Chicago Business* (March 2, 1992), p. 10; TAMS Consultants et al., *Site Selection Report-Abstract: Illinois-Indiana Regional Airport, State of Illinois, State of Indiana, City of Chicago* (Chicago, 1991).

11. Daniel Bluestone and Harold J. Christian, "The Ford Airport Hangar," *Historic Illinois* 8 (Aug. 1985), pp. 1-6. For early planning surveys of airports and their facilities, including depot-hangars, see Henry V. Hubbard et al., *Airports: Their Location, Administration and Legal Basis* (Cambridge, Mass., 1930), pp. 82, 84, 92; Louis M. Steuber, "Commercial Hangars," *American Architect* 136 (July 20, 1929), pp. 81-87; and Geoffrey Arend, *Great Airports Worldwide* (New York, 1988), pp. 562, 633.

12. Curtiss-Wright Corporation, *Curtiss-Wright Airports: A Nation-Wide Chain of Strategically Located Airports* (New York, [1930]); Thomas R. Shaver, "Principles of Airport Design," *American Landscape Architect* 3 (Sept. 1930), pp. 31-33.

13. The drawings and renderings of the passenger terminal given in note 12 and shown in figs. 2-4 are evidence of planned rather than completed buildings.

Photographs of the airport reproduced in the periodicals indicate that beacons and hangars were erected as planned, but no terminal. Yet, a booklet issued by the Community Affairs office of the U. S. Navy, *Naval Air Station Glenview: A Pictorial History* (Glenview, Ill., n. d.), p. 4, claims that the Navy leased part of the "Administration Building." This indicates that an "administration building" stood at the Curtiss-Reynolds Airport. This author has been unable to locate other confirming evidence.

14. John H. Thompson, "Admiral Gallery and His Prairie Flight Deck," *Chicago* (March 1954), pp. 12-19.

15. "Sky Harbor Petrushka Club," *Chicago Visitor* (Summer 1929), p. 10. The airport was the summer home of the Petrushka Club, which during other seasons entertained customers downtown at 165 North Michigan Avenue. By the time the summer "club house" opened, the Petrushka was already widely recognized for its "Russian-French cuisine specialities prepared by Yaschenko, the bewitching strains of George Stcherban's orchestra, and the soul stirring entertainment presided over by Ely Khmara as master of ceremonies."

16. Steuber (note 11), p. 88; W. D. Archer, "Practical Airports," *American Architect* 136 (July 20, 1929), p. 80; "Sky Harbor Attracts 'Air Minded Citizenry'," *Wilmette Life* (July 5, 1929), p. 10; "Sky Harbor Will Open Officially June 29," *Wilmette Life* (June 28, 1929), pp. 1, 4; and Frank Copeland, "Chicago's Wings," *Chicago Visitor* (Dec. 1929), pp. 12, 25.

17. An airport in or at the edge of Lake Michigan was a concern even twenty years later; see, for example, Wesley Hartzell, "Pilots' Chief Frowns at Our Airport in Lake," *Chicago American* (Oct. 29, 1967); "Daley Sees Airport in Lake by 1971," *Chicago Sun-Times* (Oct. 10, 1967); William Spencer, "Conservation Groups Oppose Airport in Lake," *Chicago American* (Oct. 26, 1967); Frank Sullivan, "Lake Airport Details," *Chicago Sun-Times* (Oct. 26, 1967); Wayne Thomis, "An Airport in the Lake Called Feasible but Costly," *Chicago Tribune* (June 6, 1967); Paul Gapp, "Metro-Closing Vetoed: Lakefront Meigs Field Born in Controversy and Still There," *Chicago Tribune* (Dec. 23, 1973).

18. Gapp (note 17).

19. James Ronald Wray, "Atlas of Chicago Municipal Airport" (M.S. thesis, University of Chicago, 1948), p. 137, cites Harold F. McCormick in Aero Club of Illinois, *Aviation Meet Prospectus.* Wray also details other proposals for an airport in the lake.

20. Mayer (note 5), pp. 20, 21.

21. Wayne Thomis, "City Neglecting Air Future, View of Rickenbacker," *Chicago Tribune* (Dec. 15, 1934).

22. General Airport Company, *Comprehensive Study Relating to Aeronautical Facilities for Metropolitan Area of Chicago Projected to 1970* (Stamford, Conn., 1946), p. 76.

23. Chicago Citizens Committee, *To the Preparatory Commission of the United Nations — "Northerly Isle"* (Chicago, 1945); Larry Ewing, "The Island that Lost the United Nations," *Viewpoint* (Spring 1966), pp. 10-12.

24. Gapp (note 17); Robert Bruce Tague, "Aéroports de Chicago," *Techniques et Architecture* nos. 9-12 (1947), pp. 504-05.

25. City of Chicago, Department of Aviation, *History: Chicago's Lakefront Airport, Meigs* (Chicago, [1974]); idem, *Meigs: Facts about Chicago's Lakefront Airport, Merrill C. Meigs Field* (Chicago, [c. 1988]).

26. "Let Contract on Meigs Field Terminal Unit," *Chicago Tribune* (Sept. 20, 1960); Wayne Thomis, "Dedicate Meigs Field Terminal Thursday," *Chicago Tribune* (Oct. 15, 1961); *Meigs: Facts* (note 25).

27. "Let Contract on Meigs Field" (note 26); Ray McCarthy, "New Meigs Terminal Building Opens Soon," *Chicago American* (Sept. 20, 1961).

28. Tom Leach, "Pucinski Urges Airport on Stilts Over the Lake," *Chicago American* (Oct. 3, 1966).

29. See, for example, Douglas Schroeder, "The Lake Airport — A Disaster in the Making," *Inland Architect* 13 (March 1969), pp. 30-33.

30. Ray Draper, "St. Pete-Tampa Airboat Service Was the First United States Airline," *Atlantic Flyer Aviation News* (March 1992), sec. A, p. 32, notes that the

first one-way flights between New York and Los Angeles in the late 1920s cost between $337 and $403. Today a round trip ticket on that route may be purchased for approximately the same fare or less. Moreover, "Air Transport Growing Quickly, Plays Key Role in Development," *Aviation Week and Space Technology* 136 (March 9, 1992), p. 41, states that "more efficient aircraft and airline equipment already have helped lower 'real' airfares by 68% — after adjusting for inflation — compared to 20 years ago."

31. Kirchherr, "Aviation and Airport Land Use" (note 3), pp. 36-37; "Chicago's Municipal Airport, an Institution," *Airports* 1 (July 1928), pp. 27, 38; "Chicago's Municipal Airport," *Airway Age* 10 (Jan. 1929), pp. 38-41; Wray (note 19); John A. Casey, compiler, "The First Forty Years: Chicago Aviation and Airports, 1926-1966," a manuscript available in the library of the Chicago Historical Society; "Municipal Air Field to Open this Week," *Chicago Daily News* (Oct. 3, 1922). Some minor details in these narratives conflict.

32. City of Chicago, Bureau of Parks, Recreation and Aviation, "Chicago Municipal Airport [Financial Statements], Statement E-2: Bond Funds — Expenditures for Improvements" [1931]. Other literature from the period reports conflicting information about the cost of the terminal and other airport improvements. See, for example, "Dedicate New Terminal at City Airport," *Chicago Herald* (Nov. 16, 1931), and "Chicago Municipal Airport," *Architectural Record* 71 (Feb. 1932), pp. 117-20.

33. The competition was as important to the design of airports as the Chicago Tribune competition was to the development of the skyscraper; Walter Wright, "Passenger Terminal for Chicago's Municipal Airport," *Chicago Visitor* (Dec. 1931), p. 29; Talbot F. Hamlin, "Airports as Architecture," *Pencil Points* 21 (Oct. 1940), pp. 636-46, passim. Hamlin, a proponent of austere modernism, cited several exceptional American airport terminals, including Rebori and Wentworth's Curtiss-Reynolds Airport and Paul Gerhardt's Chicago Municipal Airport.

34. D. H. Burnham, "Chicago Municipal Airport Plans," *Monthly Bulletin, Illinois Society of Architects* 27 (Feb. 1943), pp. 1-2.

35. See Klekamp and Whitmore, "Add. to Midway Airport 1934, Job # KW-1," Chicago Historical Society, Department of Architecture, Drawing Collection.

36. Burnham (note 34); Howard Lovewell Cheney, the author of the program for the Chicago Tribune competition and the supervisor of the "plan and development" of the "magnificent new" Washington National Airport, assisted Burnham and Hammond in the design of the proposed Chicago terminal.

37. Paul Gerhardt, Jr., "Terminal Bldg-Chicago Mun. Airport," Chicago Historical Society, Department of Architecture, Drawing Collection; "Standard Unit Scheme Varied to Speed Airport Traffic," *Architectural Record* 107 (Feb. 1950), pp. 90-93; descriptive text and an aerial perspective of the airport with a proposed terminal and an "architect's drawing," respectively, appear in Wayne Thomis, "Airport Work to Make Field Nation's Finest," *Chicago Tribune* (Jan. 24, 1941), and *Chicago Tribune* (Nov. 20, 1940). These two newspaper narratives, which convincingly present similar information about important aspects of the proposed terminal, conflict with Burnham's description of the project three years later. This is likely a result of changing design concepts. See also "Council Votes for Midway as Airport Name," *Chicago Tribune* (Dec. 13, 1950). But Wayne Thomis, "Midway in Jet Age Is Like Ghost Town," *Chicago Tribune* (Aug. 28, 1961), states that the completed terminal, which still stands, was merely a "temporary" building.

38. Edward B. Williams, "Outlook for Midway Bleak and Deserted," *Chicago Journal* (July 8, 1962), p. 2; Thomis (note 37); Landrum and Brown, *Airport Master Plan Study, Data Collection and Analysis: Chicago Midway Airport, Chicago, Illinois, for City of Chicago, Department of Aviation* (Chicago, 1976); David Young, "$150 Million City Plan for Midway," *Chicago Tribune* (April 28, 1981); Wayne Thomis, "Signs of Midway's Reawakening Noted," *Chicago Tribune* (Feb. 5, 1964).

39. Richard P. Doherty, "The Origin and Development of Chicago-O'Hare International Airport" (Ph.D.

diss., Ball State University, 1970), pp. 12-39, passim. See also "From the Archives," *Exchange* 11 (Nov. 1991), p. 20; John Jenkins, "Douglas Plant Built of Wood, 30,000 Tons of Metals Saved," *Chicago Daily News* (Feb. 23, 1943); "Aircraft Plant Has 150-ft. Timber Trusses," *Engineering News-Record* 114 (Oct. 21, 1943), pp. 114-19; "Chicago Skymaster Roars into Air on Successful Maiden Flight," *Chicago Sun-Times* (July 31, 1943); Jack Miehls, "Steel Saver," *Flying* (Nov. 1943), pp. 46-47, 158.

40. Special Committee Representing Chicago Association of Commerce, Chicago Plan Commission, and Chicago Regional Planning Commission, *Airport Program for Chicago and the Region of Chicago* (Chicago, 1941).

41. Burke (note 6); interview with Larry Donoghue, chairman, Ralph Burke Associates, Park Ridge, Dec. 18, 1991.

42. Doherty (note 39), pp. 43-48; Arthur Evans, "Act to Assure City Place as Aviation Hub," *Chicago Tribune* (Dec. 17, 1944).

43. Doherty (note 39), pp. 45-85, passim.

44. Ralph H. Burke, *Master Plan of Chicago Orchard (Douglas) Airport* (Chicago, 1948); idem, *O'Hare Field, Chicago International Airport: Report on First Stage for Scheduled Passenger Operation* (Chicago, [1949]); idem, *O'Hare Field, Chicago International Airport: Master Plan (6 Runway Pattern)* (Chicago, 1950); idem, *O'Hare Field, Chicago International Airport: Progress Report and Description, Stage I-Plan C* (Chicago, 1953); idem, *O'Hare Field, Chicago International Airport: Plan "C" Development—Initial Stage, Stage II, Stage III* (Chicago, 1954). A description of the evolution of the finger design and the first built concept for O'Hare are in Department of Education and Research, "Building Type Reference Guide No. 7: Airports (Part II)," *Bulletin of the American Institute of Architects* 5 (May 1951), pp. 7, 10-11; Wayne Thomis, "Two Projects Are Pushed at O'Hare," *Chicago Tribune* (July 13, 1953).

45. Doherty (note 39), pp. 136-39.

46. Cynthia Davidson-Powers, "The O'Hare Station: Last Link to the Loop," *Inland Architect* 29 (July/Aug. 1985), p. 20; David Greenspan, "We're on Our Way to O'Hare," *Inland Architect* 27 (July/Aug. 1983), pp. 28-31; Nora Richter Green, "Movement and Color as Themes: O'Hare International Airport Rapid Transit Extension, Murphy/Jahn," *Architecture: The AIA Journal* 76 (May 1987), pp. 152-55.

47. Doherty (note 39), pp. 118, 136-39, 193-97, 364, 365; Wayne Thomis, "O'Hare Plan Links Airports and Roadwork: Advanced Stages of Construction to Begin," *Chicago Tribune* (June 13, 1959); Naess and Murphy, Landrum and Brown, and James O'Donnell, *Chicago-O'Hare International Airport: Engineering Report-First Stage Development Program* (Chicago, 1958); Landrum and Brown, *O'Hare Field—Chicago International Airport*, vol. 1, *Air and Surface Traffic Studies* (Chicago, 1958); "Commercial Planes Begin Flights; Expect 250,000 at Ceremonies," *Chicago Sun-Times* (Oct. 29, 1955).

48. Landrum and Brown (note 47); "C. F. Murphy Associates, Chicago, Internationaler Flughafen Chicago-O'Hare," *Bauen und Wohnen* 17 (July 1963), pp. 281-95; "Our Two Largest Airports," *Progressive Architecture* 44 (Aug. 1963), pp. 102-11; interview with Carter Manny, Jr., Chicago, Dec. 12, 1991; interview with Christian Young, Airport Planning Consultant to Landrum and Brown, New York, March 2, 1992;

Doherty (note 39), pp. 197-99; Robert H. Cook, "Major U. S. Airports—Part 1: Walking Distance Main Airport Complaint," *Aviation Week and Space Technology* 78 (June 17, 1963), p. 45; idem, "Major U. S. Airports—Part 5: O'Hare Walking Distance Stirs Criticism," *Aviation Week and Space Technology* 79 (July 15, 1963), pp. 45, 47; "The Anatomy of a Project—Preview: 43," *Architectural and Engineering News* 4 (June 1962), pp. 65-69.

49. Interview with Francis McKelvey, Professor of Civil and Environmental Engineering, Michigan State University, Lansing, Feb. 14, 1990.

50. "Flughafen Chicago-O'Hare" (note 48), pp. 281-95; "Our Two Largest Airports" (note 48), pp. 102-111; Doherty (note 39).

51. Doherty (note 39), pp. 263-65; Peter Reich, "Airport of Future Rises at O'Hare," *Chicago American* (April 23, 1961). For information about moving walkways, first used in Chicago at the World's Columbian Exposition in 1893, see Federal Aviation Agency, Bureau of Facilities and Materiel, Airports Division, *Airport Terminal Buildings* (Washington, D.C., 1960), pp. 7, 13; Robert Horonjeff and Charles J. Hoch, "Some Facts about Horizontal Moving Sidewalks at Airports," in American Society of Civil Engineers, Carnegie-Mellon University and Metropolitan Association of Urban Designers and Environmental Planners, *Transportation Facilities Workshop: Passenger, Freight and Parking, May 22-24, 1974, New York, New York*, ed. Walter H. Kraft and John J. Fruin (New York, 1975), pp. 323-34.

52. "Flughafen Chicago-O'Hare" (note 48), pp. 281-95; "Our Two Largest Airports" (note 48), pp. 102-11; "Anatomy of a Project" (note 48), pp. 65-69.

53. Landrum and Brown and Airborne Instruments Laboratory, *Chicago O'Hare International Airport*, vol. 4, *Analysis of Capacity and Master Plan* (Chicago, 1962), p. 16; Janet Adams Strong, Director of Communications, Pei, Cobb, Freed and Partners, letter to the author with enclosures, April 27, 1992; City of Chicago, Department of Aviation, *Facts about the World's Busiest Airport: Chicago O'Hare International Airport* (Chicago, 1986).

54. "Interior Design: A Good Idea Whose Time Has Come, Again," *Progressive Architecture* 52 (Sept. 1971), pp. 122-27; "3 Jet-Age Motels for O'Hare," *Chicago American* (June 29, 1960).

55. For a description of the O'Hare International Tower Hotel, which, in addition to rooms for overnight stays, housed conference rooms, meeting facilities, and restaurants, see "Escape from and at O'Hare," *Interiors* 133 (Oct. 1973), pp. 94-99.

56. Nory Miller, "Can We Save O'Hare Field from Itself?" *Inland Architect* 17 (Aug. 1973), p. 18; Alvin Nagelberg, "Underground Pedestrian Tunnels to Link O'Hare Building Complex," *Chicago Tribune* (April 16, 1972). While designers weighed the view from the tower, they failed to consider adequately the view of the tower itself.

57. Miller (note 56), pp. 18-22.

58. David Young, "O'Hare Lays Plans to Double Traffic," *Chicago Tribune* (Oct. 20, 1980).

59. Interview with Christian Young (note 48); "Troubled Allies at O'Hare," *Inland Architect* 29 (July/Aug. 1985), p. 20; Robert Davis, "United Plans $100 Million New Terminal at O'Hare," *Chicago Tribune* (Sept. 20, 1980).

60. Robert Bruegmann, "High Flight: United Gambles

and Wins at O'Hare," *Inland Architect* 32 (Sept./Oct. 1988), pp. 32-41.

61 Interview with Barbara Hansen, Public Relations, United Airlines, Chicago, April 27, 1992.

62. Donna Green, "Chicago: Terminal of the Future," *ID* 35 (Jan./Feb. 1988), pp. 46-51; "Environments: Best of Category," *ID* 35 (July/Aug.), pp. 54-55; Paul Goldberger, "Architecture View: An Air Terminal Inspired by the Train Station," *New York Times* (Aug. 23, 1987), sec. 2, p. 25; Jim Murphy, "A Grand Gateway," *Progressive Architecture* 68 (Nov. 1987), pp. 95-105; Charles H. Thornton et al., "Innovative Engineering: United Airlines-O'Hare, Framed for Tomorrow," *Modern Steel Construction* 27 (Sept./Oct. 1987), pp. 5-12; Norma Richter Green, "Soaring Spaces that Celebrate Travel: United Airlines Terminal 1, Murphy/Jahn," *Architecture: The AIA Journal* 77 (May 1988), pp. 158-65; Deborah K. Dietsch, "High-tech Expansion," *Architectural Record* 173 (May 1985), pp. 132-39; Sylvan R. Shemitz, "Lighting the Way," *Architectural Record* 175 (Nov. 1987), pp. 148-55.

63. David Young, "Chicago to Spend $1 Billion to Rehabilitate O'Hare Airport," *Chicago Tribune* (Nov. 15, 1981); O'Hare Associates, *ORD: Chicago O'Hare International Airport Development Program* (Chicago, 1983); O'Hare Associates and Landrum and Brown, *O'Hare Development Program: 1982-1995 Master Plan* (Chicago, [c. 1985]).

64. See the press release issued by Lisa Howard, Director of Public Relations, Department of Aviation, City of Chicago, "Department of Aviation Fact Sheet: The New O'Hare International Terminal," 1989, and one by Mary Sue Kranstover, Perkins and Will, Chicago, "O'Hare's New International Terminal: Fact Sheet," 1991.

65. City of Chicago, *O'Hare Development Program: AGT Coordination Study, July 31, 1984* (Chicago, 1984); O'Hare Associates, *Chicago International Airport: Automated Guideway Transit System, Part 1 of 3, Proposal Conditions, Revision of February 21, 1986* (Chicago, [1986]).

66. City of Chicago, *O'Hare Development Program* (note 65), especially pp. 3-4; MATRA Transport, *Chicago O'Hare* (Chicago, [1991]); MATRA Transport, *VAL: Running Ahead of Expectation* ([Chicago, 1991]).

67. Interviews with Ranjit Roy and Donald J. Stolpe, Austin Company, Des Plaines, Dec. 12, 1991.

68. Special Committee (note 40); Burke (note 6); Cappo (note 10); Alverson Carlson, "3d Airport, Heavier Use of Midway Discussed," *Chicago Sun-Times* (Oct. 18, 1966); "Air Lines Push for 3d Airport: Dispute Daley View on City Capacity," *Chicago Tribune* (Jan. 1, 1970); Karwath (note 10); Landrum and Brown et al., *Lake Calumet Airport Feasibility Study* (Chicago, 1990); TAMS Consultants (note 10); City of Chicago, *Lake Calumet Airport* (note 10); Washburn (note 10), pp. 1, 14; Gillis (note 10), p. 13; Michael Gillis, "Foes of Lake Calumet Plan Blast Minority Jobs Claims," *Chicago Sun-Times* (Dec. 16, 1991), p. 13; Chris Scott, "Business Diary: Daley Wants to Shut Down Midway Airport," *Crain's Chicago Business* (March 2, 1992), p. 45; press release from City of Chicago, Mayor's Press Office, "Study Shows Future Airport Demand Favors Lake Calumet Site" (July 25, 1991); interview with Jeff Goldberg, Department of Planning, City of Chicago, Dec. 19, 1991; interview with Warren Silver, Mayor's Program and Policies Staff, City of Chicago, Dec. 19, 1991.

The Making of the Merchandise Mart, 1927-1931: Air Rights and the Plan of Chicago

Deborah Fulton Rau

Upon its completion in 1931, the Merchandise Mart, designed by Graham, Anderson, Probst and White for Marshall Field and Company, stood as a paradoxical contribution to Chicago's urbanism. Conceived as a model of modern, scientific efficiency in wholesale merchandising, the Mart's purpose was to centralize Chicago's wholesale goods trade by consolidating its vendors and activities under one roof. The wholesale trade, however, had been declining and dispersing for more than a decade. The paradoxical nature of the building's concept was paralleled by its urban form. The siting of the Merchandise Mart on air rights along the Chicago River resulted directly from recommendations in Daniel H. Burnham and Edward H. Bennett's 1909 *Plan of Chicago.* But the building's enormous size—at four million square feet it was the largest in the world—and its city-within-a-city program, which catered exclusively to the wholesale trade, isolated the Mart from its urban context (figs. 1-3).

The building's inherent contradictions were completely consistent with the impulses of its era. The creation of the Merchandise Mart epitomized the business and building boom of the frenzied years of the 1920s, which was characterized, on one hand, by an ambivalent combination of megalomaniacal building tendencies, and, on the other, by a traditional view of civic decorum in architecture and planning, codified and perpetuated by Burnham and Bennett's Plan. Compounding this was yet another ambivalence: the progressive belief in scientific efficiency in all endeavors was countered by a nostalgic clinging to time-honored tradition in business practices.[1]

The concept of the Merchandise Mart failed to save Marshall Field's wholesale trade, but Graham, Anderson, Probst and White's dignified design and inherently flexible plan proved adaptable to change from the time of its inception. The building continues to accommodate a diversity of shifting factors, including changes in ownership, marketing strategies, distribution chains, and urban demographics.

Chicago in the 1920s

A consideration of the urban climate in Chicago in the 1920s from the dual perspective of real estate speculation and the implementation of Burnham and Bennett's Plan renders the Merchandise Mart the inevitable outcome of these trends. The business boom that expanded American cities in the 1920s resulted from a rapid rise in population caused by the flood of World War I veterans into urban centers and the concomitant demand for services, luxury items, and housing.

Between 1919 and 1926 real estate profits increased while actual construction and maintenance costs decreased, making it profitable to erect new buildings. Although urban land values doubled in the same period, the underwriting of development ventures through real estate bond issues made it possible for developers and builders to finance the entire cost of a building with little substantial investment of their personal or corporate funds.[2] In 1927 the boom began to wane, but the downward trend was so slight, even by 1929, that it little prepared the nation for the October crash.

Chicago's Central Business District rapidly surged upward and outward. The Chicago Zoning Ordinance of 1923, which removed restrictions that had previously limited building heights to 264 feet, precipitated an almost immediate increase in the vertical scale of the city.[3] The skyline was soon crowned and illuminated with robust, glowing tower tops such as the pyramid of the thirty-two-story Straus Building (now Britannica Center; see Willis, fig. 20) in 1924 and the domed belvedere of the forty-story Jewelers Building in 1926 (see Sennott, fig. 15). At the same time, the horizontal scale grew to enormous proportions. The American Furniture Mart (now 680 North Lake Shore Place), one of the largest reinforced concrete structures in the world, opened in 1924. The gargantuan Stevens Hotel (now Chicago Hilton and Towers), completed in 1927 with the largest construction contract ever awarded, had 3,000 guest rooms, a

Fig. 1 Graham, Anderson, Probst and White, Merchandise Mart, North bank of the Chicago River between Wells and Orleans streets, Perspective rendering of proposed bas-relief at entrance; from The Architectural Work of Graham, Anderson, Probst, and White *(London, 1933).*

Fig. 2 Hugh Ferriss,
Perspective rendering of
the Merchandise Mart,
c. 1929.

Fig. 3 Graham,
Anderson, Probst and
White, Merchandise
Mart, 1927-31, aerial
view.

4,000-seat auditorium, and the city's biggest convention hall.[4]

The lateral expansion of Chicago's business district beyond the orbit of the elevated lines that defined the Loop was directly tied to the implementation of schemes recommended in Burnham and Bennett's *Plan of Chicago* and carried out under the tutelage of Edward H. Bennett himself, who served as consulting architect to the Chicago Plan Commission from 1913 to 1930.[5] The widening of Michigan Avenue and the erection of the bi-level Michigan Avenue Bridge (1918-20) promoted northward expansion. By 1925 three of Chicago's most famous landmarks—the Wrigley Building, the London Guarantee and Accident Building (now Stone Container Building), and the Chicago Tribune Tower—graced the view from the south. The completion of the first portion of the double-deck Wacker Drive in 1926, extending westward from the bridge along the river, opened up the south riverbank to development (fig. 4).[6] In 1927 Marshall Field and Company announced its plans to build on the north bank opposite Wacker Drive.

James Simpson and the Chicago Plan Commission

The Merchandise Mart was the brainchild of James Simpson, president of Marshall Field and Company from 1923 to 1930 and chairman of the Chicago Plan Commission from 1926 to 1935. Simpson emerged as a powerful force in the shaping of Chicago's urbanism in the 1920s and 1930s by integrating his roles as businessman and civic leader. Born in 1874, the son of Scottish immigrants who came to Chicago in 1880, Simpson rose rapidly in Field's organization. In 1892, just a year after taking his first position as clerk, the energetic and confident young Simpson was appointed personal secretary to Marshall Field himself and soon became his close friend and protégé. Simpson is said to have acquired the "Field viewpoint" more thoroughly than any of his contemporaries.[7] The classic late-nineteenth-century "go-getter," Simpson attributed his rise in the company to "enthusiasm," which he believed was "everything in business, for business is not prosaic, as some believe. It's just the opposite."[8] Simpson's

Fig. 4 Wacker Drive, showing development along south bank of Chicago River, c. 1931.

career was anything but prosaic. Appointed vice-president after Field's death in 1906, his enthusiasm made him a high-profile public relations man for the company, and much of his time and energy was spent representing Chicago's department stores in civic affairs.[9]

Simpson exemplified the civic-minded businessmen of the Commercial Club who sponsored the *Plan of Chicago* and on whom the long-range implementation of the Plan relied. From the time of the inception of the Plan in 1906, he served on special committees and helped to finance its development with personal contributions. When Mayor Fred Busse established the Chicago Plan Commission in 1909, Simpson was appointed a member of the Executive Committee under Chairman Charles Wacker.[10] The first few years of the Commission's activities were devoted in large part to promoting the Plan to the citizens of Chicago. Wacker appointed Walter Dwight Moody as managing director of a public relations campaign that included a textbook for schoolchildren entitled *Wacker's Manual of the Plan of Chicago: Municipal Economy*. Authored by Moody, *Wacker's Manual* was a more sophisticated document than the level of its audience implies. As Thomas Schlereth has pointed out, the text placed the goals of the Plan in a broad social perspective by promoting key ideas of the era: "belief in mass education, progressivism, the efficiency movement, and environmentalism."[11] Moody's rhetoric, infused with a hyperbolic civic patriotism, asserted that the Plan would make Chicago the "center of the modern world" and "the most convenient, healthful and attractive city on earth."[12] Simpson shared Moody's progressive idealism and civic patriotism, but his own beliefs were tempered by an intense, no-nonsense pragmatism. When he characterized the members of the Commission as "practical citizens, the kind who have the ability to make dreams come true," he could have been speaking of himself. Indeed, no dream was too grand for Simpson, who postured: "if Chicago had to be taken apart and reassembled ... well, why not? The difficulties were by no means insurmountable. Legal proceedings, pick axes, steam shovels, and cement mixers could toss them aside."[13]

In the early 1920s Simpson rose in his business and civic vocations to head the organizations in which he had been a key player. Between 1927 and 1930 he merged his overlapping roles in directing the development of the concept and design of the Merchandise Mart. The completion of Wacker Drive was Simpson's first project as chairman of the Chicago Plan Commission, and he believed that the city's "most urgent problem was the reclamation of the waterfronts, lake and river, and their conversion into esplanades and parkways."[14] Consequently, when plans for Marshall Field's new building on the north bank were announced in March 1927, the *Chicago Tribune* reported that the company would "voluntarily set their huge building back from the river far enough to allow the construction of the first unit of a north bank boulevard, the companion of the newly opened Wacker Drive."[15] The announcement was accompanied not only by a rendering of Graham, Anderson, Probst and White's design for the building, but also by a conceptual sketch drawn by the firm for the Chicago Plan Commission and captioned "How the Chicago River will look when North Wacker Drive balances the present Wacker Drive along the south bank."[16] This view of the river to the east, which showed wide, double-deck boulevards on each bank lined with buildings of uniform height and setback, was simply another perspective of the scheme for the Chicago River illustrated by Jules Guérin for the *Plan of Chicago* (fig. 5). The Plan, which charged that the Chicago River had become "a dumping spot and a cesspool," recommended that

the opportunity ... be seized to plan a comprehensive and adequate development of the river banks, so that the commercial facilities shall be extended, while at the same time the aesthetic side of the problem shall be worked out. Boulevards should extend from the mouth of the river along the North and South branches and on both sides.[17]

Comparison of the details in the drawing of 1909 and the later drawing of 1927 reveals the single most important change in city life during the intervening years: while Guérin's drawing includes horse-drawn carriages, the drawing by Graham, Anderson, Probst and White depicts automobiles. In 1908, at the time of the completion of the *Plan of Chicago,* there were 5,000 automobiles in Chicago; by 1925 the number had escalated to 293,206.[18] Simpson's nine-year tenure as chairman of the Chicago Plan Commission was consumed by the issues of urban transportation and congestion: the extension and erection of streets, avenues, bridges, and expressways, and, after 1930, plans for the proposed subway. The new North Bank Drive, thought to be assured by Field's decision to donate land in front of its building, was to be part of a larger network of arteries designed by Hugh Young, the Commission's chief engineer, and Edward Bennett. The bi-level drive, designed to

*Fig. 5   Jules Guérin,
View looking north from
south branch of Chicago
River; from Daniel H.
Burnham and Edward
H. Bennett,* Plan of
Chicago *(Chicago, 1909),
pl. 107.*

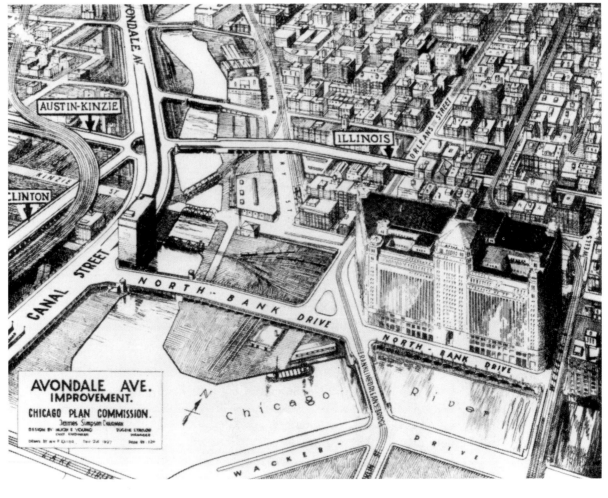

*Fig. 6   Hugh E. Young
and Edward H. Bennett,
Proposal for the
Avondale Avenue
improvement, 1927;
from Glenn A. Bishop
and Paul T. Gilbert,*
Chicago's Accomplish-
ments and Leaders
(Chicago, 1932), p. 534.

match Wacker Drive, would link up on the west with the proposed Avondale Avenue, a double-deck superhighway extending ten miles between the suburbs and the Loop (fig. 6). To the east, the drive would continue along the river to State Street, turn northeast to sweep past the north face of the Wrigley Building "twin," intersect with Michigan Avenue, then pass the south face of the Tribune Tower. From that point, the drive would turn back to follow along the river and connect with Lake Shore Drive at the proposed Outer Drive Bridge. Thus, the Marshall Field's building would share the riverfront with the city and would benefit from its position on a major boulevard.

Simpson's selection of a two-block site just east of Wolf Point, bordered by Orleans, Wells, and Kinzie Streets, held further significance for the aesthetic development of the waterfront. The site comprised the Chicago and North Western Railroad's Wells Street Station complex, consisting of the tracks and numerous buildings that had accumulated over the years since W. W. Boyington's Chicago and North Western Depot was completed in 1881 (figs. 7-8). The building would be erected on the railroad's air rights, which provided Simpson with a site big enough to accommodate "the largest building in the world." At the same time, the unsightly train yard would be removed from view, thus furthering the Chicago Plan Commission's intent to develop and beautify the riverfront.

The Development of Air Rights in Chicago

The Merchandise Mart, Chicago's second air rights project, followed closely upon the first: Holabird and Root's Chicago Daily News Building (now Riverside Plaza Building), completed a year earlier in 1929. The concept of air rights today, which includes unused, zoned air space above a building, differs from the concept in the 1920s, which pertained solely to air space above railroad tracks and facilities. In 1927 Joshua D'Esposito, the consulting engineer for the Daily News Building, succinctly defined air rights as "the space above a plane of clearance over railroad tracks and facilities, capable of utilization for the construction of streets and buildings in the same manner as if the railroad facilities did not exist."[19]

Railroads had employed the idea of air rights for their own incidental purposes in the nineteenth century.[20] The idea of utilizing air rights for unrelated development, as well as the term "air rights" itself, gained national attention in the early twentieth century when, in 1902, William Wilgus, engineer for the New York Central and Hudson River Railroad, included the concept as a fundamental part of his scheme for the electrification of Grand Central Terminal. Between about 1910 and 1930 railroad-owned air rights above the underground tracks stretching north from the new terminal beneath Lexington, Park, and Madison avenues in New York City were leased for the development of the Grand Central Zone, the most extensive City Beautiful project ever realized (fig. 9).[21] The economic and aesthetic advantages of the Grand Central air rights development were incalculable, adding an entirely new dimension to railroad economics and to City Beautiful aesthetics. The advantages of early air rights unions were threefold: the railroads benefited economically through the leasing or sale of their unused air space and ground area, and developers profited by their ability to purchase very large sites without the costly and time-consuming acquisition of contiguous parcels. The city benefited from the elimination of train yards and noisy railroad activities.

The example of New York's Grand Central Terminal project promulgated air rights-related legislation in other cities. The proposed electrification of the Illinois Central Railroad's suburban lines along the lakefront prompted the Illinois state legislature to pass a law in 1922 that allowed railroad companies to sell or lease their air space.[22] In 1923 Eliel Saarinen proposed a design for a hotel and office park complex over a multi-level, subterranean transportation center at the lakefront location. Saarinen's unrealized plan was Chicago's only air rights proposal until early 1927, when representatives of the Chicago Daily News Company and Marshall Field's applied to the Illinois Commerce Commission for the final approval needed to undertake their respective air rights projects. At a public hearing on the issue finally held before the Commission late in that year, representatives of various civic organizations who had been studying the feasibility of air rights developments voiced positive opinions on the issue. On November 23, 1927, the commission gave approval for the two projects to proceed.[23]

No two air rights projects were—or ever will be—alike. The decision of the railroad company and the developer whether to enter into a purchase or lease contract, and whether to retain or permit an easement or right-of-way, depended on whether all or a portion of the air rights were needed. These variables in turn depended upon, and were further complicated by, the exigencies

Fig. 7   Site of the Merchandise Mart, looking northwest to corner of Kinzie and Orleans streets, c. 1928.

Fig. 8   W. W. Boyington, Chicago and North Western Railroad Station, corner of Wells and Kinzie streets, 1881 (now demolished).

Fig. 9   William Wilgus, Reed and Stem, and Warren and Wetmore, Cutaway perspective view of Grand Central Terminal and the Grand Central Zone, New York City, c. 1930.

of construction over operating tracks and facilities. Although D'Esposito insisted upon "one cardinal principle, viz.: that the railroad needs are always paramount, and the air rights incidental," the advantages to both sides in the long run were so interdependent as to be inseparable.[24] In Chicago the immensity of early buildings and complexes built on air rights, and the fact that the railroads were all located along the Chicago River and Lake Michigan, presented challenges to developers and architects to ensure that the large scale of their projects did not isolate the buildings from the urban context or isolate the public from the benefits of the waterfront.

Chicago's first two air rights projects differed significantly from each other. The Chicago Union Station Company–Chicago Daily News project, which seemed to have combined every variable, took lawyers one and a half years to settle. The Daily News purchased outright a thirty-foot strip of riverfront land, received a right-of-way on 85,000 square feet of trackage to erect foundations and columns, and was deeded another 25,000 square feet of the site not used by the railroad. Design and construction were complicated by the need to vent smoke from steam-powered engines through the top of the twenty-six-story building.[25] Holabird and Root's design also featured an outdoor plaza that invited the public to share the water's edge (fig. 10). The elements of the plaza—the entrances that appear as small buildings, the memorial fountain, and the balustrades with their prominent finials— reduce the scale of this large structure, which occupies an entire city block, to the level of the pedestrian. A two-story interior concourse allows pedestrians to pass through the building on their daily commute.

While the Daily News Building provided pedestrian amenities, the Merchandise Mart was designed to accommodate motor transportation. The air rights union between Marshall Field and Company and the Chicago and North Western Railroad appears to have been relatively simple in contrast to the complexity of the Daily News project. The company purchased the railroad's air space above the twenty-three-foot city datum plane over the entire five-acre site. In addition, it purchased 458 small parcels of land (each had a separate deed) in which to sink the caissons for supports, plus a number of linear strip lots on the site necessary for the building's elevator shafts, machinery room, and sundry mechanical requirements.[26] The railroad, which had not used the Wells Street Depot for passenger service

since 1911, would build an entirely new station at ground level on its remaining property within the new building for an "in-city, less-than-carload freight terminal" to be connected by elevators to the Chicago Tunnel Company's lines under the site.[27] Because the new station would not be seen or used by the public, Graham, Anderson, Probst and White's design was not compelled to indicate the railroad's facilities or provide for the pedestrian's needs in the massing or elevation of the building. The architects' approach to site planning was predetermined by Simpson's intention to fulfill the recommendations of the *Plan of Chicago* by creating a North Bank Drive to correspond to the recently completed Wacker Drive.

The designs of the Daily News Building and the Merchandise Mart supported the ideals of the Chicago Plan while accommodating their related transportation networks, but the city's next air rights project would contribute to the gradual erosion of the Plan that began after the onset of the Depression. Chicago's United States Post Office, built by the federal government but designed by Graham, Anderson, Probst and White, was erected on air rights over terminal tracks just south of Union Station and completed in 1932. This extraordinary structure was

wrapped around the earlier U.S. Mail Building (also designed by Graham's firm and completed in 1921), leaving only the original building's east facade exposed (fig. 11).[28] True to its era, the new post office was touted as "the largest building in the world devoted exclusively to postal business," and it imitated the Merchandise Mart both in its severe Art Deco style and in its comprehensive city-within-a-city program.[29]

The government's conflict with the Plan's supporters arose in 1930, when the location of the post office was changed to the air rights site to take advantage of rail delivery of mail.[30] The new site straddled the line of Congress Street which, according to Burnham and Bennett's recommendations, eventually would have been extended to provide the city with a major east-west axis. Running from the lakefront to the riverfront, Congress Street would intersect with Halsted Street at the location of the proposed civic center with its domed City Hall. The post office would block the grand vista that had become a hallmark of the Plan. Members of the Plan Commission, who had become increasingly concerned with the engineering rather than the aesthetic aspects of urban form, objected to the implications of this change of site, but voiced their concerns rather apathetically and refrained

Fig. 10 Holabird and Root, Chicago Daily News Building, 400 West Madison Street, 1929.

Fig. 11 Graham, Anderson, Probst and White, Chicago Post Office (now altered), 1931 (photo 1951).

Fig. 12 Naess and Murphy, Prudential Building, 130 East Randolph Street, 1952-55.

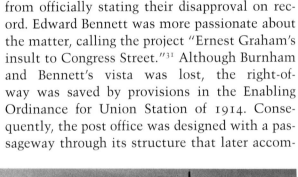
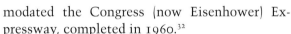

from officially stating their disapproval on record. Edward Bennett was more passionate about the matter, calling the project "Ernest Graham's insult to Congress Street."[31] Although Burnham and Bennett's vista was lost, the right-of-way was saved by provisions in the Enabling Ordinance for Union Station of 1914. Consequently, the post office was designed with a passageway through its structure that later accommodated the Congress (now Eisenhower) Expressway, completed in 1960.[32]

The post office was Chicago's last air rights project until after World War II. Plans for a huge air rights complex over the Illinois Central yards north of Randolph Street and along the river had been announced in 1929-30. Holabird and Root, as well as New York architects Ralph T. Walker and Raymond Hood, developed designs for the proposed venture, called Terminal Park, but the advent of the Depression suppressed that development.[33] After World War II, a portion of the same site was chosen for Naess and Murphy's Prudential Building, Chicago's third air rights project and the first major office tower constructed in Chicago after the war (fig. 12). As in the Daily News project, the air rights agreement between Prudential and the Illinois Central took one and a half years to negotiate, but the agreement was similar to the Merchandise Mart project in that the site consisted of a "378' x 377' block of air" plus 550 separate lots for caissons. Complicating the negotiations was Illinois Central's need to retain ownership of the portion of each lot that ran underneath the railroad's girders and the fact that the new structure was not to interfere with ongoing train operations.[34]

At forty-one stories, the Prudential was the city's tallest building upon its completion in 1955, and it remained the only structure on the undeveloped land until 1967, when construction was begun on Illinois Center, still the world's largest air rights development. The eighty acres of Illinois Central tracks were obsolete by that time, a condition that simplified air rights negotiations and construction. The development as a whole has suffered from an isolated sterility

due to a lack of pedestrian amenities such as plazas, esplanades, and overlooks that would take advantage of the waterfront location. This problem was addressed by Skidmore, Owings and Merrill in its designs for Gateway Center, an air rights development along the west bank of the Chicago River (1963-1983) that incorporated river walks with foliage, seating, and belvederes projecting over the surface of the water (see fig. 13).[35]

One of Chicago's most recent air rights projects, Perkins and Will's Morton International Building, completed in 1990, expanded the limits of air rights engineering (see pl. 69). The developer, ORIX Real Estate Equities, secured the air rights needed to erect one corner of the building over tracks on the west bank of the Chicago River, but the traditional method of sinking caissons for column support was not possible because of the dense track layout at this location. Perkins and Will's solution, which seems particularly suited to their De Stijl-inspired design, was to suspend a 25 by 120-foot corner of the thirteen-story base above the tracks by a system of five steel trusses anchored at the fourteenth floor in the building's tower. The architects' design provides public access to the waterfront site by including a river walk and a small park.[36]

Air rights unions have contributed to two related strains in twentieth-century urban development: in the aesthetic and economic realm, they fueled City Beautiful ideals and plans; in the technical realm, they furthered the horizontal layering of urban form that began with the skyscraper and found ultimate expression in the visions of Italian architect Antonio Sant'Elia and American architect and renderer Hugh Ferriss, about 1914 to 1930, where skyscrapers rise up from the multilevel transportation networks that define the city. In the late 1920s in Chicago, these strains were commingled in air rights projects such as the Daily News Building and the Merchandise Mart, the double-deck Wacker Drive and the proposed North Bank Drive-Avondale Avenue project, as well as in a proposal to make State Street a "triple-decked shopping mart" (see essay by Sennott).

The Age of Efficiency

Frank Sengstock, general superintendent of the Merchandise Mart, observed in 1930 that air rights developments marked "a new era in commercial and civic development...typifying an age of increased efficiency through consolidation

and concentration."[37] Efficiency, consolidation, and concentration were the catchwords of the age. The "search for order" that Robert Wiebe maintains took place between 1877 and 1920 found concrete expression in the architectural and planning accomplishments in the ensuing years before the Depression.[38] The quest for scientific efficiency in all human endeavors, from personal matters to business and industry to politics, coupled with the humanist, progressive belief in environmentalism—that is, that the physical nature of a city could influence the nature and activities of its citizens—made the art and science of building an exacting and noble pursuit. As Moody pithily asserted in *Wacker's Manual*, "city building means man building."[39]

When plans for its new building were revealed in 1927, Marshall Field's wholesale division had been losing money for at least seven years, and Chicago's wholesale dry goods trade in general had shown signs of obsolescence since the beginning of the century. In the nineteenth century, Field had built up his empire through the wholesale trade—largely by acting as a "jobber," or middleman, between manufacturers and merchants; only a small percentage of the company's total profits came from retail sales. That trend began to show signs of reversal at the turn of the century when, between 1886 and 1906, retail sales increased by 450 percent while wholesale sales increased by only 117 percent.[40] Field's wholesale profits continued to decrease until 1920, and thereafter losses were incurred; the ramifications of this downward trend were significant because Chicago had by far the largest market in the nation.[41]

Fig. 13   Skidmore, Owings and Merrill, Gateways I and II, 10-120 South Riverside Plaza, 1963-68.

Several factors contributed to the decline. The biggest group of wholesale customers was made up of rural or small town merchants whose businesses began to suffer when the proliferation of railroad lines, automobiles, and highways made it easy for consumers to go to the big city to shop. Department stores and chain stores, which purchased their goods directly from the manufacturer, offered wider selections at lower prices. Mail-order houses such as Montgomery Ward and Sears, Roebuck and Company began to offer a huge selection of less expensive items and delivered right to the doorstep. At the same time, manufacturers began to appeal to merchants to "buy direct" from the factory, thus eliminating the position of middleman altogether. To counter these trends, wholesalers reluctantly instituted the position of the traveling salesman; this was an effective selling method, but entailed considerable costs.

The erosion of Chicago's dry goods and apparel wholesale trade was gradual; when, as early as 1925, the wholesale division of John V. Farwell and Company collapsed, the warning sign was largely ignored. Trained by Marshall Field in the wholesale tradition, James Simpson refused to accept the impending death of the trade. As the last of Marshall Field's protégés, Simpson represented the traditional and conservative. But as the dynamic president of his company and the chairman of the Chicago Plan Commission, he was an innovator and reformer—and he believed in the power of architecture and planning to effect change. A tired, outdated wholesale trade

Fig. 14 Henry Hobson Richardson, Marshall Field Wholesale Store, Adams Street between Wells and Franklin streets, 1885-87 (now demolished).

could be revitalized and updated with an efficient new building.

Simpson's initial plan for his building, as announced on March 11, 1927, was to erect "the largest building in the world" of twelve to sixteen stories at a cost of fifteen million dollars. The purpose was to consolidate Field's wholesale activities, which were scattered about the city in thirteen different warehouses, including the thirty-year-old granite and sandstone wholesale store designed by H. H. Richardson (fig. 14).[42] Just over a year later, in May 1928, Field's announced an update of its plans. The cost had risen to $30 million, the number of stories to twenty-five, and the building, now called the Merchandise Mart, was to accommodate not only Marshall Field and Company, but "several hundred" other firms as well.[43]

Simpson's inspiration for enlarging the cost, size, and scope of the building was an urban one: State Street itself, Chicago's renowned shopping district.[44] Simpson called this concentration of department stores a "vast retail center" where "shopping is easy for buyers, profitable for sellers." By consolidating Chicago's wholesale firms, sellers would benefit from competition, and buyers would benefit from the concentration of an unprecedented number of lines in one location. But Simpson would go one step further and put them all under one roof. The buyer would be enticed to come to this wholesale mecca because the scientifically planned "department store for stores" would eliminate the "wear and tear on his energy that occurs when his wholesale sources are scattered all over town."[45] This appeal to alleviate the "wear and tear" of city life by creating an orderly, efficient environment was a recurrent promotional device used by Moody in *Wacker's Manual*, in which he related, for example, that "city life ... saps the energy of men, and makes them less efficient in the work of life."[46]

Simpson extended the urban theme of his concept by calling the Mart a "town in one building." Other published sources called the building "a veritable city of wholesale firms" and "a city with a permanent population all under one roof," where "there's no running from one side of the city to the other, no climbing up and down back stairs, or groping one's way through dark hallways." The Mart would be a planned community, a model of organization where "all merchandise needs are scientifically displayed in well lighted and comfortable showrooms and ... the arrangement of displays worked out by floors, sections, and departments, after

Fig. 15 Merchandise Mart under construction, view from southwest, 1929.

Fig. 16 Merchandise Mart, plan of first floor; from The Architectural Work of Graham, Anderson, Probst, and White (London, 1933).

Fig. 17 Merchandise Mart, typical floor plan; from The Architectural Work of Graham, Anderson, Probst, and White (London, 1933).

Fig. 18 Merchandise Mart, view of Orleans Street facade at street level, c. 1945.

months of study and research."[47] All the modern modes of transportation would be accommodated. For the seller, there would be trucking facilities with direct access to major thoroughfares, railroad lines linked to Chicago's underground tunnels, and shipping docks at the heart of a vast waterway system; for the buyer, an elevated stop, city bus stop, shuttle service, and taxi stand.

Construction and Design

James Simpson and architect Ernest Graham tossed the first shovelful of dirt on August 16, 1928, to break ground for construction.[48] In the preceding months, the Wells Street complex had been demolished and the site cleared to make way for a project in which, as Carl Condit has observed, "every part...reached an unprecedented level." The air rights union proved to be especially advantageous for construction. As in the Grand Central Terminal project, the laying of new tracks and the sinking of caissons occurred simultaneously so that materials could be delivered directly to the site by rail.[49] Railroad cranes unloaded the steel beams, columns, and girders, the heaviest of which weighed twenty tons each, and nine cranes kept on the top level of the rising structure hoisted the steel to its place (fig. 15).

New techniques developed by general contractor John W. Griffiths & Sons brought building construction into the machine age. Especially innovative was a system for mixing and placing concrete, which, as Condit described, was "ordinarily used in the construction of big dams." Cement, arriving by boat, was shot by com-

pressed air seventy-five feet up to a mammoth bin. Gravel and sand were delivered by bottom-dumping railroad cars to another bin. These ingredients were transferred by conveyors and elevators to giant mixers. The wet concrete was then elevated by skip hoists in vertical towers that were extended as the building rose. Concrete spouted from those onto portable conveyor belts by which it reached its destination.[50] The construction project, which lasted a year and a half through the first months of the Depression, employed 2,500 men throughout its duration and as many as 5,700 men altogether.

Graham, Anderson, Probst and White's *parti* was determined in part by agreements made in the air rights union (figs. 16-17). The building fills the entire site, its footprint an irregular trapezoid that results from the oblique deviation of Orleans Street from the city grid. The south, riverfront of the building predominates in plan as well as elevation. Express elevators rose directly to the seventh floor, above the point where Marshall Field and Company occupied floors three to six. The linear arrangement of the elevator and service core that extends the building's entire two-block length on this side follows the linear arrangement of the tracks below. The company's display rooms were located on the river side of the building, and passenger elevators opened to this side. Freight elevators opened to the rear, where open stock merchandise was housed. The uniform square grid of structural columns is interrupted on this side to accommodate the longer spans necessary for freight and railroad facilities on the two levels below the street.[51] The north facade, covered with fire escapes, held the entrance to the truck loading

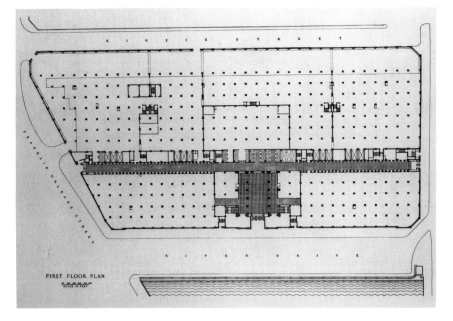

FIRST FLOOR PLAN

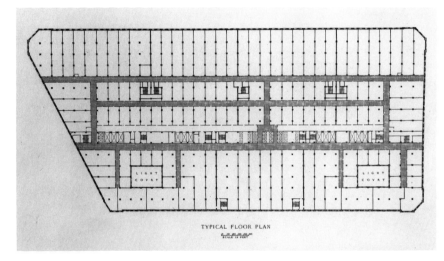

TYPICAL FLOOR PLAN

dock that occupied the entire rear portion of the first floor.

Designer Alfred Shaw conveyed the unique, modern concept of the Merchandise Mart with his suave Art Deco style and integration of elements from three building types: the warehouse, the department store, and the skyscraper office building.[52] A huge, typical warehouse block comprises the eighteen-story bulk of the building. Repetitious, unadorned ribbon piers define the fenestration pattern. The building's chamfered corners (a design element perhaps generated by the oblique angle of Orleans Street), the minimal setbacks of the roofline, and the corner pavilions serve to camouflage the edges of the basically rectilinear mass, visually reducing its weight and bulk. The functional reason given for this massing was the conception of the building as a hermetically sealed box:

The Mart was built with but two small light wells and no set-backs for ventilation or light purposes. Scientific artificial ventilation is provided for all interior spaces which are removed from windows. In showing merchandise it is much more advantageous and cleanly to be away from outside windows in as much as artificial light is used for the display of many lines of merchandise.[53]

The building opens up at pedestrian level where the two-story base is glazed with the overscaled display windows typical of a department store. Enframed in richly embossed bronze, the windows range along the length of the south, west, and east facades (fig. 18). When Graham, Anderson, Probst and White published the Merchandise Mart in their impressive, two-volume tome of 1933, the building was listed not under "Warehouses," but "Department Stores."[54]

The twenty-five-story central tower projects and rises from the main block to reveal its affinity with the corporate skyscraper. Concentrated here was the building's program of ornamental imagery. The deeply recessed and overscaled portal stands between raised panels, above which hang octagonal medallions featuring the interlocked initials of the Merchandise Mart, a logo that recurs throughout the building and on early promotional material and stationery (fig. 19). The message of the medallion is clear: although Field's built the Merchandise Mart, it was conceived not as the company's wholesale store, but as a wholesale mart, an institution in and of itself.

One early drawing, a nocturne in chiaroscuro that bespeaks the sophisticated drama of the era, indicates unrealized plans to carve the side panels in bas-relief (fig. 1). Enthroned allegorical figures appear to be holding torches that burst

forth in rays of light to illuminate surrounding figures and symbols representing industry and trade. While this classically conceived depiction would have symbolically linked activities within the building to the universal and timeless, the local origins of Chicago's trade were elevated even higher, to the tower's crown. There, fifty-six American Indian chiefs stood head, shoulder, and arms above the city, proudly and stalwartly asserting their part in Chicago's nascent trade activities (fig. 20). These terra-cotta acroteria, measuring $3^1/_2$ by 7 feet but barely visible from the street, were meant to be seen from the upper floors of the skyscrapers that would rise along the riverbank drives above the relatively low plateau of the Mart. To accommodate this view "the architects...planned a roof that'll be minus the usual galaxy of skylights, tanks, penthouses and other sky disfiguring atrocities" (see fig. 3).[55]

The lobby of the Merchandise Mart, in an overall palette of buff, bronze, and warm tones, exemplifies the understated elegance that characterizes Shaw's later designs (fig. 22). Eight square marble piers, so slightly fluted that they appear to be merely striped, define the main lobby area. Side aisles are lined with shop fronts enframed in the lavishly embossed bronze trim

found throughout this level (fig. 23). The terrazzo floor, in pale hues of green and orange, was conceived as a carpet: a lively pattern of squares and stripes bordered by overscaled chevrons inlaid with an abstraction of the Mart's initials. The chevron motif is carried out three-dimensionally in the column sconces that cast their uplight onto an ornamented cornice situated above.

The crowning feature of the lobby, Jules Guérin's frieze of murals, completes the iconographic trilogy proposed for the building. While the proposed bas-relief and acroteria on the exterior relate the mercantile activities of the Mart to the universal and the local, Guérin's murals within represent the ground between these realms in their depiction of commerce throughout the world, including the countries whence came most of the goods sold in the building. The murals depict the principal industries and products, the primary mode of transportation, and the architecture of fourteen countries; like the sculptures, they connect the modern world of the Mart with the distant and the past. Guérin executed the murals in red tones highlighted by gold leaf and, drawing upon his experience as a stage set designer, employed a compositional technique that establishes distinct layers of im-

Fig. 19 Merchandise Mart, detail of entrance; from The Architectural Work of Graham, Anderson, Probst, and White (London, 1933).

Fig. 20 Merchandise Mart, detail of acroteria on 22nd and 24th stories of the tower, 1930 (removed in 1961).

Fig. 22 Merchandise Mart, main lobby; from The Architectural Work of Graham, Anderson, Probst, and White (London, 1933).

Fig. 23 Merchandise Mart, detail of shop fronts along the perimeter of the main lobby.

Fig. 21 *Merchandise Mart, NBC television studio; from* The Architectural Work of Graham, Anderson, Probst, and White *(London, 1933).*

ters, cafés, and a restaurant to seat 1,000, as well as retail shops for everything from clothing to candy. Services included an optician, beautician and barber, stenographer and notary public, and broker's, telegraph, ticket, and railroad agent offices. The Mart had its own post office (and, later, zip code), bank, police station, and even a Chamber of Commerce.

In the Mart's upper stories, two wide 650-feet-long corridors with terrazzo floors, referred to as "business boulevards," featured six and one-half miles of display windows, all uniformly designed. Building regulations called for identical entrances along the corridors; tenants could personalize the space behind. With the exception of the corridors, elevator halls, and exhibition space on the fourth floor, the vast five acres of each upper floor was "raw space" with concrete floors and a forest of structural columns nineteen and one-half feet apart.[57] This area was limited to the tenants of the Merchandise Mart and their wholesale customers; the public was allowed access only to the retail portions of the first and second floors, exhibition space on the fourth floor, and the studios of the National Broadcasting Company (NBC), the most prestigious of the Merchandise Mart's tenants, on the nineteenth and twentieth floors of the tower. The advent of radio broadcasting in 1920, the organization of NBC in 1926, and its early support of young, innovative composers such as George Gershwin, Cole Porter, and Jerome Kern put radio at the cutting edge of the ebullient "jazz age." NBC built six studios designed by Alfred Shaw, including the largest in the world, where visitors could view performances from observation booths (fig. 21). Thus, the Merchandise Mart was crowned with the era's ultimate expression of glamour and high technology.

ages in successive planes. In the panel for Italy, vignettes of Venetian glassware seem to stand in front of fishing boats moored on the Grand Canal; the facade of the Palazzo Ducale stretches behind, and beyond rise the towers of Piazza San Marco.[56]

Between the lobby and the elevator banks, the arcade that extends the length of the building would provide the shops and services "normally found on the main street of almost any town." Here and on the second floor were lunch coun-

The Merchandise Mart opened with little fanfare on Monday, May 5, 1930, six months into the Depression. News of the opening was brief, but accompanied by a longer discussion of the closing of the revered Marshall Field Warehouse Store the previous day. The event was documented by a photograph of three veteran merchants looking up at the old building, their hats held high in a farewell gesture. As the employees nostalgically, but passively, contemplated the building's pending demolition, they related memories that seem, in retrospect, to have a remarkably prophetic character: when the erection of the structure in 1887 pioneered a new wholesale district in the city, they believed that the store's vast space would never be fully utilized. With the building's subsequent demolition in 1930 to make way for a parking lot, the rugged individualism of its architecture bowed to an age of urbane cooperation and the omnipresent automobile.[58]

No merchandising endeavor could be expected to outmaneuver the disastrous economic effects of the Depression. In 1931 Marshall Field and Company's losses amounted to five million dollars; the figure rose to eight million in 1932. Simpson, who retired from his position as chairman of the board in 1932 to direct the reorganization of Chicago's utilities companies, remained as chairman of the executive committee. In 1935, still believing that he could save Field's wholesale division, Simpson called in John O. McKinsey, one of the new breed of corporate management "efficiency experts." McKinsey dealt the final blow: Field's jobbing division, the heart and soul of wholesale trade, would have to be eliminated. Within six months of McKinsey's decision, Field's wholesale division was virtually liquidated.[59]

Marshall Field reduced its space in the Merchandise Mart from four floors to one and a half, but the building, 82 percent occupied when it opened, was still tenanted by a multitude of smaller businesses that had adapted to changes in the wholesale trade. The Mart continued to introduce current and avant-garde trends in home furnishings in its showrooms and trade shows. Promotional literature indicates that, in January 1934, its "Clinic of Modern Design" featured Frederick J. Kiesler, the Viennese-born surrealist known for his continuously curved "Endless House," and the design of Peggy Guggenheim's Art of This Century Gallery in New York City.[60]

Events in the late 1930s spurred economic recovery, and Marshall Field and Company once again began to record profit. When James Simpson died unexpectedly in November 1939, he had just completed a plan to eliminate the company's back dividends and repay its debts.[61] Later, during the years of World War II, the Merchandise Mart experienced the dreary presence of hundreds of government offices. Ironically, this was the time when the completion of the Pentagon in 1943, at 6.2 million square feet, caused a change in the Mart's title from "the largest building in the world" to "the largest *commercial* building in the world."

The war's end marked a watershed in the Mart's history, when, in 1945, ownership passed from Marshall Field and Company to Joseph P. Kennedy, former ambassador to Great Britain and father of the thirty-fifth president. Attributing his interest in the Merchandise Mart to his "faith in Chicago and the Middle West" and in Chicago's "great commercial and industrial future," Kennedy ushered in a new era of mercantile pride by reviving the original concept of the building and gradually allowing public access.[62] Kennedy's staff first undertook a programmatic renovation by creating office space on the lower floors and encouraging the use of the upper floors for home furnishing and apparel showrooms. In 1948, responding to a trend of increasing consumer interest, his staff opened up the Mart to the public by instituting daily tours given by the Merchandise Mart Guide Service (fig. 24).[63]

The Merchandise Mart underwent a modernization campaign in the late 1950s and the 1960s that reflected a broader trend of renovating older, urban buildings in those decades. In 1953 Kennedy established the Merchant's Hall of Fame, its purpose "to immortalize outstanding American merchants."[64] Those inducted into the institution—among them Marshall Field, John Wanamaker, and F. W. Woolworth—are represented in eight bronze busts, four times life size, that rise up from pillars on the river side of the plaza to face the building (see fig. 25). The individualized realism of the busts, perched on their outposts, provided a bizarre contrast to the idealized acroteria integrated into the design of the building's tower. The unfortunate Indian chiefs, unquestionably the greatest casualty of the modernization, were removed, destroyed, and replaced with "clean looking concrete plates" in 1961.[65] The aesthetic of clean concrete was rendered even more conspicuous at street level the next year when an entrance canopy was

Fig. 24 *Merchandise Mart Guide Service with a model of the Merchandise Mart, c. 1948.*

the building's superlative titles. The opening in 1977 of the annexed Apparel Center, designed by Skidmore, Owings and Merrill, increased the Mart's total square footage to 6.2 million, but that figure was surpassed by the Dallas Market Center in 1979, when additions to that complex raised the square footage to seven million. In the 1980s a boom in the development of corporate office and mixed-use buildings nurtured by President Ronald Reagan's economic policies precipitated an expansion of the contract furnishings industry. As design centers sprang up in other cities in response to the increased demand, the Mart's owners kept apace by opening the Design Center in Washington, D.C., in 1982; plans for a New York City Merchandise Mart to be erected on a site near Times Square were thwarted by politics hindering development in that area.

While the building boom of the 1980s resulted in a sudden increase of new corporate and mixed-use skyscrapers, it was also characterized by the preservation of historic buildings. The departure of some of the Mart's largest corporate office tenants—among them NBC and Quaker Oats Company, who were lured away by the new buildings and facile financing of the decade—coincided with management's decision to compete in the expanding market by exploiting the building's Art Deco cachet and opening up the Mart to serve the growing population of the expanding North Loop, River North, and River West areas. This auspicious confluence of build-

extended over the plaza to provide a vehicular drive-through, that ubiquitous architectural symbol of suburban America, ironically only possible in this urban setting because the plaza existed as the undeveloped legacy of Simpson's plans for a North Bank Drive (fig. 25).

Kennedy's modernization may have been a response to competition from merchandise markets that opened in Dallas, Atlanta, and Los Angeles in the 1950s and 1960s.[66] In the ensuing decade, the expansion of the Merchandise Mart was accompanied by a gradual diminishment of

Fig. 25 *Merchandise Mart, view of new entrance canopy and Hall of Fame, 1962.*

ing, real estate, and demographic trends resulted in a comprehensive restoration and renovation of the Mart's physical fabric. The extensive project preserved the integrity of the original concept and design while making programmatic changes that would reverse the traditionally hermetic nature of the Mart's role in Chicago's urban life and form.

The project began in 1986 with the basic necessities—a cleaning and window replacement undertaken by Graham, Anderson, Probst and White, roof repair, and upgrade of utilities systems. An enclosed pedestrian walk designed by Helmut Jahn, which bridges over Orleans Street to connect the Mart and the Apparel Center, was completed in 1988. The next year, Beyer Blinder Belle, a New York City architecture and planning firm known for its preservation work, was engaged to create a retail center on the first and second floors of the Mart. The project was deemed justified by the Mart's daily tenant and visitor population of 20,000, the enormous crowds drawn by the NEOCON trade show each year, and the growing populations of the North Loop area at Wacker Drive, the River North neighborhood at the Mart's back, and the River West area across the north branch of the river. The boom of the 1980s had provided a dense urban context around the Mart to which the building's program could finally respond.

Beyer Blinder Belle's work included opening up the building by creating additional entrances around its perimeter and restoring the display windows, main entrance, and lobby. On the south facade they removed the drive-through canopy and cut two smaller portals on either side of the main entrance, thus utilizing the lower portions of the blank side panels.[67] The overscaled display windows, painted over in the modernization campaign of the 1960s, were restored, and tenant guidelines were established to ensure that clear glass would be used in order to reveal retail activities within. The rear facade was renovated to include main and corner entrances, thus opening up the Mart to the north. The loading dock that occupied the north portion of the first floor was removed to the river level under the plaza, utilizing the bottom deck of the unrealized North Bank Drive.

On the interior, a restoration of the lobby included replication of the original glass curtain wall over the entrance, restoration of shop fronts, and even a new version of the original reception desk. The first floor north of the elevators and the entire second floor, vacated by Quaker Oats, was developed as an eighty-five-store mall. Beyer Blinder Belle's scheme included shop fronts, terrazzo floors, and wall sconces inspired by the original design. Upon its completion in 1991, the "Shops at the Mart," as the mall was trendily named, drew mixed reactions from realtors, marketing experts, and the general public who questioned the viability of a mall at this location and in this isolated building. Retailers on State Street and North Michigan Avenue expressed concern about competition and the dispersal of Chicago's retail trade in a time of recession.[68]

The Merchandise Mart has come full circle in its sixty-year history: from construction during a depression to restoration during a recession. A recent downward trend in the contract furnishings wholesale trade that resulted from the demise of the building boom of the 1980s and the onset of the ensuing recession has inspired speculation in the design world and among the Mart's tenants and management about the possibility of opening up the showrooms to retail trade, a prospect that at this writing remains studied and controversial.[69] Whatever the outcome of that surprising development, the building's elegant design, flexible plan, and evolving program no doubt will ensure its survival as a vital part of Chicago's urbanism.

NOTES

1. The application of scientific efficiency to urban form had been promoted earlier by Walter Dwight Moody, in *Wacker's Manual of the Plan of Chicago: Municipal Economy* (Chicago, 1911). For an examination of these paradoxical tendencies, see Roderick Nash, *The Nervous Generation: American Thought, 1917-1930* (Chicago, 1970; rpt., 1990). For an in-depth discussion of the relationship between Daniel H. Burnham and Edward H. Bennett's *Plan of Chicago*, ed. Charles Moore (Chicago, 1909), and *Wacker's Manual*, see Thomas Schlereth, "Burnham's Plan and Moody's Manual: City Planning as Progressive Reform," in Donald A. Krueckeberg, ed., *The American Planner: Biographies and Recollections* (New York, 1983), pp. 75-99.

2. Homer Hoyt, *One Hundred Years of Land Values in Chicago* (Chicago, 1933), pp. 236-37, 265, 445. Hoyt points out that World War I drives to sell Liberty Bonds popularized the idea of bond investments to such a degree that contractors and developers put the cart before the horse by encouraging lenders to undertake huge developments just so the banks would have the opportunity to sell the bonds.

3. Hoyt (note 2), pp. 241, 296. The ordinance did not fix a maximum height, but stated that the size of the tower could not exceed one-fourth of the lot size and that the cubic volume contained in it could not exceed one-sixth of the cubic volume of the entire building. Lot sizes in the Loop during the 1920s thus limited the height of buildings to 45 or 46 stories.

4. For a discussion of these buildings and a chronological account of the rise of the skyscraper in Chicago, see Pauline A. Saliga, ed., *The Sky's the Limit : A Century of Chicago Skyscrapers* (New York, 1990).

5. See Joan Draper, *Edward H. Bennett, Architect and City Planner, 1874-1954* (Chicago, 1982).

6. Hoyt (note 2), p. 241; John W. Stamper, *Chicago's North Michigan Avenue: Planning and Development, 1900-1930* (Chicago and London, 1991), pp. 15-21.

7. Sources of biographical information on Simpson include *Who's Who in Chicago: The Book of Chicagoans, a Biographical Dictionary of Leading Living Men and Women of the City and Environs* (Chicago, 1931), p. 896; Glenn A. Bishop and Paul T. Gilbert, *Chicago's Accomplishments and Leaders* (Chicago, 1932), pp. 437, 549; "James Simpson, Utilities Chief, Dies," *Chicago Sunday Tribune* (Nov. 26, 1939), p. 1; "Simpson Death Leaves Two Big Posts Vacant," *Chicago Sunday Tribune* (Nov. 26, 1939), pt. 2, p. 9. For the history of Marshall Field and Company, I have relied on secondary sources: Robert W. Twyman, *History of Marshall Field & Co., 1852-1906* (Philadelphia, 1954); Lloyd Wendt and Herman Kogan, *Give the Lady What She Wants! The Story of Marshall Field & Company* (Chicago, 1952); John Tebbel, *The Marshall Fields: A Study in Wealth* (New York, 1947); Stephen Becker, *Marshall Field III* (New York, 1964).

8. Daniel Boorstin, *The Americans: The Democratic Experience* (New York, 1973), pp. 3-87 passim ("go-getter"); "James Simpson, Utilities Chief, Dies" (note 7).

9. Charles Edward Merriam, *Chicago: A More Intimate View of Urban Politics* (New York, 1929; rpt., 1970), p. 109; Merriam considered department stores as a civic group: "In Chicago, the Association of Commerce, the Commercial Club, the Commonwealth Club, the Chicago and Cook County Real Estate Boards, the Department Stores, the Manufacturers, Banks, the Industrial Club, are strong factors. These groups are extremely powerful...."

10. Walter Dwight Moody, *What of the City?* (Chicago, 1919), pp. 360-61; Chicago Plan Commission, *Chicago's Greatest Issue: An Official Plan* (Chicago, 1911), p. [7]. Simpson is listed as a "subscriber" in the beginning pages of Burnham and Bennett's *Plan of Chicago*, ed. Charles Moore (note 1), n.p.; for a listing of the executive officers and chairmen of the Plan Commission, 1908-1980, see Harry Weese, "The Chicago Plan Commission," *Inland Architect* 24, no. 3 (April 1980), p. 18. I am grateful to Carroll William Westfall for calling my attention to the last source.

11. Schlereth (note 1), p. 76.

12. Moody (note 1), pp. 1, 95.

13. James Simpson, "Chicago Completes Great Civic Improvements," in Bishop and Gilbert (note 7), p. 436.

14. Ibid.

15. "Fields to Spend $15 Million for Big Mart Here," *Chicago Daily Tribune* (March 12, 1927), p. 1.

16. "How Chicago River Will Look with Banks Boulevarded," *Chicago Sunday Tribune* (March 13, 1927), pt. 3, p. 3; "$15 Million Field Project Puts North Wacker Drive on Map, Assures Start on Boulevard for River Bank," *Chicago Sunday Tribune* (March 13, 1927), pt. 3, p. 1.

17. Burnham and Bennett (note 1), p. 97.

18. Hoyt (note 2), pp. 205, 237, 485; in 1920, 89,973 automobiles were registered; in 1929, the number was 408,260. The problems of congestion related to the automobile had grown so critical that a comprehensive traffic study was undertaken in 1926; see Miller McClintock, ed., *Report and Recommendations of the Metropolitan Street Traffic Survey* (Chicago, 1926).

19. Joshua D'Esposito, "Some of the Fundamental Principles of Air Rights," *Railway Age* 83, no. 17 (Oct. 22, 1927), p. 757. Today the issue of air rights is much more complex. The transfer of air rights has become a way to circumvent zoning restrictions. Jonathan Schlefer, in "Castles in the Air," *Technology Review* 87 (July 1984), pp. 74-75, discusses the "decidedly unharmonious dealings over air rights" and quotes William Conklin's visual image: "Floating above the landmark, in its own special heaven, like a piece of yellow legal paper, is an amorphous bulk of floor levels." Schlefer continues to explain that "rather than building those extra floors allowed by the zoning, the owners can sell the 'air rights' to owners of a nearby lot. Those neighbors can use the air rights to build a tower on their own lot with more floor area than the zoning would otherwise allow."

20. D'Esposito (note 19) cites two examples of the railroads' incidental use of the idea of air rights: (1) In 1863, the Pennsylvania Railroad built the 1,325-foot Panhandle Tunnel under Granite Hill in the heart of the city and then sold the property above it while retaining an easement that covered the periphery of the tunnel structure; (2) Boston's Back Bay Station was erected directly above the tracks and platforms.

21. For an overview of the development of Grand Central Terminal and the Grand Central Zone, see Deborah Nevins, et al., *Grand Central Terminal: City within a City* (New York, 1982), and Carl Condit, *The Port of New York*, vol. 2: *From the Grand Central Electrification to the Present* (Chicago, 1980).

22. Robert Bruegmann, *Holabird and Roche and Holabird and Root: An Illustrated Catalog of Works, 1880-1940* (New York, 1991), vol. 2, p. 312; Bruegmann cites *The Economist* (Oct. 29, 1927), p. 1068 and (Nov. 26, 1927), p. 1320.

23. "State O.K.'s Air Rights Sale; Adds $330,000,000 to Values," *Chicago Daily Tribune* (Nov. 24, 1927).

24. D'Esposito (note 19), p. 758.

25. Bruegmann (note 22), vol. 2, p. 313-14. For the purposes of taxation, the Daily News air rights were valued at $1,423,827 in 1930; see "Huge Air Right [sic] Project North of Randolph," *Chicago Sunday Tribune* (May 18, 1930), p. 1.

26. Claude A. Wells, "Merchandise Mart will be the World's Largest Building," in *Chicago, The World's Youngest Great City* (Chicago, 1929), p. 141; "Merchandise Mart, Chicago," *Architecture and Building* 63 (March 1931), p. 66; "Air Rights Office Building in Chicago," *Engineering News Record* 102 (April 25, 1929), pp. 664-67. The concrete caissons, 5 to 10 feet in diameter with truncated-cone spreading bases, reached down 80-100 feet below street level.

27. Carl W. Condit, *Chicago, 1910-29: Building, Planning, and Urban Technology* (Chicago and London, 1973), p. 173, note 49. The Merchandise Mart air rights were valued at $2,307,319 in 1930; see "Huge Air Right [sic] Project North of Randolph" (note 25).

28. Sally A. Kitt Chappell, *Architecture and Planning of Graham, Anderson, Probst and White, 1912-1936: Transforming Tradition* (Chicago and London, 1992), pp. 126-27, 249-50.

29. Eugene S. Taylor, "The Chicago Plan Moves Forward," *City Planning* 8 (Oct. 1932), p. 230.

30. "City Planners Object to Site for Post Office," *Chicago Daily Tribune* (May 26, 1930), p. 6; "Post Office Site Preferred by Officials at Washington as it Appears from Air," *Chicago Daily Tribune* (May 29, 1930), p. 34; "Plan Executives Fight to Save Congress Street," *Chicago Daily Tribune* (May 30, 1930), p. 12; Letter from W. A. Dudley to Edward H. Bennett (May 24, 1930), "Story of the Purchase of the New Post Office Site," Bennett Papers, Ryerson and Burnham Libraries, The Art Institute of Chicago.

31. Draper (note 5), p. 24.

32. Condit (note 27), p. 284; Chappell (note 28), p. 250.

33. "Huge Air Right [sic] Project North of Randolph" (note 25); Bruegmann (note 22), vol. 3, p. 98; Saliga, (note 4), p. 12; and Carol Herselle Krinsky, "Chicago and New York: Plans and Parallels, 1889-1929," *Museum Studies* 10 (1983), pp. 219-35.

34. "Chicago's Prudential Building," *Architectural Forum* 97 (Aug. 1952), p. 95.

35. Saliga (note 4), pp. 209, 223.

36. "Towering Over the Tracks," *Engineering News Record* 219 (Dec. 17, 1987), p. 28; Saliga (note 4), p. 292.

37. Frank Sengstock, "The Largest Building in the World," *Western Architect* 39 (Dec. 1930), p. 206.

38. Robert Wiebe, *The Search for Order, 1877-1920* (New York, 1967).

39. Moody (note 1), p. 82.

40. Twyman (note 7), pp. 173-74.

41. Information on Chicago's wholesale trade, from 1900 to 1930, was gleaned from the following sources: Chamber of Commerce of the United States of America, *Retail and Wholesale Trade of Eleven Cities* (Washington, D.C., 1928); Hoyt (note 2), pp. 237, 410; Twyman (note 7), pp. 168-78; Wendt and Kogan (note 7), pp. 308-27; Commerce Magazine, *The Chicago Story, 1904-1954* (Chicago, 1954), pp. 36, 304, 306-08.

42. "Fields to Spend $15 Million for Big Mart Here." (note 15), pp. 1, 4, 31: "These properties are at Polk and the river, Polk and Ellsworth, the Pennsylvania Terminal, North Pier Terminal, Fulton and Desplaines, Fulton and Jefferson, 14th and Indiana, 17th and Wabash, 14 North Sangamon, 618 South Canal, 705 West Harrison, and 308 West Madison. In addition to these is the dignified old red granite wholesale warehouse on Adams, between Wells and Franklin, designed by H. H. Richardson, famous architect of Boston."

43. "Merchandise Mart to be World's Largest Building," *Chicago Sunday Tribune* (May 6, 1928).

44. See Neil Harris, "Shopping — Chicago Style," in John Zukowsky, ed., *Chicago Architecture, 1872-1922: Birth of a Metropolis* (Munich and Chicago, 1987), pp. 137-55.

45. James Simpson, "Simplifying Buying for the Merchant," *Nation's Business* 17, no. 8 (July 1929), pp. 42-43.

46. Moody (note 1), p. 95; see Schlereth (note 1) for a comparison of Moody's ideas to nineteenth-century theories of neurasthenia.

47. "Start of the Mart," *Merchandise Mart News* 1, no. 4 (Nov. 1931), p. 4.

48. "Start Work at Site of World's Largest Building," *Chicago Daily Tribune* (Aug. 17, 1928), pp. 5, 30.

49. Condit (note 27), p. 134.

50. "Machines Cut Down Man Power Used on Merchandise Mart," *Chicago Commerce* (Sept. 7, 1929), p. 16; Sengstock (note 37), p. 206.

51. Condit (note 27), p. 173, notes 49 and 50.

52. Shaw, a senior designer who became partner in 1929, introduced the Art Deco style into the firm's work; see Chappell (note 28).

53. "Merchandise Mart, Chicago" (note 26).

54. *The Architectural Work of Graham, Anderson, Probst and White, Chicago, and Their Predecessors D. H. Burnham & Co., and Graham, Burnham & Co.*, Foreword by Ernest R. Graham, 2 vols. (London, 1933).

55. "Merchandise Mart to be World's Largest Building" (note 43).

56. Information on the murals was taken from various undated and unsigned brochures prepared by the Merchandise Mart's staff over the years.

57. "The Factory Showroom," *Interiors* 102 (Oct. 1942), pp. 28-29, 61.

58. "Field Wholesale House Opens New Home Tomorrow," *Chicago Sunday Tribune* (May 4, 1930), pt. 1, p. 9; "Huge Blocks in Old Field Wholesale to Stay Where They Are," *Chicago Sunday Tribune* (May 4, 1930), pt. 2, p. 4; see James O'Gorman, "The Marshall Field Wholesale Store: Materials Toward a Monograph," *Journal of the Society of Architectural Historians* 37, no. 3 (Oct. 1978), pp. 175-94.

59. Wendt and Kogan (note 7), pp. 317-23.

60. *The Merchandiser* (Dec. 1933), a promotional bulletin now in the Archives of the Merchandise Mart.

61. "Simpson Death Leaves Two Big Posts Vacant" (note 7).

62. "Merchandise Mart Sold to Joe Kennedy," *Chicago Sun Times* (July 22, 1945); "Kennedy Takes Control of Mart," *Chicago Sun Times* (Nov. 14, 1945).

63. *Colossus of Chicago: The Merchandise Mart*, a promotional brochure, c. 1950, now in the Municipal Reference Library of Chicago, p. 3.

64. "The Merchandise Mart Hall of Fame," *Annual Awards Dinner Program* (June 24, 1954), now in the Archives of the Merchandise Mart.

65. "Indian Massacre Near Loop!" *Chicago's American* (Oct. 6, 1961).

66. The Dallas Market Center opened in 1955, the Atlanta Market Center in 1960, and the California Mart in Los Angeles in 1964.

67. It is reasonable to assume that the bas-relief sculpture originally intended for these panels was not executed because of budgetary constraints related to the advent of the Depression during the building's construction, but no documentation exists to support this thesis. It may also be reasonably proposed that the architects designed the panels in anticipation of the need for additional entrances to such a large building.

68. "Mart Mall Too Close for State Street," *Chicago Sunday Tribune* (Dec. 3, 1989), sec. 7, pp. 9-10; "Mall Frenzy in City May Spur Retail Glut," *Crain's Chicago Business* (Dec. 4, 1989).

69. Barbara Buchholz, "A Consumer Mart? Issue Gains Steam," *Crain's Chicago Business* (May 18, 1992), pp. 1, 51. I am grateful to Myron Maurer, director of building operations at the Merchandise Mart, for bringing this article to my attention and for all his help.

Light, Height, and Site: The Skyscraper in Chicago

Carol Willis

In Chicago in the summer of 1893, the critic Barr Ferree addressed the annual convention of the American Institute of Architects on the practical problems of building in the modern commercial city. In this competitive arena, he observed, the profession had little control over the basic decisions of design because factors such as height, massing, and budget were determined not just by the client, but by a mathematical equation of costs and profits. "Current American architecture is not a matter of art, but of business. A building must pay or there will be no investor ready with the money to meet its cost," Ferree argued. But he concluded with a twist: "This is at once the curse and the glory of American architecture."[1]

Indeed, no one on the congested streets of downtown Chicago in 1893 could ignore the awesome effects of the profit motive. A boom in speculative construction that preceded the World's Columbian Exposition that year had raised the standard level of new office buildings to sixteen stories, and some even higher.[2] At twenty-one stories, the majestic Masonic Temple was the tallest office building in the city and, briefly, the world. Its gabled roof supported an observation deck that allowed the public to view the urban panorama from an altitude of 302 feet, and a glass skylight covered a large interior court that penetrated the full height of the building. The lower nine floors of this atrium were planned for retail shops, while the upper floors were divided into about 540 offices.[3]

One hundred years later, tourists ascend to the 103rd-floor "Skydeck" of the Sears Tower, which at 1,454 feet remains the loftiest building on the planet. On an area only 150 percent larger than the Masonic Temple, the modern structure stacks more than 3.4 million square feet of office space, which can house a daily population of some 12,000 workers. With giants like the Sears Tower, the John Hancock Center, the Standard Oil (now Amoco) Building, and since the 1980s, more than five buildings sixty stories or taller, Chicago merits its worldwide reputation for ar-

Fig. 1 Holabird and Root, in association with Rebori, Wentworth, Dewey and McCormick, LaSalle-Wacker Building, 221 North LaSalle Street, 1929-30.

chitectural innovation, bravura engineering, and boosterish enthusiasm for great size.

Yet the history of the Chicago skyscraper has not been a steady ascent from small to tall. In fact, during the first half of this century, municipal restrictions on height shaped the city's skyline far more than bold feats of construction. In 1893, in reaction to the towering height of the Masonic Temple, the city council set a limit of 130 feet, the equivalent of ten or eleven stories, and for the next thirty years the maximum height moved up and down between 130 and 260 feet. In 1923 the city enacted a zoning law that allowed towers, but from the 1940s until 1956 the city again reduced heights, effectively to twelve stories. These height and zoning restrictions, along with other factors such as land-use patterns and rental markets, directly affected the formal development of the Chicago high-rise and of the city's skyline (figs. 2, 3).

Academic discussions of skyscraper history and the Chicago School have rarely mentioned these municipal regulations or other practical and economic considerations. They have focused instead mainly on the roles of architects, engineers, and clients, on technological and structural innovations, and on issues of style.[4] Skeletons and skins have been the fixations of modernist historians, while, more recently, others have been concerned with cultural expression.[5] Despite Louis Sullivan's famous phrase—"form follows function"—which was inspired by the tall office building, little attention has been given to the specific relationship of internal function and outward form. The practical constraints of program and plan, and their three-dimensional development in mass are key to this study.

Skyscrapers are designed from the inside out and from the smallest cell to the complex whole: a standard office unit is multiplied and arranged in an efficient floor plan. Even when the space is not partitioned, but pooled into larger areas, the "phantom" office governs the design from the dimensions of the structural bay to the fenestration pattern on the facade. Because of their de-

Fig. 2 *View of Chicago,*
c. 1935.

Fig. 3 *View of Chicago,*
c. 1927-28.

pendence on natural light, interiors changed
little from the first metal-skeleton buildings in
the 1880s until the 1940s. The rule of thumb for
first-class buildings dictated that no space be
more than 25 to 30 feet from the windows to the
innermost wall, which was the distance that
daylight could penetrate an interior. From this
constraint evolved both the dimensions of offices and the typical perimetal floor plan.

Such fundamental factors of function and economics make tall buildings in all places take
similar forms, while local conditions such as
land-use patterns, municipal codes, and rental
markets differentiate them. This play of forces
can be seen by comparing the skyscrapers and
skylines of Chicago and New York. Most previous histories have emphasized the cities' differences.[6] Commercial architecture in both, however, is formed by the same fundamental factors,
although modified by a specific urban context.
They represent, therefore, two variations on a
vernacular of capitalism.

The "Typical Chicago Office Building," 1893-1923

"If you look at our streets, you will find that the typical building of Chicago is the hollow square type," asserted architect George C. Nimmons in a paper prepared for the Zoning Committee of the Chicago Real Estate Board in 1922.[7] He was referring to the many structures erected from the 1880s through the teens that had a large light court at their centers—for example, the Rookery, Masonic Temple, Railway Exchange, Peoples Gas Company, Marshall Field Company Annex, and Conway buildings. These atrium buildings were not, in fact, the predominant type; U-shaped plans and other variations were more common, and there were, of course, many buildings on small lots. They did, however, represent many of the city's most impressive landmarks.

The hollow-square plan was the logical solution, given the city's height restrictions and the characteristically large building sites in the Loop, because in order for adequate illumination to reach all interior spaces, light courts had to be cut into the mass, usually at the center or rear of the building. In New York, by contrast, interior courts were rare because lots were generally small, and there were no restrictions on height. As a result, the typical New York high-rise was a tall, generally solid block, often towerlike in height and slenderness.

In both cities, though, the same standard office unit and the same planning strategies governed commercial development. In "Some Practical Conditions in the Design of the Modern Office Building," published in the *Architectural Record* in 1893, George Hill outlined seven basic elements of a successful building: good location; good light; good service; pleasing environment and design; maximum rentable area consistent with true economy; ease of arrangement to suit tenants; and minimum cost, consistent with true economy.[8] Summarizing these criteria in another article, Hill noted that "an office building's prime and only object is to earn the greatest possible return for its owners, which means that it must present the maximum of rentable space possible on the lot, with every portion of it fully lit."[9] To achieve the utmost rentability, Hill advised that the plan should be flexible enough to allow division for many single tenants or for large companies that might rent an entire floor. He explained that the "economical depth" for an office was determined by the fact that "after a certain point is reached, no more money can be obtained...no matter what its depth," and he reported that "the generally accepted requirement of good lighting is that every portion of the office be within 20 to 25 feet of a window."[10]

A developer received the most profit by leasing a large number of small offices. Owen Aldis, one of Chicago's most successful real estate brokers and developers, advised that the greatest income was to be reaped from buildings that were designed for intensive use by small tenants because they pay a higher rate per square foot; they do not move together and leave the building with high vacancies; and they do not overload the elevator service at time-clock hours. Aldis's point was one of eight rules he formulated while collaborating with the architects Holabird and

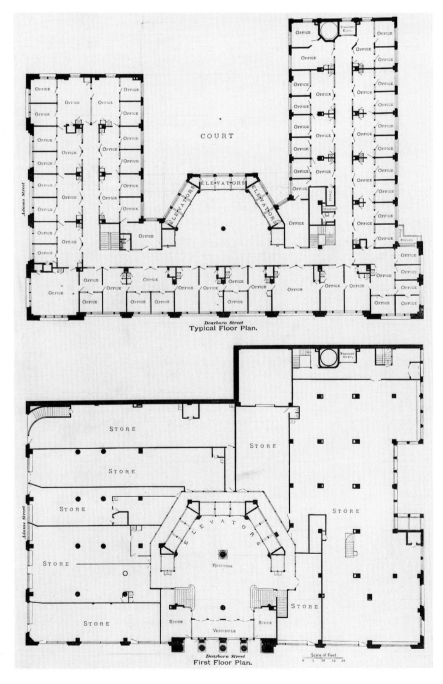

Fig. 4   Holabird and Roche, Plans of Marquette Building, 140 South Dearborn Street, 1893-95; from Prominent Buildings Erected by the George A. Fuller Company (Chicago, c. 1895), p. 42.

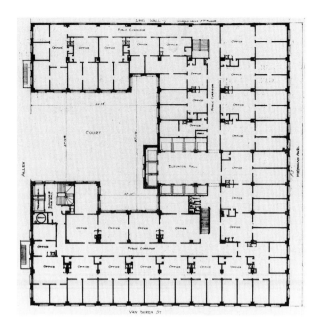

Fig. 5 Holabird and
Roche, Plan of
McCormick Building,
332 South Michigan
Avenue, 1908-12; from
Architectural Record 31
(1912), p. 321.

Fig. 6 Holabird and
Roche, McCormick
Building, 1908-12.

Roche on the Marquette Building (1895), which was widely considered a model of economic design (fig. 4). He emphasized creating only high quality layouts: "Second-class space costs as much to build as first-class space. Therefore build no second-class space." He defined quality space as no more than 24 feet from windows.[11]

The production of small offices did answer a definite demand. William Birkmire, an architect and the author of several important books on early skyscrapers, noted that offices of 10 by 12 or 15 by 20 feet rented more easily than larger ones. One of the most successful buildings in New York in the mid-1890s was the American Tract Society Building, which offered twenty floors of offices, each divided into thirty-six units, ranging in size from 9 by 11½ to 9 by 17 feet.[12] In Chicago, offices were somewhat larger, and often included built-in vaults and closets, and lavatories.[13]

Although the early 1890s was still a period of experimentation with floor plans, later in the decade and especially in the early years of the new century, an efficient office layout became quite standard and changed little through the 1920s. The depth of the space from exterior window to interior corridor was subdivided for use by multiple employees. The smallest offices had only a single room, and furniture was used to define different work areas. For larger suites, one entered from the public corridor into a large room that could serve as reception and staff areas. Off this space were the private offices, which were generally about 12 to 14 feet deep and 8 to 10 feet wide so that two fit within a standard structural bay (when used most efficiently, steel columns measured about 18 to 20 feet on center).[14] This

arrangement allowed for an anteroom, or reception area of 8 or more feet in depth, which was large enough for a stenographer, files, and a waiting area, and for two private rooms, each with a window. Examples of this layout can be seen in the plans of the Marquette (fig. 4), Old Colony (fig. 10), McCormick (figs. 5, 6), and Peoples Gas Company (fig. 11) buildings, to name but a few from the 1890s through the early teens, but it persisted throughout the 1920s, as can be seen in the Straus, Palmolive, and Board of Trade buildings (see figs. 21, 24).

The hierarchy of the office was reflected in the spatial arrangement. Executives occupied corner offices or at least a windowed room, while secretaries and other staff were relegated to the deeper, darker spaces. The arrangement was de-

Fig. 7 Holabird and
Roche, Interior of an
office in the Cable
Building (now 57 East
Jackson Street), 1899;
from Cable Building
brochure.

*Fig. 8   Map of Chicago's
Central Business
District, 1923; from
Charles M. Nichols,
Studies on Building
Height Limitations in
Large Cities (Chicago,
1923).*

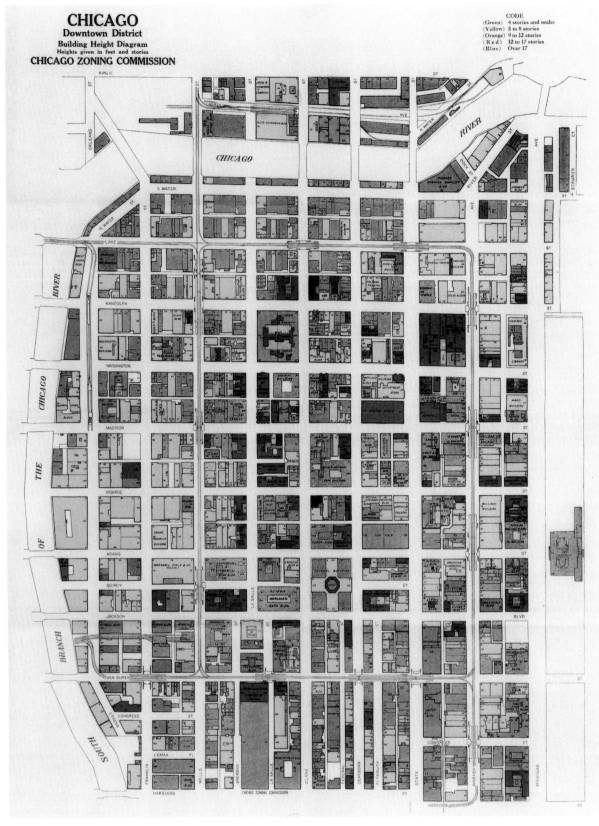

CHICAGO
Downtown District
Building Height Diagram
Heights given in feet and stories
CHICAGO ZONING COMMISSION

CODE
(Green)   4 stories and under
(Yellow)   5 to 8 stories
(Orange)   9 to 12 stories
(Red)   12 to 17 stories
(Blue)   Over 17

scribed by Earle Shultz and Walter Simmons in *Offices in the Sky*:

Of course the boss had to have his private office next to the window with the light coming in over his shoulder. In some cases his secretary worked in the office, too, but usually she and other clerical help used the reception room space between the private office and the corridor wall. To get maximum light into the reception room, the partition dividing it from the private office was glass. Sometimes this glass was opaqued to prevent people waiting in the reception room from seeing into the private office.[15]

This plan could be expanded laterally with ease, allowing the company to add as many units as it

Fig. 9   Rand McNally and Co., Bird's-eye view of Chicago, in the vicinity of Printing-House Row, from Van Buren Street, 1898; from Frank A. Randall, History of the Development of Building Construction in Chicago (Urbana, Ill., 1949), p. 179.

wanted on one floor. Small companies generally averaged only one or two staff members per private office; larger firms requiring open areas to accommodate many clerks or agents often preferred unpartitioned spaces. Over 80 percent of tenants throughout this period, however, leased suites of less than 1,000 square feet, which usually contained four or five individual offices.[16]

Tenants were willing to pay higher rents for shallow, well-lighted spaces. A 1923 survey of values in Boston, for example, showed that offices that were 15 feet deep leased for $3.00 per square foot, while space that was 25 feet deep cost $2.60 per square foot and a 50-foot space averaged $1.65 per square foot.[17] Since deep spaces cost the same to build and operate, but netted lower earnings, the logic of producing only better-quality space was clear. By 1900 the norm for first-class space was 20 to 25 feet deep, and it stretched a bit more in the later 1920s to about 28 or 30 feet.

The main reason for this standard was the dependence on daylight to illuminate work areas. Although electric wiring was universal from the 1880s, incandescent light was weak and inefficient. Desk-top lamps produced only about three to four footcandles (one footcandle is a measure of the amount of light on a surface held one foot away from a burning candle), while the average for a room with good daylight exposure was around ten, which was sufficient for reading and working.[18] In some interiors, however, daylight levels could reach from fifty to one hundred footcandles. Measures of adequate lighting varied significantly over the decades: one sanitary survey in New York in 1916 recommended eight to nine footcandles, and in the 1920s, ten to twelve footcandles was advised.[19] Indirect lighting from large ceiling lamps was considered the most desirable type of illumination since it produced the fewest and faintest shadows. In the 1930s, spurred by aggressive sales tactics of large power companies, some experts urged a new standard of twenty-five footcandles. The drawback to using more bulbs, however, was that they added heat to the room (a 500-watt bulb gave off the equivalent of one pound of steam per hour).[20] Fluorescent lighting, introduced in 1939, eliminated the problem of excessive heat, and in modernist buildings, the ceiling often became a plane of light.[21]

Before this new technology, however, in order to allow sunlight to penetrate as deeply as possible into the workspace, ceilings had to be high (at least 10 to 12 feet) and windows large—though not too big and heavy to open (fig. 7). The "Chicago window" with its large central pane and side sashes solved that problem simply.

Single windows usually measured about 4 to 5 feet wide and 6 to 8 feet high. They were often paired or grouped in multiples, which gave rhythm to the facade, but the main reason for the spacing was to allow for the partitioning of the interior. Windows were also used for ventilation, for although most buildings had mechanical systems, outside air and breezes were vital to comfort, especially in summer months (air conditioning was not available until the 1930s).

Together, the optimal economic depth for office space of about 25 feet and the dimensions of typical Chicago blocks and lots produced two characteristic floor plans favored by developers until the mid-1920s: a solid, rectangular mass with a double-loaded corridor; and a light-court building—either a hollow square, a U-shaped plan, or a truncated variation such as an L shape for corner lots. Chicago's original grid had been platted with blocks of about 320 feet square and streets 66 or 80 feet wide (fig. 8). Most of these blocks were bisected by an alley, running either north-south or east-west, which was a public right-of-way and therefore preserved some light and air on the interior of blocks and the rear of many buildings. In the 1890s there were many parcels of a full quarter-block; smaller lots were sold by front footage and were generally 160 feet deep. A map of the Central Business District published in 1923 (fig. 8) still showed about forty buildings that occupied sites that were one-quarter of a block or larger.[22] South of Van Buren Street, near the railroad stations, the area between State Street and Pacific Avenue (now LaSalle Street) was divided into long and narrow north-south blocks, which afforded through-block lots of about 70 feet and of various lengths (fig. 9).

A building with a double-loaded corridor—two rows of offices about 25 feet deep, plus a generous central circulation space—fits perfectly onto these narrow blocks. All offices had excellent light and views onto streets, rather than courts or alleys. Many of the famous early skeletal structures of the Chicago School occupied these southern sites, including the Manhattan Building (on a lot that was 68 by 150 feet) and its neighbor the Old Colony Building (68 by 148 feet; see fig. 10), as well as the Monadnock Building, the original northern building and later southern portions of which together took up an entire block (68 by 420 feet). In the heart of the Loop, Adler and Sullivan's Schiller Building was an unusual mid-block development with a short side on the street only 80 feet wide and a depth of 180 feet.[23]

Light-court plans offered the best solutions for lots of at least 80 by 100 feet—that is, where buildings could not cover the full site because the interiors would be too deep to rent as first-class space. The hollow-square was the most logical plan for the largest sites; it was used, for example, in the late 1880s and 1890s in the Rookery (on a lot of 177 by 168 feet), the Temple Court Building (100 by 180 feet), and the Chamber of Commerce Building (185 by 95 feet), among others. In the early 1900s the firm of D. H. Burnham and Company in particular exploited the hollow-square plan for many prominent structures, including the Railway Exchange, Peoples Gas Company (196 by 171 feet; see fig. 11), and Conway buildings.

Fig. 10   Holabird and Roche, Plan of Old Colony Building, 407 South Dearborn Street 1893-94; from Prominent Buildings Erected by the George A. Fuller Company *(Chicago, c. 1895), p. 30.*

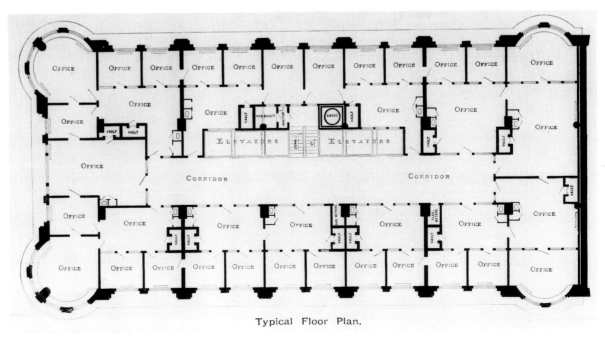

Typical Floor Plan.

In the hollow-square plan, offices could be arranged either on a double-loaded corridor with an outer and an inner ring of suites, or simply with a circulation space on the court's inner perimeter. The first solution could increase the space on each floor by 50 percent or more; the court-side offices were of secondary value, however, especially on the lower stories.[24] The building's open center was often developed as a commercial atrium, sometimes several stories high. These multistory shopping courts, like the nine commercial floors of the Masonic Temple, were a familiar feature in Chicago office buildings, and have returned in the 1970s and 1980s as the "vertical mall" (see essay by Harris). A more common use for the central court space was as a second-floor banking hall of grandiose proportions.[25]

For smaller sites, the U-shaped plan with the light court at the rear of the lot, often abutting the public alley, produced the most efficient layout. With one open end, the U allowed more light to enter the court throughout the day and saved the high costs of another exterior wall. For tenants, this plan offered better proximity to elevators. It also offered great flexibility, since a single company could take a half or full floor and incorporate the corridors into the firm's space, leaving public only the area near the elevators.[26] Examples of the U plan included the Ashland Block (on a site of 80 by 140 feet), the Unity (80 by 150 feet), Marquette (115 by 190 feet), and McCormick (101 by 172 feet) buildings (see figs. 4, 5). An L-shaped plan, which was generally used on narrower lots, as in the Tacoma Building or the Columbus Memorial, provided the same benefits.[27]

New York skyscrapers provide a useful counterpoint through which to understand the distinctiveness of Chicago during this period. Because building sites were generally smaller and land values were higher in New York than in Chicago, and because the city imposed no restrictions on height or bulk until 1916, towers proliferated in New York (fig. 12). In the Central Business District in Lower Manhattan, the area of the original colonial settlement, real estate had originally been sold as lots, rather than as frontage, with the result that ownership was broken up into many parcels, which for well over a hundred years had been occupied by profitable low-rise buildings. Large sites were difficult and expensive to assemble (no great fire conveniently cleared the way for redevelopment just as a period of rapid corporate expansion was beginning, as had happened in Chicago in 1871).

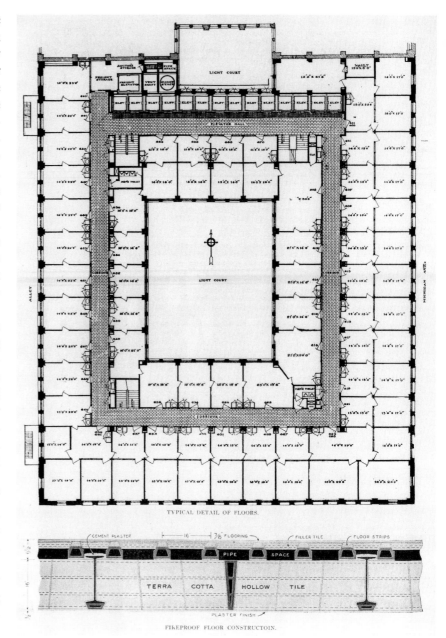

TYPICAL DETAIL OF FLOORS.

FIREPROOF FLOOR CONSTRUCTOIN.

Farther uptown in the regular grid of avenues and cross streets established by the 1811 Commissioners' Plan, the standard blocks measured 200 feet deep (north-south) and about 600 to 800 feet wide (east-west). Lots were generally 100 feet deep (half of the block) and conveniently divided for homes or shops into 25-foot frontages or multiples thereof. Despite the regularity of the blocks, therefore, parcels tended to be small.[28]

Very tall buildings rose on constricted sites, stretching high above their neighbors to capture sunlight and views. An early and extreme example was the Tower Building of 1889, which piled eleven stories on a mid-block parcel only 21½ feet wide by 108 feet deep, and on one of the world's most valuable pieces of real estate at the corner of Broadway and Wall Street, an eighteen-story tower was constructed on a 30 by 40 foot

Fig. 11   D. H. Burnham and Co., Plan of Peoples Gas Company Building (now 122 South Michigan Avenue), 1910-11; from Construction News 30 (July-Dec. 1910), p. 100.

Fig. 12 Postcard view of the skyline of New York City, 1911.

Fig. 13 Postcard view of Banker's Trust Company Building (Trowbridge and Livingston, 1912) and Equitable Building (Graham, Anderson, Probst and White, 1912-15), New York City.

Banker's Trust Co. and Equitable Buildings, New York City.

©by American Studio, N. Y.

lot. Many other skyscrapers were erected on small lots in the 1890s: the Manhattan Life Insurance Company (67 by 119 feet); the Commercial Cable Building (48 by 142 feet); and American Surety tower (85 by 85 feet). All exceeded 300 feet in height, surpassing Chicago's Masonic Temple. Later years saw even more attentuated towers: in 1912 Banker's Trust shoehorned a 540-foot-high tower onto a prime Wall Street corner about 70 feet square (fig. 13), and the campanile-like Metropolitan Life Insurance Company built on Madison Square in 1909 soared 700 feet above an area of 75 by 85 feet. Floor plans for buildings on such small sites were highly efficient because all offices could be placed on the outer perimeter, compactly arranged around a central core of circulation and services. Larger lots could also profit from a compact plan, since the additional elevators required by taller towers could occupy the otherwise unrentable center of the building.

In Chicago, however, municipal restrictions vitiated the logic of the compact core. From 1893 until the passage of a zoning law in 1923, the height limit ranged between 130 and 260 feet, or between ten and twenty-two stories.[29] This regulation, in combination with the typically large lot sizes in the Loop and the nearly inviolable custom of designing buildings that rose straight above the sidewalks (i.e., with no light courts on major facades), meant that high-rises had to be cut away at the rear or in the center in order to let adequate light into all interiors.[30] Thus, the characteristic plan in Chicago was a central *court*, while in New York it was more often a central *core*. Although the layout of an individual office was essentially the same in both cities, the full-floor plans and their projection into three-dimensional massing were entirely different due to historical patterns of land use and local codes.

The skylines of the two metropolises were likewise shaped by these conditions. Many Chicagoans had believed that height restrictions would eventually produce a harmonious streetscape as blocks were developed to the maximum. In fact, the fluctuating limit created a particu-

The Skyscraper in Chicago   127

larly motley array of flat-topped boxes, and, despite the visions of Daniel Burnham and a generation of civic efforts, the skyline never developed a strong visual order. In contrast, the distinctive silhouette of Manhattan bristled with towers. In 1913 the island boasted 997 buildings of between 11 and 20 stories, and 51 buildings ranging from 21 to 60 stories in height; the Woolworth Building soared to 792 feet. Even ten years later, Chicago had only 49 buildings of between 11 and 16 stories and 43 more of between 17 and 22 floors.[31] New York's laissez-faire environment seemed to spawn towers, for, while the city had about double the population of Chicago, it contained more than ten times the number of tall buildings.

Did Chicago's height restrictions discourage investment in high-rise construction? Impending changes in the code clearly affected short-term decisions to file building plans before a deadline or to forestall a project until the height limit might be raised, but it may be that such actions affected only the timing, not the amount of construction. Another issue that is far more debatable is whether capital that might have been invested in Loop office buildings moved instead into other types of construction outside the Central Business District, or even to other cities. To pursue this question, we must return to the definition of skyscrapers as machines of profit and to the idea of *economic height*. The economic height of a building is the number of stories that will return the highest rate of income for the money invested. Many factors figure in the equation for each site, including the costs of land and construction, rates of financing, and market rents. Tall buildings are more expensive to erect and operate, so a small building sometimes produces a higher rate of return than a more costly (and risky) project. In a high-demand market, though, bigger buildings are the most profitable.

As part of a 1922 study for the Committee on Building Height Limitations of the Chicago Real Estate Board, George C. Nimmons compared the estimated costs and returns for six buildings of different heights (5 to 30 stories) designed for a typical Chicago lot of 160 by 172 feet. His conservative analysis concluded that a 20-story structure would be the best investment, returning a rate of 7.05 percent; 30 stories produced only 5.65 percent and 15 stories, 6.82 percent.[32] Earle Shultz, then president of the National Association of Building Owners and Managers, presented another paper to the same committee in which he argued that the taller an office build-

Fig. 14   D. H. Burnham and Company, Carbide and Carbon Building, 230 North Michigan Avenue, 1929.

ing, the more profitable it would be, up to certain limits that he felt exceeded 25 to 30 stories.[33]

Whatever the optimal height, some minimum number of stories was clearly necessary to generate a sufficient return to make a project attractive; otherwise an owner would simply erect what is known as a "tax-payer" until the property was sold or the equation changed. In 1922 Shultz argued that the 130-foot height limit that was in effect from 1893 to 1902 "practically stopped building" and that when the limit was doubled to 260 feet in 1902, office construction revived.[34] In a later study, he strengthened his criticism and charged that the city's height restrictions at times had "crippled" its economic growth. A chart depicting the annual production of office space, the changing maximum heights, and the index of industrial production showed

Fig. 15 Graham,
Anderson, Probst and
White, Foreman State
National Bank Building
(now American National
Bank Building), 33
North LaSalle Street,
1928-30.

that, at certain points, new development lagged way behind the national economy.[35]

Between the Great Fire in 1871 and 1923, about 14 to 16 million square feet of office space was created in the Loop. During the same period New York constructed about 74 million square feet. Certainly one important factor in Manhattan's success as a business center in the early twentieth century was its vast supply of commercial space, most of it built by speculators, which ensured that rents were highly competitive. In Chicago, where height restrictions at times discouraged speculative development, the rate of construction—compared to the population and economic growth—was much lower than in New York. One wonders, then, how the Loop might have looked if there had been no limits on the frontier in the sky.

Twenties Towers

The Chicago skyline changed dramatically during the 1920s as slender towers punctured the old 260-foot limit. Tallest of these was the 612-foot Board of Trade, but there were also eight buildings of more than 500 feet and eleven exceeding 400 feet. This proliferation of towers was the product of two factors: the real estate boom that began in 1923 and continued in force until 1929, and the passage of the city's first zoning ordinance, also in 1923.

Historically, the Chicago real estate market was characterized by cycles of boom and bust that were "like tidal waves in their magnitude."[36] In his classic study of 1933, *One Hundred Years of Land Values in Chicago*, Homer Hoyt identified five major cycles of growth and decline since the city's founding in the 1830s. The cycle that saw the rise of the first skyscrapers began in 1879 and reached its peak between 1889 and 1892. The oversupply of office space produced during those years, along with the national depression of 1893, resulted in a decline of construction and land values that reached a nadir in 1898. Recovery began around the turn of the century, and until 1918, real estate values in Chicago showed an uncharacteristic pattern of gradual and sustained growth.[37] When World War I diverted materials and labor to the military effort, development was stanched at the same time that businesses were expanding, putting great pressures on existing rents, which increased by 80 to 100 percent between 1919 and 1924.[38]

This situation fueled a new cycle of development. As building costs began to fall after the war, many developers rushed to fill the demand. New buildings rented quickly and were extremely profitable, attracting more investors, and easy financing through banks, insurance companies, and mortgage bond houses fueled the speculation. Real estate bonds, which were sold to the public like stocks, became a popular form of investment and greatly increased funds available for new construction.[39] In addition, "shoestring financing" made it possible in many cases to undertake a project with only a small cash down payment and allowed 100 percent mortgage financing based on the future value of the building. With hindsight, the inevitable fate of such financial bubbles seems obvious. What began as an answer to a real demand, ended in frenzied speculation and a collapse in land and building values. By 1928 the financing of many projects was already in trouble, and after the stock mar-

ket crash in October 1929, the situation grew steadily worse.[40]

From the perspective of the mid-1920s, though, the phenomenal growth seemed a continuous spiral of prosperity. Land values in the Loop doubled between 1920 and 1928, which in turn put pressure on owners to capitalize land costs with bigger buildings. During the peak years of construction from 1923 to 1929, the supply of office space in the city nearly doubled.[41] The new buildings were widely distributed throughout the Central Business District, including west of the Loop and along the river, and on the developing commercial strip of North Michigan Avenue. For several years the additional space was absorbed by the expanding economy. An October 1927 survey by the Building Owners and Managers Association showed that during the previous year there had been an increase in rented space in both new and old buildings of 1,300,481 square feet and that the overall vacancy rate was a relatively low 8.6 percent.[42]

The 1923 zoning ordinance responded to the pressures of expansion by increasing the cubic volume permitted for high-rise buildings. In this sense, it had the opposite aim of the New York City law of 1916, which, after a completely laissez-faire condition, greatly reduced the height and bulk of a building that could be erected on a given site.[43] Although Chicago's guidelines were modeled on New York's, the specific formulas differed substantially, as will be discussed below.

The major effect of zoning in the Central Business District was that towers were allowed. A revision in 1920 permitted ornamental structures to rise above 264 feet, as long as they were not occupied.[44] The Wrigley Building, Chicago Temple, and London Guarantee and Accident Building (now Stone Container Building) were designed under this regulation, which also governed the Tribune Tower competition program. Under the new zoning laws, the vertical limit above the sidewalk was 264 feet for the Loop and North Michigan Avenue. Above that height, a tower could be erected on up to 25 percent of the lot, although this upper section could not exceed one-sixth of the maximum cubic area of the main building.[45] The volume restriction severely limited the height of commercially viable towers. About seventeen to twenty stories of additional tower floors was the maximum number possible for a quarter-block site such as that of the Rookery (168 by 171 feet). While the 264-foot limit for the base section of the building was the highest in any American city with regulations, the limit on the volume for the tower kept it

quite small, especially compared to the buildings in New York, where a tower could rise to unlimited height on 25 percent of the lot. The seventy-story Chrysler Building, for example, stands on a lot of 200 by 205 feet.

The new regulations tended to produce an awkward hybrid—a large blocklike base with a puny tower. An extreme example is the Jewelers Building, with its slender seventeen-story tower placed at the center of the massive twenty-four-story base, thereby diminishing its visual impact from street level (see Sennott, fig. 15). In other buildings on medium-sized lots, such as the Steuben Club (pl. 41), Willoughby Tower, Pittsfield, and Carbide and Carbon buildings (see fig. 14), the tower section was pushed toward the major facade to create a more emphatic verticality. Yet all these towers seem truncated—too small in proportion to their bases, especially when seen from a high vantage point. Larger sites afforded greater opportunity to create a somewhat more imposing tower, as in the Foreman State National Bank (see fig. 15) and Civic

Fig. 16   Left foreground, Graham, Anderson, Probst and White, Foreman State National Bank Building, 1928-30; Vitzhum and Burns, One North LaSalle, 1 North LaSalle Street, 1930; right background, Holabird and Root, Chicago Board of Trade Building, 141 West Jackson Boulevard, 1929-30.

Fig. 17   D. H. Burnham and Company, Banker's Building, 105 West Adams Street, 1926.

Fig. 18   Postcard view of the Chicago Board of Trade Building, 1929-30 (Photo 1948).

Opera (see Miller, "Helmut Jahn," fig. 2) buildings, both by the firm of Graham, Anderson, Probst and White. Nevertheless, in these monumental structures, the continuous plane of base and shaft and the great expanse of lime-stone cladding, punctured by hundreds of small windows, produced rather monotonous masses. The proportional relationship of base-and-tower schemes seemed distinctly bottom-heavy.

By the late 1920s a number of architects had developed an approach that better integrated the separate sections. From the street, the LaSalle-Wacker Building, One North LaSalle, the Ban-ker's Building, and the Board of Trade all gave the impression of one central tower of forty or more stories emerging from a low base of four to six stories, flanked by tall wings of about twenty-three or twenty-four stories, the maximum height allowed under the zoning law (see figs. 1, 16-18). On the lower floors, these buildings were configured in an H or U plan with a light court that opened onto the major street, rather than the back alley, as in the 1890s and early 1900s. Because of the height of these buildings, elevators could be placed in a compact central core, as in New York skyscrapers.[46]

Some architects and clients, nevertheless, continued to prefer the traditional hollow-square plans. The conservative firm of Graham, Anderson, Probst and White, successors of the office of Daniel Burnham, reprised the classical box with an interior court in several large bank and office buildings. Although the Federal Reserve Bank was completed just before the passage of zoning and the Illinois Merchants Bank (now Continental Illinois National Bank) shortly

The Skyscraper in Chicago   131

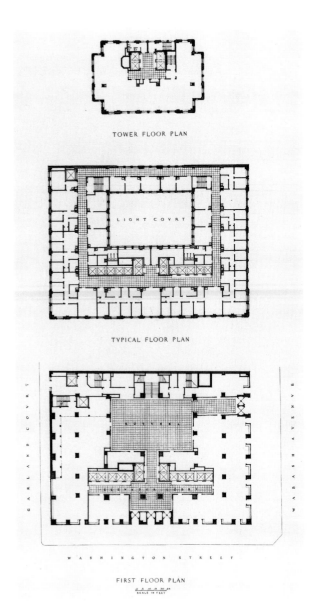

TOWER FLOOR PLAN

LIGHT COVRT

TYPICAL FLOOR PLAN

FIRST FLOOR PLAN
SCALE IN FEET

WASHINGTON STREET

thereafter, the buildings were near twins. Both featured temple-front entrances that signaled the presence of a second-floor banking hall within the central court area. A similar design by the same firm completed in 1927 was the Builders Building.[47] Its central court featured another Chicago tradition, an atrium with four floors of showrooms for the display and sale of construction materials and equipment. The same year, Graham, Anderson, Probst and White completed another structure with a court plan and a commercial atrium, as well as a seventeen-story tower. The Pittsfield Building capitalized on its location in the heart of the retail district with a five-story shopping court.[48] Like the Marshall Field Annex across the street, built in 1914 by the same clients and architects, it was marketed as offices for doctors and dentists, a use that generated considerable numbers of potential shoppers.[49] The design, however, broke with the conventional classical cube and employed a gothic

vocabulary that accentuated the verticality of its tower. The standard base rose straight up to the maximum height of twenty-one stories, above which a slender shaft in the center of the Washington Street facade continued the sheer plane, then stepped back at the top floors in a series of finials, dormers, and an ornamental copper roof. The light court and commercial atrium were positioned behind the tower, which allowed the elevator banks to be brought closer to the entrance (see fig. 19); this was a significant change from their customary position on a rear or side wall in hollow-square plans.[50]

The combination of the central court plan with a tower was unusual, but not unique. The Straus Building of 1923-24 (now the Britannica Center) was an imposing twenty-one-story block with a nine-story tower surmounted by a solid stepped-pyramid and heraldic sculpture that extended its total height to 475 feet (fig. 20). The building combined corporate headquarters for the investment banking company S. W. Straus and an income-producing property. Concerned to create a corporate symbol, the owners and architects, again Graham, Anderson, Probst and White, chose a monumental, classical character that they felt communicated strength and stability. An image of quality was also important to the speculative aspect of the project, the 80 percent of the building that was leasable space, marketed as "Chicago's finest office building."

As one of the country's most successful lenders to large construction projects, S. W. Straus Company was a savvy and demanding client. From the outset, the plans for the building were developed through a collaboration of the company's expert building committee and the architects. More than sixty different schemes were developed and considered, and before finalized, the proposed design was submitted to a special advisory panel of the National Association of Building Owners and Managers (NABOM) for analysis.[51] Various suggestions were made and adopted, and the final plans were deemed "a development of the site as nearly perfect as it was humanly possible to make it."[52]

Their analysis, which was documented in detail, supplied the economic logic behind nearly every decision of the design. Their problem was to achieve the highest ratio of rentable area to the cubic contents of the building and enclosing walls. The site was large (comparable to the Rookery), with 171 feet on Michigan Avenue and 160 feet on Jackson. The plot solution that fulfilled this goal was a hollow square (fig. 21); it produced more square feet of rentable space than

Fig. 19   Graham, Anderson, Probst and White, Plans of Pittsfield Building, 55 East Washington Street, 1927.

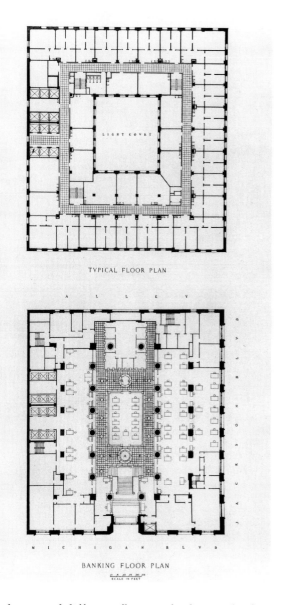

TYPICAL FLOOR PLAN

BANKING FLOOR PLAN

Fig. 20 Graham, Anderson, Probst and White, Straus Building (now the Britannica Center), 310 South Michigan Avenue, 1923-24.

Fig. 21 Graham, Anderson, Probst and White, Typical floor plan and banking floor plan of Straus Building, 1923-24; from The Architectural Work of Graham, Anderson, Probst and White *(London, 1933).*

a U-shaped plan and afforded greater flexibility in the placement of elevators and other services. The committee advised that the spacing of structural columns be 17 feet, with a depth from windows to corridor of 25 to 30 feet. These dimensions paired two windowed private offices with a reception area that was roughly 8 feet deep and 17 feet wide.[53]

Another key decision was the number of elevators, since the quality of service directly affected rents. The standard for a first-class building was a maximum waiting time during peak periods of twenty-five to thirty seconds. By projecting the total population of the building (some 4,000 to 5,000 tenants and their visitors) and the daily traffic pattern, experts determined that twelve cars were needed for public use.[54] These were placed on the south side of the property, principally because of the possibility of future expansion, and arranged in two banks with three cars on each side of the corridor. The separate

banks served different floors, which was the first time such a system had been adopted in Chicago. The nine-story tower was truly a separate section of the building, accessed by its own elevators that began on the twenty-first floor.

Although the Straus Building took some advantage of the additional volume allowed by the new ordinance, it was in essence a hollow-square building of the pre-zoning type.[55] The endurance of this plan may have been a function of the conservative nature of the clients' business or of the traditional values of the architects. In contrast, a different idea was ventured in the comparably scaled and nearly contemporary Jewelers Building. Although oddly old-fashioned in its ornament, the building was radically modern at the core, for its center was used as a mechanized parking garage that occupied the middle of the building from the basement level through the twenty-third floor (see essay by Sennott).[56] But while the garage was an efficient use of

The Skyscraper in Chicago 133

space, in economic terms, the empty center of the Straus Building was a superior use, since on a balance sheet of profits, well-lit offices on a central court produced much higher rents than did parking spaces.

The money spent by S. W. Straus in creating a Class-A property was well invested. Although the value of the building as an advertisement is impossible to quantify, there was certainly some benefit. The company occupied the impressive banking hall on the second floor of central court space (now altered) and about four floors of offices. The remaining floors were leased to tenants at some of the highest rates in the city, ranging from $7.00 per square foot in the tower (a rate comparable to premium Wall Street prices in New York) to $3.00 per square foot for the lower floors of the interior court; the average was about $5.00 per square foot. The total rentable area of the building was 440,000, the area per floor 17,068 square feet. Because of the building's carefully considered floor plan, almost 75 percent of the gross floor area was income-producing—a very high rate of return. The building's overall success can be judged by the fact that, despite a flood of new buildings during 1924, 85 percent of the rentable space was leased in the first year.[57]

In striking contrast to the Straus Building's traditional plan and conservative styling was the modernistic design of the Palmolive Building, another combined corporate headquarters and rental property that opened in 1929 at the northern end of the developing commercial strip of North Michigan Avenue (fig. 22). Designed by Holabird and Root, the thirty-seven-story building rose in a series of setbacks from which emerged a central tower.[58] The pyramidal form was both richly plastic and emphatically vertical with projecting bays alternating with the banding of windows to accentuate the building's height. Due to low-rise neighbors and the building's proximity to the lake, the tower was a distinctive sculptural presence on the skyline, and all offices enjoyed superb light and views. The dimensions of the site, 108 by 231 feet, produced a somewhat flattened tower that expanded the area for the outer ring of offices. Rental brochures extolled the convenience and modernity of this layout: "There is no circling corridor around an inner court to confuse the stranger. One walks straight from the elevators in one direction to any office door."[59]

The tower offices were the building's *raison d'être*. "High above the 'dust and fly line' of the city," noted the advertisements, its "executive

Fig. 23   Postcard view
of mid-town Manhattan,
with 500 Fifth Avenue
building in left fore-
ground.

chambers" were perfect for "estates, capitalists, and retired business men," while general office space was provided in the more capacious lower stories.[60] The main tower section began at the twenty-second floor. Working within the maximum volume allowed by zoning, Holabird and Root created a tower plan with dimensions of only 46 by 130 feet (fig. 24). After subtracting the space required for elevators and services, the net rentable area per floor was only about 4,000 square feet.

Within this small floor plan, the architects proposed a division into eight offices, ranging in size from 255 to 900 square feet; these units could be combined into larger suites and were partitioned only as they were leased. The marketing strategy was to create the maximum number of small, high-rent units, rather than large expanses of flexible floor space. This was possible because of the building's distant location from the highly competitive rental market in the Loop and the calculated effort of the client, the Colgate-Palmolive-Peet Company, to create a building of distinction that could serve as a symbol of its corporate success, as well as attract high-paying tenants.

The Palmolive Building was unique among Chicago high-rises for its "New York-style" massing. Under the formulas of New York's 1916 zoning law, the first setback began at a lower level than in Chicago, generally about 150 or 200 feet. Above that point, the building was required to step back within a prescribed diagonal plane projected from the center of the street. This base could be surmounted by a tower which, as in Chicago, could cover no more than 25 percent of the lot; however, there was no limit on the height of the tower. The typical New York skyscraper thus had a base section, a transitional zone consisting of a series of shallow setbacks, and a tower that was slender and often very tall.[61] A comparison of the Palmolive Building and 500 Fifth Avenue illustrates the resulting differences in proportion under the two cities' zoning laws (see fig. 23). Although the site of 500 Fifth Avenue (101 by 208 feet) was in fact smaller than that of the Chicago building, its tower rose twenty-two stories higher. In addition, the New York building sacrificed symme-

Fig. 24   Holabird and
Root, Plans of Palmolive
Building, 1927-29; from
Palmolive Building
brochure.

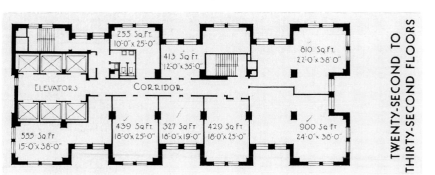

try to profit; the setbacks were different on its east and west shoulders because the owner wanted to exploit the maximum bulk allowed by the formulas that governed each side of the corner lot.

The typical massing solutions that evolved from Chicago's zoning ordinance were, as described earlier, the composite of a big base plus a small tower and the integrated central tower with flanking wings. There was also the persistent popularity of the traditional interior-court plans, in part because they were familiar, but also because they could be highly profitable. Increasingly, though, in the later twenties, the compact-core arrangement became the preferred plan, especially for its efficiency of elevator access and service. Of the two formal approaches, the central tower was the one adopted for buildings that were stylistically most modern. The LaSalle-Wacker Building and the Board of Trade represented the "stripped style" that emphasized simplified, hard-edged forms with restrained ornament carved in low relief within the plane of the walls (figs. 1, 18). The Field Building was even more austere, with the only decorative treatment being the alternating vertical bands of light limestone panels and dark windows and spandrels (fig. 25). Stretching the length of an entire block, the enormous Field Building gave the impression of a simple rectangular slab sandwiched between four similarly proportioned wings. Contracts for the 1,000,000-square-foot project were signed in 1929, and construction went forward in stages through the early years of the Depression. The Field Building was the afterbirth of the twenties' increase in building. After its completion in 1934, no new office space was undertaken until 1952 when work began on the Prudential Building (see Rau, fig. 12).

Postwar Postscript

The more than twenty-year halt in construction, caused by the oversupply of the 1920s and made worse by the Depression economy, was sustained by shortages of materials and labor during World War II. These conditions affected all cities, but the hiatus lasted longer in Chicago than in most places. In New York, recovery began almost immediately after the war, and by 1959, 54 million square feet of new office space had either been completed or was in development. During the same period, only 2.6 million square feet of new space was constructed in Chicago.[62]

What caused the slow growth? It was not low demand. Although the vacancy rate had been 19.2 percent in 1931, and the market bottomed out in 1937, by the early 1940s, not only had the space been absorbed, but 2.7 million square feet in semiloft buildings had been converted to office use.[63] Stringent zoning restrictions seem to have been a major factor inhibiting new construction. In 1942 the city again reduced the maximum size of a building; under the new formula, high-rise buildings were limited to a gross volume of 144 times the area of the lot, or if the building covered the full site, up to twelve stories.[64] To pile up several dozen floors in a high-rise, therefore, the site had to be very large, and most of it would be left empty. The developers of the forty-one-story Prudential Building, constructed over the tracks of the Illinois Central Railroad, had to lease three-and-a-half acres of air rights in order to erect the size building they desired. Under the earlier ordinance, the building could have contained more than twice the volume.[65]

In an analysis of the market conditions in 1959, Earle Shultz maintained that the new limit on height and volume was lower than what most developers or companies believed to be the economic height. Without the hope of an attractive return, their money found more lucrative areas of investment. Shultz argued further that corporations that would have preferred to build Chicago headquarters in income-producing structures like the Straus or Palmolive buildings were discouraged from doing so by the restrictions and instead moved to other cities, in particular to New York.[66] Although his theory cannot be tested, the data are consistent with such an explanation. In any case, the most significant fact about the Chicago skyscraper in the postwar decade was its absence.

New York high-rises constructed in the late 1940s and the 1950s were, with notable exceptions such as Lever House and the Seagram Building, architecturally undistinguished. They followed the setback massing of the twenties (which remained standard until the revision of the zoning law in 1961), but the pyramidal forms were clad, not in stone, but in an International Style aesthetic of banded windows or curtain walls of metal and glass. The more important change in these buildings, though, was in their plans, which featured larger floor areas—some 50 feet or more deep.

Businesses had prospered during the war years and needed additional space for their growing workforce and new types of office machinery. From 1940 to 1960 employment of office workers doubled and the size of the average office in-

Fig. 25   Graham, Anderson, Probst and White, Field Building (now LaSalle National Bank Building), 135 North LaSalle Street, 1928-34.

creased twofold, as did rents.[67] Companies often preferred to consolidate operations on large, full floors, and improved technology made the deep floors viable. Fluorescent lighting provided high levels of illumination without excessive heat to all interior spaces, and air conditioning ensured ventilation. In 1950 Lee Thompson Smith, president of the Real Estate Board of New York, summarized the advantages of postwar structures as follows:

These buildings are modern. Primarily because they are air conditioned. But one salient characteristic of the new buildings that cannot be adapted to old buildings at any price is their basic planning. They provide large blocks of space on one floor, with great glass areas, better lighting, fewer courts, less waste space and new automatic elevator arrangements, with fewer cars and faster service. Deeper floor areas, among the other developments in design, result in as much as 80 percent of the space on each floor being rentable space, as compared with 65 percent in the buildings that were conventional 20 years ago.[68]

Such buildings were modern in terms of program and function, but less so in terms of style. Yet the advantages they offered were attractive to large companies, and, as a result, pre-Depression buildings became less desirable to many tenants.

In the postwar era, technology liberated the interior from its dependence on external light and air. In theory, this situation freed architects to invent bold new expressions of plan and massing. Ironically, though, when office buildings could take any shape, they began to look more alike than ever before. By the 1960s, the typical skyscraper in Chicago and New York was a pristine rectangle of metal and glass. The new orthodoxy reflected the triumph of the Modern Movement. The open plan and the tower in the plaza were concepts realized in paradigmatic buildings such as the United Nations Secretariat, Lever House, and Inland Steel—all commissions that were relatively independent of the commercial market—and in other Chicago skyscrapers such as the Equitable Building, the Civic Center (now Richard J. Daley Center), and the Federal Center, which expanded upon the same principles (see Miller, "City Hall," figs. 14, 15). The influences on the form and function of buildings like these is a different chapter of skyscraper history.

Although this essay has argued that, above all, economics determined the forms of skyscrapers, the influence of aesthetics and ideology, especially in the postwar period, cannot be denied. But the contributions of great architects and engineers or the importance of schools or styles should be understood and appreciated in the context of the parameters of commercial architecture. In 1894 the straight-talking Barr Ferree noted:

The design of a high building is a definite problem which may be expressed in a very few words. It is the arrangement of the largest number of windows of the greatest possible size in a limited space, which is fixed by external circumstances, such as the width of the lot and the number of stories high the owner is intending to build.[69]

The art of skyscraper design, one might say, is no more and no less.

NOTES

Many thanks to Robert Bruegmann for his comments on this essay.

1.   Barr Ferree, "Economic Conditions of Architecture in America," *Proceedings of the Twenty-Seventh Annual Convention of the American Institute of Architects* (Chicago, 1893), pp. 228-41.
2.   For example, the Schiller, Ashland, Columbus Memorial, Unity, Monadnock, and Old Colony buildings all rose sixteen or more stories.
3.   Frank A. Randall, *History of the Development of Building Construction in Chicago* (Urbana, Ill., 1949), p. 198. For illustrations and discussions of the Masonic Temple, including the usually neglected interiors, see Daniel Bluestone, *Constructing Chicago* (New Haven, Conn., 1991), pp. 137-41.
4.   One long-standing debate concerns the "first skyscraper"—that is, whether the type developed first in Chicago or New York. This historiography has been neatly summarized by Rosemarie Haag Bletter in "The Invention of the Skyscraper: Notes on its Diverse Histories," *Assemblage*, no. 2 (Feb. 1987), pp. 110-17. The chief historian of the Chicago skyscraper is Carl Condit, who has written a series of books on the subject: *The Rise of the Skyscraper* (Chicago, 1952),

later revised as *The Chicago School of Architecture* (Chicago, 1964); *Chicago, 1910-1929: Building, Planning, and Urban Technology* (Chicago, 1973); and *Chicago, 1930-1970: Building, Planning, and Urban Technology* (Chicago, 1974). There are no plans in these books.
5.   For example, on the "construction of meaning" through the skyscraper in the late nineteenth century, see Bluestone (note 3), pp. 104-51. In a very different way, Thomas P. van Leeuwen, in *The Skyward Trend of Thought* (The Hague, 1986), discusses the conflicts of American culture as represented in the skyscraper form.
6.   A notable exception to the emphasis on differences can be found in the catalogue of The Art Institute of Chicago's exhibition, *Chicago and New York: Architectural Interactions* (Chicago, 1984).
7.   Charles M. Nichols, ed., *Studies on Building Height Limitations in Large Cities with Special Reference to Conditions in Chicago* (Chicago, 1923), p. 70. Similarly, in their 1959 history of the office building industry, Earle Shultz and Walter Simmons noted that the majority of the city's buildings erected up to 1920 were of the O-shaped plan; see *Offices in the Sky* (Indianapolis, 1959), p. 132.
8.   In 1893 George Hill published a number of articles on economical design, which were among the first to

appear in professional journals; they included "Some Practical Conditions in the Design of the Modern Office Building," *Architectural Record* 2 (1893), pp. 444-68; and "Wasted Opportunities, No. III," *Architectural Record* 3 (1893), pp. 436-38.
9.   Hill, "Wasted Opportunities" (note 8), p. 436.
10. Hill, "Some Practical Conditions" (note 8), p. 471; and idem, "Wasted Opportunities" (note 8), p. 437.
11. Aldis began his career as the financial agent for the Boston investors Peter and Shepherd Brooks, and as the founder of a successful management and development organization, Aldis and Company. His eight fundamentals are reprinted in Shultz and Simmons (note 7), pp. 33-35. In general, Aldis's points paralleled Hill's, with an added emphasis on good maintenance, service, and staff.
12. William Birkmire, *The Planning and Construction of High Office Buildings* (New York, 1900), p. 70. There was really no standard office size in New York in this period, in particular because sites in Lower Manhattan were often irregular. Generally, however, rooms were about 10 by 20 or 15 by 20 feet. The American Tract Society Building was designed by R. H. Robertson and was built in 1894.
13. For example, the Masonic Temple presented a wide range of offices, from 14 by 21 to 18 by 32 feet for some corner suites, and rooms of 10 by 11 feet on the

inner court. Floor plans, especially with dimensions of rooms, are often difficult to obtain. In addition to rental brochures of individual buildings, some of this type of information can be found in journals; an especially good source is the trade journal *Buildings and Building Management*. The most easily accessible sources for dimensioned plans are Birkmire (note 12) and Barr Ferree, "The Modern Office Building," *The Journal of the Franklin Institute* 141 (Jan./Feb. 1896), nos. 841-42.

14. Shultz and Simmons (note 7), p. 130.

15. Ibid.

16. Ibid.

17. A chart of average rents for spaces of various depths was prepared by Boston building manager W. H. Ballard in 1923 and was reprinted by Shultz and Simmons (note 7), p. 131.

18. Statistics are quoted from an article by Kirk M. Reid, an illuminating engineer at Nela Park, Cleveland, a research center for General Electric; see "Artificial Light in Office and Stores," *Buildings and Building Management* 25 (June 8, 1925), pp. 43-46.

19. In contrast to the attention of sanitary surveys of tenement conditions or factories, there were few studies of working conditions in office buildings. According to Charles B. Ball, chief sanitary inspector of Chicago, there were no studies of the Loop. In a paper he delivered to the Zoning Committee of the Chicago Real Estate Board, Ball used statistics from an August 1916 report by the New York City Department of Health of a survey of light and ventilation in offices located in a densely built block in the Wall Street district. The report found that no standard existed for the quantity of light and recommended eight or nine footcandles. See Nichols (note 7), pp. 34-36. The Illuminating Engineering Society's official recommendation in 1917 was only five footcandles. Statistics from the 1920s come from Reid (note 18), pp. 43-44.

20. Shultz and Simmons (note 7), pp. 202-03.

21. Fluorescents were continuously perfected to emit more lumens per watt; by 1952 the Illuminating Engineering Society standard for lighting levels in offices was fifty footcandles and in 1960 it rose to 100; Richard S. Wissoker, "More Light for Less," *Buildings* 66 (April 1966), p. 79.

22. Nichols (note 7), see foldout map insert.

23. Sources for dimensions include Randall (note 3) and Birkmire (note 12).

24. Shultz and Simmons (note 7), p. 132.

25. Examples of large second-floor banking halls can be found in the Continental Illinois National Bank and the Federal Reserve Bank, both by Graham, Anderson, Probst and White. The internal light court was also a feature in apartment plans and in some department stores, most spectacularly at Marshall Field's on State Street.

26. Shultz and Simmons (note 7), p. 133.

27. There were, of course, numerous buildings erected on narrow lots that did not require light courts. A good, general idea of the various plans can be gained from a map of the Loop showing lot coverage and building heights, which was prepared by the Chicago Zoning Commission around 1922 and reproduced in a foldout in Nichols (note 7).

28. Some lots were 15 feet wide, but 25 feet was most common; this was a good size for residential construction, which at the time was the use envisioned.

29. The city council moved the limit up or down chiefly in response to real estate pressures — that is, the limit was raised when there was high demand for office space and lowered when there was an oversupply. The best source on height regulation in Chicago is Nichols (note 7); see also Shultz and Simmons (note 7).

30. Architects in Chicago did not experiment much with other types of plan such as the H or cruciform shape. Louis Sullivan proposed a partial cruciform for the Odd Fellows' Hall in 1891, and Burnham and Root's Women's Temple had light courts on the street facade; there were a few other examples, but in general, Chicagoans seemed to prefer the appearance of a monumental block.

31. New York statistics come from the *Report of the Heights of Buildings Commission* (New York, 1913), p. 15. For figures on Chicago, see Nichols (note 7) and Shultz and Simmons (note 7), p. 284.

32. For Nimmons's study, see "Comparative Statement of Earnings of First-Class Modern Office Buildings," in Nichols (note 7), pp. 60-61. Nimmons assumed a traditional light-court plan; changes in the plan, for a taller building, could have produced more rental space.

33. For Shultz's full study, see "The Economic Height of Office Buildings," in Nichols (note 7), pp. 62-64.

34. Nichols (note 7), pp. 65, 75. Since the rise and fall in Chicago's rate of construction corresponded to broad national trends, his contention was difficult to prove.

35. See chart in Schultz and Simmons (note 7), p. 285.

36. Homer Hoyt, *One Hundred Years of Land Values in Chicago* (Chicago, 1933), p. 372.

37. This growth was interrupted by a few minor recessions and spurts of activity, as the chart of office space production demonstrates; see Schultz and Simmons (note 7), p. 285.

38. See Hoyt (note 36), p. 238, on rising rents. Hoyt's fifth cycle spanned the years between 1917 and 1933 (the lows of the curve), with the most vigorous construction during the period from 1923 to 1929.

39. For a simplified discussion of financing methods, see William A. Starrett, *Skyscrapers and the Men Who Build Them* (New York, 1928), pp. 115-16; for Chicago, see Hoyt (note 36), pp. 237, 285, and 445-46. As Hoyt noted, the credit operations of banks and bond houses tended to exaggerate the extravagances of real estate booms and depressions rather than countervail them.

40. This cycle of speculative development in the twenties simply repeated the pattern of the four earlier real estate cycles that Hoyt had charted. For the explanation of the collapse of bond financing in Chicago, which actually began in 1928, even before the stock market crash, see Hoyt (note 36), pp. 445-46.

41. From 1920 to 1929 nearly 13 million square feet of floor space was constructed in downtown Chicago, most of it between 1923 and 1929. Before 1920 rentable space totaled somewhere between 14 million and 17 million square feet, depending on the source of the figures; see Urban Land Institute, *The Boom in Office Buildings: An Economic Study of the Past Two Decades*, Technical Bulletin 58 (1969), p. 22, table 1 and p. 14, chart 3; other figures in this study suggest that the total volume of square feet in new office buildings added to the Loop from 1890 to 1910 was approximately 10.5 million.

42. Survey records of the Building Owners and Managers Association of Chicago. By January 1928, however, the vacancy rate had risen to 11 percent and in 1930, it was 17.6 percent.

43. Before 1916 the height and bulk of commercial buildings were unregulated in New York; see Marc A. Weiss, "Skyscraper Zoning: New York's Pioneering Role," *Journal of the American Planning Association* 58 (Spring 1992), pp. 201-12.

44. City of Chicago, *Building Ordinances, with Amendments up to and including January 16, 1928* (Chicago, 1928), p. 219.

45. The architect Andrew Rebori described the new law in "Zoning Skyscrapers in Chicago," *Architectural Record* 58 (July 1925), p. 89: "In a commercial district: If the area of a building is reduced so that above the street line height limit it covers in the aggregate not more than 25 percent of the area of the premises, the building above such height shall be exempted from the volume and street line height regulations. The aggregate volume in cubic feet of all such portions of the building shall not exceed one-sixth of the volume of the building as permitted by this ordinance on the premises upon which such portions are erected: provided that each 1 percent of the width of the lot on the street line height limit is greater in length than 50 percent of the width of the lot, such wall shall be erected not nearer to such street line than 1 foot; and further provided that for each 10 feet in height that any such portion of the building is erected above the street line height limit, such portion of the building shall be set back 1 foot from all lines of adjacent premises."

46. The influence of New York buildings is clear and would seem obvious. The influence cited more often in many recent histories, however, is that of Eliel Saarinen's entry to the Chicago Tribune competition; as a formal model for these Chicago towers, it has been emphasized far too much.

47. All three buildings are illustrated and discussed in Pauline Saliga, ed., *The Sky's the Limit: A Century of Chicago Skyscrapers* (New York, 1990).

48. Stores were perfectly suited to exploit the court space since they did not require exterior windows and generally brought higher rates than offices.

49. For a good description of the building, see "The Pittsfield Building," *Buildings and Building Management* 26 (Aug. 2, 1926), pp. 31-36.

50. Ibid.; the interior court was suited to the needs of medical professionals who preferred well-lit, quiet, and relatively shallow offices; all space in the building was 22 feet or less from a window.

51. The designs for the Straus Building were the first submitted to a newly created body of NABOM, the Building Planning Service, which produced a series of articles that appeared in *Buildings and Building Management* during 1925. The one that documents the various experiments with massing, facade treatments, and plan is by Leo J. Sheridan and W. C. Clark, "Perfecting the Plans of the New Straus Building," *Buildings and Building Management* 25 (Feb. 16, 1925), pp. 32-43.

52. Leo J. Sheridan and W. C. Clark, "Developing the Organization for Planning, Constructing, Renting, and Operating the Straus Building, Chicago," *Buildings and Building Management* 25 (Jan. 5, 1925), p. 31.

53. Lot dimensions were 171.8 by 160.8 feet and the area was 27,625 square feet; see Sheridan and Clark (note 51), p. 38.

54. Sheridan and Clark (note 52), p. 40; for number of tenants, p. 31.

55. The decision to keep the tower relatively low seemed to have been principally aesthetic. The owners chose the classical style — they called it Florentine — for its sense of monumentality and stability. The proportions of the short tower segment with its pyramidal roof may also have been designed with an eye to visual stability, for the whole top section can be inscribed within a triangle. See Sheridan and Clark (note 51).

56. See Saliga (note 47), p. 113; the garage was closed in 1940.

57. Leo J. Sheridan and W. C. Clark, "The Advertising and Educational Campaign, Straus Building, Chicago," *Buildings and Building Management* 25 (Aug. 31, 1925), pp. 25-32.

58. On the Palmolive Building, see Robert Bruegmann, *Holabird and Roche and Holabird and Root: An Illustrated Catalog of Works, 1880-1940*, 3 vols. (New York, 1991), vol. 2, pp. 414-24.

59. "The Palmolive Building," rental brochure, uncatalogued files, Ryerson and Burnham Libraries, The Art Institute of Chicago.

60. Ibid.

61. The Palmolive Building's setbacks at floors three, eleven, and eighteen were not required by the zoning law; the base could have risen straight up to the twenty-third floor. For details on the formula of the New York law, see Carol Willis, "A 3-DCBD: How zoning shaped Manhattan's Central Business District," in *Planning and Zoning New York City: Yesterday, Today, and Tomorrow* (New Brunswick, NJ, 1993).

62. Urban Land Institute (note 41), p. 6. The proportions of the overbuilding had been even greater in Manhattan than in Chicago: from 1925 to 1931 Manhattan had increased its total volume of office space by 92 percent; Chicago had grown by 74 percent. See the table in Shultz and Simmons (note 7), p. 162.

63. Shultz and Simmons (note 7), p. 286.

64. Ibid., p. 287.

65. Ibid.

66. Shultz wrote, "During the period [of the late 1940s and early 1950s], New York could and did build office buildings to house the great expansion of business. Some of this business wanted to come to Chicago and would have if it could have been accommodated there"; ibid., pp. 286-87.

67. In 1965 the average tenant occupied 2,622 square feet, double the average of 1952, which was the year the figure was reported for the first time. Urban Land Institute (note 41), p. 32.

68. Shultz and Simmons (note 7), p. 247.

69. Barr Ferree, "The High Building in Art," *Scribners Magazine* (March 1894), p. 300.

Mies van der Rohe in America

Franz Schulze

By nature taciturn and phlegmatic, Ludwig Mies van der Rohe had little if anything of record to say about the intellectual and psychological adjustment he was obliged to make when he departed Germany in 1938 to take up residence in Chicago. It is certain, however, that by that time he had witnessed his once considerable stature within the European architectural world diminish, as the German national government grew more consolidated under the National Socialist German Workers' Party, whose attitude toward him and his work had fluctuated between indifference and outright hostility. Moreover, Mies was fifty-two years old. He spoke no English and had little taste for long trips, even less for the prospect of permanent exile from his homeland. He was just sophisticated enough to take for granted that Berlin and Europe were culturally well advanced of Chicago and the United States, but he lacked the worldly experience to recognize that this belief was a prejudice, not to mention one of little advantage to his future. Even so, if he were to move to America at all, he first would have to travel five thousand miles to a place he must have regarded as even more alien than Chicago: Wyoming, where he had been granted a commission in 1937 to design a country residence whose requirements were as frustrating as they were promising. The clients, Mr. and Mrs. Stanley Resor of New York, had made it clear that Mies was to accommodate his design to a fragment of the house already constructed but abandoned by its previous architect. When completed, it would have stood on pylons, athwart a mountain stream. Mrs. Resor knew of Frank Lloyd Wright's spectacular new creation, Fallingwater, and she nursed the hope that she might have something at least roughly akin to it. Mies did not share her dream, preferring to build on solid land. Once at the proposed site, near Jackson Hole, he spent several lonely weeks sketching, with one unexpectedly happy interruption, an evening in the company of the painter Grant Wood, with whom he communicated solely but cordially through the medium of a bottle of Scotch. The Resor House, for which he did at least 850 drawings, was never built.

In the fall of 1938 Mies did go on to assume the directorship of the School of Architecture of the Armour Institute of Technology, later the Illinois Institute of Technology, and he passed the remaining thirty-one years of his life in Chicago. He designed the master plan for IIT and erected twenty-two buildings there, producing the first all-modern university campus in America. He built no fewer than fourteen other structures in Chicago, including the twin apartment towers at 860-880 North Lake Shore Drive that contributed signally to the establishment of a new formula for the form of the modern highrise building (see pls. 114-17). Several other works of historic importance developed on his American drawing boards. He not only regained all his former professional authority, but broadened its base, becoming a legend in the annals of Chicago building and assuming a high place among the most influential architects of the post-World War II world.

On the other hand, notwithstanding the outward success with which he was able to make

Fig. 1 Ludwig Mies van der Rohe, Conceptual representation of the Convention Hall project, Chicago, 1953-54, detail of photo collage.

Fig. 2 Mies van der Rohe, Adam Department Store project, Berlin, 1928, Perspective collage.

Fig. 3   Mies van der Rohe, Alexanderplatz project, Berlin, 1928, Perspective collage.

Fig. 4   Mies van der Rohe, Friedrichstrasse Office Building project, Berlin, 1921, Perspective collage.

Fig. 5   Mies van der Rohe, Glass Skyscraper project, 1922, Model.

the transition from Germany to America, it is hard to believe that the personal experiences he endured on both sides of the Atlantic during the 1930s would have had no impact on his later architecture and the goals he set for it. Out of the combination of that subjective effect and the demonstrably different objective conditions that he found in the U.S., Mies's American architecture took its form and its rationale.

Formally speaking, the American buildings tend to be more geometrically compact and less freely composed than those that Mies had conceived and realized in Europe. Leaving aside comparisons with his early traditionalist work, whose overt traces he left behind when he suddenly embraced modernism after World War I, there is nothing in the American oeuvre as close to Expressionism as his skyscraper projects of 1921 and 1922. Nor do his American buildings search out space, either within a structure or surrounding it, as they did in his European modernist houses. Instead he favored the rectangular parallelepiped, obvious in the high-rise slabs for which he is most popularly known, as well as in a number of low-rise buildings that he designed with the same basic cubic form. In several instances, he attached a spine to the rear elevation of a tall structure, but the front invariably projected a slablike character. Even when he recessed the building volume behind a row of columns supporting a roof, the shape of the structure was rectangularly prismatic. Several of his European projects provide precedents for these later efforts: one thinks of the Stuttgart bank, the Adam Department Store in Berlin (fig. 2), and the row of slabs that made up his proposal for the remodeling of the Berlin Alexanderplatz (fig. 3), all designed in 1928.

None of these, however, was built. In fact, in view of the abundance and magnitude of his American works, it is worth reflecting that the tallest building he completed in Europe, and probably the largest in terms of cubic footage, was the Verseidag factory in Krefeld, constructed during the first half of the 1930s. It stood four stories high and was one of the few buildings of his European oeuvre in which he employed a skeletal structure, a fact that points up certain further significant differences between the European and the American works. Despite the esteem in which he is now held as a master of structure, his European work indicates little that bears out that exalted reputation. While much has been made of his decision to relieve the walls in the Barcelona Pavilion of 1928-29 of their bearing function, the columnar system

Fig. 6   Mies van der Rohe, Alumni Memorial Hall, Illinois Institute of Technology, Chicago, 1945-46.

Fig. 7   Corner detail of Alumni Memorial Hall.

used there afforded only the simplest way of holding the roof up, yet it was no more adventurous than anything else he tried in Europe. (Moreover, some of the walls in fact had columns buried in them that performed a bearing function after all.) In his first published article, dating from 1922, he argued the primacy of structure in a skyscraper.[1] Yet the work he had in mind when he said this, the so-called Friedrichstrasse Office Building (fig. 4), he most likely never expected to build, nor did he show in any drawings or models or explain in any textual detail precisely what sort of structure he would have applied to it. In that building, in fact, as well as in the Glass Skyscraper (fig. 5), the structure was far too gossamer to be realized by the technology of the time. Both buildings as we know them turned out to be aesthetic manifestos rather than buildable architecture. Mies in Europe may have been a singular master of space, of massing, of proportions, and of materials, but in effective terms, hardly of structure.

In his American work, on the other hand, structure became an inarguably vital concern in practical fact, as well as in symbolic expression. It is not the strikingly inventive kind of structure that one associates with a Pier Luigi Nervi or a Felix Candela, but it was a major determining factor as early as the first classroom buildings at IIT, in which he took the most scrupulous pains to express the skeleton that holds the building up. The famous corner detail of Alumni Memorial Hall (1945-46; figs. 6, 7) was, as I have written elsewhere,

his way of distinguishing between the primary structure of the building and the secondary structure of the skin. The former consisted of wide-flange columns encased in fireproofing concrete and covered with steel plates, the latter, of I-beams welded to the steel plates. Each of these components and their connections were *expressively* exposed at the corners, while a reveal between I-beam and brick infill avoided a possible untrue adjacency between the edges of the materials.[2]

The corner is an abstraction of structure, a symbolic apotheosis of it. Comparably, the Farnsworth House (1946-51) is an aestheticization of the wide-flange column (fig. 8).

In turn, the apartment buildings at 860-880 North Lake Shore Drive (1948-51) are before all else structural objects, in which Mies pared down to "beinahe nichts" ("almost nothing"), as he liked to put it, the components of the steel cage so that structure and architecture became virtually identical. To this system he later added the outer curtain wall that was hung in front of the structure, although it seems fair to say that

structure in any such instance was, again, symbolized but not disguised.

Meanwhile, his most impressive contribution to an architecture of structure was the clear-span pavilion, a genre that compelled his attention more than any other during his American career. Certainly it was the building type to which he gave his most concerted personal energies in the last ten to fifteen years of his life, by which time he had decided that the problem of the high-rise office/apartment building had been "solved" and could be turned over mostly to his assistants. Even as early as the 1920s, when he was still in Europe, he had become absorbed by a plan prefigurative of clear-span space, namely leaving whole floor areas of a multistory building free of functionally differentiating forms because, as he wrote in a letter in 1928 to the Adam Company of Berlin, "the exceptional variability of uses to which your building would be put requires maximally open spaces on all floors."[3]

Mies resumed his study of clear-span structure in Chicago, assigning it as a problem for his classes at IIT. One of his earliest American projects, dating from 1942, grew out of a photograph found by a student, Paul Campagna, and later studied in detail by another, Daniel Brenner. It showed Albert Kahn's Martin Bomber Plant in Baltimore, in which gigantic steel trusses spanned a space far larger than anything Mies had conceived in Germany. Mies used the photo as the backdrop of a design for a Concert Hall (fig. 9), following it with the first clear-span structure of his own devising, the Museum for a Small City of the same year, 1942, in which the roof covering the space for an auditorium was hung from overhead trusses. These suspending elements were relatively inconspicuous in that design, but they formed the dominant feature of the project for the Cantor Drive-In Restaurant of 1946. There the decision to span the restaurant longitudinally required trusses nearly as deep as the column-free interior was high. In a series of pavilions designed between the late 1940s and the late 1960s, Mies proposed a variety of structural systems: the 50 by 50 House project of 1950-51, notable for a two-way stressed roof that rested on four columns, each midway between cantilevered corners (fig. 10); S. R. Crown Hall of 1950-56, in Chicago, with its four lateral overhead plate girders (see pl. 24); the Convention Hall project of 1953-54, in which the load of a stupendous three-dimensional roof truss was transferred to the ground via ranks of three-dimensional triangular trusses (figs. 1, 12); and the Bacardi Corporation headquarters project in

Fig. 8   Mies van der
Rohe, Farnsworth
House, Plano, Illinois,
1946-51.

Fig. 9   Mies van der
Rohe, Concert Hall
project, 1942, Collage.

Fig. 10   Mies van der
Rohe, 50 by 50 House
project, 1950-51, Model
by Phil Hart and others.

Mies van der Rohe in America   145

Cuba, in which the weight of another two-way roof was meant to pass through pin joints to eight columns, two to each side of a square-plan building. These are only the prototypes of several structural systems that Mies employed in variation and quantity in other American projects. Saying as little as this about them leaves unremarked much that pertains to the often audacious and painstakingly detailed structural solutions of his American career.

These various structural works notwithstanding, a case may be made that structure, whether practical or symbolic, was not only a factor of smaller consequence in Mies's European than in his American architecture but something less than the primary expressive objective even in the work he did in this country. The belief persists that structure was the means to other ends, either to the rigorously compacted forms mentioned earlier, or to a noteworthy and special kind of space. In fact, Mies's American work appears to have been, if anything, devoted more to space than to structure, or more precisely to space and structure together and inseparable—but distinguishable—with structure serving space. This contention itself begs a further question, the ultimate question, of why, for what purpose, he worked as he did in the U. S.

It is a matter of record that Mies was fascinated by the photograph of the Martin Bomber Plant, and surely there was more than one thing about it that arrested his attention. The structure of the plant undoubtedly appealed to him, since he said so often and so credibly that he liked architecture when it was stripped to its tectonic parts. His favorite building in New York City, he affirmed in an interview the year before he died, was the George Washington Bridge, and in that same conversation he cited the much-published engraving of William Le Baron Jenney's 1891 Fair Store in Chicago (fig. 11), commenting that he found it regrettable that "the part on the right had to develop into the part on the left."[4]

No less certainly he was seized by the potential of a material, steel, that he had had little prior opportunity, given the character of his German projects, to use in any notable quantity. Now he was in America, where that magical stuff, the essential building substance of the modern technology that forever claimed his attention, seemed more likely to be available, certainly after the war and especially in the large institutional and commercial work he had reason to anticipate in Chicago. At the same time, it follows that if steel could provide what for him was a new kind of structure, structure must

yield space, again of a dimension, in the case of the Bomber Plant or the Convention Hall project, that he had never been able to realize in his European works. And like his treatment of structure and form, Mies's way with interior space in America was unlike his way with it in Europe, and he began to cultivate the difference even before he encountered the possibilities of a new structure through steel.

In Mies's final proposal for the Resor House in Wyoming, he managed to retain the aforementioned existing fragment by attaching to it, in a manner visually independent of it, a compact, rectangularly prismatic volume that prefigured the building form we have already observed to be his eventual American building type. No less important was his treatment of the single dominant space within, a living/dining area flanked by picture windows on the long sides, with bedrooms set behind a freestanding fireplace at one end and the kitchen and service area at the other (figs. 13-15). The space was itself a negative rectangular prism, uninterrupted and unarticulated by any architectural element, more specifically, by nothing like the walls that had subdivided space in his best-known European houses. In Europe, as we have been told over and over, those walls did not enclose space but rather defined it. Moreover, because of their informal asymmetrical composition, sometimes sliding past each other, they created a dynamic flow of interior space. Space in the Resor House interior, however, did not flow. The living room was essentially an empty volume, symmetrically serene, a

Fig. 11 William Le Baron Jenney, The Fair Department Store under construction; from Inland Architect and News Record *18 (1891).*

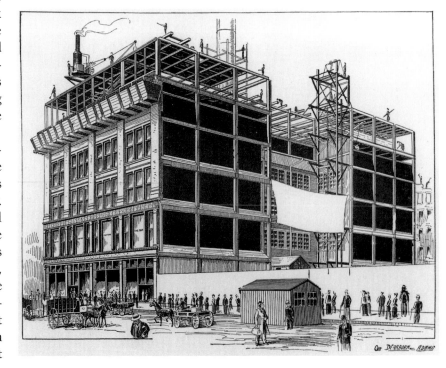

Fig. 12 Mies van der
Rohe, Convention Hall
project, 1953-54.

space less to move through than to sit in and gaze out of, contemplatively. The structure of the Resor House was a simple matter that in no significant way foretokened either the frame of Mies's columnar grid buildings or the roof systems of his clear-span structures. The interior space, on the other hand, set the stage for the stasis and unarticulated freedom of the later clear-span buildings.

The effects of this space vary, depending on the size and the function of Mies's buildings, but several shared qualities may be discerned in most of them. In large structures like Crown Hall and the Neue Nationalgalerie in Berlin, which were built, the height of the elevations and the breadth of the plans create in the viewer a sensation of spatial vastness that is one of the most exhilarating attributes of the buildings. That Mies himself knew this and actively sought it, even at the expense of functional commodity, may be inferred from the oft-quoted statement he made about the main hall of the Berlin museum, a space notorious for its tendency to crush all art exhibitions installed within it, except those of comparably outsize dimensions. He said: "It is such a huge hall that of course it means great difficulties for the exhibiting of art. I am fully aware of that. But it has such potential that I simply cannot take those difficulties into account."[5]

The quality of space in smaller column-free buildings is something else again, obvious from contrasting the experience of the intimate and personal Farnsworth House with that of Crown Hall or the Berlin museum, formal, public, and huge as the latter spaces are. But the sensation of transparency that the Farnsworth House produces so vividly recalls the effect of another material, glass, that Mies used reciprocally with steel and more single-mindedly in his American than in his European spaces. All of these clear-span buildings have glass walls that ring them, either completely, or at floor level or at the level of a *piano nobile*. The glass wall fulfills the simple necessity of protecting the interior of the building from the outdoor elements, but in Mies's hands it does so minimally, and in a figurative sense, immaterially, as if the internal space were intended to escape the confines of its borders so that vastness might transcend to infiniteness. Infinity suggests a consciousness of space, rather than of substance.

Mies did indeed reflect a desire to express or to reach for infinity in his European buildings. The three radiating walls of the Brick Country House project of 1924 are one sign of the impulse, but so are the windows of the 1928-30 Tugendhat House in Brno, Czechoslovakia (now the Czech Republic), that appeared to "dissolve" when they

4 copies

Fig. 13   Mies van der Rohe, Resor House project, Jackson Hole, Wyoming, 1937-38, Interior perspective.

Fig. 14   Resor House, First-floor plan, delineated by J. B. Rodgers, March 21, 1938.

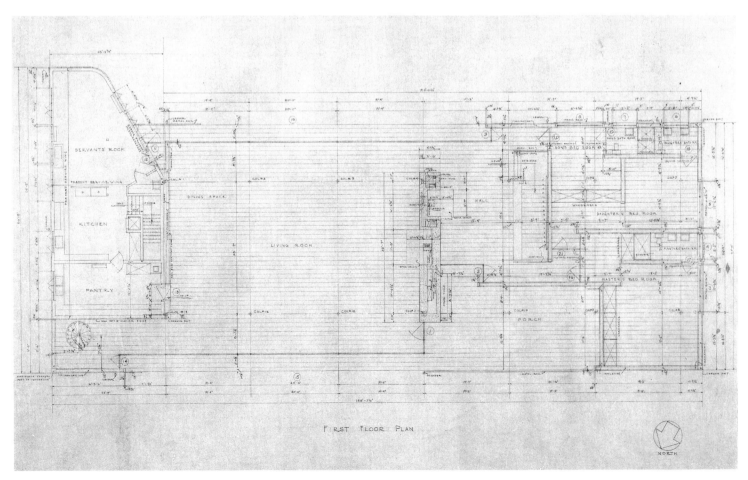

FIRST FLOOR PLAN

NORTH

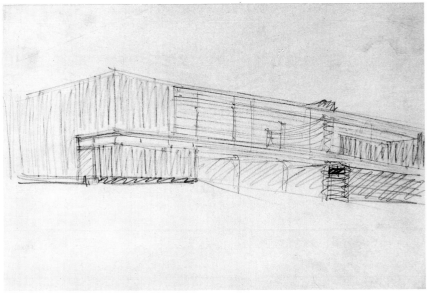

Fig. 15   Resor House,
c. 1937-38, Preliminary
perspective studies.

It is the consensus of current scholarship that by the end of the 1920s Mies had become disenchanted with functionalism in modern architecture and had adopted instead a more idealized belief in an architecture expressive of spiritual aspirations. Wolf Tegethoff perceives "a certain mystic and ethereal quality" in the Barcelona Pavilion, which he connects with Mies's yearning to equate the materiality of architecture with the immateriality of philosophy.[6] The late Richard Pommer likewise took up the issue of spirit in Mies's work of the later Weimar years, although the key terms he employed in defining it are freedom—of a personal and metaphorical rather than political sort—and order.[7] By 1929, Pommer argued, Mies had been persuaded that modern society was threatened, on the one hand by mechanization, which he saw as an ill-disciplined child of the Industrial Revolution—that is, as technology unbridled—and on the other, by a gulf between "hyper-individualism" and the mass culture, a condition he traced to the Renaissance.[8] The chaos of modern architecture could be overcome, Mies believed, only by the preservation of a coherent set of values that would at the same time ensure man the liberty of his own movement and encourage his sovereign interaction with nature. Pommer saw this view "with its potential significance of freedom and order and of tradition and modernity" worked out in Mies's manner of design, in which organization based on classical principles was married to an abstract steel-and-glass building technique.[9] Analogously, Fritz Neumeyer depicts Mies as a creative spirit who sought to balance the expression of subjective will in art with a discipline based upon the search for objective and immutable truth. (Hence Mies's constant inquiry into the nature of architecture.)[10]

Pommer, however, claimed to note a change in the architect's view of freedom and order at the time he arrived in the United States:

In his inaugural address as director of architecture at the Armour Institute of Technology in November 1938, [Mies] said, "The long path from material through function to creative work has only a single goal: to create order out of the desperate confusion of our time." Neither then nor later did he speak again of freedom as a value in itself. When Peter Blake asked him in 1961, "Do you think that in a free enterprise democracy, where everyone is free to do just about what he wants within very slight limitations, that it is possible to create architectural order?," Mies replied, "Yes, I think it would be an order in freedom." Freedom was left to American politics; the task of architecture was order.[11]

Given Mies's nautilus-like nature and the life he lived in the 1930s, it is not unreasonable to sup-

were mechanically retracted into the floor. These works, however, were animated chiefly by the interior spatial dynamism that we have already distinguished from the more static, emptied-out spaces of his American work.

Why Mies's work changed in America is as engrossing a question as how it changed. If the answer points in part to the social and technological differences between Weimar Germany and post-World War II America, it is similarly reflective of shifts and developments in Mies's personal understanding of the objectives of architecture, about which he talked and wrote with such steady conviction that they must be taken seriously as factors central to the genesis of his work.

Fig. 16 Mies van der Rohe, Promontory Apartments, 5530 South Shore Drive, Chicago, 1949.

Fig. 17 Mies van der Rohe, Perspective study and plans for a high-rise building, c. 1938-40.

Fig. 18 Mies van der
Rohe, The Arts Club
of Chicago, 109 East
Ontario Street, 1948-52,
Four elevations.

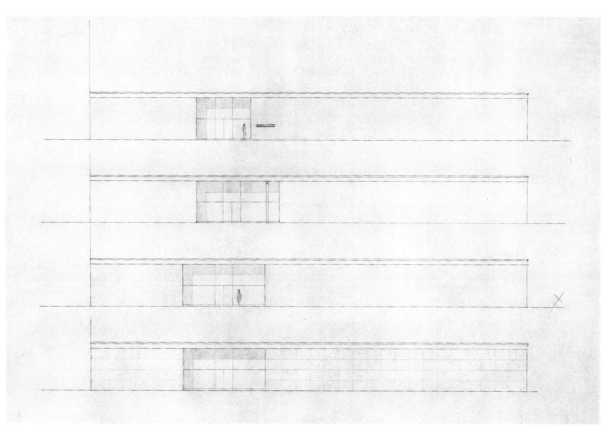

Fig. 19 The Arts Club
of Chicago, Plan.

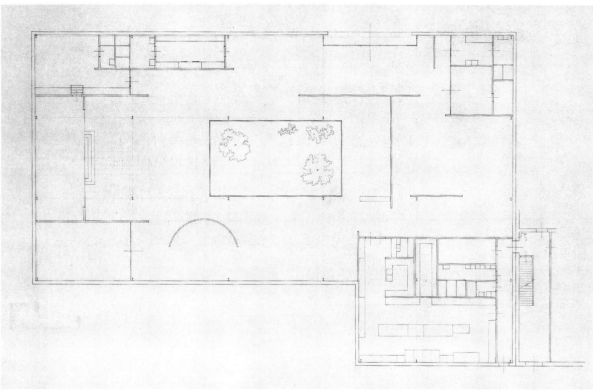

pose that he saw America in two lights, on the one hand, as a place where he could take anxiety-free refuge from the storm of politics—a realm he had never cared much for even in the freewheeling atmosphere of 1920s Berlin—and on the other, as a setting that was eternally foreign to him and he to it. "Ich bin immer ein stiller Deutscher" ("I am forever a silent German"), Philip Johnson has reported Mies as having said to him in a moment of candor in America.[12] Mies was never an eager socializer in Germany or the U.S., preferring his own company always at the close of the day, and as he grew older in Chicago, he took greater sustenance from the

Mies van der Rohe in America   151

Figs. 20, 21 Mies van
der Rohe, Sketches of
sculpture for the Joseph
E. Seagram and Sons
Office Building, New
York, 1954-58.

communion with his books—and himself—than from the people around him, who may have revered him but almost never followed him, or cared to, on his endless philosophical expeditions.

He was more solitary in America than he had been in Europe, and like many aging artists, he concentrated his energies more narrowly and more intensely on the goals of the idealized architecture that he had begun in Germany. We know from Fritz Neumeyer the extent and character of his reading prior to his emigration. Neumeyer suggests that

the preference for an empty, silent room, may have had its ideological-religious impulse in the writings of [Romano] Guardini and the church buildings of Rudolf Schwarz. Guardini described "fear of empty space and silence... as a fear of being alone with God and the forlorn

standing in front of him," a confrontation man attempts to avoid: "That is why he always wants to have things, pictures, words and sounds around himself."

Rudolf Schwarz, who claims that the idea of a large, pure, almost empty space is his idea, created in his church structures, which were highly valued by Mies, ascetic rooms in which Guardini's postulate assumed architectonic form: "We must again rediscover the emptiness of God's house, and the silence in his service; man is in need of it."

"In the silence of the large rooms," of which Rudolf Schwarz had spoken, arises "not the longing to become lost, but the hope of finding oneself."[13]

In America Mies was able to create those rooms, supporting them with an appropriately minimal structure of steel and enclosing them in a suitably cubic glass envelope. Space and structure were together reduced to "beinahe nichts," an architecture optimally dematerialized. Yet if we find in Mies's yearnings after a higher, immaterial order traces of his Catholic upbringing, we must also recall another aspect of his makeup. For he was the son of a stonemason, and he learned about architecture, more properly building, as an apprentice on construction sites around his native Aachen. There was a practical side to him, which enabled him to make the most of the riches America had to offer. It is no accident that he struck up a relationship with the Chicago rabbinical-student-turned-developer Herbert Greenwald that led to the commissions for all those apartment buildings on the Chicago lakefront and the various commercial structures that grew out of them. American confidence in modern technology, elevated by the country's resounding victory in World War II, which was taken as proof of the imperative of technology, granted Mies assignments that were most conveniently solved by the compacted modular prismatic forms and columnar grids — and even the clear-span structures — of his American career.

Moreover, in affirming the differences between the two major phases of his career, we would be well advised to remember that the line separating them is both blurred and crooked. Mies of the Berlin years is recognizable as the old Mies in Chicago, and vice versa. The slab forms of the Alexanderplatz remodeling project of 1928 were revived as soon as he set about working in 1946 on his first high-rise commission in

Fig. 22   Myron Goldsmith, Republic Building, Columbus, Indiana, 1971.

Chicago, the Promontory Apartments (fig. 16).
No less intriguing, however, are sketches of tall
buildings of a strikingly dissimilar sort that he
made around 1940, well before the early American commissions were conceived (see fig. 17).
They are not prismatic so much as multilobed
structures with vertically slotted elevations,
vaguely but not at all exactly akin to the 1921-22
skyscraper projects. Similarly, notwithstanding
his fascination with the empty spaces of the
clear-span pavilions, he did not altogether forsake
the open plans of his European houses. He would
have employed them in the 860-880 North Lake
Shore Drive towers had it not been for Greenwald's insistence that American apartment
dwellers prefer the privacy implicit in cubicu-
larly subdivided plans. Furthermore, one of the
most engaging recent discoveries among his
American drawings is a design for the Arts Club
of Chicago in which he postulated not just an
interior space, as in the finished work, but an
entire and independent building, proposed for
the same location on Rush and Ontario streets
(figs. 18, 19). It would have assumed the American outer form of a parallelepiped, but its interior
would have been a faithful reprise of the wander-
ing walls so typical of his European spaces.

He produced this last project, most likely for
his own delectation, at the very same time he
was working on such emptied-out pavilions as
the Farnsworth House and Crown Hall. And,
almost as if to confound anyone hoping to find
a steady evolution of form and content in the
work of so apparently methodical a thinker,
Mies left a group of drawings of large abstract
sculptures for the plaza of the Seagram Building
(1954-58) in New York City (figs. 20, 21). They
are startling not only in their spontaneity of
attack but in the unfettered expressionism of
their shapes.

As with the Arts Club project, Mies never
meant or expected these sketchbook fantasies to
be realized in material form. Even so, since they
are so obviously improvisations, by a man who
so often and so publicly deplored improvisation
as an accidental and unrational way of arriving
at a finished work, they are further evidence that
Mies, before he was a maker of systems or an
unbending follower of principles, was an artist,
prepared, at least when the spirit moved him, to
prefer the meandering nonlinear path characteristic of the creative process to the straight line
and rhythmic pulse associated with rational
analysis. He could fool even himself. "Sometimes late at night when I am tired," he once told
his student and colleague Louis Rocah, "I am

Fig. 23 George
Schipporeit and John
Heinrich; Graham,
Anderson, Probst and
White, associate
architects, Lake Point
Tower, 505 North Lake
Shore Drive, 1968.

Fig. 24 David Haid,
Rose Studio Pavilion,
Highland Park, Illinois,
1974.

overcome with a desire to do something just because I like it. Then I know it is too late. I've been
waiting too long. You don't do a thing because
you like to do it, but because it is right."[14] There
is a covert vanity in that remark; it was the
speaker, not the substance of what he said, that
lent it credibility. The attribute that resolved the
Miesian contradictions was a charisma derived
more from the man's olympian image than from
his fundamentally retiring personality, and the
image, of course, was dependent on the palpable
excellence of his work. Well before Mies ever
arrived, the Chicago architectural community
had known other masterly figures with strong

philosophical biases; Louis Sullivan and Frank
Lloyd Wright are outstanding among them. But
since the city's building tradition was manifestly
commercial and pragmatic, its practitioners were
better prepared to admire the look and logic of
Mies's buildings than to pursue him into the rar-
efied atmosphere of German idealist philosophy.

It took until the mid-1950s, a decade after
World War II, for Chicago to begin the rebuilding
of its downtown area. By then Mies was firmly
established as a local presence, with the IIT campus mostly reconstituted and the 860-880 North
Lake Shore Drive Apartments finished and functioning. Indeed, the following decade was the

Fig. 25   Haid, Rose
Studio Pavilion, interior.

most active of his career, not only in the quantity of work that emerged from his office, but in the material evidence of a flourishing local Miesian school. Among his own students who rose to prominence in Chicago during the 1950s, 1960s, and 1970s were Jacques Brownson and Gene Summers of C. F. Murphy Associates, chief designers, respectively, of the Civic Center (1965; now Richard J. Daley Center; see Miller, "City Hall," fig. 1) and the McCormick Place convention center (1967-71; see Miller, "Helmut Jahn," figs. 7, 8); Myron Goldsmith of Skidmore, Owings and Merrill (SOM), primarily responsible for the Brunswick Building (1961-65; see Miller, "City Hall," fig. 17) and the Republic Building (1971), a newspaper plant in Columbus, Indiana (fig. 22); George Schipporeit and John Heinrich, who together designed Lake Point Tower (1968; fig. 23); and David Haid, creator of the Dyett Middle School (1972) and the Rose Studio Pavilion (1974; figs. 24, 25). In turn, Bruce Graham and Fazlur Khan of SOM did not study with Mies, but both architects acknowledged a debt to him, notable especially in their design of the John Hancock Center (1965-69) and Baxter Travenol Laboratories in Deerfield (1975; fig. 26; pls. 90, 91). Similarly, the early terminals of Chicago

O'Hare International Airport (1957-63; see Brodherson, figs. 17-19), credited principally to Stanislaw Gladych of C. F. Murphy Associates, suggest origins in Miesian form. An emphasis on structural reductiveness is common to all these buildings, while the long span deriving from Mies's example is evident at large scale in McCormick Place and Baxter Travenol, and in smaller dimension in the Rose Pavilion.

Mies's sway over the local community of designers lasted long enough to reestablish Chicago as the leading center of American commercial architecture during the 1950s and most of the 1960s. In fact, it is frequently argued that it lasted too long, since the various perceived failings of modernist architecture and by extension of Miesianism—such as an indifference to physical and social context, a rejection of historical form, and a reliance on formal absolutes even as the urban environment grew irreversibly heterogeneous—were only tardily acknowledged in a city so corporately proud of its modernist tradition.

Surely Mies did not seek to combat heterogeneity or to yield to it, preferring to call it confusion and chaos. And indeed he concentrated his energies principally on the building as artwork,

Fig. 26 Bruce Graham and Fazlur Kahn, Baxter Travenol Laboratories, Deerfield, Illinois, 1975.

an object that might approach the condition of an aesthetic and spiritual distillate as it grew increasingly self-referential. This is true even of the multipart endeavors like the IIT campus, the Chicago Federal Center (see Miller, "City Hall," figs. 14, 15) and the 860-880 and 900-910 North Lake Shore Drive apartment complexes. In these instances, the "sliding walls" of Europe have been transformed into whole buildings, composed in his famous "occult balance." It is as if he had responded in this way to an American scale.

Yet, if in the process of this accommodation, his architecture also proved only too well suited to the mid-century American corporate mentality, it must be said on his behalf that that occurrence was in significant part an accidental symbiosis. Mies was hardly a corporate creature in his own right. He reduced his buildings to primary structural forms evocative of spatial infinitude less to serve the needs of IBM than the imperatives of a universal order and a sensibility to form that has had no more than a handful of equals during this century. The détente that developed between an artist of profound solitude and a country of openhanded pragmatism is one of the most remarkable and ironical marriages in all modern culture.

NOTES

1. Mies van der Rohe, "Hochhaus-Projekt für Bahnhof Friedrichstrasse, Berlin," *Frühlicht* 1 (Summer 1922), pp. 122-24.
2. Franz Schulze, *Mies van der Rohe: A Critical Biography* (Chicago, 1985), p. 226.
3. Mies van der Rohe, letter to S. Adam Company, Berlin, July 2, 1928, Mies van der Rohe Archive, The Museum of Modern Art, New York.
4. Franz Schulze, "I Always Wanted to Know About Truth," *Chicago Daily News* (April 27, 1968).

5. Mies van der Rohe, quoted in "Mies van der Rohe," a documentary film directed by Georgia van der Rohe, sponsored by Knoll International and Zweites Deutsches Fernsehen, Mainz, and produced by IFAGE Filmproduktion, Wiesbaden; English version, 1979, German version, 1980.
6. Wolf Tegethoff, "From Obscurity to Maturity: Mies van der Rohe's Breakthrough to Modernism," in Franz Schulze, ed., *Mies van der Rohe: Critical Essays* (New York, 1989), p. 84.
7. Richard Pommer, "Mies van der Rohe and the Political Ideology of the Modern Movement in Architecture," in Schulze (note 6), pp. 97-145.

8. Ibid., p. 111.
9. Ibid., p. 113.
10. Fritz Neumeyer, "Space for Reflection: Block versus Pavilion," in Schulze (note 6), pp. 148-71.
11. Pommer (note 7), p. 134.
12. Personal conversation with Philip Johnson, June 11, 1987.
13. Fritz Neumeyer, *The Artless Word: Mies van der Rohe on the Building Art* (Cambridge, Mass., 1991), pp. 228-31.
14. Schulze (note 2), pp. 313-15.

Schaumburg, Oak Brook, Rosemont, and the Recentering of the Chicago Metropolitan Area

Robert Bruegmann

Near the intersection of I-90 and I-290, some twenty-five miles northwest of Chicago's Loop, a set of gleaming office towers marks the business center of Schaumburg. These towers seem to have sprung up overnight. In 1956 this site was still largely covered with fields, and the nearby village of Schaumburg counted only 130 people. Today downtown Schaumburg boasts over ten million square feet of office space and six million square feet of retail space, making it one of the largest business centers in the Midwest, surpassing downtown Rockford, Illinois, for example, or downtown Milwaukee, Wisconsin, or St. Paul, Minnesota, according to a number of key business indicators (see figs. 2, 3).[1]

The appearance of Schaumburg is symptomatic of some fundamental changes that have dramatically reshaped the business landscape of the Chicago metropolitan area as well as that of almost every other major city in the world.[2] Like other traditional city centers, Chicago's Loop, while remaining a major business center, has ceased to dominate the region. Since World War II, the Loop's share of office and retail space in the metropolitan area has declined rapidly, as new concentrations of business activity have emerged along the region's superhighways (fig. 4).[3] For the most part these zones follow the roads north and west of the city, especially the Tri-State Tollway (I-294) north of O'Hare International Airport; the East-West Tollway (I-88) between Oak Brook and Aurora; the Northwest Tollway (I-90) from O'Hare to Elgin; and, most recently, the North-South Tollway (I-355). The most important concentrations tend to occur where superhighways intersect, notably at Oak Brook to the west, at Rosemont just east of O'Hare, and in the Woodfield area of Schaumburg and the surrounding communities to the northwest.

The move of business away from the traditional center toward the periphery has had an enormous impact on the political, economic, and social life of the region. As industry and population have moved out, the city of Chicago's share of the region's taxes has declined, while, at the same time, the remaining population has become older and poorer. As the jobs have dispersed across the metropolitan area, the city's transportation network, which was built to get workers from the periphery to the Loop and back, has become increasingly inefficient. Finally, with the rapid population growth of suburban areas, the city of Chicago has been forced to share its political power in the state with the outlying municipalities.

Despite the importance of this business shift, most scholars and urban planners until quite recently either ignored the phenomenon or examined it only long enough to lament it.[4] On the rare occasions when architectural and planning journals discussed it, for example, they rarely paused to analyze or even describe what they found before coming to a negative judgment.[5] In the last few years, however, the new business centers have received a sudden burst of attention. In 1986 developer Christopher B. Leinberger coauthored a widely read article in *Atlantic* in which he discussed the rise of cities like Schaumburg, places he called "urban villages." Historian Robert Fishman looked at the same places in his book *Bourgeois Utopias* and labeled them "technoburbs." Finally, in 1991 journalist Joel Garreau issued by far the most popular study to date of what he calls the "Edge City."[6]

These authors differ widely in their descriptions of what has happened and in their judgments of the new business centers. Fishman is rather negative; Leinberger and Garreau considerably more positive. In all three cases, however, the authors use a similar plot to explain what happened: the traditional city, which had been built up in the era of railroads and mass transit, suddenly exploded outward with the development of the automobile. Middle-class Americans, particularly after World War II, fled the central city and its problems and took up residence in homogeneous bedroom communities in the suburbs. Finally, within the last several

Fig. 1 Victor L. Charn, Motorola, Inc., headquarters, 4545 West Augusta Boulevard, 1937, detail of entrance.

159

Fig. 2 Aerial view of
Schaumburg, looking
north, October 1989.

Fig. 2 Aerial view of
Schaumburg, looking
north, October 1989.

Fig. 5 Location of
industries employing
100 or more people; from
Miller McClintock,
Report and
Recommendations of the
Metropolitan Street
Traffic Survey (Chicago,
1926).

Fig. 3 Map of
Schaumburg, showing
location of office
buildings and shopping
centers, by Dennis
McClendon, 1992.

Fig. 4 Map of Chicago
metropolitan area,
showing major
expressways and
tollways and outlying
business centers, by
Dennis McClendon,
1992.

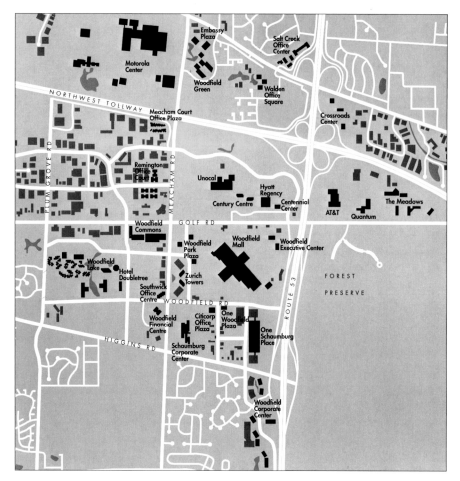

decades, jobs have started to move out to where the people are, as businesses have followed the residences out to the edge of the metropolitan area. Here, these authors believe, business enterprises have constituted new centers that are quite different from the old downtown since they are more spread out, more dependent on the automobile, and more highly privatized.

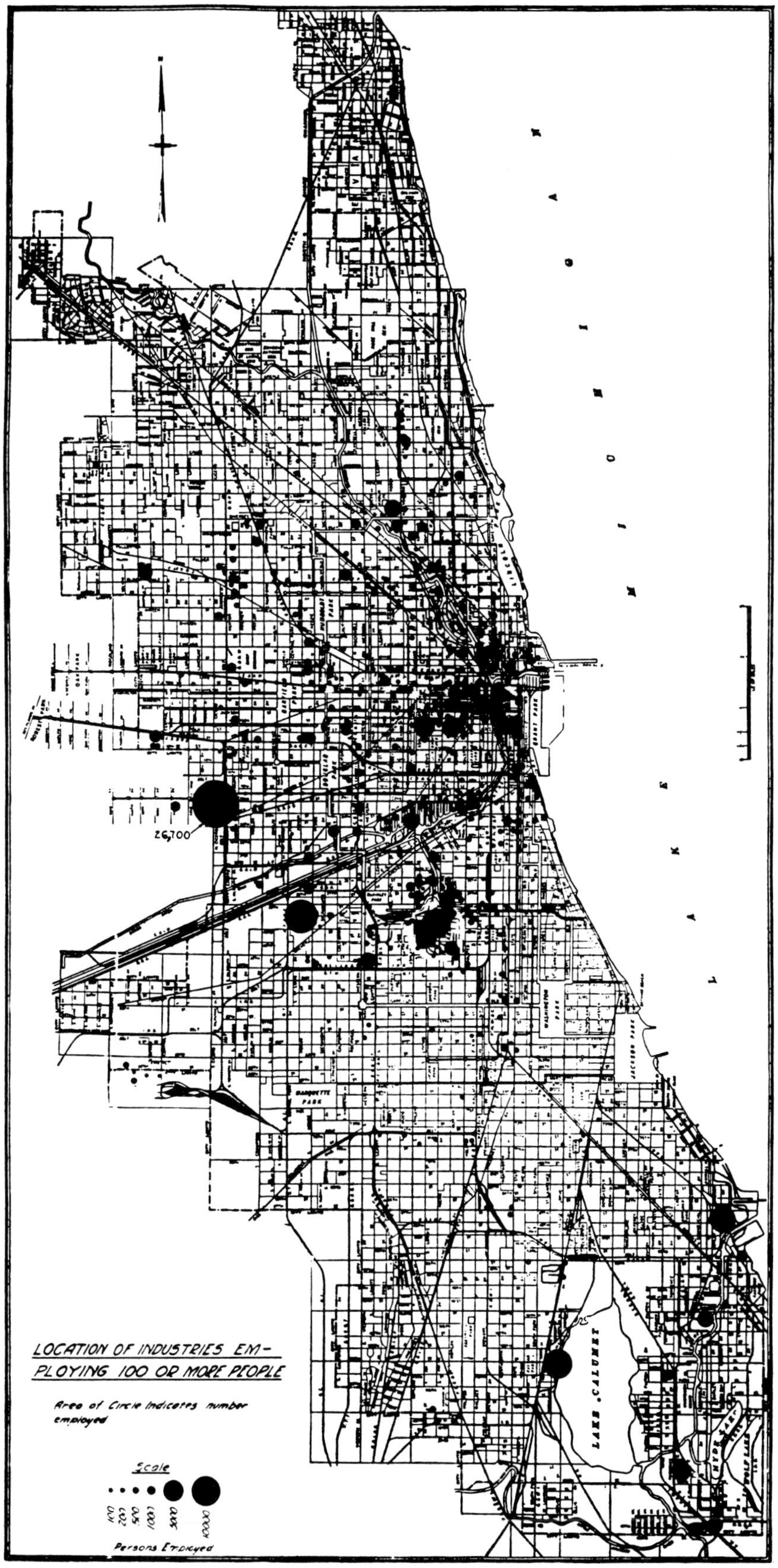

At first glance this explanation seems to work. It offers a plausible explanation of the sudden appearance of places like Schaumburg and Oak Brook. It also helps explain why central Schaumburg and Oak Brook share many features with other places across the country, like Tyson's Corner outside Washington, D. C., Perimeter Center outside Atlanta, the Post Oak/Galleria District of Houston, or Costa Mesa-Irvine in Orange County south of Los Angeles. Furthermore, it seems to explain why these centers look so different from pre-World War I cities, and it accords nicely with most of what has been written about the history of the American suburbs.

Ultimately, however, the explanation fails to satisfy. I will argue, using three key business activities—retail, manufacturing, and office work—as examples, that the new business centers, as novel as they at first seem, are not a wholly new phenomenon, but are, instead, the latest manifestation of a complex, reciprocal relationship between center and periphery that has been going on since the birth of the city. Chicago provides a particularly revealing example, since the flat, unobstructed terrain offers few obstacles to growth in any direction except east.

I. Commercial Centers in the Chicago Area before World War II

Chicago, like all American cities, has been engaged since its founding in a process of constant movement as means of transportation have changed and as land prices have risen and fallen. From their initial location near the mouth of the Chicago River in the city's early days, retail, wholesale, manufacturing, and office activities tended to move outward and segregate themselves, first in the Loop and then increasingly throughout the Chicago metropolitan area.[7] From the first, this pattern of movement and relocation has involved not just decentralization but also recentering.

Manufacturing

As manufacturers moved out from the old Central Business District, they found themselves far from the services that they and their employees needed (fig. 5). Very early these companies started to reconstitute the new industrial areas into small cities unto themselves, duplicating many of the features of the old downtown.

LOCATION OF INDUSTRIES EMPLOYING 100 OR MORE PEOPLE

Area of Circle Indicates number employed

Scale

Persons Employed

26,700

The Recentering of the Metropolitan Area 161

Fig. 6   J. B. Jorgensen (listed on building permit), Mars Candy factory, 2019 North Oak Park Avenue, 1928-29.

Fig. 7   Aerial view of Motorola, Inc., headquarters and plant, 4545 West Augusta Boulevard, c. 1960.

This was true in towns like Joliet, Aurora, Elgin, and Waukegan that were substantial cities in their own right, in planned industrial districts like the Union Stock Yard (1865), in planned industrial towns like Pullman (1879-95), in large factory complexes like the great Western Electric Hawthorne Works in Cicero (1903), and in industrial parks like the Central Manufacturing District and the Clearing Industrial District.[8] In addition to the actual manufacturing facilities, each of these places reproduced on a small scale many of the characteristics of the Chicago Loop, containing commercial buildings, banks, and hotels, and in the case of the Stockyards, even its own loop of the Chicago elevated transit system.

The peripheral locations offered more efficient transportation and cheaper land. These savings in cost allowed the manufacturers to construct freestanding industrial buildings that were more efficient, better lighted, and healthier for workers than the old multistory lofts downtown. Increasingly, lighter industry sought out loca-tions in or near residential neighborhoods, and tried to blend in through architecture and land-scaping, as, for example, at the beautifully land-scaped Spanish colonial Mars Candy factory at 2019 North Oak Park Avenue in Chicago, con-structed by Frank Mars in 1928-29 on the site of a former golf course (fig. 6).

Although already underway in the nineteenth century, the outward movement accelerated in the twentieth, and the buildings became larger and lower the farther they got from the Loop. The Galvin Manufacturing Corporation (later Motorola, Inc.) provides a good example. Starting in rented space in a seven-story building at 847 West Harrison Street, the company built a large, low facility housing a production plant and of-fices on a spacious site at 4545 West Augusta Boulevard on the West Side of Chicago in 1937 (fig. 1). The company selected this site because it was in a residential neighborhood that could pro-vide a substantial, stable work force. By the end of World War II, Motorola had expanded at Augusta Boulevard and bought or leased other

Fig. 8 Aerial view of
Englewood business
district, 63rd and
Halsted streets, 1941.

facilities totaling nearly 500,000 square feet of space (fig. 7).[9] Motorola's experience was typical: by 1945 many of Chicago's manufacturing plants had made a substantial move from the Loop. As in the case of other trends examined in this essay, this shift is much more apparent from an examination of the existing built environment than it is from examining statistics.[10]

This outward move of manufacturing centers was greatly facilitated by the increased use of the automobile and the truck and by an improved road system. During the teens and twenties, a large amount of money was spent on upgrading highways and removing grade crossings, and the first schemes for Chicago superhighways appeared. The first limited access highways were built in the 1930s,[11] and by 1945 the major lines of what eventually became the superhighway system of the Chicago region had been drawn.[12]

Retail

Even more dramatic to the casual observer than the outward movement of industry in the inter-

war years was a shift in retail activity. In Chicago, as in a number of other cities, the nineteenth-century shopping district was forced to yield a substantial piece of its most prestigious trade to new, automobile-oriented streets.[13] In Chicago, North Michigan Avenue played the leading role. Located outside the immediate area served by the old mass-transit rail lines, North Michigan Avenue was in great measure a product of the automobile and the bus.[14]

Outside the Central Business District were the neighborhood centers. Although these had long existed, before 1910 they were usually relatively small. During the next two decades efficient streetcar transportation made possible a major decentralization of retail trade, best exemplified in the rapid rise of the chain store and the outlying department store.[15] As a result, in the 1920s some of the outlying business areas became really important commercial centers in their own right. The Englewood business district, located at 63rd and Halsted streets, was the largest of these, boasting both Wieboldt's and

Sears department stores and hundreds of other shops (fig. 8).[16] Englewood counted more retail sales than all but a handful of American cities, and it continued to be the largest retail center outside the Loop well into the postwar years, easily surpassing all the early postwar shopping centers in size.[17] Other large retail concentrations were found outside the Chicago city limits in such places as Evanston and Oak Park.[18] In all of these, department stores, smaller shops, movie theaters, and professional offices together created dense concentrations of commercial activity.

One of the most interesting developments of the interwar years was a jump in scale in commercial development and the accommodation of automobiles. Where the earlier streetcar strips had consisted of single stores and small retail blocks, the interwar years saw the rise of a new kind of shopping center, in which a single developer constructed buildings that could house many shops and often some offices, sometimes with substantial amounts of automobile parking. Chicago appears to have made an important early contribution to this history at Market Square in Lake Forest, but after this initial step, nothing in the Chicago area seems to have matched places like the Country Club Plaza in Kansas City, Westwood Village in Los Angeles, Highland Park Village in Dallas, or Suburban Square in Philadelphia.[19] The only major automobile-oriented shopping center in the Chicago area appears to have been Spanish Court (later, Plaza del Lago) in Wilmette.[20]

Fig. 9 Perkins, Chatten and Hammond, Northwest Tower, Milwaukee, Damen, and North avenues, 1928-29 (photo c. 1956).

Fig. 11 Holabird and Root, Jewel Tea Company, Barrington, 1929.

Fig. 10 Herbert G. Banse, G. D. Searle Laboratories, Skokie, 1942.

Offices

Recent accounts of the rise of the "Edge City" tend to perpetuate a popular misconception of the American city: that downtown housed a large percentage of the metropolitan area's non-manufacturing jobs until the suburbs fairly recently started to siphon them off. In fact, it appears that at no time in the twentieth century did the Loop house anything near a majority of jobs, even of those within the city itself. The Central Business District was only dominant in a few key areas, notably the upper end of office work. Here, too, substantial shifts took place during the interwar years, although, again, available statistics tend to obscure rather than illuminate this trend.[21]

In the Central Business District itself, the newly opened Wacker Drive and Michigan Avenue siphoned off some of the most prestigious office tenants away from the central Loop. The availability of these new commercial developments allowed Chicago's central district to expand easily, and they probably made it unnecessary to establish new, more remote commercial districts as happened in New York City and Detroit, where ambitious new midtowns were established several miles away from the old core.

Many of Chicago's regional centers experienced a pronounced increase in available office space, primarily for professional services. A good index of this increase in space needs can be seen in the jump in size of the buildings that banks built for themselves and for speculative rental purposes at the corners of the city's principal arteries. Major examples include the Hyde Park State Bank on 53rd Street in Hyde Park, the National Bank of Commerce at Madison and Pulaski streets, and the Uptown National Bank at Broadway and Lawrence. Even more dramatic was the appearance of mini-skyscrapers, for example, the 1929 Northwest Tower at the business center at the intersection of Milwaukee, Damen, and North avenues (fig. 9).

In a certain number of cases companies moved their offices out beyond the city altogether. Usually these were companies in which the offices were attached to laboratories or production facilities that required large numbers of well-paid workers. The 1930s and 1940s witnessed a number of architecturally distinguished examples, among them, the G. D. Searle and Company offices and laboratories in Skokie (fig. 10) and the Jewel Tea Company plant and offices in Barrington, some fifty miles northwest of the Loop (fig. 11).[22]

II. The Postwar Decades

In many histories of the American city, the postwar years are said to mark the beginning of a wholly unprecedented move of city dwellers out to the periphery, where the automobile allowed the formation of vast and homogeneous middle-class bedroom suburbs. This characterization does not adequately reflect what actually happened. The term "suburb," to begin with, is almost useless in any such discussion. What was within the municipal boundary of any given city and what was outside it changed constantly and differed markedly from city to city. Contrary to the stereotypes created by many postwar "urban historians," suburbs were not at all homogeneous. There were affluent suburbs and modest ones, bedroom suburbs and industrial ones, white suburbs and black ones. The outer part of the metropolitan area was just as complex as the inner (fig. 12).[23]

Furthermore, the changes that occurred in the 1950s were not different in kind from those that had taken place before. It seems more useful to consider them as continuations of processes that had started at least by the 1920s and that were merely delayed by the Depression and World War II.[24] A final myth concerns the role of the automobile. In the postwar shifts in population and business, the automobile did play a role, but it was not a prime mover. In fact, the increasing importance of the automobile was probably more a result of geographical shifts than a cause.[25]

Manufacturing

Postwar manufacturing continued to move outward at an ever accelerating pace. The chief gains in the postwar years were made at the very edge of the city and in the band of suburbs immediately around it, particularly to the north around Skokie and the northwest around O'Hare Airport. By 1959 the city of Chicago was virtually ringed by a series of dense industrial belts along the area's major belt railway lines, including the Belt Railway of Chicago, which ran from the area around Lake Calumet past the Clearing Industrial District and the Hawthorne Works, north through industrial areas on the West Side of Chicago. The Indiana Harbor Belt Railway ran in a wider arc, taking in industrial areas of the near west suburbs. Finally, there was the Elgin, Joliet and Eastern Railroad, extending from the steel mills of Gary, Indiana, and the Standard Oil refinery of Whiting, Indiana, in a huge semicircular arc all the way around to the

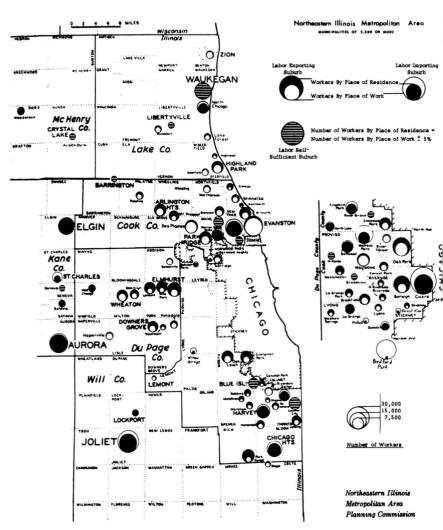

Abbott Laboratories in North Chicago.[26] These belt railways, constructed before 1900, prefigured the postwar circumferential highways.

Once again, Motorola can serve as an example of a specific organization moving outward. Although the company continued to buy and lease space near the center of Chicago, the majority of its new construction was either considerably farther out, if not beyond the Chicago region altogether, as, for example, in the case of a semiconductor facility in Phoenix. In the Chicago area the company opened a plant in Franklin Park in 1953, and in 1959 completed a new headquarters in front of it along Grand Avenue (fig. 13).[27] Already looking to the future, Motorola was buying land still farther out. It purchased a site for further expansion in Niles, but it ultimately swapped this land for a much larger tract along the newly opened Northwest Tollway in what is now Schaumburg. In 1967 the Communications Division moved to this site, and in 1976 the company's corporate headquarters moved into a twelve-story office tower (fig. 14).[28]

In addition to buildings constructed by companies for their own use, there were speculative

Fig. 12 Distribution of labor force by place of work and residence, 1957; from Northeastern Illinois Metropolitan Area Planning Commission, A Social Geography of Metropolitan Chicago (Chicago, 1960), map 15.

Fig. 13 Shaw, Metz and Associates, Motorola, Inc., headquarters and plant, 9401 West Grand Avenue, Franklin Park, 1959.

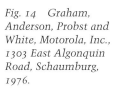

Fig. 14 Graham, Anderson, Probst and White, Motorola, Inc., 1303 East Algonquin Road, Schaumburg, 1976.

manufacturing buildings and industrial parks. While postwar parks dwarfed in scale any that had preceded them, they were surprisingly similar in form and appearance to earlier ones.[29] The largest of the immediate postwar parks was the giant Centex Industrial Park, at Elk Grove Village, just west of O'Hare Airport. It started with 650 acres in the early 1950s as a complement to the residential development that the Centex Company was doing nearby and expanded rapidly.[30] Other industrial parks appeared on all sides of the city.

Retail

In the retail area, most postwar shopping centers in Chicago, as in the United States generally, continued patterns established in the interwar periods. Most common was the strip of shops with parking on the street in front. As the scale increased, the single bar of shops gave way to an L or U shape with off-street parking in front. Sometimes these "strip centers" were rearranged in more complex configurations. This was the case at Lincoln Village, just north of the city, where the shops were concentrated in an L-shaped block with a lower triangular block set in the angle. Between the buildings were internal pedestrian streets and around them a large parking lot.[31]

Also L-shaped but much larger and accessible from two levels was Evergreen Plaza, located just southwest of the city. Opened in 1952 with some 500,000 square feet of retail space and 1,200 parking places, Evergreen Plaza served as a transition between the prewar neighborhood

centers and the regional centers of the mid-1950s, and it boasted a number of design and service innovations.[32]

A different kind of design was used almost simultaneously at the earliest large-scale postwar center, Park Forest Plaza, at the heart of the famous planned community (see Harris, fig. 9). Here architects Loebl, Schlossman and Bennett placed a landscaped court at the center of a ring of shops and surrounded the entire complex with parking. The court was conceived of as a modern analogy to the old village green.[33]

Nationwide, however, the model used at most of the large centers of the early postwar years was the city street. This was the case at the earliest really ambitious project for a regional center in the Chicago area. In 1951 Marshall Field and Company announced the results of a competition among four invited architectural firms for a site in Skokie. Each of the schemes included a "mall," a long, narrow central space with shops to either side, the whole surrounded by parking (fig. 15). Although historians have stressed how different the postwar shopping area was from earlier shopping configurations, the four projects indicate to what extent they, like all the other retail types of the postwar years, were continuations on a larger scale of earlier patterns. Here the model was clearly State Street.[34]

If it had been built, this center would have been the largest in the world, surpassing the pioneer American regional shopping centers such as Shoppers' World outside Boston or Northgate in Seattle, and surpassing the largest of the second generation of regional shopping centers, Northland in Detroit. In the end, however, none of the four schemes was built. When Marshall Field's and its partners could not agree upon a design, two competing centers—Old Orchard and Edens Plaza—were built in close proximity.[35] The larger of the two, Old Orchard Shopping Center, was built on the original competition site in Skokie but to new designs by Loebl, Schlossman and Bennett. Although designed with landscaped interior spaces like Park Forest Plaza, the spaces at Old Orchard were smaller and tighter, more reminiscent of an urban square than a village square. The courtyards featured sprightly landscape designs by California landscape architect Lawrence Halprin (see Harris, figs. 11, 12).[36] Before long, Old Orchard was itself surpassed in size when the more elegant Oakbrook Center, a product of the same design team, opened in 1962 (see Harris, fig. 13). In their single, uncluttered buildings and superb landscapes, Old Orchard and Oakbrook were among the most successful designs for postwar American centers.[37]

Fig. 15   Ketchum, Gina, and Sharp, Proposed scheme for Marshall Field's shopping center, Skokie; from Architectural Forum 95 (Dec. 1951), p. 189.

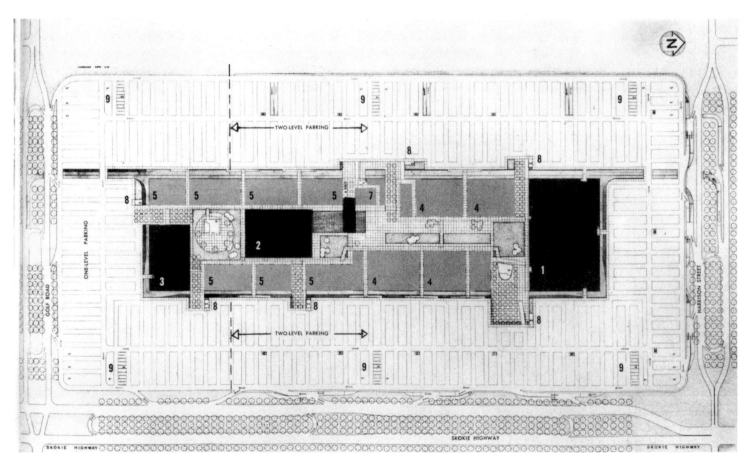

Fig. 16   Perkins and
Will, Pure Oil, Inc. (now
Unocal, Inc.),
Schaumburg, 1959-60.

Yet these early open-air centers were quickly considered old-fashioned once the new enclosed malls appeared in Chicago. At Southdale outside Minneapolis and at subsequent enclosed malls throughout the country, the streets and courts of earlier centers were made still tighter, more focused, and consciously more urban.[38] In Chicago by far the largest of these enclosed malls was Woodfield Mall in Schaumburg, which opened in 1971. With four department stores and over two hundred shops on its three levels, Woodfield remained for a number of years the largest shopping center in the world (see Harris, figs. 1, 18).[39]

Offices

During these same years the city witnessed the start of a major outward move of office activity. Although there was precedent for this kind of move in the interwar years in the case of offices or research laboratories connected to factories or other production facilities, many observers found it rather startling when large corporations with predominately white-collar workers, notably insurance companies, started to move their headquarters out of downtown office buildings into locations far from downtown. A major wave

Fig. 17   Aerial view of
central Oak Brook,
looking east, May 1989.

of corporate relocations in the mid-1950s was concentrated along Peterson Avenue on Chicago's Northwest Side and along Grand and North avenues in the near west suburbs.[40]

The second wave of headquarters moves followed hard on the heels of the completion of a number of the region's interstate highways in the late 1950s and early 1960s. Among the most prominent examples included the International Mining and Manufacturing Co. along the Tri-State Tollway in Skokie, the Sperry and Hutchinson Co. regional offices and Chicago Bridge and Iron Co. along the East-West Tollway in Hillside and Oak Brook, respectively, and United Airlines, near the Northwest Tollway in what is now Elk Grove Village.[41]

The move of Pure Oil (later Unocal) can provide a typical example. After extensive research on the costs of continuing to operate their large downtown headquarters building, on outlying alternatives, on what similar moves had done for other companies, and on the possible impact of the move on the existing employees, the company commissioned from architects Perkins and Will a spacious, one-story structure on a large tract of landscaped land with ample adjacent parking at the intersection of the new Northwest Tollway and Illinois 53 (later the I-290 extension) (fig. 16).[42]

The architects of most major outlying headquarters buildings were usually prominent local firms also heavily involved with prestigious buildings downtown. The landscaping was often entrusted to leading landscape architects, although not usually from the Chicago area. In the best examples, the results of the marriage of building and landscape have been spectacular. At the offices of Kemper Corporation in Long Grove, the low buildings were set into a landscaped park and a golf course.[43] At Baxter Travenol along the Tri-State in Deerfield, an elegant office block with a dramatic tension structure roof, designed by Skidmore, Owings and Merrill, was set into a splendid English park designed by Sasaki Associates (see pls. 90, 91).[44]

As large corporations started to move out along the superhighways, many other companies wanted to join them, creating a market for speculative office space. From early single buildings, these developments soon grew to clusters of two, three, and four buildings and more, and finally, by the early 1970s, into large, planned office parks that included linked office buildings, hotels, garages, and other amenities. Among the earliest of these multi-building complexes were the Concourse near the Edens Expressway in Skokie, the Oak Brook Executive Plaza in Oak Brook, and O'Hare Plaza near O'Hare Airport.[45]

Like the headquarters, speculative office development came in overlapping waves. The first wave included the Edens corridor between the city and Glencoe, the O'Hare area, and Oak Brook.[46] The most important center was Oak Brook (fig. 17). This business center was largely the creation of a single family, the Butlers, who over the previous decades had established substantial land holdings in the area.[47] When it was apparent that the Tri-State and East-West tollways would cross within or near the Butler properties, Paul Butler negotiated with the tollway authority to establish the route and commissioned a master plan to guide development. Oak Brook was intended from the start as a high-end, exclusive business address in keeping with the character of the planned neighboring residential areas.[48]

In 1958, the year the toll roads were finished, the village of Oak Brook was incorporated. Major corporations soon opened offices in the village, and Chicago Bridge and Iron established its headquarters there. Oakbrook Center followed in 1962. The entry of the Del E. Webb Co., a major contracting firm, into a partnership in 1964 marked the beginning of the intense phase of development in which some of Chicago's largest corporations were joined by hundreds of smaller firms (fig. 18). Oak Brook's business center has been immensely successful, so successful that it has spilled over into adjacent communities like Oakbrook Terrace and Downers Grove.[49]

The second wave of construction has followed the Tri-State Tollway north from Northbrook, the Northwest Tollway beyond O'Hare, and I-88 west of Oak Brook. The largest center in this wave was Schaumburg, and its growth has been even more meteoric than Oak Brook's.[50] Following Pure Oil was Motorola, which built an enormous complex just north of the tollway; Woodfield Mall; and many smaller industrial, retail, and office developments.[51]

Unlike Oak Brook, but like most fast-growing American business centers in the postwar years, Schaumburg was initially more a result of market forces than of conscious planning. But as in almost all these centers, once growth started to occur, planning by the municipality, the county, and regional planning bodies generally followed, in theory to guide long-term growth, though in actual practice merely to avoid the worst consequences of the erratic development patterns, excessive traffic congestion, and the other problems that have accompanied rapid growth in

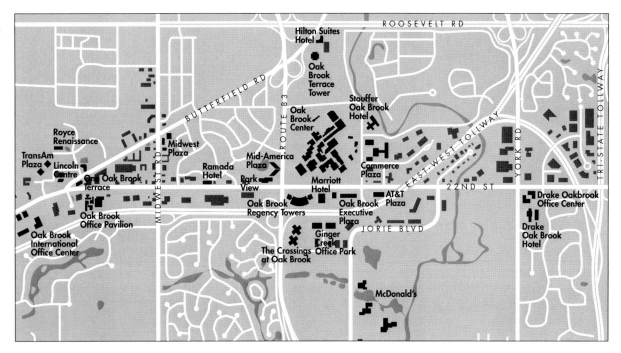

Fig. 18   Map of Oak Brook, showing location of office buildings and shopping centers, by Dennis McClendon, 1992.

almost every really successful urban area since the rise of the modern city.[52]

In addition to Oak Brook and Schaumburg, other metropolitan business centers have developed their own characters. In the area around O'Hare International Airport, in the northwest corner of the city of Chicago, and in adjacent Des Plaines and Rosemont, many developers have, not surprisingly, concentrated on businesses that need immediate access to the airport, as well as on hotels and convention trade (fig. 19). Along the I-88 corridor between Oak Brook and Aurora, on the other hand, particularly in the area of Naperville, so many of the region's high-tech firms have clustered that they have given Chicago its own "technoburb" (fig. 20).[53]

Periphery and Center

One of the most interesting results of the decentralization of the metropolitan area in the post-war years was its impact on the old central district. Partly because of conscious planning, but mostly as a result of complex market forces, the old central city in many ways started to emulate what was happening at the periphery. The urban

Fig. 19   Map of Rosemont/O'Hare area, showing location of office buildings and hotels, by Dennis McClendon, 1990.

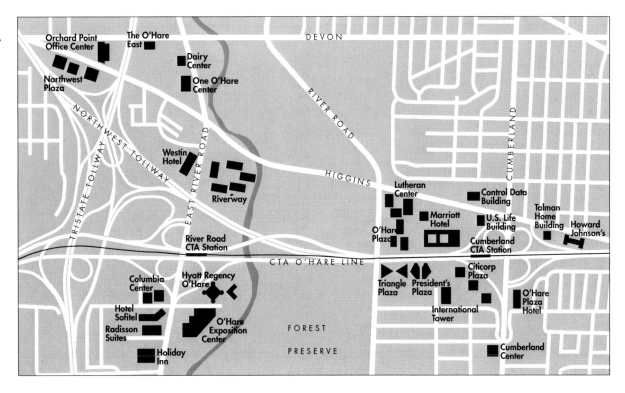

The Recentering of the Metropolitan Area   171

Fig. 20   Aerial view, looking east from West Street, Naperville, along the East-West Tollway (I-88), October 1988.

renewal and highway programs of the 1950s and 1960s were deliberate attempts to remake the fabric of the city center so that it could be more competitive with the outlying areas.[54] However much these programs have been criticized, it is quite likely that in many cases they ultimately achieved their intended goal, although often in ways that no one could have foreseen. The consolidation of property and the demolition of large areas of substandard buildings in and near the old Central Business District opened up new sites for development, and the creation of a network of new highways connected them to the airports and new centers farther out. It is also likely that these "urban removal" programs and the construction of highways into the existing fabric were prerequisites for the gentrification process that was also just starting to get underway in neighborhoods near the core. Without the removal of the "blighted" areas around the old core and without the highways that link the gentrifying neighborhoods to the airport and the rest of the region, it is unlikely that many middle-class professionals would have stayed in the city or that suburbanites would have joined them.

Other developments were even more specifically targeted at keeping downtown competitive with the outlying areas. The movement across the country to turn downtown shopping streets into pedestrian malls was a direct reaction to the

earliest suburban shopping centers. Perhaps the most dramatic of the early attempts in the Chicago area involved the Englewood shopping area at 63rd and Halsted streets where planners hoped that an efficient ring road carrying traffic

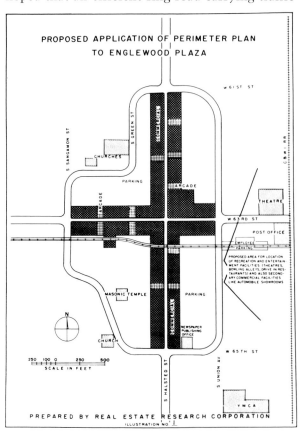

Fig. 21   Proposed application of Perimeter Plan to Englewood Plaza, 1953; from Real Estate Research Corporation, Perimeter Plan for Englewood Plaza: Economic and Legal Analysis (Chicago, 1953), opp. p.1.

around the shopping center, provision for increased parking at the periphery, and an interior
pedestrian core would revive the fortunes of what
had once been the largest shopping center outside the Loop (see fig. 21).[55] The plan's main features—the ring road, parking at the periphery,
and a pedestrian core—were all, not surprisingly,
similar to those found at outlying centers. Oak
Park put in a mall in 1974. Chicago's State Street
itself was malled in 1979, although it served as a
transit, rather than a purely pedestrian, mall.
None of these efforts, which were aimed at physical form rather than underlying ownership and
management patterns, proved to be successful.
Indeed, by reducing the hustle and bustle characteristic of the city street, they probably had a
detrimental effect.[56]

Chicago developers, on the other hand, seem
to have been successful in their response to the
second wave of outlying shopping centers. When
Water Tower Place opened in 1976 it represented
one of the earliest large downtown versions of
the suburban enclosed mall (see Harris, figs. 19-
22). Its ultimate source was an urban one, the
nineteenth-century arcade or galleria, but the
direct inspiration was the arcade as it had been
transformed at the periphery of the American
city in the 1960s and 1970s. It is likely that
Water Tower Place was successful in part because its developers and architects had worked

on outlying centers and had learned from them,
but also because they recognized that the new
downtown had to fill a different, more specialized market niche than it had in the earlier
twentieth century.[57]

III. Recent Decades

What has happened since the end of the economic downturn of the 1970s represents a speeding up and playing out on a larger scale of the
themes visible for at least a half century. Manufacturing plants, because they depend less and
less on rail lines and more on the superhighway
network, have tended to scatter. Some of the
largest new facilities are being built in what was
recently the country, but which has increasingly
come to be a zone that is neither urban nor rural
by traditional definitions. As heavy industry has
declined and high technology production has
taken its place, the need to separate industry
from other land uses has weakened. One result
has been the "business park," which houses
light manufacturing, warehousing, offices, and
retail establishments. In a way, the circle has
been closed. At the turn of the century, all of
these activities were housed in nearly identical
loft buildings near the center of downtown.
During the diaspora from the city, in the decades
before and after World War II, they segregated

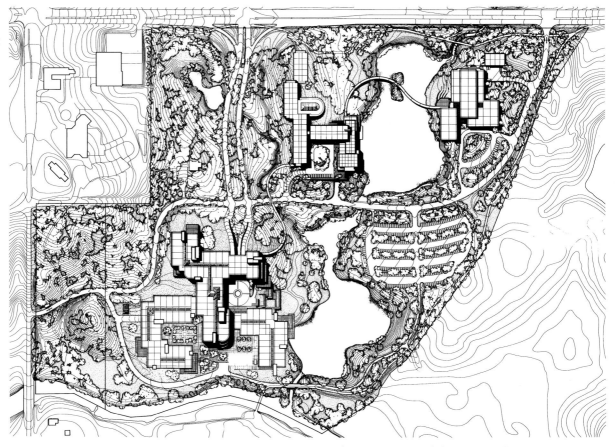

*Fig. 22 Lohan
Associates, McDonald's
Corporate Campus, Oak
Brook, site plan, 1979.*

The Recentering of the Metropolitan Area 173

themselves into office parks, industrial areas, and so on. Now, in many of the more recent business parks vast one- and two-story buildings have witnessed a return to multipurpose usage. The most impressive of the new business parks—Meridien Business Park in Aurora, for example—are enormous in size and often boast much higher levels of architectural and landscape design than any previous parks.[58]

Retail since the 1970s has continued its outward move but has tended to diversify. In some cases existing shopping centers have gotten larger and denser. The most remarkable example in the Chicago metropolitan area is Oakbrook Center, where the latest round of additions includes three shopping levels and structured parking of up to six levels. This has brought it an intensity of land use rivaling or even surpassing some of the country's largest downtown shopping districts. If at some shopping centers density has increased dramatically in much of the market the opposite has happened. Following the same logic that drove shopping out of the old downtowns, in the 1980s and early 1990s many shoppers started to find the regional malls too big and too crowded. They preferred driving to smaller shopping areas closer to home, especially the strip center, which had been popular in the early postwar period and has revived in popularity over the last decade. In fact, the strip center and the townhouse together best exemplify the convergence of periphery and center. Looking conspicuously similar whether two miles or forty-two miles from the Loop, they now constitute a great deal of the new fabric in the metropolitan area.

Construction for office purposes has followed the same path as retail. In many cases corporations have pushed for even larger, more heavily landscaped complexes. McDonald's, for example, on a prime site in Oak Brook, has commissioned a low, spreading set of buildings placed in a splendidly redesigned prairie and forest landscape (fig. 22).[59] Other companies are now jumping over Oak Brook and Schaumburg for still larger, less congested sites farther from the Loop. The forthcoming move of Spiegel's from Oak Brook to a bold high-rise building farther west along the I-88 tollway and the move of Ameritech (figs. 23, 24) and Sears from the city to enormous, lavishly landscaped campuses beyond Schaumburg on the I-90 corridor are symptomatic.

Although decentralization continues, a countervailing trend is also visible toward more urban-looking configurations. Perhaps the most

striking example of this is the thirty-one-story Oakbrook Terrace Tower, adjacent to Oak Brook. Here a telling sign of increasing land values is the extensive underground parking garage. Likewise, while many of the largest of the new office parks are farther out and less dense than ever, some have taken the opposite approach and have become more citylike and dense. At the Chancellory at Hamilton Lakes in Itasca, for example, the tight clustering of high-rise office buildings and hotels is clearly intended as an evocation of imagery from the traditional downtown.[60]

As with retail, the outlying office parks have had a major effect on developments downtown. The emphasis on new open space, fountains and trees, the addition of large parking decks, even the widespread use of reflecting glass, have all

Figs. 23, 24 Lohan Associates, Ameritech Center, Hoffman Estates, 1987-91.

made downtowns come to resemble the new outlying centers. Although they are intended by their designers to be specifically urban, projects like Cityfront Center, for example, are often strikingly similar in site plan and imagery to the largest and most intensive developments at the periphery. In both cases a mix of high- and low-rise buildings housing office, hotel, and related uses stands in a carefully managed, coordinated landscape.

The result of this complex process of decentralization and recentering has been to make the outlying areas more citylike and the old central district more like the new centers at the periphery. Although many observers might feel that this is a betrayal of the character of each, it is probably more accurate to say that it is merely the latest result of the process of continuous change and reciprocal relationships between center and periphery that is the American city.

NOTES

1. Among the individuals who read a manuscript version of this essay and provided me with important advice were Dennis McClendon of the American Planning Association, Wim Wiewel of the University of Illinois at Chicago, and Richard Longstreth of George Washington University. Tim Samuelson of the Chicago Commission on Historical and Architectural Landmarks was also very helpful. Information on Schaumburg is taken from the Chicago Fact Book Consortium, *Local Community Fact Book* (Chicago, 1984), and Village of Schaumburg, *Woodfield Regional Concept Plan* (1990). Office statistics here and elsewhere are from Frain, Camins and Swartchild, *Office Market Report* (Spring 1992). I am grateful to John Juroe of this company for providing me with this information.
2. The author's forthcoming book *The Center and the Park: The Decentralization and Reshaping of the City* will treat this subject in more detail, using examples from cities across the country and the world.
3. As recently as 1967, Chicago's Loop dominated the region in office space. At that time the Central Business District contained slightly over 43 million square feet of space, according to the Building Owners and Managers Association of Chicago. The figure for the entire

suburban metropolitan area was about just over 2 million, according to Continental Illinois National Bank and Trust Co., *Suburban Metropolitan Chicago Office Space* (Chicago, 1972). By the end of 1991 the figure for Chicago's Central Business District had jumped to just under 114 million, while the figures for the outlying areas had reached nearly 80 million with some 20 million in the Northwest, 15 million in the North, 4 million in the Southwest, 12.5 million near O'Hare, and 26 million in the West.
4. Serious studies appeared, particularly by geographers, but they did not reach a wide audience. Among the best were those concentrating on specific areas: for example, E. W. Kersten and D. R. Ross, "Clayton: A New Metropolitan Focus in the St. Louis Area," *Annals of the Association of American Geographers* 58 (Dec. 1968), pp. 637-49; and Thomas Baerwald, "Emergence of a New 'Downtown,'" *Geographical Review* 68 (Jan. 1978), pp. 308-18, on Bloomington, outside Minneapolis. The pioneer attempt to provide a framework for the new business centers was Peter O. Muller, "The Outer City: Geographical Consequences of the Urbanization of the Suburbs," *Association of American Geographers Resource Paper* 75, no. 2 (1976). Also good is Michael P. Conzen, "The Changing Character of Metropolitan Chicago," *Journal of Geography* (Sept./

Oct. 1986), pp. 224-36, and idem, "American Cities in Profound Transition: The New City Geography of the 1980s," *Journal of Geography* (May/June 1983).
5. More recently this has changed. Probably the best design magazine coverage has come from an issue of *Landscape Architecture* 78 (Dec. 1988) on "Edge Cities." *Architecture* 80 (Dec. 1991) also published an interesting issue on the topic.
6. Christopher B. Leinberger and Charles Lockwood, "How Business is Reshaping America," *Atlantic* (Oct. 1986), pp. 43-52; Robert Fishman, *Bourgeois Utopias: The Rise and Fall of Suburbia* (New York, 1987); Joel Garreau, *Edge City: Life on the New Frontier* (New York, 1991).
7. The main retail area located itself on State and Wabash streets; offices and government agencies settled on Dearborn, Clark, and LaSalle streets; and wholesale and light manufacturing took over the central area west of Wells Street.
8. In the development of these large industrial districts and industrial parks, Chicago led the world in much of the late nineteenth and early twentieth centuries. On Chicago's industrial parks, see the entries for the Central Manufacturing District and the Clearing Industrial District in Urban Land Institute, "Planned Industrial Districts," *Technical Bulletin*, no. 19 (Oct.

1952). On the Clearing Industrial District, see also "The Richest Subdivision in the U.S.," *Architectural Forum* 65 (July 1936), pp. 66-70. The Central Manufacturing District was located south of Pershing Road between Ashland and Western avenues; the Clearing Industrial District was located in an area that is just outside the city limits of Chicago, south of 65th Street between Cicero and Harlem avenues, now Bedford Park.

9. Information on Motorola facilities was generously supplied by Eric Schuster, researcher at the Motorola Museum of Electronics. The blue and white terra-cotta building at 4545 West Augusta Boulevard provided 85,000 square feet of space for the manufacture of automobile and household radios; see *Chicago Sunday Tribune* (Dec. 27, 1936), p. 44. According to Schuster, the inspiration for the design came from a trip that founder Paul Galvin made to the 1933-34 Century of Progress Exposition. For further information on Motorola buildings before World War II, see *The Facilities of Motorola*, issued by the company in 1947, a copy of which is in the Motorola Museum of Electronics in Schaumburg.

10. The way statistics are collected usually reflects the prevailing attitudes of the organizations that collect them. Industrial jobs, for example, have usually been counted by municipality, but this gives little indication of how these jobs moved in the city or how they grouped themselves outside it. The obsession of urban historians with urban-suburban rivalries in the postwar years has exacerbated this problem. For the situation in Chicago in the 1940s, see Leonard Z. Breen, "Separation of Place of Work from Place of Residence in the City of Chicago" (Ph.D. diss., University of Chicago, 1950). A very good summary of information on what we know about job locations from 1947 to 1980 can be found in Marcus Alexis and John F. McDonald, "The Changing Economy of Metropolitan Chicago: Past, Present, and Future," in P. Nardulli, ed., *Diversity, Conflict, and State Politics* (Urbana, Ill., 1989), pp. 146-75. According to the authors' calculations, there were 668,000 manufacturing jobs in the city in 1947 and 189,000 in the suburbs. By 1980 this had changed dramatically, with the city counting only 314,000 and the suburbs 494,000. But these raw numbers give little indication of where these jobs were. Several attempts at graphic presentation are more helpful. Figure 5, above, for example, from Miller McClintock, *Report and Recommendations of the Metropolitan Street Traffic Survey* (Chicago, 1926), shows large job concentrations in the city.

11. Chicago City Council, Committee on Traffic Regulation and Public Safety, *A Memorandum and Preliminary Report with Reference to Elevated Highways for the Chicago Metropolitan Area* (Chicago, 1928); Chicago City Council, Committee on Traffic Regulation and Public Safety, *A Limited Way Plan for the Greater Chicago Traffic Area* (Chicago, 1933).

12. The story of Chicago's expressways has never been adequately documented. There is a sketch in Chicago Department of Public Works, *Chicago Public Works: A History* (Chicago, 1973), pp. 155-68. The best sources remain two expressway studies: Chicago Department of Superhighways, *A Comprehensive Superhighway Plan for the City of Chicago* (Chicago, 1939); Chicago Plan Commission, *Proposed Expressway Development Program (Initial Stage) for the City of Chicago* (Chicago, Dec. 1943). See also the essay by R. Stephen Sennott in the present volume.

13. The most famous of these was Wilshire Boulevard in Los Angeles with its branch of Bullock's Department store and the Miracle Mile.

14. On North Michigan Avenue, see John W. Stamper, *Chicago's North Michigan Avenue: Planning and Development, 1900-1930* (Chicago, 1991).

15. The most vigorous of the early chain stores were F. W. Woolworth and S. S. Kresge, but chain stores of all kinds burgeoned in the 1920s. Some department stores, notably moderately priced Goldblatt Brothers and Wieboldt's, were primarily regional stores that opened up downtown branches only later. According to Richard Longstreth of George Washington University, these stores were exceptional among American regional stores in size and importance. Very interesting figures for retail sales at outlying centers can be found in Gerald William Breese, "The Daytime Population of the Central Business District of Chicago" (Ph.D. diss., University of Chicago, 1947), p. 26.

16. On Englewood, see "Englewood," *Chicago Daily News* (July 4, 1929), p. 31; and "Englewood a Merchandising Center," *Economist* (2nd half, 1928), p. 689. On the history of city and suburban neighborhood shopping centers before World War II, see also Morton Bodfish and Homer Hoyt, "The New Shopping Centers in the Chicago Region" in *Savings and Homeownership* (Sept. 1955), a newsletter issued by First Federal Savings; and Malcolm J. Proudfoot, "The Major Outlying Business Centers of Chicago" (Ph.D. diss., University of Chicago, 1936).

17. Homer Hoyt, "Sales in Leading Shopping Centers and Shopping Districts in the United States," *Urban Land* (Sept. 1961). The regional shopping areas in the city together had a larger volume of business and number of employees than the Loop. According to Alexis and McDonald (note 10), the Central Business District in 1948 accounted for only 65,000 jobs in retail compared to 184,000 for the rest of the city.

18. Both Marshall Field's and Wieboldt's opened stores in Evanston and Oak Park in the late 1920s. Oak Park also had a branch of The Fair store.

19. On Market Square, see Susan Dart, *Market Square* (Lake Forest, Ill., 1984).

20. Spanish Court was designed in 1926 as a group of shops, restaurants, apartments, and a theater. The developers and their architect, Edwin H. Clark, consciously designed the Spanish colonial-style complex as an exclusive retail area with provision for a high percentage of customers arriving by automobile. A history of Plaza del Lago can be found in Robert Shea, *From No Man's Land to Plaza del Lago* (Chicago, 1987), pp. 32-46.

21. Unfortunately, as stated above (see note 10), statistics for employment in the Loop as opposed to outside the Loop are very sporadic before the postwar years. From 1972 onward there are statistics in Lawrence B. Joseph, ed., *Creating Jobs, Creating Workers* (Chicago, 1990), table 6.

22. The strikingly modernistic Searle factory, designed by architect Herbert G. Banse, was built to aid medical research in new areas like chemotherapy, and also included executive offices; see Kenneth Reid, ed., *Industrial Buildings: The Architectural Record of a Decade* (New York, 1951), p. 187. According to Geoff Fleet of Searle's Central File Department, the company had started out on Wells Street in the Loop and had moved to Ravenswood in the 1920s before constructing this building on Searle Parkway. Plans and drawings, as well as a short history and description of the building, are contained in a special issue of the company's publication, *The Searle Circle* 4, no. 4 (July 1941). The Jewel building is described in Robert Bruegmann, *Holabird and Roche and Holabird and Root: An Illustrated Catalog of Works, 1880-1940* (New York and London, 1991), vol. 3, p. 7. These volumes contain a great many projects, many of them built, for new industrial and commercial buildings in the outlying areas of Chicago.

23. The stereotype that the postwar suburbs were homogeneous was a creation of city dwellers. From the point of view of many informed observers of the postwar years, one of the major problems with the suburbs was just how diverse they had become. In its 1960 report entitled *A Social Geography of Metropolitan Chicago*, the Northeastern Illinois Metropolitan Area Planning Commission noted that a mass of new commuters added to the already existing residents had created hybrid communities: "Until 1940," the report continued, "suburbs were, by and large, remarkably stable and relatively homogeneous communities, with a nice mixture of local and metropolitan functions. This stable and homogeneous social structure has been rudely shaken, whether by the massive infusion of new residents without a parallel growth of services and facilities, or the introduction of large industrial plants and shopping centers in dormant residential communities." The report went on to create six classifications of suburbs, ranging from dormitory suburbs to manufacturing suburbs.

24. In fact, the effects of these two events, while very dramatic in Chicago and other old industrial cities of the Northeast and Midwest, were much less clearly felt in the newer cities of the South and West, where, despite the slowdown caused by economic crisis and war, the outward movement of population and business did not stop. On the continuity of decentralization, see Homer Hoyt, "Forces of Decentralization in Chicago," *Savings and Homeownership* (July 1953).

25. While it is true that the automobile had an effect on development patterns, the notion that the postwar outlying communities became possible because the family wage-earner could drive to work and thus no longer needed to live near public transit lines is misleading. Most Americans in major cities in the postwar period did not drive from home into the old Central Business Districts. If they worked downtown they were more likely to take public transit. When they drove to work they were more often driving to jobs that were located well outside the Loop. An excellent documentation of this process can be found in Robert Blythe, "Morton Grove, Illinois, and 1950s Metropolitan Development" (Master's thesis, University of Illinois at Chicago, 1992).

26. On postwar industry, see City of Chicago, Department of City Planning, *Industrial Movements and Expansions, 1947-1957*, Economic Base Study Series, no. 3 (Chicago, 1961). A good survey of some of the new industrial plants can be found in "Chicago Industrial Growth to Continue at Record Pace," *Commerce* (June 1957), pp. 52ff.

27. The administration building was designed by Shaw, Metz and Dolio. At the time of its completion Motorola believed that the building was the largest combined development/production headquarters facility in the United States. See pamphlet issued by the company entitled *Administration Building*, in the collections of the Motorola Museum. The Franklin Park facility is now owned by the Matsuhita Company.

28. The Motorola headquarters was designed by Graham, Anderson, Probst and White.

29. Although prefabricated parts, tilt-up concrete panels, and open bar joists replaced the old masonry structures, the general configuration of the buildings and the layout of the parks were similar to those built before the war.

30. Very little has been published on Centex Industrial Park despite the frequently made claim that it was the largest of its type in the world. According to Louis Kahnweiler, partner of the real estate brokerage firm of Bennett and Kahnweiler, his firm brought together Centex and the Pritzker family of Chicago to develop the park, the original portion of which was located between Busse Highway and Elmhurst Road, from Devon Avenue on the south to Landmeier Road on the north. Eventually, land acquired by General Electric was added. Interview with Louis Kahnweiler, May 9, 1991. Together with other parks in the area, Centex forms part of an immense belt of low industrial buildings around the south and west sides of O'Hare. On Centex, see Harold M. Mayer, "Centex Industrial Park: An Organized Industrial District," in Richard S. Thoman and Donald J. Patton, eds., *Focus on Geographic Activity: A Collection of Original Studies* (New York, 1964).

31. On Lincoln Village, designed by Howard T. Fisher and Associates and opened in 1951, see Geoffrey Baker and Bruno Funaro, *Shopping Centers: Design and Operation* (New York, 1952), p. 137. Good lists and statistics on Chicago's postwar shopping centers can be found in publications issued by the city's newspapers, for example, *Chicago's Major Shopping Areas*, published by the *Chicago Tribune* in 1971.

32. Evergreen Plaza was developed by Arthur Rubloff, who reportedly had conceived the idea in 1936 and spent $100,000 in studies before settling on the site at 95th Street and Western Avenue. The center contained branches of The Fair store and Carson, Pirie, Scott and Company, offered long opening hours, and featured a conveyor belt that delivered groceries from the supermarkets to a parking-area kiosk. On Evergreen Plaza, see "This One Stop Center Drew More than a Million Shoppers in the First Six Weeks," *Journal of Property Management* (Dec. 1952), pp. 85-91; and Baker and Funaro (note 31), pp. 118-21. See also Arthur W. Rubloff, "The Problem of Organizing a Shopping Center," and Howard T. Fisher, "The Development of Planned

Shopping Centers," in Chicago Chapter, American Institute of Planners, *Regional Shopping Centers* (Chicago, 1952), pp. 1-7, 23-30.

33. On Park Forest Plaza, constructed between 1947 and 1950, there has been surprisingly little written. See "Park Forest Illinois: Proving Ground for Community Planning Techniques," *Architectural Record* 109 (May 1951), pp. 95-115; and Rita Caviglia, *Design for Better Living: The Architecture of Richard Marsh Bennett, 1937-1973* (Cambridge, Mass., 1984) pp. 42-43. The best source of information consists of a number of transcribed interviews, one with Richard Bennett in August 1980 at the Park Forest Library, another in December 1978 between Tom McDade and Norman Schlossman in the files of Loebl, Schlossman and Hackl.

34. According to "Marshall Field's New Shopping Center," *Architectural Forum* (Dec. 1951), pp. 185-99, the four invited architects for the new Marshall Field's center, after all of their studies and calculations, produced designs that "turned out to be State Street all over again: their carefully studied pattern of store location (which gently graded from high-priced stores on the north to low-priced stores on the south) turned out to duplicate, to an amazing degree, the retailing pattern set up in downtown Chicago by a century of natural competition. But it was State Street with snarling traffic replaced by grass and trees, and, by every economy and artifice of contemporary design, cut down to half the weary length a determined comparative shopper would have to traverse downtown" (p. 185).

35. Carson, Pirie, Scott and Company went into the Edens Plaza in Wilmette just north of the Marshall Field's site.

36. On Old Orchard, see Victor Gruen and Larry Smith, *Shopping Towns USA: The Planning of Shopping Centers* (New York, 1960), pp. 224-25. For comparative figures as of 1958, see Homer Hoyt, "Sales in Leading Shopping Centers and Shopping Districts in the United States," *Urban Land* (Sept. 1961). Sales at Old Orchard in this year still fell short of those at established regional shopping districts such as Englewood.

37. On Richard Bennett's architectural designs, see Caviglia (note 33), pp. 42-51. On the landscape design, see San Francisco Museum of Art, *Lawrence Halprin: Changing Places* (San Francisco, 1986), pp. 120, 123.

38. On the urban character of the enclosed mall, see the testimony of Victor Gruen, the designer of Southdale and the most important architect in the development of this kind of center, in Gruen and Smith (note 36).

39. On Woodfield, designed by Jickling and Lyman of Detroit, see Louis G. Redstone, *New Dimensions in Shopping Centers and Stores* (New York, 1973), pp. 18-19; and Franz Schulze, "Enormous Woodfield Mall, Super-Package With Parking," *Inland Architect* 17 (Jan. 1973), pp. 8-11. In 1980 Woodfield registered $348 million in sales compared to $242 million at Oak Brook, the area's second largest center, $169 million at Old Orchard, which had fallen to sixth place, and $145 million at Evergreen Plaza, according to the *Directory of Shopping Centers in the United States*, 21st ed. (Chicago, 1980).

40. Among the important new corporate headquarters on the Northwest Side of Chicago were Commerce Clearing House and Walgreen Drugs, both on Peterson Avenue. In the near west and north suburbs were Universal Oil Products in Des Plaines by Olsen and Urbain and Jewel Tea Company in Melrose Park by A. Epstein and Sons. Among the most prominent speculative buildings was Edens Plaza near the interchange of the Edens Expressway and Peterson Avenue. Insurance companies were widely spread around the metropolitan area. An excellent example is the Aetna Life Insurance Company's regional offices on Northwest Highway in Park Ridge.

41. The International Mining and Manufacturing buildings were by Perkins and Will; the Sperry and Hutchinson complex by A. Epstein and Sons; and the United Airlines Headquarters by Skidmore, Owings and Merrill. On the latter, see Skidmore, Owings and Merrill, *Architecture of Skidmore, Owings and Merrill, 1950-1962* (New York, 1963), p. 186. Both the International Mining and United buildings are discussed in chapter 3 of Carl W. Condit, *Chicago, 1930-1970:*

Building, Planning, and Urban Technology (Chicago, 1974).

42. Unocal company archives in Schaumburg contain detailed records of all the studies. According to a popular misconception, companies often moved at the whim of a chief executive who wanted to be nearer his country club. This might have happened in the case of one or two companies, but the Pure Oil experience is almost certainly the norm.

43. Kemper, which opened in one building in 1971, was designed by Chicago architects Childs and Smith, with the landscape by Clauss Brothers of Roselle. According to Chuck Meinhardt, director of community relations, the company moved to the site because it was to have been adjacent to the Illinois 53 superhighway. Subsequently, road opponents blocked this stretch of road for decades. The Kemper site involved a pioneer case of wetlands conservation, according to Ian Stevenson of Clauss.

44. On Baxter Travenol, see Skidmore, Owings and Merrill, *Skidmore, Owings and Merrill: Architecture and Urbanism, 1973-1983* (New York, 1983), p. 130.

45. *Suburban Metropolitan Chicago Office Space* (note 3).

46. The two waves discussed here follow the major divisions used by Continental Illinois National Bank in its *Suburban Metropolitan Chicago Office Space* (note 3).

47. There is amazingly little literature on most postwar suburbs. For Oak Brook there is even less than usual since it was so tightly controlled by private individuals. There is a brief history of the village and planning in the current plan, "Comprehensive Plan, Village of Oak Brook," June 1990, and in an interesting manuscript history, "Notes on the History of Oak Brook," by Richard Alan Barton.

48. The village of Oak Brook does not appear to own this plan. Presumably copies still exist in private hands. According to "Oak Brook: The Spectacular 200 Million Dollar Suburb," a magazine insert in the *Chicago Tribune* (Sept. 17, 1961), the plan was the work of Col. Raulin B. Wight, an officer in the U. S. Army Corps of Engineers and an engineering consultant; Carl L. Gardner, former director of the Chicago Plan Commission, then a city planning and site planning consultant; James C. Downs, chairman of the board of Real Estate Research Corp.; and Alfred Shaw, a partner at the Chicago firm of Shaw, Metz and Associates. Surprisingly little has been written about the founding or the planning of Oak Brook. One good anecdotal source of information can be found in Barton (note 47); see also Robert Cassidy, "Planning for Polo, Not People," *Planning* (April/May 1974), pp. 34-37.

49. In 1992 Oak Brook itself had slightly over 6 million square feet of office space, Oakbrook Terrace over 3 million, and Downers Grove 2.5 million. Among the companies headquartered there, according to the *Chicago Tribune's* listing of Chicago's top 100 companies (with their ranking among Chicago corporations) were: Waste Management (3), McDonald's Corp. (5), Chemical Waste Management Inc. (15), Wheelabrator Technologies (25), CBI Industries (42), Spiegel Inc. (55), and Federal Signal (59). The forthcoming move of Spiegel to a dramatic new headquarters building further west along the tollway is a good indication of the challenge Oak Brook faces as it has become largely built out.

50. The best history of Schaumburg yet written is Connie Fletcher, "We Have Seen the Future and it is Schaumburg," *Chicago* (Nov. 1978), pp. 156ff. See also Village of Schaumburg and Camiros Ltd., *Managing the Growth of Schaumburg* (1980); Anthony Monahan, "Schaumburg — The View from Supersuburb," *Chicago Sun-Times Midwest Magazine* (Feb. 27, 1972), pp. 13ff; and "A New Kind of Town, Fiercely Independent, Thrives Near Chicago," *Wall Street Journal* (Feb. 10, 1978), p. 1.

51. Schaumburg has attracted a somewhat different set of users than Oak Brook. Although it counts Motorola, one of America's largest companies, among its companies, for example, it is conspicuous that the Motorola offices adjoin a large manufacturing facility that would not have been allowed in Oak Brook. In addition to Motorola, according to the *Chicago Tribune*

list of the 100 largest Chicago area companies, Schaumburg is listed as headquarters for Santa Fe Pacific Corp. (27).

52. Planning in the Chicago region has been notoriously fragmented since there are so many governmental entities. The Chicago area has had a regional planning body, the Northeast Illinois Planning Council, for decades, but this group is an advisory body. While it has proved effective at some issues of coordination, its major planning initiatives, for example, the well known document, *Diversity within Order: Coordinated Development for a Better Environment* (Chicago, 1967), have not been influential. This plan advocated fingers of development following the old rail lines. This plan was probably obsolete before it was even issued since development has tended to ignore the railroads and follow the superhighways.

53. The development of this corridor has been studied by Michael Ebner of Lake Forest College. See his unpublished paper, "Creating Chicago's Technoburb in Naperville, 1945-90," delivered at the annual meeting of the American Historical Association, December 1990.

54. On this, see City of Chicago, Department of City Planning, *Development Plan for the Central Area of Chicago* (Chicago, 1958). Plans were produced for many areas of the city. Among the flood of documents produced by the Chicago Plan Commission and other official bodies, see, for example, Chicago Plan Commission, *Calumet Industrial District: A Preface to a Comprehensive Development Plan* (Chicago, 1942), or South Side Planning Board, *An Opportunity to Rebuild Chicago through Industrial Development on the Central South Side* (Chicago, 1953).

55. Englewood managed to maintain its importance for over a decade into the postwar period, but it started to slip badly in the 1960s. Although competition from outlying shopping centers had a major impact, it is also likely that the establishment of the pedestrian mall by the city helped speed its decline. The racial disturbances of the late 1960s sealed its fate. In 1958 it had $75 million in annual sales and was the largest business center outside the Loop, surpassing all the early suburban centers. By 1972 its sales had barely increased to $79 million, while those at Evergreen Plaza had reached $130 million. By that time Englewood had slipped well behind many suburban centers and was on the verge of losing its position in Chicago. Continental Bank, Area Development Division, *Neighborhood Shopping Facilities, City of Chicago* (Chicago, 1979). On the Englewood renewal project, see Chicago Plan Commission, *Perimeter Plan for Rehabilitation of Major Shopping Centers* (Chicago, June 1953); see also Real Estate Research Corporation, *Perimeter Plan for Englewood Plaza: Economic and Legal Analysis* (Chicago, 1953).

56. For a summary of current thinking on the pedestrian mall, see Lawrence O. Houstoun, Jr., "From Street to Mall and Back Again," *Planning* (June 1990), pp. 4-10.

57. The developers of Water Tower Place were Marshall Field and Company and the Urban Investment and Development Co., two of the most active players in Chicago's outlying malls, and the architects were Loebl, Schlossman, Bennett and Dart, the firm that had been responsible for Park Forest Plaza, Oakbrook, and Old Orchard. Associated architects at Water Tower Place were C. F. Murphy Associates and, for the interiors, Warren Platner Associates. See "The Seven Level Shopping Mall at Water Tower Place: A Try for a Revolution in Retailing," *Architectural Record* 159 (April 1976), pp. 136-40.

58. The master planning and lush landscaping for the 660-acre Meridien Business Park was done by the SWA Group of Sausalito, California.

59. On McDonald's, see Robert Bruegmann, "The Corporate Landscape," *Inland Architect* 33 (Sept./Oct. 1989), pp. 33-42.

60. On the evolution of the denser office park, see Robert Bruegmann, "The New Main Street," *Inland Architect* 34 (Nov./Dec. 1990), pp. 34-41. On Oakbrook Terrace Tower, see Blair Kamin, "Shall We Dance? The Suburban Context of Oakbrook Terrace Tower," *Inland Architect* 32 (Nov./Dec. 1988), pp. 52-57.

The City That Shops:
Chicago's Retailing Landscape

Neil Harris

The retail store is the jazzman, the hawker, the pitch-man, the titillator—the essence of a capitalistic, materialistic society. It is satiating, entertaining, and subservient to the physical, social, and psychological needs of the shopping public. It is expected to be pretentious, frivolous, and fun.

William R. Green, *The Retail Store* (1986)[1]

Statistics tell much of the story. In the Roaring Twenties, when the proverbial Chicago of gangster violence, jazz, and exuberant growth epitomized much in the national mood, the city contained 75% of the residents in the metropolitan area. But decennial census data have revealed Chicago's steadily eroding central population base: 71% in 1930, 69% in 1940, 64% in 1950, 52% in 1960, and only 44% in 1970. Retail sales have followed the same direction. Just before the Great Crash, the city of Chicago accounted for some 78% of the $2.7 billion generated annually by retailing; twenty years later it was 71%; by 1965, barely over 50%; and by 1972, approximately 40%. If before World War II retail sales had somewhat exaggerated the city's population, now they began to understate it.[2]

Such an enormous shift of people, capital, and merchandising over a fifty-year period sounded the broadest themes of local history and established many of the basic conditions for the development of its landscape. The relative decline of the city was most dramatic, however, within a tighter time frame; between 1950 and the mid-1970s, Chicago's share of many economic activities was cut in half. During this same period, while suburban retail sales increased six times, city retailing did not even manage to double.

The drama—and the dream—of retailing captured postwar America's uneasy infatuation with the credit card and the shopping mall (fig. 1). On the national scene they set much of the social agenda, and the steadily enlarged cultural role of consuming in American life can be tracked in the dominant status accorded shopping places in debates over urban renewal. The massive investments and striking settings that exploited the shopping habit in the 1960s and 1970s served as a rhetorical rehearsal for the America of the 1980s, forecasting the apparent triumph of a new political sensibility. For this reason alone, but for others also, the evolution of Chicago's retail landscape merits attention.

There had been writing on the walls even in the 1920s, by which time Chicago retailing had divided into three main sectors.[3] First of all, there was the nationally celebrated strip of department stores lining State Street, a series of mercantile palaces largely completed before the outbreak of World War I (fig. 2). Straddling the hub of a great mass-transit web, abutting specialized centers on neighboring streets—for jewelry, furniture, or musical instruments (fig. 3)—close by financial, media, entertainment, and professional districts, the big stores exemplified American urban life and helped set the physical pattern for hundreds of others on the country's major shopping streets.

A second sector of smaller centers and ribbon strips served many of the city's neighborhoods. Exploiting their relationship to rapid transit, particularly to streetcars and the "El," these clusters of department stores, bakeries, restaurants, clothiers, food markets, shoe stores, cinemas, pharmacies, and furniture, hardware, and specialty shops met the basic needs of large numbers of Chicagoans, who saw no reason to travel downtown regularly to make their purchases (see Bouman, fig. 5). In 1936 Malcolm J. Proudfoot identified twenty major neighborhood centers, widely spaced throughout the city, and he estimated that 50% of the city's population lived within a mile of at least one of them.[4] Halsted and 63rd, Broadway and Wilson, Madison and Crawford, and 63rd and Cottage Grove were bustling nodes of commercial activity (figs. 4, 5). Generally less self-conscious architecturally than the great downtown retailers, these neighborhood centers grew by accretion, incorporating mass-produced ornament and standardized store fronts into their building complexes.

In this they contrasted with a third, more recent zone, largely confined to a new luxury

Fig. 1   Jickling, Lyman and Powell, Woodfield Mall, Schaumburg, 1970-71.

shopping strip that was making its appearance on North Michigan Avenue. Encouraged by construction of the Michigan Avenue Bridge (part of Daniel H. Burnham's great 1909 Plan for the city), the elegant hotels, apartment houses, restaurants, and specialty shops that multiplied in the twenties recalled to some the pleasures of London, Paris, and Vienna (figs. 6, 7).[5] Extending all the way north on Michigan Avenue to the Drake Hotel and south to the Congress and Stevens hotels, were fine shops with famous names and elaborate facades. Many caught the sumptuous look of the moderne style.

On the eve of the Great Depression, Chicago merchants had thus achieved three principal retailing modes: working-class and mass taste served in convenient neighborhood centers; wealthier, socially self-conscious clients handled in Michigan Avenue's specialty shops; and, for purchases large and small, classes and masses, the State Street department stores. These last, combining competitive prices and handsome appointments, were particularly successful. In 1923, when Stevens Brothers purchased the Columbus Memorial and Venetian buildings on the southeast corner of State and Washington streets at a rate of more than $300 a square foot, the Loop proclaimed itself America's most valuable retail location, surpassing even the northwest corner of Fifth Avenue and 42nd Street in New York.[6]

Of the three sectors, the Loop was the most vulnerable as well as the most valuable, because of its intimate linkage to fixed transportation networks. But when automobiles began to replace trains, buses, and streetcars as favored instruments of travel, problems surfaced. The most dramatic of these was the parking crisis. In 1911 Chicago contained only 12,000 licensed automobiles; fifteen years later almost 100,000 vehicles were entering the central area in a single twelve-hour day.[7] Even the Depression could not halt the explosion. By 1940 the ratio of cars to people in Chicago was approximately 1:6.

Responses were made, however. Central Chicago offered 14,000 garage spaces in 1929; a year earlier the city had actually prohibited Loop parking during working days, encouraging use of the new Chicago Park District lots.[8] Compared with what came later, the streets were not so terrible, but the popularity of the automobile indicated that customers of choice might change their shopping habits if habitually inconvenienced.

Retailers made adjustments as well. Sears, Roebuck and Company, the great mail-order house that began its retailing operations as late as 1925, initiated a series of neighborhood branches. Its eighth Chicago store, 220,000 square feet in size, opened in the fall of 1938 in Irving Park, at the intersection of Milwaukee, Cicero, and Irving Park Road. With what Sears declared to be the "largest display window in the city," forty by twenty-three feet, the poured-concrete store eschewed elaborate ornamental detail in favor of a rather austere frame that relied upon the merchandise display to make its argument (see pl. 94).[9] Wieboldt's opened its sixth Chicago-area store in River Forest in 1937—claimed as the largest suburban store in the world (fig. 8) —while Montgomery Ward, another merchandiser catering to price-conscious consumers, also expanded its department store operations.[10]

But these policies were not typical, and they certainly did not concentrate on the center city. Stagnation was a more general rule. The Great Depression and World War II disguised changes in the urban landscape. While auto ownership increased, highway construction and new commercial buildings were delayed, and gas rationing curtailed full exploitation of the car. Planners and architects were aware that something fundamental was happening, but they did not always agree about what it was. In 1945 William T. Snaith of Raymond Loewy Associates acknowledged that there was significant movement from city to suburb, but he argued that urban departures would "have nowhere near the acceleration of the shift to the city, and in a great many cases will not be very appreciable." Cities, he predicted, stood an excellent chance of holding on to their wartime growth—principally from rural areas—and he foresaw suburban branches that would be outpost or ambassador stores, subordinates of the main downtown centers.[11]

Others saw the changes differently. Thus, *Architectural Forum* in May 1943 featured twenty proposals for a town center's Main Street. "Downtown merchants are becoming concerned with the loss of trade to new shopping areas where parking is less of a problem," it observed. "Tax officials and investors are disturbed by the likelihood of further declines in downtown real estate."[12] These two thoughts would be repeated with some frequency and increasing desperation during the next several decades. The *Architectural Forum* program requirement, providing all structures with "adequate off-street parking," suggested an awareness of things to come, as did Victor Gruen's prescient proposal to create large shopping centers with covered walks and "protection from automobile traffic."[13]

Fig. 2   View of State Street, looking south from Jackson Street, c. 1920, showing the Rothschild (later Goldblatt's) Store (Holabird and Roche, 1912).

Fig. 3   View of Wabash Avenue music district, including Baldwin Piano Co. and Rudolph Wurlitzer Co., 323-25 and 329-31 South Wabash Avenue, c. 1918.

Fig. 4   Dubin and Dubin, Marks Clothing Store, 6409 South Halsted Street, 1935.

Fig. 5   Dubin and Dubin, Newart Clothing Store, 6345 South Halsted Street, 1935.

Fig. 6   View of North
Michigan Avenue,
c. 1929, showing at right
the Michigan-Superior
Building, 737 North
Michigan Avenue,
1928-29, designed by
Andrew N. Rebori.

Fig. 7   Holabird and
Root, Michigan Square
Building, 540 North
Michigan Avenue,
1928-29 (photo 1955).

By the early 1950s the stage was set throughout the country for a struggle whose broad implications were clearly understood, not only by many merchants but by other urban business interests. In the first five years of the decade, a total of seven plaza shopping centers was opened in the Chicago metropolitan region; but between 1955 and 1960 thirty-five came on the scene. Between 1950 and 1959 planned centers in the United States grew from 100 to 4,500, and in Chicago from 1 to 42. Two years later there were more than 60.[14]

Among the first urban institutions to acknowledge publicly the gravity of the changes were the city's daily newspapers, the ancient partners of the downtown stores. The big department stores had been the mainstays of advertising linage; in 1934, during the depths of the Depression, the downtown stores were spending more than $7 million annually on Chicago newspaper advertising.[15] Twenty years later metropolitan dailies saw with dismay their bastions crumbling. The issue was whether to oppose or make their peace with the suburban centers. "No greater challenge has ever faced newspaper promotion departments," wrote *Editor and Publisher* in 1954, than that thrown up "by the tremendous growth and development of suburban shopping centers. The challenge is to do what they can to keep downtown shopping centers alive."[16] In Detroit, Cincinnati, Louisville, and Boston, newspapers sponsored research into consumer buying patterns, and they jointly sponsored (with Central Business District associations) aggressive campaigns to focus public attention on the appeals of the downtown. Special festivals garnered lots of free advertising to emphasize downtown's concentrated varieties.[17]

The new suburban centers were not yet heavy advertisers; indeed, some writers suggested they were free-loading on the backs of downtown merchants.[18] This charge was partly true because the big downtown stores, sensing the future, were opening large branches to form their own competition. In Detroit the paradox was particularly acute: its major commercial institution, Hudson's, was simultaneously leading a crusade to save the downtown and profiting from the suburban exodus by developing several of Victor Gruen's influential new suburban complexes.

Like the Detroit merchants, Chicagoans also expressed anxiety about their downtown investments and an interest in covering their losses by expanding into the population-rich suburbs. Before World War II this process had begun in older communities like Evanston and Oak Park, where Marshall Field's, for example, had opened branches in 1929. After the war, others, like Lytton's, followed suit.[19] But these were freestanding structures, often located in mini-downtowns, projecting rather urbane values. The early 1950s introduced something rather different. The new branches did not enter the centers of existing communities, nor did they resemble traditional commercial structures. Their design, location, and larger orientation were now part of carefully calibrated merchandising experiments in the hands of real estate developers who coordinated these large-scale projects. Retailers were about to become partners in one of the most influential environmental planning movements in twentieth-century America.[20]

Chicago's first regional shopping mall was, appropriately enough, associated with a planned community, the celebrated and much studied Park Forest Plaza, south of the city (fig. 9). Opened in 1951 on a sixty-acre site, with Marshall Field's as a featured tenant, this shopping complex would soon contain more than one hundred stores. However innovative it was as a concept, the mall itself—designed by the firm of Loebl, Schlossman and Bennett, the first of six major malls the firm would create locally during the next two decades—constituted something of a false start.[21] It had a rather formal placement, for one thing, extending a major street, Victor Boulevard, and its splayed, irregular building pattern made at least metaphorical reference to the older idea of a village green. The whole project was spatially integrated with the new community.[22] Like some other early shopping centers, it included within its spaces a series of bureaucratic and civic services, among them, a post office. Such functions would soon be stripped away from the commercial centers, which increasingly would be massive and clearly

Fig. 8   Holabird and Root, Wieboldt's Store, River Forest, 1937.

Fig. 9   Loebl, Schlossman and Bennett, Park Forest Plaza, Park Forest, 1947-51, aerial view.

Fig. 10   Victor Gruen, Northland Center, Detroit, 1954, aerial view.

Figs. 11, 12   Loebl, Schlossman and Bennett, Old Orchard Shopping Center, Skokie, 1955-56.

defined complexes of their own, relating not to any particular community but to networks of roads that would bring in customers, merchandise, and employees.

By the early 1950s a number of other cities offered more obvious models for developers to imitate. John Graham's Northgate, a $15 million complex with 800,000 square feet of selling space anchored by the Bon Marché department store, opened in the spring of 1950 in Seattle; Shoppers' World at Framingham, Massachusetts, an innovative two-story mall, began operations a year later, about the same time as Park Forest. And then there was Detroit's Northland, designed by the philosopher of the mall movement, Victor Gruen, an enormous, carefully landscaped center that opened in March 1954 with more than a million square feet of retailing (fig. 10).[23] Of this group, it was Gruen's Northland, with its full basement, its special graphics (by Alvin Lustig), its modernist architecture, landscaped courtyards, deployment of contemporary sculpture, and, above all, its carefully planned parking lots, that quickly emerged as an instant classic and an influential forecast of things to come.[24] Unlike John Graham's barrack-like Northgate with its long pedestrian mall, the stores all facing one another on axis, Northland varied and scaled down many of its open spaces. In this it was quite different from Gruen's original plan—a circular Hudson's amid a 1,300-foot-long oval of stores—and it gained immediate recognition as a conceptual breakthrough.[25] Ele-

gant, tightly controlled, and extremely efficient, Northland proved immediately and immensely profitable, far beyond the developer's dreams. This alone would have brought it universal attention.

Similar design principles shaped Chicago's second significant suburban regional mall, the Old Orchard Shopping Center, opened two and a half years later, in the autumn of 1956, in Skokie. Also created by Loebl, Schlossman and Bennett, Old Orchard, like Park Forest, was broken into a number of small courts, but unlike Park Forest it made no effort at visual connection with a local community. Supported by the landscape architecture of Lawrence Halprin and Associates, and developed by its anchor store, Marshall Field's, which was searching for a "suburban State Street," this would be metropolitan Chicago's most expensive and extravagantly planned center for some years to come.

Old Orchard was soon featured by *Architectural Record*, which praised its "charming and unusual" personality. As the visitor "strolls about he becomes pleasantly aware of a scene that changes refreshingly—he finds change of pace, of scale, of direction, of shape, of surface.... The lure of around-the-corner urges the shopper on.... Here is clever planning for business and a delightful environment for humans" (fig. 11).[26] Carefully integrated parking lots employed pylons as identifying aids for confused motorists. The center featured a series of separate buildings, many of them one story; a

Fig. 13 Loebl, Schlossman and Bennett, Oakbrook Center, Oak Brook, 1959-61.

second department store, The Fair; a super-market, fountains, and a serpentine pool; a seven-story professional building; brick and pebbled paving; and low walls of fieldstone surrounding various plantings to emphasize a country-like irregularity (fig. 12). "One's view is constantly limited, but never confined," *Architectural Record* concluded.[27]

Only a few months earlier, one of Marshall Field's major downtown competitors, Carson, Pirie, Scott and Company, had participated in the opening of another mall a few miles to the north in Wilmette, the Edens Plaza. But with little more than 200,000 square feet of selling space and only two dozen stores, this was a far less elaborate and innovative center, despite its design by a well-known local firm, Graham, Anderson, Probst and White.

The early 1960s brought continued development in the suburbs. Despite its one million square feet of selling space, Old Orchard became Chicago's second largest shopping center in 1962, giving pride of place to another complex designed by Loebl, Schlossman and Bennett, Oakbrook Center. Much of the same team was in place: the landscape architects, Lawrence Halprin and Associates; Marshall Field and Company as major anchor (joined now by Sears, Roebuck); and many of the engineering firms who had worked on the earlier project.[28]

Oakbrook represented a more sophisticated exercise in harmonizing store architecture, land-scaping, pavement, parking, and lighting than its

sister complex of six years earlier (fig. 13). The scale of the half-dozen buildings was larger and the varieties greater. There were now two levels of parking. Marshall Field's built a three-story structure, employing a substantial, mansard-like tile roof overhang to disguise its bulk. Sears's store projected a very different character, appearing circular from certain angles, with an over-hanging roof supported by thin pylons and entries on two levels (see pls. 95, 96).

The two centers had many resemblances. As at Old Orchard, the placement of sunken flower beds, benches, lamps, fountains, and brick pavements at Oakbrook projected a total environment of village-like features. Efforts were made to reduce the sense of distance separating the major buildings; terraces provided ample room for shoppers to sit down and watch the passing scene. Using its different levels and buildings to create more spatial variety than a linear, single-spine mall possessed, Oakbrook clearly belonged to its larger suburban environment, twenty-five miles west of Chicago.

These shopping centers did not escape the eyes of downtown merchants. By this time Chicago could boast more than a decade of replies. Indeed, the city's nearest planned mall sat literally on the border of Western Avenue. Evergreen Park's Evergreen Plaza (by Holabird and Root and Burgee) opened in the summer of 1952, one year after Park Forest but four years ahead of Old Orchard. While it contained "only" 500,000 square feet of selling space, less than half the

Fig. 14, 15 Ford City
Shopping Center, Cicero
Avenue at 73rd Street,
1963-65, housed in the
converted factory
buildings of the former
Dodge Chicago Plant;
Ford City was renovated
in 1987-88 by Loebl,
Schlossman and Hackl.

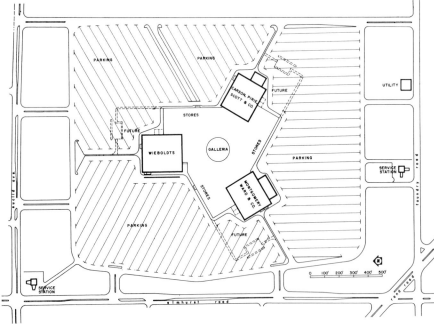

*Figs. 16, 17 Victor
Gruen Associates,
Randhurst Shopping
Center, Mount Prospect,
1962, model and plan.*

capacity of Old Orchard, Evergreen Plaza featured two department store outlets and almost seventy stores. Regimented, uniform, and linear in character, its design offered nothing new and excited little commentary; nor did the much smaller Lincoln Village, opened the previous year and dominated by a medical center and almost twenty additional stores. These newer complexes competed with already existing neighborhood nodes rather than with downtown, but they demonstrated that urban merchants could respond actively to their new competition.

By the early 1950s city government had also indicated some sense of the stakes and a determination to do something. Thus, the Chicago Plan Commission, in 1953, suggested protecting the major shopping districts outside the Loop by improving their traffic flow.[29] The Commission proposed to eliminate local streets within the neighborhood centers and surround them with one-way roads that would carry traffic around the perimeters of the shopping areas (see Bruegmann, fig. 21). Parking lots would occupy the newly cleared land, and there would be improvements in signage and local services. Funding for these changes was premised upon

fuel taxes, revenue bonds, special assessments, and private investment. The program was a self-conscious response to the success of the new suburban malls and an attempt to beat them at their own game. Some of the clearance powers were available through federal legislation, for urban renewal was a much-discussed issue in the

Fig. 18   Jickling, Lyman
and Powell, Woodfield
Mall, Schaumburg,
1970-71.

built in the city for a full decade, and none would surpass it in size.

The suburbs, however, continued to attract a whole string of regional malls.[31] By 1980 Chicago was girdled by at least fourteen suburban shopping centers of more than one million square feet. But these were no longer cast in the mold of Loebl, Schlossman and Bennett's garden ensembles: the big, austere, tightly massed structures set in open air amid carefully landscaped courtyards. Suburban malls were now going urban for their inspiration.[32] Again, Victor Gruen provided much of the stimulus and some of the philosophy. The mother ship sat, this time, near Minneapolis. The 1955 opening of Southdale—the first large, fully enclosed, climate-controlled, multi-level mall—inaugurated a new era for shopping centers.[33] Its concentrated drama suggested the excitement of downtown activity, and could be read as a repudiation of the manicured placidity associated with suburbia. Density of people and services, cosmopolitan design, and convenient access, all were featured. In the temperature extremes of the Midwest, enclosed malls proved especially popular, but even milder climates took up the atrium form.

Chicago was relatively slow to adopt the new model. The first local version opened in 1962, seven years after Southdale: the Randhurst Shopping Center in Mount Prospect. With three levels, 7,000 parking spaces, a cost exceeding $20 million, and the imprimatur of Victor Gruen Associates, Randhurst was Carson's answer (in conjunction with Wieboldt's and Montgomery Ward) to the challenge of Marshall Field's. Its 1.2 million square feet of selling space made it (briefly) the largest enclosed mall in the United States. The three department store anchors were set in what *Architectural Forum* called a "Big Pinwheel on the Prairie" (figs. 16, 17).[34] Its central dome covered a spacious "Galleria," and its various levels were adorned with specially commissioned sculpture and furniture. Randhurst stood practically alone as the area's enclosed regional mall for a half-dozen years until the Yorktown Shopping Center in Lombard opened in 1968. Larger than Randhurst and still more expensive (at some $50 million), Yorktown had four major stores—Carson's, Ward's, Wieboldt's, and Penney's—that took up well over half the center's 800,000 square feet of selling space.

By the standards of the day, both Yorktown and Randhurst were impressive, exporting what *Architectural Forum* termed "a huge chunk of downtown" into the suburbs. But their interior effects looked relatively banal when placed

early years of the first Eisenhower administration.

But the perimeter scheme came to nothing. Like many other urbanites, Chicagoans could effectively diagnose their problems, but they had not yet devised solutions. Despite the attention the federal government was giving to deteriorating city cores, its immense highway subsidy programs more significantly reshaped traditional urban centers than did any of its direct intervention into the existing building stock.

In the 1960s Chicago entrepreneurs made still further efforts to compete with the suburban giants. Although a fourth huge Loebl, Schlossman and Bennett shopping center, River Oaks in Calumet City, appeared in 1966, its 1.3 million square feet of selling space were challenged by what soon became the city's largest mall. Built on the site of an abandoned factory on Cicero Avenue—once the source of World War II bomber engines and later of Tucker cars—Ford City, anchored by Wieboldt's, Montgomery Ward, and J. C. Penney, opened in 1965 (figs. 14, 15).[30] Ford City was large and successful, but, in terms of its scale and form, almost inimitable within Chicago. It was the last true regional center to be

beside some of the new enclosed centers completed in the early and mid-1970s. Two, in particular, showed just how dramatic spatial arrangements could become. These were Hawthorn Center, in Vernon Hills, with 1.4 million square feet, the first enclosed mall that Loebl, Schlossman produced, and the largest center of all, the Taubman Company's Woodfield Mall, designed by the Michigan firm of Jickling, Lyman and Powell, which soon made available more than two million square feet for selling.[35]

Woodfield was extravagant in every way: it contained more than two hundred stores and was surrounded by 10,000 parking spaces. Its major anchors, Field's and Sears, operated stores as big as regional centers themselves. The great court now dwarfed, in scale and impact, the proudest malls of an earlier decade like Gruen's Southdale. It was clearly a significant civic space, home to concerts, meetings, and public events (figs. 1, 18). Hard colors, glass, strong lights, dramatically placed escalators and elevators, and the sight of dozens of storefronts produced more animation than many city streets. There were quiet nooks here and there in Woodfield, but the emphasis lay on recapturing the feel of a city downtown, only an improved-upon downtown—safe, dry, cool (or warm depending on the season), clean, and dedicated to one single-minded purpose: shopping. By its concentrated dynamism Woodfield projected a self-contained and self-absorbed totality; it belied the image of suburbia as centerless, diffuse, and anomic—precisely the impression Gruen had sought to counter with his first enclosed mall.

During holiday seasons the shopping center's easy assumption of festive dress suggested how naturally it had become the focus for almost every social activity. Theaters, gourmet restaurants, and skating rinks, all now seemed natural tenants.[36] "Already the shopping center has begun to replace the courthouse square as the center of the community's cultural and recreational life," *Time* reported a decade earlier in 1962. "The rattle of bowling pins is accompanied by the scrunch of ice skates, the twang of archers' bows. There are fashion shows, cooking schools, art shows, and folk-dancing classes."[37]

Despite the undeniable appeal of closed malls, many of their open-air predecessors continued to thrive. In the early 1970s, for example, Oakbrook, with only 75% of Woodfield's space, was doing almost 20% more business; and Old Orchard, even smaller, was almost equaling Woodfield. But the next generation of large regionals would be almost exclusively examples

of the enclosed genre; once experienced, they simply made other choices impossible. Their scale also made clear to everyone that suburban centers were now the dominant forces in modern retailing.

City authorities, not fully resigned to their dwindling share of shopping, still hoped to do something positive. In the early 1970s Mayor Richard J. Daley appointed a commission headed by a local realtor, Harry Chaddick, to make some proposals. Chaddick himself, aside from being a good friend of the mayor, had been the developer of Ford City. After a series of press announcements, the Chaddick commission issued its report in November 1973.[38] Pointing out that between 1947 and 1960 the number of Chicagoans working in retailing had fallen from 247,000 to 214,000, and reemphasizing the fact that since 1952 the city's percentage of total sales had shrunk from 65% to 40%, the commission blamed the Interstate and Defense Housing Act of 1956 as a primary villain. But it also admitted that the huge enclosed malls had de-

Figs. 19, 20 Loebl, Schlossman, Bennett and Dart, Water Tower Place, 845 North Michigan Avenue, 1975-76.

passed the appropriate enabling legislation and funded supportive services like traffic changes and public utilities.

Nonetheless, despite the air of crisis, the specific analyses, and the recommended designs —modular, concrete-frame structures, Plexiglass skylights, and balcony railings of textured concrete and tempered glass panels; tile, terrazzo, and carpeting; and public spaces so "designed as to create outdoor characteristics with maximum natural lighting, landscaping, ponds, fountains, art objects, aviaries, and group seating arrangements"—the commission report went largely nowhere.[39] In 1975 construction began at the Brickyard, one of the sites the commission had proposed. But the Brickyard would be the only mall built.[40] Support from the major local department stores, already heavily invested in suburban malls, was mild at best. Land assemblage was difficult.[41] Indeed, one of Mayor Daley's successors actively opposed a Chaddick shopping center.[42] The widely dispersed regional malls proved an illusory dream.[43]

But not the enclosed center. For just as the Chaddick scheme was being discussed and dissipated, Loebl, Schlossman, Bennett and Dart were bringing to the central city what was undoubtedly their most spectacular and influential mall, in a move that was as significant as Gruen's Southdale had been twenty years earlier. That mall, of course, was to become Water Tower Place.

For several years journalists, planners, developers, and political leaders had been talking about city centers in accents rather different from the depressed tones of the 1960s. Changes in American life-styles promised "rejuvenation—instead of lingering death—for the downtown areas of major cities," as one typical *U.S. News and World Report* story noted in 1973.[44] While recognizing that "the suburban shopping center is here to stay," cities, large and small, had begun pouring money into core areas: hotels, office buildings, stadiums, theaters, arenas, townhouses, apartments, and shopping malls were part of the building boom. The reasons were multiple. Demographics suggested an aging population, for one thing, "empty nesters" who, having raised their children, wished to return to city centers. The energy shortage was another source; the costs of commuting suggested the greater efficiencies of urban concentration. There appeared hints of nostalgia as well, fond memories of growing up in city neighborhoods, distantly recalled pleasures of street life, window shopping, ethnic variety, old buildings, and

veloped into community centers with powerful cultural appeals of their own. Without such concentrated shopping facilities, city retailers, other than the big State Street and Michigan Avenue stores, apparently could not compete. As a response, the commission recommended construction of five regional centers within the city of Chicago, each to cover more than fifty acres and include 150 to 200 stores. The five sites—Humboldt Square, a Milwaukee Road railroad yard near Grand and Sacramento; Green Acres, host to a Municipal Tuberculosis Sanitarium, at Peterson and Pulaski; the Stockyards, near 43rd and Halsted; Diversey-Narragansett, located on a former brickyard; and Lake Calumet—could generate $722 million in retail sales after five years, the commission promised, as well as add 20,000 jobs and produce millions of dollars in tax revenues. It also proposed ten new community shopping centers. All of them, declared the Chaddick commission, despite land and development costs exceeding $250 million, could be privately developed, provided the city council

Fig. 21 Interior view of entrance atrium of Water Tower Place.

Fig. 22 Glass-walled elevators in the central atrium of Water Tower Place.

skyscrapers—none of which the suburbs could offer.

Master planners, moreover, had demonstrated the power of organized leisure settings. Atrium hotels, convention centers, theme parks, and, above all, markets appeared to be competing with and even supplanting older civic spaces. Privately built, managed, and supervised (although often with hefty public subsidies), they suggested a public happiest when consuming, either commodities or experiences.[45] If suburban malls and Disneyland could manage it, why not city centers? A burgeoning architectural preservation movement testified to the rising level of interest in historic settings, and some developers, notably James Rouse, would exploit this taste with major effectiveness.[46] From San Francisco's Embarcadero Center and Ghirardelli Square to Philadelphia's Society Hill and Market East Gallery, the mid- and late 1970s bore witness to extensive efforts at downtown revitalization, through both new construction and restoration. "The strongest location for major retailing is in the heart of the city," James Rouse insisted.

The multi-storied atria that had been featured by turn-of-the-century office buildings, department stores, banks, post offices, and hotels, along with the grand interiors of railroad stations, stock exchanges, markets, and courthouses, were now reclaimed in the interests of downtown commerce.

While Philip Johnson's 1973 Crystal Court at the IDS Center in Minneapolis was seen by some as an initial statement of the new commercial atria, plans for Water Tower Place were already in place by then.[47] Again, the development-architect team was one that had been working together for two decades, supplemented now by extensive development participation by Mafco, a subsidiary of Marshall Field and Company, and retailing design by Warren Platner Associates.[48] But this project was a bigger gamble than any of their earlier efforts; the cost of the combined shopping atrium, hotel, and luxury apartment tower would come close to $200 million (figs. 19, 20). Landscaping proved an even more important element than it had been earlier, but now it was interior rather than exterior.

The atrium itself was far from the largest space that Loebl, Schlossman had designed; about half of its 660,000 square feet was shared by 100 smaller shops; the other half by Marshall Field's and Lord and Taylor. But the seven levels of Water Tower Place far exceeded the verticality of any previous mall. The challenge of moving shoppers through the entire center was a real one. The water cascades and bright vegetation of the entrance atrium (fig. 21) served to pull visitors past the mezzanine to the second floor, where they could catch a glimpse of the brilliantly lit interior, and have a choice of escalators or the popular glass-enclosed elevators that were becoming hallmarks of many contemporary atria (fig. 22). No attempt was made to regulate the facades of the interior specialty shops; Warren Platner argued that "the individual store's identity is the essence of retail life— variety and competition. We've handled the malls as if they were city streets."[49]

The external appearance of Water Tower Place did not excite universal admiration. Paul Gapp's description of the building as an "animated mausoleum," a reference to its extensive marble facing, built on his observation that the windowless complex would have seemed more appropriately centered in a suburban parking lot (fig. 20).[50] The loss of Michigan Avenue's human scale and the eclipse of its low, elegant buildings (fig. 24) in favor of colossal multi-use skyscrapers would be a theme of his columns for the next decade. But Gapp's disappointment in the interior, where he found a lack of drama and excitement, was not representative. Water Tower Place proved to be an incredible draw. After an initial period of nervousness, the center filled up rapidly with high-end, luxury stores, catering to the well-heeled market that was the basis for the center's very existence.

Water Tower also had an impact on the Loop.[51] The strengthening of the North Michigan Avenue high-fashion strip—by 1990 it offered 2.3 million square feet of retailing space—undoubtedly contributed to the further economic decline of State Street, even as it stimulated the older section to affirmative action. Marshall Field's started a major renovation of its main floor, transforming what one executive called a "closed case mahogany look" into open merchandising and upgraded lighting.[52] Furthermore, within a year of the completion of Water Tower Place came another significant step in what could be called the suburbanization of downtown retailing: the push for the State Street Mall.

Just as the transfer of the enclosed mall represented one response to suburban flight, so the introduction of open pedestrian malls, which barred some or all vehicular traffic, formed another. By the early 1970s a whole series of cities (and some suburban downtowns) had more than fifteen years of mall experience.[53] Kalamazoo, Michigan, established one of the first such permanent installations in 1958. Miami Beach's Lincoln Road Mall and Minneapolis's Nicollet Mall became famous and successful, while Dallas, Providence, Burbank, Santa Monica, Fresno, and Knoxville were among dozens of cities and small towns with pedestrian malls in the 1960s. Pittsburgh, Seattle, Oak Park, Baltimore, Louisville, Philadelphia, Galveston, and many others would follow as Chicago was making its plans.[54] The State Street Mall, financed partly with federal funds, was first proposed in 1974. Four years later, work began on the $17 million project, and after several years of reconstruction, the widened sidewalks, tree

Fig. 23   Skidmore, Owings and Merrill, Ground-floor shopping concourse within Continental Illinois National Bank and Trust Co. (Graham, Anderson, Probst and White; 1924), 231 South LaSalle Street, 1991-92.

planters, bus shelters, and vehicular limitations awaited downtown shoppers.[55]

The planners of the State Street Mall assumed that reduced traffic intensity, more space for promenading, and some added creature comforts—like the bus shelters—would make the street more inviting. As Paul Gapp observed in 1978, State Street, when finished, would host the longest such mall in the country, "plus the means of battling suburban merchandisers with their esthetic weapons: trees, flowers, miniplazas, sidewalk cafes, space for arts and crafts shows, and the slickest line of street furniture money can buy." It was, Gapp declared, a calculated risk, but it "could be the start of the strip's biggest renaissance since the fire of 1871."[56] Newspaper hoopla, as well as the extensive restoration of Carson, Pirie, Scott, added to the ambitious hopes.[57]

In fact, State Street was soon threatened by a precipitate decline. Shortly after the mall's completion, in 1981, Goldblatt's closed its main store; the next year Sears announced it would shut its most famous local outlet; in 1984 Montgomery Ward decided to leave; and in the summer of 1987 Wieboldt's declared an end to its State Street retailing.[58] Only two department stores, albeit the two largest and best known, remained. The decline of State Street retailing was not produced by architects or by design decisions, but the mall was clearly an inadequate response, and its flaws were quickly seized upon by critics as evidence of incapacity.[59] While comments singled out failures quite specifically, the more general view found it a basic denial of the Loop's traditional character and an assault on the vitality of the street. If Water Tower Place represented a useful lesson learned from suburban experience, the State Street Mall seemed just its opposite—a misguided and wrongheaded effort to apply palliatives that would appeal neither to city residents nor suburbanites.

At just the same time, one other, somewhat more successful, effort was made to marry suburban practice with urban form and exploit the growing architectural nostalgia that was sweeping older cities like Chicago. Part of the argument for the presence of an urban renaissance was a new popular enthusiasm for premodern eclecticism, for structures whose ornamentation, scale, and public areas symbolized both a lost era of hospitality and self-confidence and a repudiation of the more disciplined austerities championed by classic modernism. The struggle to save or restore movie palaces exemplified this sensibility. Thus, the 1974 conversion of Lakeview's 3,300-seat Century Theater, with its gaudy, terra-cotta facade, into a seven-level center of more than fifty shops and five restaurants, seemed specially potent.[60] Although it was attached to a specially prepared, seven-level parking deck, by recent standards this was a relatively small center, with only 120,000 square feet of retail selling space. Yet the Century Theater project signified the adaptive reuse strategy that was being applied to a number of older Chicago buildings in this period, as well as the combination of nostalgia and self-indulgence that would characterize the coming era. Anxiety about hedonism would soon mark both the White House and the academy in the late 1970s, but these misgivings would be overwhelmed by fast-breaking developments in the 1980s.

In this decade Chicago shoppers moved far beyond conditions that had been in place just a few years earlier. For one thing, they had available longer hours and longer weeks. Stores, particularly those located in the new indoor malls, were now open every day. The last blue laws collapsed in the face of changing life-styles and consumer demands. Furthermore, the new urban-suburban mixture spread rapidly. Within blocks of Water Tower Place would come, by the late 1980s, two other multi-story indoor malls, Chicago Place and 900 North Michigan Avenue. Each represented a different, and perhaps less persuasive, version of the prototype. Chicago Place colorized the vertical space, softened and lightened it, bringing a little more of California to the avenue and suburbanizing the harder edges (fig. 25). On the other hand, 900 North

Fig. 24 Shaw and Associates, Bonwit Teller store, 820 North Michigan Avenue, 1949 (later remodeled).

Michigan Avenue produced a somewhat more austere effect, employing rich traditional materials like marble and etched glass, suggesting, indeed, the light court of some older department stores (see pl. 97). Neither of these two vertical malls, secure in the knowledge that the type worked, required or displayed the elaborate landscaped entry of their predecessor.

It did not end here. Having developed, in Water Tower Place, an urban translation of a suburban translation of an urban form, Marshall Field's moved this complex system of cross-referencing one step further. Its own flagship, part of the idealized center city that originally inspired Gruen's Southdale, was now partially transformed into a suburban mall itself.[61] The old store, with its ninety-year-old atria, opened in 1991 an additional light court clad in the vocabulary of the suburban complexes (fig. 26). Completing the building program that Daniel H.

Burnham began at the very start of the century, Marshall Field's made its entire structure contiguous, incorporating the Holden Court alley within a sleek new atrium. The State Street store was now virtually a museum of shopping spaces, a source of imitation for architectural epigones.

Other downtown Chicago buildings from the State of Illinois to the Merchandise Mart now made their own gestures toward the new benchmark of urbanity: the retail arcade. Illinois Center already housed an extensive underground shopping concourse, and from North Pier to the Continental Bank (fig. 23) shopping facilities became central markers of gentrification, as well as ways to revitalize unused space.

Away from downtown the story was different. The City That Shops did not offer stores everywhere. As the 1990s began, many Chicagoans had no easy access to retail establishments, cinemas, good restaurants, or neatly landscaped plazas. Here and there centers were created and merchants were encouraged to invest. But the thriving system of dispersed retailing, that hallmark of seventy years earlier, had largely disappeared. To enjoy these amenities, most Chicagoans had to become internal tourists. The planned shopping center made traditional theories of retail development almost irrelevant.[62] Population itself no longer guaranteed retailing significance; assembling the land packages to support large regional centers was difficult within cities, as the Chaddick commission had discovered several decades earlier.[63] With so much sense of personal worth and identity tied to shopping power, and so much investment going into shopping settings, the parts of the city that lacked significant retail diversion were only likely to feel more alienated and angry. North Michigan Avenue had become one vast regional mall, lined with the kind of luxury stores and boutiques that spilled forth from Chicago Place and 900 North Michigan, and it featured new flagship stores representing Crate and Barrel (fig. 27), Nike, Sony, and Banana Republic (see pls. 103-05). The Loop still hung on, buoyed by new residential and employment patterns, and a few ambitious corridors found happy buyers.[64] But their glitter and the splendor of the suburban centers were contradicted by the mercantile devastation elsewhere. In its shopping, as in its housing, Chicago remained a city of contrasts. The delights of consumption, which seemed to promise an urban renaissance, did not solve fundamental problems. In the long run, a City That Works was far more important a goal than The City That Shops, but also, alas, far more elusive.

Fig. 25   Skidmore, Owings and Merrill, Chicago Place, 700 North Michigan Avenue, 1988.

Fig. 26   HTI Space Design International, interior view of atrium within Marshall Field and Co. Store (D. H. Burnham and Co.; 1902-14), State Street between Randolph and Washington streets, 1990-91.

Fig. 27   Solomon Cordwell Buenz and Associates, Crate and Barrel Store, 646 North Michigan Avenue, 1989-90.

NOTES

1. William R. Green, *The Retail Store: Design and Construction* (New York, 1986), p. vii.
2. These figures are taken from *Chicago Tribune/ Chicago Today*, Research Division Services Data, and the United States Census of Population, as reprinted in Mayor's Committee on Shopping Centers, *Report and Recommendations* (Chicago, 1973). This was the commission appointed by Mayor Richard J. Daley and chaired by Harry F. Chaddick.
3. For a description of Chicago shopping and its development through the 1920s, see Neil Harris, "Shopping — Chicago Style," in John Zukowsky, ed., *Chicago Architecture, 1872-1922: Birth of a Metropolis* (Munich and Chicago, 1987), pp. 137-56.
4. Malcolm J. Proudfoot, "The Major Outlying Business Centers of Chicago" (Ph.D. diss., University of Chicago, 1936).

5. For more on this and the development of the entire area, see John W. Stamper, *Chicago's North Michigan Avenue: Planning and Development, 1900-1930* (Chicago and London, 1991).
6. "State — Washington: Largest Sale in the History of the City," *Realtor* 70 (Dec. 1, 1923), p. 1237.
7. Homer Hoyt, *One Hundred Years of Land Values in Chicago* (Chicago, 1933), pp. 205, 237, summarizes the automobile statistics.
8. Theodora Kimball Hubbard and Henry Vincent Hubbard, *Our Cities To-Day and To-Morrow* (Cambridge, Mass., 1929), pp. 225-26.
9. A photograph of the store, designed by Nimmons, Carr and Wright, can be seen in *Architectural Concrete* 6 (1938), p. 6. To celebrate its fiftieth anniversary, Sears issued a fact sheet on the store's construction; see *News from Sears* (Oct. 19, 1988).
10. See Robert Bruegmann, *Holabird and Roche and Holabird and Root: An Illustrated Catalog of Works, 1880-1940* (New York, 1991), vol. 3, pp. 280-81.

11. William T. Snaith, "Serving the Suburban Customer Through Branch Stores," in *Planning the Store of To-Morrow* (New York, 1945), p. 102.
12. "New Buildings for 194X," *Architectural Forum* 78 (May 1943), p. 70.
13. Years later Gruen quoted proudly from his essay in that issue; see Victor Gruen, *Centers for the Urban Environment: Survival of the Cities* (New York, 1973), p. 17.
14. James Simmons, *The Changing Pattern of Retail Location* (Chicago, 1964), p. 103.
15. George A. Brandenburg, "Ads Built State Street Stores," *Editor and Publisher* 68 (June 8, 1935), p. 11.
16. T. S. Irwin, "Suburban Shopping Offers No. 1 Challenge," *Editor and Publisher* 87 (Dec. 18, 1954), p. 44.
17. See, for example, *Editor and Publisher* 87 (Sept. 18, 1954), p. 28; 88 (Aug. 9, 1955), p. 16; 89 (April 21, 1956), pp. 27-28; 91 (Dec. 19, 1959), pp. 7, 20; 91 (Dec. 26, 1959), pp. 17, 24, 26; 92 (Jan. 2, 1960),

p. 22, all of which describe how newspapers, in co-operation with downtown merchants, were trying to highlight the pleasures and efficiencies of downtown to counter the appeal of suburban malls.

18. Campbell Watson, "Shopping Centers Forcing Broadened Linage Areas," *Editor and Publisher* 86 (June 13, 1953), pp. 9, 46.

19. See Harris (note 3), p. 151; and Sally A. Kitt Chappell, *Architecture and Planning of Graham, Anderson, Probst and White, 1912-1936: Transforming Tradition* (Chicago and London, 1992), pp. 233-35. Field's had stores in Evanston, Oak Park, and Lake Forest, all opened in 1929.

20. There has been a considerable and impressive recent literature on the growth of the American shopping center. I have found helpful Geoffrey Baker and Bruno Funaro, *Shopping Centers: Design and Operation* (New York, 1951); Meredith L. Clausen, "Shopping Centers," in Joseph A. Wilkes, ed., *Encyclopedia of Architecture: Design, Engineering, and Construction* (New York, 1989), vol. 4, pp. 406-21; Margaret Crawford, "The World in a Shopping Mall," in Michael Sorkin, ed., *Variations on a Theme Park: The New American City and the End of Public Space* (New York, 1992), pp. 3-30; Howard Gillette, Jr., "The Evolution of the Planned Shopping Center in Suburb and City," *Journal of the American Planning Association* 51 (Summer 1985), pp. 449-60; Gruen (note 13); William Severini Kowinski, *The Malling of America: An Inside Look at the Great Consumer Paradise* (New York, 1985); Richard Longstreth, "The Neighborhood Shopping Center in Washington, D.C., 1930-1941," *Journal of the Society of Architectural Historians* 51 (March 1992), pp. 5-34; Louis G. Redstone, *New Dimensions in Shopping Centers and Stores* (New York, 1973); Peter G. Rowe, *Making a Middle Landscape* (Cambridge, Mass., and London, 1990), chap. 4, pp. 109-46; William G. Worley, *J. C. Nichols and the Shaping of Kansas City* (Columbia, Mo., and London, 1990), chap. 8, pp. 232-63. There are also a number of bibliographies on malls, downtowns, pedestrian malls, and shopping centers that have been published by Vance Bibliographies of Monticello, Illinois.

21. The firm name changed in the course of the next two decades. Richard Bennett, the architect who was given charge of Park Forest, retired from the firm; Edward Dart joined it; and Donald Hackl would become a partner. For a useful review of their work and Chicago shopping center history, see Paul Gapp, *Chicago Tribune* (Nov. 25, 1984), sec. 13, pp. 20-22.

22. See Rowe (note 20), p. 124; see also Baker and Funaro (note 20), pp. 267-69; and for an updating, George Lazarus, "Smyth Moving to Park Forest," *Chicago Tribune* (Feb. 9, 1977), sec. 4, p. 13.

23. For Northgate, see one of the first scholarly studies of a single shopping center, Meredith L. Clausen, "Northgate Regional Shopping Center — Paradigm from the Prairies," *Journal of the Society of Architectural Historians* 43 (May 1984), pp. 144-61.

24. See the extraordinarily glowing essay on Northland in *Architectural Forum* 100 (June 1954), pp. 102-19. Almost all the early studies on the shopping center (and most of the recent ones as well) paid special attention to Northland; see also *Architectural Record* 133 (June 1963), pp. 166-71.

25. Gruen (note 13) described the building of Northland, his relationship to his client, and his original design, which he labeled the "biggest egg" he ever laid but which luckily "was never hatched" (p. 24).

26. "Garden Setting Lends Charm to Chicago's Newest Center," *Architectural Record* 122 (Sept. 1957), p. 221.

27. Ibid.

28. Oakbrook is described in "Unified Variety in a Fountained Mall," *Architectural Record* 135 (June 1964), pp. 166-69.

29. Chicago Plan Commission, *The Perimeter Plan* (Chicago, 1953). See the approving coverage of the proposal in "New Thinking on Shopping Centers," *Architectural Forum* 98 (March 1953), pp. 122-23.

30. For an updating and review of Ford City's history, see "Ford City is New Wave in Malling of America," *Chicago Tribune* (Oct. 2, 1988), Real Estate, p. 1. By this

date Ford City hosted 1.65 million square feet of retailing.

31. The growth of area malls can be documented through the *Directory of Shopping Centers in the United States and Canada*, published annually by the National Research Bureau, Inc., starting in 1957. Dates of establishment, sizes, numbers of stores, ownership, etc., are all presented in this directory. By the 1970s the number of shopping centers had become so great that the directory was being issued in regional editions.

32. For comments, chosen almost at random, of the broad ambitions of the new malls, see *Chicago Tribune* (April 7, 1981), sec. 2, p. 2; and (June 28, 1981), sec. 14, p. 2.

33. For Southdale, see Gruen (note 13), pp. 33-39; *Architectural Forum* 98 (March 1953), pp. 126-33; "A Break-Through for Two-Level Shopping Centers," *Architectural Forum* 105 (Dec. 1956), pp. 114-27; and Neil Harris, "Spaced Out at the Shopping Center," *New Republic* (Dec. 13, 1975), pp. 23-26. The 1953 *Architectural Forum* piece, written while Southdale was being planned, speaks of the scheme as "air conditioning a public square," and categorizes it as a "market-square scheme." The urban implications would become clearer after its completion. But the essay reveals popular confusion about the form; Gruen reassured visitors that they would know whether it was "day or night, clear or cloudy."

34. "Randhurst Center: Big Pinwheel on the Prairie," *Architectural Forum* 117 (Nov. 1962), pp. 106-11.

35. Woodfield Mall, developed by the Taubman Company, opened in September 1971. For more on Woodfield and the big new centers of the period, see "Shopping Centers Grown into Shopping Cities," *Business Week* (Sept. 4, 1971), pp. 34-38. "With Woodfield, we are not competing against other centers or suburban business districts," Taubman told an interviewer. "We are competing against downtown Chicago." For more on Jickling, Lyman and Powell, and particularly Robert Powell, see Paul Gapp, *Chicago Tribune* (Nov. 25, 1984), sec. 13, pp. 20-22.

36. Curiously enough, fifteen or twenty years later, mall observers thought centers were now inventing the hosting of public activities; see Thomas Fisher, "Inquiry Remaking Malls," *Progressive Architecture* (Nov. 1988), pp. 96-101, for the notion that "the people developing shopping malls a generation ago did not have to go out of their way to attract the public, since there were so few other malls.... We now see shopping as a form of entertainment." All this was quite securely in place by the early 1970s. For more on social activities at malls, see Jerry Jacobs, *The Mall: An Attempted Escape from Everyday Life* (Prospect Heights, Ill., 1984).

37. *Time* 80 (Nov. 16, 1962), p. 73. Robert Jensen, "Shopping Malls in Suburbia," *Architectural Record* (March 1972), argued that "suburban shopping malls are taking on all the best urban characteristics of central cities ... achieving some of the idealized techniques of urban life that central cities have achieved.... Perhaps they show that it is time we recognize in suburbia the same human tendencies that have always led people to busy places: a need for social exchange in conversation, the presence of choices that make daily life interesting, the stimulation to our imagination that comes from watching crowds of different people" (p. 113). The attached article considered two of the new "urbane" malls, The Mall at Columbia, Maryland, and Eastridge Regional Mall in San Jose, California.

38. Mayor's Committee on Shopping Centers (note 2). See also the "Tower Ticker" columns, *Chicago Tribune* (June 9, 1972), sec. 1, p. 10; (June 10, 1973), sec. 1, p. 5; (June 13, 1972), sec. 3, p. 7; (Nov. 13, 1973), sec. 1, p. 1.

39. Mayor's Committee on Shopping Centers (note 2), p. 24.

40. *Chicago Tribune* (Aug. 28, 1977), sec. 12, p. 1.

41. Indeed, the *Chicago Tribune* suggested that it ran against public policy for the government to promote large shopping centers in urban residential neighborhoods, particularly when using the power to condemn private property; see "Big Shopping Centers Lose One," *Chicago Tribune* (Dec. 30, 1979), sec. 2, p. 4.

42. This was Mayor Jane Byrne, responding to community sentiment on the Northwest Side; see *Chicago Tribune* (Dec. 27, 1979), sec. 6, p. 1.

43. See "Chicago's Center Plans Lag," *Chain Store Age Executive* 53 (June 1977), p. 46.

44. "Revival of Downtowns," *U.S. News and World Report* 75 (Aug. 20, 1973), pp. 58-60. Hundreds of articles in the early and mid-1970s projected the same message: see "Downtown," *U.S. News and World Report* 78 (May 19, 1975), pp. 31-33; "Are All Big Cities Doomed?" *U.S. News and World Report* 80 (April 5, 1976), pp. 49-64; "Saving Downtown: Government Courts Retailers," *Chain Store Age Executive* 54 (Sept. 1978), pp. 21-24. The belief in an "urban renaissance" is examined and evaluated most fully in Jon. C. Teaford, *The Rough Road to Renaissance: Urban Revitalization in America, 1940-1985* (Baltimore and London, 1990), especially chap. 7, pp. 253-307. For an earlier, skeptical account, see Malcolm C. D. MacDonald, *America's Cities: A Report on the Myth of the Urban Renaissance* (New York, 1984).

45. For a later critique of such spaces, see the various essays in Sorkin (note 20).

46. For a typical Rouse profile of the era, see Gurney Breckenfeld, "Jim Rouse Shows How to Give Downtown Retailing New Life," *Fortune* 97 (April 10, 1978), pp. 84-87.

47. See the newspaper reports on the coming center: *Chicago Tribune* (June 8, 1972), sec. 3, p. 1; (July 9, 1972) sec. 2a, p. 1; and (June 19, 1973), sec. 3, p. 6.

48. For the Water Tower Place development itself, see *Architectural Record* 159 (April 1976), pp. 136-40; and *Chain Store Age Executive* 52 (Feb. 1976), pp. 25-30.

49. *Architectural Record* 159 (April 1976), p. 138.

50. Paul Gapp, "A Marble Block Mars the Magnificent Mile," *Chicago Tribune* (Nov. 30, 1975).

51. And on its neighborhood, almost at once. See *Chicago Tribune* (July 31, 1977), sec. 12, p. 1a, for the mini-mall of 14,000 square feet that it inspired at 840 North Michigan Avenue across the street.

52. *Chain Store Age Executive* 51 (Feb. 1976), p. 29.

53. See the extensive bibliography compiled by James F. Orr, *Malls, Pedestrian Malls, and Shopping Centers*, Vance Bibliographies, Architecture Series, Bibliography A38 (Monticello, Ill., 1979). For more on both pedestrian malls and the new central city shopping centers, see Bernard J. Frieden and Lynne B. Sagalyn, *Downtown, Inc.: How America Rebuilds Cities* (Cambridge, Mass., 1989).

54. See the exhibition catalogue and essays on pedestrian planning in Robert Brambilla, Gianni Longo, and Virginia Dzurinko, *American Urban Malls: A Compendium* (Washington, D. C., 1977). This was an outgrowth of the public information program More Streets for People.

55. See Stanley Ziemba, "City Planners O.K. Turning State St. into Shopping Mall," *Chicago Tribune* (Dec. 13, 1974), sec. 2, p. 1. The mall was dedicated in the fall of 1979, although not completed until the following year; see *Chicago Tribune* (Oct. 29, 1979), sec. 16, p. 6; and (Oct. 30, 1979), sec. 3, p. 1.

56. *Chicago Tribune* (June 18, 1978), p. 20.

57. See *Chicago Tribune* (Nov. 14, 1978), sec. 4, p. 14, and (Oct. 28, 1979), sec. 16, p. 6, for the celebration of State Street; and (July 31, 1979), sec. 2, p. 1, and (Aug. 15, 1979), sec. 1, p. 3, for the Carson's project.

58. The decline of State Street department stores is summarized in Teaford (note 44), pp. 292-93.

59. *Chicago Tribune* (June 10, 1975), sec. 2, p. 5.

60. *Chicago Tribune* (Aug. 19, 1973), sec. 12, p. 1; and (Jan. 13, 1977), sec. 6, pp. 3, 7.

61. For comments on department store interior spaces, see Chappell (note 19), pp. 63-69.

62. See the fascinating comments, based on some *Chicago Tribune* studies, in Pierre D. Martineau, "Customers' Shopping Center Habits Change Retailing," *Editor and Publisher* 96 (Oct. 26, 1963), pp. 16, 56. Mobility "has some shattering effects on some of the myths of retailing.... Convenience means something entirely different." See also Simmons (note 14), passim.

63. Simmons (note 14), pp. 147-48.

64. Particularly on the Northwest Side; see *Chicago Tribune* (Jan. 21, 1981), sec. 4, p. 1, for the survival of the Belmont-Central business district, even after the opening of the Brickyard Mall.

The Postwar Modern House in Chicago

Sidney K. Robinson

In the years immediately following World War II architects of the modern American house had to adjust to the changes brought about by the recent conflict. The war had created the need and the means both to capitalize on the disruption and move in new directions, and to reestablish continuity and recover tradition. Architects working around Chicago during the years of recovery, 1945 to 1953, incorporated both responses into their designs. They could not, however, realistically move completely in the direction of, for example, the ultramodern House of Tomorrow and Crystal House designed by the brothers George Fred Keck and William Keck for the 1933-34 Century of Progress Exposition in Chicago (fig. 2; see also Saliga, fig. 6), or follow the technological examples of other homes exhibited at the fair that were made wholly with industrial materials; these included the Stran-Steel House (fig. 3) and the "Design for Living" House (see Doordan, fig. 5). Nor could postwar architects ignore the real social and economic changes and slide back into a Cape Cod fog. In a period of shortages and retrenchment, architects who kept the modernist faith adjusted a hard-edged vision of a new tomorrow by including more traditional (and available) components and materials. As a result of the overwhelming need for housing and the complex interaction of material shortages and the desire for domestic stability, these years concentrated attention on the modern house to an unprecedented degree.

Technological advances, the driving force of the disruption, produced new appliances, structural forms, and materials that generated feelings of amazement as well as fear. Because foreign aggression had forced the development of the technology to begin with, foreign ideas about houses, such as the International Style of the 1930s, were somewhat suspect. Soldiers coming home from the war brought with them intensified memories of home, and their arrival generated new ideas about housing design. A 1948 house in Lake Forest by George Fred Keck was singled out for its "emotional content," a clear reminder of a need that Frank Lloyd Wright had summed up in the aphorism "a house is a machine only in so far as a heart is a suction pump" (fig. 1).[1] A review of George Nelson and Henry Wright's book *Tomorrow's House* that appeared in *Architectural Forum* in October 1945 reminded readers how the home, more than any other building type, should include both up-to-date advances in housing design and appliances and traditional domestic imagery. The reviewer noted that the book's introduction "explains the home as a technical, social, and psychological fact. Here, from a fresh viewpoint, is an analysis of why people cling to traditional designs."[2] The editors of *Progressive Architecture* emphasized the same point in 1947 by selecting modern houses that were "livable homes," homes that created a "congenial environment, appropriate to this country and to these times."[3] Finding a way to bring modern conveniences and emotions into a harmonious, domestic balance informed much of the postwar modern house design.

On a basic level, the average home buyer in the 1940s considered machines to be portable objects made of metal, like those used in the war, and they considered them to be incompatible with houses, which were wooden and immobile—that is, the new materials and forms could be successfully transferred to automobiles, as General Motors stylist Harley Earl knew, but home was a place of refuge and traditional comfort. Wood siding, stone, and brick were now to be used to delineate volumes that architects in the desperately modern 1930s had thought could only be appropriately expressed in steel and stucco.

Economic necessity forced a reconciliation between forward and backward thinkers. It became imperative to include the powerful associational content of home without the cost previously required to produce the effect. As is so often the case, technology and economy were called upon to carry off this sleight of hand. New technology propping up old images is as contemporary as fiberglass cornices. Postwar conditions, however, made economic necessity an energizing motive to gain the maximum psycho-

Fig. 1   George Fred Keck and William Keck, Abel E. Fagen House, Lake Forest, 1948, interior.

logical reassurance with the least material and spatial means. It was an economy of hope, not desperation.

In the postwar years the ideal of the modern house that had originated in the twenties and thirties evolved from high utopianism, on the one hand, and desperate collectivism, on the other, toward a pragmatic use of economic realities to interpret tradition rather than approximate its form. In most discussions of the postwar modern house economic pressures supplied the argument modernist designers needed to replace the traditional image with an efficient notion of how to live.

The marked display of industrial materials and processes that had been such a salient part of prewar modern houses had to be set aside. Steel was in short supply, and houses that were designed to be made of glass and steel could not, in fact, be produced. Until the materials shortage ended, more traditional materials had to be used. This necessity gave force to the ameliorating counsels of Joseph Hudnut, whose article on the "Post-Modern House" in 1945, and a later essay in 1948, urged that the modern house could incorporate the beauty of elements from both art and science. Hudnut vowed that such a combination, rather than being a cowardly compromise, would produce a "new candor and freedom."[4]

The most outstanding efforts of the building industry to use the disruption of the war to strike out in new directions were its attempts to gear up for the production of industrialized housing. Soon after being set up, these attempts failed. Numerous companies had optimistically begun to produce whole houses of modular, engineered components. Panels, trusses, and porcelain skins were all integrated into compact living units associated with names like Carl Koch, Konrad Wachsmann, and Lustron. Unfortunately, the model of automobile marketing and financing fell short when it was applied to housing. None of the industrialized housing companies was sufficiently funded to maintain production levels until long-term financing became available, and the image of the modern house suffered from these efforts, primarily due to sloppy production and the public's negative associations with modular building. These failures fed the suspicion that the proper response to changes was not to forge ahead in risky, new territory, but to return to the tried and true. An indication of this retrenchment was an increase, albeit small, in the percentage of houses with pitched roofs compared to flat roofs between

1940 and 1950, according to a Housing and Home Finance Agency survey. Technical and economic pressures over the decade caused changes in the construction of houses, however, including a significant increase in the use of copper plumbing, asphalt shingles, natural gas heating, concrete slab foundations, wood-truss roof construction, and aluminum window framing.[5]

Components of houses, of course, could be made by industrial processes without revolutionizing the whole industry and conventional expectations. America has a long tradition of the industrialized vernacular, in which prefabricated parts of houses—windows, molding, cabinetry, and appliances—are coordinated on a case-by-case basis.[6] This individual combination of technological elements allowed a traditional image to be supported by the most up-to-date components, and some form of rationalized dimensioning, as in industrialized materials, such as wood, plywood, and masonry units, was easy to achieve.

In addition to Frank Lloyd Wright's unit system, which provided a way to create plan and elevation within a dimensional discipline, the housing industry also proposed "engineered" houses after the war. The Producers Council and the National Retail Lumber Dealers Association, in cooperation with the University of Illinois Small Homes Council, presented eight houses that were designed to "integrate and coordinate, not revolutionize" house construction. A four-foot unit was used for planning both horizontally and vertically and a four-inch unit was used for details. The eight perspective views published in 1947 included only one non-traditional model, whose flat roof and banded windows recalled prewar modernist forms. As drawn by Gordon Lorimer, these industry proposals applied technology and rational production methods in creating a variety of images.[7] In a typically American fashion these pragmatic geometric systems were free of ideal proportioning ratios or cosmic magic numbers. Instead, they combined the virtue of discipline and the flexibility of convenience.

Various technological components met with resistance from the housing industry itself. The Borg Warner Corporation's Ingersol utilities unit, for example, which combined the furnace, water heater, and plumbing, and which served as the core for six architects' interpretation of the postwar house in Kalamazoo, Michigan, in 1950, never gained acceptance. In the long term, the tightly engineered unit made repairs difficult. But the immediate resistance to the idea came

Fig. 2   George Fred Keck and William Keck, House of Tomorrow, Century of Progress Exposition, 1933.

Fig. 3   O'Dell and Rowland, Stran Steel House, Century of Progress Exposition, 1933-34.

The Postwar Modern House   203

Fig. 4 Paul Schweikher, Schweikher Home and Studio, 645 Meacham Road, Roselle (now Schaumburg), 1938 (enlarged 1947), exterior.

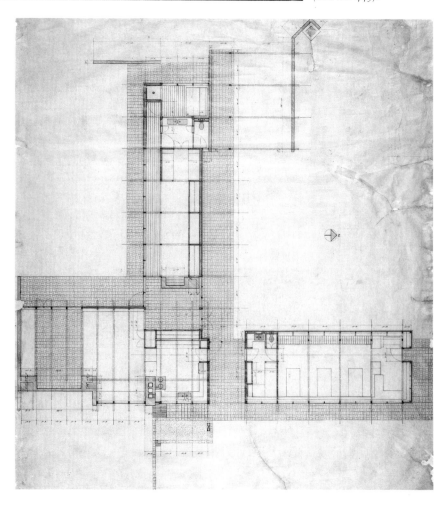

Fig. 5 Schweikher, Plan of the Schweikher Home and Studio, 1938 (cat. no. 445).

from the unions.[8] Their desire to preserve prewar construction processes arose from an understandable fear that the skilled trades would lose work on the building site to a factory system. It seemed that new-fangled industrial units would only take work away from union members. Interestingly, the hollow, clay floor tiles that distributed hot air in a heating system that was developed by the Keck brothers, although it was much more traditional in material and process, failed to gain acceptance for exactly the opposite reason: installation by the tradesmen on the site required too great a degree of craftsmanship. These two new ways of supplying utilities and services failed to find an acceptable middle ground in the housing industry so that the methods were familiar enough to fit in easily, yet sufficiently modern to provide an increased level of comfort and convenience.

Architects of the postwar American modern house turned to two sources for ideas on how to accommodate the home owner's conflicting desires for a house that was warm and comfortable, as well as efficient and economical. European models were not popular after the war, and they were difficult to achieve because of shortages in industrial materials. America, however, had its own forms of modernism in the Usonian houses

Fig. 6 Schweikher Home, interior.

Fig. 6 Schweikher Home, interior.

Fig. 7 Schweikher Home, interior.

that Frank Lloyd Wright had developed before the war, and in the casual California-style dwelling, which was becoming increasingly popular. The discovery before the war of the California life-style, in both Los Angeles and the Bay Area, evoked images of pavilionlike living originating not in a utopian/technological dream but in a real place in America. The more informal California house benefited from an efficiency that replaced a rigid distinction of propriety. These homes were characterized by glass walls, a slender structure, flowing continuity between the interior and garden, and an open plan that allowed multiple uses within the same space. Such homes seemed to offer the realistic means to live the "good life" immediately, not in a morally uplifting future. This merging of house and landscape was common to both American sources, and it was distinctive when compared to European models. As L. Morgan Yost put it in later life, the house dissolved on its edges so that "you couldn't tell where the garden ended and the house began."[9]

In their postwar modern house designs architects working around Chicago adapted earlier industrial modernism to the material shortages and the new interest in the comforts of tradition. Paul Schweikher and William and George Fred Keck produced houses that were modern in their forms, but traditional in their materials. The presence of Frank Lloyd Wright in nearby Wisconsin contributed to their awareness of a regional, as well as an international, modernism.

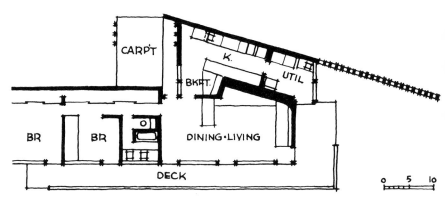

In 1947 Paul Schweikher enlarged his home and architectural studio in Roselle (now Schaumburg; figs. 4, 5). He connected the two separate wood-and-masonry structures with an open-air passageway much like one Wright had used at Taliesin. For the buildings' dimensions, Schweikher employed a four-by-eight-foot structural and spatial module. The "natural" material palette used throughout the buildings included heavy timber structural elements, a brick floor that continued through to exterior terraces, and redwood siding and battens (figs. 6, 7). In this project the traditional materials were brought into the discipline of structure. The rationalized crafts tradition of Japan that Schweikher saw in 1937, just before designing his own house and studio, clearly contributed to this combination. The contrast could not be greater than between this variety of modernism and his Eliason House of 1932, whose client, an astronomer, appreciated an inhabitable instrument of open-webbed steel joists and corrugated metal.[10]

Fig. 8   Paul Schweikher, Plan of the Harring House, Highland Park, early 1950s.

Fig. 9   George Fred Keck and William Keck, Abel Fagen House, 1581 Old Mill Road, Lake Forest, 1948.

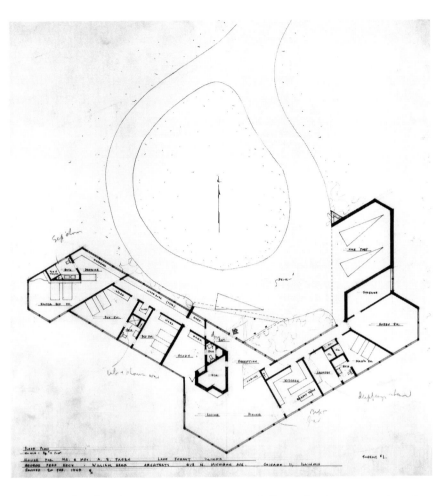

Fig. 10 Keck and Keck, Plan of the Abel Fagen House, Feb. 20, 1948.

Schweikher also followed a heavy timber discipline in the early 1950s Harring House in Highland Park, but he altered the plan by shifting the masonry fireplace mass off the orthogonal grid (fig. 8). The powerful sculptural sweep

of the fireplace reoriented the kitchen and the service spaces behind it. Using redwood, brick, and cedar plywood on the interior, the architect once again combined natural elements with modern planning to make the efficient arrangement of living spaces seem warm and comfortable.[11] A continuous deck and wall of windows allowed for contact with the site and also drew the context of the natural world into the house. Such houses did not require gardens, since they brought the world of trees and earth, which indirectly supplied the materials for the construction of the house, in direct contact with the inhabitants.

Schweikher's responses to a wide range of modern architecture prepared him to discover ways to exploit the latest technological principles of efficiency while reassuring his clients that a house was still a place of peaceful comfort. After spending two years working in the office of architect David Adler, Schweikher was exposed to modern architecture in 1936, when he visited the Van Nelle factory in Rotterdam while on a traveling fellowship from Yale. Aircraft designer Lee Atwood introduced Schweikher to the ideas of modern inventor and architect R. Buckminster Fuller and to Ludwig Mies van der Rohe's German Pavilion at Barcelona. Schweikher had met Atwood when both men were working in architect Russell Walcott's office in Chicago.

In addition, Schweikher was aware of Frank Lloyd Wright's designs. In 1940 he worked with William Beye Fyfe, a former Wright apprentice,

Fig. 11 Keck and Keck, Abel Fagen House, interior.

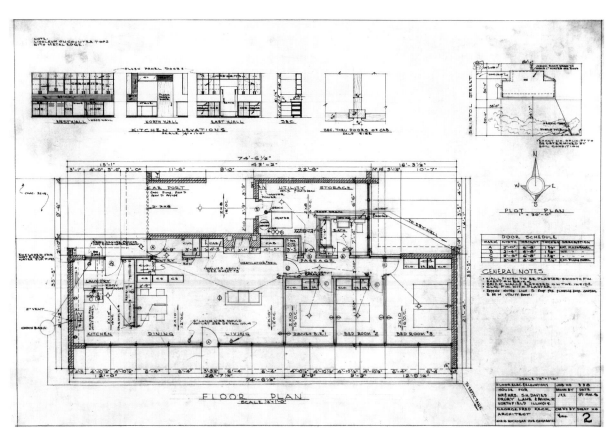

on the Lewis House, which was named "House of the Year" in 1941. This experience focused Schweikher's attention on the work of this American modern master.[12] Schweikher saw in detail how a modern house in the Usonian mode was put together. The predominant ideals that guided the work were a straightforward use of materials, a direct approach to planning, and an emphasis on simplicity. Schweikher's rereading of Henry David Thoreau also reminded him of these virtues, but from an American perspective of pragmatic simplicity rather than from one of European minimalist ideology.

The seven houses that Schweikher designed for the North Shore Cooperative Society, based in Evanston, Illinois, extended the forms and materials he had explored in the Lewis House. The group chose Schweikher to design a unified plan that could accommodate the different needs of the families who invested in the project. The architect again chose natural materials for the structures, using beveled redwood siding, red cedar shingles on sloped roof planes, and brick (and, in one case, stone) chimneys to create modest, efficient, but comfortable houses, which were built on five-and-a-half acres in Glenview, Illinois, beginning in 1941. By chance, the carpenters who built these houses were members of a Finnish co-op group who understood the ideals and did their best to make the experiment work.[13]

The sixty-degree geometry of Wright's Hanna House appeared in Schweikher's 1947 John R. Stone House in Topeka, Kansas, also designed with William Beye Fyfe,[14] and the platforms and piers of "desert concrete" from Wright's Taliesin West occurred in Schweikher's Louis C. Upton House in Paradise Valley, Arizona, of 1950, whose rectilinear plan had first appeared as one of his four postwar houses published in the December 1946 issue of *Architectural Record*.[15] These four proposals for postwar houses clearly show Schweikher's use of wood, stone, and concrete (both site cast and industrial units) within an industrial discipline. Although in his prewar houses the architect had reinterpreted available industrial materials to produce custom work, in these later projects he treated industrial equipment as an established constant and designed within its limitations. Concrete block, for instance, was to be detailed to avoid splitting. The blockish massing of these houses also emphasized their independence from the site; the buildings did not appear to merge with the site. The architect of the "house with a lawn for a roof" began with the stark rectilinear geometry of prewar modernism, added stone masonry masses for chimneys, and, on the roof of a lower wing, planted a floating lawn off the living room.

The work of George Fred and William Keck in the years after the war probably best exemplifies the way in which modern architects adjusted to

Fig. 13 George Fred
Keck and William
Keck, Sydney H. Davies
House, Drury Lane and
Bristol Street,
Northfield, 1946.

Fig. 14 Keck and Keck,
Sydney H. Davies
House, interior.

changed conditions. After taking a bold stand on
industrial modernism before the war, the Kecks
accepted the home owner's need for some reassurance of domestic tradition even as they continued to explore new designs for houses and efficient ways to live in them. George Fred Keck
also contributed to the new domestic environment by designing clean, but certainly not eccentric, table and floor lamps for Victor Pearl-
man and Company. Their simple cylindrical

fabric shades topped straight metal poles anchored by disc-shaped bases.[16]

The design of the Kecks' Abel Fagen House in
Lake Forest, built in 1948, went through three
changes, beginning with a severe, rectilinear
scheme and ending with an elaborate sixty-degree pinwheel scheme that rotated off a masonry
fireplace mass (figs. 9, 10). Of the latter version
the *Architectural Record* said, "Recently those
once-heretical words, 'warmth' and 'emotional
content' have appeared more frequently in with-
in-the-family discussions of architecture."[17] The
Wrightian features of the third scheme include
the stepped fascia of the Usonian houses, the triangular grid of the Hanna House, and the abstract combination of wood and stone.

The Kecks pursued the mechanics of making
the house a comfortable living environment.
They addressed the climatic necessities of heating and cooling by reconfiguring the walls and
roofs, rather than by installing appliances that
were produced by advanced technology (see figs.
1, 11). Their interest in radiant heat, created
when hot air moves through hollow floor tiles,
and their elaboration of various ventilating
panels over, under, or alongside fixed insulating
glass, identified their work during the postwar
years. By integrating these climatic control features into the enclosures of wall, floor, and roof,
the Kecks extended a traditional ideal that architecture could incorporate all the requirements of

habitation within structural elements, thereby eliminating the need for separate appliances. Integration, rather than installation, seemed to carry with it a sense of efficiency and economy that had intellectual and compositional origins as much as economic ones. In the Fagen house, for example, the louvered panels that were placed next to the windows looked like shutters, not technological devices. The *Architectural Record* asserted, however, with reference to the Kecks' house, which was on the cover of the September 1948 issue, that "it is debatable whether such a system would completely replace operating sash [windows] in the affections of the public."[18]

A further Keck design, the Sydney H. Davies House in Northfield, constructed in 1946, incorporated all these features in a linear room arrangement, another recurrent feature in Keck homes (figs. 12-14). Major rooms lined up along the southerly exposure could take advantage of winter solar heating. This long facade of modular insulating glass was articulated by louvers both above and below the windows.[19] The Goldman House in Aurora (1951) extended this simple arrangment by articulating communal and private areas by means of differing ceiling heights and alignments with respect to the fireplace masonry. All these wood and masonry houses with walls of glass obeyed a strictly rectilinear pattern. A much freer arrangement appeared in the 1947 house for Jerrold T. Kelly in Barrington, the steel roof structure and stucco walls of which followed a gentle compound curve along the top of a ridge overlooking The Lake of the Woods. When asked to describe its functional aspects, George Fred Keck replied, "I wouldn't describe it primarily in those terms. I drew it that way because I liked it, and what's more, the clients liked it too."[20] Personal and expressive reasons were clearly being permitted in a modernism that had earlier sought to transcend particular conditions and human desires in favor of universal necessities and methods.

One might believe that the Kecks, who designed such buildings as the International Style Miralago Ballroom in 1929 and the aggressively undomestic stucco-and-glass-block Cahn House in Lake Forest in 1937, as well as the House of Tomorrow and Crystal House for the 1933-34 Century of Progress Exposition, were simply imitating whatever style was most current and realistic. In the Edward McCormick Blair House in Lake Bluff (1954) the Kecks returned to prewar modernism, employing steel bar joists, metal stairs, aluminum trim, pipe flues, and travertine

sills.[21] These materials and the resulting tightness of form signaled the increasing influence of Mies van der Rohe's modernism and the impact of his Farnsworth House in Plano, Illinois (see Schulze, fig. 8). The return to an industrial modernism in the mid-fifties isolates the special character of the modern American house in the immediate postwar years.

William Deknatel carried forward the Wrightian interpretation of the modern house both before and after the war. His Newton S. Noble, Jr., House, published in 1947, was part of this tradition (fig. 15).[22] The architect emphasized warmth and intimacy in his choice of cypress siding, red cedar shingles, and a waxed oak interior. The ornamental cast detail of the fireplace demonstrates the architect's continued use of varied small-scale elements, a practice that stood in contrast to an ascetic, repetitive ideal of modernism (fig. 16). The plan of the Noble

Fig. 15 William Deknatel, Newton S. Noble, Jr., House, Bateman Road, Barrington, 1940-41.

Fig. 16 Deknatel, Newton S. Noble, Jr., House, interior.

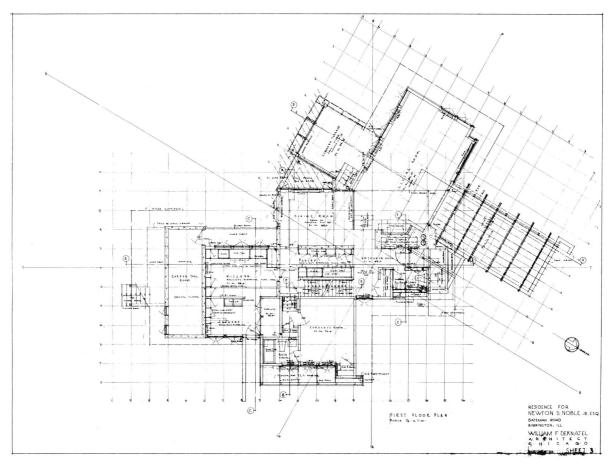

House introduces the combination of two orthogonal grid patterns that Wright also was beginning to experiment with (fig. 17). The living room is placed at an angle relative to the rest of the house, in response to site considerations. This interruption of geometric continuity is more abrupt than the gentle shift in plan that Schweikher used in the Harring House (fig. 8).

Deknatel's continued use of the Wrightian idiom derived from his direct contact with the ideals of the Taliesin Fellowship as a charter applicant in 1932, and it set him apart from those architects who occasionally worked in that idiom for more tactical reasons. His response to European formal reductionism caused him to reinterpret Wright in a way that converged from the opposite direction with other architects' reinterpretations of European modernism, which they made in response to Wright. After material shortages and wartime anxiety had passed, these architects immediately returned to prewar forms.

Most architects of postwar houses managed not to become encumbered with too many ideals. The entries of three of the top winners of the *Chicago Tribune* Chicagoland Prize Homes Competition of 1945 were only moderately modern. The designs of Ray Steurmer, D. Coder Taylor, and C. W. Schroeder showed that low,

spreading roofs had won out over crisp geometric, two-story boxes with banded windows (see pls. 107-12).[23] L. Morgan Yost specifically eschewed such tacking and trimming and concentrated on providing houses for many people. In his account of his career, Yost asserted that he thought that a "democratic architecture would be an architecture that people could do, could afford, could appreciate."[24] Yost took the housing industry procedures and the notions that most people held about houses and gave them a contemporary twist. He could not ignore the structure of the housing and material supply industry, yet he realized that the industrial housing proposals of architects like Konrad Wachsmann "didn't always produce the thing that people would want," and he rejected the ideological purity of industrial modernism because it resulted in houses that were "too much effect and not enough hominess."[25] That is not to say that he simply reproduced what the lowest common denominator desired. By considering methods to economize on materials and space, Yost made changes in the way people actually lived without making them conscious of the change. He described his method by saying "we changed people's habits of living by designing better homes."[26] He realized, for instance, that a better

house could be constructed for the same amount of money by including built-in features such as closets, shelves, and desks, because these features could be paid for as part of the long-term mortgage on the house rather than through short-term financing of furniture.[27]

Yost's Norman C. Deno House in Highland Park of 1951 incorporated advances in a mild way (figs. 18, 19).[28] The pitched roof, cedar and pink buff brick exterior, and the oak parquet floor and plaster interior fit in comfortably with convention. But he also employed the large fixed glass panels bordered by ventilating louvers that the Kecks so often used. Yost's contact with developers, building trades magazines, and other aspects of finance, construction, and economy, along with his appreciation of the ideas of Wright and Wrightian architects, allowed him to blend together many concepts without emphasizing any single one.

A far more ideological traditionalism motivated architect Royal Barry Wills to make his acid comments on the modernist creed in 1949. In an article entitled "Confessions of a Cape Codder," Wills complained that "we never became rabid enough to wage an unholy war against the inherent desires of our clients." As he urged a more subtle campaign of compromise, he inserted a sharp rhetorical aside, "if you can imagine a modernist compromising."[29] Such attacks made the task of the modernist architects much more difficult as they tried to distance themselves from the polemics of prewar architecture and move closer to at least some of

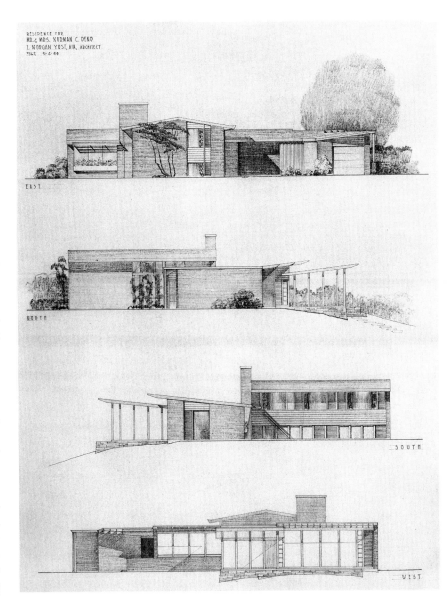

Fig. 18   Lloyd Morgan Yost, Four elevations of the Norman C. Deno House, Highland Park, Sept. 6, 1944 (cat. no. 455).

Fig. 19   Yost, Norman C. Deno House, interior.

*Fig. 20 Bruce Goff,
Ruth Ford House, 404
South Edgelawn, Aurora,
1947-49.*

*Fig. 21 Goff, Ruth Ford
House, interior.*

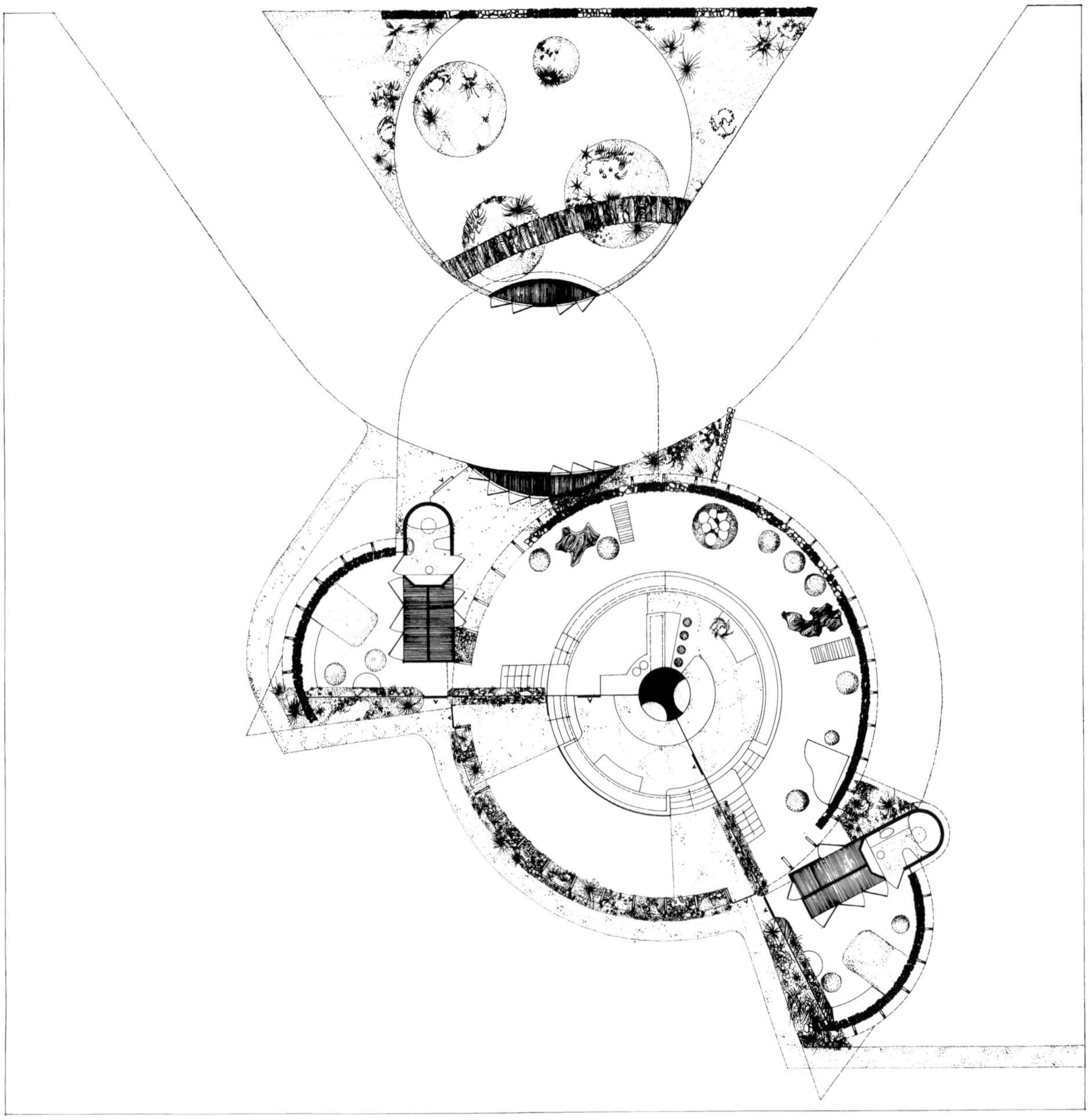

Fig. 22 Goff, Plan of
the Ruth Ford House,
1947 (cat. no. 471).

the values that architects like Wills staked out as exclusively their own.

The combination of industrial modernism and traditional materials and forms could not be more strikingly represented than in a house built in Aurora in 1949: Bruce Goff's Ruth Ford House (figs. 20-22). A 1,700-square-foot, two-bedroom, two-bath house seems a traditional program for a couple with one adult child living away from home. But Mrs. Ford was an artist with specific ideas; she wanted an appropriate setting for her watercolor paintings and a studio to work in. Her request for a black gallery wall prompted Goff to choose a most unexpected material: anthracite coal. Traditional, even primordial, elements included natural materials: cypress and cedar, hemp rope, ashlar coal (disposed around a hearth in the center of the circular plan), and many interior plants. Modern elements included a steel structure (war surplus Quonset hut ribs), hot water radiant heat, neon lighting, and steel window frames. Copper sheathing around the chimney and the ten-inch steel central support column, built-in cabinets, black terrazzo bathtubs, and chunks of raw glass embedded in the coal wall seemed to be part of both worlds. This "Quonset hut mansion," or "Umbrella house," received extensive coverage in *Life* magazine and in the architectural press in 1951.[30] What makes it such a striking combination of the two forces shaping modern American houses after the war is its close relation to two quintessential examples of industrial and natural modernism: R. Buckminster Fuller's Dymaxion House of 1946 and Frank Lloyd Wright's second Jacobs House of 1947.[31]

Fuller's Dymaxion House of 1946 was a development of his 1927 proposal for a suspended

Fig. 23   R. Buckminster
Fuller, Dymaxion House,
1946.

Fig. 24   Fuller,
Dymaxion House, plan;
from "The 8000 Lb.
House," Architectural
Forum 84 (April 1946),
p. 136.

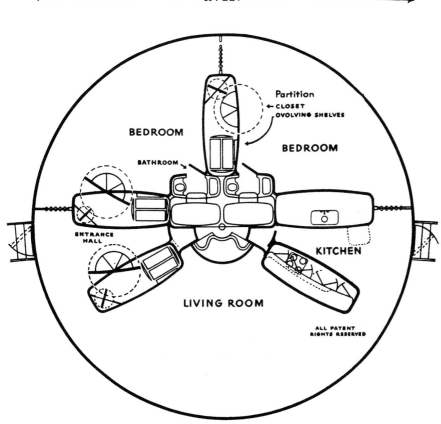

inhabitable prototype. The circular plan and
domical section were in accordance with Fuller's
insistence that, in order to achieve an efficient
use of materials, structural elements and services must be placed at a common point in the
center of the building. Suspended by cables from
a cluster of seven steel tubes surrounded by various utilities outlets, the structure is thirty-six
feet in diameter and twenty-two feet high. A list
of materials clearly indicates that this modern
house took full advantage of the wartime disruption in material availability to strike out in a
new direction: aluminum, Plexiglass, lucite, plastic, rubberized fabrics, synthetic rubber extru-
sions, fiberglass, chrome, molybdenum steel,
magnesium, and nylon. The unfamiliar aluminum roof, exterior and interior walls, and ceilings dominated the appearance of the structure
despite the central fireplace and the aggressively
traditional furnishings from a local Wichita
department store.

Besides the circular plan and domical section,
in his Ford House Goff used several other features of the Dymaxion House. Each building has
a balcony/mezzanine overlooking the main space
and service pods in elliptical shapes that contain
closets and bathrooms. Both homes have folding
accordion screens that separate private from public areas, and a valence at the base of the dome in
each structure holds lights that illuminate the
curved ceilings. Molded bathroom fixtures were
installed as a unit in both houses. Both Fuller
and Goff used steel for the structural frame and
central support. In the Ford House, however, this

hexagonal living unit constructed of metal and
glass (figs. 23, 24). Structural and material considerations, as well as the location of electrical,
mechanical, and plumbing equipment, so dominated the house design that any memory of tradition was completely banished. A postwar proposal, made with the collaboration of the Beech
Aircraft company in Wichita, Kansas, updated
various features and actually appeared to be an

use of surplus steel was not determined by economic necessity. The bases of the Quonset hut ribs were welded to I-beams, whose inward curve was obviously not determined by criteria of structural efficiency. There were some efficient translations of the Quonset hut structure that appeared after the war: Stran-Steel actually offered "arch-rib framing units" in 1947, and Campbell and Wong in California used the original Quonset hut material in a house for Dr. Felton.[32] Goff, however, simply used the Quonset hut steel for poetic purposes, incorporating the curved steel into a reinterpretation of an ancient domical form.

Frank Lloyd Wright's second Jacobs House outside Madison, Wisconsin, also known as the "solar hemicycle," is modern in a natural way. Its curved ring of space is backed into a berm with only the narrowest windows at the top exposed to the northwest (fig. 25). A curved stone wall encloses the back of the house and faces a glass wall opposite (fig. 26). Planters are located along the glass wall. The mezzanine above is a balcony screened from the bedrooms by walls of diagonal wood sheathing. The earthy roughness and solar orientation make this house wholly unindustrial. The fact that the Jacobs built much of it themselves indicates that its materials and techniques were anything but technologically sophisticated. Like the Jacobs House, Goff's Ford House has a seventy-foot-long circumferential wall (in this case, made of anthracite coal laid up in random ashlar) that surrounds the two steel-framed glass walls located on twenty-five-foot radii of the circle. Floor-level planters with rubber and fig trees line the glass walls of the Ford House, and Goff created his arched cypress ceiling from alternating diagonal segments. Finally, the floor contains hot water radiant tubes like those used in the Jacobs house.

In the Ford House Goff fused the forms and some of the materials of industrial production into a purely poetic conception that resonates as cave and tent, as both a technological and primordial dwelling. His imaginative leap was so great, however, that the house became a puzzling anomoly to most people, who still see it as a curiosity rather than as an amazing synthesis of disparate elements.

The attempts at synthesis that these architects made in the postwar modern house in the Chicago area quickly became unnecessary as the economy and tastes changed. The most salient shift occurred when the Kecks, and even Schweikher, produced "Miesian" steel-and-glass houses in 1952 and 1954. The Keck's Blair House mentioned above and Schweikher's Frazel project, which became the Ross J. Beatty, Jr., House in Lake Forest, seem to indicate that postwar adjustments, although in some ways useful, were later swept aside in celebration of new-found strength and clear horizons. For a few years, the

Fig. 25 Frank Lloyd Wright, Solar Hemicycle, Jacobs House II, Middleton, Wisconsin, 1947.

Fig. 26 Wright, Jacobs House II, interior.

conjunction of necessity and desire resulted in a group of houses around Chicago that strived to make, in Paul Schweikher's words, "a radical architecture: essential, fundamental, thorough, and underived."[33] These adjectives describe in large measure the crosscurrents of modern domestic architecture that characterized America in relation to its land, technology, and society. Chicago as an industrial and urban center, on the edge of the heartland that was now agricultural if no longer the frontier, was itself poised between the energy of new horizons and the comfort of rooted stability. The architects of modern houses in the immediate postwar years tried to bring these two images into harmony, much as the proponents of the Prairie Style had tried to do forty years earlier. Although both these balancing acts could support the proposition for only a few years, the products of their attempts sustain our interest in them.

NOTES

1. "A House with Emotional Content," *Architectural Record* 109 (March 1951), pp. 105-10.
2. "Books," *Architectural Forum* 98 (Oct. 1945), pp. 142, 146.
3. Thomas H. Creighton, Frank Lopez, Charles Magruder, and George Sanderson, eds., *Homes Selected by the Editors of Progressive Architecture* (New York, 1947), Introduction.
4. Joseph Hudnut, "The Post-Modern House," *Architectural Record* 97 (May 1945), pp. 70-75; idem, "What Buildings Are Beautiful," *Architectural Record* 103 (May 1948), pp. 88-90.
5. "Today's Typical House," *Architectural Forum* 95 (Oct. 1951), pp. 274, 278, 282.
6. Herbert Gottfried and Jan Jennings, *American Vernacular Architecture, 1870-1940: An Illustrated Glossary* (New York, 1985).
7. Gordon Lorimer, "The Industry Engineered House," *Architectural Record* 102 (Sept. 1947), pp. 74-79.
8. *Oral History of L. Morgan Yost,* interviewed by Betty J. Blum (Chicago, 1986), p. 65.
9. Ibid., p. 77.
10. *Oral History of Paul Schweikher,* interviewed by Betty J. Blum (Chicago, 1984), p. 48.

11. Katherine Morrow Ford and Thomas H. Creighton, eds., *Quality Budget Houses* (New York, 1954), pp. 108-09.
12. Creighton et al. (note 3), pp. 16-17.
13. "Co-op Houses," *Architectural Forum* 84 (Jan. 1946), pp. 89-95.
14. "Ideas Born of Wind and Weather," *Architectural Record* 87 (July 1947), pp. 84-89; *Oral History* (note 8), p. 112.
15. Henry Russell Hitchcock and Arthur Drexler, eds., *Built in U.S.A.: Post-war Architecture* (New York, 1952); *Architectural Record* 100 (Dec. 1946), pp. 73-79.
16. "Architects Design for Industry," *Architectural Record* 105 (June 1949), p. 107.
17. "Emotional Content," *Architectural Record* 107 (March 1950), pp. 105-10.
18. "Broad in Vision Though Narrow in Land," *Architectural Record* 104 (Sept. 1948), pp. 93-96.
19. "This Midwest House...Masters a Difficult Climate," *Architectural Forum* 87 (Sept. 1947), pp. 107-09.
20. "Straight Lines or Panoramic Curves," *Architectural Record* 101 (May 1947), pp. 132-35.
21. Keck Archives at the State Historical Society of Wisconsin, Job number 500.
22. "A Solid, Sturdy Design is Typical of the Middlewest," *Architectural Forum* 87 (Aug. 1947), pp. 72-74.

23. "Ten Prize-Winning Houses," *Architectural Forum* 84 (April 1946), pp. 112-16; see also Stanley Tigerman, *The Postwar American Dream,* exhibition catalogue in The Art Institute of Chicago's *Architecture in Context* series (Chicago, 1985).
24. *Oral History* (note 8), p. 8. See also *Prize Homes* (Chicago, 1948), which reproduces twenty-four prize-winning entries, as well as sixty-eight other designs.
25. *Oral History* (note 8), pp. 9, 20.
26. Ibid., p. 48.
27. Ibid., p. 60.
28. "Residence for Mr. and Mrs. Norman C. Deno," *Architectural Record* 110 (July 1951), pp. 110-12.
29. Royal Barry Wills, "Confessions of a Cape Codder," *Architectural Record* 105 (April 1949), pp. 132-34.
30. *Life* (March 19, 1951), pp. 70-75; "Umbrella House," *Architectural Forum* 94 (April 1951), pp. 118-21.
31. "Industrializing Shelter: The Fuller House," *Architectural Record* 99 (May 1946), pp. 118-20, 134; "The 8,000 Lb. House," *Architectural Forum* 84 (April 1946), pp. 70, 129-36.
32. See "Products for Better Building," *Architectural Record* 101 (May 1947), p. 147; see also Creighton et al. (note 3), pp. 52-54.
33. "Behind the Scenes with Forum Contributors," *Architectural Forum* 86 (May 1947), p. 52.

Exhibiting Progress: Italy's Contribution to the Century of Progress Exposition

Dennis P. Doordan

Speeding along South Lake Shore Drive, motorists may easily miss a two-thousand-year-old column by the side of the road. This ancient Corinthian column is almost lost against the expansive lakeshore vista to the east and dwarfed by the massive colonnade of Soldier Field to the west. When this column from the ancient Roman port of Ostia arrived in Chicago in July 1934, however, the setting was very different. Then the site was home to the 1933-34 Century of Progress Exposition. The fairgrounds stretched along the lakeshore from 12th Street south to 39th Street (figs. 2-4), and the column was erected in front of the Italian Pavilion at the fair. The inscription on its base celebrates one of the most dramatic and popular events of the 1933 season of the Century of Progress Exposition: the transoceanic flight of twenty-four seaplanes led by the Italian aviator and Fascist leader Italo Balbo.[1]

The Balbo Memorial is not the only trace on the city left in the wake of Italy's participation at the fair. Swept up in the enthusiasm of Balbo's flight, the Chicago City Council renamed 7th Street Balbo Drive. And nearby, across from the Field Museum of Natural History, stands the figure of Christopher Columbus. A gift to Chicago from the city's Italian-American community, the statue was dedicated by Balbo himself during his triumphal visit to the Century of Progress Exposition.[2]

More than a simple retelling of the colorful story behind local landmarks, an account of Italy's participation brings into sharp focus a whole series of issues central to our understanding of the Century of Progress Exposition, beginning with the theme of the fair itself. Documents preserved in the exposition archives reveal how fair organizers proposed to structure their vision of the progress of civilization during the century that followed the incorporation of Chicago in 1833. The design of the Italian Pavilion at the fair reveals how the Italian government rejected the role that was originally proposed for Italy by the American organizers (fig. 1). The epic flight of Balbo and the events surrounding his reception in Chicago demonstrate how the Fascist regime attempted to use the fair's celebration of scientific and technological progress to promote a positive image of Fascism among citizens of the United States. Finally, an analysis of the official Italian Pavilion at the fair and of the so-called Italian Village that opened for the 1934 fair season illustrates the way in which different design strategies operated to reinforce or subvert cultural stereotypes.

Science Finds—Industry Applies—Man Conforms

In his account of the Century of Progress Exposition, Lenox Lohr, vice-president and general manager of the fair, described the fair's theme as "the dramatization of the progress of civilization during the hundred years of Chicago's existence."[3] Fair literature linked the specific story of Chicago's development as a metropolis with the universal phenomena of science and technology in the modern era. The official guide to the fair noted that

Fig. 1 Adalberto Libera, Mario De Renzi, Antonio Valente with Alexander V. Capraro, Italian Pavilion, Century of Progress Exposition, 1933.

Fig. 2 Skyride at the Century of Progress Exposition, 1933-34.

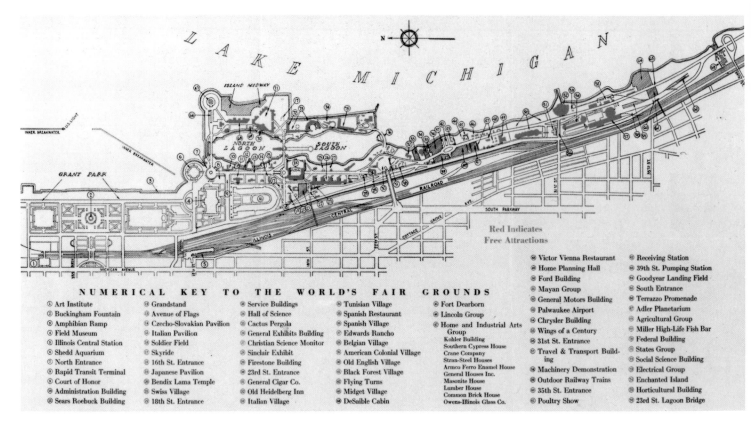

NUMERICAL KEY TO THE WORLD'S FAIR GROUNDS

① Art Institute
② Buckingham Fountain
③ Amphibian Ramp
④ Field Museum
⑤ Illinois Central Station
⑥ Shedd Aquarium
⑦ North Entrance
⑧ Rapid Transit Terminal
⑨ Court of Honor
⑩ Administration Building
⑪ Sears Roebuck Building

⑫ Grandstand
⑬ Avenue of Flags
⑭ Czecho-Slovakian Pavilion
⑮ Italian Pavilion
⑯ Soldier Field
⑰ Skyride
⑱ 16th St. Entrance
⑲ Japanese Pavilion
⑳ Bendix Lama Temple
㉑ Swiss Village
㉒ 18th St. Entrance

㉓ Service Buildings
㉔ Hall of Science
㉕ Cactus Pergola
㉖ General Exhibits Building
㉗ Christian Science Monitor
㉘ Sinclair Exhibit
㉙ Firestone Building
㉚ 23rd St. Entrance
㉛ General Cigar Co.
㉜ Old Heidelberg Inn
㉝ Italian Village

㉞ Tunisian Village
㉟ Spanish Restaurant
㊱ Spanish Village
㊲ Edwards Rancho
㊳ Belgian Village
㊴ American Colonial Village
㊵ Old English Village
㊶ Black Forest Village
㊷ Flying Turns
㊸ Midget Village
㊹ DeSaible Cabin

㊺ Fort Dearborn
㊻ Lincoln Group
㊼ Home and Industrial Arts Group
  Kohler Building
  Southern Cypress House
  Crane Company
  Stran-Steel Houses
  Armco Ferro Enamel House
  General Houses Inc.
  Masonite House
  Lumber House
  Common Brick House
  Owens-Illinois Glass Co.

㊽ Victor Vienna Restaurant
㊾ Home Planning Hall
㊿ Ford Building
Ⓜ Mayan Group
Ⓜ General Motors Building
Ⓜ Palwaukee Airport
Ⓜ Chrysler Building
Ⓜ Wings of a Century
Ⓜ 31st St. Entrance
Ⓜ Travel & Transport Building
Ⓜ Machinery Demonstration
Ⓜ Outdoor Railway Trains
Ⓜ 35th St. Entrance
Ⓜ Poultry Show

Ⓜ Receiving Station
Ⓜ 39th St. Pumping Station
Ⓜ Goodyear Landing Field
Ⓜ South Entrance
Ⓜ Terrazzo Promenade
Ⓜ Adler Planetarium
Ⓜ Agricultural Group
Ⓜ Miller High-Life Fish Bar
Ⓜ Federal Building
Ⓜ States Group
Ⓜ Social Science Building
Ⓜ Electrical Group
Ⓜ Enchanted Island
Ⓜ Horticultural Building
Ⓜ 23rd St. Lagoon Bridge

Red Indicates
Free Attractions

Fig. 3   Plan of the Century of Progress Exposition, 1934 season.

Fig. 4   View of the Century of Progress Exposition, looking south, 1933.

Chicago's corporate birth as a village, and the dawn of an unprecedented era of discovery, invention, and development of things to effect the comfort, convenience, and welfare of mankind, are strikingly associated.[4]

With the cooperation of a host of consultants, corporations, and special advisory boards, fair organizers planned exhibits covering new developments in every field of human endeavor—scientific, industrial, social, and aesthetic—to illustrate the theme neatly summed up in one popular fair slogan: Science Finds—Industry Applies—Man Conforms.[5]

Having settled on a theme, fair organizers were faced with the question of how to exhibit the concept of progress. Individual displays in housing (fig. 5), the Hall of Science (fig. 8), the General Exhibits Pavilion, and the Travel and Transport Building (fig. 6) reviewed advancements in discrete areas of knowledge and experience.

Fig. 5 John C. B. Moore, Richard C. Wood, and S. Clements Horsley, "Design for Living" House, Century of Progress Exposition, 1933.

Fig. 6 Edward H. Bennett, John Holabird, and Hubert Burnham, Travel and Transport Building, Century of Progress Exposition, 1933.

But merely presenting a series of didactic exhibits was not enough; the promoters, organizers, and designers of the Century of Progress Exposition wished to produce an exposition that engaged the visitor in a visceral experience as well as in the cerebral contemplation of progress.[6] If the fair were to be more than the sum of its individual parts, some vivid image (or, better yet, a set of images) was needed that could serve as an unmistakable point of departure from which the progress of Chicago, specifically, and civilization, generally, could be felt and measured. The star Arcturus provided one such point. Each evening fairgoers gathered in the Court of the Hall of Science for the "Arcturus Ceremony," in which light from the star that was focused on a photoelectric cell provided the current necessary to turn on the fair's illumination system. Forty light-years from earth, the light of Arcturus captured at the 1933 fair had begun its long journey to Chicago during the World's Columbian Exposition of 1893. Thus, past and present were linked through the modern magic of science and technology (see Bouman, figs. 18-20).

South of the colorful, modern main exhibition pavilions, another kind of architectural design appeared linking Chicago's present to its past. Reconstructions of historic Fort Dearborn and Du Sable's cabin resurrected the setting for the beginning of Chicago's one hundred years of progress. Before they entered Fort Dearborn, fair visitors were advised to:

Look back and scan the Chicago skyline with its towering skyscrapers; drink deep the scene about you that voices a century of progress. For the next moment you are carried back a hundred years and more.... Here is contrast almost breathtaking—a century spanned with a few short steps, and with little need for imaginative aid.[7]

If the stars above Chicago and the legendary sites of the city's origin could be pressed into service to animate the fair's theme of Chicago's century of progress, could not the same thing be done for the dramatization of the larger theme of the progress of modern scientific and technological civilization?

Old Europe

In February 1931 John S. Sewell, director of the Exhibits Department for the Century of Progress, sent two long memoranda to Henry Cole, director of the fair's London office, outlining the desired format for foreign participation.[8] Sewell favored the creation of a series of European villages, each ranging from one to three and a half

acres in area, depicting the traditional styles of Old World architecture. Such villages had proven to be popular attractions at earlier World's Fairs.[9] Sewell envisioned the Old Europe villages making their own distinctive contribution to the fair's iconographic program. Just as Fort Dearborn provided a necessary starting point for Chicago's century of progress, so too, the premodern image of "Old Europe" was to be pressed into service as the natural foil for the vibrant new world spawned by modern science and technology.

Sewell proposed to cluster the villages together in an Old Europe exhibit near the 23rd Street entrance to the fairgrounds (fig. 7). The proposed location stood roughly at the midpoint between the scientific exhibits clustered at the north end of the site and the carnival atmosphere of the Midway to the south. Sewell wrote to Cole:

At this point Old Europe will mark the transition from matters of purely intellectual and commercial interest to those in which what is ordinarily known as human interest begins to predominate. Everything else north of Twenty-third Street will be modernistic in character. Old Europe, situated at Twenty-third Street, sets alongside the beginning of a new art the culmination of an older one.... To me, considering the underlying philosophy of this exposition, there is a peculiar fitness in setting what I hope will be a fine example of this European architecture alongside of the budding effort of the modernistic.[10]

Sewell elaborated on this theme four days later in a second memorandum to Cole.

Underlying economic conditions have changed and the old style of architecture, beautiful as it is, is no longer suited to the changed conditions. Modern architects have started to develop a new style.... In this matter we are at the turning point or perhaps better we should say we are at the parting of the ways.... Everything north of Twenty-third Street will be modernistic. Should not those nations which brought the old order of things to such a point of perfection take pride in setting alongside of this modernistic effort a worthy example of the old order which is passing.... This Old Europe idea is probably the last singularly fitting opportunity for Europe to record the great achievements of its past generations.[11]

Cole dutifully tried to solicit foreign support for Sewell's proposal. Official fair brochures describing the plan for "Old Europe" were sent to potential foreign participants, and pamphlets distributed by the fair's London office clearly articulated the role of the villages in the larger scheme of the Century of Progress.[12]

Not surprisingly, foreign nations displayed little enthusiasm for playing the role of quaint custodians of a picturesque past. In addition to resistance to the Old Europe concept, fair organizers faced other obstacles. As the Great De-

pression spread worldwide in the early 1930s, many countries decided they could not afford the cost of participating in a major World's Fair. Later, Lenox Lohr reluctantly admitted :

In the face of opposition to the high tariff policy of the United States, it was useless to suggest to foreign coun-

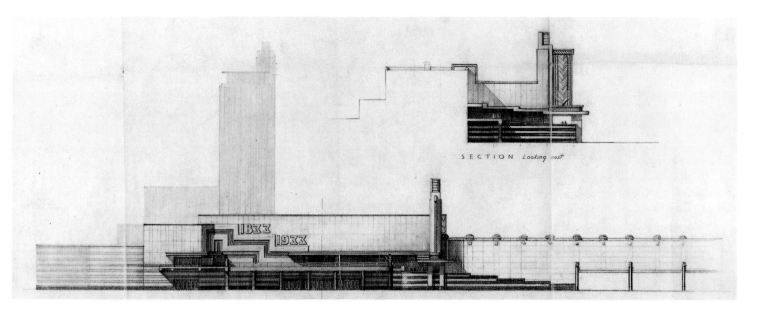

SECTION *Looking east*

Fig. 9   Office of Paul Cret, South elevation and partial section of the Hall of Science, Century of Progress Exposition, 1933.

Fig. 7   View of the Century of Progress Exposition, looking south from 23rd Street, 1934 season.

Fig. 8   Italian Scientific Exhibit, Hall of Science, Century of Progress Exposition, 1933.

tries that an exhibition of their products at the Fair would result in a greatly increased demand for them in America.[13]

Searching for any persuasive rationale for foreign participation, fair promoters argued that the charm of the foreign villages would awaken a nostalgic desire on the part of Americans of foreign descent to visit their ancestral homelands and thus promote tourism. When the Century of Progress Exposition opened in May 1933, however, only a handful of countries sponsored official national pavilions.[14]

Italy Comes to the Fair

In March 1931 fair officials visited Rome and pitched the concept of Old Europe to Italian officials in the Foreign Office without success. The Italians declined, citing American tariff policy as the chief obstacle and expressing doubts that, given economic conditions in the United States, the fair would actually happen.[15] Political rather than commercial or tourist concerns prompted the Fascist regime to change its mind and participate in the fair. The Century of Progress Exposition offered Italy an excellent opportunity to promote a positive image for Mussolini and the Fascist regime at a time when the regime's image in the United States desperately needed some attention.

On the whole, Mussolini and Fascism enjoyed good press in the United States during the 1920s.[16] In November 1929, however, *Harpers Magazine* published a long article critical of Mussolini's efforts to organize the huge Italian-American community in the United States. Italy's Duce, the article charged, had established Fascist organizations to rally support for Fascism

and suppress criticism of the regime among Italians in the United States.[17] In the wake of the *Harpers Magazine* exposé, there were calls by members of the United States Congress for a congressional investigation of the Fascist League of North America (FLNA), an organization created in 1925 to coordinate the programs of various Italian-American organizations.[18] In order to avoid such an investigation, the FLNA was disbanded in late December 1929.[19] This was not the end of Fascist efforts to promote the regime's interests in the United States, but it did force the Italians to reconsider their approach to propaganda abroad.

In March 1932 Felix Streyckmans, director of the fair's Office of Foreign Participation, and Major O. J. F. Keatinge, an advisor to Lenox Lohr, visited Rome to confer with Foreign Office officials. In a memorandum to his superiors in Chicago, Keatinge reported the new Italian position:

The idea is to erect a small pavilion which will shelter exhibits demonstrating such matters as education, communications, hygiene, etc., in fact all activities of the government with a special emphasis on the benefits and development attained under the present regime. The government would insist that this display should be entirely modern in character and that it was no use thinking they would go in for a reproduction of old buildings which would give a false impression of the high degree of modern efficiency which has been reached by the Italian state.[20]

The Italians planned to supplement the display housed in a small pavilion with other exhibits installed in the General Exhibits Pavilion and the Hall of Science.

When the fair opened, the Hall of Science included lavish displays outlining the Italian contributions to modern energy, transportation,

and communications technologies (fig. 8). This century of Italian progress was presented against the background of two millennia of Italian contributions to civilization. Models of ancient Roman ports and roads, surgical instruments from Pompeii, and the discoveries of explorers, scientists, and artists, such as Marco Polo, Christopher Columbus, Leonardo da Vinci, and Galileo, were acknowledged in different exhibits.[21] By the time the fair opened, however, the "small pavilion" had grown to become one of the most dramatic architectural designs at the exposition, and plans were underway for Italy to seize center stage at this mammoth celebration of civilization's advancements over one hundred years.

The Italian Pavilion

According to the official guidebook published by the fair:

The voice of modern Italy, vibrant with the heroic deeds of Fascism, speaks more resoundingly, more intelligently and more forcefully to the World's Fair visitor than that of any other foreign nation participating in A Century of Progress.[22]

Propaganda, rather than commercial opportunities, explains why Italy came to Chicago in 1933. In order to appreciate how Italy "spoke" so forcefully, it is necessary to examine the Italian Pavilion in light of architectural and exhibition design at the fair. As early as May 1928, the Architectural Commission, chaired by Harvey Wiley Corbett, rejected the classical architecture characteristic of the 1893 Columbian Exposition

and recommended that the fair be designed in a modern style expressive of the spirit of the times.[23] Buildings like Paul Cret's Hall of Science abandoned overt references to specific historical precedents in favor of a modernist abstraction of architectural form (fig. 9). These pavilions articulated the progressive spirit in asymmetrical compositions of windowless volumes, smooth surfaces, and novel materials animated by Joseph Urban's extraordinary color scheme. The result was described by one contemporary critic as "containers to house temporary exhibits...wrapped in lively colors or labels."[24]

The Italian Pavilion, designed by Adalberto Libera, Mario De Renzi, and Antonio Valente, with local supervision by Chicago architect Alexander V. Capraro, demonstrated another design strategy (figs. 10, 11).[25] The designers selected easily recognizable symbols, inflated their size, and incorporated them into the design as independent architectural elements. The impact of the Italian Pavilion was due, in great part, to the skillful juxtaposition of two potent symbols: an aircraft wing, emblematic of recent Italian aviation triumphs, and the fascio littorio, the symbol of the Italian Fascist Party.[26] A huge aircraft wing with the word "Italia" across its leading edge served as the entrance canopy for the Italian Pavilion.[27] The word "Italia" appeared again atop an eighty-foot-high tower rendered as a stylized fascio sheathed in metal with the ax blade fabricated of Aurora Prism Glass set in steel sash.[28] The Italian Pavilion conflated the technological triumph of modern aviation with the political

Figs. 10, 11   Italian Pavilion, Century of Progress Exposition, 1933, exterior.

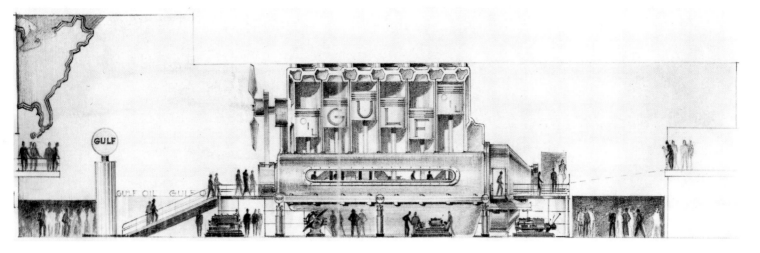

Fig. 12 Holabird and Root, Gulf Oil Exhibit, Century of Progress Exposition, 1933.

identity of Mussolini's Fascism in a manner typical of the period.

Propaganda and advertising design emerged in the 1920s as a distinctive form of design practice.[29] The design strategy employed in the Italian Pavilion has obvious parallels with some of the corporate pavilions and exhibits designed for the fair and reflected the latest in exhibition design.[30] A gigantic Havoline Thermometer towered two hundred feet over the fairgrounds, and Holabird and Root proposed a huge combustion engine, which the visitor would be able to walk through, as part of the Gulf Oil Exhibit (fig. 12).[31] This type of advertising and propaganda design did more than provide an efficient medium for conveying corporate or political messages. The imaginative manipulation of scale and dramatic juxtaposition of forms reduced complex phenomena like manufacturing processes or political ideologies to easily grasped, popular symbols. Propaganda design captured the (often jaded) public's attention and encouraged the visitor to experience the promoter's message literally by walking through the exhibit. This design strategy features dynamic images rather than explanatory texts and emphasizes the immediacy and excitement of novel sensations and experiences over more erudite and pedantic forms of presentation.

Inside the Italian Pavilion, the visitor encountered exhibits outlining ambitious public works projects, such as the extensive campaign of land reclamation that was underway in the Pontine Marshes, southwest of Rome. But the essence of the message Fascist Italy wished to convey to an American audience was set out in the decorative program of the basilica-like main reception hall (fig. 13). Murals filling the upper register of the wall and models on display in the hall hailed Mussolini's development of a modern transpor-

Figs. 13, 14 Reception Hall, Italian Pavilion.

Fig. 15   Photo panel in
the Reception Hall,
Italian Pavilion.

Fig. 16   View of Italo
Balbo's flight to
Chicago, 1933.

tation infrastructure. The mural's central motif included a fascio flanked on one side by a profile of Mussolini and on the other by the Latin word *dux*. Superimposed on the bottom of the fascio appeared a mile marker with the inscription *Roma Caput Mundi* and the roman numeral XI (a reference to the eleventh year of the Fascist regime, that is, 1933). To either side of this central area, political maps depicting new Italian rail lines, highways, and maritime and aviation routes filled the rest of the walls. An eighteen-foot-long model of the latest Italian luxury liner, the *Rex*, occupied the center of the hall. Opposite the great curved end wall of the hall and on axis with the *Rex*, a smaller model of a Savoia-Marchetti seaplane was also exhibited (fig. 14).

The celebration of modern transportation was entirely appropriate to the theme of the Century of Progress Exposition and a source of justifiable pride for Italians. The five large photo panels illustrating contemporary views of Rome conveyed one of the central themes of Fascist propaganda: Mussolini's revival of the triumphal spirit of Rome's imperial past. The first photo panel on the left showed the Colosseum (fig. 15). In the foreground stood a single commemorative column erected in 1932 to mark the inauguration of the Via dell'Impero. This new street (today known as the Via dei Fori Imperiali) linked the

Colosseum with the Piazza Venezia (the site of Mussolini's office in Rome) and represented one of the regime's most important urban interventions in the capital. Then came views of the Roman Forum and the Capitoline Hill—sites associated with civil authority in the city's history. The fourth panel showed the vista from the foot of the Capitoline Hill along the Via del Mare (the present Via del Teatro di Marcello) toward the ancient Theater of Marcellus. In the Fascist plan for Rome, this area marked the point of departure for an ambitious new extension of the city of Rome toward the sea. The sequence concluded with the modern equivalent of the ancient Colosseum and Forum: the recently completed stadium in the new Forum Mussolini (today called the Foro Italico) on the northern edge of the capital.

A brochure available to fair visitors extolled the achievements of a decade of Fascist rule:

Thanks to Benito Mussolini's enthusiasm for Rome, the city is reacquiring the aspect described by historians during the most glorious period of Roman history. New quarters have arisen and are developing rapidly, new and magnificent public buildings are being put up, great modern urban undertakings are decided upon and carried out with remarkable rapidity, while in the streets the new life of Rome flows with ever increasing steadiness.[32]

Italy's most dramatic contribution to the fair, however, was not its pavilion or the scientific

exhibits, but its decision to include Chicago and the fair in one of the epic flights of the decade.

Italo Balbo's Transoceanic Flight

Late in the afternoon of Saturday, July 15th, 1933, an estimated one million people lined Chicago's lakeshore awaiting the arrival of an aerial armada led by the Fascist Italo Balbo. At approximately 5:45 p.m., twenty-four Savoia-Marchetti S.55X seaplanes swooped low past the fairgrounds, landed on the lake, and taxied to their moorings at Navy Pier having completed a 6,100-mile flight from their air base at Orbetello, near Rome (fig. 16).[33] Overhead, forty-two U.S. Army planes provided an escort for the Italian squadron. The American aircraft formed the word "Italia" in the sky while fair officials, politicians, and civic leaders greeted Balbo and his ninety-six airmen at Navy Pier. The Italians were whisked to a reception at Soldier Field, where a crowd estimated at some 75,000 to 100,000 people awaited the new heroes. Sounding a familiar fair theme, Illinois Governor Henry Horner told the crowd that the flight "epitomizes, dramatically and forcefully, the progress of the world in the last hundred years."[34] Chicago's Mayor Kelly announced the renaming of 7th Street to Balbo Drive.

The mastermind of the epic flight and the center of attention in Chicago was Italo Balbo himself. A charismatic figure, Balbo was one of the organizers of the 1922 Fascist March on Rome. Ruthless in his suppression of antifascist forces, he rose rapidly in the new regime, becoming Minister of Aviation in 1929. In the early 1930s Balbo was considered Mussolini's heir-apparent.[35] Under Balbo's leadership, Italian aviation enjoyed enormous prestige at home and abroad. The popular fascination with aviation meant that record-setting flights by Fascist pilots could serve as ideal vehicles for promoting a dynamic image of Fascism. In one historian's words:

Fascism proclaimed itself to be a new and revolutionary political movement, a break with the past, a path to the future; so was aviation. Fascism exalted courage, youth, speed, power, heroism; so did flying.... Mussolini sensed aviation's potential for propaganda. The wonders of fascism could literally be written in the skies.[36]

Called the *Crociera Aerea del Decennale* (Decennial Air Cruise), the flight was conceived as part of the national celebration of the first decade of Fascist rule and as a gesture of goodwill between Italy and the United States (fig. 17).

The bold venture was a smashing success. Descriptions in the American press of Balbo's

Fig. 17 Luigi Martinati, Crociera Aerea del Decennale (Decennial Air Cruise), poster, 1933.

flight were filled with superlatives. The *New York Times* called the Rome to Chicago flight "the greatest mass flight in aviation history."[37] *Time* magazine hailed the arrival in Chicago as "the glorious end of a glorious flight."[38] The *Chicago Tribune* called it the most notable landing in America since Columbus's arrival and added:

From the historical perspective it was memorable, for these men came out of Rome, the world's oldest capital and scene of a civilization 3,000 years old, as ambassadors of goodwill to the world's youngest capital, with a history of 100 years.[39]

The parallel between Balbo and Columbus was one of the favorite themes in coverage of the event. When the Balbo squadron left Orbetello, for example, the *Chicago Herald and Examiner* published an editorial cartoon with the caption "Centuries of Progress." The cartoon depicted Columbus's ship, the Santa Maria, sailing on the ocean, with Balbo's plane soaring overhead, and was accompanied by a map that traced the intrepid Italians' routes.[40]

While Balbo participated in the unveiling of a new statue of Columbus at the south end of Grant Park during his stay, Mussolini, rather than Columbus, figured most prominently in the aviator's public statements.[41] In remarks, delivered in Italian, Balbo described the flight as

Fig. 18 View of entrance to the Italian Village.

proof of a "new spirit which urges us toward progress," and he was careful to attribute the success of his flight to the inspiring leadership of Mussolini:

The Italian airmen are soldiers in the service of a nation which has a great inspiration at its head, Mussolini.... I owe also to him and his inspiration as a leader my unshakable faith in victory.[42]

Balbo and his airmen spent three days in Chicago, and wherever they went they were greeted by large and enthusiastic crowds. On Sunday morning, 40,000 people gathered outside Holy Name Cathedral to catch a glimpse of the Italians as they arrived to attend services.[43] That evening, 3,500 people attended a banquet at the Stevens Hotel in their honor. The next day, the Italians visited the fair, where it was noted that "they were especially interested in the [Italian] pavilion since its architecture is symbolic of their aeronautic achievement."[44] On Tuesday, July 18th, a crowd of people, ten deep, lined Michigan Avenue from 8th Street to the Chicago River to watch a parade honoring Balbo and his airmen.[45] A scattering of anti-Fascist circulars appeared among the crowds, but few journalists raised any embarrassing questions about Balbo's role in the bloody suppression of political dissidents at home.[46] In the summer of 1933 Chicago was satisfied to entertain an authentic aviation hero and bask in the warm glow of an epic aerial voyage.

The year 1933 proved to be a good one for Italy. Following Balbo's aerial conquest of the Atlantic Ocean, the Italian liner *Rex* captured the prestigious Blue Ribbon with a record-setting crossing of the Atlantic. The Italian boxer

Fig. 19 Schmidt, Garden and Erikson, Italian Village, Century of Progress Exposition, 1934.

Fig. 20   Holabird and
Root with Andrew
Rebori, Bird's-eye view
of Streets of Paris,
Century of Progress
Exposition, 1933
(cat. no. 590).

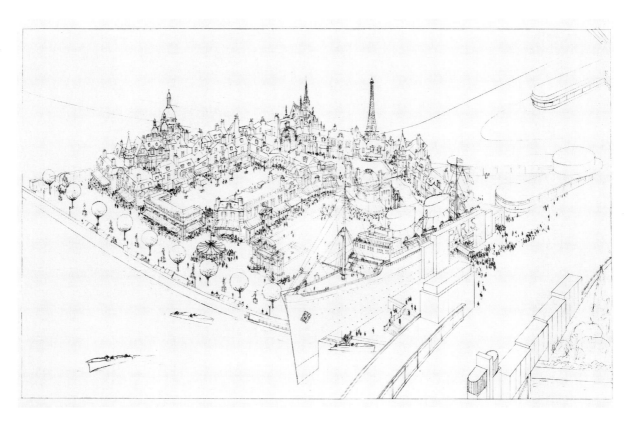

Primo Carnera reigned as the heavyweight champion of the world, and the great inventor Guglielmo Marconi was honored by the Century of Progress Exposition for his development of wireless telegraphy and radio.[47] Press accounts of Italian exploits were filled with adjectives like "modern," "daring," "athletic," and "inventive." The star Arcturus was even forced to defer to the Italians one evening. As part of the ceremonies honoring Marconi, a beam from the star Capella was transmitted to Chicago via wireless telegraphy from an observatory in Florence, Italy, to light the fair.[48]

The Villages

The success of the 1933 season prompted fair organizers to extend the exposition for a second season. Italy returned for the 1934 edition of the Century of Progress with a new emphasis on commercial considerations. Encouraged by the recent repeal of Prohibition, Italian wine merchants sponsored an exhibit and display booths promoting glassware, foodstuffs, and arts and crafts.[49] Italy tried to revive the memory of its dramatic success the previous summer. "Italian Day" at the fair was scheduled to coincide with the first anniversary of Balbo's arrival in Chicago, and a marble column commemorating the Rome to Chicago flight was unveiled in front of the Italian Pavilion. Balbo addressed the crowd again, this time by radio from Rome.[50]

Fairgoers encountered another version of Italy at the 1934 fair, one at odds with the dynamic modernism signalled by the fascio and wings of the official pavilion. The Italian Village offered visitors a chance to explore a simulated medieval walled town. In place of the official Italian Pavilion's emphasis on modern transportation networks and public works projects, the Italian Village simulated the picturesque qualities of narrow winding streets, medieval towers, fountains, and ancient ruins.[51] This was an American portrait of an Italy of picture postcard views and old-world charm (see figs. 18, 19).

A group of Chicago-area investors, headed by Joseph Imburgio, formed the Italian Village, Inc., and commissioned the Chicago architectural firm of Schmidt, Garden and Erikson to design the village.[52] Nothing about the village challenged the visitor to reconsider his or her image of Italy. Instead, the village reinforced stereotypes of Italy as a nation of narrow streets, ancient monuments, and singing waiters. Amid the reproductions of medieval towers and broken columns, the only references to contemporary Italy consisted of street signs identifying the Via Marconi, the Piazza Mussolini, and the Cortile Balbo.

The Italian Village was the progeny of two very popular and lucrative attractions of the 1933 fair: the Streets of Paris (fig. 20) and the Belgian Village (fig. 21). Operated as private concessions rather than official national pavilions

Italy at the Century of Progress Exposition   229

during the 1933 fair season, they provided shops, restaurants, and entertainment facilities (and, in the case of the Streets of Paris, income for Chicago's own architects) in settings that simulated historic architecture and popular street scenes in their respective countries.[53] The Belgian Village featured folk dancing and craft demonstrations while the Streets of Paris quickly acquired a reputation for offering some of the most risqué revues at the fair.[54] Their success spawned, the following year, a whole series of new villages clustered along the Midway south of the 23rd Street entrance to the fairgrounds (see fig. 22).[55]

In 1933 Mussolini's Fascist Italy, literally carried on the wings of modern technology, came to Chicago and staked its claim to a place of honor at the celebration of a century of progress. But this was not the role that fair organizers initially projected for Italy. What Fascist Italy refused to do, the Italian Village, Inc., was only too happy to produce—a quaint and familiar image of an Italy untouched by progress. So, the next year, a second, American-inspired Italy appeared, competing not for the world's respect but for the tourist's dollar.

Six decades later, neither Italy can bear careful scrutiny. Mussolini ultimately led his Italy not to new heights of international prestige but to ruin. The Italian Village recreated Italy as a charming Disneyland-like theme park, not a country struggling through the process of modernization and industrialization. Ironically, this Italy was as unfamiliar and foreign to most Italian-Americans as it was to non-Italians visiting the fair. The vast majority of the Italians who emigrated to the Chicago area arrived from Italy's rural south and not from the towns recalled in Schmidt, Garden and Erikson's *tableau vivant* of northern sites. Nor were the personalities behind these two Italys admirable models of progressive-minded men. Italo Balbo, whose flight to Chicago did so much to animate the Italian presence at the fair, actively participated in the organized curtailment of civil liberties in Fascist Italy, and when Joseph Imburgio died in a plane crash in 1966, Chicago newspapers referred to him as a "wealthy hoodlum lawyer."

World's Fairs are, by their very nature, ephemeral events. For the student of history they offer snapshots, not just of a moment in time, but of all the aspirations and ideals that give each era its particular identity. The Balbo Memorial on Lake Shore Drive records one of the epic feats of aviation during the 1930s. A more appropriate inscription might read, *Sic Transit Gloria.*

Fig. 21   View of Belgian Village, Century of Progress Exposition, 1933.

Fig. 22   View of Black Forest Village, Century of Progress Exposition, 1934.

NOTES

1.   The inscription reads "This column/Twenty centuries old/erected on the beach of Ostia/The port of Imperial Rome/To watch over the fortunes and victories/Of the Roman triremes/Fascist Italy with the sponsorship of Benito/Mussolini/Presents to Chicago/ As a symbol and memorial in honor/Of the Atlantic Squadron led by Balbo/Which with Roman daring flew across the ocean/In the Eleventh year/Of the Fascist era." Ira J. Bach and Mary Lackritz Gray, *A Guide to Chicago's Public Sculpture* (Chicago, 1983), p. 1. Balbo's flight took place at a time when many countries, including the Soviet Union and Great Britain, were attempting to break world records in flight speeds and distances.

2.   Ibid., pp. 9-10.

3. Lenox R. Lohr, *Fair Management: The Story of a Century of Progress* (Chicago, 1952), p. 14.

4. *Official Guide, Book of the Fair, 1933, with 1934 Supplement* (Chicago, 1934), p. 11.

5. Ibid.

6. For an excellent discussion of the distinctive character of American fairs in the 1930s, see Warren Susman, "The People's Fair: Cultural Contradictions of a Consumer Society," in *Culture as History: The Transformation of American Society in the Twentieth Century* (New York, 1933), pp. 211-30.

7. *Official Guide* (note 4), p. 128.

8. In September 1930 the fair opened an office in London to publicize the exposition in Europe. In late March 1931 the London office was closed and its responsibilities were transferred to the Office of Foreign Participation under the direction of Felix Streyckmans, who was headquartered in Chicago. The correspondence of both offices is preserved in the Century of Progress Exposition Archive at the University of Illinois at Chicago (hereafter cited as CPE-UIC).

9. For a discussion of the phenomenon of architectural villages at earlier fairs, see Edward N. Kaufman, "The Architectural Museum from World's Fair to Restoration Village," *Assemblage* 9 (June 1989), pp. 20-39. See also Paul Greenhalgh, *Ephemeral Vistas: The Expositions Universelles, Great Exhibitions and World Fairs, 1851-1939* (Manchester, 1988), pp. 112-42.

10. Memorandum from John S. Sewell to Henry Cole, Feb. 20, 1931; CPE-UIC, Foreign Participation Series, Folder 11-144.

11. Memorandum from John S. Sewell to Henry Cole, Feb. 24, 1931; CPE-UIC, Foreign Participation Series, Folder 11-144.

12. One brochure, for example, offered the following rationale for the villages: "It will enable American citizens of European descent to see for themselves how their European ancestors lived. This in itself, in contrast to the modern cities in which they now live, will give them a good idea of the changes that have occurred during the last hundred years"; *Century of Progress Exposition, Old Europe* (Antwerp, n.d.), p. 6.

13. Lohr (note 3), p. 154. A typical example of the fair's reception abroad is contained in a memorandum from Hallet Johnson, American chargé d'affaires in The Hague, to fair officials, reporting in April 1931 that Dutch participation was highly unlikely "as long as the possibilities for the exportation of many Dutch products is out of the question owing to the high American tariffs"; CPE-UIC, Foreign Participation Series, Folder 11-124. Similar messages were conveyed to fair officials by American consular officials in Greece and Denmark. The fair's representative in Europe, Henry Cole, reported much the same message to his employers in Chicago. See, for example, a memorandum from Henry Cole to John S. Sewell (Feb. 26, 1931) regarding Belgium's resistance to participation due to American tariff policy; CPE-UIC, Foreign Participation Series, Folder 11-157.

14. Czechoslovakia, Italy, Japan, and Sweden erected national pavilions. Other countries sponsored small exhibits installed in various exposition pavilions or sanctioned private trade and tourist organizations to present industrial and travel displays. For a list of foreign participants, see Lohr (note 3), pp. 155-58.

15. The relevant correspondence is preserved in the CPE-UIC, Government Correspondence Series, Folder 2-1106.

16. For a discussion of American perceptions of Italian Fascism during the 1920s and 1930s, see John P. Diggins, *Mussolini and Fascism: The View from America* (Princeton, 1972), pp. 93-94.

17. Marcus Duffield, "Mussolini's American Empire: The Fascist Invasion of the United States," *Harpers Magazine* 159 (Nov. 1929), p. 672.

18. For the activities of the Fascist League of North America, see Alan Cassels, "Fascism for Export: Italy and the United States in the Twenties," *American Historical Review* 69 (April 1964), pp. 707-12; and Gaetano Salvemini, *Italian Fascist Activities in the United States* (New York, 1977).

19. For a discussion of Duffield's article and its aftermath, see Salvemini (note 18), pp. 73-74; and Diggins (note 16), pp. 93-94.

20. Memorandum from O. J. F. Keatinge to Henry Cole, March 10, 1932; CPE-UIC, Government Correspondence Series, Folder 2-1106. Upon his return to Chicago, Felix Streyckmans communicated the same information to the Italian consul in Chicago, Giuseppe Castruccio; Letter from Felix Streyckmans to Giuseppe Castruccio, May 3, 1933; CPE-UIC, Government Correspondence Series, Folder 2-1097.

21. One of the most complete descriptions of the Italian exhibit in the Hall of Science appeared in the 1934 edition of the fair guide, the *Official Guide Book of the World's Fair of 1934* (Chicago, 1934), p. 30.

22. *Official Guide* (note 4), p. 93.

23. For a description of the Architectural Commission's deliberations, see Lohr (note 3), chap. 6, "Architecture Interprets the Theme"; and Forrest Crissey, "Why the Century of Progress Architecture?" *Saturday Evening Post* 205 (June 19, 1933), pp. 16-17, 60-64. Crissey's article is based on a long interview with Allen D. Albert, secretary to the Architectural Commission.

24. Arthur F. Woltersdorf, "Carnival Architecture," *American Architect* 143 (July 1933), p. 11.

25. Alexander V. Capraro was born in Campobasso, Italy, emigrated to the United States in 1899, and studied at the Armour Institute of Technology (now the Illinois Institute of Technology), in 1912-14. For additional information on Capraro, see Giovanni Schiavo, *The Italians in Chicago* (Chicago, 1928), p. 168. For background on the Italian designers, see Giacomo Polin and Giovanni Marzari, *Adalberto Libera* (Milan, 1989); Dennis P. Doordan, *Building Modern Italy: Italian Architecture, 1914-1936* (New York, 1988); and Richard Etlin, *Modernism in Italian Architecture, 1890-1940* (Cambridge, Mass., 1991).

26. The fascio, a bundle of rods bound together around an ax with the blade projecting, was an ancient Roman symbol of authority, revived by the Fascists as the party's symbol; see Philip V. Cannistraro, ed., *Historical Dictionary of Fascist Italy* (Westport, Conn., 1982), p. 205.

27. A set of six blueprints for the Italian Pavilion signed by Alexander V. Capraro is preserved in the architecture collection of the Chicago Historical Society (see cat. no. 600).

28. The giant fascio of the Italian Pavilion repeated an idea that had proved immensely popular in the important Mostra della Rivoluzione Fascista staged in Rome the previous year. For this exhibition celebrating the tenth anniversary of the Fascist March on Rome, Libera and De Renzi erected four huge fasci across the facade of the Palazzo delle Rivoluzione Fascista; see Diane Ghirardo, "Architecture and Culture in Fascist Italy," *Journal of Architectural Education* 45 (Feb. 1992), pp. 67-75. Libera used the same motif for the Italian Pavilion at the international exposition staged in Brussels in 1935; see Polin and Marzari (note 25), p. 152.

29. For more on the theme of advertising architecture, see John Gloag, "Advertising in Three Dimensions," *Architectural Review* 74 (Sept. 1933), pp. 107-16; and Dennis P. Doordan, "The Advertising Architecture of Fortunato Depero," *The Journal of Decorative and Propaganda Arts* 12 (Spring 1989), pp. 46-55.

30. The historian Roland Marchand has argued that the Chicago fair marked a significant moment in the history of corporate exhibits at World's Fairs; see Roland Marchand, "The Designers Go to the Fair, Part I: Walter Dorwin Teague and the Professionalization of Corporate Industrial Exhibits, 1933-1940," *Design Issues* 8 (Fall 1991), pp. 4-17. See also Roland Marchand, "The Designers Go to the Fair, Part II: Norman Bel Geddes, The General Motors 'Futurama' and the Visit-to-the-Factory Transformed," *Design Issues* 8 (Spring 1992), pp. 23-40.

31. For the Havoline Thermometer, see *Official Guide* (note 4), p. 103; and *Official Pictures of A Century of Progress Exposition* (Chicago, 1933), p. 24. For the Gulf Oil Exhibit, see Robert Bruegmann, *Holabird and Roche and Holabird and Root: An Illustrated Catalog of Works, 1880-1940* (New York, 1991), vol. 3, pp. 247-48.

32. *Ten Years of Italian Progress* (Milan, 1933), p. 26.

33. The Italian fliers departed Orbetello on July 2nd. En route, the squadron stopped at Amsterdam (where one airman was killed when his plane crashed upon landing), Londonderry (where the Italians were delayed by bad weather), Reykjavik (another lengthy weather delay), Cartwright in Labrador, Shediac in Newfoundland, and Montreal (where the Italian ambassador to the United States, August Rosso, joined the flight as a passenger). Total flight time amounted to 47 hours, 52 minutes.

34. Philip Kinsley, "Italy's Intrepid Flyers Reach Goal of Victory," *Chicago Tribune* (July 16, 1933), p. 2.

35. Claudio G. Segre, *Italo Balbo: A Fascist Life* (Berkeley, 1987).

36. Ibid., p. 149.

37. "100,000 at Chicago Greet Balbo Fleet," *New York Times* (July 16, 1933), p. 1.

38. "Viva Balbo," *Time* 22 (July 24, 1933), p. 22.

39. "Chicago Hails Balbo Fleet," *Chicago Tribune* (July 16, 1933), p. 2.

40. *Chicago Herald and Examiner* (July 1, 1933), p. 5.

41. James O'Donnell Bennett, "Flyers Parade Thrills City on Departure Eve," *Chicago Tribune* (July 19, 1933), p. 1. The Columbus statue, a gift to the city from Chicago's Italian-American community, was dedicated a second time on August 3rd as part of the fair's "Italian Day" celebration; see "25,000 Italians Join in Colorful Program at Fair," *Chicago Tribune* (Aug. 4, 1933), p. 13.

42. "Balbo's Own Story of Amazing Flight," *Chicago Tribune* (July 16, 1933), p. 6.

43. James O'Donnell Bennett, "Chicago Fetes Balbo Heroes in Heroic Style," *Chicago Tribune* (July 17, 1933), p. 1.

44. "Cheers for Il Duce Greet Balbo at Fair," *Chicago Herald and Examiner* (July 17, 1933), p. 2.

45. Bennett (note 41).

46. One of the few journalists to voice any criticism of Balbo was George Seldes, the former Rome correspondent for the *Chicago Tribune*; see George Seldes, "Hero Balbo," *The Nation* 137 (Aug. 2, 1933), p. 131.

47. "Marconi Praises Radio Financing," *New York Times* (Oct. 3, 1933), p. 20; and "Marconi Slips into the Fair and Tries the Wireless," *New York Times* (Oct. 3, 1933), p. 7.

48. Earl Mullin, "Italy Transmits a Starbeam to Illuminate Fair," *Chicago Tribune* (Oct. 3, 1933), p. 7.

49. For a description of the Italian commercial display at the 1934 fair, see *Padiglione alla Esposizione Mondiale di Chicago* (Rome, 1934). A copy of this brochure is preserved in the Century of Progress Exposition Papers, Chicago Public Library, Box 2, Folder 20.

50. Earl Mullin, "Record Throng Jams Fair for Italians' Day," *Chicago Tribune* (July 16, 1934), p. 8; "Over 100,000 Pay Homage to Balbo at Fair,'" *Chicago Herald and Examiner* (July 16, 1934), p. 7.

51. For a detailed description of the various historic monuments reproduced in the Italian Village, see *Colorful Italian Village*, a promotional pamphlet preserved in the Century of Progress Exposition Papers, Chicago Public Library, Box 1, Folder 9.

52. In the 1920s Joseph Imburgio amassed a fortune through real estate and insurance investments. In the early 1930s he was mayor of Melrose Park. He later earned a law degree from John Marshall Law School, changed his name to Joseph Bulger, and became one of the top lawyers for the Chicago crime syndicate. For biographical information, see Frank Maier, Donald Barlett, and William Clements, "Bulger's Mysterious Double Life," *Chicago Daily News* (Aug. 23, 1967), p. 1; Umberto Nelli, *Italians in Chicago, 1880-1930* (New York, 1970), pp. 208-09.

53. Andrew Rebori and John Root conceived the Streets of Paris as an opportunity to aid unemployed architects by allowing them to run the Streets of Paris concessions; see Bruegmann (note 31), pp. 242-47.

54. *Official Guide* (note 4), pp. 124-25.

55. In addition to the Belgian Village and the Streets of Paris, the 1934 Century of Progress Exposition included the American, Colonial, Black Forest (that is, German), Dutch, English, Irish, Italian, Mexican, Spanish, Swiss, and Tunisian villages, the Streets of Shangai, and the Oasis (that is, North African Village). Both 1933 and 1934 editions of the fair included a Midget Village as well. The Midget Village reproduced in miniature a typical Bavarian town and was home to over one hundred midgets during the fair.

The Rise of Public Housing in Chicago, 1930-1960

Wim de Wit

Anyone traveling on Chicago's Dan Ryan Expressway necessarily encounters, if only at a distance, one of the city's most infamous public housing developments. The sight of this vast expanse of 1960s high-rise towers with many burned out and boarded-up apartments makes an unforgettable impression. These are the Robert Taylor Homes (fig. 1). Together with other public housing developments such as Cabrini Green and Stateway Gardens, the Robert Taylor Homes represent just about everything that has gone wrong with public housing in Chicago. Living in one of these buildings today means facing the constant threat of gangs, shoot-outs, and drug-related violence.[1]

In a powerful and disturbing account of life in the Henry Horner Homes, Alex Kotlowitz documents a housing project that, only thirty years after completion, is in total disrepair because its owner, the Chicago Housing Authority (CHA), long ago decided not to spend money on its maintenance. This, too, is a place where at a very early age every resident has to learn to live with violence and, therefore, is forced to forego the pleasures of childhood.[2]

Public housing in Chicago has not always had a bad reputation. In fact, Vince Lane, the current chairman of the Chicago Housing Authority, has said on several occasions that when he was growing up he "envied the kids in public housing" for their "front- and backyards, heat, hot water, [and] basketball courts."[3] This essay examines the underlying reasons for the changes in Chicago's public housing and in the attitude of its landlord, the Chicago Housing Authority, during the first twenty years of its existence. Clearly, one cannot construct a meaningful history of public housing in Chicago without considering the ways in which architectural configurations have been determined by the interrelated issues of economics and race.

The CHA began in 1937 with high ideals about the positive effect decent housing could have on people's lives. By the late 1940s that idealism had been almost destroyed by Chicago politics. Public housing had become the object of tumul-

tuous debates in the city council, as the city's aldermen sought to influence where new housing would be built. Although never explicit about their motivations, white aldermen apparently feared that these subsidized housing complexes would be erected in their predominantly white neighborhoods and that the real estate value of these neighborhoods would consequently experience a marked decline.

While the city council had no power over the CHA during the first decade of its existence, in the late 1940s aldermen managed to force the CHA to build its projects only in slum clearance areas, far away from their own wards. The aldermen claimed that public housing was a way to revitalize the city, and slum clearance was one of the two goals articulated by the CHA. Revitalization, however, appears to have been far from the aldermen's minds. What they tried to achieve, instead, was racial segregation, and they were remarkably successful. The predominantly black slums on Chicago's South and West sides, which provided the sites for the most prominent public housing projects, were far removed from white, blue-collar, and middle-class neighborhoods at that time. In fact, there was so little connection between Chicago's slums and the rest of the city that the public housing that replaced these slums ironically wound up creating new ghettos. Instead of making the city healthier, the aldermen effectively pulled the city apart by isolating public housing, thus creating many of the social problems evident in urban life.

In Chicago and the rest of the United States, as in many other countries, public housing was introduced at a time when construction of low-cost housing by private enterprise had ceased. Several early attempts to provide public housing through private funds were not financially successful. Julius Rosenthal, an important Chicago philanthropist, built the Michigan Boulevard Garden Apartments in 1929 in a black neighborhood on the South Side (fig. 2). Designed by Ernest Grunsfeld, Jr., the architect of the Adler Planetarium, this development was humanly scaled and had some amenities, including on-

Fig. 1 Shaw, Metz and Associates, Robert Taylor Homes and the Dan Ryan Expressway, looking north from 47th Street, 1960-62 (photo 1964).

site nursery schools. The Marshall Field Garden Apartments, developed by the Estate of Marshall Field and designed by New York architect Andrew J. Thomas, was the largest moderate-income housing development in the country when it was built in 1929-30 (fig. 3).[4] Its near North Side location attracted lower-income white residents. Neither development, however, provided a reasonable return on the developers' investments, as was the case with the city's two other privately subsidized housing developments. Private funding of subsidized housing subsequently ended, and, during the Depression, construction of any kind was at a standstill. Housing shortages, homelessness, and unsanitary conditions in poor neighborhoods became threats to entire urban communities. Overcoming the fear that government involvement in public housing would constitute a first step towards socialism, Franklin D. Roosevelt in 1933 introduced a Housing Division as part of his Public Works Administration (PWA). At the same time he appropriated funds for the construction of fifty-one projects, three of them in Chicago: the Jane Addams Houses, Julia C. Lathrop Homes, and Trumbull Park Homes.[5]

The circumstances in Chicago were certainly no better than those in the rest of the country. The number of dwellings built in Chicago had dropped from 18,837 in 1929 to 2,741 in 1930, 966 in 1931, and 221 in 1932. By 1934-35 there was a shortage of 60,799 homes.[6] These trends would not be reversed until 1936, when the PWA projects were begun. Housing starts were certainly too low for a city that had been growing exponentially because of a constant influx of immigrants from all over Europe, and the arrival of black people who were fleeing discrimination in the South and hoped to find a better life in the cities of the North.

Most of the people coming from the South found places to live in the many old houses and apartment buildings on Chicago's near South Side which, beginning around 1920, had been deserted by its original upper-middle-class inhabitants when the area began to change in character. Because of its proximity to the Loop and to the railroads, the near South Side had become attractive to industry and other commercial enterprises. Once the quality of this neighborhood had started to deteriorate, other areas on the South Side followed, and many residences ended up in the hands of landlords who wanted them to produce income without any significant investment. Houses were subdivided into small units called kitchenette apartments (an attractive name that masked an appalling life-style: one or two rooms with a hotplate in a closet, or with the use of a common kitchen); little was done to provide acceptable sanitary conditions, and these areas quickly turned into slums.

By the 1930s the conditions in the South Side slums had become so bad that they were considered to be a threat to the rest of the city. Not only were they a health hazard, they also had a negative effect on the real estate values of surrounding neighborhoods; moreover, they were a hotbed of crime. In a memorandum of 1931 entitled "How to Build Low Cost Housing: A Study of the Slum Problem," architect Henry K.

Fig. 2   Ernest Grunsfeld, Jr., Michigan Boulevard Garden Apartments, 54 East 47th Street, 1929 (photo 1951).

Fig. 3   Andrew J. Thomas, project architect; Ernest R. Graham of Graham, Anderson, Probst and White, associate architect, Marshall Field Garden Apartments, 1500 North Sedgwick Street, 1929-30 (photo 1946).

Fig. 4 Alfred Shaw of
Shaw, Naess and
Murphy, in association
with three firms:
Thielbar and Fugard;
Nimmons, Carr and
Wright; Metz and
Gunderson, Ida B. Wells
Homes, 454 East
39th Street, 1941 (photo
1951).

Holsman made some pointed remarks about this problem. He first defined a slum as "a festering spot which is not unlike a quagmire or an opium habit, easy to get into but hard to get out—a moral, political, social, and sanitary blemish, detrimental to all citizens in many insidious ways." Holsman then continued, "These babies, by the way, are our babies—American citizens, our aldermen, presidents, captains of industry, and teachers, or our gangsters and brothel keepers, depending mostly on how we feed them and house them."[7]

In spite of his passionate plea for decent housing, Holsman had to wait six years for the problems of housing and urban blight to be tackled in a coordinated manner by government agencies rather than private individuals. The passage of a federal Housing Act in 1937 allowed for the establishment of local housing authorities, which could in turn build housing projects with the assistance of local, state, or federal money. The Chicago Housing Authority was established in the same year with an idealistic program devoted to improving the quality of the city by clearing slums, and to improving people's lives by building subsidized housing "for low-income urban families unable to obtain 'decent, safe, and sanitary' dwelling units within their income-paying ability."[8]

Elizabeth Wood, appointed in 1937 to head the CHA, was sufficiently idealistic to endorse these goals. Wood came to the job from a background in social work, which in itself indicates a great deal about the CHA's priorities in its early years. None of her successors would have similar training or experience in dealing with social problems at a basic level. Moreover, prior to her appointment to the position of executive secretary, Wood, a daughter of lay missionaries in Japan, had held numerous jobs that had prepared her in various ways not only to become the "City's Biggest Landlord," but also to be very much in favor of racial integration, an attitude that was not generally accepted at the time.[9] She had learned about the building trade as a secretary director of the home modernizing bureau of the Building Industries of Chicago. She had also been employed as a case worker at United Charities, where she had seen the negative effects of poor housing on the people who lived in it. Finally, she had been the head of a housing committee established by the Council of Social Agencies. In that position she had drawn the attention of some assistants of Mayor Edward Kelly, who appointed her the CHA's first executive secretary.

World War II prevented Wood from furthering racial integration in the first years of her tenure, but the situation changed soon after the war was over. Her efforts undoubtedly received some support from the man who had become chairman of the CHA's board in 1943, the black building manager Robert Taylor. Together, Wood and Taylor worked hard on keeping the CHA's early ideals alive. They could do this without too many problems as long as Mayor Kelly was in power (until 1947), because Kelly was strong enough to keep the city's aldermen away from the CHA.

The first buildings operated by the CHA were the three projects built by the Public Works Administration: the Jane Addams Houses, the Julia C. Lathrop Homes, and the Trumbull Park Homes, a total of 2,414 dwelling units. Upon their completion in 1937-38, control of these projects was transferred to the CHA, which leased them from the United States Housing Authority. They were completely transferred to the CHA in the late 1940s. Before the start of World War II, the CHA managed to build only one project: the Ida B. Wells Homes (fig. 4). Originally planned by the PWA, which had already purchased and cleared the site, the Ida B. Wells Homes were intended exclusively for "Colored Families," whose housing needs had gone largely unaddressed in the PWA projects.[10] In an article in the *Chicago Tribune* of June 25, 1939, Elizabeth Wood admitted that only thirty-five black families had found homes in the first projects, all in the Addams Houses. The reason for such a low number, Wood insisted, was not that the CHA tried to maintain a "color line,"

Fig. 5 West Side
Housing Project
Associated Architects
(John Armstrong,
Melville Chatten, Ernest
Grunsfeld, Jr., Frederick
Hodgdon, John
Holabird, Ralph
Huszagh, Elmer Jensen,
Philip Maher, John
Merrill, and Chester
Walcott), Jane Addams
Houses, Roosevelt Road
between Racine Avenue
and Loomis Street, 1938,
view of entrance with
sculpture by Edgar
Miller (photo 1951).

but that the city was extremely segregated. Most black families lived on the city's South Side and applied for public housing in that area, because it was familiar to them. The 1,662 units in Wells Homes (completed in 1941) were intended to ameliorate this imbalance.

The design of these four projects was partially inspired by European housing projects of the 1920s, although the communities designed by New York regional planners Henry Wright and Clarence Stein appear to have been equally important.[11] In all four projects, for example, the buildings are in a parklike setting (about 25 percent of the site is occupied by buildings). The open areas surrounding the buildings were used for playgrounds, sports fields, and places to sit. Attempts were made to achieve liveliness in design by including a mix of building heights: two-story row houses and apartment buildings of three and four floors. Yet, the emphasis on creating a healthy, attractive living environment did not necessar-ily mean that the projects were innovative in design. In fact, the projects were rather stark; they looked more like industrial buildings than residential buildings. Interesting detailing was, in general, impossible as the buildings had to be inexpensive and sturdy so that they would withstand many families.

Of the four projects, the starkest in design are the Jane Addams Houses, which were designed by a consortium of architects led by John Holabird and including Ernest A. Grunsfeld, Melville

Chatten, Chester Walcott, and Ralph Huszagh. The buildings are square, brick blocks without much articulation; they rise rather abruptly out of the ground and end equally abruptly with a horizontal coping of stone or tile (fig. 5). The only interruption in the roofline occurs where the stairwell protrudes through the roof to allow for access to this area. As the stairwells are located immediately behind the doors on the first floor, these roof-level projections are placed perpendicularly above the door openings and thus serve as markers in the otherwise monotonous

Fig. 6 Diversey
Housing Project
Associated Architects
(Robert DeGolyer, chief
architect; Hugh Garden,
Hubert Burnham,
Vernon Watson, Thomas
Tallmadge, Israel
Loewenberg, Max
Loewenberg, E. E.
Roberts, Elmer Roberts,
Roy Christiansen,
Everett Quinn, Charles
White, Bertram Weber,
Edwin Clark, Earnest
Mayo, and Peter Mao),
Julia C. Lathrop Homes,
2000 West Diversey,
c. 1938, aerial view.

Fig. 7 Julia C. Lathrop
Homes, exterior.

Fig. 8 Floor plan of one
of the buildings in Julia
C. Lathrop Homes, 1936.

facades to indicate where the entrance to each building can be found. Balconies on the second and third floors above each door opening further call attention to the location of entrances. Inside, the apartments are rather small. The complex has dwelling units with two, three, four, and even five rooms; most apartments (618 of 1,027) have three rooms. The kitchens have wooden cabinets, a gas range, a refrigerator, and a sink.

In comparison with the sturdy simplicity of the Jane Addams Houses, the Julia C. Lathrop Homes show much more attention to decorative detail. Designed by Robert S. DeGolyer, in association with Everett Quinn, Thomas Tallmadge, Vernon Watson, Hubert Burnham, Roy Christiansen, Bertram Weber, and Hugh Garden, among others, the project consists of a mix of three-story apartments, two-flats, and two-story row houses (figs. 6, 8). The project is the largest after the Wells Homes, covering thirty-five acres that had been vacant before construction. The buildings are arranged in U shapes alternating with cross shapes, except for the row houses, which are in straight lines along the Damen Avenue border and in the northwest corner of the project. The site is divided into two halves by Diversey Avenue. South of Diversey the buildings are set parallel to the site's eastern border, Damen Avenue, providing a large stretch of open land along the river on the project's west side; the northern half is laid out more symmetrically, with open green spaces between the buildings. The corners of the buildings are articulated by rusticated brickwork and topped by concrete urns; the bases of the buildings also have a rusticated articulation (fig. 7). Some of the buildings are connected by arches. The complex has seven recreation rooms for children and seven social units for adults.

In spite of their spare design, these buildings were thought to be a first step in the CHA's effort to provide an environment that would have a positive impact on those living in public hous-

ing. The other principal means toward that end was thought to be in the area of management. The role of the individual project manager was adapted from the earlier model of the settlement house worker. As Elizabeth Wood noted, the settlement house experience was more or less the only example available for emulation by the housing managers.

One of the important aspects of the influence of the settlement house movement was the requirement that housing managers live in their projects, just as the settlement house workers lived in theirs. The workers were expected to be available evenings and weekends both for on-going activities and the numerous emergencies that were part of the daily routine. They were expected not only to stimulate tenant activities, but to participate in them.

This policy assumed that the workers could influence the tenants only through closeness and neighborliness. The fact that the manager lived in the dwelling verified the quality of the home.[12]

Very soon after the completion of the first public housing projects, the United States became involved in World War II, which put intense and unforeseen pressures on public housing. Indeed, one might reasonably argue that the war was responsible for the appearance of the first crack in the CHA's smooth surface of idealism. The United States Housing Authority determined very soon after the start of the war that new public housing could be built only if it would be used to house war workers. In Chicago so much emphasis was placed on building quickly in order to house workers engaged in industries converted to war production that the original standard of high-quality housing was significantly diluted. In Wood's opinion, this lowering of quality had a lasting impact on postwar housing: the standards were never raised again.[13] The war also delayed the slum clearance program, which had barely begun. Because there would not have been sufficient housing for people displaced from the slums, this program was put on hold until after 1945.

Altgeld Gardens, a public housing development that was begun in 1943 and finished in 1945, is unusual in that it was constructed according to higher quality standards than other public housing built during the war years (figs. 9, 10). The CHA, the National Housing Association, and the Federal Public Housing Authority, the agencies in charge of the project, built the development on a 157-acre site at 130th Street and Ellis Avenue, where it would accommodate black workers who could not find affordable housing on the far South Side. Because Altgeld Gardens was far from the city and public transportation, architects Naess and Murphy de-signed the development as a self-contained unit, with a health clinic, a library, a shopping center, and nursery, elementary, and high school facilities.[14]

Ironically, the end of World War II only added new facets to existing problems in the field of public housing. Now the veterans returning from Europe and Asia also needed housing. As the CHA's *Annual Report* of 1945 noted:

Immediately after V-J Day, and continuing throughout the remaining months of 1945, the Authority worked with equal haste to "re-tool" for peace – a process which involved setting up new standards for tenant selection, converting plans for war housing to plans for low rent housing, and launching a program of temporary housing to meet a portion of the crucial need for homes on the part of returning veterans and their families.[15]

The CHA anticipated that by early 1946 there would be 32,500 homeless veteran families. To meet their needs, all kinds of new solutions were introduced: prefabricated houses and temporary houses, as well as trailers and the so-called Quonset huts (semi-circular structures of corrugated steel). Most of these temporary housing facilities remained in use until the mid-1950s.[16]

The scale on which the CHA could build new projects after World War II was much larger than before and during the war. Indeed, the CHA seemed to grow so fast that many Chicagoans felt threatened by it. Already in 1946, the white residents of Edison Park on the far Northwest Side protested the placement of temporary veterans' housing in their neighborhood, voicing the concern that the value of their real estate would depreciate.[17] Behind their protest there doubtless lay the fear that, as a result of such housing construction, blacks might come to live in their neighborhood. When Elizabeth Wood continued to speak up for integration, she angered many people. Indeed, several riots occurred in the late forties and early fifties when blacks moved into new public housing in areas that were considered to be white neighborhoods.[18]

Many white people in Chicago wanted to keep the city in a state of de facto segregation. The city's white aldermen, aware of this desire, were unable to do much for their constituencies as long as Edward Kelly was mayor. When Kelly was replaced in 1947 by Martin Kennelly, the aldermen seized their chance. Only six months after Kennelly's installation as mayor of Chicago, several council members started to attack the Chicago Housing Authority for "gross inefficiencies" and demanded an investigation. Both Robert Taylor and Elizabeth Wood responded that they would welcome an investigation to

Fig. 9 Naess and Murphy, Altgeld Gardens, 130th Street and Ellis Avenue, 1943-45, exterior.

clear the air.[19] Indeed, they realized that the complaints were not so much about how the CHA was run, but were instead an expression of frustration on the part of the aldermen about their persistent inability to gain control over the CHA. Kennelly protested such an investigation but eventually conceded.

The processes that the aldermen sought to influence were site selection for CHA projects and the related designation of areas to be cleared of slums. These issues became the subject of a major confrontation between the aldermen and

the CHA in 1948, when, with Mayor Kennelly's tacit approval, the city council took responsibility for granting official approval of any site proposed by the CHA as a potential location for new public housing. The first test of the city council's new powers with regard to site selection occurred in 1949, when CHA Chairman Robert Taylor submitted a list of seven sites to the mayor and city council. The aldermen rejected most of these sites because they were too close to white neighborhoods. Ready for a battle, the CHA board demanded public hearings, which the

Fig. 10 Aerial view of Altgeld Gardens.

The Rise of Public Housing   239

Fig. 11 Loebl, Schlossman and Bennett, Dearborn Homes, 2960 South Federal Street, 1948-50 (photo 1951).

city council's housing committee held in February 1950. Devereux Bowly gave a lively report of what happened in the wake of these hearings:

After the hearings were over the City Council Housing Committee recommended approval of only two sites, both slum-clearance extensions of existing projects. They refused to recommend the remainder of the sites in the package, and then delegated the site selection problem to a subcommittee of nine aldermen. In March the subcommittee made tours of forty sites that had been proposed by one source or another. The subcommittee came up with its own list of thirteen sites, some of which were ridiculous, such as one in the path of a planned expressway. CHA then proposed a new package of sites, including some of the vacant sites from its first list. The new package, in fact, had two-thirds of its units on vacant land sites. Kennelly refused to take any position on it. Alderman John J. Duffy, chairman of the Finance Committee, and Alderman Lancaster [chairman of the Housing Committee] called an informal meeting of a few of the most influential aldermen, and worked out what came to be referred to as the Duffy-Lancaster compromise. It provided for only 2,000 units on vacant land, and over 10,000 on slum-clearance sites. It had eight slum sites, all in black ghettos, and seven small vacant sites to accommodate from 300 to 588 units each.[20]

This confrontation constituted a turning point in the history of the Chicago Housing Authority: from that moment on, its developments were going to be hidden away in blighted areas that, although cleared of their slums, would remain unconnected to the rest of the city. In November 1950 Robert Taylor resigned in protest.

A major problem faced by the CHA in the context of slum clearance was the rehousing of people living in the blighted areas that were slated for clearance. In order to create space for these residents, people living in public housing whose income had risen above a certain level

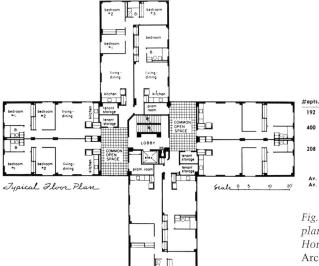

#apts.	#rms.	Room sizes (sq. ft.)	
192	3½	LR, D A, K	270
		#1 BR	130
400	4½	LR, DA, K	307
		#1 BR	123
		#2 BR	110
208	5½	LR, DA, K	319
		#1 BR	130
		#2 BR	129
		#3 BR	91
Av. rooms per family			4.51
Av. gross sq. ft. per rm.			217

Fig. 12 Typical floor plan of Dearborn Homes; from Progressive Architecture 32 (April 1951), p. 58.

were told to evacuate their apartments. Elizabeth Wood had tried to stave off evacuation, arguing that there was not enough housing available in the private market to accommodate these tenants. She also had another reason: her awareness that the residents whose incomes had become too high were very often community leaders in their housing developments. They were now going to be replaced by people who had lived under the worst circumstances and who had never learned to take care of a dwelling of their own. The latter group was, in Wood's estimation "a microcosm of all the statistics on the prevalence of social, physical and moral disabilities among slum dwellers."[21] The careful selection process that the CHA had applied in filling its first housing developments was undermined.

One of the earliest public housing developments to be built on land cleared of slums was Dearborn Homes, constructed between 1948 and

1950 (at the height of the CHA's conflict with the city council) (fig. 11). Located in an area between 27th and 30th streets and between State Street and the Pennsylvania Railroad tracks, this project was designed to house a maximum of eight hundred families in sixteen cross-shaped towers of six, seven, or nine stories. (Dearborn Homes was the first CHA project to incorporate apartment buildings of more than four stories.) The architects, Loebl, Schlossman and Bennett, included several features intended to soften the unpleasantness attached to living in a high-rise building with an elevator. Every floor (with eight apartments each) had two "common open spaces," which could, for example, be used as play areas for smaller children who needed supervision and were too young to play by themselves on the green grounds surrounding the buildings (fig. 12). Moreover, knowing that many young families would live in these buildings, the architects put two pram rooms on each floor, in addition to tenant storage spaces. These seemingly negligible elements were actually quite important and they drew national attention.[22] Yet the apartments themselves were very small; a three-bedroom apartment occupied less than seven hundred square feet.

The new sites that became available after the Duffy-Lancaster compromise were barely big enough to rehouse the people evacuated from the slum areas in which the projects were slated to be built. If the CHA seriously wanted to attack the problems of homelessness, overcrowding, and slums, it would have to build more dwelling units per area than it had been building in the previous years. What appeared as an exception in Dearborn Homes (high-rise buildings with elevators) soon became the general tendency. New apartment buildings were built at an average height of seven floors, at least three floors more than the average height in the projects of the 1930s and 1940s. Elizabeth Wood was opposed to high-rise buildings, but, as she told William Mullen of the *Chicago Tribune* in 1985, "I was so undercut politically that I was feeble, I was floundering around. . .we had very little space to work with, so we had to go to the high-rises, though we tried to come up with imaginative designs that could accommodate family living."[23] The "imaginative designs" to which she referred were probably the common open spaces and pram rooms already included in Dearborn Homes. Presumably, Wood was also thinking of the outside galleries, which were to become a characteristic feature of all public housing of the 1950s and 1960s.

In an April 1951 article in *Progressive Architecture*, Julian Whittlesey suggested that the introduction of the high-rise apartment building was not only the result of the CHA's need to build more densely on the areas it had available, but could also be attributed to the architects hired by the CHA to design the apartment buildings of the early 1950s. This should come as no surprise. The architects hired at that time—Skidmore, Owings and Merrill, Loebl, Schlossman and Bennett, Loewenberg and Loewenberg, Keck and Keck—had all shown in their other work that they were committed to modernist styles in architecture. They had obviously felt the impact of Mies van der Rohe's 860-880 North Lake Shore Drive apartments (1948-51), buildings that set the tone for a whole generation to come (see pls. 114-17). Similar high-rise buildings, set back from the street's lot line to create a small plaza, and with a steel or concrete structure and a skin made mostly of glass, became the oft-repeated fashion regardless of whether the building was designed for apartments, offices, or a hospital. It is no wonder that public housing projects were assimilated to this fashion, especially when one considers that the standardization and repeatability of building elements promoted by modernist architects significantly reduced the unit cost of these dwellings.

At least one major problem with respect to high-rise building in the modernist style, à la Mies van der Rohe, very quickly emerged: such buildings often do not relate well to their environment. Because they are set back from the street and have plazas in front or on all sides around them, they are more like isolated islands than integrated components of a city street. High-rise apartments designed for public housing were no exception to this problem. Some of the characteristics of these new projects, such as the geometric arrangement of the buildings over the available land, and the playgrounds and other recreational areas that surrounded them, were no different from the earliest CHA projects. But in a project such as the Jane Addams Houses, which was only four stories high, a resident could still relate to the open areas surrounding the buildings; in high-rise buildings of seven or more stories, this was no longer possible. Even starker in design than the 1930s buildings, the high-rise towers of the 1950s and 1960s did not foster the development of a sense of community among the tenants, in spite of the many programs set up by building managers to encourage people to feel proud of their apartment, their building, and the project as a whole. In addition,

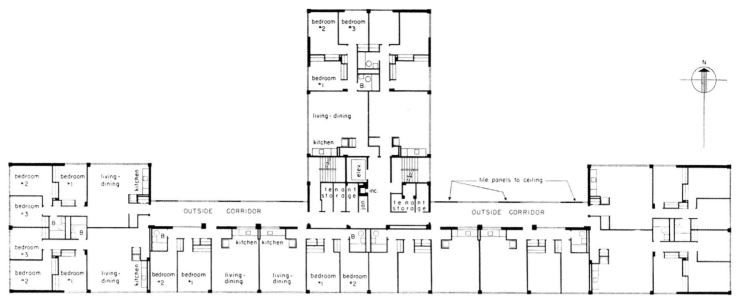

Typical Floor Plan   Scale 0 5 10   20   30'

Fig. 13   Typical floor plan of Ogden Courts; from Progressive Architecture 32 (April 1951), p. 60.

Fig. 14   Site plan of Henry Horner Homes, 1952.

integration of high-rise buildings with the rest of the city was more or less impossible because they were placed in slum-cleared areas, areas that had lost any trace of the old city fabric, areas without a heart. Thus, the old ghettos on the city's South and West sides were cleared of existing structures and simply replaced by new ghettos.

Initially, the new housing projects of the 1950s were welcomed enthusiastically, especially by architects. *Architectural Forum*, for example, published the Skidmore, Owings and Merrill designs for Ogden Courts—two buildings located on Ogden Avenue between Fairfield and Talman avenues, which were constructed for the relocation of people living in the path of the Congress Expressway—and judged them to be a "best 'look in the future' [by] top-flight architects" (figs. 13, 15).[24] The article praised the two T-shaped buildings with their open corridors and

use of unfinished concrete as great cost savers. The CHA also lavished praise on this project, claiming that it was its "most efficient and economical high-rise plan."[25] In one of its announcements the CHA proudly proclaimed that the buildings would occupy only 16 percent of the total site. Even the tenants were happy; one of them wrote to Elizabeth Wood: "Moving into the Ogden Courts marked the happiest event in my life. Compared to the places I was forced to live in before, this seems like 'paradise regained.'"[26]

Because of its initial success, Ogden Courts became something of a prototype, components of which would be seen over and over again in subsequent buildings. For example, the eight-foot-wide open corridors or galleries on one side of the building became very popular: they allowed fresh air and light to enter the apartments from two sides (as the interior corridor from

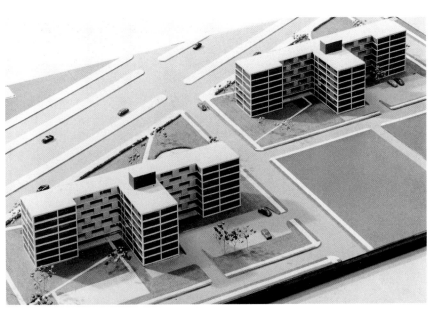

Fig. 15 Skidmore, Owings and Merrill, Model of Ogden Courts, Ogden and Fairfield avenues, 1950-52.

Fig. 16 Skidmore, Owings and Merrill, Henry Horner Homes, 1834 West Washington Street, 1957.

which one could enter the apartments was no longer necessary), and they also could be cleaned much more easily than inside corridors. In addition, they provided something like a sidewalk for the apartments and were in that sense a variation of the common, open spaces in the Dearborn Homes. Many of the big projects of the late 1950s were outfitted with such galleries. Similarly, Ogden Courts's exposed frame of unfinished concrete with red brick infill must have appealed not only to the CHA's desire to save costs, but also to its sense of modernistic, austere aesthetics. Several later projects would look quite similar.

Henry Horner Homes is one of this group. Again, Alex Kotlowitz has shown how the CHA's optimism about efficient design, cost saving, and a pleasant living environment turned into a major disappointment for the Horner Homes tenants. Located on the near West Side in

an area bounded by Lake Street and Washington Boulevard and Damen and Hermitage avenues, the Horner Homes consists of nine apartment buildings (seven buildings of seven stories and two buildings of fifteen stories), a community building, a maintenance building, and a management building (fig. 16).[27] The area is subdivided into three blocks by two north-south streets (Wolcott and Wood avenues); an east-west street that originally ran through these blocks was reduced to a walking path. Within each block the buildings are arranged around a recreation area or playing field. A drawing by Skidmore, Owings and Merrill suggests that the arrangement of the buildings on the site was determined by the desire that no building cast a shadow over any other building (fig. 14). While the drawing is actually no more than a regular site plan showing the footprint of each building and the suggested landscaping, the (white) footprints are outlined by black shadows that, first of all, provide an idea of how tall each T-shaped building is and, second, show that, at least on a summer day when the sun is high enough, no building will be overshadowed by another. The ideals of modern planners of sufficient air, light, and recreational green area seemed to be met in this plan.

While the layout of the site may have been designed according to the modernistic book, the modern movement's ideals were unable to prevent the rapid decay of the Horner Homes. Maintenance very soon became the budget item on which the CHA wanted to save money and, since the project was sufficiently isolated from the rest of the city, nobody seemed to care about the effects of such negligence. In his book Alex Kotlowitz shows how isolated and neglected the residents really feel. The desolate area surrounding the Horner Homes is experienced as a barrier between the project and the center of the city; consequently, City Hall seems to have forgotten about the needs of the people here.

By the time this project opened to its first residents in 1957, the CHA had changed. Elizabeth Wood, who—in spite of the aldermen's successful efforts to segregate the city—had continued to strive for racial integration, was fired as the CHA's executive secretary in 1954. The reason for this action, according to the CHA board, led by architect John R. Fugard, was that the Authority had to be run in a more businesslike manner and that social welfare considerations could no longer play a primary role. Everybody assumed, however, that there was another reason as well: Wood was too liberal with regard to integration. In particular, she was blamed for a number of

Fig. 17 Holabird and Root and Burgee, Stateway Gardens (1958-59) and the houses that the development replaced along Dearborn Street, near 39th Street.

Fig. 18 Slum clearance on South Federal Street for Stateway Gardens.

Fig. 19 Robert Taylor Homes, 4410 South State Street, 1960-62.

Fig. 20 Site plan of Robert Taylor Homes.

ROBERT R. TAYLOR HOMES   39TH TO 55TH AND STATE STREETS   CHICAGO HOUSING AUTHORITY   SHAW METZ & ASSOCIATES   ARCHITECTS-ENGINEERS

race riots resulting from the CHA's attempt to settle black families in public housing projects located in predominantly white neighborhoods. The worst of these riots occurred in Trumbull Park in the summer of 1953; it continued intermittently for more than one-and-a-half years and was still ongoing when Wood was fired.[28]

Wood was replaced by a retired Lieutenant General William B. Kean. During Kean's short tenure as executive director (until 1957), and during that of his successor, the CHA started to build higher and higher. As the city wanted to build only in slum-clearance areas and had to find housing both for the people who were displaced by slum clearance and for those large numbers of others looking for housing, it had to go up to heights of fifteen to twenty stories. This period saw the creation of such gigantic projects as Stateway Gardens, built in 1958 and consisting of two ten-story buildings and six seven-

teen-story buildings (figs. 17, 18), and Robert Taylor Homes, twenty-eight towers of sixteen stories each, which made it the largest public housing development in the world when it was constructed in 1960-62 (figs. 19, 20).[29] Through these mega-projects, the city sought to solve its need for inexpensive housing. At the same time, however, a new problem was created: as old slums were replaced by substandard housing that the CHA failed to maintain, blighted areas became crime-generating ghettos. The city's aldermen of the 1950s thought that their constituents would sleep more soundly if public housing were kept out of their neighborhoods. These aldermen did not realize, however, that by isolating public housing from the rest of Chicago, they stunted the potential growth and vitality of whole communities, and this, in turn, would eventually threaten the well-being of the entire city.

NOTES

In the production of this essay I have relied on the careful attention to detail of Amy Mooney, who was an untiring research assistant. I am also grateful to those who generously provided access to their archives or collections: the staff of the Municipal Reference Library; Katie Kellie, Director of the Office of External Affairs, Maxine Mitchum, Manager of the Office of External Affairs, and Andre Gardner, Media Specialist of the Office of External Affairs of the Chicago Housing Authority; and Michelle Grunau and Diane McCormick and their staff at Skidmore, Owings and Merrill. Finally, I want to thank my wife, Nancy Troy, who, as always, has offered valuable support during the writing of this essay.

1. This essay deals with only a few aspects of the much larger subject of public housing in Chicago. For a more detailed account, see Harvey Warren Zorbaugh, *The Gold Coast and the Slum* (Chicago, 1929); Martin Meyerson and Edward C. Banfield, *Politics, Planning, and the Public Interest* (London and New York, 1955); Devereux Bowly, Jr., *The Poorhouse: Subsidized Housing in Chicago, 1895-1976* (Carbondale and Edwardsville, 1978); Thomas Lee Philpott, *The Slum and the Ghetto: Neighborhood Deterioration and Middle-Class Reform, Chicago, 1880-1930* (New York, 1978); and Arnold R. Hirsch, *Making the Second Ghetto: Race and Housing in Chicago, 1940-1960* (New York, 1983). Some general sources of information about race relations and black history in Chicago include Alan Spear, *Black Chicago: The Making of a Negro Ghetto, 1890-1920* (Chicago, 1967); and St. Clair Drake and Horace R. Cayton, *Black Metropolis: A Study of Negro Life in a Northern City*, 2 vols. (New York, 1945). For a detailed account of housing issues in Chicago after World War II, see The Chicago Plan Commission, *Housing Goals for Chicago* (Chicago, 1946).
2. Hence the title of Alex Kotlowitz's book, *There Are No Children Here: The Story of Two Boys Growing up in the Other America* (New York, 1991).
3. Jorge Casuso, "High hopes, many think that public housing is a lost cause; Vince Lane doesn't agree," *Chicago Tribune Magazine* (July 22, 1990), pp. 12-16, 34. Lane reiterated this statement in a presentation to the Architecture Alliance, Chicago Historical Society, in May 1989.

4. Bowly (note 1), p. 12.
5. Bowly (note 1), p. 18. The Jane Addams Houses are located in an area between Cabrini Street, Roosevelt Road, Racine Avenue, and Loomis Street. The Julia C. Lathrop Homes are on the east side of the north branch of the Chicago River, with Clybourn and Damen avenues forming eastern boundaries; Diversey Avenue, an east-west street, bisects the site. The Trumbull Park Homes are located on the Southeast Side at 105th Street and Oglesby Avenue.
6. Chicago Plan Commission (note 1), p. 215; see also Chicago Housing Authority, *Annual Report, 1937-39* (Chicago, 1939), p. 7.
7. Henry K. Holsman, 1931 memorandum entitled "How to Build Low Cost Housing: A Study of the Slum Problem," pp. 2-3, Chicago Historical Society, Archives and Manuscripts Collection, Mary McDowell Papers, folder 14.
8. Chicago Plan Commission (note 1), p. 179.
9. Anton Remenih, "City's biggest landlord is a busy woman," *Chicago Tribune* (April 19, 1942).
10. The site is bounded by Martin Luther King, Jr. Drive, Pershing Road, Cottage Grove Avenue, and 37th Street.
11. In her book *The Beautiful Beginnings, The Failure to Learn: Fifty Years of Public Housing in America* (Washington, D.C., 1982), pp. 2-3, Wood mentions that Sir Raymond Unwin and several other public housing experts were invited by the National Association of Housing Officials in 1934 to visit the United States and draft a proposal for a public housing program to be implemented in the U. S.
In his popular book *Towards New Towns for America* (1951), regional planner/architect Clarence Stein discusses Chatham Village (Pittsburgh, 1930), one of the New Deal Greenbelt Towns that he and town planner/landscape architect Henry Wright designed. Stein and Wright, along with Lewis Mumford, Edith Elmer Wood, Robert D. Kohn, and Benton McKaye, formed the Regional Planning Association of America. The group was highly influenced by British garden city principles, and Stein and Wright planned two other American communities according to the British guidelines, Sunnyside Gardens, Queens, New York (1924), a residential complex, and Radburn, New Jersey (1926), planned as a complete town. These communities were innovative in their extensive use of community parks and gardens.

12. Wood (note 11), p. 6.
13. Ibid., p. 16.
14. Bowly (note 1), p. 42; Bowly states that Altgeld Gardens was "the most self-contained and comprehensive public housing project ever constructed in Chicago."
15. Chicago Housing Authority, *Annual Report, 1945* (Chicago, 1945), p. 1.
16. Bowly (note 1), pp. 47-48.
17. Wayne McMillen, "Public Housing in Chicago," *Social Service Review* 20, no. 2 (June 1946), pp. 150-64. For the Edison Park riots, see p. 163.
18. For further discussion of the riots brought about by integration efforts in the late 1940s and the 1950s, see Hirsch (note 1), pp. 40-99; and see note 28 below.
19. Thomas Drennan, "Council to Probe CHA," *Daily Times* (Oct. 15, 1947).
20. Bowly (note 1), pp. 78-79; see also Meyerson and Banfield (note 1), p. 136 et passim.
21. Wood (note 11), p. 30.
22. For a contemporary critique of Dearborn Homes, see Julian Whittlesey, "New Dimensions in Housing Design," *Progressive Architecture* 32 (April 1951), pp. 57-65.
23. William Mullen, "Cabrini-Green: The Road to Hell," *Chicago Tribune Magazine* (March 31, 1985), p. 16; see also Whittlesey (note 22), p. 57.
24. *Architectural Forum* (Jan. 1950), p. 84.
25. Whittlesey (note 22), p. 60.
26. From Chicago Housing Authority, *Monthly Report* (Aug. 1951); courtesy Skidmore, Owings and Merrill.
27. In 1961 the project was expanded with seven new buildings (four of fourteen stories and three of eight stories).
28. See Robert Gruenberg, "Trumbull Park: Act II, Elizabeth Wood Story," *The Nation* (Sept. 1954); Chicago Commission on Human Relations, *The Trumbull Park Homes Disturbances: A Chronological Report, August 4, 1953 to June 30, 1955* (Chicago, n.d.); Frank Brown, *Trumbull Park* (Chicago, 1959).
29. Bowly (note 1), p. 124. Stateway Gardens, designed by Holabird and Root and Burgee, is located between 35th Street and Pershing Road, and Robert Taylor Homes is between State Street and the Rock Island Railroad tracks and runs from Pershing Road to 54th Street, a distance of two miles; the architects were Shaw, Metz and Associates.

City Hall and the Architecture of Power:
The Rise and Fall of the Dearborn Corridor

Ross Miller

On four key sites in the center of Chicago, an activist mayor brought local and federal government together with private capital to rebuild a city. Within months of taking office in April 1955, for what would be the first of his six consecutive terms as mayor, Richard J. Daley began plans for a new Civic Center. Consolidating city and county offices that were scattered all over town, Chicago's Civic Center (1965; fig. 1) was the municipal equal of the three new buildings that constituted the Federal Center (1959-75) four blocks south on Dearborn Street. Meanwhile, the new building for the First National Bank of Chicago (1964-69) went up right between the two. Only one of the four sites frustrated the new mayor's plans, and it remains "unimproved" twenty-five years after his death.

This leftover block, at the crossing of streets where the city first developed, with all of its accumulated architecture removed, is little more than a giant crack in the pavement. In 1989 the City of Chicago paid over $40 million to buy three-quarters of this once lively place, and then resold it for a little less than $13 million to developers who owned the other one-quarter. To the new owners of this square block of land, who thought that they would already be open for business with two office towers taking in top rents on Dearborn Street and with a low-rise retail mall along State Street attracting the richest shoppers, this is a sweet deal gone sour. Having spent a fortune since they took title in 1989 just to keep their bargain land ready to build, the developers of Block 37—as this site is designated—bear melancholy witness to the civic failure of miscalculated growth.

By the end of 1991, the empty block had consumed nearly $20 million in taxes, debt service, and development costs. Such a valuable, undeveloped piece of land, right under the noses of the politicians and businessmen who engineered its speedy demolition, provides a vivid contrast to the nearby successes up and down Dearborn Street.

Only one building remains on this flat and empty site, three deserted acres in the center of

Fig. 1   C. F. Murphy Associates; Jacques Brownson, designer; with Loebl, Schlossman and Bennett, and Skidmore, Owings and Merrill, Richard J. Daley Center (formerly Chicago Civic Center), block bounded by Dearborn, Washington, Clark, and Randolph streets, 1965.

Fig. 2   Aerial view of Block 37, bounded by Dearborn, Randolph, State, and Washington streets, November 1990; the only remaining building on this block is the Commonwealth Edison Substation (Holabird and Root, 1929-31).

Chicago (fig. 2). Once hemmed in by neighboring buildings, all of which were demolished in the winter of 1989-90 and hauled away as rubble, an electrical substation operated by Commonwealth Edison survives alone on what was until recently a typical, crowded city block. Thick-walled with only one detailed elevation to conceal the automated machinery behind, this tomb-like substation—designed in 1929 to replace the 1898 Chemical Bank Building—is after sixty years the block's newest building, still distributing one half of the downtown's ration of electricity.

The substation's Dearborn Street facade of quarried stone, ornamented high above the door-less entrance with a heroic bas-relief, is architectural camouflage for a utilitarian brick box that was slotted into a 60-by-80-foot lot, the footprint originally of a four-story post-fire-era structure, the Williams Building by J. R. Willett, an obscure local architect. Carefully proportioned by architects Holabird and Root to fit in with its neighboring buildings, now suddenly absent, the un-tenanted structure at 121 North Dearborn Street lies exposed on a piece of land that is bare again for the third time in only 150 years. Neatly parceled into its own 124,441 square feet in 1830, Block 37 is older than the original town of Chicago. It is only a single, carefully calibrated piece cut from millions of identical square-mile sections that constituted the Northwest following the 1785 Federal Land Ordinance.

Using surveyor James Thompson's 1830 calculations, mapmakers long ago further divided this wild place into eight equal portions of land called lots, which were to be traded first in their original 15,500-square-foot sections and then quickly subdivided again. This land, which surveyors pacing the soggy prairie had ordered with their instruments, was, until things began to go bad in the 1960s and downtown blight was declared, the destination of thousands of daily office workers and nighttime visitors to its two first-run movie theaters, bars, and restaurants.

On this desolated site were also landmark buildings, two examples erected one year after the Great Fire on two of the best corners, separated by the long diagonal through the middle of the block. The two buildings lasted until 1990, stubborn survivors from the time when this address was one of the city's proudest. On the northeast corner of the block, at State and Randolph streets, opposite Marshall Field's, stood the Bay State Building (fig. 3), designed by Peter B. Wight of Carter, Drake and Wight, assisted by the young draftsmen Daniel H. Burnham and

John Wellborn Root. In the Bay State Building were fine specialty shops and two old establishments selling Viennese pastries and ice cream to the carriage trade. The building's upper floors contained offices for doctors and other established professionals, including a hair specialist, Mrs. Burnham, who "invented" the permanent wave. On the southwest corner of Block 37, at Dearborn and Washington streets, was the McCarthy Building (fig. 4), the last remaining example of the popular five-story type that architect John M. Van Osdel set onto many prominent corners in the Loop. A dense-use building up to its last days, the McCarthy Building was the only example of Chicago's historic architec-

Fig. 3   Carter, Drake and Wight, Bay State Building (formerly the Springer Block), southwest corner of State and Randolph streets, 1872, with later additions by Adler and Sullivan, 1888 (photo 1964; now demolished).

Fig. 4   John M. Van Osdel, McCarthy Building, northeast corner of Dearborn and Washington streets, 1872 (photo c. 1950; now demolished).

Fig. 5   Clinton J.
Warren, Unity Building
(later the American
Bond and Mortgage
Company Building), 127
North Dearborn Street,
1892 (now demolished);
at right, Chemical Bank
Building, 121 North
Dearborn Street, 1898
(now demolished; site of
Commonwealth Edison
Substation, 1929-31).

ture ever to have rescinded its official city council designation as a "landmark."

Like Block 37 at its head, the rest of Dearborn Street had experienced a long decline from as early as the 1890s, when it was the city's main office zone. That decline lasted until Mayor Daley made plans to reverse it. There had not been a new commercial building anywhere in the Loop since 1934, when the Field Building on LaSalle Street was completed, right before the Depression entirely froze the real estate market. In the 1950s, when Daley took over, Chicago was still the country's youngest major city, but with no new buildings it looked old and tawdry.[1] For the mayor, already middle-aged and eager

to get things done, the sad agglomeration of structures on Block 37 represented the decay at the center of town. Only a football field away from his office, this old block with its honky tonks and its human disorder gave him a fixed target that could register all the changes he had planned for the city.

For thirty years, Richard Daley had risen patiently from job to job, from party hack to positions of power, until he was at last at the top. Controlled and unexpectedly silent in company, he knew how to be effective. The radicals, hangers-on, hustlers, and other low-life professionals who left their Sam Spade offices in the Unity Building (fig. 5) and its near neighbor, the New World Building (1914; 109 North Dearborn Street) on Block 37, to chase cases in his City Hall were the wrong kind of people to advertise his new downtown. Mayor Daley was a builder, and one by one he would get rid of these awful dark places and replace them with gleaming, tax-paying glass-and-steel towers with their richer clientele. To show everyone how it was done, he would begin methodically in his own backyard and build the city's long-planned Civic Center across the street from the City Hall—County Building. Block 37, an early contender for the site of the new building, would have to wait its turn.

The new mayor was trying by the force of his own will to reactivate a process of renewal that the city had experienced haphazardly before through conquest and natural disaster. While the land had been cleared first by settlers and then in 1871 by fire, Richard J. Daley would use bulldozers. Although he was an unlikely figure to play the role of Baron Georges-Eugene Haussmann, who had remade Paris, or Peter the Great, who had forced a new capital city of St. Petersburg out of the swamps, Daley nonetheless used architecture to direct development exactly where he wanted it.[2]

In recognizing that architecture was one of his city's unique resources, Daley attempted to reverse the traditional route of urban development. Where factories and grain elevators had industrialized the mouth of the river at the lakefront and its riverbanks, bankers and developers later colonized the interior streets of the downtown with office buildings. In both cases, specific areas of the city prospered as building followed money. Daley made capital follow buildings. He started the process by getting the best architects in the city teamed with the biggest banks to build the first monuments to his city and himself. By siting the new Civic Center

City Hall and the Dearborn Corridor   249

(now named the Richard J. Daley Center) right in the middle of the downtown, between his office and Block 37, Daley changed the rules. His consolidation of the Cook County Circuit Court, the state Appellate and Supreme courts, and other city and county offices in a stunning new skyscraper—at its completion the tallest building in the city—created a bull's-eye for developers to aim at, right where the mayor wanted the money invested.

By providing a secure environment for investment with a top municipal bond rating and a liberal zoning ordinance that encouraged giant downtown buildings, the mayor kept business happy by reducing expensive competition. From the perspective of a banker active in the 1960s, development was a game of "who you knew and how well you knew him." Deals were made directly with the city and Daley spread around the loot. There "was no bidding for deposits."[3] The mayor saw to it personally that each big bank got its fair share of city business. Daley controlled the downtown as effortlessly as the mayors before him had lorded over the patronage-dominated neighborhoods. The plan was to direct billions of dollars of private investment to precisely those areas of the city where it would be of most benefit and continue to enhance Daley's prestige. The downtown 1st Ward, which produced over one-third of the city's tax base, was Daley's Paris and St. Petersburg.

Daley saw the fall of Dearborn Street as an opportunity to rebuild to his advantage. Daley's focus on the downtown was still, at best, a rearguard action. Redevelopment of the Loop was a financial necessity: it was the only possible growth area for city revenues. Bigger, newer buildings would pay more taxes. Like every other established American city, Chicago was losing population and jobs to the new postwar suburbs. In 1960 Chicago's population was 3,550,000, and it would decline another 5.2 percent by 1970 (3,369,000), while the metropolitan area increased its size by 12.2 percent, from 6,220,000 to 6,977,000. The mayor's job of reviving the city economically was further complicated by the fact that those leaving Chicago were being replaced by an increasingly poorer population. For example, between 1960 and 1970, the white population declined by over 470,000 and the black increased by 288,000, settling in the destitute West Side ghetto rather than the more stable Blackbelt, running directly south of the Loop. The Central Business District (CBD) assumed an ever greater tax burden as taxpayers were replaced by tax consumers.[4]

Daley had grown up just north of the Stockyards on the near South Side, in an insular Irish neighborhood called Bridgeport where Chicago's leaders were trained—a politician's Sandhurst or West Point that prepared officers to lead the city's vast patronage army that numbered nearly 40,000 troops at its height. Despite his ties to the neighborhood where he lived his entire life, Daley loved the downtown. In silent recognition of its rules and formalities, the squat, jowly mayor of Chicago, who never lost his wheezing malaprop Bridgeport stammer, sported dark conservative LaSalle Street suits. An only son, rare for a neighborhood of large immigrant families, Richard Daley had big ambition focused all on him. A bulldog in a CEO's suit, Daley, once he was mayor, started immediately to consolidate the city's bureaucracy—controlling the city's purse. An obsessive detailer, an accountant with a law degree that he earned after hours at DePaul University, the new mayor moved methodically to reoccupy the center of his neglected city.

During the day, as a young man in the 1920s, Richard Daley had balanced the books at Dolan and Ludeman, a stockyard commission house, and at night he worked for the local Democratic club, where he helped process 11th Ward patronage checks for Alderman Big Joe McDonough. No small political boss himself, McDonough got the young Daley his first downtown job as a clerk in City Hall. In 1936, at the age of thirty-four, he became a state representative and after only one term a state senator, rising to minority leader down in Springfield, where he represented the interests of Chicago Mayor Edward J. Kelly and developed a reputation as a reliable ally who kept his mouth shut and had a way with numbers. In 1937, after making the switch from the lower to the upper house, he was appointed chief deputy county controller, a sensitive political job that gave him intimate knowledge of the patronage lists. In 1949, he became county controller, and only four years later, chairman of the Cook County Central Committee: boss of the country's best-organized big-city machine. Already on two payrolls, before he was ready to run the city of Chicago, Daley got the last of his postgraduate education when Governor Adlai Stevenson chose him to be in his state cabinet as revenue director.

By the time Richard Daley was inaugurated mayor on April 20, 1955, and added the position of head of the city government to the equally powerful post of leader of the Democratic Party, he needed no help with budgets and managing money. He could do it all alone under the new

guidelines proposed by the Home Rule Commission, set up by previous mayor, Martin Kennelly, which provided the mayor with wider taxing jurisdiction without prior legislative approval. After quickly taking the budgetary powers out of the hands of the aldermen, Daley had personal control over every dollar that came into City Hall.

The third Irish mayor in a row, he wanted quickly to be known as the best and not confused with his predecessors, the ineffectual Kennelly and the corrupt Kelly. His ticket was to "convert programs into action" by making the bureaucracy work for him. Using the Department of Streets and Sanitation and the Department of Public Works as his infantry, Daley achieved an immediate effect: garbage was collected, street lights were repaired, potholes were filled, and alleys lighted, so the people back in the wards knew that he was at work. At the same time, with money from the federal government, the new mayor widened his scope. First, he secured the city's perimeter. Multilane highways slashed through neighborhoods, splitting the formerly consolidated power bases of his political rivals, as public housing projects extended the old South Side ghetto and anchored a new one on the West Side. In increasing numbers, poor Chicagoans filtered into the apartments and subdivided single-family homes as quickly as the white middle-class abandoned them in their flight out of town. Others, who were thought luckier at the time, moved into the new public housing high-rises that were marching in long straight lines to the south and west along the right-of-ways of the new interstate highways.[5]

The highways that provided newly affluent suburbanites with an easy in and out of the city were as forbidding as moats with crocodiles for public housing residents, who had seen the old fabric of their neighborhoods — their stores, their churches, and the very streets themselves — bulldozed to accommodate the new wide roads and the tower housing. This new style of redevelopment through relocation reached its apotheosis with the construction of the Robert Taylor Homes (1960-62; see de Wit, figs. 1, 19, 20). On a quarter-mile-wide strip, two-miles long, built on the boundary of the old South Side ghetto, the Robert Taylor Homes housed the black poor, who were kept isolated from Daley's Bridgeport by railroad tracks and the Dan Ryan Expressway.[6] Stacking and concentrating people in minimalist spaces — rooms without closet doors, bathrooms without showers — worked not only to segregate poverty away from gentrifying areas but also to pacify the population. Black politicians loyal to the Daley organization had their constituents coraled into tight, easily controlled mini-wards where they were totally dependent and thankful for small favors. When the 1968 riots ripped up the high-rise-free West Side, the South Side gulags of public housing in the old Black Belt were calm.[7]

With the poor out of his downtown and isolated from the white wards that represented a majority of the city council, Daley turned his attention to the center of town, where his larger ambitions could take form. Thomas Keane, one-time chairman of the city council's Finance Committee, and imprisoned in the 1970s for fixing real estate deals, has said that the difference between himself and Daley was that he was interested in making money, while the mayor was interested only in power. Daley's rare concentration of ambition made him especially dangerous in a city where the players always had the ultimate security of a rival's marker. No one ever had anything on Daley. The mayor went to Mass each morning, stayed out of taverns, and sat down to dinner with his family every evening. Being personally incorruptible, identifying in a regal way his own interests so completely with the city's, made Daley free to muscle the politicians that he needed to carry out his orders. In addition, he was never personally in debt to the businessmen whose resources he would so deftly direct.

The creation of a Civic Center in Chicago was supposed to be convincing proof of a resuscitated downtown ever since Daniel H. Burnham and Edward H. Bennett had first conceived of a vast concentration of public buildings, a flattened Acropolis on the near West Side at Halsted and Congress streets. The centerpiece of their 1909 Chicago Plan was a bloated, overscaled version of Richard Morris Hunt's Administration Building at the 1893 World's Columbian Exposition; it was planned to terminate a long ceremonial axis from Lake Michigan down Congress Street to the Haussmannized West Side where all buildings were substantial and regularized by a uniform cornice height. Essentially, Burnham abandoned the old center; a new one was scientifically planned to take its place. Yet, even with powerful advocates like Daniel Burnham and the Commercial Club, the promise of a Civic Center remained unfulfilled until Daley took office.

Daley succeeded where others had failed because he rejected the move west and instead

reaffirmed the center: the city's traditional civic axis that extended from the original Court House site, between Clark and Dearborn, Randolph and Washington streets, east on Court House Place through Block 37 to State Street. To accomplish this transformation that his other, more celebrated predecessors would not even have attempted, Daley thoroughly reformed the way business would be done in the city, creating a public/private cartel with himself completely in charge. In this way, the mayor bypassed the traditional ward-based political alliances, which, as Democratic Party chairman, he controlled as a matter of right, and he concentrated a new sort of patronage on the downtown Republican business elite.[8]

Business in Chicago was concentrated to an unusual degree by an anachronistic Illinois state law that prohibited branch banking. Thus, huge national banks were forced to contain all their activities in one centrally located building near the narrow strip of State Street where the city's retailers had always conducted business. Added to these captives were the usually fixed downtown tourist businesses and utilities. Daley recruited them all as part of a new "non-partisan" constituency and ran the show through two inventions: the Public Building Commission (PBC), established in 1955, and Central Area Committee (CAC), organized in 1956.[9] By these and other smaller, blue-ribbon organizations fronted by the city's biggest private employers, Daley created a sham planning apparatus that allowed business to validate policies he had already decided on.[10] The PBC and CAC were used by the mayor to support his proposals to increase the density of the Loop and to counter any competing schemes. Before he took office, several serious private ventures, with old-time machine backing, had lobbied for large public subsidies to relocate government outside the Loop. One proposal, supported by West Side Aldermen Harry L. Sain (27th Ward) and William J. Lancaster (37th), announced in October 1953, was to build a Civic Center, a mirror image of the huge new post office, on Congress Street near where the Burnham Plan had first located it, although that site was now luckily in the way of a superhighway (figs. 6, 8). Sain and Lancaster's site was, not coincidentally, the same as one that had appeared in the Chicago Plan Commission's *Preliminary Comprehensive City Plan of Chicago* (1946), which was reviewed first by the city council and did not enjoy wide public circulation.

Daley knew their scheme was a fraud, freelanced to raise the value of land owned by several aldermen directly adjacent to the site of the proposed public buildings. Already working on bigger plans himself, Daley would have none of this old machine-style profit sharing. His ambitions now went beyond ward politics. He could not afford the embarrassment of business as usual. As Democratic Party leader guiding the inert Mayor Kennelly, Daley would see to it personally that their land would be condemned for the Congress Expressway at the going rate. And to make sure that no sweetheart deals were made, he took his old political allies to court.[11] This nice bit of political Kabuki was aimed less at the old ward bosses, who were free to do their dealing back in the neighborhoods, than it was intended to reassure the bankers and businessmen who commuted in from Kenilworth and Lake Forest that he was not about to sell them out for any penny-ante deals. They could trust that when he became mayor he would make sure that the downtown was a place where they could do business.

At about the same time, a more serious threat to the Loop was launched by developer Arthur Rubloff. His Fort Dearborn Plan of 1954 proposed relocating government buildings north of the river as anchors for a 148-acre private residential redevelopment of blighted land to qualify for federal funding from Title I of the 1949 Housing Act. Daley eventually used the Rubloff and the Sain/Lancaster plans for his own purposes. He encouraged the idea that there was a

Fig. 6   *Chicago Plan Commission, Bird's-eye view perspective drawing of proposed Chicago Civic Center, Chicago River between Madison and Van Buren streets; from Chicago Plan Commission,* Chicago Civic Center *(Chicago, 1949), p. 35.*

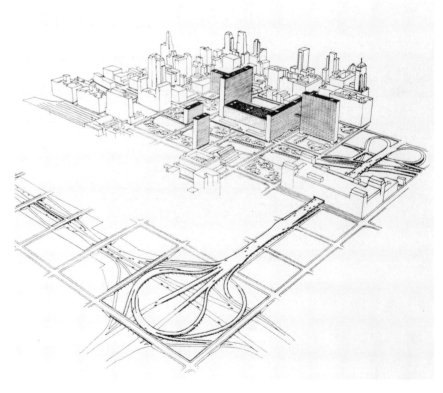

Fig. 7   C. F. Murphy Associates; with Loebl, Schlossman and Bennett, and Skidmore, Owings and Merrill, Richard J. Daley Center, detail of plaza with sculpture by Pablo Picasso.

stead of resisting the inevitable, he struck a cynical, silent bargain. The mayor agreed not to interfere with the metropolitan area's self-segregating residential patterns. In return for this, he would insist that businesses reinvest, on their own terms, in the downtown. Daley knew that if he lost a vital Central Business District—that roughly one square mile of the downtown ringed by the elevated train line—then he would lack a sufficient tax base to run the city. Therefore, to make everyone understand that he was not about to abandon the middle of the city, he would start by building the biggest building he could right in the heart of downtown.

Daley's earliest transformation of a private into a public initiative came in August 1958, when the Central Area Committee, composed of the heads of fourteen of the city's most powerful corporations, published a plan for a newly expanded central area. They argued that this "nonpartisan" plan would help encourage growth and ultimately higher tax collections. The highest priority was for a Civic Center, placed right in the middle of the Central Area, right next to City Hall and a few blocks north of Democratic Central Committee headquarters at the Morrison Hotel, a site that no planner had ever proposed before.

Daley was pleased when his architects designed a municipal building unlike any other. The radically modern architecture demonstrated that the mayor of Chicago was not simply de-

political consensus to the effect that Chicago had suffered severely from postwar demographic changes. Its core population was fleeing to the suburbs and those remaining in the inner city were progressively poorer than those who left.[12] Daley understood immediately that these changes he deplored were permanent, and in-

Fig. 8   Chicago Plan Commission, Photographic collage of proposed Chicago Civic Center, Chicago River between Madison and Van Buren streets; from Chicago Plan Commission, Chicago Civic Center (Chicago, 1949), p. 16.

City Hall and the Dearborn Corridor   253

fending old arrangements, but was doing nothing less than recasting the aging American downtown. The mayor, acting through the Public Building Commission, made certain that the Civic Center, finished in 1965, would not be a neoclassical pile but every inch a modern steel-and-glass tower, like the very best of the private office buildings that were colonizing all prosperous cities of the world. The choice of form was critical. With a building that for a time was the tallest in town and bold in its architecture, Daley gave instant parity to the public sector.

There is nothing random about any aspect of the building from the pioneering use of Cor-Ten steel that oxidized to a russet brown, to the eagle span of its immense bays (87 feet long and nearly 48 feet wide), its 18-foot floor-to-floor heights, or the Picasso sculpture in the front yard (fig. 7). At 648 feet in height, with only thirty-one stories occupying just 35 percent of its site, the Civic Center rises above the plaza like a technological colossus. The building communicates civic authority in contrast to the squat and hunched City Hall and County Building next door with its staunch Corinthian columns and Roman vaults (fig. 9). It provides a minimalist wrapping for over 120 courtrooms and office space for Cook County, the State of Illinois, and the City of Chicago.[13] The Civic Center was Daley's first public building. None would be more important or more economical in the ways it used architecture to express the city's new aggressive attitude toward downtown blight.

Prior to this, the city had been careful to designate decayed areas far from the prosperous cen-

ter.[14] Symbolically, the 65 percent of the site that was retained as open space reinforced the hygiene of urban renewal, where a once-crowded city block with fourteen separate structures was now a classical plinth, curetted and debrided: a perfected open space returned to the people through the beneficence of good government.

The change in style from Roman to Miesian represents a change in the way Chicago politicians viewed modern architecture. Daley understood how bare-bones high-rise architecture, in addition to conferring status on municipal workers, could represent publicly the raw political power he mastered in private. The Civic Center as finally conceived and built is a monument to Daley's use of architecture to extend his control of the city from the wards to the Central Business District. It was also the three-dimensional expression of the sort of changes envisioned by the mayor when he conceived the Public Building Commission during his first days in office. The PBC was a fast-track way to get his decisions implemented. The mayor presided as chairman over an eleven-person board, composed of businessmen and political heavyweights from independent city fiefdoms like the Park District, with broad powers of home rule that included the right of condemnation and the authority to issue tax-exempt bonds, without state referendum, to fund its operations.[15] With the PBC in place and with himself at the helm, Daley would not suffer the frustrations experienced by other big-city mayors, who were left to run a creaking political bureaucracy—a social welfare organization for the beneficiaries of

Fig. 9 Jacques
Brownson of C. F.
Murphy Associates,
Perspective rendering of
proposed Civic Center
plaza, delineated by
Al Francik, 1963 (cat.
no. 144); at left is the
City Hall and County
Building (Holabird and
Roche, 1911).

Fig. 10 View looking
west from the southwest
corner of Dearborn and
Randolph streets,
August 1940; this entire
block was cleared for
construction of the Civic
Center.

patronage and civil service—while the real action was being played out through new urban renewal agencies, funded through Title I of the 1949 and 1955 Federal Housing Acts.

As chairman of the Public Building Commission, Richard Daley had an independent source of funding and a handpicked group of powerful allies who were eager to please.[16] To make sure that there would be no mistaking the hierarchy of this power pyramid, the mayor engineered the election of Ira Bach, the head of the city's newly established Department of Planning (1957), as PBC secretary, and he ensured that three of the city's top architectural firms would cooperate, not compete, to build the Civic Center.[17] Even the big five downtown banks, whom no mayor before Daley could significantly influence, now fell into line by contributing proportionately, according to the size of their deposits, to underwrite the project's interim financing. Daley made sure the local banks cooperated by getting Henry Crown, who then owned both the Conrad Hilton and the Palmer House, to offer to put up the interim financing from his own personal fortune if the banks were not "patriotic" enough to do it themselves. In return for their patriotism, until the revenue bonds were issued, the largest lender, Continental Bank, was given the courtesy of holding all the PBC's reserve funds. The naked modernism of America's newest civic building—more like those corporate masterpieces in New York, the Seagram Building or Lever House, than like a seat of government— would be the Daley administration's only outward expression of the new order.

From a long list of qualified architects, he assembled the group for this sensitive commission with the same care he took when putting together an election ticket. An old time Irish firm, Naess and Murphy, would be responsible for design. Skidmore, Owings and Merrill (SOM), the corporate darling, provided additional engineering services and planning expertise, while adding an aura of priceless WASP legitimacy. Although careful to signal that he would not alter the rules completely, he included, for ethnic balance, the Jewish firm of Loebl, Schlossman and Bennett, whose responsibilities were vague enough to indicate that they were just in it for the sake of the deal.

The completed building with its sanitized plaza represented a blitzkrieged upzoning of an area that only years before was regarded as derelict and underused. While New York, Boston, Philadelphia, and New Haven with their ambitious urban renewal programs had left unfilled holes where expressways abruptly ended and scrub trees broke through the pavement, Mayor Daley had focused his activities on a single three-acre site.[18] The new Civic Center rose on a site which was formerly the home of a legendary watering hole, Henrici's (fig. 10), and the headquarters for a Mr. Rockola who ran his jukebox and arcade business out of a jumble of buildings across from City Hall.[19] Daley further showed the center of town how up-scale and highbrow it could be by encouraging William Hartmann, an SOM partner, to get Pablo Picasso to donate a fifty-foot statue for the Civic Center plaza. Hartmann, who lent his personality and an East

Coast pedigree to the formlessness of Skidmore, Owings and Merrill, spent weeks in France successfully interesting the "world's greatest artist" to create a work for the site.[20] The marriage of high art and corporate muscle was made complete when Picasso's sculpture was fabricated by the American Bridge Division of U. S. Steel in the same Cor-Ten steel that framed the tower.

The model for the PBC and Daley's use of modern architecture for direct civic gain has its roots in the development of McCormick Place, on an old railroad fair site on the lakefront, south of the Loop (figs. 11, 12). The mayor watched with admiration as Colonel Robert R. McCormick, owner of the *Chicago Tribune*, maneuvered the city council and the Illinois state legislature to build a permanent convention center.[21] Daley was less interested in the building than he was in the political know-how and the fiscal creativity that got it built with no obvious cost to the taxpayers.[22] In 1956 two bills were introduced to the legislature, supported by Republican Governor Stratton and the mayor: one established the Metropolitan Fair and Exhibition Authority (MFEA) as the municipal corporation (permitting the state and other political bodies to buy their bonds), and the second authorized the Chicago Park District to lease, for forty years, as many as 180 acres around the 23rd Street site.

Daley was not interested in helping the Republican *Tribune* immortalize Col. McCormick, who died in 1955, but he quickly came to understand how the MFEA could be used as a precedent for his Public Building Commission, which was just then beginning to plan the Civic Center.[23] The beauty of letting the *Tribune* do their own thing, through their own network in Springfield, was that Daley got the benefit of a new building without expending any political capital. In fact, Republicans in league with the *Tribune* would owe him one. He explained it to his new head of

planning, Ira Bach, who initially opposed granting the lease on lakefront property that had traditionally been kept free of building and available for public use. Daley told Bach, "The land will cost the city nothing! The Park District will give it to us," and the MFEA would build it with state money. "Top that," Daley cheered, but Bach still didn't get it. Daley, now red in the face, added the obvious, "You stick to planning, I'll stick to politics."[24]

When the black, mortar-board-flat, second McCormick Place (1967-71; fig. 13) replaced the short-lived exhibition hall that burned down in 1967, the new structure had the same severe modernist look used to clean out the core of town, particularly the old federal site straddling Dearborn between Adams and Jackson streets, where a deteriorating classical heap from 1905 housed all the federal courts and offices. The site was so critical to the rebuilding of the city that Chicago's local Picasso, Ludwig Mies van der Rohe, was asked to get involved with the project right from the beginning. He landed this plum $100 million federal commission in association with A. Epstein and Sons, C. F. Murphy Associates, and Schmidt, Garden and Erikson.

Fig. 11 Shaw, Metz and Associates, McCormick Place, South Lake Shore Drive at 23rd Street, 1960 (now demolished).

Fig. 12 Aerial view of lakefront, showing McCormick Place.

Fig. 13 C. F. Murphy Associates; Gene Summers with Helmut Jahn, designers, Perspective view of McCormick Place, photographic collage delineated by Gene Summers with Tom Burke, c. 1969 (cat. no. 153).

Mies produced a campuslike ensemble (1959-75) of two high-rise buildings—one a court house and the other an office tower—oriented to each other like his earlier residential work, most obviously at 860-880 (1949-52) and 900-910 North Lake Shore Drive (1955-58), and he added a low-rise post office that mined some of the Platonic clarity of Crown Hall at the Illinois Institute of Technology (figs. 14, 15). The complex not only helped anchor the upzoned Dearborn Street on the south, but through the steady criticism of Daley's City Plan Commission, the General Service Administration was persuaded to abandon its 1959 plan to build a single, seventy-five-story, block-hogging building in favor of creating the openness of its current site. After much study, the GSA thought it would be "inappropriate" to have their government building be the tallest building, too much like the Soviets in Cold War Eastern Europe.

Instead, they built a monument to propriety and proportion. Anchored with a bright red stabile by Alexander Calder, the Federal Center's open plaza on its northern corner was the mirror image of the open space on the Civic Center's south side. These fine public buildings, with their tasteful placement of high art and open space, subtly validated the new zoning bonuses that favored the construction of bigger skyscra-

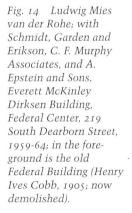

Fig. 14 Ludwig Mies van der Rohe; with Schmidt, Garden and Erikson, C. F. Murphy Associates, and A. Epstein and Sons, Everett McKinley Dirksen Building, Federal Center, 219 South Dearborn Street, 1959-64; in the foreground is the old Federal Building (Henry Ives Cobb, 1905; now demolished).

Fig. 15 Ludwig Mies van der Rohe; with Schmidt, Garden and Erikson, C. F. Murphy Associates, and A. Epstein and Sons, Federal Center, 1959-75; left to right, Dirksen Building, John C. Kluczynski Building, and United States Post Office.

City Hall and the Dearborn Corridor 257

pers to fuel the necessary inflation in downtown property values. Without a rising trend in property values to justify private investment, the redevelopment of Dearborn Street would not continue. But Daley could look to some early signs that just this very thing was happening.

Directly south of the Civic Center, across Washington Street, Arthur Rubloff had hired a design team of Bruce Graham, Myron Goldsmith, and engineer Fazlur Khan of Skidmore, Owings and Merrill to build the city's first speculative office building. Their Inland Steel Building (1954-58; fig. 16) on Dearborn Street at Monroe Street and Naess and Murphy's Prudential Insurance Company's headquarters (1952-55) on Randolph Street at Michigan Avenue had been the first new buildings since the Depression. Without being leased in advance, the Brunswick Building (1961-65; fig. 17) was built at considerable risk. The concrete, exposed-frame, thirty-seven-story tower insinuated itself with the large-scale public building going up across the street. Acknowledging the new civic style, it left more open space than was required. By making it easier to assemble small lots to make way for larger, well-ordered modern buildings, the mayor's initial de-blighting of downtown worked without new taxes.

The Brunswick Building leased up quickly at much higher rents than the land had ever produced before.[25] Soon that success was imitated by another concrete building, designed by Otto Stark at C. F. Murphy Associates, at the corner of Dearborn Street and Wacker Drive, initially the fifteen-story headquarters of Blue Cross-Blue Shield (1968). The Civic Center proved to be such an unimpeachable public reference that an elite group of big-time architectural firms would use it, for two decades, to get new work.[26] Such was the chain of connections that brought more and more select corporate architects into the game.

Yet, the construction of a new office building for the First National Bank of Chicago (1964-69; fig. 18) provided the strongest confirmation of Daley's plans for an improved downtown, capitalized through private investment. The 850-foot-high, sixty-story corporate headquarters for one of the city's two biggest banks was the culmination of a decade of planning.[27] Interested in leaving his Loop location, Homer J. Livingston, president of First National, commissioned his firm's appraiser, Gilbert H. Scribner, only recently named a director of the bank for his loyal service, to look for alternative sites.

Scribner's observations in a series of confidential letters give independent support to the

Fig. 16 Skidmore, Owings and Merrill, Inland Steel Building, 30 West Monroe Street, 1954-58.

notion that Daley's first attempts to improve downtown real estate were not lost on the private market. When Scribner gave his first appraisal at the end of March 1959, he concluded that the bank should consider improving its current site, noting that "there are few solid blocks obtainable. The Federal Building occupies the most conspicuous one, but the Government's latest plans do not abandon it. Don't overlook the fact that with your own business you have built up the esteem and prominence of your present location."[28] Just a few months later, the bank's search for an improved location or an expansion of their current facilities had progressed to the point that Scribner was concerned that land values were being adversely affected. Too many people already knew the bank was "look-

ing for property." The appraiser advised Homer Livingston, "I don't know whether your architects talk too much or whether it has gotten out through other sources, but I think an effort ought to be made to keep this more or less quiet."[29] Scribner did not want the bank's interest in downtown land to help speculators bid up the price.

On July 10, 1961, Scribner wrote a letter to Gaylord A. Freeman, Jr., the new president of the bank, in which he confirmed that the best, most economical block the bank could own was the one they already occupied. The announced improvements for the area had already taken land values, flat for over a hundred years, and begun to drive them up.[30] By staying put and doing nothing, the land around them would be improved sufficiently, through public improvements, to justify a large new investment. Daley had hooked a big one.

Scribner noted that in addition to the properties they already controlled, the bank could, for an additional $4.4 million, control the land that comprised the rest of the block under the Morrison Hotel, and the Hartford and Hamilton buildings. With the old First National Bank Building itself appraised at $10 million (fig. 19),

Fig. 17 Skidmore, Owings and Merrill, Brunswick Building, 69 West Washington Street, 1961-65.

Fig. 18 C. F. Murphy Associates; with the Perkins and Will Partnership, First National Bank Building, One First National Plaza, Madison Street between Dearborn and Clark streets, 1964-69.

the bank was in the enviable position of needing to invest as little as $15 million for the land. They had all the land required to build a four-million-square-foot tower. Gaylord Freeman was ready to build on the same public scale as the Civic and Federal centers. With a total area of 128,000 square feet to build on, all he needed were the architects to design a beautiful tower in the shape of the deal.

Daley's refusal to press recalcitrant downstate legislators for branch banking legislation compelled the First National Bank of Chicago to increase the size of its operations downtown. Expansion of postwar business had created a space crunch for banks that remained chained to a single downtown site, and First National moved cautiously to expand their operations. Daley was not yet in office when First National sought relief the old-fashioned Chicago way: through an ordinance introduced on April 22, 1953, in the city council by the alderman of the 1st Ward, the titular seat of downtown mob activities. The ordinance gave the bank, for a period of twenty years, permission to "construct and maintain a four (4) level bridge structure over the east-and-west public alley" connecting the First National Bank Building at 38 South Dearborn Street with the Hotel Chicagoan and Hamilton Hotel.

Fig. 19   D. H. Burnham and Company, First National Bank Building, 38 South Dearborn Street, northwest corner of Dearborn and Monroe streets, 1903 (now demolished).

Figs. 20, 21   C. William Brubaker of the Perkins and Will Partnership, Preliminary sketches of the First National Bank Building, 1964 (cat. no. 215).

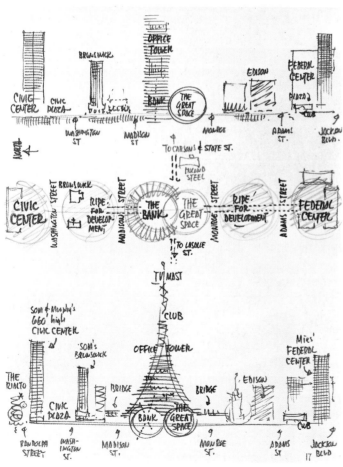

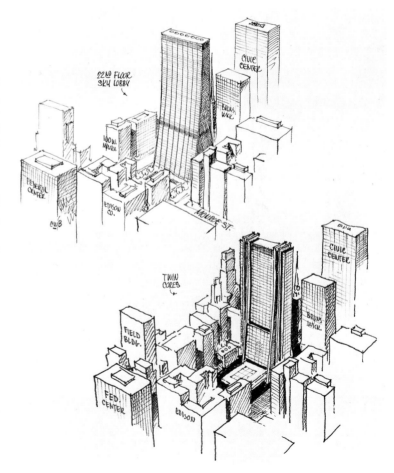

When the time came some ten years later, the very same alley that the bank had been allowed to bridge in 1953 was vacated by the city for only $77,500. Robert Wilmouth, then a vice-president of First National Bank, personally confirmed the deal for the alley over the phone with Mayor Daley, who referred him directly to an insurance firm in Evanston, where the mayor knew someone who would complete the paperwork for the transaction. The bank needed the alley if they were to control the whole block. Daley personally expedited the work. The new First National Bank of Chicago building was half completed before the appropriate city department even required a building permit. Daley had made certain that no one in his bureaucracy would get in the way of this new piece of downtown development, because he knew how much more this tower would pay in taxes than their old headquarters, while still yielding open space for the public use.[31]

At the exact geographical center of the Loop, equidistant from the two new open-plaza public projects, the First National Bank executives had recognized their unusual architectural opportunity (fig. 20). A preliminary zoning analysis for the total block, conducted in April 1964, indicated that the bank, without seeking a variance,

Fig. 22   Aerial view, looking west along Washington Street from State Street, c. 1970.

Fig. 23   C. F. Murphy Associates; with the Perkins and Will Partnership, First National Bank Building, plaza on Monroe Street, 1969-72.

could build a sixty-story tower of 4,043,500 square feet. But the bankers and their architects immediately realized that a single structure of this density would have plugged the whole block and cast a good part of the area into darkness. For an exercise the architects, led by Stanislaw Gladych of C. F. Murphy and Lawrence Perkins of the Perkins and Will Partnership, considered the idea of two towers, to be built in stages.[32] First the north half of the block was to be demolished, while the bank continued operations in its old structure on the south half.

Gaylord Freeman, however, was keen to exploit the bank's opportunity to become the most distinctive building on the city's skyline. Some of the earliest sketches include a transmitting tower reserved for the city's tallest building. Both the Hancock and Sears towers soon denied Freeman this honor, but the final spread-leg structure and castellated top, with the mechanicals and blowers differentiated, provided the building a strong image (figs. 21, 22).

Single-location banking required large-span bottom floors where all the tellers could be in the same space. This arrangement was accomplished at First National Bank by moving the elevator core out of the center and onto the building's "legs." The final tapering form of the bank, narrowing from 59,000 on the banking floors to 29,000 square feet on the typical rental floors gave the building its distinctive "swoop," first used by I. M. Pei in an unbuilt design for the New York Stock Exchange. Employing the established formula of a large tower on a generous plaza (fig. 23), the bank projected civic responsibility. Later in 1972, with its own work of art by an acknowledged master, Marc Chagall, the First National Bank of Chicago would be favorably compared with the Civic and Federal centers. No need for the moment to disclose earlier plans to build a second tower, to consume another two million square feet on the remainder of the block.[33] By being able to build a profitable skyscraper of this size, so large that it did not have to consume even one half of its permitted size, the bank was a sign to private investors that Chicago was a good place to build.

Before the decade of the 1960s had come to a close with riots, antiwar demonstrations, and the national public humiliation of a man clearly out of control at the 1968 Democratic Convention, Richard J. Daley had good reason to believe that through a mixture of political monopoly and pure bluff he was well on his way to rebuilding the city. His way. But in the end, the complicated process of urban redevelopment Daley set in motion proved to be uncontrollable. The real failures only appeared later, when the Boss who drew power to himself like a black hole was no longer around to set in balance both public and private interests in what he had once confidently called "the pure deal."

NOTES

1. Chicago delayed rebuilding its downtown. Daley moved cautiously, unlike Robert Moses in New York and the heads of other big city urban renewal efforts. See Jeanne R. Lowe, *Cities in a Race with Time: Progress and Poverty in America's Renewing Cities* (New York, 1967), pp. 45-109.
2. Earlier Chicago politicians had used this form of directed development to fund public works projects, like the creation of the Metropolitan Sanitary District (1889), or to fund and administer the construction of the Sanitary and Ship Canal (1894-99) to reverse the flow of the Chicago River. No one had ever tried to lead such intensive development downtown, which was traditionally beyond the range of the Democratic machine.
3. Interview with Robert Wilmouth, October 22, 1991. Wilmouth was a vice-president at the First National Bank and the executive in charge of the planning of the new bank building, 1963 to 1965.
4. A useful statistical profile of Chicago during the Daley years can be found in Brian J. L. Berry, Irving Cutler, Edwin H. Draine, Ying-cheng Kiang, Thomas R. Tocalis, and Pierre de Vise, *Chicago: Transformations of an Urban System* (Cambridge, Mass., 1976).
5. See Jean-Louis Cohen and Andre Lortie, *Des Fortifs au Périf: Paris les Seuils de la Ville* (Paris, 1991). The authors consider the relationship between roads, military fortifications, and social control in Paris during the nineteenth and twentieth centuries.
6. Arnold R. Hirsch, *Making the Second Ghetto: Race and Housing in Chicago, 1940-1960* (New York, 1983); Thomas Lee Philpott, *The Slum and the Ghetto: Neighborhood Deterioration and Middle-Class Reform, Chicago, 1880-1930* (New York, 1976); and Martin Meyerson and Edward C. Banfield, *Politics, Planning, and the Public Interest* (London and New York, 1955), consider the ways Chicago's public housing took the shape of vested downtown interests. Hirsch writes, "Initially comprised of 4,415 units in twenty-eight identical sixteen-story buildings, the Taylor project has cast the shadow of the original Black Belt in concrete ....the development housed, when completed, some 27,000 residents (20,000 of them children), all poor and virtually all black" (pp. 262-63).
7. Hirsch (note 6), p. 263. Preacher Davis, a black ward precinct captain, efficiently worked the Robert Taylor Homes. When in the 1960s the FBI was invited to monitor "irregular" Chicago voting, they were sent to Preacher Davis's precinct. The preacher marched his registered voters to the polls in military fashion and proudly gave the vote total to the feds, twelve hours before it was officially tallied. With over five hundred votes cast, he was only one vote off. (Interview with Thomas Foran, U.S. Attorney from 1968 to 1972, on May 12, 1992.)
8. This doubling of power was unique to Daley. He held the position of chairman of the Central Committee of the Democratic Party before he became mayor. He told his supporters that he would let someone else take over the party leadership as soon as he took office; but in twenty-one years in the job he never managed to do so. When, in 1956, he became chairman of the Public Building Commission, he held all three of the most powerful jobs in the city.
9. John R. Logan and Harvey M. Molotch, *Urban Fortunes: The Political Economy of Place* (Berkeley, 1987), explain precisely the phenomenon of captive downtown businesses.
10. Chicago did not even have a professional planning department to supplement the Chicago Plan Commission, a creation of the 1909 Plan, until 1957, when Mayor Daley handpicked Ira Bach to start a Department of Planning. Bach had been tested politically to Daley's satisfaction through his various administrative experiences in neighborhood urban renewal.
11. "Council Votes Study of Big Civic Center," *Chicago Tribune* (Oct. 23, 1953). Interview with Thomas Foran, April 28, 1992. As a young attorney in the 1950s, Foran worked for Frank Righeimer, who represented the city in condemning land for the new Congress Expressway. The federal government was holding up highway money until the city controlled the entire parcel of land where the new road was to go. A group of aldermen wanted to make a deal, asking over $5 million for the land. Righeimer took them to jury trial and they were awarded about $400,000. Interview with Earl Bush, Richard J. Daley's press secretary, March 11, 1992.
12. By 1970, 88,000 families (10.6 percent) were living below the poverty line. With the exodus of whites to the suburbs and the influx of blacks and Hispanics into the neighborhoods they vacated, the city's poverty became spatially more concentrated. In the 1960s, 128,829 units were transferred from black to white occupancy. See Berry et al. (note 4), pp. 28, 30, 69.
13. Carl Condit, *Chicago, 1930-70: Building, Planning, and Urban Technology* (Chicago, 1974), pp. 135-38; Pauline A. Saliga, ed., *The Sky's the Limit: A*

Century of Chicago Skyscrapers (New York, 1991), p. 193.

14. The Public Building Commission's initial report, *The Central Area and the Civic Center Site of the City of Chicago* (Chicago, 1958), claimed an urban renewal role for the building: "The construction of new public buildings would contribute to conservation measures in the downtown area. Dilapidated structures would be demolished and vacant land developed. The center would stimulate rehabilitation and new construction in nearby properties. This area could be acquired with a minimum displacement of essential elements" (p.5). The Civic Center was Chicago's first cautious move to transfer "conservation" efforts from its vast Black Belt, south of the Loop, to downtown.

15. The original charter passed by the City Council provided the PBC the authority to issue forty-year tax-exempt bonds. On September 20, 1956, the State's Attorney of Cook County, Illinois, brought suit in the Illinois Supreme Court, questioning this authority. This was the last effective challenge to Daley's fiscal autonomy. On March 20, 1957, the Supreme Court of Illinois upheld the constitutionality of the PBC, but it limited to twenty years the maturities of the municipal bonds. This saved face for competing politicians in Cook County, but did little more than raise slightly the low coupon on PBC bonds. Chicago Public Building Commission revenue bonds with a 4 percent coupon rate raised $67 million to cover the Civic Center's total development costs.

16. The mayor's relationship was so good with the big five Chicago banks that he had uninterrupted access to a $100 million line of credit. In turn, Daley kept the businessmen happy by maintaining an excellent credit rating that helped leverage more and more private capital. Among the original members of the PBC were Henry Crown, head of the Material Services Division of General Dynamics, Willis Gale, head of Commonwealth Edison, and Philip K. Wrigley, chairman of the family gum empire.

17. While Daley would allow less able designers but politically savvy architects Louis R. Solomon and John D. Cordwell to provide preliminary plans for the project, they were "not to be considered as being necessarily representative of an architectural and planning solution and should not be so construed." When it came time to select the final team among the nineteen that submitted proposals – including Mies van der Rohe, Harry Wesse, Perkins and Will, and Holabird and Root – Daley went with a representative team of the best the city could offer.

18. Daley had earlier signaled his interest in the redevelopment possibilities of daring architecture when he gave his blessing to Bertrand Goldberg's corkscrew-shaped Marina City (1960-64), built just north of the river between Dearborn and State streets. The slip-form concrete balconies of the twin towers and the armadillo-shaped theater suggested by their very weirdness the fact that something radical needed to be done to reshape the downtown. The new architecture captured, without needing further articulation, the audacity of the mayor's plans for the city center.

19. The mayor used the PBC's condemnation of property for the Civic Center as a way to demonstrate to his new allies in the business community and his old ones back in the wards that he would do business in his own way. No one would hold up condemnation proceedings to push up awards, and there would be no special deals downtown as he had shown earlier when Frank Righeimer went to trial to condemn land for the Congress Expressway. The owner of the Peerless Weighing and Vending Machine Company, Mr. Rockola, owned three lots, all but fifty feet of the south part of the Civic Center site. He asked for more than the city offered for his land, and he hired a politically connected law firm headed by Col. Jacob Arvey to represent him. Arvey had been Daley's predecessor as Central Committee chairman and a power in the 24th Ward. Arvey was credited with engineering the elections of Governor Adlai Stevenson and Senator Paul Douglas. The confrontation over these three lots had the look of a classic political deal, but Daley played it straight and had William Dillon, PBC legal counsel, take Arvey to trial. The jury awarded Mr. Rockola $3.9 million, a little more than half of what he sued for and less than the city had offered in a negotiated settlement that he had earlier rejected. The city ended up paying $10,979,500 for the entire fourteen-lot parcel ($95.31 per square foot for the land).

20. See Condit (note 13), pp. 139-41; and Betty J. Blum, interviewer, *Oral History of William Hartmann* (Chicago, 1991), pp. 218-52.

21. The best single source on the building of McCormick Place remains "The Exhibition Hall," in Edward C. Banfield, *Political Influence: A New Theory Of Urban Politics* (New York, 1961), pp. 190-235.

22. The original exhibition hall had none of the architectural audacity of the Civic Center. After it burned down in January 1967, Daley had direct influence over the project to rebuild it, and he guaranteed that it would be done right. Again C. F. Murphy was hired. Gene Summers headed a design team that included Helmut Jahn, and he constructed on the foundations of the old structure, a huge loft building that was as notable horizontally with its giant-span black cantilevered roof as the russet brown Civic Center was vertically. In the image of a famous unexecuted design by Ludwig Mies van der Rohe, normally cautious public buildings elsewhere, were, in Chicago, to take the most radical form possible. This tendency, begun with Daley, was taken to its limit with Helmut Jahn's flying-saucer plan for the State of Illinois Building (1985).

23. The MFEA was to be composed originally of a representative board with the governor and mayor as ex officio directors. Originally the governor was to appoint six members and the mayor five. This number was later equalized at six after a lack of enthusiasm was shown by Cook County Democrats. When it came time for Daley to create the PBC, he tilted the balance between his appointments (six) and other agencies (five) in his favor, exactly the same arrangement as that which he had opposed when the state held the upper hand with the Exposition Authority. Henry Crown, the owner of the Conrad Hilton and Palmer House and the Material Service Corporation (which in the 1950s was doing $100 million a year in business with the city), was one of the prominent businessmen on the board. Crown will also be an early key member of the PBC. He had a strong interest in keeping Daley happy, for he was almost a monopoly supplier of the aggregate that the city used to pave its roads.

24. From the unpublished papers of Ira Bach.

25. The Brunswick Building is a good example of the way the scale of the money to be made from downtown land imitated the increased size of the buildings, on larger building lots. The site has a long real estate pedigree going back to William D. Kerfoot, who did business there in the ashes of the 1871 fire. Later, it was the site of the Chicago Title and Trust Company until it was sold on July 3, 1946, for $2,650,000 to Mr. Edward E. Glatt. The 241-by-183-foot lot (including the alley) included a sixteen-story fireproof building, a four-story fireproof building, a two-story taxpayer, and two other old structures. The price equaled $62.78 per square foot. Given a low inflation rate over the twenty years the property was held by Mr. Glatt, he would be lucky to break even. The big return on the land came when Arthur Rubloff, anticipating the early benefits of the Central Area Plan, got his hands on the property. When it was resold on September 14, 1957, for $3,000,000 with Arthur Rubloff as broker, the price equaled $68.50 per square foot. In 1965 Rubloff's syndicate built a 650,000-square-foot building on the consolidated larger lot, multiplying the rentable property by sixteen times. At the end of 1991 the building was 94 percent occupied with a net square-foot rental of $18.00. *The Metro-Chicago Office Guide* 6, no. 1 (First Quarter 1991).

26. On March 14, 1961, the Public Building Commission signed a contract for architectural services with Naess and Murphy, supervising architects; Skidmore, Owings and Merrill and Loebl, Schlossman and Bennett, associate architects; see "Minutes of the Public Building Commission of Chicago," March 20, 1961. The commission had received a $1.5 million advance from the federal Community Facilities Administration of the Housing and Home Financing Agency. For this fee, the architects agreed to provide, within 420 days, all the preliminary site and design work. Once the PBC bonds were successfully floated, the architects would be paid 5 percent of construction costs. The architects' eagerness to do work under Daley is revealed by their willingness to accept the tough terms dictated by the city and to deliver on time. This arrangement had already been lucrative for Murphy in the massive construction of O'Hare Airport and other public works commissions: the public work almost inevitably led to more lucrative private jobs, like those along the Dearborn corridor.

27. When the bank decided to build a new building it is significant that they used C. F. Murphy, already viewed as a firm politically connected to the Daley administration through their work on the Civic Center. The Perkins and Will Partnership, whose U. S. Gypsum Building (1961-63) had received considerable attention with its rotated prism form, opening four small triangular plazas at the corners of the lot, was favored by Freeman and some other executives at the bank who admired their design skills.

28. Letter dated March 30, 1959, from Gilbert H. Scribner, Scribner and Co., to Homer J. Livingston, President, The First National Bank of Chicago, p. 6.

29. Letter dated August 26, 1960, from Gilbert Scribner to Homer J. Livingston, Chairman of the Board, the First National Bank of Chicago. It is clear that the bank's decision was being influenced directly by downtown land values. On June 15, 1960, Scribner made note of his $10,750,000 estimate of the "fair cash market value" for the Civic Center site then slated for demolition, and he also noted that it was his "understanding that you [Livingston] are not interested in a half block but only in obtaining a full block, within a very limited area of the downtown district." He also noted the PBC's advantage in having the powers of eminent domain to help set their price. On September 14, 1960, Scribner prepared a summary of values for Livingston, noting that earlier he had told him "that there were cases where properties in the past had sold or been leased at more than their present value." But it was still early in Daley's crusade to prop Loop values up, and Scribner did not want his client to be rash. He concluded with the caveat, "The point is not that downtown as a whole has slipped but the values of some of the properties have varied. In other words, it doesn't always go up in price."

30. See Homer Hoyt, *One Hundred Years of Chicago Land Values* (Chicago, 1933); and Richard M. Hurd, *Principles of City Land Values* (New York, 1903).

31. Undated letter from the First National Bank to Otto H. Loser, Acting City Comptroller, confirming the Bank's $77,500 offer to the city to vacate the alley, the last piece they needed to control the entire block. Interview with Robert Wilmouth (note 3); interview with Thomas Foran (note 7).

32. The architects at C. F. Murphy dominated the collaboration. On September 20, 1965, Gaylord Freeman wrote to Homer Livingston of his conviction that for the bank the architects should "use two materials of contrasting color (and possibly texture) to dramatize the structure." The vertical members would be white to "emphasize the dramatic vertical structure" and the spandrels darker. After Perkins and Will took up Freeman's cause, Carter Manny, Jr., of C. F. Murphy led a successful public crusade, soliciting expert opinion, against the two color scheme. The incident is revealing in that it shows how important the collaborating (but potentially competing) architectural firms took this building to be.

33. The care the bank took in addressing its public role is evident in a series of meetings, "The National Bank of Chicago Conference, June 25-28, 1964," which included planners, urban pundits, academics, and a journalist. William Brubaker, a principal at Perkins and Will, kept notes, now in the collections of the Department of Architecture at The Art Institute of Chicago and at The Chicago Historical Society. Throughout the proceedings, the bankers, who saw this as the first bank of the electronic age, and the architects stressed the building's importance for Chicago and the country. Professor Brown of MIT reminded the group that "in spending $100 million the bank had a great moral and cultural responsibility to the city and country."

"To Build a Better Mousetrap": Design in Chicago, 1920-1970

Pauline Saliga

As the British design historian Penny Sparke wrote in the April 1982 issue of *Design* magazine, "What chance has design got in Chicago, a city overwhelmed by the architectural profession?"[1] Her remark seems appropriate, given the city's long and distinguished history of architectural innovation, but Chicago's design tradition is, in fact, equally distinguished, although it has been less well documented. As early as the 1920s, Chicago was a major center of design, particularly in the fields of graphic and advertising design (see essay by Margolin). Some types of Chicago design, such as furniture development and manufacture, have always had a national impact, and the city dominated that industry from the late nineteenth century to the 1950s. Chicago-area manufacturers and distributors of products for homes and businesses, such as Sunbeam, Playskool, Bell and Howell, Motorola, Sears, Roebuck and Company, Montgomery Ward, and dozens of others, were without equal in size or influence in the United States. In the 1930s and subsequent decades, large industrial design offices, like those of Jean Reinecke, Dave Chapman, and Joseph Palma, opened in Chicago, producing everything from Sunbeam toasters to school furniture for the postwar baby boomers.

Although some aspects of Chicago design changed quite dramatically after World War II, the city's impact as a national and, later, an international force in the field of design continued to strengthen. The exception was the home furnishings industry, which weakened after the war and abandoned Chicago to move south. The postwar era heralded other changes, however, because in the 1950s leading Chicago designers such as Richard Latham and Jay Doblin began to concentrate on product planning, rather than styling and manufacturing. Later, in the 1960s, large Chicago design firms, like Unimark, and design schools, such as the Institute of Design, focused on global markets and commissions for large international clients.

As in architecture, designers often relied on historical and European precedents for inspiration,

and this reliance on past design concepts is evident throughout the history of Chicago design, from the early tubular steel furniture produced in Chicago in the 1930s, which was inspired by Bauhaus examples, to the invention of world-famous toys from the 1970s like Masterpiece, a board game based on some of the best-loved paintings in the collection of The Art Institute of Chicago. This essay considers the history of various aspects of design in Chicago and identifies trends in the field from the 1920s to the 1970s, after which time it becomes increasingly difficult to identify the particular characteristics of Chicago design.

Europe Shapes Chicago Design of the 1920s

In the 1920s the two primary influences on design in Chicago and the world at large were the modern skyscraper and the great industrial design exhibition held in Paris in 1925, L'Exposition Internationale des Arts Décoratifs et Industriels Modernes. It was there that the streamlined Art Deco style so closely associated with the look of the 1920s and 1930s was introduced. The impact of the exposition on decorative arts, architecture, graphics, and industrial design around the world, and in Chicago as well, was tremendous. According to historian Sharon Darling, after the 1925 exposition, furniture manufactured in Chicago took on a distinctly modern appearance.[2] The W. H. Howell Company, which was established in 1924, became the first Chicago company to mass-produce tubular metal furniture, beginning in 1929. The company's furniture line provided an important impetus for the production of tubular steel furniture in America, which had previously been manufactured only in Europe. Architects of the 1920s, including Abel Faidy, Hal Pereira, John Wellborn Root, Jr., Robert Switzer, and Philip B. Maher, designed furniture and interior details, often in the French moderne style, and leading interior designers such as Rue Winterbotham Carpenter, Lucy Blair Linn, and Marianne

Fig. 1 Motorola Incorporated, Advertisement for the walkie-talkie, 1943.

Willisch produced novel and luxurious modern interiors heavily influenced by modern French decorative arts.[3]

Furniture production for the nation was an important industry in Chicago in the 1920s. For example, 250 furniture factories in Chicago produced 20 percent of the furniture made in the U.S. in 1920.[4] During the early 1920s wholesalers and retailers, who were dispersed on Michigan and Wabash avenues in fourteen different buildings, instituted Chicago's biannual furniture shows, and the American Furniture Mart, designed by Henry Reader Associates with George C. Nimmons and N. Max Dunning, was opened in 1924 to consolidate the wholesalers into one convenient location. The success of the American Furniture Mart established Chicago as the undisputed center of the country's wholesale furniture trade.[5]

Modern decorative arts also found a home in Chicago at Secession Ltd., the first shop in Chicago to sell modern decorative arts exclusively. Founded in 1927 by two young Chicago architects, Robert Switzer and Harry O. Warner, the shop carried furniture, fabrics, pottery, metalwork, and glass that the architects brought back from Europe. Later, Switzer sold his own modern furniture designs in the shop, whose display cases and interior appointments displayed an inventive setback skyscraper influence.[6] In 1928 Marianne Willisch began bringing annual exhibitions of the Austrian Werkbund, that country's leading artists' guild, to Chicago with the help of interior designer Rue Winterbotham Carpenter. Willisch also formed Chicago Workshops, modeled after the Werkbund, and sold furniture and crafts designed by its members, including Paul Schweikher (fig. 2), in a shop in Diana Court in the Michigan Square Building at 540 North Michigan Avenue (see Harris, fig. 7). Willisch became a respected interior designer and advocate of modern design (fig. 4).

Development of the Chicago Design Profession in the 1930s

Although New York dominated the birth of the industrial design profession in the 1930s, Chicago also was an important design center in that decade, during which Dave Chapman, Jack Little, and Peter Muller-Munk developed extensive and important practices.[7] At that time, industrial design was closely associated with architecture since most designers had been trained in architectural programs. Yet, schools specializing in industrial design like the New Bauhaus (later

the Institute of Design) would not be established until later in the decade. Among the milestones in design in the 1930s was the establishment of related design "institutions," namely, the bureaus of design at Montgomery Ward; Sears, Roebuck and Company; and Container Corporation of America. Two factors were of key importance to the development of the design profession in Chicago in the 1930s: the Depression and the Century of Progress Exposition.

The Great Depression and the Century of Progress

The economic hardship of the Depression era forced a great many architects to shift in practice from architecture to industrial design. Some architectural firms, in fact, survived by designing furniture. The Bowman Brothers designed metal furniture that was manufactured under the trade name "Metalune"; Lloyd Morgan Yost designed Gothic and Art Deco-style radio cabinets and a wide variety of period and contemporary furniture; and Abel Faidy, a Swiss architect, designed elegant bent metal chairs (fig. 3). Bertrand Goldberg began designing experimental molded plywood furniture in 1937. Following the Arts and Crafts traditions that held sway throughout the Depression, Yost, Paul Schweikher, and others continued to design custom furniture, particularly built-ins, even after architectural commissions began to increase later in the 1940s and 1950s.

The 1933-34 Century of Progress Exposition, held along Chicago's lakefront just south of the Loop, was a provocative fantasy of modern buildings that had enormous impact on the fields of architecture and design in Chicago. The exposition celebrated the city's achievements since its founding one hundred years before with a theme based on scientific advancements. Exhibits focused on transportation, science, commerce, electricity, agriculture, and international cultures. Among the many innovations introduced at the fair were R. Buckminster Fuller's streamlined Dymaxion Car (fig. 5; pls. 11, 12). The teardrop-shaped vehicle had three wheels and proved to be too extreme for the American automotive industry, even though the American public had a great capacity to accept innovation.[8] In fact, the entire fair provided the opportunity for the average person to be immersed in innovative modern design and architecture in exhibits like George Fred Keck and William Keck's Crystal House (fig. 6), with tubular steel furniture designed by Leland T. Atwood and produced by the W. H.

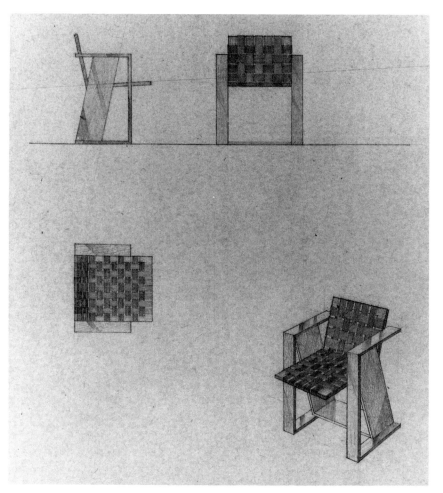

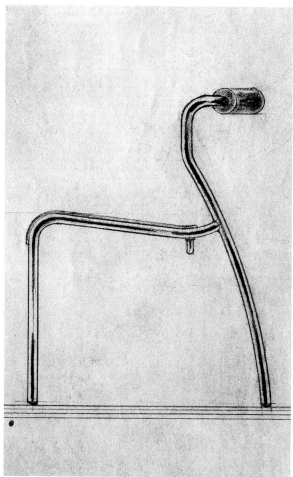

Fig. 2 Paul Schweikher,
Studies for armchair
with webbing for
Chicago Workshops,
c. 1930-35 (cat. no. 438).

Fig. 3 Abel Faidy, Side
elevation of a tubular
steel side chair, 1934
(cat. no. 313).

Fig. 4 Marianne
Willisch, Perspective
study of the proposed
living room of the
Sigmund Edelstone
apartment, c. 1965
(cat. no. 507).

Fig. 5 R. Buckminster Fuller, Dymaxion Car, Century of Progress Exposition, 1933.

Fig. 6 George Fred Keck and William Keck, Perspective rendering of the Crystal House, showing an airplane and Dymaxion Car, Century of Progress Exposition, 1934 (cat. no. 435).

Fig. 7 Leland T. Atwood, Interior design and furniture of the House of Tomorrow (George Fred Keck and William Keck), Century of Progress Exposition, 1933.

Howell Company (fig. 7). Other dramatic new buildings were proposed for the second year of the fair, such as Henry Harringer's Ziegfield Fashion Theatre (fig. 8). If the 1925 Paris exposition introduced modern design, the 1933-34 Chicago exposition popularized it. Tubular steel furnishings were used in 87 percent of the buildings at the fair, while modern furniture materials such as chrome-plated tubular steel, glass, plastic, and bent aluminum were also used extensively.[9]

Among the more fantastic pavilions created for the fair was the Radio Flyer building, designed by Alfonso Iannelli, the Italian-born artist and industrial designer who taught at the Art Institute in the 1920s (pls. 75, 77). Iannelli also designed a number of products for consumers in the 1920s and 1930s, including toasters, coffeemakers, and hair dryers for Sunbeam, and pens for Eversharp and Parker Pen Company. Iannelli's Radio Flyer pavilion featured the products of the Radio Steel and Manufacturing Company, which was founded in the teens to produce children's coaster wagons, initially made of wood and, later, steel (see pl. 76). Located on the Enchanted Island, a separate amusement area for children visiting the fair, the pavilion consisted of a small building topped by a smiling boy riding in his wagon. This symbol of youth and joy was conceived by Antonio Pasin, the founder of the Radio Steel company, and executed by Iannelli. Miniature replicas of the boy and wagon were sold by the thousands at the fair.

More important than the pavilion itself, however, was the company that designed and produced the Radio Line of wagons. The company, whose plant was on West Grand Avenue, became the world's largest exclusive manufacturer of coaster wagons and scooters by the 1950s, and today is one of the few old Chicago companies that still produces its original line of goods, providing an important link with the city's design and manufacturing history from the early years of the century.

In addition to popularizing modern architecture and design, the Century of Progress Exposition also provided unique career opportunities: through the experience and contacts they gained at the exposition, many young exhibition and display designers, architects, and industrial designers moved into industrial design careers. In the 1930s and early 1940s Chicago was also a major center of manufacturing of consumer products such as Sunbeam appliances, Ekco kitchen utensils, and Rock-ola jukeboxes. As a result, leading designers like Chapman made the conscious decision to establish their offices in Chicago, rather than New York, so they could be near the area where their products were manufactured.

In the meantime, the impact of streamlining, which had become synonymous with American industrial design of the 1930s, was appearing on other fronts. The year the fair closed, 1934, the elegant Burlington Zephyr train was produced

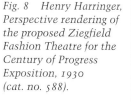

Fig. 8   Henry Harringer, Perspective rendering of the proposed Ziegfield Fashion Theatre for the Century of Progress Exposition, 1930 (cat. no. 588).

by the Chicago Burlington and Quincy Railroad (fig. 9). It had an astonishing impact when unveiled in April of that year. John Heskett noted in *Industrial Design*:

The Zephyr received over half a million visitors during a six-week-long exhibition tour. It appeared at a time when hope was beginning to revive after the hardships of the Depression, and, as with the DC3 aircraft, its radically new form was a symbol of progress renewed, and of better times to come.[10]

The Founding of In-House Corporate Design Departments

Around 1934 the giant retailer Montgomery Ward and Company hired Ann Swainson, a designer at Revere Copper and Brass, to establish a corporate design department. Although little is known about Ann Swainson, it is believed that the design department she established at Ward's was the first such in-house department established by a retailer. She transferred Dave Chapman, an Armour Institute-trained architect then at Ward's, to the new department as head of product planning. Under Swainson and Chapman, the design department grew rapidly and by 1935 eighteen designers, most of them architects, were producing custom-designed products for Ward's. Some of the designers who got important career starts under Ann Swainson were Joseph Palma, Fred Preiss, and Richard Latham, all of whom went on to become influential industrial designers in their own right.[11] Among the prod-

ucts that this new team of corporate designers produced were moderne-style products of bent plywood, sheet metal, Bakelite, and tubular steel (see fig. 10).[12]

Rival Chicago retailer Sears, Roebuck and Company also established a Bureau of Design in the 1930s that was initially headed by John Morgan.[13] One of the designers who worked in the Sears bureau was German-born architect Karl Schneider, who had studied under Walter

Fig. 9 The Burlington Zephyr of the Chicago Burlington and Quincy Railroad, shown here with a streamlined Olson Rug Company truck, 1935.

Fig. 10 Joseph Palma, Proposed design for a baby walker for Montgomery Ward, 1944.

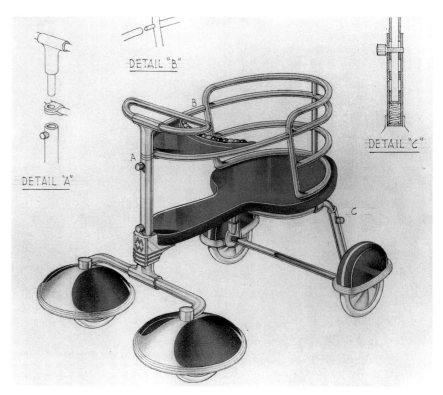

Fig. 11 Bertrand
Goldberg, Stanfab
bathroom, c. 1945-47.

Gropius and Peter Behrens in Berlin from 1912 to 1916. He established an architectural office in Hamburg in 1923, concentrating on residential work, factories, theaters, and furniture, but in 1935 he emigrated to the United States and settled in Chicago. He worked for Sears, Roebuck and Company from approximately 1938 until his death in 1945, designing a wide variety of streamlined household goods, including furniture (lawn chaise lounges), household goods (Sears food blenders), Craftsman tools, and toys. He also designed a number of International Style stores for Sears, including a "standard Sears store" in 1944. The two-story, flat-roofed building featured large ground-level display windows and prominent signage.[14] Fellow German architect Ferdinand Kramer created similar product and store designs in the 1940s for Alden's department store in Kankakee, Illinois.[15]

In 1935 Walter Paepcke established a design department at Container Corporation of America, a packaging design firm, and he named as its director Egbert Jacobson, a leader in the emerging field of advertising design. Paepcke established his design department with the intention of modernizing every aspect of the company, from its logo to its factories, and under Jacobson's direction, the company made dramatic changes in its image. Whereas relatively little information survives about the design bureaus at Montgomery Ward and Sears, the design philosophy and work of Container Corporation is well documented and has had far-reaching consequences (see Margolin, figs. 14, 20).

Design for the War and Planning for Postwar Life

Between 1942 and 1945 virtually all Chicago firms, including Container Corporation, Motorola, Chicago Roller Skate Company, and Schwinn Bicycle Company, won large contracts for the production of goods that were used in the war effort, vital products like cartons, radios, bomber parts, antennae, and rifles. These efforts were critical to the allied victory. In 1943, for example, Motorola developed the first portable FM two-way radio, called the "walkie-talkie," which, together with the hand-held "handie-talkie," developed by Motorola in 1940, revolutionized battlefield communications in Europe and the South Pacific (see fig. 1). Likewise, both Zenith and Western Electric contributed to the development of radar and sonar technology, both of which were crucial advancements during the war.[16]

Materials shortages and lack of manufacturing facilities forced Chicago manufacturers to defer the production of consumer goods until the war's end. Metal and other shortages forced some design firms, like the toy designer Marvin Glass Associates, to produce plans for paper, cardboard, and wooden toys. Since there was little opportunity to develop new products during the war years, some enterprising Chicago manufacturers hired leading New York designers to assess their products and redesign them so that their companies would be ready to capitalize on the changes in taste and trends in the postwar era. One such farsighted company, Crane plumbing supply company, commissioned Henry Dreyfuss to study its entire line of plumbing fixtures.[17] Dreyfuss set up an office in Chicago to do so, and by war's end, the company was ready to release a new line of fixtures, just in time to be installed in the thousands of homes that would be built or renovated after the war. Architects also experimented with new designs for plumbing fixtures in anticipation of a postwar building boom. Bertrand Goldberg, for instance, designed the Stanfab bathroom, which was a prefabricated unit that combined a bathtub, sink, toilet, medicine and towel cabinets, towel bar, and toilet-paper holder (fig. 11). The multi-functional unit took up a mere 7½-by-2½-foot space. By combining it with U. S. Gypsum's plasterboard walls, which were ubiquitous in postwar construction, a new bathroom could be outfitted in a single day.[18]

Fig. 12 Zenith Radio Corporation, Advertisement for the Stratosphere radio, 1935.

Similarly, Donald Deskey was contracted by the Brunswick, Balke and Collender Company to conduct research into new types of products for postwar years. He was commissioned to develop new uses for billiard tables, but instead he devised a national program for postwar recreation. From this program came the concept of family-oriented bowling centers. Proposals developed by Deskey and Edgar Lynch, Brunswick's in-house architect, "set the type-form for the hundreds of bowling centers that were built in the postwar era."[19] Crane, Brunswick, and other companies, however, were the exceptions to the rule. Most companies did not take immediate advantage of the materials and production techniques that were developed during the war, so many products were still conservative and fashioned in prewar styling. Those companies that did invest in planning during the war were wildly successful.

Furnishing the Postwar Home

In the furniture industry of the 1940s innovative production processes and materials were combined with conservative designs. When the war ended in 1945 Chicago manufacturers faced a great demand for furniture, as well as shifts in population (to the suburbs) and new materials (Formica, vinyl plastic, foam rubber, chrome-plated steel). As a result of the new economic factors that included the higher cost of labor, energy, transportation/trucking costs, and higher taxes in Chicago in the decade following the war, many old Chicago furniture firms went out of business, and by 1956 North Carolina had become the premiere state for the production of home furnishings. Some Chicago furniture manufacturers survived because they planned unusual products, decentralized their facilities, and/or simplified designs in order to utilize assembly-line techniques. In addition, Chicago furniture manufacturers found it necessary to focus on only two types of market after the war—namely, mass-produced and custom-designed furniture.[20]

Among the most outstanding successes in postwar, mass-produced furniture were bent steel dinette sets like those designed by Wolfgang Hoffman before the war. These sets became W. H. Howell Company's major product.[21] Douglas Furniture also capitalized on the postwar, mass-produced furniture market by modifying the traditional Duncan Phyfe style of dinette set and giving it a Formica top and curved chrome-plated legs.[22] The dinettes were a success because they combined the form of a "traditional" dining room set and all its familial associations with new postwar materials. By retaining the values of family and home while using popular new materials, the dinettes presented an optimistic image that the American public consumed by the thousands. Other highly successful furnishings that were mass-produced in Chicago included the Stratalounger (1952), the Barcalounger (1954), and Zenith and Motorola radios and television sets (see figs. 12, 13). These new furniture types were enormously successful because they provided comfort and preserved the image of the home as a refuge, where relaxation and recreation were valued. In 1959 Motorola produced its first all-transistor radio, a miniaturized product that provided consumers with portable entertainment (fig. 14).

After World War II local manufacturers developed not only metal furniture, but also plastic products in earnest, creating everything from plastic and plywood refrigerators to plastic sewing machines.[23] Radios also became an indispensable feature of the American home. The war had made radios a necessity, and by 1947 they were in 93 percent of American homes. Unlike the radios of the thirties, which were encased in elaborate wooden cabinets like one designed by L. Morgan Yost, postwar radios, such as the Hallicrafters radio designed by Richard Latham for Loewy Associates, were intended to look like military equipment. Likewise, other industrial designers adopted a military look for their products. Renor Faidy (son of architect Abel Faidy)

New from Motorola
ALL-TRANSISTOR

Shirt-pocket radio

with powerful built-in speaker

Slips into your pocket . . . plays with the sound of a set twice its size

ONLY $29⁹⁵

More to enjoy **MOTOROLA**

Fig. 13 Zenith Radio Corporation, Advertisement for the Viceroy television set, 1952.

Fig. 14 Motorola Incorporated, Advertisement for Motorola's first all-transistor radio, 1959.

Fig. 15 Renor Faidy, Proposed design for a General Electric range, 1954.

designed the dials and backsplash of a 1954 General Electric range to resemble the controls in the cockpit of an airplane (fig. 15). Faidy worked for noted designer Arthur Bec Var in the Appearance Design Department at General Electric from 1946 to 1964.

Although W. H. Howell Company, Douglas Furniture, and other manufacturers were selling mass-produced modern glass-and-steel and Formica furniture to the general population after the war, a market still existed for high-style modern furniture. Baldwin Kingrey was founded in the 1940s to sell American and Scandinavian modern furniture designed by leading architects. The company imported Alvar Aalto's furnishings and sold Eero Saarinen, Ray and Charles Eames, Harry Bertoia, and other high-style modern furnishings manufactured by Knoll and Herman Miller. Harry Weese also custom-designed furniture for the company, and local craftsmen constructed it. Baldwin Kingrey was the only such furniture outlet in Chicago, and it

played a key role in popularizing fine modern design nationwide, often holding exhibitions of the work of Institute of Design faculty members. Like Marianne Willisch's Werkbund shop, Baldwin Kingrey was located in the venerable, but now demolished, Art Deco Michigan Square Building, a mecca for designers in Chicago.

"Good Design" Exhibitions

In the 1940s and into the 1950s virtually every museum, gallery, and university in the U.S. held an exhibition of art in everyday living to promote modern design. Notable and influential examples included The Museum of Modern Art's "Useful Objects" exhibitions, the Walker Art Center's Everyday Art Gallery, and an exhibition of seven modern rooms designed by the country's leading designers held in 1949 at the Detroit Institute of Arts. All the exhibitions showed the renaissance of American design sensibility. Chicago also played a role in promoting modern design through exhibitions. The Art Institute of Chicago organized a pioneering exhibition of Italian crafts entitled "Italy at Work: Her Renaissance in Design Today" in 1950 (fig. 16). As Walter Dorwin Teague wrote in the exhibition catalogue, the aim was to present the "upsurge of Italian vitality that [had] stored itself up during the long, grey Fascist interim."[24] The exhibition was organized by Meyric Rogers, curator of industrial and decorative arts at the Art Institute; Charles Nagel, director of the Brooklyn Museum; designer Walter Dorwin

Teague; and Ramy Alexander, vice-president of the Italian artists' guild, Comagna Nazionale Artiginia. The organizers toured Italy for three months to find the best that postwar Italy had to offer in crafts, furniture, lighting fixtures, and mass-produced products like office machines by Olivetti and Lambretta motor scooters. Even before the exhibition was organized, eleven U.S. museums had committed to host the exhibition on its three-year tour.

The Art Institute of Chicago made other attempts to educate the public about good design. In 1954 the museum announced plans to form a new department of design and industry, which would organize a series of special design-related exhibitions, host conferences aimed at manufacturers, designers, and consumers, and publish catalogues and books, "which would spread the new concepts of design through the libraries of the entire world."[25] William Friedman, who pioneered a similar program at the Walker Arts Center in Minneapolis, was to head the department, and designer Russell Wright delivered an impassioned paper about why The Art Institute of Chicago needed such a department. The three-year program was never implemented, presumably because the $130,000 needed to fund it were not raised.

In 1950 Chicago was also the site of a series of other important "Good Design" exhibitions, which were held in the Merchandise Mart. The Merchandise Mart asked Edgar Kaufmann, Jr., curator of industrial design at The Museum of Modern Art (MoMA), to create a series of exhibi-

Fig. 16 "Italy at Work: Her Renaissance in Design Today," The Art Institute of Chicago, 1950.

Fig. 17 Palma Knapp Design, Sunbeam electric drill, 1962.

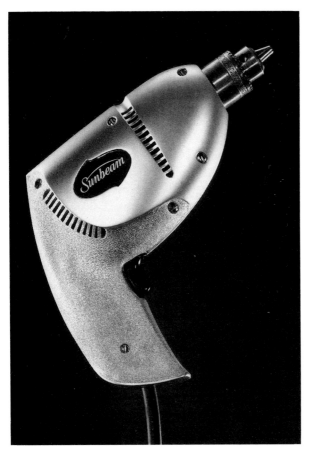

Prosperity and Growth in the 1950s

In the postwar period, "industrial design expanded rapidly into a glamorous professional career for those who saw in it opportunities for the future in creating furnishings and products for the home."[27] In order to educate all the returning veterans and prospective new designers, the program at the Institute of Design took on new importance. As a result, numerous design firms began and established firms prospered, including Morton Goldsholl, Barnes and Reinecke, and Palma Knapp (see fig. 17). The trend in design was clearly toward product planning, not just the styling of a product. Some Chicago designers, most notably Richard Latham and Jay Doblin, were leaders in this area. Latham, who became a product planner for General Electric, characterized designers of the 1950s who crossed the line from design to product planning, a functionalist approach in which products are overhauled and improved through design. In an article in a 1957 issue of Industrial Design magazine Latham summed it up succinctly: "Most designers today concentrate on styling, merchandising, and selling. These are the tail of the dog; the body is planning."[28] Product planning at General Electric led to the invention of portable appliances like electric skillets and can openers.[29]

Other leading designers in Chicago took the same approach to developing products. Dave Chapman's industrial design firm established a separate entity named Design Research, Inc., "in order to analyze factors affecting buyer motivation for the benefit of companies facing the need to invest in new or expanded plant facilities."[30] Like Latham, Chapman became one of this new breed of designer, one who planned products rather than merely designed them. As part of the product planning program, by the 1950s package design was becoming a major concern in the marketing of American products. Independent package design firms were established in New York, San Francisco, and Chicago, where Sid Dickens, Container Corporation of America, and other companies developed package designs for a long list of clients. In the postwar era, the package itself, along with the image projected by the name of the product, became an important marketing tool, designed to attract the purchaser's attention long enough to convey a message, sometimes a subliminal one. Product packages and names projected images of royalty, adventure, or romance. During this period, packages were also given new shapes to convey certain messages and promote the products contained within.[31]

tions that would bring good design to the attention of the public and to present the best examples of modern design for the home. The objects were selected from among the products available at the Mart and stressed eye appeal, function, construction, and price.[26] Two exhibitions were juried each year from 1950 to 1955, by Edgar Kaufmann, a designer, and a retailer. Over the years, the jury included such noted advocates of modern design as Meyric Rogers, designer Serge Chermayeff, William Friedman, director of the Walker Art Center, architect Harry Weese, and designers Russell Wright and Edward Wormley. The Good Design exhibitions at the Mart, which included anywhere from 250 to 500 sleek and functional objects, were designed by an equally distinguished list of architects, including Ray and Charles Eames, who designed the first exhibition in 1950, Danish architect and designer Finn Juhl, architect Paul Rudolph, Alexander Girard, and the Chicago architectural team of Daniel Brenner and A. James Speyer. The exhibition program came into existence because manufacturers and consumers needed information about the merits of modern design. The shows were initially very popular and were displayed at the Mart and MoMA, where they helped popularize modern design by showing the functional beauty of the products in the postwar home.

Institutions and Government in the 1950s

As institutions and governments reshaped themselves after the war, they too had new design needs. Changes in the postwar classroom, for example, were dramatic. From the late nineteenth century to the late 1930s, school furnishings consisted of heavy cast-iron and wood desks and seats that were bolted to the floor to prevent any chance of distraction in the rigid environment. In 1938, however, the revolutionary Crow Island School opened in suburban Winnetka. The building, designed by Eliel Saarinen and Lawrence Perkins, was planned to accommodate the progressive educational theories of Carleton Washburne, the superintendent of Winnetka's schools. His plan called for flexible classroom spaces and modular, movable furnishings (fig. 18). The furniture, molded plywood on birch legs, was produced by the Illinois Crafts Project, under the auspices of the Works Progress Administration. When the need for new schools to house the children born after the war became apparent in the 1950s, the open classroom of Crow Island School was the model that inspired school planners. The era of the flexible classroom had arrived.

The market for new school furnishings was so great that many companies, such as the Brunswick, Balke and Collender Company, that previously had not manufactured school furniture now hired designers to develop prototypes for innovative furniture. In 1952 the Brunswick company, which formerly developed sports equipment and bowling centers, hired Dave Chapman's firm to design a new line of school furnishings.[32] Based on the Crow Island philosophy, all the desks, chairs, tables, and bookcases (eleven basic units in all) were modular and interchangeable. The desks and chairs had tapered steel legs, with laminated wood and plastic surfaces. The beauty of the furnishings was in their flexibility—they could be grouped or separated to suit the activity in the classroom. In an effort to publicize its line of furniture, the Brunswick company in 1959 engineered a dramatic weekend makeover for a first-grade classroom in St. Gabriel School, a parochial school on Chicago's South Side that is best known for its adjoining Richardsonian Romanesque church designed by Burnham and Root (1887). In the classroom makeover, which was described in *Life* magazine in October 1959, the children were introduced to their Victorian-style classroom on the first day of school (fig. 19). Then, over the weekend, workers transformed the space by removing the stationary cast-iron desks, combining two classrooms, installing new lighting fixtures and drapes, and arranging the Brunswick flexible furnishings (which included drumlike bookcases, round tables, and modular, child-sized desks and chairs) into a series of arcs (fig. 20).[33] The flexible

Fig. 18   Perkins and Will with Eliel Saarinen, Crow Island School, Winnetka, Illinois, 1938.

furnishings and, by extension, the flexible approach to education, made attending school more enjoyable for the children, and the widespread use of flexible furnishings in classrooms across the country would prove to be a great leap forward in education.

The 1960s: Chicago Takes a Global Focus

In the 1950s and 1960s a trend toward international exchanges of design ideas began to develop, and it has evolved into the globalization of

design that continues into the 1990s. As early as 1959 Chapman and Doblin went to Japan to advise leaders in Japanese industry on postwar design, production, and marketing of new products. Along with other leading designers, including Raymond Loewy, Russell Wright, George Nelson, and Jean Reinecke, they essentially set up the systems that have led to Japan's enormous success today.[34] Herbert Zeller was the director of industrial design at Motorola and later for Matsushita of Japan. He claimed that America brought design to Japan, and that product design eventually enabled the Japanese to dominate the consumer electronics industry.[35] Also in the late 1950s Dave Chapman's Design Research group studied the crafts of Pakistan and Afghanistan and the Caribbean to set up institutes to train the company's craftsmen to produce high-quality products for export. These early efforts to make design an international endeavor multiplied a thousandfold in the decades that followed.[36]

Perhaps the one Chicago design firm of the 1960s that most clearly typifies the trend toward globalization is Unimark. Founded in 1964 by Jay Doblin, Massimo Vignelli, and others, Unimark soon attracted the talents of other major designers, including Ralph Eckerstrom. Unimark quickly grew to be one of the largest design firms in the world, with branch offices in Chicago, New York, Aspen, Milan, Melbourne, and many other locations. At its largest, the firm

Figs. 19, 20 St. Gabriel School, before and after the remodeling of a typical classroom, 1959; from Life *(Oct. 1959), p. 64.*

Fig. 21   Daniel Brenner,
National Design Center,
Marina City, 1965.

employed more than 400 designers in a variety of fields including graphic, interior, package, and product design. Clients included Alcoa, Gillette, Fieldcrest Mills, P. Lorillard, Standard Oil of Indiana, Olivetti, Tupperware of Australia, Rank Xerox, American Airlines, General Electric, and J. C. Penney.[37] Among Unimark's best-known projects are the signage for the Washington Metro (designed by Harry Weese and Associates, 1977) and a user-friendly, color-coded New York subway map of 1972. According to Ralph Eckerstrom, Unimark strove "to synthesize fine design and sophisticated marketing procedures for the benefit of the international business community."[38] When Unimark closed in the early 1970s, more than forty-eight design firms were spawned from the giant, thereby continuing its considerable influence around the world.

National Design Center

At the same time that Chicago's influence was expanding globally, firms outside the city increasingly took an interest in the markets that had been developed there. One such venture was the National Design Center, a 40,000-square-foot, consumer-oriented products and furniture showroom that opened in Marina City in 1965 (fig. 21). Founded by New York furniture retailer Norman Ginsberg and designed by Chicago architect Daniel Brenner, the National Design Center in Chicago was actually a branch of a showroom that Ginsberg had begun in New York in 1958. Like the New York showroom, the Na-

tional Design Center in Chicago was open to the general public, as well as to design professionals, but no selling was conducted there. Instead, it was conceived of as an information clearinghouse for design professionals and the public, with an information center that provided details about the exhibitors' products. The public also could obtain impartial information on how to engage the services of an interior designer. Both the Design Center and the information center within it were modeled after two successful European design showrooms: the Design Center in London and Den Permanente in Copenhagen. Like its New York and European predecessors, the Design Center in Chicago also had an auditorium for lectures, a design bookstore, and areas for changing exhibitions like the International Design Awards exhibition, which featured the best in contemporary home furnishings from around the world. These exhibitions were a continuation of the Good Design exhibitions that were staged in museums, the Merchandise Mart, and elsewhere in the 1950s.[39]

When the National Design Centers in New York and Chicago were founded, Norman Ginsberg had high hopes of raising the standards of the home furnishings industry, which he felt remained at the same low level as after World War II, when furniture design was overshadowed by the need to provide housing for thousands of new families. Given such an idealistic philosophy, it is unfortunate that this European-style design center closed just a few years after it opened. The primary reason is that rather than

use the center, architects and interior designers preferred to rely on the larger and more established Merchandise Mart and on Sweets Catalog, the multi-volume reference book of products and hardware, while the public seemed largely unaware of the services the Design Center offered.

Even after competition had reduced Chicago's role as a major furniture manufacturer, the city assumed a new position as the center of the contract furnishings industry, with the Merchandise Mart at its center. Instead of providing furniture primarily for homeowners, the Chicago furniture markets focused on furnishing the millions of square feet of new office space built between the 1950s and 1990s, as well as all the new schools, hospitals, and airports. Since the 1960s, the Merchandise Mart has had a tight hold on the furniture market in Chicago, and in 1969 the Mart began its annual contract furnishings convention, called NEOCON, to market furnishings to the architects and designers who specify contract furnishings internationally. The convention was founded to feed the commercial furniture market and to help Chicago maintain its leadership in the industry. Showrooms at the Mart have been able to gain attention for their product lines by hiring leading designers and architects to develop original images for their spaces. Such innovative interiors included the postmodern Hauserman showroom designed by Japanese architect Arata Isozaki in 1982 and the Dupont Resource Center executed by Eva Maddox Associates in 1991. The American Furniture Mart was unable to compete, and it closed in 1979 as other major furniture showrooms opened in Dallas, Los Angeles, and High Point, North Carolina, further dividing the furniture market and pulling interest away from Chicago.

The Toy Industry in Chicago

In *Industrial Design* John Heskett described the toy industry in the following terms:

> The history of toys is a microcosm of the evolution of industrial design, with a continuous flow of innovations, new technology, and materials constantly being introduced, yet never entirely replacing old forms, so that traditional craft-forms of wooden toys from Eastern Europe and Asia can still be found alongside the most sophisticated electronic playthings.[40]

Generally speaking, the manufacture of toys gradually had evolved from a cottage industry to a factory-based industry in Europe by 1900. In America, toys were mass-produced in tin, cast iron, and wood in the 1880s and the following decades. By the early twentieth century, many countries had well-established toy industries, with products ranging from miniatures of objects in the adult world (baby dolls, stoves, trains, houses) to building blocks and games that allowed a child to learn and experiment while playing.

The 1960s and 1970s were the high point of toy design in Chicago, primarily due to one inventive designer, Marvin Glass. Although the firm produced toy designs during the war, Marvin Glass applied for its first toy patent in 1950 for a children's utensil set. The work of the firm expanded tremendously in the postwar years to provide toys for the enormous baby-boom generation, and the company created board games, dolls, trains, and other toys. Many of its designs were innovative novelties such as over-sized sunglasses (Super Specs, 1960), plastic robots (Mr. Machine, 1960), and battery-operated board games (Operation, 1965). As a testament to the success of the company's creations, many

Fig. 22   Marvin Glass and Associates, Advertisement for Mouse Trap board game, 1963.

Here's the comic classic of the century. Is it an insane inventor's zany nightmare? No it's a hilarious three dimensional game. The object of the game is to trap the other fellow's mouse. First, players, directed by the die, take turns constructing the rickety mechanical wonder, piece by unlikely piece. When completed it is a most curious sight and the trap is set. When a player's mouse lands on the right square, a crank of a handle starts a clanking wheezing chain reaction of moving parts, rolling ball, shuttling levers, swinging "boards," until ZING! Mousetrap!

games designed by the Marvin Glass firm in the 1960s and 1970s are still in production today, including Lite-Brite (1967), a game in which transparent, colored pegs are pushed into a pegboard that is lit from behind. The pegs light up like miniature light bulbs so that a child can "create pictures with light." Another successful board game that is still manufactured is Masterpiece (1971), a variation on Monopoly, but instead of buying real estate, the players participate in an international art auction. The postcard-size paintings in the game are well-known works by Rembrandt, Picasso, Grant Wood, and others from the collection of The Art Institute of Chicago. Probably one of the most well-loved Marvin Glass board games is Mouse Trap (1963), which is based on a Rube Goldberg cartoon titled "To Build a Better Mousetrap," in which an unlikely jury-rigged contraption connects a whole series of unlikely events ending with the capture of a mouse (fig. 22). These and other inventive toys gave Marvin Glass Associates an international reputation that continued long after the founder's death in 1974. When the firm broke up in the early 1980s as a consequence of royalty disputes, it spawned a whole industry of toy designers in Chicago, including Meyer Glass Design, IDEA, and B & D Design Associates, to name only three. As a result, Chicago remains an international leader in toy design, and designs by Chicago firms are licensed in Japan, Germany, and elsewhere.

Conclusion

As the Chicago design world began expanding into global markets in the 1960s, it has become increasingly difficult to define what constitutes Chicago design. As Patrick Whitney, director of the Institute of Design, noted in a conversation in 1990, the definitions of design associated with Chicago, or with any particular place for that matter, are now blurred and much harder to identify. Product development is no longer localized, as it is often done by teams, not by individuals, and sometimes the members of the team are from different countries. Also, products are often no longer built in one place. In many cases elements are fabricated in different cities (or countries) and then assembled somewhere else. But all this is not to say that many talented designers do not still have offices in the Chicago area. On the contrary, a glance through the local directory reveals dozens of firms, some of which—KDA Industrial Design Consultants, Goldsmith, Yamasaki, Specht, and Henry P. Glass

Associates, for example—can trace their roots to firms begun in the 1930s and 1940s.

Indeed, it seems we have entered a new age with regard to design and its history. Design offices tend to be either small and very focused or large and capital intensive, because the needs of global clients can better be served that way. Large offices with branches around the world seem to thrive today in advertising and many other design fields. At the same time, the recent deaths of some of the most important figures of the postwar years—namely, Jay Doblin in 1990 and Richard Latham in 1991—have opened the way for the emergence of new leaders. Yet their legacy lives on in first-rate educational institutions, specifically the Institute of Design, which still bears the influence of Doblin's philosophy of design education, and in the products of their notable clients, companies like Land's End, Bang and Olufsen, and Rosenthal China, which still carry the mark of Latham's revolutionary product-planning philosophy. Their legacy also lives on in the new trend in Chicago toward documenting design history. In the early 1980s, for example, the University of Illinois at Chicago began offering courses in design history, established a design archive in the university library, and began publishing the scholarly journal *Design Issues*. In 1988 The Art Institute of Chicago received a grant from the Design Arts Division of the National Endowment for the Arts to study the design collections of other museums and to hold two day-long symposia with international design historians to develop a plan for integrating the history of design into its programs and exhibitions.

For Chicago institutions the time has come to consider seriously the history of twentieth-century industrial, graphic, and product design, as Britain, Holland, and the Scandinavian countries are already doing. There are many good European models to follow. Early in 1992, in fact, the Dutch government established the European Design Centre, a new industrial design archive in Eindhoven, and The Design Museum at Butler's Wharf in London has been posing intriguing questions about design since it opened in 1989.

Increasingly, design is a concern of business people, environmentalists, cultural historians, and others who believe that it must be responsive to the needs of the disabled and other special populations. Designers themselves have recognized that they must, by necessity, address those questions and issues that go beyond styling to enter the realm of design with a conscience. The

Fig. 23 KDA Industrial Design Consultants, Inc., Qwork Bench, 1991; this product is made entirely of recyled and recyclable materials.

ability to develop ecologically sound packaging, to employ manufacturing techniques that reduce the emission of chemical pollutants, and increase the use of recycled and recyclable materials are but a few of the challenges that today's designers face (see fig. 23). Just as they welcomed the utopian ideals that were attached to architecture of the 1920s, more people today are looking to design as a means of relieving some of the problems of society. Jay Doblin succinctly

characterized the trend in a 1982 interview with Penny Sparke:

The heroes of styling and marketing in the old sense are a thing of the past. What's coming through is more scientific and corporate design.... American designers have yet to learn that it's no longer about aesthetics and styling. When they do (as they have in Silicon Valley), and begin to work with abstract, scientific disciplines, like psychology and anthropology, to build up a solid base of information beneath product planning, something new will emerge.[41]

NOTES

1. Penny Sparke, "Chicago: On the Incline Again," *Design* 400 (April 1982), p. 7.
2. Sharon Darling, *Chicago Furniture: Art, Craft, and Industry, 1833-1983* (New York and London, 1983), p. 270.
3. Ibid., p. 272.
4. Ibid., p. 292.
5. Ibid., p. 294.
6. Ibid., p. 274.
7. John Heskett, *Industrial Design* (New York and Toronto, 1980), p. 109.
8. Ibid., p. 122.
9. Darling (note 2), p. 314.
10. Heskett (note 7), p. 130.
11. Arthur J. Pulos, *The American Design Adventure, 1940-1975* (Cambridge and London, 1988), p. 23.
12. "The Origin and History of KDA Industrial Design Consultants," 1987.
13. Ibid.
14. Robert Koch and Eberhard Pook, eds., *Karl Schneider: Leben und Werk (1892-1945)* (Hamburg, 1992), pp. 207-24.
15. Claude Lichtenstein, ed., *Ferdinand Kramer: Der Charme des Systematischen* (Giessen, 1991), pp. 194-233.
16. Perry R. Duis and Scott La France, *We've Got a Job to Do: Chicagoans and World War II* (Chicago, 1992), p. 67ff.
17. Pulos (note 11), p. 46.
18. "Gadgets: Two Years of Peace Produce Some Strange and Wonderful Inventions," *Life* (Dec. 15, 1947), p. 84.
19. Pulos (note 11), p. 47.
20. Darling (note 2), p. 321.
21. Ibid., p. 316.
22. Ibid., pp. 324-25.
23. Pulos (note 11), p. 45.
24. The Art Institute of Chicago, *Italy at Work: Her Renaissance in Design Today* (Chicago, 1950).
25. "Daniel Catton Rich and Russel Wright Discuss Formation of Institute's New Department," news release from The Art Institute of Chicago, June 17, 1954.
26. Pulos (note 11), p. 110.
27. Ibid., p. 59.
28. Ibid., p. 270.
29. Ibid., p. 143.
30. Ibid., p. 270.
31. Ibid., p. 283.
32. Ibid., pp. 328-29.
33. "Weekend Face-lifting for Classroom," *Life* (Oct. 19, 1959) p. 64.
34. Pulos (note 11), pp. 192-93.
35. Ibid., p. 302.
36. Ibid., p. 237ff.
37. J. Roger Guilfoyle, "Unimark International," *Industrial Design* 13, no. 6 (June 13, 1966), p. 87.
38. Ibid.
39. See "The Design Center for Interiors," *Interiors* 117, no. 8 (March 1958), p. 106ff; "National Design Center Expands to Chicago," *Interiors* 122, no. 3 (Oct. 1962), p. 58; and Ghita Cary, "A Center with Designs on the City: New Showcase for Furnishings," *Chicago Sun-Times Family Magazine* (April 25, 1963).
40. Heskett (note 7), p. 157.
41. Sparke (note 1), p. 7.

TANNHÄUSER

BY Richard Wagner (directed BY Peter Sellars)

LYRIC OPERA OF CHICAGO 88 89

This poster made possible by a deeply appreciated gift from 10 & 30 South Wacker, IMD Realty Corporation and Metropolitan Structures. Impressions. Bradley Printing Company. Color Separations: Midwest Litho Arts. Consolidated Reflections. Cover, donated by Butler Paper, Chicago Imagery: THIRST

Graphic Design in Chicago

Victor Margolin

Fig. 1   Rick Valicenti
and Michael
Giammanco, Poster
for Richard Wagner's
Tannhäuser, Lyric Opera
of Chicago, 1988.

In the emerging history of graphic design, Chicago is yet to receive due recognition, even though it has a rich and complex legacy of design practice.[1] There is, in fact, no better city in the United States within which to chart the transformations that have occurred in graphic design during the twentieth century. Although no single set of circumstances can account for the development of design in Chicago, there are, nonetheless, a number of reasons why certain forms of practice flourished in the city. Central to the initial development of the commercial and typographic arts were two factors. One was the communication needs of a large industrial metropolis as represented by the newspapers, magazines, advertising, railroad timetables, and business promotions that had to appear regularly. The other, perhaps of more significance, was the extraordinary growth of the printing industry, which spawned a number of concomitant enterprises that had national import, such as publishing and advertising. During the period from about 1900 to the end of the 1920s, the Chicago printing industry made its greatest strides, growing from an annual volume of approximately $50 million to sales of nearly $333 million a year. By the early 1930s, Chicago ranked first in the nation in the number of people employed in printing and publishing. It had the country's largest printing plants, as well as sizeable linotype businesses, well-equipped binderies, large composing rooms, and immense facilities for map printing. Besides the bigger printing firms such as R. R. Donnelley, W. F. Hall, and the Cuneo Press, there was also an enormous number of smaller printing establishments. In addition, the city was a leader in the manufacture of printing presses and related machinery. Although Chicago could not rival New York in its number of trade-book publishers or mass circulation magazines, it was, nonetheless, a major center for the publication of trade journals, of which there were more than two hundred in 1932.[2]

Volume was also matched by standards of quality that had been set before the turn of the century. In the 1890s there was a community of Chicagoans who took great interest in the finely printed books produced by the Arts and Crafts movement in England. Stone and Kimball, one of the few American publishers influenced by the English private presses and the European aesthetic movement in general, moved from Boston to Chicago in 1893, and a year later launched *The Chap-Book*, a leading "little magazine" of the 1890s. To promote the magazine, the firm sponsored a memorable series of lithographic posters by Will Bradley, Frank Hazenplug, J. C. Leyendecker, and other artists.[3] While many of these poster designers were illustrators, Bradley, who was trained in a jobbing print shop in Michigan, was distinct in the breadth of his talents; he was able to design typography and advertising layouts, as well as produce illustrations.

The first of the Chicago private presses, which was to inspire others in later years, was the Village Press, started by Frederic and Bertha Goudy in 1903.[4] At the time Fred Goudy was also doing lettering for advertising layouts and had been invited in 1899 to teach lettering design at the newly founded Frank Holme School of Illustration, where W. A. Dwiggins and Oswald Cooper had come to study. Dwiggins, who became one of America's outstanding typographers and book designers, followed Goudy to Massachusetts in 1904, but Cooper remained to establish one of Chicago's leading commercial art studios, which specialized in lettering and layouts. Cooper epitomized a type of commercial artist known as a "lettering man," who was usually hired to provide lettering for advertisements and other printed matter. Clients also found in him someone extremely knowledgeable about advertising and commercial printing, and he wrote copy as well. When designing ads, he would sometimes use available display types, but in the years before World War I, the supply of these types was limited, so he created much display lettering himself. Early on he had formed a partnership with Fred Bertsch. Known as Bertsch and Cooper, the firm was equipped to see a job through from artwork and layout to typesetting.[5]

Cooper was also in demand as a type designer, and he created a number of faces for type foundries in Chicago and elsewhere. His best-known face is Cooper Black, a fulsome round-serif face from the early 1920s that was widely used in advertising (fig. 3). Cooper Black exemplified the kind of bold lettering that was dominant in Chicago before and after World War I.[6] Many lettering men worked in that style, which Cooper invented.

The Frank Holme School of Illustration was not the only place to study commercial art in Chicago. The School of the Art Institute of Chicago also offered courses in illustration, as well as in poster and advertising design, in the years prior to World War I.[7] According to the school's catalogue for 1919-20, the latter course provided training in "taste and effectiveness in mass and color arrangements," and taught students "how 'selling' ideas are thought out." The school also had an evening course in lettering, taught by Ernst Detterer, which provided "a comprehensive study of 'built up' letters and of classic forms and the principles underlying their design and variations."[8] Other illustrators in Chicago may have been enrolled at the Chicago Academy of Fine Arts, which was founded in 1922. In addition to courses in illustration, the Academy also offered classes in packaging, advertising design, and cartooning in its curriculum.[9] One large project of the 1920s that employed a number of illustrators was the poster series commissioned by the Chicago Rapid Transit Lines and the Chicago North Shore and Milwaukee Railroad. Similar in concept to the posters done

September 1977   Field Museum of Natural History Bulletin

HOPI INDIAN BRIDE

NAVIGATO

FIELD MUSEUM
BY CHICAGO RAPID TRANSIT

Fig. 2 *Rocco Navigato, Poster for* The Field Museum of Natural History, *1920s; from* Field Museum of Natural History Bulletin *48, no. 8 (Sept. 1977), cover.*

ABCDEFGHIJKL
MNOPQRSTUVWXYZ&
abcdefghijklmnopq
rstuvwxyz
1234567890$
ˆ˘¯—·.,'':;!?[]

Fig. 3 *Oswald Cooper, Cooper Black typeface, early 1920s; from Society of Typographic Arts,* The Book of Oz Cooper *(Chicago, 1949), p. 131.*

for the London Underground, which had begun to appear much earlier, the posters for the Rapid Transit, Elevated, and North Shore Lines were designed in several different styles, ranging from the German advertising style of Lucien Bernhard and Ludwig Hohlwein to one that had strong similarities to architectural drafting. Among the illustrators who worked on this series were Rocco Navigato (fig. 2), Willard Frederic Elmes, and Oscar Hanson.

In 1921 the School of the Art Institute brought together its separate courses in lettering, illustration, and advertising design under a new Department of Printing Arts, whose aim was to "prepare designers for work in the field of printing, decorative illustration, and commercial art."[10] Headed by Ernst Detterer, who had studied at the Pennsylvania Museum School of Industrial Art, the new department offered a two-year curriculum beyond the foundation year and put more emphasis on typography and lettering than other commercial art programs had done. Courses included instruction in various printing techniques, typographic layout, and designs for advertisements, posters, and packages (see fig. 4). Detterer, who was inspired by William Morris's Kelmscott Press, as well as by the British calligrapher and type designer, Edward Johnston, began introducing courses in hand lettering and illumination. A description of the lettering course in the 1924-25 catalogue referred to both its commercial and scholarly possibilities.[11] Detterer paid special attention to the application of lettering to typography, and he gave students a strong introduction to the his-

Fig. 4   The School of the Art Institute of Chicago, Department of Printing Arts, Student poster, 1929-30; from Catalogue of the Art School of The Art Institute of Chicago, 1929-1930 (Chicago, 1929), p. 45.

ABCDEFGHIJ
abcdefghijklmn
KLMNOPQRS
&opqrstuvwxyz
TUVWXYZ

Fig. 5   R. Hunter Middleton, Tempo typeface, 1965.

tory of calligraphy and type design. By the 1925-26 school year, students were also required to take Helen Gardner's course in the history of art. In 1928 the department was expanded to become the Division of Printing Arts and Advertising Design, which existed until 1932, when it was folded into a more ambitious School of Industrial Art. Detterer left the School of the Art Institute in the early 1930s to become curator of the Rare Book Room and the John M. Wing Foundation of the History of Printing at the Newberry Library. The Wing Foundation was then and continues to be one of the few special collections devoted to typographic history and the graphic arts and has been an invaluable resource for many graphic designers in Chicago and elsewhere.

One of Detterer's outstanding pupils in the Department of Printing Arts was Robert Hunter Middleton, who best represents the development of graphic designers in Chicago from the mid-1920s through the 1950s because of his energetic involvement in all the city's design organizations during those years.[12] While a student, Middleton had assisted Detterer with his adaptation of Nicolas Jenson's typeface, considered to be one of the original Roman faces, for use by the Ludlow Typograph Company. It was through Detterer's recommendation that Middleton went to work for Ludlow when he left the Art Institute in 1923. In 1933 he became the company's director of typeface design and he remained with Ludlow until his retirement in 1971.[13] During his long tenure at Ludlow, Middleton designed almost one hundred typefaces, spanning a full range of traditional and modern styles; some examples include Record Gothic, Stellar, Radiant, Delphian, and Tempo (fig. 5). Like Goudy before him, Middleton worked at the intersection of fine and commercial printing. Through Detterer he maintained close contact with the Newberry Library, and as a founder and active member of the Society of Typographic Arts, he infused the society with a concern for fine printing and an interest in typographic history. In 1945 he established his own printing and publishing venture, the Cherryburn Press. Before his retirement from Ludlow, he worked at the press in his spare time, managing to print some exemplary volumes, and then continued to issue Cherryburn publications after his retirement. Among Middleton's most notable projects were the two portfolios of prints from original blocks cut by Thomas Bewick, the British wood engraver.[14]

Although Middleton and Cooper were both major figures in Chicago, there is a significant difference between them. Cooper had a wide knowledge of lettering styles and printing, but he did not have the devotion to the traditional printing arts that Middleton possessed. Middleton was essentially a typographer, rather than a letterer, and he brought an extensive knowledge of printing history to his work. In his various activities with the Society of Typographic Arts and other organizations, he promoted the relation of typographic tradition to contemporary design. Both Cooper and Middleton, however, had to come to terms with the demand for modern typefaces and each responded in kind. But Cooper, perhaps because he was a more retiring man, never established relations with the wide range of colleagues and organizations that Middleton did. Through his work with Ludlow, Middleton traveled widely and corresponded with many typographers, printers, and printing scholars in the United States and abroad. He was perhaps the most cosmopolitan of the Chicago designers for many years and was instrumental in bringing a large number of speakers to the city for lectures at the Society of Typographic Arts and elsewhere.

The Society of Typographic Arts (STA) was established in 1927 by a diverse group of lettering men, typographic designers, commercial artists, and printers. Some of the founding members had belonged to the American Institute of Graphic Arts (AIGA) but wished to break away and form their own organization because they felt the AIGA was biased towards its New York members.[15] As inscribed in its first constitution, the aim of the STA was

To promote high standards in the typographic arts by all possible means; to foster and encourage education in these arts; to elevate public taste in matters typographic; and to cooperate with all other organizations and institutions having similar aims.[16]

Among the first members were Middleton, Detterer, and Cooper, along with Paul Ressinger, Bill Kittredge, Rodney Chirpe, Egbert Jacobson, and Will Ransom, who had worked with the Goudys at the Village Press. Initially, the membership was almost entirely male, reflecting the general paucity of women in the printing and graphic arts professions at that time. The Society envisioned an ambitious program that included publications, exhibitions, and lectures. Despite the emphasis on typographic arts in its title, it declared itself "as much interested in good posters as in well printed books" and was "concerned with the interests of the designer and illustrator as well as those of the type de-

Fig. 6   Otis Shepard,
Wrigley's Billboard,
1940s.

signer and typographer."[17] Among the Society's most important projects was the annual Design in Chicago Printing exhibition, which became a showcase for Chicago talent and helped to promote a distinct graphic identity for the city.[18] The STA's first major project was an enterprising one. Shortly after its founding, the group proposed to the planning committee for the 1933-34 Century of Progress Exposition in Chicago that it take over the design of all the graphic material to be produced for the fair. In retrospect, the membership appears to have been overly ambitious in expecting this to come about. The fair's administration understandably was reluctant to agree to the proposition, but as a result of extended negotiations over several years, the STA was given a free space in the General Exhibits Building for an exhibition of good printing design, which it presented in both 1933 and 1934.

The STA benefited greatly from the involvement of Douglas McMurtrie, a printing scholar and publicist for the Ludlow Typograph Company, who gave a number of lectures on printing history to the group. Like Middleton, McMurtrie brought his knowledge of printing history to bear on a commercial enterprise. The author of myriad volumes on many aspects of printing and typographic history, McMurtrie realized early on that the history of printing in America was an unexplored field, and he devoted much energy to a series of studies on the early development of printing in individual Midwestern states.[19] McMurtrie also kept up with the contemporary printing and design magazines in the United States and abroad, and he became aware of the modern advertising and typographic design then being produced in Europe and in a few places in the United States. In 1929, before any articles on the new European typography and advertising had appeared in English, McMurtrie published *Modern Typography and Layout*. The book's aim was to make the American community of typographic and advertising users and providers aware of the new developments in design, and it included copious examples of type design and advertising layouts. *Modern Typography and Layout* was not an ideological argument for modern design, as was Jan Tschichold's *die neue typographie*, which had appeared in Germany the previous year. Instead, McMurtrie presented a reasoned account of the new design, being careful to note that he did not espouse everything modern but only the best work.[20] McMurtrie's strategy for assimilating modernism was reflective of America's lack of familiarity with European avant-garde movements and modern art in general. Unlike the way most critics viewed the modern art exhibited in the Armory show in New York and Chicago only a few years earlier, McMurtrie was sympathetic to modern design, yet he was unwilling to espouse it as a replacement for everything that had come before. And in Chicago his book appeared within the context of strongly held views on the importance of tradition in typographic design, as exemplified by the work of Ernst Detterer.

Although some members of the STA were sympathetic to and interested in modernism, it was the Art Directors Club of Chicago that made a more overt push to bring contemporary

Graphic Design   287

European tendencies in art and design to the attention of its members. Like the STA, which was modeled to some degree on the American Institute of Graphic Arts, the Art Directors Club of Chicago, founded in 1932, followed the precedent of the Art Directors Club in New York, which had been established in 1919. E. Willis Jones, an art director who was one of the early members of the STA, was the founder of the Chicago club.[21] The art director's role arose within the process of preparing advertising layouts for printing. As Jones noted, "Even by 1925 the term was about as familiar as aviphenologist."[22] At that time the distinction between the work of a lettering man like Oswald Cooper, who handled all phases of production, including typesetting, and an art director was not crystal clear. A general difference between the two practices might have hinged on the degree to which the art director was involved in the overall production of a printed piece, as well as the degree to which he had administrative authority. According to Jones:

Many agencies and other firms had "layout men" or art departments headed by a "manager" but they were expected to do no more than what they were told by higher-ups. These companies had to be made aware of the existence of the art director and that he could be important creatively and should have executive status.[23]

Jones's impetus to found the Chicago club came from his awareness that he was the only agency art director in the STA. Although he also designed layouts like many STA members and spent time learning about type with Oswald Cooper and Edwin Gillespie at Bertsch and Cooper on Saturday mornings, there was still a sense of difference between Jones's work as an art director and the job of a designer.[24]

In 1934 the Art Directors Club of Chicago, perhaps stimulated by the activity of the Century of Progress Exposition, sponsored a course by Joseph Binder, the Austrian poster and advertising designer whose sleek airbrush style gave his posters a distinctly modern flair. Binder's course, as it turns out, was a revelation to a number of Chicago art directors and illustrators, most notably Otis Shepard, art director for the Wrigley Company, who developed a billboard look for Wrigley that was clearly derived from Binder's style (fig. 6). As George McVicker, one of the participants in Binder's course, noted:

It was very well attended and we were quite astounded at the entirely new methods and ideas that were so different from any American art school's teaching. Stylizing of nature, figures and perspective and an "abstract symbol" approach to a problem were all new to us.[25]

The Century of Progress Exposition, and particularly the STA's participation in it, helped to establish the importance of Chicago as a printing center and spurred interest in promoting Chicago graphic designers more aggressively. To that end John Averill, who created humorous illustrations and advertising layouts, took the lead in establishing 27 Chicago Designers, a group that intended to promote the work of its members through an annual book that would be widely distributed in Chicago and elsewhere in the United States. The format for the book allowed each designer three pages in which to make an original presentation.[26] Among the designers included in the earliest volumes were Averill, Rodney Chirpe, Egbert Jacobson, Robert Hunter Middleton, Dale Nichols, Ray DaBoll, Bert Ray, Paul Ressinger, Sid Dickens, and Oswald Cooper. These men had a wide variety of talents and in no way provided a unified profile of what practitioners in the graphic arts did. Averill made

Fig. 7   László Moholy-
Nagy, New Bauhaus
catalogue cover, 1937.

Fig. 8   Morton Gold-
sholl Design Associates,
Martin-Senour Company
logo, 1951.

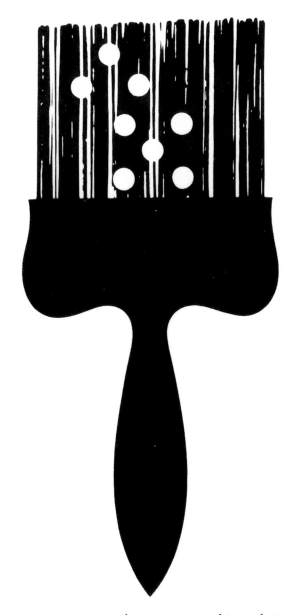

woodcut illustrations for advertising layouts, DaBoll was a calligrapher, Ray designed publications and advertising flyers, Middleton was a type designer, Jacobson was the corporate art director for the Container Corporation of America, Chirpe created package and product designs, and Dickens specialized in industrial styling, packaging, and layouts.

The diversity of this work tells us something about the formation of the graphic arts profession itself. All these designers were satisfying clients' communication needs and all had some relation to printing. As tenuous a professional relationship as that might seem, it was nonetheless sufficient to bring them together to solicit new business. As with the early industrial designers, clients were more interested in how graphic artists might meet their needs than they were in issues of certification or professional unity.[27] In general, the work of the early 27 Chicago Designers made little reference to the European Modern Movement, although one illustrator, Werner Pursell, whose work first appeared in the 1938 edition, was strongly influenced by Joseph Binder's posters. In effect, 27 Chicago Designers was more an outgrowth of the STA's aim to improve the quality of typographic and advertising design than it was the vehicle for introducing a new conceptual or stylistic model of design to Chicago. The group did, however, gain recognition for Chicago designers nationally. Its book was mailed to potential clients throughout the country and made a strong impression, helping to build a national reputation for Chicago graphic art. At the time the 27 Chicago Designers group was founded, there was hardly another city in the United States where graphic art was so extensively developed as a professional practice.

The establishment of the New Bauhaus in 1937 first brought the principles and practices of European modern design to Chicago (see fig. 7). The New Bauhaus was the result of efforts made by the Association of Arts and Industries to found a school of industrial design that would improve the quality of American products. Frustrated by lengthy negotiations with the Art Institute over several years to develop a design program that was mutually satisfying, the association decided to start its own school and engaged László Moholy-Nagy, a former Bauhaus faculty member in Germany, to be the director.[28] Shortly after Moholy-Nagy arrived at the Weimar Bauhaus in 1923, he published a strong manifesto, entitled "The New Typography," in the catalogue of the first Bauhaus exhibition the

same year. He was also instrumental in updating the graphic image of the school. He continued to write about typography and the use of photography in advertising while at the Bauhaus and after he left in 1928. When he stopped teaching, he worked as a free-lance designer in Berlin and then continued in England before he took up his new post in Chicago. Moholy-Nagy was thus experienced in the principles and techniques of the "new typography" and had, in fact, been one of the first theorists of this movement. In the initial curriculum of the New Bauhaus, he placed advertising design within a more comprehensive Light Workshop, which included photography, typography, layout, and serigraphy. The workshop was headed by Gyorgy Kepes, a fellow Hungarian who had worked with Moholy-Nagy in Berlin and London.[29]

In 1938 the Art Directors Club of Chicago invited Kepes to teach a basic course on visual design, a course that had an even greater impact

on Chicago designers and art directors than Binder's earlier course in illustration. George McVicker, who attended both courses, described Kepes's class as follows:

This course, attended by art directors, artists and designers, had more effect than anything else on the progress of design in Chicago. Previous to that, we had all been used to designing by looking through books and magazines and getting ideas — that is, taking someone else's. This whole new revolutionary concept of *thinking* — taking the required elements, the medium, the audience, the purpose, and arriving at a solution from inside out, was a real liberation, and we were just ripe for it.[30]

McVicker thought the visual fundamentals that Kepes taught could be applied to almost any design problem, and he contrasted Kepes's course sharply with the more restricted technique that Binder had brought to Chicago four years earlier.

Kepes taught first at the New Bauhaus and then at the School of Design, which Moholy-Nagy founded after the New Bauhaus closed. Kepes remained at the School of Design until 1943.[31] In 1944 Paul Theobald and Company, a new Chicago publisher dedicated to publishing books on modern architecture and design, brought out Kepes's *Language of Vision*, which made some of the principles and techniques of his teaching accessible to a wider public.[32]

Aside from the radically new curriculum at both the New Bauhaus and the School of Design, their modern spirit attracted a lot of young women to the study of design. This was a new phenomenon for Chicago and helped to change the male-dominated atmosphere in the city's graphic arts community. Among the students who took either day or night classes with Kepes or Moholy-Nagy in the 1940s were Mort and Millie Goldsholl, Bruce Beck, Elsa Kula, and Herb Pinzke. All became leaders in the Chicago graphic arts community. The Goldsholl studio, which was established in the 1940s, later introduced a type of practice that contrasted strongly with many of those developed by members of STA and 27 Chicago Designers. As the Goldsholls developed their activities, they began to focus on several areas that were relatively new to Chicago, notably corporate identity (fig. 8) and filmmaking. The firm also built a strong business in packaging that was more like the kind of practice that a number of other Chicago designers, including Sid Dickens, Rodney Chirpe, Ernest Spuehler, and DeForest Sackett, had developed. Sackett, for example, designed hundreds of packages as a designer-art director for Walgreens Drug Stores before he began a free-lance business around 1939 (see fig. 9). Dickens had started earlier with a packaging business and developed that as his specialty (fig. 10). In the 1952 edition of the 27 *Chicago Designers* book, he

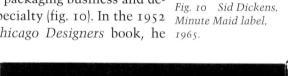

Fig. 9   DeForest Sackett, Self-promotion page; from 27 Chicago Designers (Chicago, 1940).

Fig. 10   Sid Dickens, Minute Maid label, 1965.

Fig. 11 Earl Uhl, Self-promotion page; from 27 Chicago Designers (Chicago, 1940).

published the following statement: "A designer is a specialist. A *package* designer is a specialized specialist."[33]

In the late 1930s, at the time the New Bauhaus opened, graphic arts practice in Chicago took various forms. Some designers like Dickens and Sackett specialized in packaging, but both did advertising work as well. Others, like Ray DaBoll and Earl Uhl, were lettering specialists (fig. 11), although DaBoll was particularly known for his calligraphy (fig. 12). He had studied at the School of the Art Institute and designed typographic layouts and lettering for Oswald Cooper before starting his own practice in 1929. Perhaps the majority of Chicago designers in the 1930s concentrated on general advertising layouts, posters, and some publication designs. There were also the art directors,

who worked primarily in advertising agencies, and a few typographers, such as Robert Hunter Middleton. Chicago had fewer opportunities for publication design than New York, the center of trade-book publishing as well as mass-circulation magazines. One exception was *Esquire*, which started publication in 1933 in Chicago, although it moved to New York in the early 1950s.[34]

Beginning in the 1930s, one of the biggest clients for Chicago graphic designers was Abbott Laboratories, which hired a large number of free-lancers to work on packaging, brochures, and other printed materials. Among those who worked for Abbott over the years were Rodney Chirpe, M. Martin Johnson, Bert Ray, William Fleming, Everett McNear, Mort Goldsholl, Elsa Kula, Norman Perman, and Bruce Beck. Bert Ray

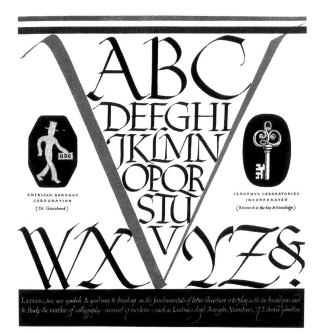

LETTERS, too, are symbols. A good way to brush up on the fundamentals of letter structure is to play with the broad pen and to study the masters of calligraphy—ancient & modern—such as Ludovico degli Arrighi Vicentino, & Edward Johnston

was the first art director of the company's house organ, *What's New*. This magazine began publication in 1935 under the aegis of Abbott's director of advertising, Charles Downs, and featured writing by such well-known authors as Jean Stafford, Carl Sandburg, and Robert Frost, and paintings that Downs commissioned from Ben Shahn, Thomas Hart Benton, Robert Gwathmey, and other prominent artists. These were used for covers, illustrations, and advertisements, and they helped to make *What's New* an exemplary visual publication (fig. 13).[35]

The other company that had an exemplary design program as early as the mid-1930s was Container Corporation of America, founded in 1926 by Walter Paepcke through a merger of several firms that manufactured paperboard boxes.[36] According to James Sloan Allen, Paepcke's patronage of good design was strongly influenced at the outset by his wife Elizabeth, who persuaded him to improve the company's graphic image by hiring an art director.[37] In 1936 Paepcke brought in Egbert Jacobson as director of the department of design. At the time Paepcke hired him, Jacobson, who had started out as an art director in New York before coming to Chicago, was a free-lance designer and president of the Art Directors Club. He had also been an early member of the STA and was one of the first 27 Chicago Designers.

Jacobson was given the unusual assignment of creating a unified visual image for Container. He was to be responsible not only for logos, stationery, invoices, annual reports, and advertising, but also for the company's office interiors, factories, and trucks. This was certainly one of the first such assignments in an American corpora-

tion, although a few other companies, such as CBS, were also beginning to think about similar identity issues around the same time.[38] One of Jacobson's initial projects was to develop a series of corporate advertisements. The planning of the series was turned over to Charles Coiner, an art director with the N. W. Ayer advertising agency in Philadelphia. Coiner hired the French poster artist A. M. Cassandre to design a group of conceptual ads promoting the company and its paperboard products. Jacobson went on to develop a number of distinguished advertising campaigns featuring well-known artists (see fig. 14). Around 1940 Paepcke established a package design laboratory, which was under the direction of Albert Kner, who had come to Chicago from Hungary, where he had been involved in his family's printing business. Over the years the nuts and bolts package designs of the Design Laboratory received considerably less attention than Container's corporate advertising, but the lab developed many novel uses of paperboard.[39] A selection of Container's corporate ads was featured in a special 1946 exhibition, "Modern Art in Advertising," at The Art Institute of

Fig. 12   Ray DaBoll, Self-promotion page; from 27 Chicago Designers (Chicago, 1942).

Fig. 13   Bert Ray, art director, cover of What's New, Abbott Laboratories company magazine, 1948.

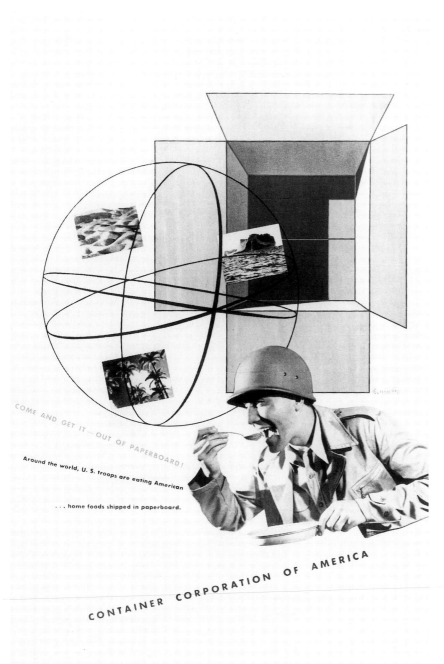

CONTAINER CORPORATION OF AMERICA

Fig. 14 Herbert Matter, "Come and Get It," newspaper advertisement for Container Corporation of America, 1943.

Fig. 15 Bruce Beck, Jewel Food Stores logo, 1950s.

subject of design and management. The International Design Conference evolved into an annual event, although Container only funded it for the first several years. Later, it was organized for some years by a group of Chicago designers that included Robert Hunter Middleton and Herb Pinzke, who was working with Albert Kner at Container's Design Laboratory.

A conceptual program in visual communication continued at the School of Design, which opened in 1939 and became the Institute of Design in 1944. After Kepes left Chicago in 1943, Moholy-Nagy took over the graphic design program. He died in 1946 and subsequently Richard Koppe became the most prominent teacher in the program, now called Visual Design. Others who taught either at the New Bauhaus, the School of Design, or the Institute of Design were Eugene Dana, Elsa Kula, Sarah Leavitt, Hubert Leckie, Irving Titel, and Frank Barr.[41] Barr produced wonderful small announcements for various events in the city that he set and printed on his own press. Hans Schleger, the German designer who had emigrated to England and become one of that country's leading postwar commercial artists, was also a visiting professor in the program in 1950-51.[42] Both Koppe and Dana later joined the faculty of the University of Illinois at Chicago and taught in the university's art department. For some time the University of Illinois also had an exemplary institutional identity program, which was created by James Axeman.

Despite the more theoretical pedagogy at the Institute of Design, the School of the Art Institute still appealed to many students, primarily because of its strong fine arts program. The head of the program in commercial art in the early 1950s was Park Phipps, a member of 27

Chicago and a catalogue was published by Paul Theobald.[40] The exhibition was designed by Herbert Bayer, who had created some ads for Container shortly after he emigrated to the United States in 1938. He did not meet Paepcke, however, until 1945, when he received the exhibition commission. Eventually, he did a great deal of design work for Paepcke in Aspen, while also functioning as a special design consultant for Container Corporation.

Paepcke's knowledge of design developed through his friendship with Moholy-Nagy and Bayer. He began to preach a doctrine of good design to the Art Directors Club of Chicago and other groups, and in 1949 he took up Jacobson's suggestion to hold a conference in Aspen on the

Chicago Designers, who had taught lettering at the school as far back as 1921, when Ernst Detterer was there. One of the city's old-timers, Phipps was primarily a teacher, but he also designed announcements for the Art Institute, Ravinia, and various commercial clients. Among the design students who graduated from the School of the Art Institute in the early 1950s and practiced graphic design in Chicago were Norman Perman and Ed Bedno. At the time, the leading studios in the city included Whitaker-Guernsey and Tempo, which was headed by Taylor Poore, and those of Bert Ray, Everett McNear, and Morton and Millie Goldsholl. The bulk of the work for most of these firms was advertising, publications, and miscellaneous printed matter. Other designers who became active in the 1950s included Randall Roth, Bruce Beck (fig. 15), Allen Porter, Ann Long, Rhodes Patterson, Franklin McMahon, Dan Smith, Susan Jackson Keig, and Carl Regehr. Regehr arrived from Denver around 1952 and became a top designer in the Bert Ray studio. It was not until 1951 that Phoebe Moore became the first woman elected to 27 Chicago Designers, to be followed shortly by Elsa Kula (fig. 16). Both women had strong backgrounds in illustration and possessed, in their different ways, a keen sense of whimsy. Kula's humor was wackier, but Moore had a gentle sense of irony that sometimes came out in the playful manipulation of female clichés, as in a hand holding a dainty handkerchief or a pair of cut-out legs on stilts (fig. 17). Her clients included Mercury Records, for which she designed a number of covers for pop and jazz albums; she

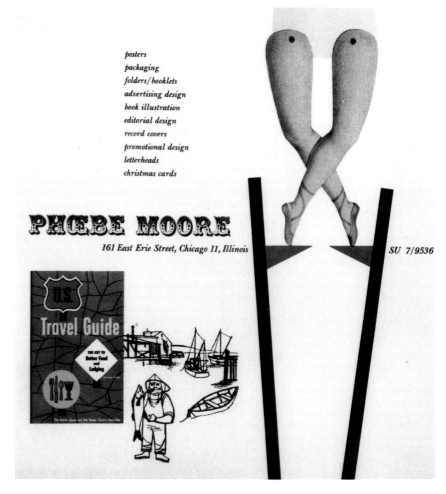

*Fig. 16   Elsa Kula,
Exhibition announce-
ment, 1965.*

*Fig. 18   Arthur Paul,
Playboy logo, 1953.*

*Fig. 17   Phoebe Moore,
Self-promotion page;
from 27 Chicago
Designers (Chicago,
1954).*

also designed the logo for one of Mercury's new labels, Emarcy.

In 1953 *Playboy* magazine hit the newstands (see fig. 18). Its art director was Arthur Paul, who had studied at the Institute of Design and then free-lanced in the city before going to work for *Playboy.* Paul had a strong interest in painting and illustration, but not in the traditional illustrative styles that pervaded most magazine advertising and layouts. The illustrator Jerome Snyder described Paul's approach as

vastly different from the prevailing illustrative mode of the early fifties, a literal, albeit skillful, translation into pictures of what had already been said in words. Paul's effort from the outset was to project a dimension of visual excitement and invention that dealt with ideas and visual idioms rather than being a banal portrayal of commonplace events.[43]

There are some Chicago precedents for Paul's style of art direction both in *Esquire* and in Abbott Laboratories' *What's New,* which commissioned many illustrations and covers from established artists. Like *What's New,* Paul published illustrations by numerous contemporary artists over the years, including Andy Warhol, George Segal, Alfred Leslie, and Larry Rivers, and he gave opportunities to young Chicago painters in the 1960s and early 1970s, including Roger Brown, Karl Wirsum, Ed Paschke, and Christina Ramberg. In addition, Paul created many striking layouts through the bold placement of typography and illustrations in relation to the texts. The kind of work he was doing at *Playboy,* particularly in the 1960s, was paralleled by that of other magazine art directors, such as Allen Hurlburt, Milton Glaser, and Herb Lubalin, although they were primarily in New York. But *Playboy* certainly ran counter to the tradition of advertising illustration and layout in Chicago and was in an especially fortunate position to bring art direction and contemporary art closer together.

The STA had an opportunity to project an image of Chicago graphic arts to designers across the nation in a special issue of *Print* magazine that appeared in March 1953 and was guest-edited by Robert Middleton. There was a modest tone of muscle-flexing in the opening article, particularly in regard to competition with New York. And yet, compared to design in New York at the time, design in Chicago was quite tame. The New York graphic arts community had benefited from the presence of a number of European modernists—Herbert Matter, Ladislav Sutnar, Walter Allner, Will Burtin, and Leo Lionni, for example—who came to the United

States from Europe because of World War II. In New York there were also the strong publication graphics of Dr. Agha at Condé Nast and Alexei Brodovitch at *Harper's Bazaar,* as well as the provocative advertising work of Paul Rand and Herb Lubalin, and the CBS corporate graphics of William Golden and Lou Dorfsman. By contrast, the Chicago work was far more representative of the tradition of typographic arts that had been a part of the STA since its inception. The work was excellent and need not be measured by some standard of modernity or innovation, but the comparison of the two cities at the time made it clear that Chicago was hardly the center of graphic innovation that New York was.

One voice that distinguished itself from the others in the STA issue of *Print* was that of Ralph Eckerstrom, the art director of the University of Illinois Press in Urbana. Reflecting on the Chicago graphics he had viewed as a judge of the most recent STA Design in Chicago Printing show, he characterized the work as representing "warmed-up Bauhaus and cleaned up traditional concepts," and further commented that it did not sufficiently recognize the selling function of design.[44] The books designed by Eckerstrom had already begun to attract national attention, and in 1955 he came to Chicago to succeed Egbert Jacobson as director of design at Container Corporation. While Walter Paepcke was still alive, Eckerstrom was able to maintain the Container Corporation tradition of quality modern design and develop his convictions about design as a selling tool (see fig. 19). By the time he arrived, one of the company's big projects was the "Great Ideas of Western Man" series of ad-

lincoln park

run jump play look walk think dream

vertisements, which featured recognized artists and designers interpreting significant quotes by great thinkers that were selected by Mortimer Adler of the University of Chicago.[45]

At the University of Illinois Press, Eckerstrom's staff included Robert Vogele and John Massey. Massey had previously worked for Herb Pinzke in Urbana on the design of a children's encyclopedia, *Our Wonderful World*.[46] Eckerstrom and his staff at the press often discussed the Bauhaus and the new rational Swiss design of Josef Müller-Brockmann and Armin Hofmann. Massey recalls being "blown away" by Hofmann's work at an Aspen Design Conference around 1954. "I really didn't know what design was while I was at the University of Illinois," he told an interviewer in 1990. "It was called advertising design and suddenly I [was] exposed to an entirely new discipline which was design. And that changed my entire life."[47] Not long after Eckerstrom arrived at Container Corporation, he hired Massey as his assistant. At the time Container's design department also included architects, interior designers, and industrial designers, and they developed a method of working as a group. Massey recalls the "phenomenal and marvelous dialogue" that occurred among these designers, who knew something about each other's disciplines as well as their own.[48] After

Paepcke's death in 1960 there was a period of ferment as the new corporate management tried to assess the value of design in the company, and the design department experimented with a number of new strategies for advertising and public relations.

Massey became Container Corporation's director of design when Eckerstrom left in 1964 to start Unimark, one of the first international interdisciplinary design offices.[49] The company, founded by a number of partners in 1965, was intended to operate on a worldwide scale with a range of disciplines that included graphics, packaging design, interiors, and product design. As a precedent for Unimark, one should not underestimate the importance of Eckerstrom's experience at Container Corporation, where he not only encountered a multidisciplinary design group for the first time but also worked on an international scale with Container's various divisions and subsidiaries abroad. Unimark grew quickly and, thanks to Eckerstrom's gift of salesmanship, garnered a variety of large corporate accounts including Ford, Gillette, Alcoa, J. C. Penney, American Airlines, and Standard Oil of Indiana. At its peak Unimark had close to five hundred employees worldwide with about sixty in the Chicago office.[50] Massimo Vignelli headed the New York office, and over the years there were offices in Cleveland, San Francisco, Denver, and Detroit. Abroad Bob Noorda was in charge in Milan, and Francois Robert managed a small Unimark operation in Johannesburg. There were additional offices for varying lengths

Fig. 19   John Massey, Poster for Lincoln Park, 1967.

Fig. 21   Carl Regehr, First Chicago magazine cover, 1964.

Fig. 20   Ralph Eckerstrom, Container Corporation of America logo, 1957.

CHICAGO

ONE DOLLAR

Carl Regehr

of time in Copenhagen, London, and Melbourne.[51]

In the United States, Unimark pushed the grid system and the Swiss typeface Helvetica for corporate clients and was thus influential in bringing a cool Swiss style to corporate communications. Massimo Vignelli, the senior graphic designer for the firm, stated his belief that "design could be a system, a basic structure that could be set up so that other people could implement it effectively," and he recounts how the company's designers "used grids all the time as a tool the way a carpenter uses a hammer."[52] By the time Unimark dissolved around 1979, it had served as a training ground for many young designers, a number of whom continued to work in Chicago after they left the firm. These included Harri Boller, Peter Teubner, Ron Coates, Ron Kovach, Tony Spadaro, and Francois Robert. Among the more seasoned designers who worked for Unimark and then went out on their own were John Greiner and Jay Doblin. Doblin, who joined Unimark while still director of the Institute of Design, established his own firm, Jay Doblin and Associates, in 1972. There he developed a focus on corporate planning, which he had begun to explore at Unimark. Doblin made the planning emphasis into a strength of his firm and began to refer to its work as "strategic planning." While it did involve graphic design, this activity was the outcome of a larger process of analyzing a company's overall internal and external communications strategies. Similar to the earlier development of corporate identity as a form of practice, strategic planning put more emphasis on planning and overall communications issues rather than just graphic identity.

Around the time that Unimark started in the mid-1960s, several other offices opened and began to play an important role in establishing Chicago as a major center of corporate design. One was the Center for Advanced Research in Design (CARD), which John Massey operated as a semi-independent subsidiary of the Container Corporation while he was still director of design there.[53] CARD carried out a number of projects that were significant in Chicago, as well as nationally. These included a series of banners and posters for the City of Chicago (fig. 19), the redesign of the identity system for the Atlantic Richfield Company, and an identity program for the U.S. Department of Labor. Together, these projects were important because, unlike Unimark, which focused on corporate clients, CARD got Chicago designers involved with the federal government and the city administration in ways that they had rarely been before.[54] The banners and posters were part of a larger civic project to improve the image of Chicago. This was conducted under the Mayor's Committee on Economic and Cultural Development, a group formed around 1955. An important effort of the project was the founding of a new city magazine, *Chicago*, proposed to the Committee by Carl Regehr, who became the art director and created a strong graphic look for the publication over a number of years (fig. 21). The committee's awareness of design stimulated other organizations to improve their public images. The Chicago Metropolitan YMCA commissioned H. B. Smith to create a new graphics program for the organization, and some of the city agencies began using outside designers for their annual reports. Another project that resulted from this momentum was the signage program for O'Hare International Airport designed by Hayward Blake.[55]

Another design office that was structured to serve the communication and marketing needs of corporate management was RVI Corporation, headed by Robert Vogele. Like Massey, Vogele also learned more about graphic design at the University of Illinois Press under Ralph Eckerstrom than he had as a student in the advertising design program at the University of Illinois, Urbana. He developed a knowledge of corporate design when he worked as director of graphics for Latham, Tyler, Jensen, an industrial design firm in Chicago. In 1958 Vogele went out on his own as a corporate identity consultant, and by 1965 he had developed the RVI Corporation as an umbrella organization that had within it separate firms to handle advertising, packaging, and graphics. RVI was also the training ground for a number of young designers who later established their own firms in Chicago, among them Wayne Webb, Jim Lienhart, and Bart Crosby.

By the late 1960s, the work of RVI, Unimark, CARD, and the Container Corporation, along with the activities of other firms such as Goldsholl Associates, Design Consultants Inc., and the Design Partnership, had begun to give Chicago a reputation for corporate graphics. The Design Partnership was formed in 1968 from four separate studios, those of Bruce Beck, Blake & Weiss, Mabrey/Kaiser, and Henry Robertz. The aim of these designers was to provide a vehicle through which they could work on larger projects than a small firm could handle alone.

In 1969 Mary Garrahan published an article in *Chicago* magazine in which she referred to Chicago's graphic designers as follows:

Fig. 22   Chris Garland, Cover of Zoetrope, *no. 3 (March 1979).*

Solving sales problems is their thing, and if that sounds stodgy, take a long look at industry today. The evidence of the designer's eye is there, for corporations want recognizable and consistent visual images for their companies.[56]

But not all designers would admit to the dominance of this quality. In the same article, Jim Lienhart was quoted as saying that Swiss graphics had spawned too many imitators in Chicago and their work at its worst had become stylistic decoration.[57] By contrast, Lienhart developed his own sense of expressive typography and playful wit that was somewhat distinct in the city during the 1960s (fig. 23). Besides corporate graphics, a number of firms, large and small, did extensive design work on textbooks, particularly for Scott Foresman, where Hall Kearney was vice-president of design. Ed and Jane Bedno, Norman Perman, and others, even Unimark for a short period, completely changed the look of school textbooks by creating strong contemporary layouts and using photography extensively. Because of Scott Foresman's tremendous influence on the school market, this new look helped to revolutionize elementary and secondary school teaching.

The work of the large corporate-oriented firms helped to propel Chicago graphic designers into a wider arena of recognition, but it also contributed to a perception that most design in the city

Fig. 23   Jim Lienhart, The Black Sheep Club logo, 1962.

**40. The Black Sheep Club, Chicago, Ill. (1962)
Designer: Jim Lienhart/Whitaker Guernsey Studio
250 E. Illinois, Chicago, Ill.**

was characterized by clean, sober graphics rather than more expressive, risk-taking work. Ed Bedno echoed this perception when he characterized New York's Push Pin Studio as being "oriented to the groovy, wild image that isn't Chicago's thing."[58] The emphasis on corporate design and planning that had given Chicago greater national recognition in the 1960s and 1970s also contributed to a broader orientation for the STA. In 1977 the society changed its annual show from a local to a national one, which was renamed the STA 100 Show. The STA also became more active in the International Council of Graphic Design Associations (ICOGRADA) and was selected to host the 1978 ICOGRADA Congress. The major responsibility for this congress was undertaken by Robert Vogele, who hired Patrick Whitney, now director of the Institute of Design, as the program director. Jay Doblin advised Vogele to present a set of case studies that would allow the congress to deal with problems of design evaluation.[59] As a result, the congress turned out to have been one of the more focused ICOGRADA events and one that tried to give more emphasis to research and theory than previous congresses had. Vogele became president of the STA after the 1978 congress, and he initiated some new proj-

ects, notably Design Chicago, an umbrella concept within which several programs were held that addressed Chicago's graphic design history, and the STA Journal, which began as a modest-size publication and was subsequently considerably enlarged.

In 1989 the STA changed its name to the American Center for Design (ACD) to acknowledge the fact that "Society of Typographic Arts" no longer explained to the public what its members did. Few were typographers or were involved with the typographic arts in the way many of the organization's founders had been, and there was a move within the STA to give greater recognition to the broad spectrum of disciplines represented in the organization.[60] In the meantime, the American Institute of Graphic Arts had become a national organization, and there was now a Chicago chapter to complement the graphic design activities of the ACD. It can be argued that the large interdisciplinary design offices which started in the mid-1960s dominated the external perception of graphic design in Chicago more than they did the actual practice. Chicago has always had many smaller offices whose work has been recognized in Chicago shows and those elsewhere, especially the work done in the 1960s and 1970s by the offices of Norman Perman, Randall Roth, Ed and Jane Bedno, Michael Reid, David Burke, John Greiner, Larry Klein, and others.[61] A new organization, Women in Design, was established in 1978 to address particular concerns of women designers. In addition to dealing with issues such as commensurate fees, the organization fulfilled a networking function and also sought more recognition for women through several exhibitions, including its tenth anniversary show, "Ten Years: Women in Design, Chicago."[62]

During the 1980s, a few of the smaller design offices tried to carve out a niche for more expressive work but succeeded only to a modest degree. A studio that introduced a New Wave look from California in the early 1980s was Xeno, whose chief designer was Chris Garland. Among his varied projects, Garland art-directed a free cultural newspaper called Zoetrope (fig. 22). But the kind of experimentation Garland was promoting has failed to take hold to any significant degree in Chicago. Xeno, in fact, eventually moved to Los Angeles. Through his studio Thirst, Rick Valicenti has built a reputation as a free spirit within a relatively conservative Chicago design community (see fig. 1). One can also mention the late 1980s work of Anthony Ma, David Frej, and Maria Grillo, for example, as representing a more experimental approach.

In the past twenty years many of the young designers who chose to begin their careers in Chicago have come from the graphic design programs at the University of Illinois campuses in Urbana and Chicago. While Carl Regehr was a professor at Urbana in the 1970s and early 1980s, he was influential in moving the program from an emphasis on traditional advertising design to modern graphic design. At the Chicago campus, former teachers and students at the Institute of Design were initially most influential in developing the program—Richard Koppe, Eugene Dana, and Tad Takano, in particular. In recent years John Massey has joined the faculty at the Chicago campus, as have others with active studios in the city, such as Michael Glass and John Greiner. In 1984 the School of Art and Design at the University of Illinois at Chicago, began to publish one of the design field's first scholarly journals, Design Issues.

Today, the graphic design scene in Chicago, as in the United States as a whole, is extremely pluralistic and difficult to characterize. To make a generalization, however, I would argue that the corporate legacy of the 1960s still remains the strongest influence on young designers in the city. Chicago design is less distinct than it once was, because designers across the country now share similar professional backgrounds and have access to the same up-to-date information and technology. Although Chicago is still a large and active center of graphic design practice, it remains to be seen whether the city's designers can reassert a strong sense of identity comparable to that which Chicago had as a graphic design center at several earlier moments in its history.

NOTES

1. The only reference to Chicago graphic design in Philip Meggs's widely used textbook A History of Graphic Design, 2nd ed. (New York, 1992) is to Container Corporation of America and several firms that were offshoots of it, Unimark and CARD.

2. Data on Chicago publishing is from Ernest T. Gundlach, "Chicago's Growing Leadership in Printing, Publishing, and Advertising," in Glenn A. Bishop and Paul T. Gilbert, Chicago's Accomplishments and Leaders (Chicago, 1932), pp. 76, 78, 80.

3. See Victor Margolin, American Poster Renaissance: The Great Age of Poster Design, 1890-1900 (New York, 1975).

4. On the Village Press, see Will Ransom, Private Presses and Their Books (New York, 1929), pp. 79-86. Frederic Goudy's life is recounted in D. J. R. Bruckner, Frederic Goudy (New York, 1990) and summarized by Sebastian Carter in Twentieth Century Type Designers (London, 1987), pp. 42-50. Bertha Goudy, who typeset nearly all the Village Press books and made bindings as well, is given special attention in the exhibition catalogue Ten Years: Women in Design, Chicago (Chicago, 1988), pp. 22-26.

5. The best reference on Cooper is The Society of Typographic Arts, *The Book of Oz Cooper* (Chicago, 1949).

6. Cooper Black and other typefaces by Cooper are discussed in Richard N. MacArthur, "On Cooper Typefaces With Some Digressions," *The Book of Oz Cooper* (note 5), pp. 71-124. One way that commercial artists earned money was to create alphabets that would be cut in metal by type foundries. Packard, a typeface sold by the American Type Foundry, originated in Cooper's lettering for Packard Motor Company ads.

7. On the early history of design training at the Art Institute, see Roger Gilmore, ed., *Over a Century: A History of The School of the Art Institute of Chicago, 1866-1891* (Chicago, 1982), pp. 80-85. Design is also mentioned in Charlotte Moser, "'In the Highest Efficiency': Art Training at The School of the Art Institute of Chicago," in Sue Ann Prince, ed., *The Old Guard and the Avant-Garde: Modernism in Chicago, 1910-1940* (Chicago and London, 1990), pp. 193-208.

8. The School of the Art Institute of Chicago, *Catalogue of the Art School of The Art Institute of Chicago, 1919-1920* (Chicago, 1919), pp. 15, 24.

9. "Recollections of an Institution: The Chicago Academy of Fine Arts," *Creative Communicator* 11, no. 1 (1980), pp. 2-5. The Chicago Academy of Fine Arts closed its doors in 1979.

10. The School of the Art Institute of Chicago, *Catalogue of the Art School of The Art Institute of Chicago, 1921-1922* (Chicago, 1921), p. 12. It is of interest to note the early use of the term "designer" rather than "commercial artist" in this catalogue copy.

11. The School of the Art Institute of Chicago, *Catalogue of the Art School of The Art Institute of Chicago, 1924-1925* (Chicago, 1924), p. 19.

12. On Middleton's role as an organizer, see Herbert Pinzke, "Organizer and Catalyst," in Bruce Beck, ed., *RHM: Robert Hunter Middleton, The Man and His Letters* (Chicago, 1985).

13. See James M. Wells, "The Man and His Career," in Beck (note 12), pp. 1-8.

14. Middleton had acquired about one hundred of Bewick's blocks for his personal collection. See Gordon Williams, "The Bewick Blocks," in Beck (note 12), pp. 51-64, and R. Russell Maylone, "Cherryburn," ibid., pp. 65-72.

15. James Wells, "Book Typography in the United States of America," in Kenneth Day, ed., *Book Typography 1815-1965 in Europe and the United States of America* (Chicago, 1965), pp. 369-70.

16. "STA Constitution," 1928, Society of Typographic Arts Records, Chicago Historical Society.

17. Statement of Submission of Constitution, Society of Typographic Arts Records, Chicago Historical Society. Some members were unhappy with the emphasis on typographic arts in the title and the name was changed to the Society of Graphic Arts before being changed back at the 1928 Annual Meeting. "Minutes of the Annual Meeting, June 12, 1928," The Society of Typographic Arts Records, Chicago Historical Society.

18. For an overview of work done by STA members, see the exhibition catalogue issued by The Society of Typographic Arts, *Fifty Years of Graphic Design in Chicago: 1927-1977* (Chicago, 1977).

19. See Frank McCaffrey, *An Informal Biography of Douglas C. McMurtrie* (San Francisco, 1939).

20. Douglas McMurtrie, *Modern Typography and Layout* (Chicago, 1929). McMurtrie's book is discussed in Lloyd Engelbrecht, "Modernism and Design in Chicago," in Prince (note 7), pp. 130-31.

21. E. Willis Jones, "How It All Started—Twenty-Five Years Ago," *ADCC News Bulletin* (early winter 1957), n. p.

22. Ibid.

23. Ibid.

24. In the 1938 edition of *27 Chicago Designers*, Jones explicitly defined himself as an art director, not a designer.

25. George McVicker, "European Influences on Chicago Designers," *Print* 7, no. 5 (March 1953), p. 27.

26. "In the Beginning," *27 Chicago Designers*, 40th anniversary edition (Chicago, 1975), n. p.

27. On the development of industrial design as a profession in America, see Jeffrey L. Meikle, *Twentieth-Century Limited: Industrial Design in America, 1925-1939* (Philadelphia, 1979); and Arthur Pulos, *American Design Ethic: A History of Industrial Design* (Cambridge, Mass., 1983), pp. 336-419.

28. The literature is growing on the New Bauhaus and its subsequent incarnations under Moholy-Nagy as the School of Design and the Institute of Design. The initial source of documentation was Sybil Moholy-Nagy's *Moholy-Nagy: An Experiment in Totality* (Cambridge, Mass., 1950). The first major exhibition on the school was mounted by the Bauhaus-Archiv in Berlin, which published a major catalogue, *50 Jahre New Bauhaus: Bauhausnachfolge in Chicago* (Berlin, 1988). An exhibition on Moholy-Nagy in Chicago included material on his pedagogical activities; see *Moholy-Nagy: A New Vision for Chicago* (Urbana and Chicago, 1991). A major study of the New Bauhaus and its subsequent forms under Moholy-Nagy has been completed by Alain Findeli but has not yet been published. Findeli has, however, published two important articles, "The Methodological and Philosophical Foundations of Moholy-Nagy's Design Pedagogy in Chicago (1937-1946)," *Design Issues* 7, no. 1 (Fall 1990), pp. 4-20; and "Design Education and Industry: The Laborious Beginnings of the Institute of Design in Chicago in 1944," *Journal of Design History* 4, no. 2 (1991), pp. 97-113.

29. Moholy-Nagy had invited Herbert Bayer to join the faculty of the New Bauhaus, but Bayer received word on his way to America by ship that the school would soon close because of financial difficulties and thus did not pursue the offer. Gwen Finkel Chanzit, *Herbert Bayer and Modernist Design in America* (Ann Arbor, 1987), p. 84.

30. McVicker (note 25), p. 28.

31. The combination of photography, photomontage, typography, and layout in the Light Workshop at the New Bauhaus had precedents in other courses taught in Europe in the 1920s and 1930s, especially those of Joost Schmidt at the Bauhaus and Max Burchartz in Essen.

32. On Paul Theobald and Company, which also published Moholy-Nagy's *Vision in Motion* in 1947 and a subsequent book by Kepes, *The New Landscape*, see Victor Margolin, "Paul Theobald and Company: Publisher with a New Vision," *Printing History* 9, no. 2 (1987), pp. 33-39.

33. *27 Chicago Designers* 14 (Chicago, 1952), n. p.

34. Celia Hilliard, "Sophistication Sells: *Esquire's* Chicago Success Story," *Chicago Magazine* (May 1980), pp. 134-36, 183, 140.

35. *What's New* lasted until the 1960s, when it was transformed into an international medical quarterly titled *Abbottempo*. For background information on Abbott Labs, with a short section on Charles Downs and the company's advertising, see Herman Kogan, *The Long White Line: The Story of Abbott Laboratories* (New York, 1963).

36. A wide range of examples from the company's design program can be seen in *The First Fifty Years: Container Corporation of America* (Chicago, 1976). For an extensive account of the program, see James Sloan Allen, *The Romance of Commerce and Culture: Capitalism, Modernism, and the Chicago-Aspen Crusade for Cultural Reform* (Chicago and London, 1983). Neil Harris discusses the design program within a larger history of American graphic arts in "Design on Demand: Art and the Modern Corporation," in *Cultural Excursions: Marketing Appetites in Cultural Tastes in Modern America* (Chicago and London, 1990); see also Philip B. Meggs, "The Rise and Fall of Design at a Great Corporation," *Print* 46, no. 3 (May/June 1992), pp. 46-55, 116, 118.

37. Allen (note 36), p. 26.

38. Dennis Doordan has noted that the architect William Lescaze was given a series of commissions by CBS between 1934 and 1949 that included responsibility for "the design of a major new broadcasting facility, the interior design of studio and office spaces, the design of a variety of studio furnishings such as microphones and clocks, the design of a mobile broadcasting vehicle, and the graphic design for CBS facilities across the country"; see Doordan's essay "William Lescaze and CBS: A Case Study in Corporate Modernism," *Syracuse University Library Associates Courier* 19, no. 1 (Spring 1984), pp. 43-55.

39. Allen (note 36), p. 33.

40. The Art Institute of Chicago, *Modern Art in Advertising: An Exhibition of Designs for Container Corporation of America*, compiled and edited by Egbert Jacobson and Katherine Chandler (Chicago, 1945).

41. For examples of work by students of Koppe and Dana, see *50 Jahre New Bauhaus* (note 28), pp. 142-45.

42. Despite the intensity of the program and the student involvement in it, some thought it was not practical enough. In the 1960s a committee from the Art Directors Club of Chicago was invited to visit the school and make suggestions that might be incorporated into the curriculum. The team perceived the curriculum as too theoretical and too far removed from practice. Among their recommendations was the recruitment of practicing art directors to teach part-time, and a greater emphasis on drawing because, as the committee rationalized, human figures were still the principal subject in advertisements and annual reports. After the report was submitted, however, no action was taken; see "ADCC and IIT Department of Design," Leonard S. Rubenstein Collection, University Library, University of Illinois at Chicago.

43. Jerome Snyder, quoted in *The Art of Playboy: An Exhibition of Illustrations Commissioned by Arthur Paul* (Chicago, 1978), n. p.

44. Ralph Eckerstrom, "STA Design in Chicago Printing Show," *Print* 7, no. 5 (March 1953), pp. 54-58.

45. Selected "Great Ideas" ads are reproduced with explanatory texts in John Massey, ed., *Great Ideas* (Chicago, 1976). The series began in 1950 and lasted until the mid-1980s.

46. Massey cites Pinzke as having introduced him to the "broad range and potential of what design is all about"; John Massey interviewed by Robert Even, *The Chicago Design Project* (interview transcripts), p. 18.

47. Ibid., pp. 16-17.

48. Ibid., p. 21.

49. The most thorough documentation of Unimark thus far is Jan Conradi Helms, "A Historical Survey of Unimark International and Its Effect on Graphic Design in the United States" (M.A. thesis, Iowa State University, 1988). See also Ralph Eckerstrom, "Unimark International: Design Team," *STA Journal* 1, no. 2 (Winter 1980), pp. 13-14; and Massimo Vignelli, "Unimark: Toward a New Language of Design," ibid., p. 15. Unimark is a shortened form of Unimarketing, an earlier suggestion by James Fogelman, one of the founding partners.

50. Helms (note 49), p. 75.

51. Ibid., pp. 13-14.

52. Vignelli (note 49), p. 15.

53. At Container, Massey continued an exemplary design program with the assistance of a staff that included Joe Hutchcroft, Bill Bonnell, and Jeff Barnes.

54. An earlier precedent for the involvement of Chicago graphic designers with the city was Robert Middleton's design of a letter form for Chicago's street signs in the late 1930s.

55. On the work of the Mayor's Committee for Economic and Cultural Development, see Robert A. Bassi, "Chicago: Still the City of 'First,'" *Print* 22, no. 2 (March/April 1968), pp. 26-33, 114, 118, 121. This issue of *Print* featured a series of articles on "Graphic Design in the Human Environment."

56. Mary Garrahan, "Conversations on Design," *Chicago* 6, no. 3 (October 1969), p. 28.

57. Ibid.

58. Ibid.

59. Robert Vogele interviewed by Robert Even, *The Chicago Design Project*, pp. 244-47.

60. The title was chosen by a committee that Vogele chaired. Telephone interview with Jane Dunne, executive director, American Center for Design, June 9, 1992.

61. Numerous examples of work from these studios can be seen in *Fifty Years of Graphic Design* (note 18).

62. See *Ten Years: Women in Design, Chicago* (note 4). As of 1988, Women in Design was one of only three graphic design organizations for women in the United States; the other two were in Phoenix and Los Angeles.

Helmut Jahn's first experiences as a Chicago architect set the tone for his entire career. In 1967, having arrived only a few months earlier from Germany to study at the Illinois Institute of Technology on a Rotary Scholarship for International Understanding, Jahn had just begun working for Gene Summers. An architect in the Office of Mies van der Rohe for over fifteen years, Summers himself was only recently out on his own. He had been on Mies's team for New York's Seagram Building (1954-58)—modern architecture's Taj Mahal—and he had the pedigree to get into the highest ranks of Chicago architects. In the same building at Ohio and St. Clair streets where Mies had his office, Gene Summers and his young assistant, Helmut Jahn, looked for work. Work, as it turned out, found them.

Fig. 1   C. F. Murphy Associates; Helmut Jahn, designer, Xerox Centre, 55 West Monroe Street, 1977-80.

Fig. 2   Graham, Anderson, Probst and White; Alfred P. Shaw, designer, Civic Opera Building, 20 North Wacker Drive, 1927-29.

In January 1967 a fire that destroyed the old McCormick Place exhibition center put a quick end to Summers's plans to go into practice on his own and tied his fate to C. F. Murphy Associates, one of Chicago's largest architectural establishments with a big share of the city's public commissions. Charles F. Murphy, who headed the firm, had been politically wired to Mayor Richard J. Daley's powerful administration since he had handled a troublesome project back in the 1950s. It was only natural that the mayor, after examining the ruins of the lakefront hall, told his friend, "Charlie, start drawing."

The trouble was that Charlie did not really draw. Instead, he headed a team of designers, managers, and engineers—a legacy from his days as Ernest R. Graham's personal assistant. During the teens and twenties, Graham, Anderson, Probst and White built on a huge scale: the Wrigley Building (1919-24), the Civic Opera Building (1927-29; fig. 2), and the Merchandise Mart (1927-31; see Rau, fig. 3), to name only a few. Strong organization, not necessarily subtlety in design, executed this work. If the mayor had wanted subtlety, Ludwig Mies van der Rohe would have been his man. But the mayor was calling Charlie Murphy, not Mies, and Murphy was not about to pass up this commission. A new McCormick Place was just the sort of *grand projet* that would further enhance his firm's reputation.

Normally, Murphy would have reassured his powerful friend and gotten the office right down to work. This was the pattern he had established long ago, during the early years of the Daley administration, when Murphy had gained the mayor's confidence with the successful completion of the Central District Filtration Plant (1952-64; fig. 3) and the master plan and terminals for O'Hare International Airport (1957-63; see Brodherson, figs. 17, 18). Richard J. Daley and Charles F. Murphy first met at the dedication of the Prudential Building in 1954, when the firm was still called Naess and Murphy. The Prudential was the first new office tower in Chicago

Fig. 3 C. F. Murphy
Associates; Stanislaw
Gladych, designer,
Central District
Filtration Plant, 1000
East Ohio Street,
1952-64.

since 1934, the year that Graham, Anderson, Probst and White completed the Field Building on LaSalle Street. Daley, then County Clerk (and less than a year away from his election as mayor of Chicago), identified with Murphy, a down-to-earth Irishman who had preceded him at De La Salle Institute and did not strike Daley as a fancy-pants architect. Murphy was like Daley himself, a guy from "the Hall" who got things done. Years later, when the two men knew each other better, a persistent rumor had it that the mayor and Charles Murphy—who was almost a generation older—had gone to grammar school together. But the Daley-Murphy connection was purely a business, not a sentimental, relationship.

Murphy was a man who reinvented himself throughout his career, beginning in 1911 as a secretary to Ernest Graham at D. H. Burnham and Company, the firm that had dominated Chicago's commercial architecture since Daniel Burnham first entered into partnership with John Wellborn Root in 1873. Graham, like his mentor Burnham, understood that a reputation for quality design and efficient project management was good for business. Murphy stayed by Graham's side at Graham, Burnham and Com-

Fig. 4 Naess and
Murphy; Sigurd E.
Naess, designer, Chicago
Sun-Times Building, 401
North Wabash Avenue,
1957.

Figs. 5, 6   C. F. Murphy Associates; Otto Stark, designer, Blue Cross–Blue Shield Building, 55 West Wacker Drive, 1968.

pany, a partnership formed with two of Burnham's sons after their father's death in 1912, and he was with him again in 1917 for the creation of Graham, Anderson, Probst and White. For the following two decades, Murphy helped Graham manage the inner workings of one of the most prolific architectural firms in the United States. Peirce Anderson was the firm's chief designer until his death in 1924. When Ernest R. Graham died in 1936, Charles F. Murphy, the former stenographer, created Shaw, Naess and Murphy along with Graham, Anderson, Probst and White's chief designer, Alfred P. Shaw, and its planning expert, Sigurd E. Naess. Murphy retained Graham's model of corporate organization, which had traditionally given engineers and managers a strong hand. Shaw departed in 1946 to open his own office, and the firm of Naess and Murphy churned out its own brand of serviceable modernism. Sigurd Naess, a confident planner but an uncertain designer, often hired outside delineators to work off his plans. While Naess strengthened the firm's reputation

with buildings for Prudential Insurance (1952-55; see Rau, fig. 12), the Chicago Sun-Times (1957; fig. 4), and the addition to the Federal Reserve Bank (1957), Murphy watched passively as his competitors, Skidmore, Owings and Merrill (SOM), and the Office of Mies van der Rohe, did better and more elegant work.

In 1959, with Naess safely in retirement and with Stanislaw Gladych, who had come over to Murphy after a fight with Walter Netsch at SOM, installed as chief of design, the firm of C. F. Murphy Associates began to change. Charles F. Murphy, Jr., who took a greater role in the 1960s, recognized that it was not enough just to get and manage large-scale work. A contemporary architectural business needed to attract designers with unusual talent and let them take the lead. An admirer of Mies, it was the younger Murphy who helped the firm on its present course. Beginning with Gladych, and using as a lure the firm's uncanny success at getting high-profile public commissions, C. F. Murphy Associates employed a succession of talented architects.

Fig. 7   C. F. Murphy
Associates; Gene
Summers, partner-in-
charge, assisted by
Helmut Jahn,
McCormick Place, South
Lake Shore Drive at 23rd
Street, 1967-71.

Fig. 8   C. F. Murphy
Associates; Gene
Summers, partner-in-
charge, assisted by
Helmut Jahn,
Perspective view of the
interior of the Exposition
Center at McCormick
Place, delineated by
Helmut Jacoby, 1969
(cat. no. 155).

Gladych led the team responsible for the Central District Filtration Plant, the O'Hare International Airport Terminals, the J. Edgar Hoover Building in Washington (1974), and, with Jim Ferris, the sunken plaza (1969-72) adjacent to the First National Bank Building (1964-69). The eccentric Otto Stark designed the brutalist Blue Cross-Blue Shield Building (1968; figs. 5, 6), and Jacques Brownson was responsible for the final form of the Civic Center (1965; see Miller, "City Hall," fig. 1), renamed the Daley Center after the mayor's death in 1976.

At the time of the McCormick Place fire, C. F. Murphy Associates had firmly established itself as one of the city's premier firms. But Charles F. Murphy was not in great shape when he took Mayor Daley's call. For the first time in years he was without a seasoned architect in charge of design. The natural choice to take the lead, Jacques Brownson, had committed himself to teach at the University of Michigan. With the city's most coveted architectural commission in hand, the Murphys needed someone who could, with distinction, get the work done. They went to the top for advice. Mies, who was the city's aging architectural pharaoh, recommended his old assistant Gene Summers. C. F. Murphy Associates quickly made Summers a partner and got his young employee, Helmut Jahn, as a bonus. Three years and three complicated schemes later, a new and widely praised McCormick Place On-the-Lake (1967-71; figs. 7, 8) was completed. Before Summers left the firm in 1973 for California, he had become partner in charge of

design and had supervised Thomas Beeby and Hans Neumann's work on Malcolm X College (1971) and John M. Novack's design of the Cook County Juvenile Center (1973).

The rebuilding of McCormick Place proved to be a critical experience for Helmut Jahn. For three years he worked with Summers in the same close way that the older architect had apprenticed with Mies van der Rohe. This was a laboratory for the rigorous technical education that Jahn had received in Munich and relearned at IIT. Jahn observed Summers closely as the rigid Miesian struggled to express himself. Recalling that time, Jahn says, "Gene, in all his jobs, changed something. Originally, he wanted the Rehabilitation Institute [1974] yellow. He turned the mullions the other way in Malcolm X. He wanted the change more in the detail, not in the big concept."[1]

Helmut Jahn encountered the Miesian absolute on that job through Gene Summers. All the mastery was there in one of Mies's star pupils, but there was also a certain paralysis in trying too hard to do things right. For the young Jahn, who sometimes stayed all night at the job working on a new problem or looking at plans of older buildings he admired, McCormick Place was his graduate school. "I learned much at that time from Gene, because working on this project we did a lot of talking," Jahn notes. "He told

1.   All quotations in this essay are drawn from an interview with Helmut Jahn, Aug. 27, 1992.

me about Mies and showed me things. It was an attitude about how you worked, because I was the next generation."

This tutorial liberated Jahn from orthodoxy, while providing him with a rigorous architectural method. He soon broke with Summers over a detail on a project in New York. Jahn had made a corner of a building round; his boss insisted that he square it off. Summers left C. F. Murphy shortly thereafter, and in 1973 Jahn became the firm's director of planning and design. He quickly made his reputation with the Kemper Arena in Kansas City (1973-74), the Michigan City, Indiana, Public Library (1974-77), St. Mary's Athletic Facility in South Bend, Indiana (1976-77), the De La Garza Career Center in East Chicago, Indiana (1975-81), and the Chicago Area 2 Police Headquarters (1977-82). Using color, rounded corners, steep-angled roofs, expressive details, and exposed structure and mechanicals, he altered Miesian details to transform the "big concept." Within the framework of C. F. Murphy's bread-and-butter civic commissions of the 1970s, Jahn methodically renewed the firm and established his own reputation.

In the previous century, Daniel Burnham put his name ahead of John Wellborn Root's and molded that partnership around the power of a single designer. Taking his lead from Burnham, in what amounted to a classic 1980s-style leveraged buyout, Jahn purchased the Murphy firm without cash in 1983, and he stopped the revolving door that had seen a succession of gifted designers work briefly and leave without making

an enduring impression. Jahn shrank the old Murphy firm from 350 people to half that number, while SOM bloated to over a thousand. In addition, he got rid of the bureaucratic baronies that divided design from production. By 1983, when Jahn was the president and CEO of the new Murphy/Jahn, he had disbanded the engineering department and put architects in charge of all projects. He was, in effect, returning to the earlier Burnham and Root model. Jahn remembers: "My perception of the firm when I entered was that it was too corporate; the people were not acting together to get the job done so much as each had their own compartment. Too many people, too many responsibilities. Things didn't go right." So Jahn reorganized the office to make architects more responsible for management and design decisions. "Some architects are more management-oriented, others are more design-oriented," he adds. The purpose was "not to interchange these people to make a manager a better designer or a designer a better manager, but [to create] building teams so they get the necessary support to support each other. Each one can do best what they like."

Helmut Jahn became a headliner, the leading man of architecture to Philip Johnson's *éminence grise*. Other chief designers in huge firms, like Bruce Graham at SOM, who had done Inland Steel (1954-58; see Miller, "City Hall," fig. 16), the John Hancock Center (1965-69; pls. 46-47), and Sears Tower (1968-74; pls. 49-50) in relative anonymity outside the insular world of architecture, looked on in amazement. Jahn was

getting noticed by a certain sleight of hand. With his German accent—the everyday reminder of Miesian rigor—his Armani suits, and his Euro hats, Jahn was the perfect architect for the 1980s. Just in time for the last American building boom, he added glamour to corporate architecture, combining the mystery of the individual artist-practitioner with the resources of a rich, politically connected corporation. His method was in evidence in his first skyscraper, a concrete speculative office building in the middle of Chicago's Loop. Instead of playing the fashionable game of putting a John Portman atrium inside an undistinguished box, like an adjacent building by Bruce Graham, Jahn disguised the box by wrapping it in a sleek glass-and-anodized-aluminum skin. A cross between Erich Mendelsohn and Louis Sullivan, the Xerox Centre (1977-80; fig. 1) elegantly turned the corner, concealing the banality of the offices inside while extroverting the image of European sophistication—a la Mendelsohn—and the most optimistic period of American commerce, represented by Sullivan's Carson, Pirie, Scott Store. Distinguishing a client's stack of downtown square footage from his competitor's became the architect's main calling. Murphy/Jahn's work of the decade, including One and Two Liberty Place in Philadelphia (1987, 1981), the Northwestern Atrium Center in Chicago (1979-87), New York's 425 and 750 Lexington Avenue (1989), the Messe Frankfurt Convention Center in Germany (1984-91; see Zukowsky, fig. 21), and the new 120 North LaSalle Street Building (1990-92; fig. 9), is the physical manifestation of the firm's eclectic approach to design.

Almost a generation after the McCormick Place fire and the Murphy-Daley alliance, the office, now firmly under Helmut Jahn's control, had another shot at a critically important Chicago building. And while the characters had changed, the large ambitions of the players were familiar. The State of Illinois Building (1979-85; pls. 31-34) would anchor the North Loop Redevelopment, an ambitious thirty-acre rebuilding project for the Central Business District. Governor James Thompson hired the nation's most flamboyant architect to design, with public money, a worthy counterpart to the classicism of Holabird and Roche's City Hall and County Building (1911) and the strict modernism of Brownson's Civic Center across Randolph Street.

Jahn obliged Governor Thompson by reconceiving the nature of public building, scooping out the core and leaving the largest possible open space at the center. Pot-bellied glass and metal, the building waddles right up to the property line except for a tiny triangular plaza to mark the entrance. As with Graham, Anderson, Probst and White's Merchandise Mart for Marshall Field, which opened its doors in time for the Great Depression and quickly went bankrupt, the architect's genius is unrestrained by practicalities. Like his predecessors Graham and Murphy, Jahn overreached.

Ambitious architects with many opportunities to build often expose themselves to public risks. In the nauseating colors of every 1950s suburban high school, Jahn created the State of Illinois Building, where workers baked in summer and froze in winter until the problems were partially corrected. The brilliance of the form is subverted by the mad ecology of the huge unsheltered spaces, happily gorging on an endless diet of electricity. No one has yet been able to get a decent accounting of the cost overruns and yearly operating expenses. Nonetheless, the architecture of glassed offices and universal surveillance remains profoundly optimistic. Everyone can watch one another from the glass-walled fun-house elevators that open on an atrium in the tapering shape of an observatory dome. The building sits in downtown Chicago like a spaceship awaiting its orders to return home. The governor, like Marshall Field, got more architecture than he bargained for.

But this hunger for the new, no matter what the price, accompanies the drive to build. Sometimes it works out perfectly. The United Airlines Terminal at O'Hare (1983-87; pls. 19-21) pushes Chicago's identity as a railroad town to an extreme. Jahn combines the Crystal Palace glorification of the railroad shed with the more prosaic reality of the jetway. At the United Airlines Terminal, the circulation is the architecture. The architect recognizes that travel in America today is not arrival but constant passage. As he did in the State of Illinois Building, Jahn frees the work to express fantasy along with utility. Architecture, not just building.

Burnham joined with Root in 1873, beginning a 120-year succession of designers—a constant passage from Anderson to Naess to Gladych, then to Stark, Brownson, Beeby, and Summers, and finally to Helmut Jahn. Over six generations through all of their various identities, these architects inherited a legacy that they, in turn, helped shape and redefine. In the modern development of the city their spirit of innovation and fantasy has never been far from the utility of Chicago's design tradition.

Fig. 9   Murphy/Jahn, 120 North LaSalle Street Building, 1990-92, detail of exterior.

Chicago Architects: Genealogy and Exegesis

Stanley Tigerman

The genealogical document that accompanies this essay has evolved almost continuously since the early 1980s.[1] It is important to understand that the architects included in this genealogy, singly and collectively, determine representatively, rather than all-inclusively, Chicago's architectural tradition from its beginnings to the present. Architects have been included on the basis of their visibility through their built work, historical documentation, publications, design awards, professional influence, and so forth. Certain practitioners were also added when it was clear that their architectural firm begot succeeding individual or collaborative practices of consequence, or even significantly sized—and influential—architectural organizations. Other than serving the obvious function of fleshing out Chicago's architectural evolution, the purpose of developing this genealogical document (as of this essay) is to ascertain the connective tissues of Chicago's architectural life, in order to delineate sequentially the impact of employment on the formal, functional, and social characteristics of what has clearly become, over time, the city's premier art form.

Because the breadth of Chicago's entire sociocultural tradition is so intertwined with its architecture, a number of time-lines have been introduced horizontally into the vertical design of this genealogical chart so that one can better understand the impact that significant events have had, at these intersections, upon the city's architecture. Events such as the Great Chicago Fire of October 1871, the 1893 World's Columbian Exposition, the 1922 Chicago Tribune tower competition, the 1933-34 Century of Progress Exposition, the end of World War II in 1945, and, finally, the death of Ludwig Mies van der Rohe in 1969—however different they may be on any other scale of comparison—are all particularly seminal, especially in light of their connection with the inexorableness of this otherwise apolitical genealogical advance.

While this essay is delimited by the time-line established for the present volume (and the exhibition it accompanies), with its focus on Chicago architecture from 1923 to 1993, the genealogical origins antedating it are significant, and they relate directly to the earlier, companion volume on Chicago architecture from 1872 to 1922 (and, naturally the exhibition it accompanied).[2] The intention to interrelate architects and the kinds of buildings that they design has been largely guided by information about "who worked for whom" and, of course, "who worked when." Together these two guiding principles require that one move vertically through the two halves of the genealogy that represent the periods covered by the two exhibitions, as well as oscillate laterally across the accompanying genealogical charts, so that one may come to appreciate the natural complexity of Chicago's temporal and sequential liaisons as they influence practitioners formally, functionally, socially, and in other ways.

If this architectural genealogy were to become the first of a series of similar efforts throughout the United States, it would not be without reason. Chicago is not only arguably the most "modern" city in America, but also one which those practitioners who have come here from far and wide—with few exceptions—never leave. Their continuation in Chicago makes this particular genealogy both complex and hermetic. Its benefactors not only result from progenitors (in the biblical sense that "Abraham begot Isaac who begot...."), but also from those new figures who arrived all the time. The Chicago fire, the two major World's Fairs, and the two World Wars all brought their share of architects to Chicago to live and to work. Perhaps seeking more direct influence, young architects have come here for the express purpose of working and/or studying with another, more established mentor: Frank Lloyd Wright (who worked for Louis Sullivan); David Adler (Howard Van Doren Shaw); Reginald Malcolmson, Daniel Brenner, Gene Summers, and others (Ludwig Mies van der Rohe); Bruce Graham and Joseph Passonneau (Holabird and Root and Burgee); Laurence Booth and James Nagle (Stanley Tigerman); Tannys Langdon and Thomas Rajkovitch (Thomas Beeby); and further examples too numerous to mention.

Continued on page 322

Fig. 1 Aerial view of Chicago, looking south, 1990.

311

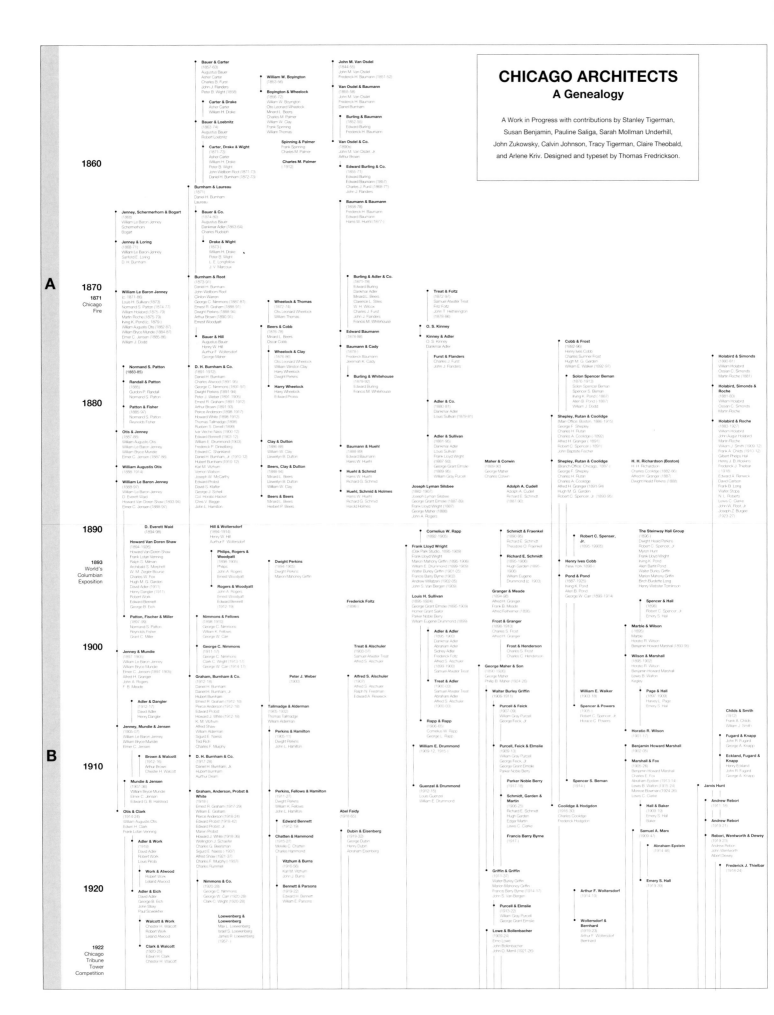

1922
Chicago Tribune Tower Competition

1930

1933
Century of Progress Exposition

C

1940

1945
World War II Ends

1950

1960

1969
Death of Mies van der Rohe

1970

D

1980

1990

Stockade Building System & 4-D Co.
(1922-32)
Buckminster Fuller

General Houses, Inc.
(1928-40)
Howard T. Fisher
Lawrence Perkins
Paul Schweikher

Howard T. Fisher & Associates
(1928-64)

Schweikher & Lamb
(1933-45)
Paul Schweikher
Theodore W. Lamb

Mundie, Jensen, Bourke & Havens
(1936-44)
William Bryce Mundie
Elmer C. Jensen
Bourke
George Havens

Winston Elting
(1937-41)

William F. Deknatel
(1937-60)
William F. Deknatel
Myron Goldsmith (1941)
Geraldine Eager

Mundie & Jensen
(1944-46)
William Bryce Mundie
Elmer C. Jensen

Jensen & McClurg
(1946-)
Elmer C. Jensen
Verne O. McClurg

William Bryce Mundie
(1946-)

Schweikher & Elting
(1945-53)
Paul Schweikher
Winston Elting
Edward H. Bennett
Ralph Rapson
I. W. Colburn
Edward D. Dart (1949-51)

Barancik Conte & Associates
(1950)
Richard Barancik
Richard Conte

I. W. Colburn & Associates
(1955-)
I. W. Colburn
Edward Noonan

Paul Schweikher
(1953-70)
Ralph Rapson
Hanno Weber

Elting & Bennett
(1953-56)
Winston Elting
Edward H. Bennett

Edward H. Bennett
(1956-)

Winston Elting
(1956-60)

Elting, Deknatel & Associates
(1960-61)
Winston Elting
William F. Deknatel

Wendell Campbell & Associates
(1966)

Sisco/Lubotsky Associates
(1975-77)
Gene Sisco
Robert Lubotsky
Andrew Metter (1977)

Sisco, Lubotsky & Stuart Cohen
(1977-81)
Gene Sisco
Robert Lubotsky
Stuart Cohen
James Law
Andrew Metter (1977-81)
Anders Nereim (1978-81)
Kathryn Quinn (1979-81)

Cohen & Nereim
(1981-88)
Stuart Cohen
Anders Nereim
Christopher Rudolph (1981-83)
Karen Johnson (1986)
Julie Hacker (1986-88)

Christopher H. Rudolph & Associates
(1983-)
Christopher H. Rudolph
Thomas N. Rajkovich (1983-84)

Sisco/Lubotsky Associates
(1981-84)
Gene Sisco
Robert Lubotsky
Andrew Metter (1981-84)
James Law (1981-84)

Lubotsky, Metter, Worthington & Law
(1984-86)
Robert Lubotsky
Andrew Metter
Wayne Worthington
James Law

Stuart Cohen & Associates
(1988-91)
Stuart Cohen
Julie Hacker (1988-91)

Anders Nereim
(1988-)

Stuart Cohen & Julie Hacker
(1991-)
Stuart Cohen
Julie Hacker

Nimmons, Carr & Wright
(1928-47)
George C. Nimmons
George W. Carr
Clark C. Wright

Burnham Brothers
(1928-33)
Daniel H. Burnham, Jr.
Hubert Burnham
Paul McCurry (1929-30)
Nathaniel Owings (1929-33)
Louis Skidmore (1930-33)

Burnham & Hammond
(1933-)
Daniel H. Burnham, Jr.
Hubert Burnham
Charles Herrick Hammond
Nathaniel Owings (1933-34)
Louis Skidmore (1933-)

Shaw, Naess & Murphy
(1937-46)
Alfred Shaw
Sigurd E. Naess
Charles F. Murphy

Bertrand Goldberg & Associates
(1937-)
Bertrand Goldberg
Gilmer Vardiman Black
(1938-61)
Floyd Magnuson (1955-)

Huszagh & Hill
Ralph Huszagh
Boyd Hill

Boyd Hill

Loebl Schlossman
(1925-46)
Jerrold Loebl
Norman J. Schlossman

Carr & Wright
(1947-)
George W. Carr
Clark C. Wright

Edward D. Dart
(1951-65)

Loebl Schlossman & Bennett
(1946-65)
Jerrold Loebl
Norman J. Schlossman
John I. Schlossman
Richard M. Bennett
Edward D. Dart
Marvin Fitch (1946-51)
Donald A. Schiller (1948-51)

Fitch, Schiller & Frank
(1951-57)
Marvin Fitch
Donald A. Schiller
Burton H. Frank

Schiller & Frank
(1957-)
Donald A. Schiller
Burton H. Frank

Fridstein & Fitch
(1957-69)
Robert B. Fridstein
Marvin Fitch
Wojciech Madeyski
(1966-68)

Loebl, Schlossman, Bennett & Dart
(1965-75)
Jerrold Loebl
John I. Schlossman
Richard M. Bennett
Edward D. Dart
David Swan (1968-70)
Philip Johnson (1973-75)

Alfred Shaw & Associates
(1966-69)

Shaw & Associates
Alfred Shaw (1969-70)
Patrick Shaw

Fitch, Larocca, Carington & Jones
(1973-)
Marvin Fitch
Frank L. Larocca
Robert W. Carington
E. Erie Jones

Loebl, Schlossman, Dart & Hackl
(1975-76)
Jerrold Loebl
John I. Schlossman
Edward D. Dart
Donald J. Hackl
Philip Johnson (1975-76)

Loebl, Schlossman & Hackl
(1976-)
Jerrold Loebl
John I. Schlossman
Donald J. Hackl
Lawrence Dieckman
Howard Decker (1977-78)
Philip Johnson (1976-78)
Steven Wright
Wojciech Lesnikowski (1988-)

Loewenberg/Fitch Partnership
James R. Loewenberg
Marvin Fitch

Johnson & Lee
(1983)
Philip Johnson
Chris Lee

William R. Hasbrouck
(1976-86)

Hasbrouck, Peterson Associates
(1986-1991)
William R. Hasbrouck
James M. Peterson
Grittip Sirattumrong

Hasbrouck, Peterson, Zimochi & Sirirattumrong
(1991-)
William R. Hasbrouck
James M. Peterson
Henry Zimoch
Grittip Sirattumrong

Voy Madeyski Architects
(1987-)
Wojciech Madeyski

Richard A. M. Potokar
(1987)

Talmadge & Watson
(1932-)
Thomas Talmadge
Vernon Watson
Paul McCurry (1926-28)

Bennett, Parsons & Frost
(1922-27)
Edward H. Bennett
Harry T. Frost

Bennett & Parsons
(1927-38)
Edward H. Bennett
William E. Parsons

Perkins, Chatten & Hammond
(1927-35)
Dwight Perkins
Melville Clark Chatten
Charles Herrick Hammond

Perkins, Wheeler & Will
(1936-44)
Lawrence Perkins
E. Todd Wheeler
Philip Will, Jr.
James W. Hammond (1939-40)

Shaw, Metz & Dolio
(1947-59)
Alfred Shaw
Karl Metz
John Dolio

C. F. Murphy Associates
(1947-81)
Charles F. Murphy
Stanislaw Gladych
Charles Rummel (1947-67)
Carter Manny (1948-)
Y. C. Wong (1958)
Jacques Brownson (1959-66)
John Hartray, Jr. (1959-61)
Andrew Heard (1964-65)
Hans Neumann (1965-)
Thomas H. Beeby (1965-71)
Gerald Horn (1966-68)
Gene Summers (1967-73)
Helmut Jahn (1967-81)
Wojciech Madeyski (1968-76)
Ronald W. Krueck (1970-71)
Keith Olsen
Peter Frisbee (1977-80)
Suzanne Underwood
Howard Decker (1978-80)
Chris Lee (1979-81)
Otto Stark
James J. Belli

Perkins & Will
(1944-)
Lawrence Perkins
Philip Will, Jr.
Hans P. Neumann
Wilmont Vickrey (1951-69)
C. W. Brubaker
Philip Kupritz (1966-62)
Neil Frankel
J. Jeffrey Conroy
Garrett Eakin (1974-78)
Wojciech Madeyski (1976-)
Martin F. Wolf
Ralph Johnson (1976-)
Richard Potokar (1979-82)
Andrew Metter (1986-89)

Milton M. Schwartz
Milton M. Schwartz
Neil Frankel
Floyd Magnuson
Stanley Tigerman (1956-57)
Arthur Myrhum (1950s)

Shaw, Metz & Associates
(1959-66)
Alfred Shaw
Karl Metz

John Dolio Mechanical Engineers
(1959-)

Metz & Train
(1966-67)
Karl Metz
Jack Train

Metz, Train, Olsen & Youngren
(1967-74)
Karl Metz
Jack Train
Ronald Olson
Ralph Youngren
Lonn Frye

Andrew Heard & Associates
(1967-)

Philip Kupritz & Associates
(1967-)

Vickrey Ovresat Awsumb
(1969-)
Wilmont Vikrey
Raymond Ovresat
John Awsumb

Metz, Train & Youngren
(1974-82)
Karl Metz
Jack Train
Ralph Youngren

Hinds, Schroeder & Whitaker
(1978-82)
George Hinds
Kenneth Schroeder
Richard Whitaker
John M. Syvertson
(1976-77)
George Pappageorge
(1979-81)
David Haymes
(1979-81)

Jack Train & Associates
(1982-)

Murphy/Jahn
(1981-)
Charles F. Murphy
Carter Manny
Helmut Jahn
Philip Castillo (1978-)
John C. Lahey (-1986)
James Goettsch (-1988)
Dennis Recek (-1989)
Chris Lee (1981-83)
Rainer Schildnicht
Martin F. Wolf

Kenneth Schroeder & Associates
(1982-88)

Schroeder Murchie Laya & Associates
(1988-)
Kenneth Schroeder
Jack Murchie
Richard J. Laya

McNally & Quinn
(1922-)
Frank McNally
James Quinn
Lewis C. Clarke
Benjamin Howard Marshall
Lawrence E. McConville
Carl Sterner
B. G. Greengard
John Story
George A. Hossack
George Eigh
A. G. Lehman
J. M. Bryant
J. J. Silverman

Hamilton, Fellows & Nedved
(1926-34)
John L. Hamilton
William K. Fellows
R. J. Nedved

Holsman & Holsman
(1928)
Henry K. Holsman
William Holsman

Klekamp & Whitmore
Bernard R. Klekamp
Whitmore

Holsman, Holsman, Klekamp, & Taylor
(1928-53)
Henry K. Hasman
William Holsman
John Holsman
Bernard R. Klekamp
Darl Coder Taylor

Dubin & Dubin
(1932-62)
Henry Dubin
Arthur D. Dubin
Martin D. Dubin

Alschuler & Friedman
(1940-46)
Alfred S. Alschuler, Jr.
Ralph N. Friedman

Alfred Caldwell
(1944-59)

A. James Speyer
(1946-)
A. James Speyer
William E. Dunlap

Friedman, Alschuler & Sincere & Grunsfeld
(1946-)
Ralph N. Friedman
Alfred S. Alschuler, Jr.
Sincere
Ernest A. Grunsfeld, Jr.
(1946-55)

Holsman & Co.
(1953-)
William Holsman
John Holsman

Bernard R. Klekamp
(1953-)

Coder Taylor Architects
(1960-)

Schipporheit & Heinrich
(1965-70)
George Schipporheit
John Heinrich

Dubin, Dubin, Black & Moutoussamy
(1963-)
Arthur D. Dubin
Martin D. Dubin
John Black
John Moutoussamy

Gelick Foran & Associates
(1969-)
Michael Gelick
Walter J. Foran
John W. Clark (1982)

George Schipporheit
(1970-)

Dubin, Dubin & Moutoussamy
(1978-)
Arthur D. Dubin
Martin D. Dubin
John Moutoussamy
Henry Zimoch

Pappageorge/Haymes Ltd.
(1981-)
George Pappageorge
David Haymes
James Plunkard (1984-86)
Ray Hartshorne (1984-86)

Hartshorne Plunkard
(1987-)
Ray Hartshorne
James Plunkard
Karen Hollander (1987-88)

Douglas A. Garafolo
(1987-)

Valerio Associates
(1987-)
Joseph Valerio

Morris Erie Myers
(1992-)
John Morris
Florence Erie Krieger
Sherrill Myers

Klaber & Grunsfeld
(1924-29)
Eugene H. Klaber
Ernest A. Grunsfeld, Jr.

Frank Lloyd Wright
(Taliesin West, 1925-59)
Frank Lloyd Wright
William F. Deknatel
Geraldine Eager

Eugene H. Klaber
(1929-39)

Ernest A. Grunsfeld, Jr.
(1929-39)

Klaber Homsey
(1942-44)
Eugene H. Klaber
Victorine Homsey

Eugene H. Klaber
(1944-)

Grunsfeld, Yerkes & Koening
(1939-46)
Ernest A. Grunsfeld, Jr.
Yerkes
Koening

Grunsfeld & Associates
(1956-)
Ernest A. Grunsfeld, Jr. (d. 1970)
Ernest A. Grunsfeld III

Ernest A. Grunsfeld

Belli & Belli
(1941-72)
Edo J. Belli (1941-1972)
Anthony Belli (1941-72)
Allen J. Belli (1965-72)
James J. Belli (1971-72)

The Office Of Mies Van Der Rohe
(1938-69)
Mies Van Der Rohe
John Heinrich
George Danforth (1939-44)
Ludwig Karl Hilbersheimer
Alfred Caldwell (1944-59)
Joseph Fujikawa (1945-69)
Myron Goldsmith (1946-53)
Reginald Malcomson (1947)
Daniel Brenner (1947-51)
Gene Summers (1950-66)
Y. C. Wong (1950 & 52-57)
David Haid (1951-60)
Peter Carter
William M. Drake, Jr.
George Schipporheit (1957-60)
William E. Dunlap (1958-60)
Jacques Brownson
Jack Bowman (1958-69)
Arthur Salzman (1960-69)
Dirk Lohan (1960-69)
Roy Kruse (1961)
Arthur Takeuchi
Charles Booher Genther
David Fix
A. James Speyer
Phyllis Lambert (-1965)
Rainer Schildnicht
Edward Duckett
Joe Burnett

Brenner & Turck
(1958-61)
Daniel Brenner
Dorothy Turck

Brenner Danforth Rockwell
(1961-69)
Daniel Brenner
George Danforth
H. P. Davis Rockwell
John Vinci (1961-69)
John C. Lahey

David Haid & Associates
(1963-)

Phyllis Lambert
(1965-72)
Phyllis Lambert
David Fix

O'Donnell, Wicklund & Pigozzi
Lawrence J. O'Donnell
Leonard S. Wicklund
Raymond A. Pigozzi

Fujikawa, Conterato, Lohan & Associates
(1969-82)
Joseph Fujikawa
Bruno Conterato
Dirk Lohan
Jack Bowman (1969-82)
Arthur Salzman (1969-82)
Gerald L. Johnson

Roy Kruse
(1972-)

Belli & Belli
(1972-)
Allen J. Belli (1972-)
James J. Belli (1972-)
Edo J. Belli (1972-)
Anthony Belli (1972-78)

Fujikawa, Johnson & Associates
(1982-)
Joseph Fujikawa
Gerald L. Johnson

Lohan Associates
(1982-)
Dirk Lohan
Jack Bowman (1982-)
Arthur Salzman (1982-1991)
Kathleen Hess (1985)

Arthur Salzman
(1991-)
Albert Salzman
Gilbert Gorski (-1989)

Gilbert Gorski
(1989)

O'Donnell, Wicklund, Pigozzi & Peterson
(1987-)
Lawrence J. O'Donnell
Leonard S. Wicklund
Raymond A. Pigozzi
Leonard A. Peterson
John Macsai (1991-)
John Syvertsen (1992-)

Daniel Wheeler Architects
(1987-89)
Daniel Wheeler
Lawrence Kearns

Wheeler Kearns
(1989-)
Daniel Wheeler
Lawrence Kearns

Legge Kemp
(1989-)
Diane Legge Kemp

George Grant Elmslie
(1922-30)

Granger, Lowe & Bollenbacher
(1924-26)
Alfred H. Granger
Elmo Lowe
John Bollenbacher
John O. Merrill (1924-26)
Paul Schweikher

Phillip B. Maher
(1926-75)
Philip B. Maher
Paul Schweikher (1930-33)

Schmidt, Garden & Erikson
(1926-)
Richard E. Schmidt
Hugh Garden
Carl Erikson
Vale Faro
Albert Bacci
Paul McCurry
(1945-76)
William E. Drummond
Dennis Recek
Richard Yoshiro Mine

Granger & Bollenbacher
(1926-39)
Alfred H. Granger
John Bollenbacher
John O. Merrill (1926-39)
Winston Elting (1934)
Frank Lotan Venning

Lewis C. Cordogan
(1951-84)
Lewis C. Cordogan
John G. Cordogan

Harry Weese & Associates
(1947-)
Harry Weese
Ezra Gordon (1954-61)
Hans P. Neumann (1954-64)
Ben Weese (1959-77)
John Buenz (1960-61)
John Hartray, Jr. (1961-76)
Stanley Tigerman (1961-62)
Thomas Hickey
Stanley Allen (1964-)
Peter Landon
William B. Bauhs (1965-74)
William Dring
Cynthia Weese (1973-75)
Frederick Phillips (1974-75)
William McBride (1980-81)
Kathryn Quinn (1977-79)
William Ketcham

Hausner & Macsai
(1955-70)
Robert O. Hausner
John Macsai

Arthur Takeuchi
(1965-)

Bauhs & Dring
(1974-)
William Bauhs
William Dring

Frederick Phillips & Associates
(1976-)

Campbell & Macsai
(1970-74)
Wendell Campbell
John Macsai
William Brazley, Jr. (1968-70)

Cynthia Weese
(1975-77)

Weese Seegers Hickey Weese
(1977-82)
Ben Weese
Arnold Seegers
Thomas Hickey
Cynthia Weese

Weese Hickey Weese
(1982-89)
Ben Weese
Thomas Hickey
Cynthia Weese
Peter Landon

Weese Langley Weese
Ben Weese
Dennis Langley
Cynthia Weese

Vinci Kenney Architects
(1970-77)
John Vinci
Lawrence C. Kenney

Eva Maddox Associates
(1975-)
Eva Maddox
Patrick Grzybek
Eileen Jones

Margaret I. McCurry
(1977-82)

The Office of John Vinci
(1978-)

Banks/Eakin Architects
John Banks
Garret Eakin

Florian Wierzbowski
(1983-)
Paul Florian
Stephen Wierzbowski
Jordan Mozer (1983-84)

Jordan Mozer & Associates
(1984-)

John Macsai & Associates
(1975-91)

Cordogan, Clark
(1984-)
John G. Cordogan
John W. Clark

Peter Landon Architects
(1987-)

DeStefano/Goettsch
(1988-91)
James R. DeStefano
James Goettsch

DeStefano & Partners
(1991-)
James R. DeStefano

Goettsch Associates
(1991)
James Goettsch
Nada Andric

Pond & Pond, Martin & Lloyd
(1925-31)
Irving K. Pond
Allen B. Pond
Edgar Martin
Alfred Lloyd

Pond & Pond & Martin
(1931-)
Irving K. Pond
Allen B. Pond
Edgar Martin

L. Morgan Yost
(1932-52)
L. Morgan Yost
Walter Netsch (1946-47)
Lewis B. Walton, Jr.
(1950-51)

Skidmore & Owings
(1936-39)
Louis Skidmore
Nathaniel Owings
John Weese (1936-39)
Ambrose Richardson (1937-39)

Skidmore, Owings & Merrill
(1939-)
Louis Skidmore
Nathaniel Owings (d. 1984)
John O. Merrill
John Weese (1939-)
Ambrose Richardson (1939-41, 1945-51)
Charles Booher Genther (1942-43)
Nathalie Dublois (1945-74)
James W. Hammond (1946-61)
Peter Roesch
Walter Netsch (1947-79)
Harry Weese (1946-47)
John Macsai (1950-53)
Joseph Passonneau (1950-52)
Bruce J. Graham (1950-90)
Robertson Ward, Jr. (1950-62)
Ralph Youngren (1950-67)
William Dunlap (1951-68)
Y. C. Wong (1951)
Stanley Allen (1955-62)
Myron Goldsmith (1955-83)
John Hartray, Jr. (1956-57)
George Schipporheit (1956)
Rainer Schildnicht
Stanley Tigerman (1957-61)
George Larson (1958-67, 1970-78)
Donald Powell
Arthur Takeuchi (1959-63)
San Utsonomiya
Edward Duckett
Donald Powell
Robert Kleinschmidt
Edward Dart
Fazlur R. Khan (1960-82)
John Vinci (1960)
Lucien LaGrange
Margaret I. McCurry (1966-1977)
Adrian D. Smith (1967-)
Gerald Horn (1968-71)
Gregory W. Landahl
Garrett Eakin (1973)
Joseph A. Gonzalez (1974-)
Stephen Wierzbowski (1975-81)
Kathleen Hess (1977-83)
Charles Fill (1977-79)
Lawrence E. Dieckmann
James R. Destefano (-1988)
William M. Drake, Jr.
Anders Nereim (1977-78)
Diane Legge Kemp (1977-89)
Hanno Weber (1980-84)
Daniel H. Wheeler (1981-87)
Kevin Kemp (1983-86)
Grittip Sirattomrong
Michel Mossessian (1987-92)
Nada Andric (1991-)

Yost & Taylor
(1952-60)
L. Morgan Yost
Darl Coder Taylor
Albert Bacci

Robertson Ward
(1962-75)

Hammond & Roesch
(1961-71)
James Hammond
Peter Roesch
James Mastro (1970-72)

Hammond Beeby & Associates
(1971-76)
James W. Hammond
Thomas Hall Beeby
Ronald Krueck (1971-76)
Keith Olsen

Hammond Beeby & Babka
(1977-)
James W. Hammond (d. 1986)
Thomas Hall Beeby
Bernard F. Babka
Phillip Castillo (1976-78)
Tannys Langdon (1978-87)
John W. Clark (1978-82)
Charles G. Young (1979-92)
Kathryn Quinn (1981-85)
Karen Johnson (1983-86)
Gary M. Ainge (1984-)
Dennis Rupert
John M. Syvertson
Thomas Rajkovich (1984-86)

Krueck & Olsen
(1978-91)
Ronald F. Krueck
Keith Olsen

Larson Associates
(1978-)
George Larson

Hanno Weber & Associates
(1984-)
Hanno Weber
Kathleen Hess (1985-)
Christopher Hale (1989-)

McBride & Kelly
(1984-)
William McBride
Jack Kelly

Lucien LaGrange & Associates
(1985-)

Quinn & Searle
(1986-90)
Kathryn Quinn
Linda Searle

Rajkovich & Mayernick
Thomas N. Rajkovich
David T. Mayernick

Krueck & Sexton
(1991-)
Ronald F. Krueck
Mark Sexton

Kathryn Quinn Architects
(1990-)

Linda Searle & Associates
(1990-)

John Syvertsen Architect
(1987-91)

Langdon & Woodhouse
(1987-91)
Tannys Langdon
David Woodhouse

Tannys Langdon & Associates
(1991-)

David Woodhouse & Associates
(1991-)

Benjamin Howard Marshall
(1926-)
Benjamin Howard Marshall
Lewis B. Walton (1926)

Marx, Flint & Schonne
(1947-)
Samuel A. Marx
Noel L. Flint
Charles W. Schonne

Walton & Kegley
(1938-51)
Lewis B. Walton
Lewis B. Walton, Jr.
Kegley

Keck & Faro
(1926-27)
George Fred Keck
Vale Faro

George Fred Keck
(1926-46)
George Fred Keck
Paul Schweikher (1930)
William Keck (1931-41)
Robert Bruce Tague (1935-37)
Ralph Rapson (1942-46)

Keck & Keck
(1946-80)
George Fred Keck
William Keck
Robert Bruce Tague (1937-56)
Clarence Rudolph (1948-49)
Michael K. Young (1948-50)
John Buenz (1962-63)
Winston Elting
Stanley Tigerman (1948-49)
Jack Levin
Ezra Gordon
John Van Der Muelen

Tigerman, Rudolph & Young
(1949-50)
Stanley Tigerman
Clarence Rudolph
Michael K. Young

Michael K. Young & Associates

Rapson & Van Der Muelen
(1950-54)
Ralph Rapson
John Van Der Muelen

Gordon & Levin
(1961-)
Ezra Gordon
Jack Levin

Walton & Walton
(1952-)
Lewis B. Walton
Lewis B. Walton, Jr.

A. Epstein & Sons
(1946-)
Abraham Epstein
Raymond Epstein
Ralph J. Epstein
Sidney Epstein
William Brazley, Jr.
(1970-73)
Christopher Hale
(1987-89)
Andrew Metter (1990-)

Tigerman & Koglin
(1962-64)
Stanley Tigerman
Norman A. Koglin
Laurence O. Booth (1962-64)

Norman Koglin & Associates
(1964-)

Powell Kleinschmidt
Donald Powell
Robert Kleinschmidt

Stanley Tigerman & Associates
(1964-82)
Laurence O. Booth (1965-66)
James L. Nagle (1965-66)
Jack Murchie
Ralph Johnson (1971-72)
David Woodhouse (1975-79)
Robert Fugman
Deborah Doyle (1976-80)

Booth/Nagle
(1966-77)
Laurence O. Booth
James L. Nagle
Marvin Ullman (1969-74)
David Swan (1971-73)
Christopher Rudolph
(1974-77)
Phillip Castillo (1975-76)
Gene Sisco
Marvin Ullman
Robert Lubotsky

David Swan Architect
(1973-)

Booth, Nagle & Hartray
(1977-79)
Laurence O. Booth
James L. Nagle
Jack Hartray, Jr.
Richard A. M. Potokar
(1977-79)
Christopher Rudolph
(1977-79)
Darcy Bonner (1978-79)

William Brazley & Associates
(1978-)

Himmel Bonner Architects
(1979-)
Scott Himmel
Darcy R. Bonner, Jr.
Dirk Dennison

Dirk Dennison

Booth/Hansen & Associates
(1980-)
Laurence O. Booth
Paul Hansen
William Ketcham
David Woodhouse (1980-87)

Tigerman Fugman McCurry
(1982-88)
Stanley Tigerman
Robert Fugman
Margaret I. McCurry
Richard Dakich
Gary M. Ainge (1982-84)
James Plunkard
Carl Darr (1985-87)
John Holbert (1985-87)
Fred Wilson (1985-88)
Karen Hollander (1986-87)
Melany Telleen (1986-88)

Holbert Hollander
(1988-)
John Holbert
Karen Hollander

Dotson & Darr
(1988-)
David Dotson
Carl Darr

Tigerman McCurry
(1988-)
Stanley Tigerman
Margaret McCurry
Melany Telleen (1986-)
Paul Gates (1988-90)
Richard Dragisic (1988-)

Fugman Dakich & Associates
(1988-)
Robert Fugman
Richard Dakich

Thielbar & Fugard
(1925-41)
Frederick J. Thielbar
John R. Fugard

Hunt & Bohasseck
(1925-27)
Jarvis Hunt
Bohasseck

Rebori, Wentworth & Dewey
(1919-23)
Andrew Rebori
John Wentworth
Albert Dewey

Rebori, Wentworth, Dewey & McCormick
(1923-30)
Andrew Rebori
John Wentworth
Albert Dewey
Leander J. McCormick
Paul McCurry

Holabird & Root
(1927-48)
John W. Root, Jr.
Joseph Z. Burgee (1927-45)
Gilbert P. Hall
Lewis C. Clarke
Helmuth Bartch (1927)
Monroe Bowman (1927-29)
Irving Bowman
Paul D. McCurry (1930)
William C. Periera (1930-32)
Winston Elting (1932-33)
Charles B. Genther (1945)
Henry J. B. Hoskins
Frank B. Long
John S. Cromelin
David Carlson
Col. Horatio Hacket

William C. Periera

Luckman & Periera
(1930s)

The Bowman Brothers
(1929-36)
Irving Bowman
Monroe Bowman

Rebori & Wentworth
(1930)
Andrew Rebori
John Wentworth

Andrew Rebori
(1930-66)

Fugard, Olson, Urbain & Neiler
(1940s)
John R. Fugard
Olson
Leon F. Urbain
Neiler

Landahl Associates
Gregory Landahl

Holabird & Root & Burgee
(1948-)
John A. Holabird
John W. Root, Jr.
Joseph Z. Burgee
John Macsai (1949-50)
Bruce Graham (1949-50)
Richard Yoshiro Mine
Joseph Passonneau
(1949-50)
John Hartray, Jr. (1958-59)
Andrew Heard (1962-64)

Solomon Cordwell
(1957-63)
Louis R. Solomon
J. D. Cordwell

Solomon Cordwell Buenz
(1963-)
Louis R. Solomon (1963-71)
J. D. Cordwell
John Buenz

Holabird & Root
Gerald Horn (1971-)
Paul G. A. Florian (1978-81)
Thomas R. Welch
Roy J. Solfsburg
Bernard Bradley
Harry Manning
James Baird
John Z. Burgee

Greenberg & Finfer
Aubrey Greenberg
Mark Finfer

Aubrey Greenberg
Aubrey Greenberg
James Mastro
Claudia Skylar

Marvin Ullman Architects
(1974-88)
Marvin Ullman
Charles Fill (1979-88)

Mastro & Skylar
(1979-)
James Mastro
Claudia Skylar

Doyle & Associates
(1981-88)
Deborah Doyle

Doyle & Ohle
(1988-91)
Deborah Doyle
James L. Ohle

Doyle & Associates
(1991-)
Deborah Doyle

Nagle, Hartray & Associates
(1980-)
James L. Nagle
John Hartray, Jr.
Howard Decker (1980-86)
Linda Searle (1980-86)
Dirk Danker (1988-)
Howard A. Kagan
Donald McKay

Decker & Kemp
(1986-)
Howard Decker
Kevin Kemp

Newman/Lustig & Associates
Newman
Michael Lustig

Michael Lustig & Associates
(1987-)

Johnson & Rogatz
(1986-88)
Karen Scott Johnson
Janet Rogatz

Ullman & Fill
(1988-)
Marvin Ullman
Charles Fill

Johnson Rogatz Wilson
(1988-89)
Karen Scott Johnson
Janet Rogatz
Frederick H. Wilson

Johnson & Wilson
(1989-)
Karen Scott Johnson
Frederick H. Wilson

1860

1870

1871
Chicago
Fire

1880

1890

Bauer & Carter
(1857-63)
Augustus Bauer
Asher Carter
Charles B. Furst
John J. Flanders
Peter B. Wight (1858)

Carter & Drake
Asher Carter
William H. Drake

Bauer & Loebnitz
(1863-74)
Augustus Bauer
Robert Loebnitz

Carter, Drake & Wight
(1871-73)
Asher Carter
William H. Drake
Peter B. Wight
John Wellborn Root (1871-73)
Daniel H. Burnham (1872-73)

Burnham & Laureau
(1871)
Daniel H. Burnham
Laureau

Bauer & Co.
(1874-80)
Augustus Bauer
Dankmar Adler (1863-64)
Charles Rudolph

Drake & Wight
(1873-)
William H. Drake
Peter B. Wight
L. E. Longfellow
J. V. Marcoux

Burnham & Root
(1873-91)
Daniel H. Burnham
John Wellborn Root
Clinton Warren
George C. Nimmons (1887-81)
Ernest R. Graham (1888-91)
Dwight Perkins (1888-94)
Arthur Brown (1890-91)
Ernest Woodyatt

Bauer & Hill
Augustus Bauer
Henry W. Hill
Aurthur F. Woltersdorf
George Maher

D. H. Burnham & Co.
(1891-1912)
Daniel H. Burnham
Charles Atwood (1891-95)
George C. Nimmons (1891-97)
Dwight Perkins (1891-94)
Peter J. Weber (1891-1905)
Arthur Brown (1891-93)
Ernest R. Graham (1891-1912)
Peirce Anderson (1898-1917)
Howard White (1898-1912)
Thomas Tallmadge (1898)
Rueben S. Denell (1899)
Ivar Vieche-Nass (1900-12)
Edward Bennett (1903-12)
William E. Drummond (1903)
Frederick P. Dinkelberg
Edward C. Shankland
Daniel H. Burnham, Jr. (1910-12)
Hubert Burnham (1910-12)
Karl M. Vitzhum
Vernon Watson
Joseph W. McCarthy
Edward Probst
David S. Klafter
George J. Schell
Col. Horatio Hacket
Chris V. Bagge
John L. Hamilton

Jenney, Schermerhorn & Bogart
(1868)
William Le Baron Jenney
Schermerhorn
Bogart

Jenney & Loring
(1868-71)
William Le Baron Jenney
Sanford E. Loring
D. H. Burnham

William Le Baron Jenney
(c. 1871-86)
Louis H. Sullivan (1873)
Normand S. Patton (1874-77)
William Holabird (1875-79)
Martin Roche (1875-79)
Irving K. Pond (c. 1879-)
William Augustis Otis (1882-87)
William Bryce Mundie (1884-87)
Elmer C. Jensen (1885-86)
William J. Dodd

Normand S. Patton
(1883-85)

Randall & Patton
(1885)
Gurdon P. Randall
Normand S. Patton

Patton & Fisher
(1885-97)
Normand S. Patton
Reynolds Fisher

Otis & Jenney
(1887-88)
William Augustis Otis
William Le Baron Jenney
William Bryce Mundie
Elmer C. Jensen (1887-88)

William Augustis Otis
(1888-1914)

William Le Baron Jenney
(1888-97)
William Le Baron Jenney
D. Everett Waid
Howard Van Doren Shaw (1893-94)
Elmer C. Jensen (1888-97)

William W. Boyington
(1853-56)

Boyington & Wheelock
(1856-72)
William W. Boyington
Otis Leonard Wheelock
Minard L. Beers
Charles M. Palmer
William W. Clay
Frank Spinning
William Thomas

Spinning & Palmer
Frank Spinning
Charles M. Palmer

Charles M. Palmer
(-1912)

Wheelock & Thomas
(1872-74)
Otis Leonard Wheelock
William Thomas

Beers & Cobb
(1876-78)
Minard L. Beers
Oscar Cobb

Wheelock & Clay
(1876-86)
Otis Leonard Wheelock
William Winston Clay
Harry Wheelock
Dwight Perkins

Harry Wheelock
Harry Wheelock
Edward Proissi

Clay & Dutton
(1886-88)
William W. Clay
Llewellyn B. Dutton

Beers, Clay & Dutton
(1888-94)
Minard L. Beers
Llewellyn B. Dutton
William W. Clay

Beers & Beers
Minard L. Beers
Herbert P. Beers

John M. Van Osdel
(1844-55)
John M. Van Osdel
Frederick H. Baumann (1851-52)

Van Osdel & Baumann
(1855-58)
John M. Van Osdel
Frederick H. Baumann
Daniel Burnham

Burling & Baumann
(1852-55)
Edward Burling
Frederick H. Baumann

Van Osdel & Co.
(1890s)
John M. Van Osdel, Jr.
Arthur Brown

Edward Burling & Co.
(1855-71)
Edward Burling
Edward Baumann (1857)
Charles J. Furst (1868-71)
John J. Flanders

Baumann & Baumann
(1858-78)
Frederick H. Baumann
Edward Baumann
Harris W. Huehl (1877-)

Burling & Adler & Co.
(1871-78)
Edward Burling
Dankmar Adler
Minard L. Beers
Clarence L. Stiles
W. H. Wilcox
Charles J. Furst
John J. Flanders
Francis M. Whitehouse

Edward Baumann
(1878-88)

Baumann & Cady
(1878-)
Frederick Baumann
Jeremiah K. Cady

Burling & Whitehouse
(1879-92)
Edward Burling
Francis M. Whitehouse

Baumann & Huehl
(1888-89)
Edward Baumann
Harris W. Huehl

Huehl & Schmid
Harris W. Huehl
Richard G. Schmid

Huehl, Schmid & Holmes
Harris W. Huehl
Richard G. Schmid
Harold Holmes

Treat & Foltz
(1872-97)
Samuel Atwater Treat
Fritz Foltz
John T. Hetherington
(1878-86)

O. S. Kinney

Kinney & Adler
O. S. Kinney
Dankmar Adler

Furst & Flanders
Charles J. Furst
John J. Flanders

Adler & Co.
(1880-81)
Dankmar Adler
Louis Sullivan (1879-81)

Adler & Sullivan
(1881-95)
Dankmar Adler
Louis Sullivan
Frank Lloyd Wright
(1887-93)
George Grant Elmslie
(1889-95)
William Gray Purcell

Maher & Corwin
(1889-90)
George Maher
Charles Corwin

Joseph Lyman Silsbee
(1882-1907)
Joseph Lyman Silsbee
George Grant Elmslie (1887-89)
Frank Lloyd Wright (1887)
George Maher (1888)
John A. Rogers

Adolph A. Cudell
Adolph A. Cudell
Richard E. Schmidt
(1887-90)

Cobb & Frost
(1882-96)
Henry Ives Cobb
Charles Sumner Frost
Hugh M. G. Garden
William E. Walker (1892-97)

Solon Spencer Beman
(1876-1913)
Solon Spencer Beman
Spencer S. Beman
Irving K. Pond (-1887)
Allen B. Pond (-1887)
William J. Dodd

Shepley, Rutan & Coolidge
(Main Office: Boston, 1886-1915)
George F. Shepley
Charles H. Rutan
Charles A. Coolidge (-1892)
Alfred H. Granger (-1891)
Robert C. Spencer (-1891)
John Baptiste Fischer

Shepley, Rutan & Coolidge
(Branch Office: Chicago, 1887-)
George F. Shepley
Charles H. Rutan
Charles A. Coolidge
Alfred H. Granger (1891-94)
Hugh M. G. Garden
Robert C. Spencer, Jr. (1893-95)

H. H. Richardson (Boston)
H. H. Richardson
Charles Coolidge (1882-86)
Alfred H. Granger (1887)
Dwight Heald Perkins (1888)

Holabird & Simonds
(1880-81)
William Holabird
Ossian C. Simonds
Martin Roche (1881)

Holabird, Simonds & Roche
(1881-83)
William Holabird
Ossian C. Simonds
Martin Roche

Holabird & Roche
(1883-1927)
William Holabird
John Augur Holabird
Martin Roche
William J. Smith (1909-12)
Frank A. Childs (1910-12)
Gilbert Phelps Hall
Henry J. B. Hoskins
Frederick J. Thielbar
(-1918)
Edward A. Renwick
David Carlson
Frank B. Long
Walter Stopa
N. L. Roberts
Lewis C. Clarke
John W. Root, Jr.
Joseph Z. Burgee
(1923-27)

B

1890

1893
World's
Columbian
Exposition

1900

1910

1920

1922
Chicago
Tribune Tower
Competition

D. Everett Waid
(1894-98)

Howard Van Doren Shaw
(1894-1926)
Howard Van Doren Shaw
Frank Lotan Venning
Ralph S. Milman
Archibald S. Morphett
W. M. Ziegler Bourse
Charles W. Fox
Hugh M. G. Garden
David Adler (1911)
Henry Dangler (1911)
Robert Work
Edward Bennett
George B. Eich

Patton, Fischer & Miller
(1897-99)
Normand S. Patton
Reynolds Fisher
Grant C. Miller

Jenney & Mundie
(1897-1905)
William Le Baron Jenney
William Bryce Mundie
Elmer C. Jensen (1897-1905)
Alfred H. Granger
John A. Rogers
F. B. Meade

Adler & Dangler
(1912-17)
David Adler
Henry Dangler

Jenney, Mundie & Jensen
(1905-07)
William Le Baron Jenney
William Bryce Mundie
Elmer C. Jensen

Brown & Walcott
(1912-16)
Arthur Brown
Chester H. Walcott

Mundie & Jensen
(1907-36)
William Bryce Mundie
Elmer C. Jensen
Edward G. B. Halstead

Otis & Clark
(1914-24)
William Augustis Otis
Edwin H. Clark
Frank Lotan Venning

Adler & Work
(1918)
David Adler
Robert Work
Louis Pirola

Work & Atwood
Robert Work
Leland Atwood

Adler & Eich
David Adler
George B. Eich
John Story
Paul Scweikher

Walcott & Work
Chester H. Walcott
Robert Work
Leland Atwood

Clark & Walcott
(1920-25)
Edwin H. Clark
Chester H. Walcott

Hill & Woltersdorf
(1894-1914)
Henry W. Hill
Aurthur F. Woltersdorf

**Philips, Rogers &
Woodyatt**
(1898-1905)
Philips
John A. Rogers
Ernest Woodyatt

Rogers & Woodyatt
John A. Rogers
Ernest Woodyatt
Edward Bennett
(1912-19)

Nimmons & Fellows
(1898-1910)
George C. Nimmons
William K. Fellows
George W. Carr

George C. Nimmons
(1911-17)
George C. Nimmons
Clark C. Wright (1913-17)
George W. Carr (1914-17)

Graham, Burnham & Co.
(1912-18)
Daniel H. Burnham
Daniel H. Burnham, Jr.
Hubert Burnham
Ernest R. Graham (1912-18)
Peirce Anderson (1912-18)
Edward Probst
Howard J. White (1912-18)
K. M. Vitzhum
Alfred Shaw
William Alderman
Sigurd E. Naess
Ted Rich
Charles F. Murphy

D. H. Burnham & Co.
(1917-28)
Daniel H. Burnham, Jr.
Hubert Burnham
Aurthur Deam

**Graham, Anderson, Probst &
White**
(1918-)
Ernest R. Graham (1917-29)
William E. Graham
Peirce Anderson (1918-24)
Edward Probst (1918-42)
Edward Probst, Jr.
Marvin Probst
Howard J. White (1918-36)
Wellington J. Schaefer
Charles G. Beersman
Sigurd E. Naess (-1937)
Alfred Shaw (1921-37)
Charles F. Murphy (-1937)
Charles Rummell

Nimmons & Co.
(1920-28)
George C. Nimmons
George W. Carr (1920-28)
Clark C. Wright (1920-28)

**Loewenberg &
Loewenberg**
Max L. Loewenberg
Israel S. Loewenberg
James R. Loewenberg
(1957-)

Dwight Perkins
(1894-1905)
Dwight Perkins
Marion Mahoney Griffin

Peter J. Weber
(1900)

Tallmadge & Alderman
(1905-1932)
Thomas Tallmadge
William Alderman

Perkins & Hamilton
(1905-11)
Dwight Perkins
John L. Hamilton

Perkins, Fellows & Hamilton
(1911-27)
Dwight Perkins
William K. Fellows
John L. Hamilton

Edward Bennett
(1912-19)

Chatten & Hammond
(1915-27)
Melville C. Chatten
Charles Hammond

Vitzhum & Burns
(1916-56)
Karl M. Vitzhum
John J. Burns

Bennett & Parsons
(1919-22)
Edward H. Bennett
William E. Parsons

Frederick Foltz
(1898-)

Treat & Alschuler
(1903-07)
Samuel Atwater Treat
Alfred S. Alschuler

Alfred S. Alschuler
(1907)
Alfred S. Alschuler
Ralph N. Friedman
Edward A. Rewwick

Abel Faidy
(1918-65)

Dubin & Eisenberg
(1919-32)
George Dubin
Henry Dubin
Abraham Eisenberg

Cornelius W. Rapp
(1892-1905)

Frank Lloyd Wright
(Oak Park Studio, 1895-1909)
Frank Lloyd Wright
Marion Mahony Griffin (1895-1906)
William E. Drummond (1899-1909)
Walter Burley Griffin (1901-05)
Francis Barry Byrne (1902)
Andrew Willatzen (1902-05)
John S. Van Bergen (1909)

Louis H. Sullivan
(1895-1924)
George Grant Elmslie (1895-1909)
Homer Grant Sailor
Parker Noble Berry
William Eugene Drummond (1899)

Adler & Adler
(1895-1900)
Dankmar Adler
Abraham Adler
Sidney Adler
Frederick Foltz
Alfred S. Alschuler
(1899-1900)
Samuel Atwater Treat

Treat & Adler
(1900-03)
Samuel Atwater Treat
Abraham Adler
Alfred S. Alschuler
(1900-03)

Rapp & Rapp
(1906-65)
Cornelius W. Rapp
George L. Rapp

William E. Drummond
(1909-12, 1915-)

Guenzel & Drummond
(1912-15)
Louis Guenzel
William E. Drummond

Schmidt & Fraenkel
(1890-95)
Richard E. Schmidt
Theodore O. Fraenkel

Richard E. Schmidt
(1895-1906)
Hugh Garden (1895-1906)
William Eugene Drummond (c. 1903)

Granger & Meade
(1894-98)
Alfred H. Granger
Frank B. Meade
Alfred Fellheimer (1896)

Frost & Granger
(1898-1910)
Charles S. Frost
Alfred H. Granger

Frost & Henderson
Charles S. Frost
Charles C. Henderson

George Maher & Son
(1890-1926)
George Maher
Phillip B. Maher (1924-26)

Walter Burley Griffin
(1906-1911)

Purcell & Feick
(1907-09)
William Gray Purcell
George Feick, Jr.

Purcell, Feick & Elmslie
(1909-13)
William Gray Purcell
George Feick, Jr.
George Grant Elmslie
Parker Noble Berry

Parker Noble Berry
(1917-18)

Schmidt, Garden & Martin
(1906-25)
Richard E. Schmidt
Hugh Garden
Edgar Martin
Lewis C. Clarke

Francis Barry Byrne
(1917-)

Griffin & Griffin
(1911-37)
Walter Burley Griffin
Marion Mahoney Griffin
Francis Barry Byrne (1914-17)
John S. Van Bergen

Purcell & Elmslie
(1913-22)
William Gray Purcell
George Grant Elmslie

Lowe & Bollenbacher
(1909-24)
Elmo Lowe
John Bollenbacher
John O. Merrill (1921-26)

Robert C. Spenser, Jr.
(1895-1905)

Henry Ives Cobb
(New York:1898-)

Pond & Pond
(1887-1925)
Irving K. Pond
Allen B. Pond
George W. Carr (1899-1914)

William E. Walker
(1903-18)

Spencer & Powers
(1905-)
Robert C. Spencer, Jr.
Horace C. Powers

Spencer S. Beman
(1914-)

Coolidge & Hodgdon
(1916-30)
Charles Coolidge
Frederick Hodgdon

Arthur F. Woltersdorf
(1914-19)

Woltersdorf & Bernhard
(1919-23)
Arthur F. Woltersdorf
Bernhard

The Steinway Hall Group
(1896-)
Dwight Heald Perkins
Robert C. Spencer, Jr.
Myron Hunt
Frank Lloyd Wright
Irving K. Pond
Allen Bartlit Pond
Walter Burley Griffin
Marion Mahony Griffin
Birch Burdette Long
Henry Webster Tomlinson

Spencer & Hall
(1896)
Robert C. Spencer, Jr.
Emery S. Hall

Marble & Wilson
(-1895)
Marble
Horatio R. Wilson
Benjamin Howard Marshall (1893-95)

Wilson & Marshall
(1895-1902)
Horatio R. Wilson
Benjamin Howard Marshall
Lewis B. Walton
Kegley

Page & Hall
(1897-1909)
Harvey L. Page
Emery S. Hall

Horatio R. Wilson
(1901-17)

Benjamin Howard Marshall
(1902-05)

Marshall & Fox
(1905-26)
Benjamin Howard Marshall
Charles E. Fox
Abraham Epstein (1913-14)
Lewis B. Walton (1915-24)
Monroe Bowman (1924-26)
Lewis C. Clarke

Hall & Baker
(1909-19)
Emery S. Hall
Baker

Samuel A. Marx
(1909-47)

Abraham Epstein
(1914-46)

Emery S. Hall
(1919-39)

Childs & Smith
(1912)
Frank A. Childs
William J. Smith

Fugard & Knapp
John R. Fugard
George A. Knapp

Eckland, Fugard & Knapp
Henry Eckland
John R. Fugard
George A. Knapp

Jarvis Hunt

Andrew Rebori
(1911-18)

Andrew Rebori
(1919-21)

Rebori, Wentworth & Dewey
(1919-23)
Andrew Rebori
John Wentworth
Albert Dewey

Frederick J. Thielbar
(1918-24)

C

1922
Chicago
Tribune Tower
Competition

1930

1933
Century of
Progress
Exposition

1940

1945
World War II
Ends

1950

1960

Stockade Building System & 4-D Co.
(1922-32)
Buckminster Fuller

General Houses, Inc.
(1928-40)
Howard T. Fisher
Lawrence Perkins
Paul Schweikher

Howard T. Fisher & Associates
(1928-64)

Schweikher & Lamb
(1933-45)
Paul Schweikher
Theodore W. Lamb

Mundie, Jensen, Bourke & Havens
(1936-44)
William Bryce Mundie
Elmer C. Jensen
Bourke
George Havens

Winston Elting
(1937-41)

William F. Deknatel
(1937-60)
William F. Deknatel
Myron Goldsmith (1941)
Geraldine Eager

Mundie & Jensen
(1944-46)
William Bryce Mundie
Elmer C. Jensen

Jensen & McClurg
(1946-)
Elmer C. Jensen
Verne O. McClurg

William Bryce Mundie
(1946-)

Schweikher & Elting
(1945-53)
Paul Schweikher
Winston Elting
Edward H. Bennett
Ralph Rapson
I. W. Colburn
Edward D. Dart (1949-51)

Barancik Conte & Associates
(1950)
Richard Barancik
Richard Conte

I. W. Colburn & Associates
(1955-)
I. W. Colburn
Edward Noonan

Paul Schweikher
(1953-70)
Ralph Rapson
Hanno Weber (1963-67)

Elting & Bennett
(1953-56)
Winston Elting
Edward H. Bennett

Edward H. Bennett
(1956-)

Winston Elting
(1956-60)

Nimmons, Carr & Wright
(1928-47)
George C. Nimmons
George W. Carr
Clark C. Wright

Burnham Brothers
(1928-33)
Daniel H. Burnham, Jr.
Hubert Burnham
Paul McCurry (1929-30)
Nathaniel Owings (1929-33)
Louis Skidmore (1930-33)

Burnham & Hammond
(1933-)
Daniel H. Burnham, Jr.
Hubert Burnham
Charles Herrick Hammond
Nathaniel Owings (1933-34)
Louis Skidmore (1933-)

Shaw, Naess & Murphy
(1937-46)
Alfred Shaw
Sigurd E. Naess
Charles F. Murphy

Bertrand Goldberg & Associates
(1937-)
Bertrand Goldberg
Gilmer Vardiman Black
(1938-61)
Floyd Magnuson (1955-)

Huszagh & Hill
Ralph Huszagh
Boyd Hill

Boyd Hill

Loebl Schlossman
(1925-46)
Jerrold Loebl
Norman J. Schlossman

Carr & Wright
(1947-)
George W. Carr
Clark C. Wright

Edward D. Dart
(1951-65)

Loebl Schlossman & Bennett
(1946-65)
Jerrold Loebl
Norman J. Schlossman
John I. Schlossman
Richard M. Bennett
Edward D. Dart
Marvin Fitch (1946-51)
Donald A. Schiller (1948-51)

Fitch, Schiller & Frank
(1951-57)
Marvin Fitch
Donald A. Schiller
Burton H. Frank

Schiller & Frank
(1957-)
Donald A. Schiller
Burton H. Frank

Fridstein & Fitch
(1957-69)
Robert B. Fridstein
Marvin Fitch
Wojciech Madeyski
(1966-68)

Talmadge & Watson
(1932-)
Thomas Talmadge
Vernon Watson
Paul McCurry (1926-28)

Bennett, Parsons & Frost
(1922-27)
Edward H. Bennett
Harry T. Frost

Bennett & Parsons
(1927-38)
Edward H. Bennett
William E. Parsons

Perkins, Chatten & Hammond
(1927-35)
Dwight Perkins
Melville Clark Chatten
Charles Herrick Hammond

Perkins, Wheeler & Will
(1936-44)
Lawrence Perkins
E. Todd Wheeler
Phillip Will, Jr.
James W. Hammond (1939-40)

Shaw, Metz & Dolio
(1947-59)
Alfred Shaw
Karl Metz
John Dolio

C. F. Murphy Associates
(1947-81)
Charles F. Murphy
Stanislaw Gladych
Charles Rummel (1947-67)
Carter Manny (1948-)
Y. C. Wong (1958)
Jacques Brownson (1959-66)
John Hartray, Jr. (1959-61)
Andrew Heard (1964-65)
Hans Neumann (1965-)
Thomas H. Beeby (1965-71)
Gerald Horn (1966-68)
Gene Summers (1967-73)
Helmut Jahn (1967-81)
Wojciech Madeyski (1968-76)
Ronald W. Krueck (1970-71)
Keith Olsen
Peter Frisbee (1977-80)
Suzanne Underwood
Howard Decker (1978-80)
Chris Lee (1979-81)
Otto Stark
James J. Belli

Perkins & Will
(1944-)
Lawrence Perkins
Phillip Will, Jr.
Hans P. Neumann
Wilmont Vickrey (1951-69)
C. W. Brubaker
Philip Kupritz (1962-66)
Neil Frankel
J. Jeffrey Conroy
Garrett Eakin (1974-78)
Wojciech Madeyski (1976-)
Martin F. Wolf
Ralph Johnson (1976-)
Richard Potokar (1979-82)
Andrew Metter (1986-89)

Milton M. Schwartz
Milton M. Schwartz
Neil Frankel
Floyd Magnuson
Stanley Tigerman (1956-57)
Arthur Myrhum (1950s)

Shaw, Metz & Associates
(1959-66)
Alfred Shaw
Karl Metz

John Dolio Mechanical Engineers
(1959-)

McNally & Quinn
(1922-)
Frank McNally
James Quinn
Lewis C. Clarke
Benjamin Howard Marshall
Lawrence E. McConville
Carl Sterner
B. G. Greengard
John Story
George A. Hossack
George Elgh
A. G. Lehman
J. M. Bryant
J. J. Silverman

Hamilton, Fellows & Nedved
(1926-34)
John L. Hamilton
William K. Fellows
R. J. Nedved

Holsman & Holsman
(1928)
Henry K. Holsman
William Holsman

Klekamp & Whitmore
Bernard R. Klekamp
Whitmore

Holsman, Holsman, Klekamp, & Taylor
(1928-53)
Henry K. Holsman
William Holsman
John Holsman
Bernard R. Klekamp
Darl Coder Taylor

Dubin & Dubin
(1932-62)
Henry Dubin
Arthur D. Dubin
Martin D. Dubin

Alschuler & Friedman
(1940-46)
Alfred S. Alschuler, Jr.
Ralph N. Friedman

Alfred Caldwell
(1944-59)

A. James Speyer
(1946-)
A. James Speyer
William E. Dunlap

Friedman, Alschuler & Sincere & Grunsfeld
(1946-)
Ralph N. Friedman
Alfred S. Alschuler, Jr.
Sincere
Ernest A. Grunsfeld, Jr.
(1946-55)

Holsman & Co.
(1953-)
William Holsman
John Holsman

Bernard R. Klekamp
(1953-)

Klaber & Grunsfeld
(1924-29)
Eugene H. Klaber
Ernest A. Grunsfeld, Jr.

Frank Lloyd Wright
(Taliesin West, 1925-59)
Frank Lloyd Wright
William F. Deknatel
Geraldine Eager

Eugene H. Klaber
(1929-39)

Ernest A. Grunsfeld, Jr.
(1929-39)

Klaber Homsey
(1942-44)
Eugene H. Klaber
Victorine Homsey

Eugene H. Klaber
(1944-)

Grunsfeld, Yerkes & Koening
(1939-46)
Ernest A. Grunsfeld, Jr.
Yerkes
Koening

Grunsfeld & Associates
(1956-)
Ernest A. Grunsfeld, Jr.
(d. 1970)
Ernest A. Grunsfeld III

Ernest A. Grunsfeld

Belli & Belli
(1941-72)
Edo J. Belli (1941-1972)
Anthony Belli (1941-72)
Allen J. Belli (1965-72)
James J. Belli (1971-72)

The Office Of Mies Van Der Rohe
(1938-69)
Mies Van Der Rohe
John Heinrich
George Danforth (1939-44)
Ludwig Karl Hilbersheimer
Alfred Caldwell (1944-59)
Joseph Fujikawa (1945-69)
Myron Goldsmith (1946-53)
Reginald Malcomson (1947)
Daniel Brenner (1947-51)
Gene Summers (1950-66)
Y. C. Wong (1950 &52-57)
David Haid (1951-60)
Jacques Brownson
William M. Drake, Jr.
Peter Carter
George Schipporheit (1957-60)
William E. Dunlap (1958-60)
Jack Bowman (1958-69)
Arthur Salzman (1960-69)
Dirk Lohan (1960-69)
Roy Kruse (1961)
Arthur Takeuchi
Charles Booher Genther
David Fix
A. James Speyer
Phyllis Lambert (-1965)
Rainer Schildnicht
Edward Duckett
Joe Burnett

Brenner & Turck
(1958-61)
Daniel Brenner
Dorothy Turck

George Grant Elmslie
(1922-30)

Granger, Lowe & Bollenbacher
(1924-26)
Alfred H. Granger
Elmo Lowe
John Bollenbacher
John O. Merrill (1924-26)
Paul Schweikher

Phillip B. Maher
(1926-75)
Phillip B. Maher
Paul Schweikher (1930-33)

Schmidt, Garden & Erikson
(1926-)
Richard E. Schmidt
Hugh Garden
Carl Erikson
Vale Faro
Albert Bacci
Paul McCurry
(1945-76)
William E. Drummond
Dennis Recek
Richard Yoshiro Mine

Granger & Bollenbacher
(1926-39)
Alfred H. Granger
John Bollenbacher
John O. Merrill (1926-39)
Winston Elting (1934)
Frank Lotan Venning

Lewis C. Cordogan
(1951-84)
Lewis C. Cordogan
John G. Cordogan

Harry Weese & Associates
(1947-)
Harry Weese
Ezra Gordon (1954-61)
Hans P. Neumann (1954-64)
Ben Weese (1959-77)
John Buenz (1960-61)
John Hartray, Jr. (1961-76)
Stanley Tigerman (1961-62)
Thomas Hickey
Stanley Allen (1964-)
Peter Landon
William B. Bauhs (1965-74)
Cynthia Weese (1973-75)
Frederick Phillips (1974-75)
William McBride (1980-81)
Kathryn Quinn (1977-79)
William Ketcham

Hausner & Macsai
(1955-70)
Robert O. Hausner
John Macsai

Arthur Takeuchi
(1965-)

Pond & Pond, Martin & Lloyd
(1925-31)
Irving K. Pond
Allen B. Pond
Edgar Martin
Alfred Lloyd

Pond & Pond & Martin
(1931-)
Irving K. Pond
Allen B. Pond
Edgar Martin

L. Morgan Yost
(1932-52)
L. Morgan Yost
Walter Netsch (1946-47)
Lewis B. Walton, Jr.
(1950-51)

Skidmore & Owings
(1936-39)
Louis Skidmore
Nathaniel Owings
John Weese (1936-39)
Ambrose Richardson (1937-39)

Skidmore, Owings & Merrill
(1939-)
Louis Skidmore
Nathaniel Owings (d. 1984)
John O. Merrill
John Weese (1939-)
Ambrose Richardson (1939-41; 1945-51)
Charles Booher Genther (1942-43)
Nathalie Dublois (1945-74)
James W. Hammond (1946-61)
Peter Roesch
Walter Netsch (1947-79)
Harry Weese (1946-47)
John Macsai (1950-53)
Joseph Passonneau (1950-52)
Bruce J. Graham (1950-90)
Robertson Ward, Jr. (1950-62)
Ralph Youngren (1950-67)
William Dunlap (1951-68)
Y. C. Wong (1951)
Stanley Allen (1955-62)
Myron Goldsmith (1955-83)
John Hartray, Jr. (1956-57)
George Schipporheit (1956)
Rainer Schildnicht
Stanley Tigerman (1957-61)
George Larson (1958-67; 1970-78)
Donald Powell
Arthur Takeuchi (1959-63)
San Utsonomiya
Edward Duckett
Donald Powell
Robert Kleinschmidt
Edward Dart
Fazlur R. Khan (1960-82)
John Vinci (1960)
Lucien LaGrange
Margaret I. McCurry (1966-77)
Adrian D. Smith (1967-)
Gerald Horn (1968-71)
Gregory W. Landahl
Garrett Eakin (1973)
Joseph A. Gonzalez (1974-)
Stephen Wierzbowski (1975-81)
Charles Fill (1977-79)
Kathleen Hess (1977-83)
Lawrence E. Dieckmann
James R. Destefano (-1988)
William M. Drake, Jr.
Anders Nereim (1977-78)
Diane Legge Kemp (1977-89)
Hanno Weber (1980-84)
Daniel H. Wheeler (1981-87)
Kevin Kemp (1983-86)
Grittip Sirirattomrong
Michel Mossessian (1987-92)
Nada Andric (1991-)

Yost & Taylor
(1952-60)
L. Morgan Yost
Darl Coder Taylor
Albert Bacci

Benjamin Howard Marshall
(1926-)
Benjamin Howard Marshall
Lewis B. Walton (1926)

Marx, Flint & Schonne
(1947-)
Samuel A. Marx
Noel L. Flint
Charles W. Schonne

Walton & Kegley
(1938-51)
Lewis B. Walton
Lewis B. Walton, Jr.
Kegley

Keck & Faro
(1926-27)
George Fred Keck
Vale Faro

George Fred Keck
(1926-46)
George Fred Keck
Paul Schweikher (1930)
William Keck (1931-41)
Robert Bruce Tague (1935-37)
Ralph Rapson (1942-46)

Keck & Keck
(1946-80)
George Fred Keck
William Keck
Robert Bruce Tague (1937-56)
Clarence Rudolph (1948-49)
Stanley Tigerman (1948-49)
Michael K. Young (1948-50)
John Buenz (1962-63)
Winston Elting
Jack Levin
Ezra Gordon
John Van Der Muelen

Tigerman, Rudolph & Young
(1949-50)
Stanley Tigerman
Clarence Rudolph
Michael K. Young

Michael K. Young & Associates

Rapson & Van Der Muelen
(1950-54)
Ralph Rapson
John Van Der Muelen

Gordon & Levin
(1961-)
Ezra Gordon
Jack Levin

Walton & Walton
(1952-)
Lewis B. Walton
Lewis B. Walton, Jr.

A. Epstein & Sons
(1946-)
Abraham Epstein
Raymond Epstein
Ralph J. Epstein
Sidney Epstein
William Brazley, Jr.
(1970-73)
Christopher Hale
(1987-89)
Andrew Metter (1990-)

Tigerman & Koglin
(1962-64)
Stanley Tigerman
Norman A. Koglin
Laurence O. Booth (1962-64)

Norman Koglin & Associates
(1964-)

Powell Kleinschmidt
Donald Powell
Robert Kleinschmidt

Thielbar & Fugard
(1925-41)
Frederick J. Thielbar
John R. Fugard

Hunt & Bohasseck
(1925-27)
Jarvis Hunt
Bohasseck

Rebori, Wentworth & Dewey
(1919-23)
Andrew Rebori
John Wentworth
Albert Dewey

Rebori, Wentworth, Dewey & McCormick
(1923-30)
Andrew Rebori
John Wentworth
Albert Dewey
Leander J. McCormick
Paul McCurry

Holabird & Root
(1927-48)
John W. Root, Jr.
Joseph Z. Burgee (1927-45)
Gilbert P. Hall
Lewis C. Clarke
Helmuth Bartch (1927)
Monroe Bowman (1927-29)
Irving Bowman
Paul D. McCurry (1930)
William C. Periera (1930-32)
Winston Elting (1932-33)
Charles B. Genther (1945)
Henry J. B. Hoskins
Frank B. Long
John S. Cromelin
David Carlson
Col. Horatio Hacket

William C. Periera

Luckman & Periera
(1930s)

The Bowman Brothers
(1929-36)
Irving Bowman
Monroe Bowman

Rebori & Wentworth
(1930)
Andrew Rebori
John Wentworth

Andrew Rebori
(1930-66)

Fugard, Olson, Urbain & Neiler
(1940s)
John R. Fugard
Olson
Leon F. Urbain
Neiler

Landahl Associates
Gregory Landahl

Holabird & Root & Burgee
(1948-)
John A. Holabird
John W. Root, Jr.
Joseph Z. Burgee
John Macsai (1949-50)
Bruce Graham (1949-50)
Richard Yoshiro Mine
Joseph Passonneau
(1949-50)
John Hartray, Jr. (1958-59)
Andrew Heard (1962-64)

Solomon Cordwell
(1957-63)
Louis R. Solomon
J. D. Cordwell

1960

Elting, Deknatel &
Associates
(1960-61)
Winston Elting
William F. Deknatel

Wendell Cambell & Associates
(1966-)

Loebl, Schlossman, Bennett &
Dart
(1965-75)
Jerrold Loebl
John I. Schlossman
Richard M. Bennett
Edward D. Dart
David Swan (1968-70)
Philip Johnson (1973-75)

Alfred Shaw &
Associates
(1966-69)

Shaw & Associates
Alfred Shaw (1969-70)
Patrick Shaw

1969
Death of Mies
van der Rohe

1970

Fitch, Larocca,
Carington & Jones
(1973-)
Marvin Fitch
Frank L. Larocca
Robert W. Carington
E. Erie Jones

Metz & Train
(1966-67)
Karl Metz
Jack Train

Metz, Train, Olsen &
Youngren
(1967-74)
Karl Metz
Jack Train
Ronald Olson
Ralph Youngren
Lonn Frye

Andrew Heard & Associates
(1967-)

Philip Kupritz & Associates
(1968-)

Vickrey Ovresat Awsumb
(1969-)
Wilmont Vickrey
Raymond Ovresat
John Awsumb

Metz, Train & Youngren
(1974-82)
Karl Metz
Jack Train
Ralph Youngren

Coder Taylor Architects
(1960-)

Schipporheit & Heinrich
(1965-70)
George Schipporheit
John Heinrich

Dubin, Dubin, Black &
Moutoussamy
(1963-)
Arthur D. Dubin
Martin D. Dubin
John Black
John Moutoussamy

Gelick Foran &
Associates
(1969-)
Michael Gelick
Walter J. Foran
John W. Clark (1982)

George Schipporheit
(1970-)

1975

Sisco/Lubotsky Associates
(1975-77)
Gene Sisco
Robert Lubotsky
Andrew Metter (1977)

Sisco, Lubotsky & Stuart Cohen
(1977-81)
Gene Sisco
Robert Lubotsky
Stuart Cohen
James Law
Andrew Metter (1977-81)
Anders Nereim (1978-81)
Kathryn Quinn (1979-81)

Loebl, Schlossman, Dart & Hackl
(1975-76)
Jerrold Loebl
John I. Schlossman
Edward D. Dart
Donald J. Hackl
Philip Johnson (1975-76)

Loebl, Schlossman & Hackl
(1976-)
Jerrold Loebl
John I. Schlossman
Donald J. Hackl
Lawrence Dieckman
Philip Johnson (1976-78)
Howard Decker (1977-78)
Steven Wright
Wojciech Lesnikowski (1988-)

Hinds, Schroeder &
Whitaker
(1978-82)
George Hinds
Kenneth Schroeder
Richard Whitaker
John M. Syvertson
(1976-77)
George Pappageorge
(1979-81)
David Haymes (1979-81)

Jack Train & Associates
(1982-)

Dubin, Dubin &
Moutoussamy
(1978-)
Arthur D. Dubin
Martin D. Dubin
John Moutoussamy
Henry Zimoch

1980

Cohen & Nereim
(1981-88)
Stuart Cohen
Anders Nereim
Christopher Rudolph (1981-83)
Karen Johnson (1986)
Julie Hacker (1986-88)

Christopher H. Rudolph &
Associates
(1983-)
Christopher H. Rudolph
Thomas N. Rajkovich (1983-84)

Sisco/Lubotsky Associates
(1981-84)
Gene Sisco
Robert Lubotsky
Andrew Metter (1981-84)
James Law (1981-84)

Lubotsky, Metter, Worthington &
Law
(1984-86)
Robert Lubotsky
Andrew Metter
Wayne Worthington
James Law

Loewenberg/Fitch
Partnership
James R. Loewenberg
Marvin Fitch

Johnson & Lee
(1983-)
Philip Johnson
Chris Lee

William R. Hasbrouck
(1976-86)

Hasbrouck, Peterson Associates
(1986-1991)
William R. Hasbrouck
James M. Peterson
Grittip Sirirattumrong

Hasbrouck, Peterson, Zimochi &
Sirirattumrong
(1991-)
William R. Hasbrouck
James M. Peterson
Henry Zimoch
Grittip Sirirattumrong

Murphy/Jahn
(1981-)
Charles F. Murphy
Carter Manny
Helmut Jahn
Phillip Castillo (1978-)
John C. Lahey (-1986)
James Goettsch (-1988)
Dennis Recek (-1989)
Chris Lee (1981-83)
Rainer Schildnicht
Martin F. Wolf

Kenneth Schroeder &
Associates
(1982-88)

Schroeder Murchie
Laya & Associates
(1988-)
Kenneth Schroeder
Jack Murchie
Richard J. Laya

Pappageorge/Haymes Ltd.
(1981-)
George Pappageorge
David Haymes
James Plunkard (1984-86)
Ray Hartshorne (1984-86)

Hartshorne Plunkard
(1987-)
Ray Hartshorne
James Plunkard
Karen Hollander (1987-88)

Douglas A. Garafolo
(1987-)

Valerio Associates
(1987-)
Joseph Valerio

1990

Stuart Cohen & Associates
(1988-91)
Stuart Cohen
Julie Hacker (1988-91)

Anders Nereim
(1988-)

Stuart Cohen & Julie Hacker
(1991-)
Stuart Cohen
Julie Hacker

Voy Madeyski
Architects
(1987-)
Wojciech Madeyski

Richard A. M. Potokar
(1987)

Morris Erie Myers
(1992-)
John Morris
Florence Erie Krieger
Sherrill Myers

D

Brenner Danforth Rockwell
(1961-69)
Daniel Brenner
George Danforth
H. P. Davis Rockwell
John Vinci (1961-69)
John C. Lahey

David Haid & Associates
(1963-)

Phyllis Lambert
(1965-72)
Phyllis Lambert
David Fix

O'Donnell, Wicklund & Pigozzi
Lawrence J. O'Donnell
Leonard S. Wicklund
Raymond A. Pigozzi

Fujikawa, Conterato, Lohan & Associates
(1969-82)
Joseph Fujikawa
Bruno Conterato
Dirk Lohan
Jack Bowman (1969-82)
Arthur Salzman (1969-82)
Gerald L. Johnson

Roy Kruse
(1972-)

Belli & Belli
(1972-)
Allen J. Belli (1972-)
James J. Belli (1972-)
Edo J. Belli (1972-)
Anthony Belli (1972-78)

Fujikawa, Johnson & Associates
(1982-)
Joseph Fujikawa
Gerald L. Johnson

Lohan Associates
(1982-)
Dirk Lohan
Jack Bowman (1982-)
Arthur Salzman (1982-1991)
Kathleen Hess (1985)

Arthur Salzman
(1991-)
Arthur Salzman
Gilbert Gorski (- 1989)

Gilbert Gorski
(1989)

O'Donnell, Wicklund, Pigozzi & Peterson
(1987-)
Lawrence J. O'Donnell
Leonard S. Wicklund
Raymond A. Pigozzi
Leonard A. Peterson
John Macsai (1991-)
John Syvertsen (1992-)

Daniel Wheeler Architects
(1987-89)
Daniel Wheeler
Lawrence Kearns

Wheeler Kearns
(1989-)
Daniel Wheeler
Lawrence Kearns

Legge Kemp
(1989-)
Diane Legge Kemp

Bauhs & Dring
(1974-)
William Bauhs
William Dring

Frederick Phillips & Associates
(1976-)

Campbell & Macsai
(1970-74)
Wendell Campbell
John Macsai
William Brazley, Jr. (1968-70)

Cynthia Weese
(1975-77)

Weese Seegers Hickey Weese
(1977-82)
Ben Weese
Arnold Seegers
Thomas Hickey
Cynthia Weese

Weese Hickey Weese
(1982-89)
Ben Weese
Thomas Hickey
Cynthia Weese
Peter Landon

Weese Langley Weese
Ben Weese
Dennis Langley
Cynthia Weese

Vinci Kenney Architects
(1970-77)
John Vinci
Lawrence C. Kenney

Eva Maddox Associates
(1975-)
Eva Maddox
Patrick Grzybek
Eileen Jones

Margaret I. McCurry
(1977-82)

The Office of John Vinci
(1978-)

Banks/Eakin Architects
John Banks
Garret Eakin

Florian Wierzbowski
(1983-)
Paul Florian
Stephen Wierzbowski
Jordan Mozer (1983-84)

Jordan Mozer & Associates
(1984-)

John Macsai & Associates
(1975-91)

Cordogan, Clark
(1984-)
John G. Cordogan
John W. Clark

Peter Landon Architects
(1987-)

DeStefano/Goettsch
(1988-91)
James R. DeStefano
James Goettsch

DeStefano & Partners
(1991-)
James R. DeStefano

Goettsch Associates
(1991)
James Goettsch
Nada Andric

Robertson Ward
(1962-75)

Hammond & Roesch
(1961-71)
James Hammond
Peter Roesch
James Mastro (1970-72)

Hammond Beeby & Associates
(1971-76)
James W. Hammond
Thomas Hall Beeby
Ronald Krueck (1971-76)
Keith Olsen

Hammond Beeby & Babka
(1977-)
James W. Hammond (d. 1986)
Thomas Hall Beeby
Bernard F. Babka
Phillip Castillo (1976-78)
Tannys Langdon (1978-87)
John W. Clark (1978-82)
Charles G. Young (1979-92)
Kathryn Quinn (1981-85)
Karen Johnson (1983-86)
Gary M. Ainge (1984-)
Dennis Rupert
John M. Syvertson
Thomas Rajkovich (1984-86)

Krueck & Olsen
(1978-91)
Ronald F. Krueck
Keith Olsen

Larson Associates
(1978-)
George Larson

Hanno Weber & Associates
(1984-)
Hanno Weber
Kathleen Hess (1985-)
Christopher Hale (1989-)

McBride & Kelly
(1984-)
William McBride
Jack Kelly

Lucien LaGrange & Associates
(1985-)

Quinn & Searle
(1986-90)
Kathryn Quinn
Linda Searle

Rajkovich & Mayernick
Thomas N. Rajkovich
David T. Mayernick

Krueck & Sexton
(1991-)
Ronald F. Krueck
Mark Sexton

Kathryn Quinn Architects
(1990-)

Linda Searle & Associates
(1990-)

John Syvertsen Architect
(1987-91)

Langdon & Woodhouse
(1987-91)
Tannys Langdon
David Woodhouse

Tannys Langdon & Associates
(1991-)

David Woodhouse & Associates
(1991-)

Stanley Tigerman & Associates
(1964-82)
Laurence O. Booth (1965-66)
James L. Nagle (1965-66)
Jack Murchie
Ralph Johnson (1971-72)
David Woodhouse (1975-79)
Robert Fugman
Deborah Doyle (1976-80)

Booth/Nagle
(1966-77)
Laurence O. Booth
James L. Nagle
Marvin Ullman (1969-74)
David Swan (1971-73)
Christopher Rudolph (1974-77)
Phillip Castillo (1975-76)
Gene Sisco
Marvin Ullman
Robert Lubotsky

David Swan Architect
(1973-)

Booth, Nagle & Hartray
(1977-79)
Laurence O. Booth
James L. Nagle
Jack Hartray, Jr.
Richard A. M. Potokar (1977-79)
Christopher Rudolph (1977-79)
Darcy Bonner (1978-79)

William Brazley & Associates
(1978-)

Himmel Bonner Architects
(1979-)
Scott Himmel
Darcy R. Bonner, Jr.
Dirk Dennison

Dirk Dennison

Booth/Hansen & Associates
(1980-)
Laurence O. Booth
Paul Hansen
William Ketcham
David Woodhouse (1980-87)

Tigerman Fugman McCurry
(1982-88)
Stanley Tigerman
Robert Fugman
Margaret I. McCurry
Richard Dakich
Gary M. Ainge (1982-84)
James Plunkard
Carl Darr (1985-87)
John Holbert (1985-87)
Fred Wilson (1985-88)
Karen Hollander (1986-87)
Melany Telleen (1986-88)

Holbert Hollander
(1988-)
John Holbert
Karen Hollander

Dotson & Darr
(1988-)
David Dotson
Carl Darr

Tigerman McCurry
(1988-)
Stanley Tigerman
Margaret McCurry
Melany Telleen (1986-)
Paul Gates (1988-90)
Richard Dragisic (1988-)

Fugman Dakich & Associates
(1988-)
Robert Fugman
Richard Dakich

Solomon Cordwell Buenz
(1963-)
Louis R. Solomon (1963-71)
J. D. Cordwell
John Buenz

Holabird & Root
Gerald Horn (1971-)
Paul G. A. Florian (1978-81)
Thomas R. Welch
Roy J. Solfisburg
Bernard Bradley
Harry Manning
James Baird
John Z. Burgee

Greenberg & Finfer
Aubrey Greenberg
Mark Finfer

Aubrey Greenberg
Aubrey Greenberg
James Mastro
Claudia Skylar

Marvin Ullman Architects
(1974-88)
Marvin Ullman
Charles Fill (1979-88)

Mastro & Skylar
(1979-)
James Mastro
Claudia Skylar

Doyle & Associates
(1981-88)
Deborah Doyle

Doyle & Ohle
(1988-91)
Deborah Doyle
James L. Ohle

Doyle & Associates
(1991-)
Deborah Doyle

Nagle, Hartray & Associates
(1980-)
James L. Nagle
John Hartray, Jr.
Howard Decker (1980-86)
Linda Searle (1980-86)
Dirk Danker (1988-)
Howard A. Kagan
Donald McKay

Decker & Kemp
(1986-)
Howard Decker
Kevin Kemp

Newman/Lustig & Associates
Newman
Michael Lustig

Michael Lustig & Associates
(1987-)

Johnson & Rogatz
(1986-88)
Karen Scott Johnson
Janet Rogatz

Ullman & Fill
(1988-)
Marvin Ullman
Charles Fill

Johnson Rogatz Wilson
(1988-89)
Karen Scott Johnson
Janet Rogatz
Frederick H. Wilson

Johnson & Wilson
(1989-)
Karen Scott Johnson
Frederick H. Wilson

One of the methods of reading this genealogical chart may be to examine the several strains that evolved in Chicago as a by-product of architectural collaborations (together with the educational training of architects) during the latter part of the nineteenth century. For example, there is, for lack of a better description, the no-nonsense, structurally driven "William Le Baron Jenney strain." Jenney, whose training in engineering dominated his decision-making process, began his Chicago practice in 1868 as Jenney, Schermerhorn and Bogart. Through the several incarnations of his professional career, ending with Jenney, Mundie and Jensen (1905-07), his architectural production had a predictably rational cast to it, as did his descendant firm, beginning with Mundie and Jensen (1907-36) and ending with the split in 1946 into William Bryce Mundie, and Jensen and McClurg.

And yet, any number of classically inclined architects, some of whom were trained at the Ecole des Beaux-Arts in Paris, were employed at one time or another by various Jenney-named firms: influential architects such as D. H. Burnham, Louis Sullivan, Irving Pond, Alfred Granger, and Howard Van Doren Shaw. These important professionals in turn spawned their own, very different organizations, which, at least in part, represented their apprenticeship and/or professional training. What part, if any, did their training with Jenney play in influencing each of their separate careers as they unfolded? For example, did Charles Atwood's stylistic ambivalence as represented by the sharp contrast between the Reliance Building at 32 North State Street (1890; enlarged 1895) and the Palace of Fine Arts at the 1893 World's Columbian Exposition result from disparate pressures put on him by his employer, D. H. Burnham, and did that ambivalence result in any way from Burnham's own training with Jenney, which in turn was ameliorated by Burnham's understanding of the need for a reinvigoration of the classical zeitgeist?

Louis Sullivan is another interesting case, insofar as his architectural production appears to have reflected Jenney's rationalism (perhaps reinforced by the practicality that Dankmar Adler's own engineering bias brought to their partnership) combined with the enriched decorative treatment that Sullivan's official training at the Ecole des Beaux-Arts (as well as the "unofficial" drawing courses that he took at the Ecole de Dessin Gratuité) may have given him. Likewise, the work of Irving Pond (together with that of his brother Allen) conceivably represented Jenney's understanding of the skeleton frame combined with an idiosyncratic sense of contextualism, as might be seen in the office buildings designed by the Pond brothers. On the other hand, the classically inspired work of Alfred Granger seems to betray little influence emanating from Granger's term of employment with Jenney.

It is, however, possible that Howard Van Doren Shaw managed to synthesize his training with Jenney by employing a personal interpretation of the English Arts and Crafts movement, particularly as he saw it relating to the development of the Chicago exurban villa he helped to evolve. In all events, causality of influence is central to my argument that the nature of architectural production (stylistically and constructionally) is, in some ways, influenced by who works for whom, every bit as much as it is influenced by architectural education, interpretation of the environment, or other similar factors.

In terms of Chicago's several architectural traditions, then, it is useful to probe generally into causality, understanding that major movements (evolving modernism, neo-Miesianism, postmodernism, and deconstructivism) are also powerful forces that inform the ways that architects are influenced.[3] The formalist or classical typology, the rationalist or modernist typology, the romantic or organic typology, and the structural or constructional typology are the four most obvious categorizations that are worth scrutinizing from a genealogical point of view.

The Formalist or Classical Typology

The binary origins of what we might call the formalist or classical typology begin, on the one hand, with two Boston architectural firms—namely, the office of Henry Hobson Richardson and the Shepley, Rutan and Coolidge organization—and on the other hand, with the D. H. Burnham organization in Chicago. The former, especially after Shepley, Rutan and Coolidge, having completed Richardson's three Chicago projects—the Glessner and MacVeagh houses and the Marshall Field Wholesale Store—established an office in Chicago in 1887, gave way to Frost and Granger, Marshall and Fox, Jarvis Hunt, Andrew Rebori, and Samuel Marx. The Burnham legacy has been almost equally prolific, having begotten Graham, Anderson, Probst and White, the Burnham Brothers, Howard Van Doren Shaw, David Adler, and Tallmadge and Watson. All this occurred generally before the time-line marking the beginning of this present volume, and thus, these architects stand as antecedent figures for others to follow.

The Depression and the war years were not a particularly hospitable environment for the continuous evolution of what had begun shortly after the 1871 fire and been brought to full flower at the time of the 1893 fair, and with certain exceptions, little transpired in the lean decades of the 1930s and 1940s. Samuel Marx and Andrew Rebori were two who carried forth the formalist ideals that had begun in Boston three-quarters of a century earlier. The strain that began with Daniel Burnham, however, continued apace with Graham, Anderson, Probst and White, which practices still today. Huszagh and Hill, Edward H. Bennett, and I. W. Colburn worked in this manner right through the 1950s and 1960s.

The most recent practitioners to further the cause of formalistic studiousness include the twenty-year descendancy that began with Sisco/Lubotsky and carries on today with Stuart Cohen and Julie Hacker; the Hammond, Beeby and Babka organization that has spun off Tannys Langdon, John Syvertsen, and Thomas Rajkovitch; the Tigerman, Fugman and McCurry firm, from which James Plunkard, Dotson and Darr, Holbert and Hollander, Deborah Doyle, Fred Wilson, and Fugman Dakich and Associates have emerged; and Booth, Nagle and Hartray, from which Howard Decker was begotten.

But what of the case of influence-through-employment? There is little doubt that Stuart Cohen cross-fertilized the Sisco/Lubotsky firm. There is equally no question that Langdon and Syvertsen were influenced by their association with Thomas Beeby, and it is also clear that in the postmodernist era Plunkard, Doyle, Wilson, and Fugman were informed by the nature of the work that they engaged in while in the employ of Tigerman, Fugman and McCurry. On the other hand, Rajkovitch and McCurry both brought formalist concerns with them to their respective associations, and Booth and Nagle, separately, changed their "spots" in the decade of the 1980s from anything they had done earlier. In a word, the influence emanating from employment is not the only force at work in an architect's changing career.

Nonetheless, employment is a factor in career evolution, perhaps even transcending education; but this is not to say that practice is not influenced by the nature of the times. For the seed of intentionality is sometimes unexpectedly fertilized. For example, Thomas Beeby's career does not seem to have been particularly influenced by his association with C. F. Murphy Associates generally, or with Gene Summers specifically. But if one considers that Northwestern Memorial Hospital's Rehabilitation Institute (on which Beeby labored) represented a more classically formalist intention than Summers's work with Mies van der Rohe, then it is clear that all that was needed was for the times to be more sympathetic to Beeby's concerns (and postmodernism provided just the sort of encouragement that Beeby needed) to understand how the Murphy experience helped to flesh out Beeby's basis for design influenced by precedent.

On the other hand, when Laurence Booth and James Nagle were partners, their work was visibly more rationalist than formalist. After 1980, when the partners went their separate ways, each became more formalistically driven. Did that change reflect the times, or was it, perhaps, the influence of their own employees (for employees, needless to say, can also have an impact on their employers)—especially if one notes that before 1980 the Booth and Nagle staff represented great diversity (not unlike the work they produced), while after 1980 each of the former partners had a more homogeneous employee cadre (Ketchum, Woodhouse, and others on the Booth side; Decker, Searle, Danker, and others on the Nagle side).

Often, a lack of resonance can produce subsequent vulnerabilities to the pressures of the day. When Gene Sisco and Robert Lubotsky, for example, worked for Booth and Nagle, the work by that firm did not have an overridingly authoritative direction that was made manifest in building. The effect was such that when Sisco and Lubotsky established their own partnership, the shift in values denoted by postmodernism combined with the influence of employee/associates who bore some commitment to the order of the day (Cohen, Metter, Nereim, Quinn) and helped to impart a very different character to the architectural production of the descendant firm.

Sometimes, individual employees or associates (and even partners) try to alter the trajectory of a firm from its initial course. Results are predictably mixed, depending on the relative strengths of the individuals and firms in question. For example, Edward Bennett's classicism had little effect on his employees Paul Schweikher and Winston Elting. Thomas Rajkovitch did little to deflect Christopher Rudolph away from his obsession with organic architecture. Howard Decker tried unsuccessfully to influence Loebl, Schlossman and Hackl, and both Hartshorne and Plunkard had to leave Pappageorge/Haymes to go into private practice in order to establish themselves, formally speaking. It is too early to tell if John Syvertsen will have any impact on

O'Donnell, Wicklund, Pigozzi and Peterson. On the other hand, Ralph Johnson to an impressive degree, and Rich Potokar and Andrew Metter in a much less measurable way, have clearly changed Perkins and Will's course. Adrian Smith and Joseph Gonzalez defined the stylistic trajectory of Skidmore, Owings and Merrill during the late 1980s, but Diane Legge-Kemp, Margaret McCurry, and Kevin Kemp had to find more receptive venues for their formalistic concerns. Roy Solfisburg has had limited success in influencing Holabird and Root's direction away from its century-long rationalist course, and Deborah Doyle, Sisco/Lubotsky, and Rich Potokar had to leave (or remake) their respective firms in order to practice unrestrainedly within their classically inclined visions. Wojciech Lesnikowski's influence on Loebl, Schlossman and Hackl is unresolved at this writing. In the context of the times in which these individuals labored within larger organizations, it is safe to say that the degree of success each has had is based on a number of factors, but the potential for influence remains undeniable between employer and employee, and is often quite striking in reciprocal relationships.

The Rationalist or Modernist Typology

Antecedent figures and firms for a rationalist or modernist typology include the Holabird and Roche, and Schmidt, Garden and Martin organizations, as well as Dankmar Adler and Louis Sullivan both individually and as partners. The precedent for this typology arises out of the pragmatic necessity that results directly from the need to build simply and quickly. Apart from the concept of structure-as-art, this typology is at once modern and practical. For every poet (Sullivan) there was a practical counterpart (Adler); for every designer (Hugh M. G. Garden), a manager (Richard Schmidt); and for every visionary (John Wellborn Root, Jr.), an engineer (Colonel John A. Holabird). One may have chemically neutralized—or indeed stabilized—the other, depending on your point of view.

This typology continues uninterrupted throughout the entirety of Chicago's relatively short history. Its descendants within this timeline are both design driven and pragmatic practitioners. Singly and severally, they represent the synthesis of Chicago's "I will" work ethic and spirit. The Holabird organization, for example, continues today much as it always has. Its architectural production is solid and vanguard by turns with flashes of brilliance, and above all

practical. A great diversity of leaders in the profession grace its alumni roster, not all of whom exercised the same degree of hyper-rationalism for which the firm is noted: Monroe and Irving Bowman, William C. Pereira, Winston Elting, Charles Genther, Bruce Graham, Joseph Passonneau, and Paul Florian. Now directed by Gerald Horn, a new generation committed to the firm's tradition is representative of the current organization.

The modernist tradition begun by George Fred Keck in 1926-27 (soon joined by his brother William) includes among its alumni Paul Schweikher, Robert Bruce Tague, Ralph Rapson, Winston Elting, and John van der Muelen. Although always a small practice, the Kecks brought rationalism to a new level. Hammond and Roesch (both Skidmore, Owings and Merrill alumni) and later Hammond and Beeby, along with Booth and Nagle (and later David Swan), represented rationalism as a design generator. On the other hand, Schmidt, Garden and Erikson, and A. Epstein and Sons made rationalism work for them in practical terms. Practicum, practice, practical...firms such as the Dubin organization, Loebl, Schlossman and Hackl, Greenberg and Finfer, Shaw, Metz and Dolio, O'Donnell, Wicklund, Pigozzi and Peterson, Loewenberg and Loewenberg, Milton Schwartz, and others too numerous to mention gave rationalism its most widespread representation in the realm of practice. In quite another way, Howard Fisher, L. Morgan Yost, Schweikher and Elting, Banks/Eakin, Wheeler Kearns, Mastro and Skylar, and many, many others saw rationalism as a means to elevate a hybridized society that was driven to better understand its collective desire to seek pragmatic answers to its needs.

The Romantic or Organic Typology

A romantic or organic typology may trace its antecedent strain back to the time of Louis Sullivan's arrival in Chicago from Boston. It evolved with Joseph Silsbee and the "Steinway Hall" group, reached its zenith with Frank Lloyd Wright, and went into overdrive with Elmslie, Purcell, Drummond, Dwight Perkins, and the Griffins—collectively identified as the Prairie School architects of the day. In fact, the precedent group reached such stature that its descendancy from 1923 forward can only be perceived in decline. Its destiny as this century comes to a close has resulted in eccentricity, over and against the noble vision trumpeted by its seminal chronicler, Frank Lloyd Wright.

As has been noted earlier, from the Depression throughout the years of World War II, from a romantic point of view, nothing much occurred in Chicago. Frank Lloyd Wright had long since departed, and the two bleak decades of the 1930s and 1940s produced little to be romantic about, at least in Chicago. But the strain re-emerged when Harry Weese returned home from World War II. He heralded his intrinsic belief in mid-western values by the use of exaggeration and hyperbole, and he bred a lineage that includes Thomas Hickey, Ben and later Cynthia Weese, Peter Landon, William Bauhs, William Dring, and Rick Phillips, all of whom proliferate an inexplicably mysterious architectural production, not at all assured of attracting sycophants.

The more literally Wright-indebted descendants, William Deknatel and Christopher Rudolph, tried unsuccessfully to keep alive values that are no longer in sync with the changing times. Meanwhile, the eccentric Hinds, Schroeder and Whitaker organization has begotten Pappageorge/Haymes and finally Schroeder, Murchie, Laya and Associates. Always admittedly outside the mainstream of American architectural development, the proponents of the romantic typology speak to an American dream long perverted by wars, insensitivity to pressing issues of underclass, and more. Dramatically reduced in its influence over the seventy years explored in this volume, this small gathering huddles together looking backward to a time before our collective fall from grace.

The Structurally or Constructionally Expressive Typology

The fourth and final strain that might be charted through this genealogy is the structurally or constructionally expressive typology. Its single, most authoritative predecessor for twentieth-century descendants is William Le Baron Jenney. But the elevation of engineering to an art form was heralded by this century's architectural historians in order to valorize adherents of the Modern Movement by giving them legitimate antecedents. Jenney-as-engineer became the kind of understandable father-figure that Louis Sullivan could not be, precisely because Jenney's practical nature was more immediately acceptable in the context of the ennoblement of the skeleton frame than was Sullivan's flowery rhetoric. Nonetheless, the fullness of structural expressionism was only to be realized in the 1930s—a realization so vast as to escape predictability. It was to begin with the 1933-34 Century of Progress Exposition, and it manifested itself precisely because of employer/employee relationships.

When Daniel H. Burnham, Jr., inherited a role in the planning of the Century of Progress fair that was similar to the one played by his father in the Columbian Exposition forty years earlier, he turned to two of his young associates, Nathaniel Owings and Louis Skidmore, to perform a central role in administering that fair. Brothers-in-law (they married sisters), Skidmore and Owings capitalized on the many client contacts they made during the project, and they opened their own practice in 1936, which, with the addition of the engineer John Merrill in 1939, continues nominally today. Their practice coincided almost precisely with the emergence of modernist values worldwide, and it enjoyed the surprising coincidence of the arrival of Ludwig Mies van der Rohe in Chicago in 1938. While employees migrated between the two firms (Haid, Dunlap, Drake, Goldsmith, Wong, Duckett), Mies's students from the Illinois Institute of Technology also inseminated the Skidmore, Owings and Merrill (SOM) organization (Hammond, Roesch, Dunlap, Wong, Goldsmith, Schipporeit, Heinrich, Takeuchi, Vinci, DeStefano). Thus was SOM's trajectory made parallel with that of Mies. When the C. F. Murphy organization began to be populated by IIT-trained and IIT-influenced employees as well (Manny, Wong, Brownson, Summers, Jahn, Krueck), the die was cast for a renaissance of the initial Chicago School: the fascination with the structural and technical domains of architecture had returned to Chicago with a vengeance.

Former employees of Mies perpetuated his structural expression in numerous subsequent practices: Alfred Caldwell, Phyllis Lambert, Arthur Takeuchi, Y. C. Wong, Schipporeit and Heinrich, Pace Associates, and Brenner Danforth Rockwell (which in turn begot John Vinci's practice). Even SOM, itself thoroughly influenced by Mies's authority, spun off neo-Miesian firms: Powell/Kleinschmidt, Greg Landahl, and even begot Krueck and Olsen, through SOM alumnus James Hammond and his Hammond, Beeby organization. C. F. Murphy begot Murphy/Jahn, which in turn begot James Goettsch's practice. Sometimes the lineage of structo-constructivist expression is not simply the result of employment descendancies: Eva Maddox's work of the 1990s is one example; but the accomplishments of such firms as Florian Wierzbowski, Himmel Bonner, or Tigerman McCurry in the late 1980s and 1990s are others. Nonetheless, the over-

whelming evidence in this typology suggests that influence through employment—of course, valorized by public acceptance—is a factor of major consequence in influencing strategies of design.

The four typologies gleaned from this genealogical chart represent only one of the many possible interpretations suggested by the raw data. Other than stylistic tendencies, for instance, building types are, in part, the product of liaisons formed in practice between architects, just as they are also in part the result of their contact with a particular client. A recent example of this might be the work of DeStefano/Goettsch, whose highrise experience—and contacts—has enabled them to continue what they had begun at SOM and Murphy/Jahn, respectively. Another example might begin with the largely residential practice begun by George Fred Keck, and extend logically to the equally domestically inclined work of such Keck alumni as Paul Schweikher, Robert Bruce Tague, Ralph Rapson, Winston Elting, John van der Muelen, and Ezra Gordon and Jack Levin. It may be that particular expertise gained through employment suggests a convenient extension through subsequent practice. It may also be that reputations formed within organizations continue apace after associations dissolve, with ongoing practitioners capitalizing on the building types that they know best.

Another use of this chart emanates from the linkages that become apparent and that enable one to challenge an architect's ambiguity and/or unwillingness to acknowledge shared origins of authorship. For example, a long-standing conundrum has been the uncertainty connected with many of the details developed for the Charnley House. Sullivan had the commission, but his employee Wright worked on the project at home at night, bringing drawings in for approval. The flowery woodcarving presages Sullivan's later designs in his *System of Architectural Ornament* (1924), while the stairscreen can be seen in various ways in later projects by Wright.

Within the time-line of this book, Paul Schweikher's reluctance to acknowledge design participation by his partner Ted Lamb ranks with Bertrand Goldberg's unwillingness to acknowledge Gilmer Vardiman Black's early role in the work of his firm, or more importantly, Floyd Magnuson's impact on Goldberg's well-known use of circular geometry.[4] Equally interesting is the case of the shared authorship of the Inland Steel Building (Walter Netsch's concept, Bruce Graham's development), as each of the authors has long been unwilling to acknowledge the role of the other. Graham is particularly interesting here, since he also refuses to credit either Diane Legge-Kemp with the Chicago Tribune Printing Plant, or Natalie de Blois with the Equitable Building, and he has diminished Fazlur Khan's part in the design concept of the John Hancock Center.[5] The chart is useful in this way in order to excavate information emanating from professional relationships. In other words, "Who worked for whom?" can lead to "Who worked on what project?" or "What role did the various participants play in the evolution of a project?" There are, doubtless, other insights that can be gleaned from genealogical exploration. Clearly, this is a work-in-progress that requires periodic updating and corrections—of that I am certain. The existence of such information derived from a single, albeit seminal, location such as Chicago may encourage others throughout the United States to excavate their own architectural past and assemble similar genealogies. The particular interpretations suggested here are necessarily subjectively limited ways of understanding Chicago's own architectural legacy. The lasting value of this genealogy will only be ascertained over time, and it is hoped that its publication here will prompt further scholarship.

NOTES

1. The genealogy has been a work-in-progress; it has been reviewed by and received contributions from a number of individuals: Susan Benjamin, Calvin Johnson, Arlene Kriv, Pauline Saliga, Claire Theobald, Tracy Tigerman, Sarah Mollman Underhill, and John Zukowsky. The author is also grateful to Thomas Fredrickson for his computer-assisted layout of the information contained in the genealogy.

2. John Zukowsky, ed., *Chicago Architecture, 1872-1922: Birth of a Metropolis* (Munich and Chicago, 1987).
3. See Stanley Tigerman, *Halftime: Celebrating 75 Years of Chicago Architecture* (Chicago, 1992), the catalogue accompanying an exhibition at the Arts Club of Chicago.
4. For a discussion of these examples, see Stuart Cohen, *Chicago Architects*, introduction by Stanley Tigerman (Chicago, 1976).
5. Bruce Graham made corresponding remarks publicly to the author on the occasion of the publication of *Halftime* (note 3).

Plates

329   Urban Images

332   Transportation

342   Institutions and Government

349   Commerce and Business

368   Industry

376   Shopping

387   Houses and Housing

401   Recreation

The annotations in the plates section were contributed by Mark Bouman, David Brodherson, Robert Bruegmann, Jane Clarke, Dennis Doordan, Victor Margolin, Ross Miller, Pauline Saliga, Franz Schulze, Stephen Sennott, Robert V. Sharp, Stanley Tigerman, Carol Willis, Wim de Wit, Mary Woolever, and John Zukowsky.

Urban Images

1 SKIDMORE, OWINGS AND MERRILL. Bird's-eye view for the Central Area Plan,
showing proposed development and public lakefront amenities, delineated by
Carlos Diniz Associates, 1985 (cat. no. 29).

2-5 Aerial photographs of Chicago, 1989-92.

Transportation

6   Steam engines of the Illinois Central Railroad with the skyscrapers of Michigan Avenue in the background, c. 1929.

7   LESLIE RAGAN. "For the Public Service," a view of the LaSalle Street Station showing the Twentieth Century Limited and other New York Central trains, c. 1939 (cat no. 41).

The New York Central's streamlined Twentieth Century Limited, designed by Henry Dreyfuss, leads the way out of the LaSalle Street Station, while the LaGrange-built diesel and the steam-powered Empire State Express keep a demure distance. The smoke-caressed Board of Trade Building seems to ride in the rear car of the "most beautiful train in the world." New York and Wall Street are but seventeen hours away. Chicago's steely grasp on its hinterland is also seen along the lakefront, where five locomotives of the Illinois Central Railroad are ready for another run to the deep South. The IC carried a heavily northbound passenger traffic in the postwar years; between 1940 and 1970, it contributed mightily to the quadrupling of the city's African-American population.   M. B.

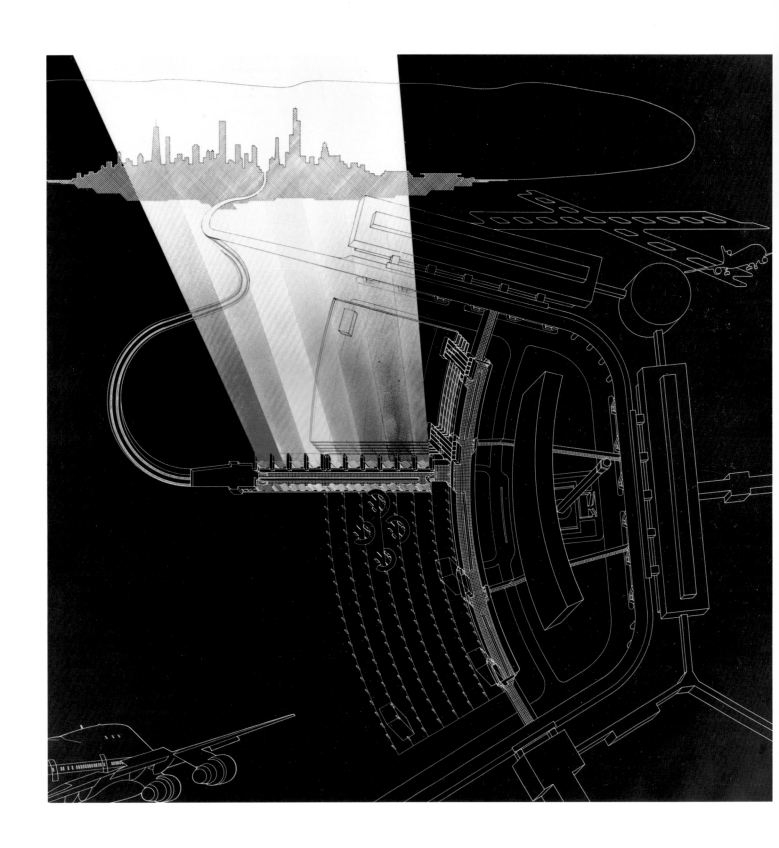

8-9 MURPHY/JAHN ARCHITECTS.
Axonometric view (cat. no. 46) and photograph
of the Chicago Transit Authority subway station
at O'Hare International Airport, c. 1981-82.

With the completion of the rapid transit station at O'Hare in 1984, previously distinct air and high-speed surface transportation systems became extensions of each other. Curved walls of glass block, backlit with lights and painted in different colors, illuminate the train platforms and absorb sound in the station, which is a gateway to both the city and the airport. Escalators and stairs rise from the subway platforms through a gray metal fenestrated wall that mimics an aircraft fuselage. Passengers moving in the opposite direction enter the rapid transit station in an equally dramatic procession past bold postmodern forms.   D. B.

10-12   HUGH FERRISS. Highways of the Future, 1943 (cat. no. 61), with sectional views of Dymaxion Cars designed by R. Buckminster Fuller, 1933 and 1943 (cat. nos. 56 and 60).

Famous for his 1929 book, *Metropolis of Tomorrow*, delineator Hugh Ferriss envisioned high-speed, limited-access highways for travel across the country or between major metropolitan centers. During the 1920s, Ferriss collaborated with New York architect Harvey Corbett to propose multi-level streets and sidewalks for New York City, one of many futuristic views of urban landscapes dominated by the automobile. Just as Ferriss's elevated, reinforced concrete highways had abandoned existing outmoded street prototypes previously suited to slower horsedrawn traffic, industrial designer R. Buckminster Fuller's Dymaxion Car — first exhibited at Chicago's 1933 Century of Progress Exposition — rejected horsedrawn vehicles in favor of modern machines designed for high-speed travel. While it was never mass-produced, Fuller's experimental aerodynamic design was notable for its three-wheel system. Aerodynamic styling was subsequently used in many production automobile designs of the 1930s, from the famed Chrysler Airflow of 1934 to the 1935 Volkswagen.   S. S.

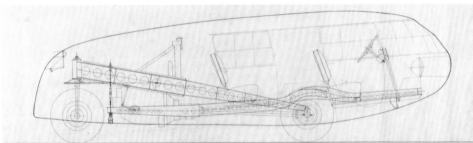

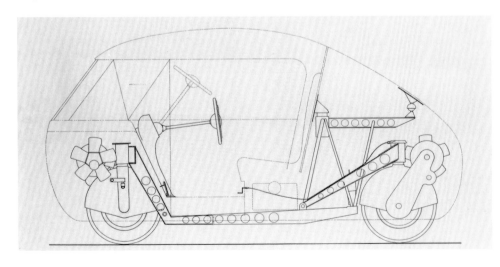

13-14   Restoration of the first McDonald's drive-in restaurant of 1955, 100 Lee Street, Des Plaines, with a perspective study of the McDonald's System Building of 1957-58 (cat. no. 80).

Regarded as roadside eyesores by many critics, hamburger restaurant chains had provided drive-in service to motorists for decades before Chicagoan Ray Kroc's first franchised McDonald's opened in April 1955. In 1952, just before they hired Kroc to sell franchises, drive-in operators Richard and Maurice McDonald had collaborated with architects Stanley Meston and Charles Fish to conceive of a standardized restaurant made eye-catching to passing motorists by parabolic arches, contrasting red- and white-tiled walls, and a slanted, wedge-shaped roof illuminated at night with neon lights. Part of popular culture's absorption of modernism's dynamic abstract forms, McDonald's parabolic arch represented one of many uses for this symbolic form, demonstrated in large scale by Eero Saarinen's 1948 Jefferson Westward Expansion Memorial Arch in St. Louis (completed in 1964). In response to demands to harmonize their units with surrounding building traditions, McDonald's has, over the years, replaced identical modular restaurants with varied buildings employing local materials and traditional styles.
S. S.

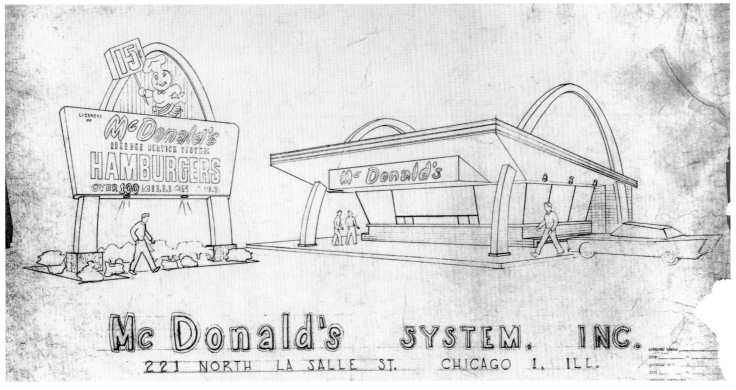

As part of the redevelopment of the North Loop begun in 1973, the Greyhound Bus Station — designed by Skidmore, Owings and Merrill with a functional modern shed for a waiting room and a series of ramps for buses below grade — was condemned and removed to a less central location southwest of the Loop. The old Greyhound depot and a smaller terminal for its competitor Trailways were both on Randolph Street, Chicago's version of Times Square. The new consolidated facility by Nagle, Hartray and Associates is now tangential to the downtown. A post-and-tension-wire roof provides the building with a pleasant modern anonymity of the sort SOM first accomplished on Randolph Street.

R. M.

15 SKIDMORE, OWINGS AND MERRILL. Cutaway perspective view of the Greyhound Bus Station, northeast corner of Randolph and Clark streets, 1953 (now demolished).

16 NAGLE, HARTRAY AND ASSOCIATES. The Greyhound-Trailways Bus Station, 631 West Congress Street, 1988-90.

17-18 I. M. Pei and Associates.
The control tower at O'Hare International
Airport, with a detail of a working drawing
for the control tower, 1966 (cat. no. 103).

In 1962, in response to a Congressional
mandate, the Federal Aviation Administration employed I. M. Pei and Associates to design a standardized air traffic control tower.
The tower at O'Hare International Airport is
one of fifty similar forms erected at airports
throughout the United States. The design
program divided the tower into three component parts, with variations in all three: two
types or sizes of control cab at the top of the
tower for visual flight control; two kinds of
pentagonal tower shafts in an array of sizes,
most of which are of reinforced concrete; and
an underground base of varying sizes housing
equipment for instrument flight control and
other functions.   D. B.

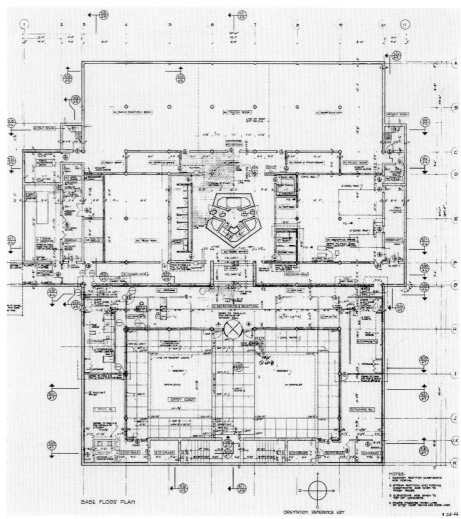

19-21 MURPHY/JAHN ARCHITECTS.
The United Airlines Terminal at O'Hare
International Airport, 1983-88, with a view
of the underground tunnel connecting
Concourses B and C, and a perspective
cutaway drawing of the entire terminal
(cat. no. 108).

The original layout at O'Hare International
Airport was a classic example of a compact
horseshoe plan. The two original terminal
buildings were simple, but elegantly
designed, steel-and-glass boxes with more
utilitarian concourses extending from the
rear to the gates. When it came time to replace a temporary structure along the inner
loop, increasing demands on the airport
made it desirable to change this configuration. Instead of a single building with concourses, two long rectangular buildings
connected by an underground tunnel allowed

for more gates and produced a more compact
building footprint. Murphy/Jahn used a sleek
steel-and-glass envelope to enclose a pair of
dramatic concourses. Impressive in their
dimensions and full of light, they are among
the most memorable transportation spaces
ever created.   R. B.

Institutions and Government

22 VOORHEES, GMELIN AND WALKER. Perspective rendering of a proposed Chicago War Memorial, delineated by John Wenrich, 1931 (cat. no. 119).

In February 1919, Edward H. Bennett conceived of a war memorial for Grant Park at Congress Street. Nearly ten years later, the War Memorial Committee of Chicago announced a competition for such a monument, and the jury invited eleven architectural firms to enter, including the prominent New York firm of Voorhees, Gmelin and Walker. They also opened the competition to all American architects, and drew an additional 103 entries, including the winning, but unbuilt, design of Eric Gugler and Roger Bailey of New York. Ralph Walker's entry, selected as one of the four finalists, was, in his own words, "an attempt to express the chaos [of war] and the ideal of man looking out between the dominant forces surrounding him to a vision of his hopes". For Chicago, Walker prepared designs for Terminal Park, a proposed large-scale office development over the Illinois Central freight yards north of Grant Park (1929-30); an aluminum tower in the central lagoon at the Century of Progess Exposition (1933-34); and a 1934 competitive design for the enlargement of the Art Institute. All these designs were unexecuted.   M. W.

23-24 LUDWIG MIES VAN DER ROHE. Perspective study for a proposed library or administration building, Illinois Institute of Technology, 1944 (cat. no. 130), with a detail of a photograph of Crown Hall (1955; cat. no. 132), which houses IIT's School of Architecture.

Holy of holies, ground zero for modern architecture in Chicago, Crown Hall was Mies van der Rohe's centerpiece for the new campus of the Armour Institute of Technology (now the Illinois Institute of

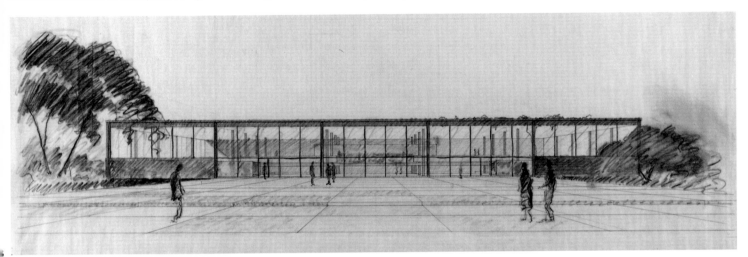

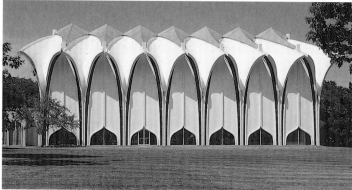

Technology). Constructed in 1955-56 to house the departments of architecture, design, and planning, this building was the ultimate refinement of a Miesian type first raised to the status of an international icon with his German Pavilion at the World Exhibition in Barcelona, 1929, and the Tugendhat House in Brno, Czechoslovakia, 1930. The transformation of a domestic type into an institutional one parallels Mies's rising status as the corporate world's darling, able to provide a sufficiently elegant setting for postwar American business culture. Mies himself said of Crown Hall, "I think it is the clearest structure we have done, the best to express our philosophy."   R. M.

25-27 MINORU YAMASAKI AND ASSOCIATES. Entrance to North Shore Congregation Israel (cat. no. 142), Glencoe, 1963, with a detail of the side elevation, and the 1982 addition to the synagogue complex by Hammond, Beeby and Babka.

Twenty years lie between the design of the temple and its addition, each project responding to a very different program set forth by the congregation. Yamasaki's temple and the adjacent Memorial Hall were planned to serve the overflow crowds on the high holidays. Suffused with light from ogival windows at ground level, the sanctuary seats 800 in a space that is 50 feet high and 126 feet long. Taking full advantage of the spectacular site on a bluff overlooking Lake

Michigan, the design of the temple was, according to the architect, generated by plant forms, especially exemplified by the "unfolding lily" vaults of the sanctuary. The congregation's requirements for the 1982 addition were to provide "a sense of intimacy, warmth, and community" for the modest attendance at regular Friday night services, and to include a social hall for the communal gathering that traditionally follows. The small sanctuary is an enclosed, circular space with natural light entering through an oculus, while the social hall is rectangular with large windows overlooking the lake.

J. C.

28-30 HAMMOND, BEEBY AND BABKA. Exterior and interior views of the Harold Washington Library Center, 1988-91, with the 1988 competitive model showing pedimental sculpture.

This full-block structure is the product of a competition with five design-build teams. The winning scheme, by Hammond, Beeby and Babka with A. Epstein and Sons, is a massive masonry behemoth, looking backwards in spiritual homage to Henri Labrouste's Bibliothèque Nationale in Paris. The architects' rationale for not providing public space outside the library is the desire to reiterate the State Street corridor as it intersects Congress Street. The interior spaces are negotiated by escalators that are unclearly located, in ways not dissimilar to other State Street department stores, and they ascend ultimately to a Winter Garden, whose primary function seems to be in providing rental income from social functions. The small, three-story entrance rotunda passes for what public space there is in this massive structure. The abrupt displacement of the exterior stone-and-brick container with an aluminum grid on the rear Plymouth Court facade is unexplained, and it may raise unnecessary questions about "the emperor's new clothes" of Chicago's newest leviathan.

S. T.

31-34 MURPHY/JAHN, with LESTER B. KNIGHT AND ASSOCIATES. Exterior and interior views of the State of Illinois Building, Randolph, LaSalle, Lake, and Clark streets, 1985, with early study models (cat. no. 164).

Under Mayor Richard J. Daley, Chicago began to rebuild its downtown core using the best contemporary architects. The Civic Center (1965), later renamed the Richard J. Daley Center, established the type of a tower in a plaza. When an equally ambitious politician, Republican Governor James Thompson, needed to build a state office building, he had a splendid site, directly north of the City Hall and County Building, and an audacious architect ready to design a monumental building. Helmut Jahn took the opportunity to reconfigure civic architecture. He essentially inverted Chicago's tower-and-plaza formula by putting the public space inside a giant belly-shaped atrium and squashing the tower into a polychrome-paneled, flying saucer form. State offices are opened to the multistory atrium and glass-walled elevators ride up and down with funhouse precision. Completed in 1985, it is an optimistic architecture where government is exposed, and the classical detail, like the thin alloy columns on the south side, is simply there for show.   R. M.

35-36 PERKINS AND WILL.
Orland Park Village Center, 1987-89,
with a drawing of the west elevation
(cat. no. 169).

Orland Park, like many other rapidly
expanding communities at the outer edge of
the metropolitan area, has been confronted
with the task of defining itself. Larger and
more self-sufficient than the railroad suburbs
of a previous era, but determined to avoid
the problems of the densely packed city, this
community found itself confronted by fundamental questions of image when it needed a
set of new public buildings. Ralph Johnson
and his colleagues at Perkins and Will
responded to the challenge by creating an
impressive ensemble of buildings that manages to be at once friendly in appearance and
compatible with the residential neighborhoods nearby, but monumental enough to
provide a civic focal point to the community
and to avoid being dwarfed by the boisterous
vitality of the adjacent commercial strip.

R. B.

Commerce and Business

37   FRANK LLOYD WRIGHT.
Perspective rendering of the proposed
National Life Insurance Building, 1923
(cat. no. 193).

In 1923-24, Frank Lloyd Wright was commissioned by the president of the National Life Insurance Company, Albert M. Johnson, to propose an office building for a site on the newly developing extension of Michigan Avenue north of the Chicago River. Wright's unbuilt and, for the time, probably unbuildable project overturned the conventions of skyscraper design as a masonry-clad steel skeleton. He replaced column-and-beam construction with a system of reinforced-concrete supports from which were cantilevered floor slabs; these carried the screen walls of glass and copper. The building was composed of four identical wings, separated by light courts that projected asymmetrically from its narrow spine. In spite of Wright's radical rethinking of massing, skeleton, and skin, his scheme conformed to the city's new zoning regulations, and Wright seriously promoted his visionary design as "a standardization along industrial lines to lighten and cheapen and make more humanly effective the skyscraper."   C. W.

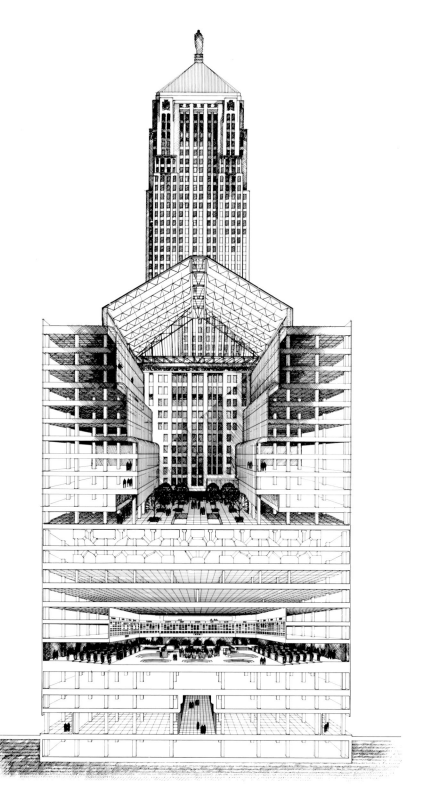

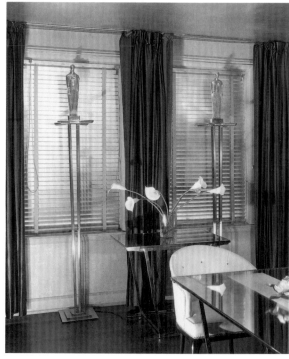

38-40 JOHN STORRS. Maquette for *Ceres* (cat. no. 198), the 1928 statue atop the Chicago Board of Trade Building by Holabird and Root, with a 1931 photograph of John Wellborn Root, Jr.'s apartment showing *Ceres* maquettes and a cutaway section of the 1978 addition to the original building by Murphy/Jahn (cat. no. 197).

Chicago has always been, first and foremost, a city known for business, so it is perhaps fitting that no building dominated the skyline for such a long time as the present Board of Trade, designed by Holabird and Root in the late 1920s. The site, at the foot of LaSalle Street, is certainly more impressive than that enjoyed by any religious or governmental structure, and it is conspicuous that the crowning feature commemorates no civic leader or saint but Ceres, the Roman goddess of the harvest. This figure, somewhat abstracted and modernistic, but still clearly human and female, provides a fitting termi-

nation to the dramatic stepped-back silhouette of the building mass. This silhouette in turn provided inspiration for the addition by Murphy/Jahn, where it was most potently reinterpreted as interior space in the great atrium.   R. B.

41 THIELBAR AND FUGARD. Perspective
rendering of the Trustee System Service
Building (later the Corn Exchange),
201 North Wells Street, delineated by
F. Holcomb, 1930 (cat. no. 204).

42 VITZTHUM AND BURNS. Perspective
rendering of the Steuben Club Building, 188
West Randolph Street, delineated by
E. Tronnes, c. 1928 (cat. no. 203).

Thielbar and Fugard developed their
expertise in the design of large commercial
and residential buildings in the teens and
twenties. Their 201 North Wells Street tower
of 1930, at the western edge of Chicago's
famous Loop elevated municipal transit line,
is their most famous and largest pre-
Depression building. The firm of Vitzthum
and Burns also executed high-rise buildings
of comparable scale before the Great
Depression, the two most important being
the One North LaSalle Building of 1930 and
the Steuben Club Building of 1929 at 188
West Randolph Street. The Great Depression
and World War II took their toll on both
these firms: neither was to build commercial
skyscrapers such as these afterward. In fact,
large high-rises in the West Loop were not to
be seen again until a building boom there in
the 1970s and early 1980s was spawned by
construction of the Sears Tower of 1974.

J. Z.

43-44 HARRY WEESE AND ASSOCIATES. Perspective study of the Time-Life Building, 541 North Fairbanks Court, delineated by Robert E. Bell, 1966 (cat. no. 220), with a photograph of the building.

This orthodox Miesian skyscraper, constructed from 1966 to 1968 for the subscription services of *Time* and *Life* magazines, was a surprise from the unorthodox firm of Harry Weese and Associates. The exterior infill of tinted mirror glass was unusual in a skyscraper at the time, and for the interior Weese's firm introduced a pioneering concept in the design of double-deck elevators that stop at two floors simultaneously, an innovation that has been widely copied. This efficient use of space also reduced the number of elevator shafts required for the building and made possible the generously proportioned lobbies that Time-Life devoted to exhibitions when the skyscraper was opened.   J. C.

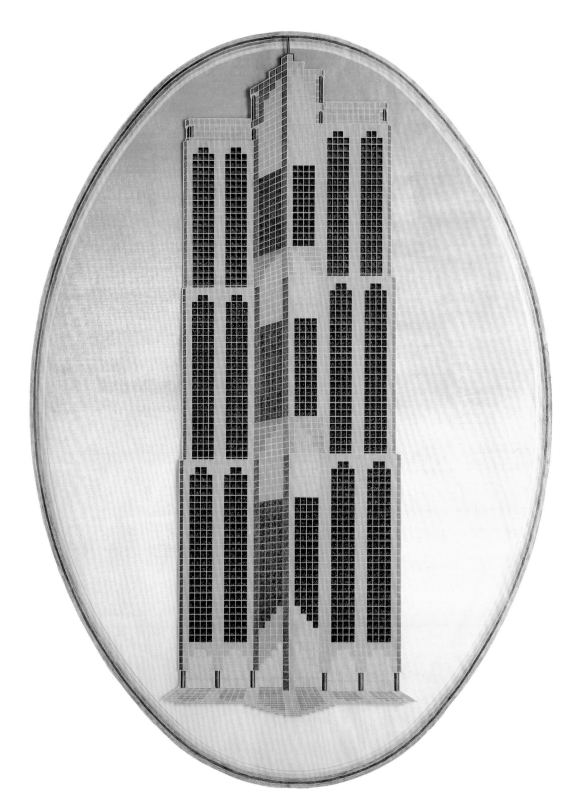

This skyscraper, designed by Helmut Jahn with the assistance of James Goettsch, consciously evokes the excitement of American architecture of the 1920s in its use of set-back, ziggurat-like forms in the massing and decoration of this reflective-glass building. Each of the angular spaces that project on the building's center houses an atrium. The building was one of many that were con-

45   C. F. MURPHY ASSOCIATES.
Elevation of One South Wacker Drive, 1981 (cat. no. 238).

structed on the western edge of the business district — the West Loop area adjacent to Wacker Drive — following the completion of the Sears Tower. This drawing, itself a distinctive oval presentation, was shown before the building was completed, in the "New Chicago Architecture" exhibition at the Museo di Castelvecchio in Verona, 1981.   J. Z.

46-48 SKIDMORE, OWINGS AND MERRILL. The John Hancock Center and Garage, 875 North Michigan Avenue, 1965-69, with "Tops" entry to the Chicago Architectural Club Competition by Peggy Smolka Wolff, 1983 (cat. no. 245).

One of the most curious features of the Chicago skyline is the pairing, on the extreme opposite sides of the central business district, of the Sears Tower and the John Hancock Center. Chicago's two tallest buildings, both massive, dark presences on the skyline, were built almost simultaneously and are both the product of the firm of Skidmore, Owings and Merrill. Here the resemblance ends. The Sears Tower, for all its height (110 stories; 1,454 feet), looks almost small, like a model blown up to great scale. The Hancock Center, on the other

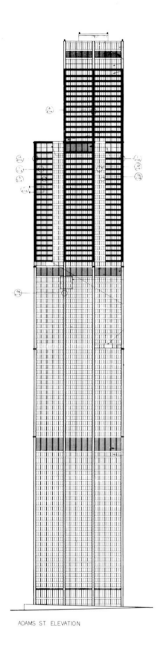

ADAMS ST ELEVATION

hand (100 stories; 1,107 feet), is one of the few postwar skyscrapers that actually looks tall, the result of its elegant tapering form and the huge cross braces. Although it meets its site somewhat awkwardly at the bottom, the Hancock soars above all its neighbors in a confident, almost swaggering way that is very much in the Chicago tradition. Sears recently began leaving its tower behind, when it embarked on a move to suburban Hoffman Estates in November 1992, relocating 5,000 employees of its merchandise group to a new campus headquarters.   R. B.

49-50   SKIDMORE, OWINGS
AND MERRILL.
Construction photograph
of the Sears Tower,
233 South Wacker Drive,
1974, with a drawing of a
proposed fiberglass window
wall for the upper levels
(cat. no. 224).

51   PERKINS AND WILL.
Perspective view of the lobby
of the Sears Merchandise
Group Home Office,
Hoffman Estates, 1990
(cat. no. 290).

Commerce and Business   355

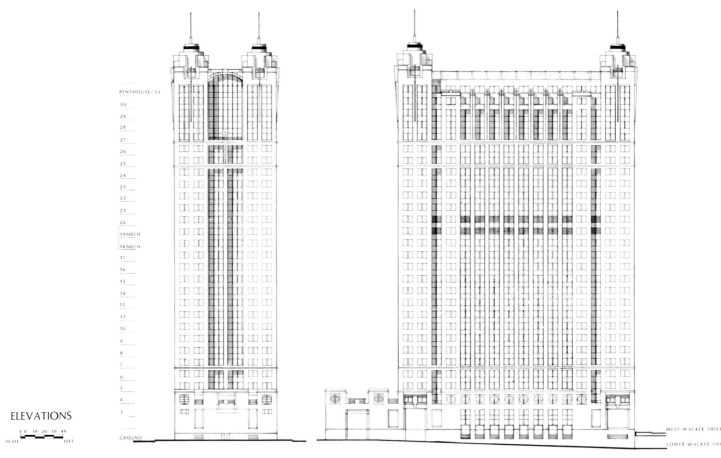

ELEVATIONS

PENTHOUSE/31
30
29
28
27
26
25
24
23
22
21
20
19 MECH
18 MECH
17
16
15
14
12
11
10
9
8
7
6
5
4
3
GROUND

SCALE 5 0 10 20 30 40 FEET

WEST LAKE STREET

NORTH POST PLACE

WEST WACKER DRIVE

LOWER WACKER DRIVE

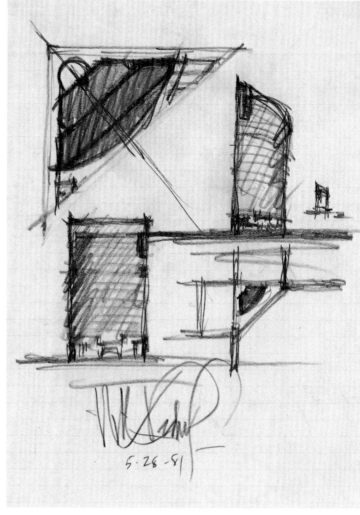

5·28·81

356   Commerce and Business

52-56 KOHN PEDERSEN FOX ASSOCIATES.
333 West Wacker Drive, 1983, with a detail
of the base of the building, a 1981 sketch by
William Pedersen (cat. no. 249), and two
elevations for 225 West Wacker Drive,
c. 1989 (upper left; cat. no. 279).

Of all the skyscrapers constructed in Chicago
during the 1980s, perhaps the most beautiful
is 333 West Wacker Drive. Located on the
Chicago River at the point where it veers
sharply to the south, the building has a
curved green glass facade that is keenly responsive to its dramatic river site. Likewise,
the three-story marble and granite base of the
building is responsive to the neighboring
buildings. The base features an arcade
linking the river with the historic Loop, and
ground-floor octagonal columns that pay
subtle homage to the towers of the
Merchandise Mart directly across the river.
The deliberate contrast in materials from the
masonry base to the sheer glass wall of the
tower and penthouse was intended to give
the building a base, shaft, and top — a design
concept explored extensively by nineteenth-
century architects, particularly Louis
Sullivan. The same firm designed 225 West
Wacker in 1989, which has base elements
that echo those of 333 West Wacker.   P. S.

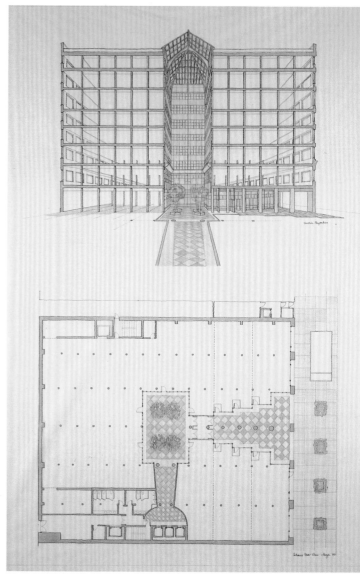

57-58 NAGLE, HARTRAY AND ASSOCIATES. Perspective elevations (cat. no. 244), cutaway perspective view, and plan of the remodeling of 20 North Michigan Avenue, 1983.

atrium spaces in this and other office buildings, such as the Lumberman's Mutual Casualty Company (pls. 59-60), became a trademark of design in the 1980s.   J. Z.

The eight-story commercial building at 20 North Michigan Avenue (1885-92) by Beers, Clay and Dutton — formerly the John M. Smyth Furniture Store — became part of the Montgomery Ward complex when retailing giant A. Montgomery Ward attached a tower building designed by architect Richard Schmidt to the south at 6 North Michigan Avenue in 1898. But since the sale of this complex in 1908, after Montgomery Ward moved its headquarters to its present Chicago Avenue location, the low-rise block of 14-20 North Michigan Avenue has experienced a variety of tenants and alterations. Consistent with the interest in the 1980s in contextual design, James Nagle and Jack Hartray renovated this retail and showroom facility into an office building by providing a cut-stone base and decorated cornice, and creating an atrium space within the layered floors of this former loft building. The use of

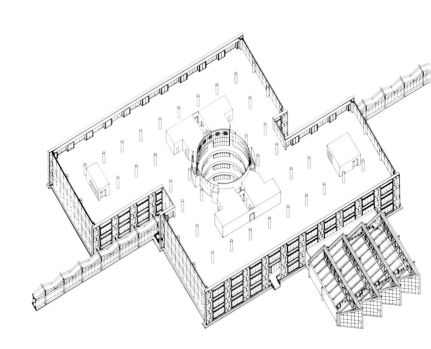

59-60 HOLABIRD AND ROOT.
Axonometric view (cat. no. 289) and interior
of the atrium of the Lumberman's Mutual
Casualty Company, Long Grove, 1990.

61-64 JOHN BURGEE with PHILIP JOHNSON; SHAW AND ASSOCIATES, associate architects; POWELL/KLEINSCHMIDT, associate architects for the interiors.
Interior view of the lobby and detail of the exterior of 190 South LaSalle Street, c. 1983-86, with photographs of the preliminary model of the lobby (cat. no. 254) and the library for Mayer, Brown and Platt.

Since its completion in 1987, the forty-story office building at 190 South LaSalle Street has been both applauded and criticized for its overt references to historic architecture. After exploring a variety of building styles, the architects, in the final version, settled on a five-story red granite base and a distinctive gabled roof that draw inspiration from two well-known nineteenth-century Chicago office buildings designed by John Wellborn Root — the recently restored Rookery of 1888 and the Masonic Temple of 1892 (now demolished). The LaSalle Street lobby, an opulent public space 180 feet long and 40 feet wide, features marble walls and pilasters topped by a lavish, gold-leafed barrel vault. The lobby is further enriched by two artworks — an abstract sculpture by British artist Anthony Caro, and a site-specific tapestry by Helena Hernmark, which is based on a Jules Guérin rendering for the 1909 *Plan of Chicago.*   P. S.

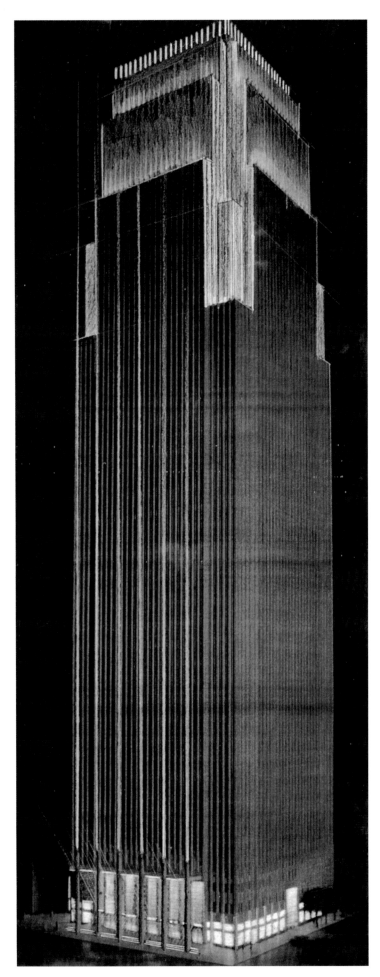

65-67 CESAR PELLI. Perspective rendering of 181 West Madison Street, c. 1990 (cat. no. 285), with views of the lobby and the office of J. Paul Beitler, Miglin-Beitler Development, designed by the Landahl Group.

68 MOORE, RUBLE AND YUDELL. Perspective view of a Late Entry to the Chicago Tribune Tower Competition, 1980 (cat. no. 227).

Charles Moore's "late entry" to the 1980 revival of the Tribune Tower Competition suggested a return to the telescoping form and fanciful lighting of the romantic skyscraper of the 1920s and 1930s. Cesar Pelli's elegant 181 West Madison Street follows through on this notion — with nods to Eliel Saarinen's 1922 Tribune Tower entry — through its thoughtful massing, mullion tracery, finials, and its five-story lobby as Renaissance loggia (complete with Frank Stella art on the wall), as well as through its illuminated nocturnal profile. Meanwhile, upstairs, on the table in the Miglin-Beitler corporate offices, sits a model of the architect's proposed 125-story Miglin-Beitler Tower, like a snow scene waiting to be shaken to life.   M. B.

69-70 PERKINS AND WILL.
The Morton International Building,
100 North Riverside Plaza, 1987-90, with a
perspective view of the lobby, 1988-89
(cat. no. 273).

The Morton Building represents a solution to
a difficult set of design constraints. The site
itself, directly on the Chicago River, had the
potential for monumental treatment, but it
was irregular in shape and slashed diagonally
by railroad tracks that were still in use. The
building also had to accommodate a complex
program that called for enormous floor plates
on the lower levels with more conventional
office floors above, as well as a whole set of
pedestrian and vehicular entrances and exits
along a very restricted street frontage. The
solution of Ralph Johnson and his associates
at Perkins and Will was to create a base
building that was partly suspended over the
tracks from a great roof truss, then to
surmount this with a tower, integrating the
whole through a complicated meshing of
horizontals and verticals in the steel, glass,
and granite skin.   R. B.

71-72   SKIDMORE, OWINGS AND MERRILL.
The NBC Tower, 454 North Columbus
Drive, 1986-90, with a preliminary design
study, 1986 (cat. no. 261).

The NBC Tower is one of the growing
number of chess pieces filling the board of
Cityfront Center, a planned private
development of commercial and residential
high-rises occupying some sixty acres on the
site of the city's first settlement. The forty-
story tower is a corporate monument in the
postmodern style of the quintessential corporate firm, Skidmore, Owings and Merrill.
It was designed by partner Adrian Smith,
with John S. Burcher and Leonard Claggett as
studio heads. The obvious inspiration was
the RCA Building, the centerpiece of New
York's great urban ensemble of Rockefeller
Center and the home of the NBC network's
offices and studios. Like the 1930s building,
the NBC Tower has at least two distinctly
different aspects: the narrow west facade
reads as a tower, while the long north and
south sides do not disguise the project's bulk.
The east facade is treated in a series of
setbacks that recall the massing on the rear
of the New York Daily News Building. In
sum, the design seems an homage to
Raymond Hood, the chief designer of the
RCA Building, the Daily News, and NBC's
near neighbor, the Tribune Tower.   C. W.

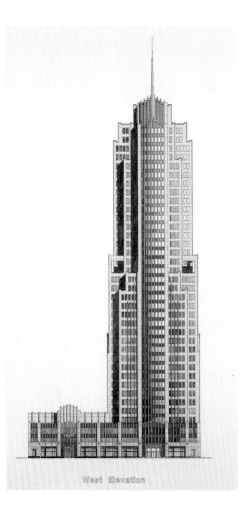

West Elevation

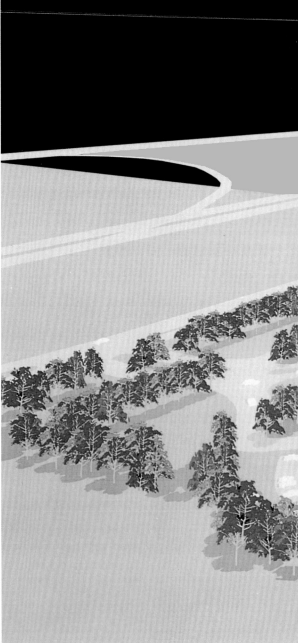

73-74 SKIDMORE, OWINGS AND MERRILL. Computer-generated renderings of One North Franklin Street, 1989 (cat. no. 267), and the proposed Spiegel Corporate Headquarters in Downers Grove, 1991 (cat. no. 293).

The Janus-faced quality of the first phase of the Spiegel Corporate Headquarters can be explained as the architects' response to the disparate nature of its setting: Interstate highway I-355 lies to the east of the site, and the Hidden Lake Forest Preserve faces it on the west. The formal facade facing the expressway presents a rectilinear grid of precast concrete and light gray granite panels, with an aluminum and glass curtain wall. The west facade eschews the grid in favor of a gently curved curtain wall with green-tinted glass and bands of ceramic coated glass spandrels. Both this computer-generated rendering and one illustrating Skidmore, Owings and Merrill's office building One North Franklin Street represent the product of the Architecture and Engineering Series (AES) software package, initially written and devel-

oped by SOM and currently marketed by IBM. Initially, AES serves as a graphic study tool to examine broad design issues such as building exteriors and materials, as a project progresses from early massing models into schematic design. As design development proceeds, AES becomes an information resource, retaining all the design and engineering data to be used in the production of working drawings and construction documents.   M. W.

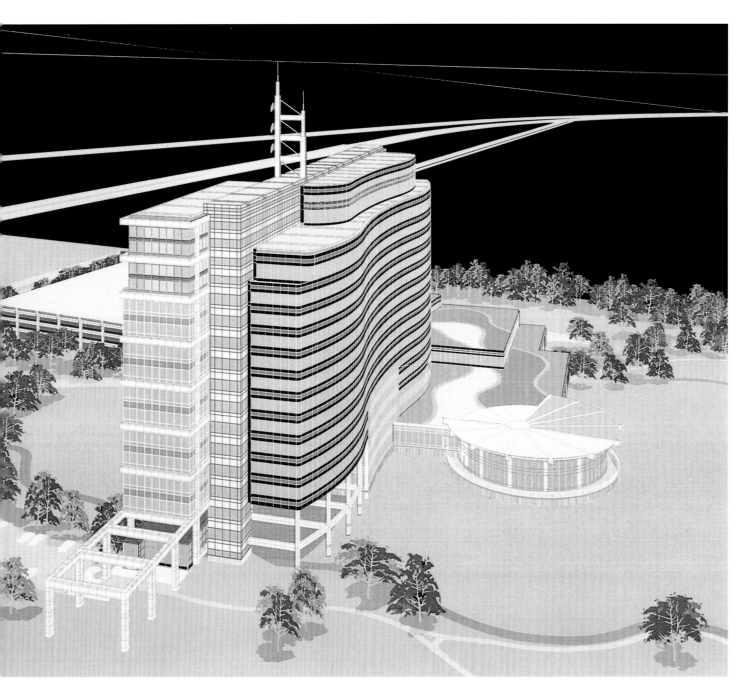

Industry

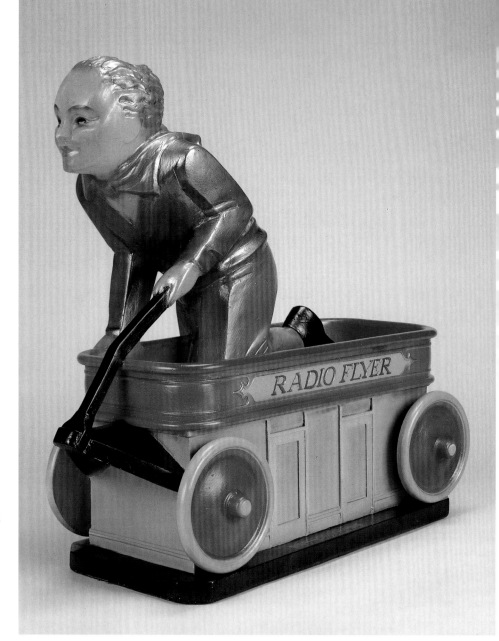

75-77 ALFONSO IANNELLI. Maquette for the Radio Flyer Pavilion, Century of Progress Exposition, 1933 (cat. no. 318), with a photograph of the Pavilion and a classic Radio Flyer wagon.

The Italian-born artist and industrial designer Alfonso Iannelli engaged in a playful exercise of design for the Radio Flyer Pavilion at the Century of Progress Exposition on behalf of the Radio Steel Manufacturing Company. Iannelli also designed the Havoline Motor Oil Thermometer Tower at the fair, as well as five relief panels recording the history of radio for the Social Science Hall.   R. V. S.

78-79 ALBERT KAHN. Exterior and interior views of the Lady Esther Factory, 7171 West 65th Street, 1938, facade later altered (see cat. no. 321).

When the famous, Detroit-based industrial architect Albert Kahn designed this Chicago factory, his firm was among the foremost ones in industrial building. His office of over six hundred people is thought to have designed almost twenty percent of the American industrial facilities that were planned by architects. Kahn is best remembered for his automobile factories, many of which were clustered around Detroit. Nonetheless, his firm also exported their talents to places as far away as the Soviet Union, assisting in the design of more than five hundred factories there following the construction of a tractor plant in Stalingrad in 1930. By the time the Lady Esther cosmetics firm hired him to design their stylish, Art Moderne plant, Kahn had already worked in Chicago, on his model factory and exposition buildings for General Motors and Ford at the 1933-34 Century of Progress Exposition.

J. Z.

80-85 ALBERT KAHN. Chicago's wartime factories in 1943: Amertorp (left), American Steel Foundries (cat. no. 324), and Dodge (far right; cat. no. 325).

World War II brought Albert Kahn's firm the opportunity and challenge to construct large industrial facilities rapidly. The most famous of these plants were near his own Detroit base for automobile industry clients, such as the 1941 Chrysler Corporation Tank Arsenal in Warren, Michigan, and the 1942-43 Willow Run Bomber Plant in Ypsilanti, built for the Ford Motor Company. Yet Kahn had similar projects throughout the country, including three Chicago-area projects that are tangible evidence of his contributions to local industrial facilities that supported the

war effort. Of these, the Amertorp facility for torpedo production (later recycled into the Forest Park Mall at 7600 West Roosevelt Road) is among the most famous. Kahn's work for weapons facilities earned him a special commendation from the United States Navy, posthumously awarded after his 1942 death.   J. Z.

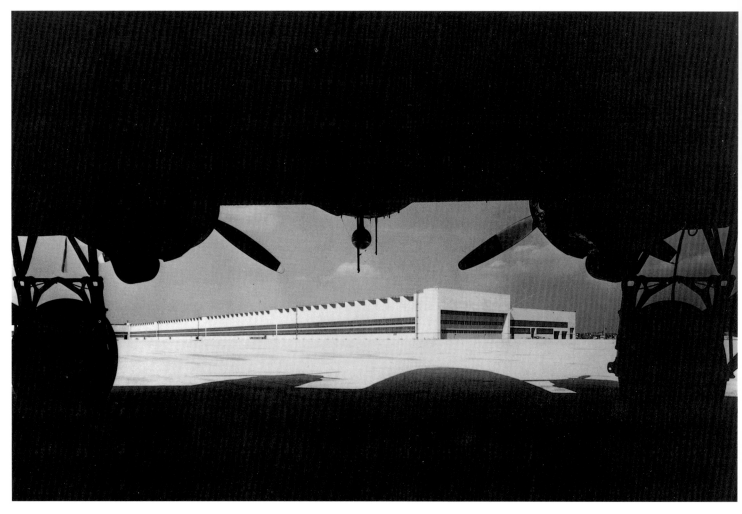

86-87 THE AUSTIN COMPANY.
Chicago Plant of the Douglas Aircraft
Company, 1943.

The Cleveland-based Austin Company is a
long-established industrial architecture firm
with extensive experience in the design of
aircraft facilities and airport construction.

During World War II they erected a number
of aircraft plants, such as the Boeing facilities
in Seattle. Their Douglas Plant in Chicago
was reported by *Flying Magazine* (November
1943) to have been the world's largest cargo
plane factory, as well as the world's largest
wooden structure. For the roof trusses of the
Douglas Plant the Austin Company used

30,000,000 feet of lumber — enough to build
4,500 homes — instead of what would have
been 30,000 tons of a strategic material like
steel. Other critical materials were saved in
the use of plastic pipe, wooden manhole
covers, non-metallic ventilation ducts, and
cement and asbestos siding. Although most
of their industrial structures here were
demolished at the war's end, some buildings
still remain, such as the two-story brick
structure that serves as the administration
building for the Air National Guard facility
on Higgins Road near O'Hare International
Airport.   J. Z.

The Chicago Bridge and Iron Company began building water towers in 1904 for the Canadian Pacific Railroad. From the 1920s through the 1950s, the company developed and patented a series of large, elevated, water-storage tanks. These include the "radial cone" tank, first built in 1929 in Brooklyn, and the all-welded "watersphere" tank, first built in 1939 in Longmont, Colorado. As a further development of the watersphere tank and the company's pioneering work on nuclear containment vessels and liquid hydrogen storage tanks for NASA, Chicago Bridge and Iron developed the "waterspheroid" tank, first built in the Chicago suburbs of Northbrook and Elmhurst in 1954 and replicated throughout the country.   J. Z.

88-89   CHICAGO BRIDGE AND IRON COMPANY.
A waterspheroid tank in Elmhurst, 1954, with specification sheets for the company's 1947 radial cone and its 1949 watersphere tanks (cat. no. 308).

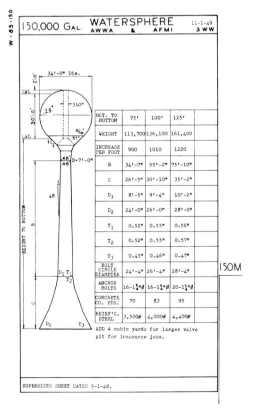

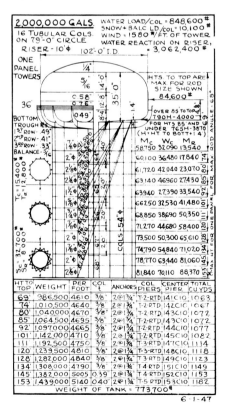

90-91　SKIDMORE, OWINGS AND MERRILL. Baxter Travenol Laboratories, Deerfield, 1975, with a section of the building (cat. no. 342).

The master plan for the corporate headquarters of the pharmaceutical firm Baxter Travenol provided for an initial construction phase of five low-rise buildings, two garages, and a central facilities building. Additional office and parking modules would be designed in clusters as the company expanded. The surrounding low-rise buildings and the prairie terrain north of Chicago formed the background for the dramatic profile of the central facilities building, with its cable-hung suspension roof. At grade level are the reception area and the service functions; a 1,000-seat cafeteria is located in the 24-foot-high second level, interrupted only by the two steel pylons supporting the cables. This design solution, the result of the architectural and engineering collaboration of Bruce Graham and Fazlur Khan, would be employed again in Skidmore, Owings and Merrill's 1984-86 McCormick Place North Building. Together, Graham and Khan also developed the tube structure of the Brunswick Building (1965), the diagonal tube of the John Hancock Center (1965-69), and the clustered tubes of the Sears Tower (1970-74).　M. W.

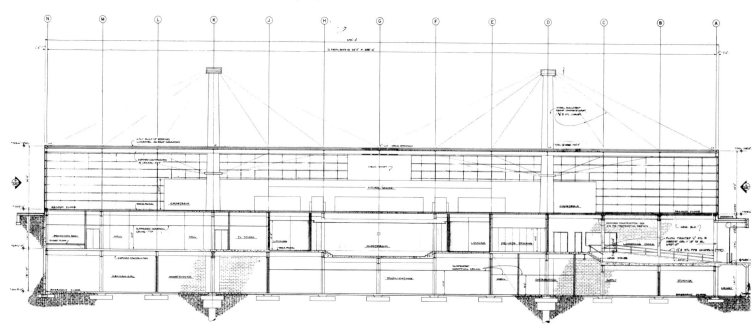

ʌʌ SECTION LOOKING WEST

92   ARQUITECTONICA CHICAGO; DANA TERP, designer. Entrance to Tang Industries, Elk Grove Village, 1989.

The project for Tang Industries called for the dramatic renovation of the client's existing warehouse dating from the 1950s into the headquarters of a growing, diversified company that deals with a variety of concerns from pharmaceuticals to the coating of industrial tools. To increase space within the structure, Arquitectonica constructed a mezzanine in one portion of the building,

with private offices and a conference room set in underneath. On the facade, round windows indicate the location of the office/ conference area. To change the image of the building even further, the architects added a new central entry and canopy, and the brick facade was clad in stripes of black and white granite.   P. S.

Shopping

93 HARRINGER-JACOBSON-COLVIN.
Perspective study of the Store for Tomorrow,
delineated by Henry Harringer for *Apparel
Arts* 1, no. 2 (1932), p. 44 (cat. no. 366).

The Store for Tomorrow was featured in the
Spring 1932 issue of the trade magazine
Apparel Arts. Henry Harringer of Harringer-
Jacobson-Colvin was a designer of interior
spaces, both in his native city of Hamburg
during the 1920s and in Chicago after his
move here in 1927. Harringer intended this
design project to represent the principle of
"suggestive selling through maximum

utilization of display space," and he hoped
that it would illustrate his belief that
"business is a fight rather than a frolic and
that stores should be functional rather than
fancy." The sleek, yet simple, facade
depicted here acts as a "shining face" for the
display of merchandise to be found within.

J. Z.

94 NIMMONS, CARR AND WRIGHT.
Night view of the Sears, Roebuck and Co.
store on Cicero Avenue and Irving Park
Road, 1937.

95-96 LOEBL, SCHLOSSMAN AND BENNETT.
Sears Store at Oakbrook Center, 22nd Street
and Route 83, Oak Brook, 1962.

Enormous, lighted plate-glass displays invited pedestrians and streetcar riders who might happen by for an evening of shopping at the "family store," one of many that Sears built in the 1920s and 1930s when it decided to move into retailing directly. Behind the building, however — which here seems so observant of the lot line at this "six corners" intersection of Irving Park Road, Milwaukee Avenue, and Cicero Avenue — is a huge parking lot, testimony to Sears's sensitivity to the change in shopping habits at the major outlying retail districts. By 1962, when Oakbrook Center opened, the change was complete: one just does not "happen by" Oakbrook; one makes a definite decision to drive there to shop. Passengers alight by car at the front door; while they might stroll through the outdoor mall at Oakbrook, Sears's presence is announced less through the understated signage and window display than through its sheer mass. The gravity of retailing reached its apogee in 1971 with the opening of the Sears-developed Woodfield Mall; at the time, it was the country's largest indoor mall. In a not unrelated move, Sears closed its flagship store on the State Street pedestrian mall in 1983.   M. B.

97   KOHN PEDERSEN FOX ASSOCIATES.
Detail of the mall at 900 North Michigan
Avenue, 1989.

98-100   FLORIAN-WIERZBOWSKI. Oilily,
900 North Michigan Avenue, 1988-89, with
two preliminary design sketches, 1988
(cat. no. 390).

Vertical shopping malls are the late-twen-
tieth-century version of the elegant retail
atriums of great, much earlier, department
stores such as Bon Marché (1869-76) and
Printemps (1881) in Paris and Marshall
Field's (1892, 1902-14) in Chicago. The 1989
mall at 900 North Michigan Avenue is
anchored by Bloomingdale's department
store, which is sited at the rear of a six-story
interior court. Escalators rise through the
space in a pattern that requires riders to
pass alluring specialty shops on each level
before reaching Bloomingdale's entrance or
continuing their ascent. Neutral colors and a
simplicity of line predominate in the Art
Deco-inspired atrium, allowing the richly
varied signage of the individual shops to
provide life and color.   J. C.

KURT SCHWITTERS CASH
WRAP

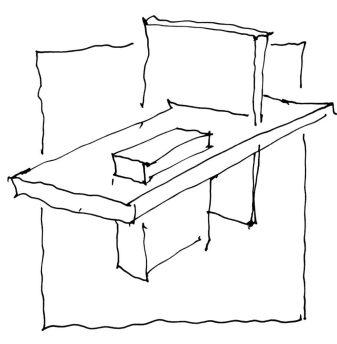

INTERSECTING
PLANES FOR CASH
WRAD.

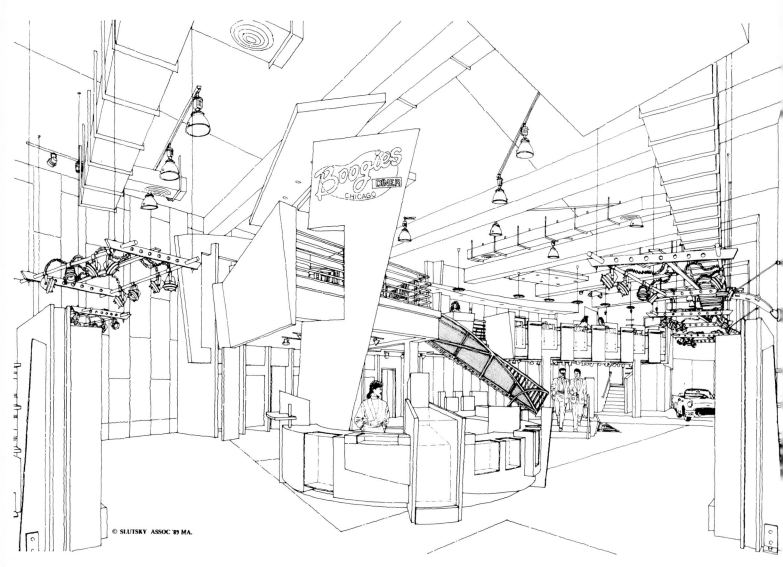

© SLUTSKY ASSOC '89 MA.

The asymmetrical, gridded design of Oilily on the fifth level of the retail mall at 900 North Michigan Avenue recalls De Stijl forms, appropriate for the first American store of a Dutch chain selling women's and children's apparel (pls. 98-100). An off-center "street" divides the shop and opens onto miniature "plazas" that are bordered by groupings of merchandise. In a radical depar- ture from this aesthetic, the Himmel Bonner architectural firm gave Boogie's Diner an energetic, upbeat look, with angular walls, a red, non-skid vinyl stair carpet, and neon signs that are arresting details in the eat-and- shop hangout, which incorporates design elements from the 1930s through the 1990s. The result, however, is not chaos, but clarity, and customers have no trouble finding the perfect T-shirt or making their way up to the soda fountain with its authentic diner stools.

J. C.

101-02   HIMMEL BONNER.
Boogie's Diner and Store,
900 North Michigan Avenue, 1988-89,
with a perspective rendering of the interior,
delineated by Rael Slutsky (cat. no. 391).

NORTH MICHIGAN AVENUE ELEVATION

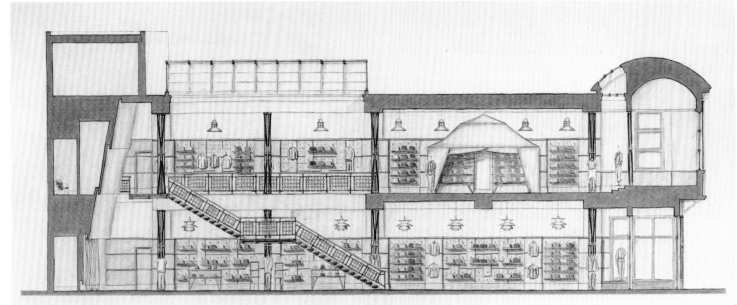

103-05   ROBERT A. M. STERN.
Elevation and section of the Banana Republic Store,
744 North Michigan Avenue, 1990 (cat. no. 410),
with a view of the central staircase.

When the Banana Republic retail chain decided to move from its safari image toward a more sophisticated concept, its managers opted for a free-standing store on North Michigan Avenue as a Chicago venue. The firm of Robert A. M. Stern of New York made its first Chicago appearance with this vaguely tropical two-story structure. Representative of this exotic reference are elegant bundles of bamboo — made of lead-coated copper — which frame the exterior display windows and reappear decoratively in the interior. Inside, the skylit atrium, an open staircase with treads of glass into which rice paper has been laminated, a cowhide floor for the women's apparel section, and still other tentlike boutique areas provide the shopper with a rich visual environment.

J. C.

106 EVA MADDOX ASSOCIATES.
T. W. Best Newsstand in the Chicago and
Northwestern Terminal Building atrium,
Madison and Canal streets, 1988-89
(see cat. no. 406).

The T. W. Best Newsstand at the busy
Chicago and Northwestern train station was
designed predominantly in black and gray
with focal points of architectural interest in
strong primary colors. The newsstand is one
of a series of such shops designed by Eva
Maddox Associates. The dramatic interior of
the shop in the Northwestern atrium contrasts sharply with the wood-paneled T. W.
Best Newsstand that Maddox designed for
the Hotel Nikko. Although they serve the
same function, each newsstand has an appearance and image that are in keeping with
the nature of the larger building in which
it is located.   P. S.

Houses and Housing

107-12 Prize-winning entries to the Chicagoland Prize Homes Competition, sponsored by the *Chicago Tribune,* 1945 (cat. nos. 460-67).

The *Chicago Tribune* organized this competition for the design of the postwar home in the spirit of its earlier competition for its own high-rise headquarters in 1922, and another in 1926 for the design of small homes. Contestants sent in 967 entries, but the *Chicago Tribune* published only 92 of them in its 1948 catalogue of the competition. Twenty-four prizes of $1,000 each were awarded to the most distinguished designs, and 172 entries were exhibited at The Art Institute of Chicago between February 8 and March 8, 1946, drawing over 90,000 visitors. The competition was so popular that several entries were constructed (cat. nos. 460-61, 463-64, 466-67) on the Northwest Side of Chicago, and 212,000 people viewed the model homes during a thirty-day open house. Many of these houses show the influence of Frank Lloyd Wright's low, rambling spaces in the Prairie School style and his inexpensive Usonian planning, while others are hybrids of these and more conservative prewar tendencies.   J. Z.

113 PHILIP MAHER. Perspective rendering of proposed apartment building, 1350 North Astor Street, c. 1938-40 (cat. no. 442).

Philip Maher (1894-1981), the son of famed Prairie School architect George Maher, was a successful architect during the pre- and post-war periods. His specialty in both eras was the luxury private home and apartment building. This project for an apartment house on Astor Street would have been built near earlier apartments he designed for the Gold Coast location of urban villas: 1301 North Astor Street of 1928 and 1260 North Astor Street of 1931. This later design of stark masses decorated only by rectilinear window frames relates to other buildings from the mid- to late 1930s that were popular in Europe and North America, and it prefigures some of the modernistic masonry high-rises that Maher designed after the war, such as 1445 North State Parkway.   J. Z.

114-17 LUDWIG MIES VAN DER ROHE. Two views of 860-880 North Lake Shore Drive, 1952, with a perspective sketch of a high-rise apartment, c. 1946-48 (cat. no. 476), possibly for 860-880 North Lake Shore Drive, and a site plan of the project.

Ludwig Mies van der Rohe's twin apartment buildings at 860-880 North Lake Shore Drive were among the first definitive examples of the rectangularly prismatic slab that Mies made the standard form of the high-rise buildings he designed during his American career. Notable for their straightforward revelation of the structural steel frame, with spaces between the horizontal and vertical members fully taken up by floor-to-ceiling glass, these towers exerted an immense in-fluence on the tall buildings that redefined American city skylines of the 1950s and 1960s. The compactness and symmetry of each of the two towers recalls Mies's devo-tion to a classical ideal, while the informal balance of their siting is the most evident vestige of the asymmetries of many of his European plans and compositions.   F. S.

PHILIP B MAHER - ARCHITECT

115

116

118-19   NAGLE, HARTRAY AND ASSOCIATES.
Rosenberg House, Highland Park, 1985-87,
with an axonometric view (cat. no. 527).

This large suburban house of 10,000 square
feet is covered in cement stucco. It is L-
shaped in plan and was designed for a family
with four grown children. The image of an
all-white house, the client's request, evokes
others of comparable modernist and neo-
modernist homes. One thinks of Richard
Meier's houses, or their ultimate prototypes,
Le Corbusier's 1920s villas. In addition, the
architects, Nagle, Hartray and Associates,
see this house as an extension of their
interests in De Stijl forms of the 1920s. By
contrast with the geometric clarity of this
architecture, the surrounding landscape is
considerably less formal.   J. Z.

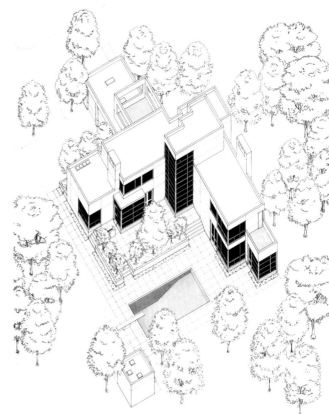

120-22 KRUECK AND SEXTON.
Axonometric view of the Nadler Apartment,
1988-89 (cat. no. 533), with a prototype side
chair (cat. no. 534) and a view of the interior.

Krueck and Sexton (formerly Krueck and
Olsen) are well known for the complex, yet
beautifully detailed, finishes within their
residential spaces, and this apartment is certainly no exception. This 3,100-square-foot
residence utilizes over twenty-five colors and
thirty tones of metallic paint, within spaces
defined by curvilinear walls and planes. The
tonal differences are extremely subtle, reflecting the architects' training at the Illinois
Institute of Technology in the niceties of
color and the manipulation of planes. The
final result here, as in many of their other interior designs, is one of reflective luxuriance
and machinelike precision.   J. Z.

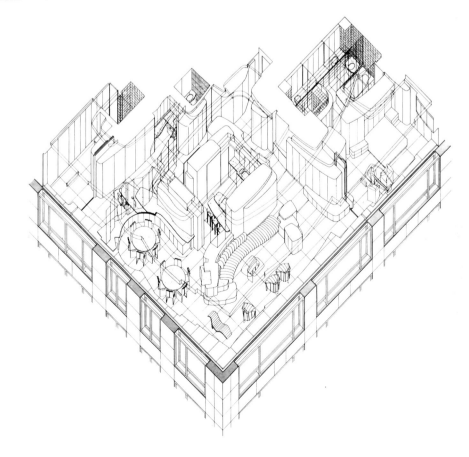

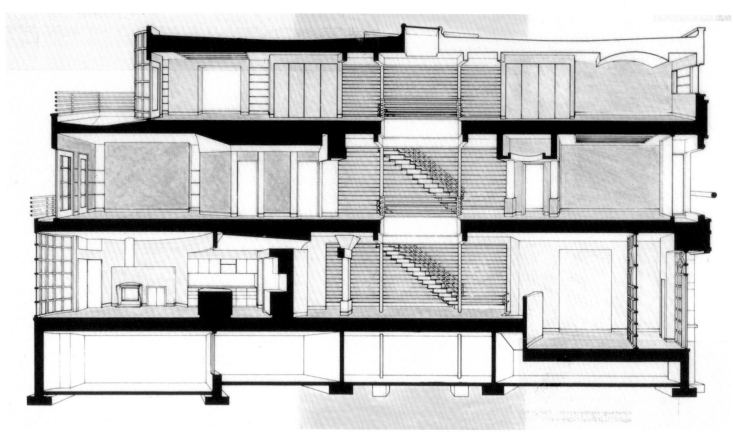

123-25   BOOTH/HANSEN AND ASSOCIATES.
Exterior and interior views with the House of
Light, 1828 North Orleans Street, 1981, with
a longitudinal section (cat. no. 517).

Booth/Hansen and Associates' House
of Light is typical of the upscale gentrification that occurred in some Chicago neighborhoods during the 1980s. Intended to express an urbane form of townhouse
consumerism, set off from the conspicuous
consumption in the suburbs by its assertion
of good taste and elevated sensibility, this
house and the more modest three-flat on
North Mohawk Street by Frederick Phillips
and Associates (pls. 129-30) were part of a
recolonizing of the downtown. Affluent
people were cautiously returning to a city
abandoned a generation before. Tannys
Langdon's audiovisual cabinet for a Gothic
apartment is a good example of the sort of
cabinetry and detailed interior work —
micro-architecture — produced during
the decade (pls. 126-28).   R. M.

126-28 TANNYS LANGDON. Interior studies of a Gothic Apartment, 20 East Cedar Street, 1989-92 (cat. no. 543), with an audiovisual cabinet for it (cat. no. 544).

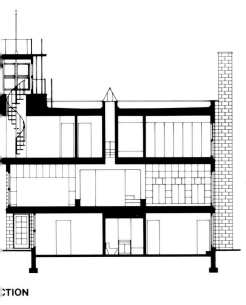

129-30 FREDERICK PHILLIPS AND ASSOCIATES.
Three-flat house at 1518 North Mohawk Street,
1989, with a sectional view (cat. no. 558).

131-32 WEESE LANGLEY WEESE.
Perspective study (cat. no. 559) and view of
the Bickerdyke CHA scattered-site public
housing, phase II, near Humboldt Park, 1989.

West Town Housing was built in 1989 for the
Bickerdyke Redevelopment Corporation, a
private, nonprofit company set up to develop
thirty vacant lots in three neighborhoods
(West Town, Humboldt Park, and Wicker
Park) and to organize each community for
the purpose of ensuring that the design of the
houses would be tailored to its needs and desires. The project consists of both new townhouse construction and the rehabilitation of
existing structures: there are 113 new townhouses (65 with three bedrooms and 48 with
four bedrooms) and 65 rehabbed units (two
and three bedrooms) in eight previously
existing apartment buildings. The input of
the community in the development of the
project is reflected in the design of the new
townhouses. A separate entry for each townhouse emphasizes the family's individual
character, while the spatial relationship
between the rows of houses creates a sense of
neighborhood. Because this housing project
is integrated into the rest of the city, it
represents a good alternative to the isolated,
high-rise public housing projects of the 1950s
and 1960s.   W. W.

Recreation

133 VOORHEES, GMELIN AND WALKER; RALPH WALKER, designer. Perspective rendering of the final design of the proposed Tower of Water and Light, for the 1933-34 Century of Progress Exposition, delineated by John Wenrich, 1930 (cat. no. 587).

New York architect Ralph Walker, the designer of numerous Art Deco skyscrapers, served as a member of the planning commission for the Century of Progress Exposition. Beginning in 1929, the group held numerous meetings to develop a scheme for the fairgrounds, themes for the major buildings, and a centerpiece of inspirational proportions. Walker's own Tower of Water and Light was a skyscraper-scale sculpture of abstract and faceted forms somewhat reminiscent of German Expressionism, especially as interpreted by the well-known delineator John Wenrich. Water cascades down the three richly colored glass and concrete sides of Walker's tower. The Depression, however, scaled down the commission's ambitions, and the tower's minimal rentable space and the technical feats required to build it meant that the more functional and lucrative Skyride — an aerial gondola that traversed the site — replaced it as the centerpiece of the Century of Progress Exposition.

M. B., C. W.

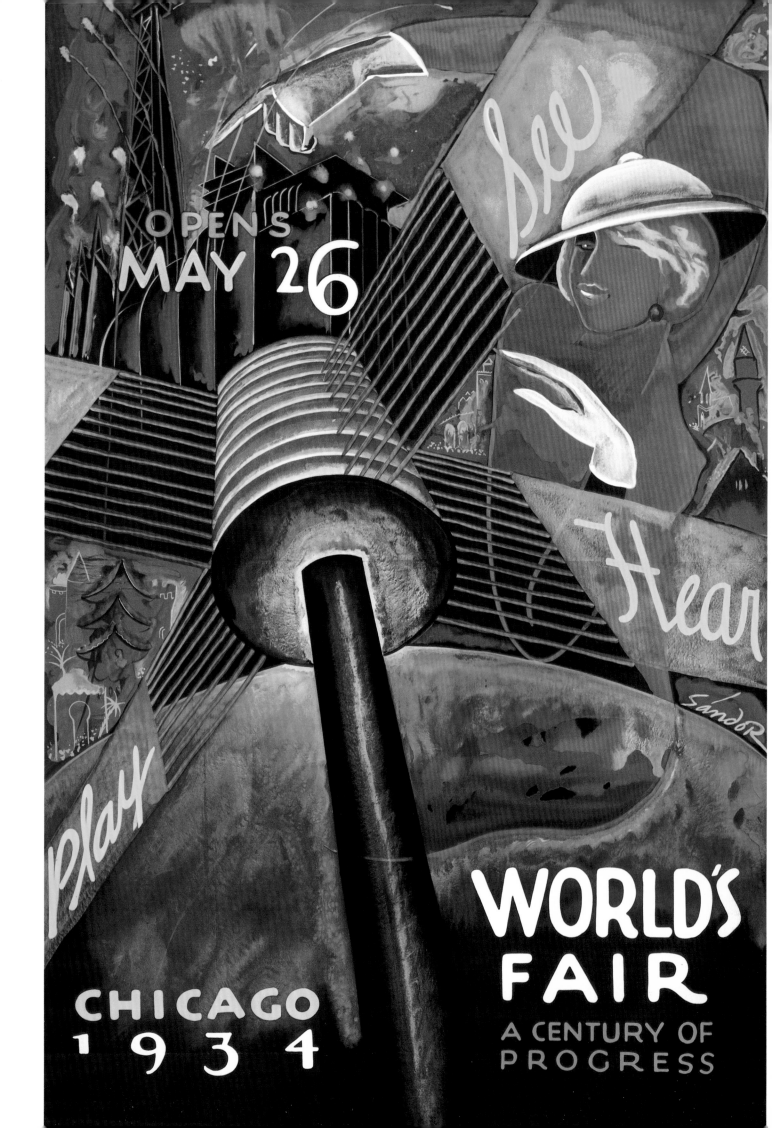

134 Poster for the Century of Progress Exposition, designed by SÁNDOR, 1934 (cat. no. 602).

The collage-like image on this poster was not at all typical of Chicago's more realistic illustrative style in the 1930s. The references are rather to Cubism, photomontage, and the unusual views of the "new photography" in Germany. The point was to employ visual devices that could clearly be read as modern. Nonetheless, the artist produced a poster that is loose and painterly rather than controlled and objective, as were most modern posters in Europe, such as those by A. M. Cassandre.   V. M.

135-37 WILLIAM PEREIRA. Esquire Theater, 58 East Oak Street, 1938; remodeled by Gelick Foran Associates, 1990. Photograph of the restored exterior, with a section and a plan for remodeling, 1990 (cat. no. 630).

The movie theater is one of the most pervasive and important arenas for popular entertainment in the twentieth century, and the evolution of theater design documents the changing way in which people experience the movies. When it opened in 1938, the Esquire Theater (named after the swank men's magazine) catered to the wealthy and sophisticated clientele of Chicago's fashionable Gold Coast neighborhood. Designed in a sleek moderne style by Chicago architect William Pereira for the Balaban and Katz theater chain, the Esquire included lobby space for musicians, small receptions, and art exhibitions. In the late 1980s, Gelick Foran Associates transformed Pereira's theater into the Esquire Center; six small screening rooms — ranging from 193 to 237 seats — replaced the original 1,400-seat auditorium, and a two-story commercial space was added. The original Esquire Theater signaled the acceptance of modern styling as synonymous with urbane sophistication, while the renovated Esquire Center testifies to the changing form in which movies are consumed by the general public.   D. D.

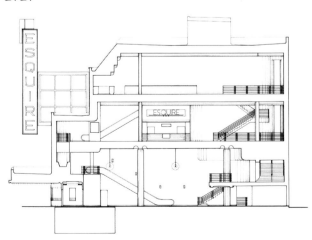

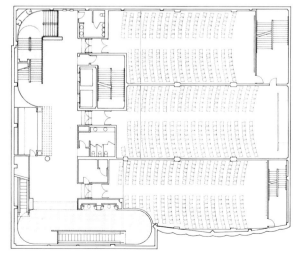

138-39 NAGLE, HARTRAY AND ASSOCIATES.
Remodeling for Oprah Winfrey of the Fred
Niles Film Studios into Harpo Studios,
110 North Carpenter Street, 1989, with an
axonometric view (cat. no. 628).

Originally the home of an early twentieth-
century film studio, these buildings have
now been remodeled and enlarged in order to
create a high-tech television studio. Beyond
containing the latest in equipment and
production facilities, as well as the studio for
Oprah Winfrey's current television show, the
structure houses her company's corporate
headquarters. The curvilinear shapes and the
extensive use of glass block in the building
consciously evoke the imagery of Art Deco
film sets from the golden age of Hollywood
movies.   J. Z.

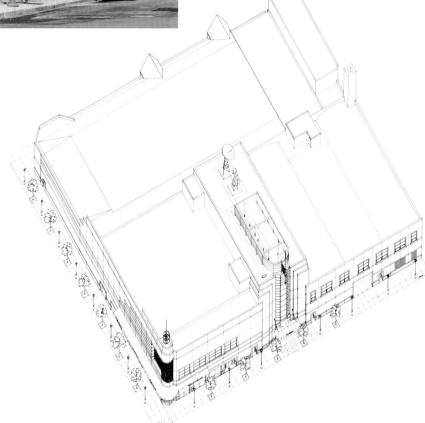

140-41   LAURENCE BOOTH. Two exterior
views of the "Chicken Coop" summer studio
for the architect, Lake Bluff, 1988.

This small summer home represents the
ultimate in rural recycling. A chicken coop
stood on the site of the home, and architect
Laurence Booth used part of its structure and
the vernacular imagery of that former building as his point of departure in designing this
1,100-square-foot house for himself and his
wife. The building is testimony to his sense
of American, democratic architecture.

J. Z.

142-44 JORDAN MOZER AND ASSOCIATES.
Interior views of Vivere in the Italian Village,
71 West Monroe Street, 1990, with a typical
chair (cat. no. 638).

Jordan Mozer's Vivere manages to evoke two
entirely different moods. It seems, on the one
hand, reassuringly warm and familiar, like
some favorite eating place once highly fashionable but now settled into a solidly comfortable existence. At the same time, nothing
is quite like what one might expect. As in a
funhouse, every surface is slightly warped,
distorted, or made of an unusual material. In
fact, every object in sight has been subjected
to a whimsical remaking at the hands of the
architect and an entire team of highly
talented artist-craftsmen.   R. B.

145 CORDOGAN, CLARK AND ASSOCIATES. Night view of the Fox River Casino, Aurora, 1991 (cat. no. 652).

The shimmering lights of the vast midwestern sky here receive the beacon of a new entertainment enterprise that joins postmodern design with post-industrial economy. John Clark's rendering of North Point Pavilion on Aurora's Stolp Island is an apse of restaurant chapels, part Aurora roundhouse, part Navy Pier on the Fox River. This former railroad city, whose economy braked and then reignited on the banks of the East-West Tollway, now hopes for another new dawn as a casino gambling center evoking nostalgia for long-past riverboat excitement.

M. B.

Catalogue

John Zukowsky

A Note on the Exhibition

The objects on display represent a broad spectrum of original drawings, prints, artifacts, furnishings, and architectural models related to the development of Chicago architecture and design over the past seventy years. The majority of these objects have been drawn from the permanent collections of The Art Institute of Chicago, but more than seventy lenders have also contributed to this exhibition. Our goal has been to examine how architecture differs before and after the Great Depression of the 1930s and World War II, and to simplify this presentation, we have organized these objects into eight building typologies, or land-use categories, and have listed them in this catalogue, in general, chronologically within each section. Despite the scope of this large selection, there will invariably be some important projects or favorite buildings that are not represented. These shortcomings may be due to the fact that no original or ex-

hibitable objects could be located to represent these buildings. It may also be a case of oversight. Nevertheless, we have tried to provide as large a sample as possible to indicate the wealth of architectural design from Chicago's not too distant past. Several other aspects should be noted here in relation to the themes of this project.

First, items included here could, in some instances, be put in several of the eight categories. The interrelationship of categories and the blurring of lines between them corresponds to the complex nature of modern society. Second, in most of the categories of the exhibition there are usually more items drawn from the forty years that have followed World War II than there are from the 1920s and 1930s. Third, and most important, is the fact that the density of objects increases as the checklist approaches the 1980s and 1990s, to the point that the number of items repre-

sented and, by implication, produced in the last decade becomes almost overwhelming. The abundance of new objects displayed is intentional: it is representative of the wide range of choices and options that we face in contemporary society, and emblematic, therefore, of the awesome variety and increasing intensity of life at the end of this millennium. The buildings discussed in the following typological summaries were, like those dealt with in the essays, often the source of controversy during their construction. The organization and composition of the checklist strives to give at least some feeling of the controversy behind these various architectural choices and issues. In so doing, we hope to inform the reader that architectural decisions can cause as many problems as they solve, and that there are no definitive ways to execute a building and no absolute solutions to urban or suburban architectural problems.

This checklist of the exhibition was prepared by John Zukowsky, Sarah Mollman Underhill, and Amy Gold, with the advice and assistance of Robert Bruegmann, Victor Margolin, Luigi Mumford, Pauline Saliga, and Stanley Tigerman. All items listed as gifts are in the permanent collection of the Department of Architecture in The Art Institute of Chicago. With the exception of the autographed photographs from the Signature Collection of Hedrich-Blessing, almost all items are architectural models, furnishings, architectural drawings, or prints made from drawings. Unless otherwise stated, all locations are understood to be Chicago.

Urban Fragments

Since the 1909 publication of *Plan of Chicago* by Daniel H. Burnham and Edward H. Bennett, Chicago has had very strong associations with comprehensive urban planning. Public initiatives before and after both world wars implemented a number of aspects of the Plan, such as the widening of Michigan Avenue and the extension of Congress Street as a major throughway. Other plans that succeeded the 1909 Plan tried to shape the character of greater Chicago in the spirit of that earlier plan, namely, the 1956 document called *Planning the Region of Chicago* and even the *Chicago Central Area Plan* of 1983.

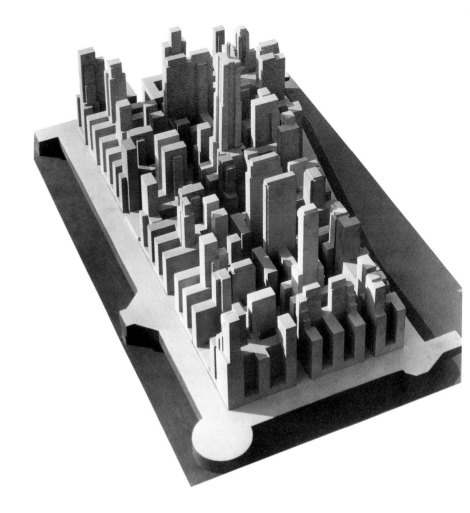

Holabird and Root.
Model for Terminal Park, c. 1928-29.

The buildings of Illinois Center on the Chicago River. Originally planned by the Office of Mies van der Rohe in 1967, these buildings have been realized by that firm and others.

Although one might assume that planning is a public process sponsored by taxpayers' dollars, it is worth noting that planning initiatives are often privately funded, at least in the pre-implementation stages, as befits our free market system. Because the impact of planning on urban and suburban situations is conceived on such a great scale, it is also often easier to implement urban changes on a smaller, almost neighborhood, scale, whether using public or private monies. Two adjacent urban fragments deserve to be compared in this regard: Illinois Center and Cityfront Center, lying east of Michigan Avenue opposite each other on the Chicago River. Both of these developments could be created once freight traffic along the river banks was eventually eliminated, in part because it had gradually been moved south to Lake Calumet and the new Port District Terminal facilities there in the 1960s and 1970s.

Plans for the development of Illinois Center began with Terminal Park in the 1920s, but the Depression and World War II halted the construction of what would have been a complex like New York's Rockefeller Center, a city within a city, set above the Illinois Central Railroad tracks. The Prudential Building, constructed from 1952 to 1955, was the first postwar development above those railroad tracks and its success paved the way for the office, hotel, and apartment spaces that now constitute Illinois

Schipporeit-Heinrich Associates, with Graham, Anderson, Probst and White. Lake Point Tower, 505 North Lake Shore Drive, 1968. This photograph, taken in 1991, shows still undeveloped land in Cityfront Center along the Chicago River.

Center, presently the world's largest air-rights development, on some eighty acres of disused railroad land.

Although not built on railroad land, Cityfront Center, a development of sixty acres, occupies land formerly used by freight warehouses. This development was first begun by the Chicago Dock and Canal Company in the late 1960s and early 1970s with the demolition, in 1972, of fifteen structures and the clearance of twenty-two acres of land. Even before this, however, Shaw and Associates had planned in 1967 a multi-use city within a city that would have bridged the space between the Tribune Tower and Equitable Building on Michigan Avenue and the towers that were planned by Schipporeit-Heinrich Associates for the lakefront at the same time. But, while three towers were actually planned, only one was built: Lake Point Tower. The Y-shaped plans of the proposed Lake Point Towers and Shaw's buildings were common in other apartments of the time. For instance, Loewenberg and Loewenberg designed similarly planned buildings at 1130 South Michigan Avenue in 1965 and at 2626 Lakeview Avenue in 1969. The Y-shaped building plan offered apartment residents better views and ventilation than either the T-shaped or H-shaped plans.

Alfred Shaw's master plan was never realized, and other architects, such as Harry Weese, a Chicagoan with a keen sense of Burnham's "big picture," have tried their hands at providing plans for multi-use developments on this site. The opening of the Columbus Drive Bridge in 1982 increased access to the area. Development eventually took off in the late 1980s through the efforts of a variety of architects with a final master plan by Alexander Cooper and Dirk Lohan. Lohan successfully implemented public space within the overall plan — public spaces that are still lacking in Illinois Center on the opposite bank.

Planning

1. Holabird and Root. Aerial perspective sketch of the proposed Illinois Central Air Rights Development at Randolph Street, Michigan Avenue, and Wacker Drive, c. 1928. Pencil on tracing paper, 62.5 x 51 cm. Gift of Carol Herselle Krinsky, 1980.

2. Holabird and Root. Proposed plan of the Illinois Central Air Rights Development north of Randolph Street, c. 1928. Pencil and wash on tracing paper, approx. 64 x 50 cm. Gift of Carol Herselle Krinsky, 1980.

3. Illinois Central Railroad, Office of Division Engineer. Illinois Central Railroad tracks and facilities, Adams Street to Chicago River, with possible air rights development superimposed, n.d. Blueline print, 93.6 x 133.5 cm. Gift of J. Edwin Quinn, 1980.

4. Bennett, Parsons and Frost. Bird's-eye view of Congress Street extension and Post Office site, with future public buildings as suggested, 1926. Photostat, 64.3 x 46 cm. Gift of Edward H. Bennett, Jr., 1953.

5. Bennett, Parsons and Frost, consulting architects, and I.F. Stern, consulting engineer. Chicago, Congress Street, bird's-eye view of the proposed development between the lake and the river, December 1929. Photostat, 21.3 x 64.7 cm. Gift of Edward H. Bennett, Jr., 1953.

6. Burnham Brothers. Plan of the lakefront showing proposed landfills, lagoons, yacht basin, and extended Lake Shore Drive for Evanston Lakefront Proposals/Studies, 1931. Pencil and colored pencil on tracing paper, 91 x 505 cm. Restricted gift of the Friends of the Library and the Architecture Society in honor of the Seventy-Fifth Anniversary of the Burnham Library of Architecture, 1987.

7. Burnham Brothers. Plan of the lakefront showing existing street system with expanded park for the Evanston lakefront, 1931. Graphite on tracing paper, 71 x 304 cm. Restricted gift of the Friends of the Library and the Architecture Society in honor of the Seventy-Fifth Anniversary of the Burnham Library of Architecture, 1987.

8. Paul Philippe Cret. Preliminary site plan study, Century of Progress Exposition, June 24, 1929. Graphite on tracing paper, 66.3 x 126.5 cm. Restricted gift of Benefactors of Architecture, Harold Schiff and Richard Stein, 1987.

9. Paul Philippe Cret. Preliminary site plan study, Century of Progress Exposition, March 12, 1930. Graphite and colored pencil on red ink grid on tracing paper, 49.2 x 54.6 cm. Restricted gift of William B. Alter, Balcor Company, and Mr. and Mrs. David C. Hilliard, 1987.

10. Paul Philippe Cret. Preliminary site plan study at Lief Ericson Drive and 16th Street, Century of Progress Exposition, May 15, 1930. Pencil and colored pencil on tracing paper, 57 x 61 cm. Restricted gifts of Charles F. Gardner and Sandra L. Miller, Benefactors of Architecture, 1987.

11. Paul Philippe Cret. Preliminary site plan study showing entrances on 16th, 23rd, and 31st streets, Century of Progress Exposition, c. 1930. Graphite and colored pencil on tracing paper, 68 x 127 cm. Restricted gift of Richard Stein, Benefactor of Architecture, 1987.

12. Paul Philippe Cret. Preliminary site plan, Hall of Science, Century of Progress Exposition, October 1, 1930. Graphite and colored pencil on red ink grid on tracing paper, 87 x 106.5 cm. Restricted gift of Miglin-Beitler Development, Inc., 1988.

13. Daniel H. Burnham, Jr. General plan for the Century of Progress Exposition, c. 1930. Ink on sepia print mounted on linen, 73.6 x 228.6 cm. Lent by the Chicago Historical Society.

14. Voorhees, Gmelin and Walker. Plan schemes "B" and "C" for the Century of Progress Exposition, Chicago, c. 1930. Pencil on tracing paper, 44.9 x 77.8 and 44.9 x 78 cm. Gifts of the Auxiliary Board of The Art Institute of Chicago, 1980.

15. Voorhees, Gmelin and Walker. Site plan study for the Century of Progress Exposition, c. 1930. Pencil on tracing paper, 47.7 x 93.4 cm. Gift of the Auxiliary Board of The Art Institute of Chicago, 1980.

16. Bennett, Parsons and Frost. General circulation plan of the Century of Progress Exposition, April 19, 1930. Ink on linen, 79 x 342 cm. Gift of Edward H. Bennett, Jr., 1953.

17. William F. Deknatel. Aerial perspective sketch of general community plan, West Side Redevelopment Project; Central Chicago Redevelopment Corp., September 23, 1952. Pencil and colored pencil on paper, taped to board, 46.8 x 47.5 cm. Gift of Diane Deknatel Pierson, 1984.

18. Arthur R. Myhrum. Two bird's-eye view studies for urban redevelopment scheme for blocks near the intersection of Ashland and Chicago avenues, c. 1950. Pencil on yellow tracing paper, 35.5 x 45.5 cm, and pencil on yellow tracing paper with white highlights, 32 x 42.5 cm. Gifts of Charlotte W. Myhrum, 1991.

19. Ludwig Karl Hilberseimer. Chicago Near North and West Loop study, bird's-eye view to east, c. 1960-63. Ink and pencil on tracing paper, 52.8 x 28 cm. Gift of George E. Danforth, 1983.

20. Chicago Plan Commission, Department of City Planning. Three sheets: Section A-Zoning-Preferential Street System; Section A-Public Improvements in the City of Chicago; Section 11-Public Improvements in the City of Chicago, 1961. Printed in black, blue, and red ink, each 62.5 x 90.2 cm. Gift of J. Edwin Quinn, 1980.

21. Chicago Plan Commission, Department of City Planning. Reference Atlas: Generalized land-use according to districts, public improvements, zoning, 1961. Softcover portfolio, 63.5 x 95 cm. Gift of J. Edwin Quinn, 1980.

22. Richard Yoshijiro Mine. Two drawings for the Carson, Pirie, Scott and Company Centennial Competition for Loop remodeling, c. 1954. Ink, pencil, and watercolor on line print, mounted on board, each approx. 74.5 x 101.7 cm. Gift of Richard Yoshijiro Mine, 1980.

23. Harry Weese. Proposals for city improvements, for *Esquire Magazine* (June 1968). Ink and pencil on tracing paper, 68.5 x 105 cm. Gift of Harry Weese and Associates, 1982.

24. Harry Weese. "Harbor Island," a bird's-eye view of an alternative proposal for the South Loop New Town Development, 1975. Ink, marker, and watercolor on tracing paper, 25.8 x 20 cm. Gift of Harry Weese and Associates, 1980.

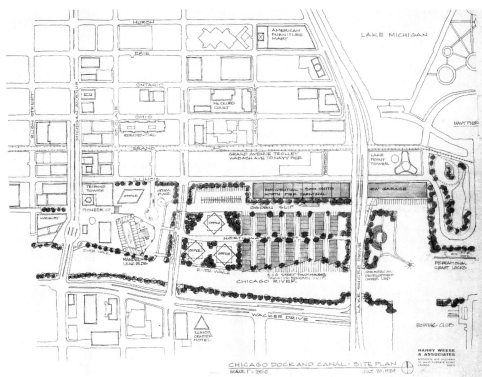

34

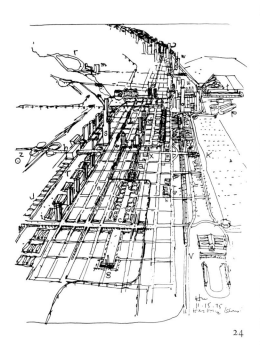

24

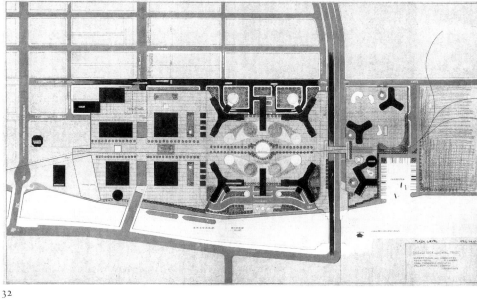

32

37

25. Harry Weese. Perspective view looking west from the lake toward the Sears Tower, showing the Navy Pier site for the 1992 World's Fair, 1977. Marker and ink on tracing paper, 21.5 x 27.8 cm. Gift of Harry Weese and Associates, 1982.

26. Harry Weese. Perspective view of the site at Navy Pier for the 1992 World's Fair, c. 1977. Pencil and oil pastel on tracing paper, 30.8 x 56.5 cm. Gift of Harry Weese and Associates, 1982.

27. Harry Weese. Site plan for the 1992 World's Fair at Navy Pier, c. 1977. Pencil on tracing paper collage, 30 x 56 cm. Gift of Harry Weese and Associates, 1982.

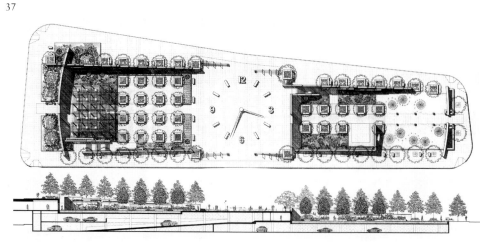

28. Harry Weese. View looking west from the lake toward Buckingham Fountain, showing proposed lakefront developments at Navy Pier for the 1992 World's Fair, c. 1977. Markers and ink on tracing paper, 21.5 x 27.8 cm. Gift of Harry Weese and Associates, 1982.

29. Skidmore, Owings and Merrill. Bird's-eye view for the Central Area Plan, showing proposed development and public lakefront amenities, delineated by Carlos Diniz Associates, 1985. Ink and colored wash on paper mounted on wood, 106.4 x 143 cm. Lent by Skidmore, Owings and Merrill. (See plate 1.)

30. Booth/Hansen and Associates. Site plan with elevations of townhouses in Dearborn Park, 1988-93. Printed Mylar with colored pencil, approx. 76 x 101.5 cm. Lent by Booth/Hansen and Associates, Ltd.

31. Lohan Associates. Development plan for Old Mill Creek, Tempel Farms, bounded by Interstate 94 and Routes 45, 132, and 173, north of Gurnee, April 1990. Ink, marker, and colored pencil on paper, 234 x 153 cm. Lent by Lohan Associates.

32. Alfred Shaw. Color study of plaza level for Chicago Dock and Canal Trust, April 24, 1967. Colored pencil on blueline print, 110.5 x 63 cm. Lent by the Chicago Dock and Canal Trust.

33. Alfred Shaw. Proposed traffic circulation, Chicago Dock and Canal Trust, May 1968. Colored sepia print, 122.7 x 77 cm. Lent by the Chicago Dock and Canal Trust.

34. Harry Weese and Associates. Proposal for Odgen Slip, July 23, 1984. Watercolor on blueline print, 59.5 x 45.8 cm. Lent by the Chicago Dock and Canal Trust.

35. Alexander Cooper; Skidmore, Owings and Merrill; and Lohan Associates. Master plan for Cityfront Center, c. 1987-91. Photograph, 35.6 x 45.7 cm. Lent by the Chicago Dock and Canal Trust.

36. Gilbert Gorski, delineator. Rendering of Cityfront Center, Odgen Slip, and North Pier, looking west, 1986. Watercolor and ink on paper, 68.6 x 48.3 cm. Lent by Amy R. Hecker.

37. Lohan Associates. Site plan and section of Mayor Ogden Plaza, showing Clock Sculpture by Vito Acconci, in Cityfront Center, bounded by Columbus Drive, Park Drive, Illinois Street, and North Water Street, 1990. Ink and watercolor on paper, 101.5 x 127 cm. Lent by Lohan Associates.

38. Gelick Foran Associates. Preliminary studies and final versions of the site plan for, and southeast elevation of, apartments at Cityfront Center, 1991. Printed paper with pastel, 127 x 101.5 cm. Lent by Gelick Foran Associates.

City of Chicago, Bureau of Architecture, with Perkins and Will, design consultants. Cumberland Station of the Chicago Transit Authority, on the line to O'Hare Airport, 1983-84.

Transportation

The completion of the Illinois and Michigan Canal in 1848 and the subsequent creation of a dense railroad network here, the 1865 consolidation of the Stockyards and the development of refrigerated railroad cars, and the linkup of the Transcontinental Railroad of 1869, all helped to make Chicago the transportation hub of the nation. The railroad remained central to Chicago even after World War II. The image of streamlined trains like the Burlington Zephyr captured the public's imagination through displays at the Century of Progress Exposition in 1933-34, as well as through adventure films such as *The Silver Streak* (1935). This same fascination with the aerodynamic industrial forms of the mid-1930s, including the Burlington Zephyr, the Douglas DC3 airplane, and the Chrysler Airflow automobile, inspired Helmut Jahn's 1982 design for an office building to replace the Chicago and Northwestern Railroad's terminal in Chicago. Jahn's project was eventually built, despite the protests of preservationists who wished to save the classical station by Frost and Granger (1906-11). Commuter rail lines continue to function from this and three other stations in Chicago, including the consolidation of Amtrak lines in Union Station. In addition, Chicago's rapid transit lines have expanded to serve growing neighborhoods at the city's fringe and, more recently, Midway and O'Hare airports.

After the war, architect Bertrand Goldberg applied his creative talents to the design of the Unicel Refrigerator Box Car, made of lightweight materials such as molded plywood. But the postwar years would witness the decline of railroads, especially as long-distance lines were increasingly relegated to freight service by the construction of superhighways. The highway system itself, constructed in the Chicago area during the 1950s and 1960s, made news in the late 1980s and early 1990s as it has required extensive redesign and rebuilding. The reconstruction of the area's tollways and throughways has caused added strain on commuters and alternative transit systems alike. Throughout the postwar period architects concentrated on opportunities for structures related to the territory encompassed by the expressways, from service stations and fast food restaurants to motels.

But even more than the changes brought by the interstate highways and the new roads that connect city to suburb, Chicago's place

Bertrand Goldberg. Unicel Refrigerator Box Car, 1951.

as a transportation hub of the nation rests upon its importance as the air capital of the country through the construction of the Municipal (now Midway) Airport of 1927 and of O'Hare International Airport in 1965. During World War II, architects and architectural artists such as Hugh Ferriss dreamt of the airport of the future, linked by highways and accessible by personal and commuter helicopters. Before the war's end, when the site was only a Douglas Aircraft Factory at Orchard Field (hence the ORD abbreviation on its current luggage tags), O'Hare was projected to support Chicago's role as the nation's air hub. On July 30, 1943, when the first airplane built there lifted off on its maiden flight, Major General Harold George stated that "Chicago sits at the crossroads of the air transport of the world." Little did he know that within forty years that very site would become the world's busiest airport. It now has more than 2,200 flights with 238,000 passengers on its busiest days. Although O'Hare has expanded with new terminals soon to be interconnected via a narrow-gauge rail line, or "people mover," continued demands on its facilities have caused air travelers increased concern over safety and inconvenience. Mayor Richard M. Daley has made the need for an additional airport in Chicago a high priority for his administration, and he has kept the topic prominently before the public for almost two years. The proposed Lake Calumet site was first suggested as a possible airport site in the 1940s and, then as now, it has provoked protest from the residents there. Likewise, proposals for further expansion of O'Hare Airport have aroused residents of the suburbs adjacent to it, as did the suggestion that Chicago's smaller Midway Airport be closed even before the Lake Calumet Airport is opened to traffic sometime in the next century. An airport at Lake Calumet may well help the region's economy, especially since the industrial base on the South Side of the city continues to shrink. Still, the final solution of the site for any new airport and any extensions to existing airports will be increasingly complicated processes that involve greater and greater concerns about environmental issues.

Railroads and Subways

39. Holabird and Root. Scheme for the Rock Island Railroad exhibit at the second year of the Century of Progress Exposition, 1934. Pencil on tracing paper, 36.8 x 86.7 cm. Lent by the Chicago Historical Society.

40. Holabird and Root. Interior of a Rock Island Railroad lounge car, 1936. Pencil on tracing paper, 45.3 x 88.7 cm. Lent by the Chicago Historical Society.

41. Leslie Ragan. "For the Public Service," a view of the LaSalle Street Station showing the Twentieth Century Limited and other New York Central trains, c. 1939. Oil on canvas, 106.7 x 91.4 cm. Lent by Arthur Dubin Collection. (See plate 7.)

42. John Reed Fugard. Exterior and interior perspective views of a typical passenger and freight station for the Rock Island and Pacific Railway, 1944. Pencil on tracing paper, 44.5 x 59.7 and 36.8 x 56.5 cm. Lent by the Chicago Historical Society.

43. Bertrand Goldberg Associates. Proposed plywood freight car, 1952. Cutaway view, 67.5 x 100.2 cm. Lent by Bertrand Goldberg Associates.

44. City of Chicago. Overall plan and profile of subway, route 1, Chicago subway system, 1959. Photostats, each 55.9 x 89.4 cm. Lent by the Chicago Historical Society.

45. Perkins and Will. Rendering of the Cumberland Avenue Station for the Chicago Transit Authority (CTA) extension to O'Hare International Airport, delineated by Frank Nelson, 1979. Casein on paper, 105.4 x 76.3 cm. Lent by the Chicago Department of Transportation.

46. Murphy/Jahn; Helmut Jahn, designer, with James Stevenson. Axonometric view of the O'Hare CTA Station, c. 1980. Airbrushed ink on resin-coated photographic paper, 60 x 60.2 cm. Gift of Laurence Booth, 1981. (See plate 8.)

47. Gannet/SIH Joint Venture and Dubin, Dubin and Moutoussamy, Architects. Proposed Addison Island Station for the CTA, delineated by Voss, 1981. Marker on illustration board, 101.6 x 76.2 cm. Lent by Capital Planning and Construction, Chicago Transit Authority.

48. Loebl, Schlossman and Hackl. Perspective rendering of the proposed 49th Street and Western Avenue Station for the southwest line of the CTA, 1988. Computer drawing with marker, 92.7 x 62.3 cm. Lent by the Chicago Department of Transportation.

49. Solomon, Cordwell and Buenz. Perspective rendering of the Adams and Jackson streets mezzanine for the State Street subway renovation, delineated by Frank Nelson,

50

53

1988. Casein on paper, 69.8 x 102.9 cm. Lent by the Chicago Department of Transportation.

50.   Castro Buchel Architects and Planners. Perspective rendering of the Ashland and Archer Station for the southwest line of the CTA, rendered by Steve Bugay, 1990. Pen and ink and watercolor on paper, 115 x 62.3 cm. Lent by the Chicago Department of Transportation.

51.   Kendall Fleming, City Architect. Perspective rendering of the Clark and Lake transit complex, showing platform replacement, rendered by Frank Nelson, 1980. Casein on paper, 105.4 x 76.3 cm. Lent by the Chicago Department of Transportation.

52.   Harry Weese and Associates. Perspective rendering of the Midway Airport Station for the southwest line of the CTA, rendered by Gene Streett, 1991. Pen and ink, marker, and Prismacolor on paper, 107.4 x 80 cm. Lent by the Chicago Department of Transportation.

53.   Murphy/Jahn; Helmut Jahn, designer. Perspective plan and Madison Street elevation of the Chicago and Northwestern Terminal Building, Madison and Canal streets, delineated by Helmut Jahn and Michael Budilovsky, 1982. Airbrushed ink on resin-coated paper, 162.88 x 104.14 cm. Anonymous gift, 1982.

Automobiles and Highways

54.   Edwin H. Clark. Floor plan of, and gasoline pump for, a service station, 1928-30. Colored pencil on tracing paper, 45.7 x 81.3 cm. Lent by the Chicago Historical Society.

55.   Edwin H. Clark. Elevation of the Crane Building Service Station, 1928-30. Colored pencil on tracing paper, 45.7 x 84 cm. Lent by the Chicago Historical Society.

56.   R. Buckminster Fuller. Sectional view and plan of the Dymaxion Car, c. 1933. Ink on tracing paper; sectional view, 34.2 x 91; plan, 27.7 x 90.2 cm. Through prior gift of Three Oaks Wrecking Company, 1990. (See plate 11.)

57.   Holabird and Root. Elevation and perspective of the Gulf Oil Station Pavilion, Century of Progress Exposition, 1933. Graphite and colored pencil on photostat, 59.2 x 45.7, and graphite on tracing paper, 64.1 x 69.2 cm. Lent by the Chicago Historical Society.

58.   Andrew Rebori. Bird's-eye view of the Coast to Coast Chain of Small Hotels, October 1939. Photostat, 35.9 x 45.7 cm. Lent by the Chicago Historical Society.

59.   J. Edwin Quinn, architect. Facade perspective of Community Motors automobile showroom, 7740 South Stony Island Avenue, delineated by George A. Hossack, 1940 (now

demolished). Pencil and pastel on paper, 30.5 x 44.3 cm. Gift of J. Edwin Quinn, 1980.

60.   R. Buckminster Fuller. Longitudinal section through proposed Dymaxion Car for Henry Kaiser, c. 1943. Ink on tracing paper, approx. 83.4 x 92.3 cm. Through prior gift of Carson, Pirie, Scott and Company and Three Oaks Wrecking Company, 1991. (See plate 12.)

61.   Hugh Ferriss. Highways of the Future, 1943. Promotional lithograph by Trinity Portland Cement Company, 38.3 x 30.5 cm. Gift of J. Edwin Quinn, 1980. (See plate 10.)

62.   Double-leaf trunnion bascule bridge at North State Street over the Chicago River. General plan and elevation of proposed bridge, December 1940. Drawing no. 12801, 106.7 x 68.6 cm. Lent by City of Chicago Department of Public Works, Bureau of Bridges.

63.   J. Edwin Quinn. Presentation perspective drawing and photograph of the 159th Street Bridge over the Calumet Parkway, 1945. Hand-tinted photographs, each 8.7 x 23.6 cm. Gift of J. Edwin Quinn, 1980.

64.   Cook County Highway Department; J. Edwin Quinn, architect. Perspective sketch of the Calumet Parkway, Little Calumet River Bridge, c. 1948 (now demolished). Pencil, colored pencil, and ink on paper, 40.4 x 53.6 cm. Gift of J. Edwin Quinn, 1980.

57

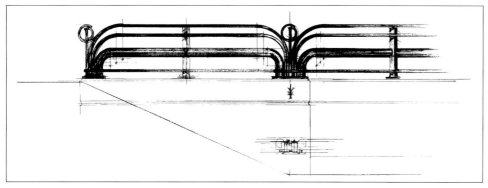

67

65. Cook County Highway Department; J. Edwin Quinn, architect. Aerial perspective of the Congress Parkway at Oak Park Avenue, delineated by Al Burnes, 1945. Pencil, watercolor, and airbrush on board, 50.7 x 86.3 cm. Gift of J. Edwin Quinn, 1980.

66. Cook County Highway Department; J. Edwin Quinn. Aerial perspective of the Congress Street Expressway between Canal Street and Jefferson Street, 1950. Hand-tinted photograph of presentation drawing, 24.2 x 35.4 cm. Gift of J. Edwin Quinn, 1980.

67. Cook County Highway Department; J. Edwin Quinn. Partial elevation of a bridge study, probably for the Congress Parkway, c. 1950. Pencil and colored pencil on vellum, 44.5 x 92 cm. Gift of J. Edwin Quinn, 1980.

68. Cook County Highway Department; J. Edwin Quinn. Aerial perspective of a section of the Congress Street Expressway between Chicago and Oak Park, 1951. Hand-tinted photographs of presentation drawings, 2 sheets, each 25 x. 49.2 cm. Gift of J. Edwin Quinn, 1980.

69. Cook County Highway Department; J. Edwin Quinn. Aerial perspectives of existing Illinois and Michigan Canal and proposed canal parkway west of Kedzie Avenue, n. d. Hand-tinted photographs of sketches, each 21.7 x 28 cm. Gift of J. Edwin Quinn, 1980.

70. Cook Highway Department; J. Edwin Quinn. Presentation perspective drawing and photograph of the bridge on the Edens Expressway over Forest Glenn Avenue, 1947 (later altered). Hand-tinted photographs, each 12 x 23.9 cm. Gift of J. Edwin Quinn, 1980.

71. Cook Highway Department; J. Edwin Quinn. Presentation perspective drawing and photograph of the bridge on the Edens Expressway over the north branch of the Chicago River, 1949 (later altered). Hand-tinted photographs, each 7.6 x 23.6 cm. Gift of J. Edwin Quinn, 1980.

72. Cook Highway Department; J. Edwin Quinn. Presentation perspective drawing and photograph of the Caldwell Avenue Bridge over the Edens Expressway, 1950. (later altered). Hand-tinted photographs, each 8 x 22.9 cm. Gift of J. Edwin Quinn, 1980.

73. Cook Highway Department; J. Edwin Quinn. Aerial view of the Edens Expressway between Winnetka Road and Lake Cook Road, c. 1950-55. Hand-tinted photograph mounted on board, 76 x 101.2 cm. Gift of J. Edwin Quinn, 1980.

74. J. Edwin Quinn. Comprehensive map of toll roads in the northeastern quadrant of the United States, 1954. Ink on linen, 28.1 x 40.7 cm. Gift of J. Edwin Quinn, 1980.

75. Milton M. Schwartz and Associates. Elevations and sections of the Chicago Airways Hotel, 5433 South Cicero Avenue, January 29, 1957 (now demolished). Pencil on tracing paper (sheet A-5), 88.3 x 119.5 cm. Lent by Milton M. Schwartz.

76. Milton M. Schwartz and Associates. Rendered elevation of the entrance pylon for the Chicago Airways Hotel, 1957. Ink and watercolor on sepia print, 77.5 x 51.5 cm. Lent by Milton M. Schwartz.

77. Milton M. Schwartz and Associates. First-floor plan and perspective view of proposed addition to the Chicago Airways Hotel, December 11, 1958. Pencil on tracing paper, each 68.5 x 91.5 cm. Lent by Milton M. Schwartz.

78. Double-leaf trunnion bascule bridge at North Dearborn Street over the Chicago River. General plan and elevation and bridge lighting, February 1958. Drawing no. 19970, 106.7 x 68.6 cm. Lent by City of Chicago Department of Transportation, Bureau of Bridges.

79. Sections and details of the McDonald's System Building, drawn by M.F.E., January 3, 1956. Blueline print mounted on board, 58.7 x 87.8 cm. Lent by the McDonald's Corporation Archives.

80. Perspective study of the McDonald's System Building, dated June 24, 1957, with later revisions. Blueline print of tracing paper drawing, 61 x 91.5 cm. Lent by the McDonald's Corporation Archives. (See plate 14.)

81. Elevations of two pylon signs for McDonald's, drawn by Gene Schroer, January 10, 1960. Blueline print annotated with colored pencil, 53 x 74.5 cm. Lent by the McDonald's Corporation Archives.

82. Perspective view of McDonald's Building and the newly designed double-arch sign of the 1962 series slab building, drawn by M. Martin, December 30, 1962. Blueline print, 61 x 91.5 cm. Lent by the McDonald's Corporation Archives.

83. Blueprint handbook for standard McDonald's Building design (Mansard-roofed), 1974. Blueprint paper, approx. 21.5 x 28 cm. Lent by the McDonald's Corporation Archives.

84. James Wines of SITE. Elevation and layout for Floating McDonald's Restaurant,

72

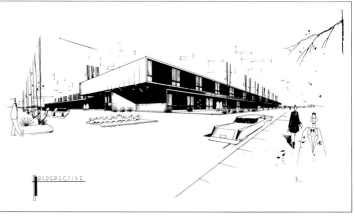

77

using reworked standard system building components; Cermak Plaza, Cermak Road and Harlem Avenue, Berwyn, 1983. Ink on Mylar, 102.1 x 74.4 cm. Lent by SITE.

85. James Wines of SITE. Floating Big Mac ideas for Floating McDonald's Restaurant, Berwyn, 1983. Pen and ink wash on paper, 35 x 42.5 cm. Lent by SITE.

86. James Wines of SITE. Exterior and interior views of Floating McDonald's Restaurant, Berwyn, 1982. Pen and ink on paper, 35 x 42.5 cm. Lent by SITE.

87. David Haid and Associates. Elevation study, Abraham Lincoln Oasis, Tristate Tollway, South Holland, 1965. Pencil, conté, and charcoal on paper, 91 x 217.5 cm. Gift of David Haid, 1985.

88. Laurence Booth of Booth and Nagle. ARCO Service Station prototype, 1972. Ink on Mylar, 76.5 x 114.3 cm. Lent by the Chicago Historical Society.

89. Double-leaf trunnion bascule bridge at Columbus Drive over the Chicago River. General arrangements, October 1974. Drawing no. 34804, 106.7 x 68.6 cm. Lent by City of Chicago Department of Public Works, Bureau of Bridges.

90. Outer Drive improvements for the bascule bridge over the Chicago River. Drawing no. 42576, 106.7 x 68.6 cm. Lent by City of Chicago Department of Public Works, Bureau of Bridges.

91. Double-leaf trunnion bascule bridge, Lake Shore Drive over the Chicago River. Alteration general plan and elevation, proposed alteration, February 1983. Drawing no. 41106, 106.7 x 68.6 cm. Lent by City of Chicago Department of Public Works, Bureau of Bridges.

92. Tigerman McCurry; Stanley Tigerman, designer. Rendered elevation of the Parking Garage, 60 East Lake Street, 1986. Watercolor on paper, 66.6 x 116.9 cm. Lent by Tigerman McCurry Architects.

93. Nagle, Hartray and Associates. Model of the Greyhound Bus Station, 631 West Congress Street, 1988-90. Glued foamcore and paper, 78 x 60 x 31 cm. Lent by Nagle, Hartray and Associates.

94. Nagle, Hartray and Associates. First-floor plan and cross section of the Greyhound Bus Station, 1988-90. Printed Mylar, 76 x 101.5 cm. Lent by Nagle, Hartray and Associates.

95. Lohan Associates. Longitudinal section and plan of the Illinois State Tollway Authority Building, intersection of the North/South and East/West tollways, Downers Grove, 1991. Airbrushed watercolor and colored pencil on paper, approx. 107 x 188 cm. Lent by Lohan Associates.

Airplanes and Airports

96. Paul Gerhardt, Jr., City Architect. Elevations of the Terminal Building at Chicago Municipal Airport (now Midway Airport), 5700 South Cicero Avenue, 1945. Blueprints, each 61.1 x 108 cm. Lent by the Chicago Historical Society.

97. Klekamp and Whitmore. Elevations and plan of proposed additions to the aviation buildings at Municipal Airport (now Midway Airport), 6048 South Cicero Avenue, for the Illinois National Guard 33rd Aviation Division, March 1934. Ink on linen, 78.1 x 108.5 and 76.6 x 106 cm. Lent by the Chicago Historical Society.

98. Voorhees, Gmelin and Walker. Proposed site plan of the Century of Progress Exposition showing an airport to be constructed in conjunction with the fair, c. 1930. Pencil on tracing paper, 47.7 x 93.4 cm. Gift of the Auxiliary Board of The Art Institute of Chicago, 1980.

99. Hugh Ferriss. Airports of the Future, 1943. Promotional lithograph by the Portland Cement Company, 38.3 x 30.5 cm. Gift of J. Edwin Quinn, 1980.

100. Andrew Rebori. Bird's-eye view of proposed Chicago Harbor Airport, 1945, done for the Global Air Meet, 1949. Pencil on tracing paper, 27.9 x 58.9 cm. Lent by the Chicago Historical Society.

101. J. Edwin Quinn. Bird's-eye view of superhighways at proposed Orchard Airport,

delineated by Al Burnes, 1948. Colored print, 21.5 x 28 cm. Gift of J. Edwin Quinn, 1980.

102. Ralph Burke Associates. O'Hare Field Master Plan, delineated by William F. Kaiser, 1952. Oil on canvas, 101.6 x 127 cm. Lent by Ralph Burke Associates.

103. I. M. Pei and Associates. Working drawings for the plans and section of the Air Traffic Control Tower, Federal Aviation Agency, O'Hare Field, 1966. Printed Mylar, each 76 x 101.5 cm. Lent by Pei Cobb Freed and Partners. (See plate 18.)

104. Aerial photograph of O'Hare International Airport in the late 1960s or early 1970s, prior to the construction of the Hilton Hotel and parking garage. Photoprint mounted on foamcore, 76 x 101.5 cm. Lent by Murphy/Jahn Architects.

105. Murphy/Jahn; Helmut Jahn, designer. Sixteen sketches for the United Airlines Terminal, delineated by Helmut Jahn, mostly March 28, 1983. Ink and colored pencil on note paper, each 14 x 11 cm. Lent by Murphy/Jahn Architects.

106. Murphy/Jahn; Helmut Jahn, designer. Two interior perspective views of the United Airlines Terminal, O'Hare International Airport, delineated by Rael Slutsky, 1985. Ink and colored pencil on paper, each approx. 44 x 63 cm. Lent by Murphy/Jahn Architects.

107. Murphy/Jahn; Helmut Jahn, designer. Model of the tunnel between Concourses B and C of the United Airlines Terminal,

111

O'Hare International Airport, 1987. Mixed media, two sections, each 227.3 x 50 x 45.7 cm. Lent by Murphy/Jahn Architects.

108. Murphy/Jahn; Helmut Jahn, designer. Cutaway perspective view of Concourse B and C of the United Airlines Terminal,

O'Hare International Airport, 1987. Printed paper, 101.5 x 127 cm. Lent by Murphy/Jahn Architects. (See plate 21.)

109. The Austin Company. Elevations and sections of the United Airlines Hangar, O'Hare International Airport, 1987. Ink on

Mylar, 76.2 x 106.7 cm. Lent by The Austin Company.

110. Perkins and Will; Ralph Johnson, design principal. Model of the International Terminal at O'Hare International Airport, 1989-92. Mixed media, approx. 138 x 91 cm. Lent by Perkins and Will.

111. Perkins and Will; Ralph Johnson, design principal. Section perspective of the interior of the International Terminal, O'Hare International Airport, 1989. Printed Mylar, approx. 75 x 102 cm. Lent by Perkins and Will.

112. Perkins and Will; Ralph Johnson, design principal. Interior perspective views of the International Terminal, O'Hare International Airport, 1989. Five printed Mylar sheets, approx. 34 x 189 cm. Lent by Perkins and Will.

113. Gelick Foran Associates. Study site plan, floor plan, and elevations for a corporate hangar and office for the American Hospital Supply Corporation (now Baxter Travenol) at the Waukegan Airport, 1984. Printed paper and pastel, 71 x 56 cm. Lent by Gelick Foran Associates.

Institutions and Government

When one thinks of Chicago and its architecture, the skyscraper comes first to mind as the city's most innovative architectural expression. Governmental and institutional buildings are frequently overlooked in the hierarchy of Chicago's buildings, except for those, naturally, that are famous skyscrapers, such as the Federal Center or the Civic Center. But we should remember that, by their very nature, buildings for government and institutions are often highly controversial because they must satisfy a wide audience, may be

built with public funds, and face limited budgets with, almost invariably, cost overruns. It becomes a nearly impossible task to find any creative solution that will not be controversial. Such was the case with the State of Illinois Building by Helmut Jahn of Murphy/Jahn, the Harold Washington Library by Thomas Beeby of Hammond, Beeby and Babka (pls. 28-30, 31-34), and the University of Illinois at Chicago by Walter Netsch of Skidmore, Owings and Merrill. Yet, because governmental and institutional services are

always needed and constantly expanding, there are an overwhelming number of buildings that fall into this category, which is not as subject to the vagaries of economic recessions and depressions as are commercial structures.

Institutional and governmental buildings run the gamut from fire and police stations, to schools, museums, planetaria, hospitals, universities, and libraries, as well as commemorative monuments, courthouses, jails, and office buildings. Conservative style, usually

Stanley Tigerman. Anti-Cruelty Society Building, 157 West Grand Avenue, 1976-78.

Zook and Taylor. Municipal Center, Route 64 at the Fox River, St. Charles, 1939.

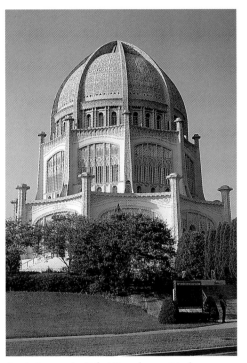

Louis Bourgeois. Bahai Temple, 100 Linden Avenue, Wilmette, 1929-53.

classical, characterizes most governmental buildings done before World War II, with corporate, conservative modernism taking its place after the war and, predictably, restrained historicist buildings of the postmodern era superseding them. Despite this conservatism, however, we can find a variety of distinctive expressions. Notable examples include the individualistic Bahai Temple in Wilmette by Louis Bourgeois, begun in 1929 (after his entry to the 1906 Hague Peace Palace competition) and completed in the early 1950s; the classically moderne Adler Planetarium of 1929-30 by Ernest A. Grunsfeld, Jr.; Zook and Taylor's Art Deco Municipal Center of 1939 in St. Charles; the modernist Crow Island School in Winnetka from 1940 by Eliel Saarinen and Perkins and Will; the expressionistic St. Joseph's Hospital by Belli and Belli in 1961; Minoru Yamasaki's expressive North Shore Congregation Israel from 1963 (see pls. 25-27); and the neighborhood scale of Stanley Tigerman's Anti-Cruelty Society Building of 1976-78.

114.   Alfred S. Alschuler. Front elevation of the Congregation Am Echod, Waukegan, 1927. Ink with graphite and crayon on linen, 66 x 94.8 cm. Lent by the Chicago Historical Society.

115.   Alfred S. Alschuler. Entrance bay elevation detail, section, and interior elevations for a fire engine house for the Chicago Fire Department, 324 South Desplaines, at the southwest corner of Boston Avenue, 1928. Ink on linen (sheet 8), 93 x 61.7 cm. Gift of Friedman, Alschuler and Sincere, 1980.

116.   Chester Howe Walcott. Perspective rendering of the Young Men's Christian Association Building, Evanston, 1928. Pencil on heavy paper, 27.9 x 35.6 cm. Gift of Julie Walcott Gallagher, 1986.

117.   Ernest A. Grunsfeld, Jr. First-floor plan and elevations of the Adler Planetarium, delineated by J. R. Ross, April 20, 1929. Ink and colored ink on linen; plan, 86 x 94, and elevations, 94 x 86 cm. Gifts of Ernest A. Grunsfeld, Jr., 1968.

118.   Perkins, Chatten and Hammond; Anderson and Tricknor Associate Architects; Phillmore N. Jacobson, designer and delineator. Elevation rendering of the proposed Lake Forest High School, c. 1930. Pencil and colored pencil on tracing paper, mounted on board, 29.7 x 51.2 cm. Gift of Mrs. Phillmore N. Jacobson, 1983.

119.   Voorhees, Gmelin and Walker; Ralph Walker, designer. Perspective rendering of a proposed Chicago War Memorial, delineated by John Wenrich, 1931. Pencil and watercolor on paper on illustration board, 56.5 x 41.5 cm. Gift of Haines, Lundberg, Waehler in honor of their centennial, 1983. (See plate 22.)

120.   Holabird and Root. Design study for their winning competitive entry for a Ferguson Building addition to The Art Institute of Chicago, 1934. Graphite on tracing paper, 29 x 44 cm. Lent by the Chicago Historical Society.

121.   Eliel Saarinen. Perspective night view of the proposed Alexander Hamilton Memorial, for the Midway, University of Chicago, 1932-37. Pencil, colored pencil, and watercolor on paper, 64 x 55.6 cm. Gift of the Kate S. Buckingham Fund, 1988.

122.   Marx, Flint and Schonne; Samuel Abraham Marx, designer. Perspective view of the Alexander Hamilton Memorial, Lincoln Park, 1950. Pencil on tracing paper, 54 x 89 cm. Gift of the Kate S. Buckingham Fund.

123.   Paul Schweikher. South and west elevations of the Third Unitarian Church of Chicago, 301 North Mayfield, 1935. Pencil on tracing paper, 24.9 x 30.7 cm and 18 x 26.5 cm. Gift of Dorothy and Paul Schweikher, 1984.

124.   Holabird and Root. Perspective sketch of Passavant Pavilion, Northwestern Memo-

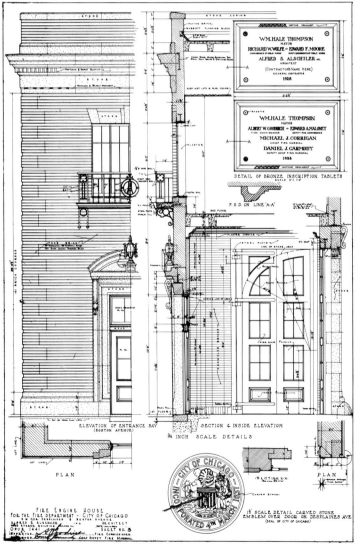

125

135

rial Hospital, 303 East Superior Street, c. 1925-29. Pencil on tracing paper, approx. 64.8 x 57.2 cm. Lent by the Chicago Historical Society.

125. Thielbar and Fugard. Perspective study of Wesley Memorial Hospital (now Wesley Pavilion at Northwestern Memorial Hospital), Superior Street at Fairbanks Court, delineated by F. Holcomb, c. 1935. Pencil and watercolor on paper, mounted on illustration board, 55 x 41.4 cm. Gift of Fugard, Orth and Associates, 1982.

126. Perkins and Will with Eliel Saarinen. Photograph of Crow Island School, 1112 Willow Road, Winnetka, 1940, signed by Lawrence Perkins and Philip Will, Jr. Photoprint on paper, 76 x 101.5 cm. Lent by Hedrich-Blessing, Photographers.

127. Ludwig Mies van der Rohe. Presentation study of a typical classroom, laboratory, or faculty office building prototype, Illinois Institute of Technology, partly de-

lineated by George Danforth, c. 1940-41. Crayon and pencil on illustration board, 50.7 x 76.2 cm. Gift of A. James Speyer, 1980.

128. George Danforth. Presentation perspective of the interior, small art museum project, 1941-42. Collage of photograph, halftone color print, ink, and paper on board, 76.7 x 101.5 cm. Gift of George E. Danforth, 1981.

129. Ludwig Mies van der Rohe. Perspective rendering of the proposed Chemistry or Metallurgy Building, Illinois Institute of Technology, c. 1944. Pencil and charcoal on illustration board, 76.9 x 101.8 cm. Gift of A. James Speyer, 1980.

130. Ludwig Mies van der Rohe. Preliminary study of a proposed library or administration building, Illinois Institute of Technology, 1944. Pencil, colored pencil, and charcoal on tracing paper, 72 x 106.7 cm. Restricted gift of the Auxiliary Board of The Art Institute of Chicago, 1987. (See plate 23.)

131. Ludwig Mies van der Rohe. Perspective rendering of the chapel, Illinois Institute of Technology, 65 East 32nd Street, c. 1949-52. Pencil and charcoal on illustration board, 75.7 x 100.2 cm. Gift of A. James Speyer, 1980.

132. Ludwig Mies van der Rohe with Pace

Associates. Photograph of Crown Hall, Illinois Institute of Technology, 1955, signed by Mies van der Rohe. Photoprint on paper, 89 x 117 cm. Lent by Hedrich-Blessing, Photographers. (See plate 24.)

133. Holabird and Root; Gerald Horn, designer. Details for the Kent College of Law of Illinois Institute of Technology, 565 West Adams Street, 1991. Colored printed paper, 76 x 101.5 cm. Lent by Holabird and Root.

134. Powell/Kleinschmidt. Model of the library in Holabird and Root's new building for the Kent College of Law, Illinois Institute of Technology, 1991. Mixed media, approx. 63.5 x 29.5 x 32.5 cm. Lent by Powell/Kleinschmidt.

135. Fugard, Olsen, Urbain and Neiler. Perspective rendering of the Veterans' Administration Hospital, Iron Mountain, Michigan, 1947. Pencil on illustration board, 53.5 x 72.6 cm. Gift of Fugard, Orth and Associates, 1982.

136. Schmidt, Garden and Erikson. Portico elevation and details for the Veterans' Administration Hospital, 333 East Huron Street (within Northwestern University Hospital complex), 1955. Screen PMT, 45.7 x 55.9 cm. Courtesy of Schmidt, Garden and Erikson.

126

129

137. Belli and Belli; Edo J. Belli, designer. Working drawings for St. Patrick's Academy, northeast corner of Austin Boulevard and Belmont Avenue, 1952; addition, 1955. Site plan with bird's-eye view; elevations (east and south) with section detail, November 21, 1952; sections of gymnasium and entry, November 27, 1952; plot plan for addition and roof plan with north and east elevations, April 28, 1955. Printed Mylar, each approx. 45.7 x 55.9 cm. Lent by Belli and Belli Architects and Engineers.

138. Yost and Taylor. Preliminary perspective study of the Unity Center of Christianity, 3434 Central Street (near the intersection of Gross Point, Wellington, and Central streets), Evanston, c. 1959. Pencil and colored pencil on tracing paper, mounted on board, 35.3 x 50.2 cm. Gift of L. Morgan Yost, 1978.

139. Belli and Belli of Missouri. Bird's-eye view rendering of St. Joseph Hospital for the Daughters of Charity, 2900 Lake Shore Drive, delineated by F. B., 1961. Watercolor and

139

tempera on board, approx. 83.5 x 109.5 cm. Lent by Belli and Belli Architects and Engineers.

140. Gertrude E. Kuh. Landscape plan and north elevation for the inner court of Children's Memorial Hospital, designed by Schmidt, Garden and Erikson, 1963. Graphite on tracing paper, 61 x 62.7 cm. Gift of John E. Deimel, 1991.

141. Minoru Yamasaki and Associates. Elevations and plans of the North Shore Congregation Israel, 1185 North Sheridan Road, Glencoe, 1962. Sepia prints, each 74.7 x 107.1 cm. Hammond, Beeby and Babka. Floor plan of additions to the synagogue, 1982. Ink and colored pencil on tracing paper, 76.2 x 108 cm. Both projects lent by the Chicago Historical Society. (See plate 26.)

142. Minoru Yamasaki. Photograph of the North Shore Congregation Israel, Glencoe, 1963, signed by Minoru Yamasaki. Photoprint on paper, 76 x 101.5 cm. Lent by Hedrich-Blessing, Photographers. (See plate 25.)

150

143. Ludwig Mies van der Rohe. Model of the Federal Center, 1959-63, with addition designed by Fujikawa Johnson and Associates, 1990. Mixed media, approx. 100 x 100 cm. Lent by the U.S. General Services Administration.

144. Jacques Brownson, designer; C. F. Murphy, supervising architect; Skidmore, Owings and Merrill, and Loebl, Schlossman, Bennett and Dart, associate architects. Perspective view of the plaza and Chicago Civic Center (now Richard J. Daley Center), bounded by Dearborn, Washington, Clark and Randolph streets, delineated by Al Francik, 1963. Watercolor and ink on board, 106.7 x 213.5 cm. Gift of Helmut Jahn, 1982.

145. Jacques Brownson, designer. Photograph of the Chicago Civic Center, 1965, signed by Jacques Brownson. Photoprint on paper, 76 x 101.5 cm. Lent by Hedrich-Blessing, Photographers.

146. Brenner Danforth Rockwell. Entrance elevation of the Museum of Contemporary Art, 237 East Ontario, c. 1967. Collage: papers and photoprint on board, 76.3 x 101.7 cm. Gift

of George E. Danforth and H. P. Davis Rockwell, 1988.

147. Coder Taylor Associates. Perspective rendering of the Glenview Public Library addition, 1930 Glenview Road, delineated by David Laughlin, 1965-69. Oil on board, 49 x 102 cm. Gift of D. Coder Taylor, 1981.

148. Harry Weese. Exterior perspective of the Seventeenth Church of Christ, Scientist, 55 East Wacker Drive, c. 1968. Pencil on yellow tracing paper, collage, 36 x 61 cm. Gift of Harry Weese and Associates, 1982.

149. Harry Weese. Interior perspective sketch of the Seventeenth Church of Christ, Scientist, 55 East Wacker Drive, c. 1968. Pencil and white crayon on paper, 54 x 57 cm. Gift of Harry Weese and Associates, 1982.

150. Skidmore, Owings and Merrill. Photograph of the University of Illinois at Chicago, 1970, signed by Walter A. Netsch. Photoprint on paper, 78.6 x 99.1 cm. Lent by Hedrich-Blessing, Photographers.

151. Edward Durrell Stone. Preliminary project sketches for the first McCormick Place Building, c. 1958-60 (now demolished).

143

148

Three sketches on Sheraton Blackstone Hotel stationery, each 12.8 x 16.5 cm. Gift of Thomas F. Sturr, 1976.

152. C. F. Murphy and Associates; Gene Summers with Helmut Jahn, designers. Two perspective sketches of McCormick Place, 2301 South Lake Shore Drive, c. 1967-69. Colored ink on photographic print, each 50.5 x 70.6 cm. Gift of Helmut Jahn, 1982.

153. C. F. Murphy and Associates; Gene Summers with Helmut Jahn, designers. Perspective view of McCormick Place, delineated by Gene Summers with Tom Burke, c. 1965. Photographic collage with line drawing, 91.5 x 91.5 cm. Gift of Helmut Jahn, 1982.

154. C. F. Murphy and Associates; Gene Summers, partner-in-charge, assisted by Helmut Jahn. Perspective view of main entrance of McCormick Place, delineated by Helmut Jacoby, 1969. Ink and watercolor on board, 32.3 x 58.4 cm. Gift of Helmut Jahn, 1982.

155. C. F. Murphy and Associates; Gene Summers, partner-in-charge, assisted by Helmut Jahn. Perspective view of the interior of the Exposition Center at McCormick Place, delineated by Helmut Jacoby, 1969. Ink and watercolor on board, 33.1 x 71.4 cm. Gift of Helmut Jahn, 1982.

156. C. F. Murphy and Associates; Gene Summers, partner-in-charge, assisted by Helmut Jahn. Perspective rendering of the interior of the Arie Crown Theater, McCormick Place, delineated by Helmut Jacoby, 1969. Ink and watercolor on board, 49 x 56.6 cm. Gift of Helmut Jahn, 1982.

157. Skidmore, Owings and Merrill; Diane Legge, designer. Building elevations and sections of McCormick Place Expansion, c. 1984. Printed Mylar, 91.2 x 138.3 cm. Lent by Skidmore, Owings and Merrill.

158. A. Epstein and Sons International, in association with Thompson, Ventulett,

Stainback and Associates. Composite rendering of exterior elevation and interior view of McCormick Place Expansion Project, delineated by Rael Slutsky and Associates, 1992. Blackline print on sepia paper, 45.7 x 55.9 cm. Printed from a Hedrich-Blessing photograph, courtesy the Chicago Historical Society.

159. David Haid and Associates. Section detail for the Walter H. Dyett Middle School, Martin Luther King Drive and 51st Street, 1973. Blackline print on polyester film, 45.7 x 55.8 cm. Printed from a Hedrich-Blessing photograph, courtesy the Chicago Historical Society.

160. The City of Chicago Bureau of Architecture; Lynn Meyers, designer. Axonometric view of the Third District Police Station, 71st Street and Cottage Grove Avenue, 1981. Printed Mylar, 101.5 x 76 cm. Lent by Terp Meyers Architects.

161. Holabird and Root; Gerald Horn, designer. Northwestern University School of Law Library, Lake Shore Drive and Chicago Avenue, 1982. Ink, graphite, and colored paper mounted on paper, 66 x 90.5 cm. Gift of Gerald Horn, 1982.

162. Holabird and Root; Gerald Horn, designer, assisted by James Baird. Exploded axonometric view of the Kersten Physics Teaching Center, University of Chicago 5720 South Ellis Avenue, 1985. Colored printed paper, 76 x 101.5 cm. Lent by Holabird and Root.

165

163. Murphy/Jahn, with Lester B. Knight and Associates. Model of the State of Illinois Building, Randolph, LaSalle, Lake, and Clark streets, 1979-85. Mixed media, approx. 121 x 130 x 71 cm. Lent by Murphy/Jahn Architects.

164. Murphy/Jahn; Helmut Jahn, designer. Photographs of the study models for the State of Illinois Building: eight preliminary study models; three final models, 1979. Photocopied paper photographs, each 76 x 101.5 cm. Lent by Murphy/Jahn Architects. (See plates 32-33.)

165. Murphy/Jahn; Helmut Jahn, designer. Two perspective renderings of the exterior and interior of the State of Illinois Building, 1979-85. Watercolor on printed paper, mounted on masonite; exterior, 76.5 x 101, interior, 101 x 76.5 cm. Lent by Murphy/Jahn Architects.

166. Murphy/Jahn; Helmut Jahn, designer. Three elevation studies of the State of Illinois Building, c. 1979. Pencil and colored pencil on printed paper, each 76.5 x 77 cm. Lent by Murphy/Jahn Architects.

167. SEBUS Group, Hammond, Beeby and Babka. Two renderings of the winning design for the Harold Washington Library Center, 400 South State Street, 1988. Colored pencil on paper, each 185.5 x 94 cm. Lent by the Chicago Public Library, Special Collections Department.

168. Booth/Hansen and Associates. Grace Place, 720 South Dearborn Street, 1984. Printed Mylar with colored pencil, approx. 56 x 71 cm. Lent by Booth/Hansen and Associates, Ltd.

169. Perkins and Will; Ralph Johnson, designer. West elevation of the Orland Park Village Center, 147th Street and Ravinia Avenue, Orland Park, c. 1987. Ink and colored pencil on vellum, 84.5 x 145.5 cm. Lent by Perkins and Will. (See plate 36.)

170. Lohan Associates. East elevation of the Shedd Oceanarium, South Lake Shore and Solidarity drives, 1987. Airbrushed watercolor and colored pencil on paper, 112 x 204 cm. Lent by Lohan Associates.

171. Lubotsky Metter Worthington and Law; Andrew Metter, principal designer. Drawing for Municipal Fueling Facility, 1313 Shermer Road, Glenview, 1988. Ink on Mylar, 76.2 x 106.7 cm. Lent by Andrew Metter.

172. Decker and Kemp. Perspective views of the main entry and boardroom wing of the Northbrook Village Hall, 1225 Cedar Lane, Northbrook, delineated by Bruce Bondy, 1989. Printed Mylar views of ink renderings, each approx. 71 x 56 cm. Lent by Decker and Kemp Architecture and Urban Design.

173. Bertrand Goldberg Associates. Sche-

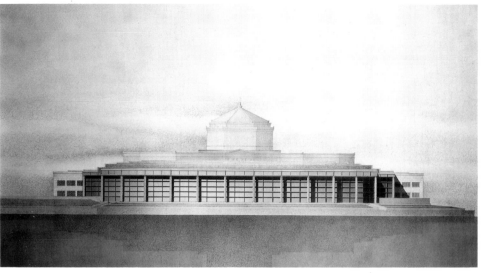

170

matic diagram for Wright College, Montrose and Narragansett avenues, 1989-91, showing the legislated five-foot modular system developed into three dimensions. Collaged and printed paper, 127 x 101.5 cm. Lent by Bertrand Goldberg Associates.

174. Belli and Belli. Perspective rendering of St. Benedict the African Church, 66th Street and Stewart Avenue, delineated by Radler, 1989. Watercolor on paper. Lent by St. Benedict the African Church.

175. Weese Langley Weese Architects; Ben Weese, designer. Sketches of the Westminster Presbyterian Church, 1420 West Moss Avenue, Peoria, delineated by Ben Weese, c. 1990. Pencil and ink on paper, various sizes. Lent by Weese Langley Weese Architects.

176. Weese Langley Weese Architects; Ben Weese, designer. Plan, section, and elevation of the Westminster Presbyterian Church, 1420 West Moss Avenue, Peoria, 1990. Printed Mylar, approx. 71 x 91.5 cm. Lent by Weese Langley Weese Architects.

177. Booth/Hansen and Associates. Axonometric view of the additions to the Walsh School, Canalport Avenue and Peoria Street, 1991. Printed Mylar, approx. 71 x 56 cm. Lent by Booth/Hansen and Associates, Ltd.

178. Weese Langley Weese Architects; Cynthia Weese, designer. Perspective study for the Business, Mathematics, and Computer Sciences Building, Luther College, Decorah, Iowa, 1991. Pencil on paper, 45.8 x 66 cm. Lent by Weese Langley Weese Architects.

179. Holabird and Root; Gerald Horn, designer. Exploded axonometric view of the addition for Digital Computer Laboratories, University of Illinois, Champaign-Urbana, Illinois, 1991. Colored printed paper, 101.5 x 76 cm. Lent by Holabird and Root.

180. Holabird and Root; Roy Solfisburg, designer, assisted by Michael Murphy. Exterior elevation and details of the Loyola University

School of Business, southwest corner of Pearson Street and Wabash Avenue, 1991. Colored printed paper, 101.5 x 76 cm. Lent by Holabird and Root.

181. Perkins and Will, Ralph Johnson, designer. Perspective rendering of the Temple Buell Hall, University of Illinois, Champaign-Urbana, 1991. Ink on Mylar, 76 x 101.5 cm. Lent by Perkins and Will.

182. Schmidt, Garden and Erikson. Perspective view, sections, and key plan for the Cook County Juvenile Center Expansion, Roosevelt Road and Hamilton Avenue, 1990-93. Printed paper, 71 x 91.5 cm. Lent by Schmidt, Garden and Erikson.

183. Tigerman McCurry. Model for the Chicago Bar Association, 321 South Plymouth Court, 1989-90. Painted plastic, 35.5 x 50.5 x 97 cm. Lent by Miglin-Beitler, Inc.

184. Tigerman McCurry; Stanley Tigerman, designer. Model of "The Powerhouse," an energy education resource center for Commonwealth Edison, 100 Shiloh Boulevard, Zion, 1988-92. Glued wood, 22 x 111 x 24 cm. Lent by Tigerman McCurry Architects.

185. A. Epstein and Sons International; Andrew Metter, principal designer. Model of the Municipal Center, Northfield, 1992. Strathmore board with silk-screened plexiglas cover, 76.2 x 30.5 x 12.7 cm. Lent by Andrew Metter for A. Epstein and Sons International.

186. Tigerman McCurry; Margaret McCurry, designer. Axonometric view of the remodeling of the Juvenile Protection Association, 3655 North Ashland Avenue, 1991. Colored pencil on paper, 91.5 x 71 cm. Lent by Tigerman McCurry Architects.

187. David Woodhouse. Plan and elevation for the Lake County Museum addition and renovation, Lakewood Forest Preserve, Wauconda, 1991. Marker and Prismacolor on yellow tracing paper, approx. 101.6 x 53.4 cm. Lent by David Woodhouse.

Commerce and Business

Skyscrapers have captured the imagination of architectural professionals and lay enthusiasts alike, and, since the early twentieth century, they have become a symbol of urban growth. Of Chicago's ornate skyscrapers of the 1920s, most people instantly recognize the Wrigley Building or the Tribune Tower. But numerous others filled out the cityscape, often with equally elaborate ornamental details.

As these ornate high-rises gave way to the painful realities of the Great Depression, however, architects who survived in practice could, at best, hope for small five- or six-story commercial jobs. The post-World War II boom witnessed new high-rise office buildings evincing various approaches to modern design, such as the Prudential Building of 1952-55 by Naess and Murphy and the Inland Steel Building of 1954-55 by Skidmore, Owings and Merrill. In addition to these newer and higher urban monuments, architects turned to modernizing the famous Chicago skyscrapers from the turn of the century.

As more and more Chicago School buildings were being demolished and altered in the 1950s and 1960s, the preservation movement took hold in Chicago. Preservationists pushed building owners to restore and renovate their historic skyscrapers sensitively, and their efforts were given a boost by the introduction of tax incentives in the 1970s and 1980s that favored restoration.

Concurrent with this renewed interest in historic structures came a wider interest in historicism and contextualism. These trends found expression in high-rises, as well as in those imaginary projects included in the exhibition "Late Entries to the Chicago Tribune Competition," organized by Chicago's Museum of Contemporary Art in 1980, and in the 1983 "Tops Competition," sponsored by the Chicago Architectural Club.

But the commercial high-rise did more than repopulate the central city after World War II. Commercial office structures of varying scale made their way into the suburbs via extended transportation systems, whether highway or commuter rail lines. Corporate headquarters spread throughout suburban locations near these transportation systems. Now, as with Lohan Associates' 1991 Safety Kleen Building near Interstate 90 in Elgin, they are beginning to be designed with more sensitivity to the open woodland they often inhabit. At Safety Kleen, a company concerned with environmental clean-up, the employees' automobiles are discreetly tucked inside the building in parking lots conveniently located near the offices themselves.

Shaw and Associates. Presidents' Plaza I and II, 1978.

Aerial photograph showing Presidents' Plaza, the Cumberland CTA Station-Cumberland Avenue and Pueblo Avenue at Interstate 90, the Kennedy Expressway, and River Road, with the skyline of Chicago in the background. The two buildings in the foreground are from 1983, whereas the two buildings to their immediate left date from 1978.

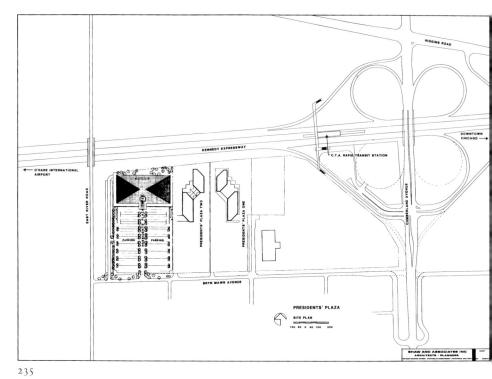

235

188. Graham, Anderson, Probst and White. Plan and elevations for Samuel Insull's private office in the Peoples Gas Building, 122 South Michigan Avenue, 1922. Graphite and colored pencil on white tracing paper, 64.5 x 99 cm. Gift of Allen W. Prusis, in honor of his graduation from Princeton University, 1980.

189. Aerial Survey Company. Aerial view of Chicago looking east along the Chicago River, 1927-28. Photograph, 49.5 x 63.5 cm. Lent by Ryerson Library, Special Collections.

190. Howells and Hood. North elevation of the 18th to 34th floors of the Chicago Tribune Tower, 435 North Michigan Avenue, October 1, 1923. Blueprint (sheet 36), 104 x 90 cm. Gift of Howells and Hood, 1925.

191. John Vinci. Axonometric view of the restoration of the lobby for the Chicago Tribune Tower, March 4, 1985. Ink and zipa-tone on Mylar (sheet A-0), 76.2 x 106.8 cm. Lent by the Office of John Vinci.

192. Andrew Rebori. Proposed setback sky-scraper on Michigan Avenue, 1923. Ink on linen, 68.7 x 33 cm. Lent by the Chicago Historical Society.

193. Frank Lloyd Wright. Perspective rendering of the proposed National Life Insurance Building, 1923. Graphite and red pencil on paper, 117.6 x 100.1 cm. Lent by Seymour H. Persky. (See plate 37.)

194. Holabird and Root. Elevation of the Palmolive Building (later the Playboy Building), 919 North Michigan Avenue, June 1, 1928. Ink on linen, 94.4 x 98.4 cm. Lent by the Chicago Historical Society.

195. Enrique Alvarez. Bas-relief designs for the elevator cab interiors of the Palmolive Building, c. 1930. Pencil on drawing paper, each 35.8 x 26.8 cm. Architecture Department purchase, 1985.

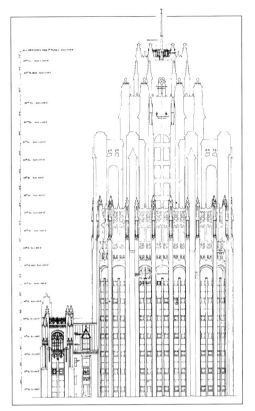

190

196. Holabird and Root. Working drawings of the north elevation and lobby plan, Chicago Board of Trade Building, Jackson Boulevard and LaSalle Street, 1928. Ink on linen, 101.8 x 84.8 and 105.3 x 88.3 cm. Lent by the Chicago Historical Society.

197. Murphy/Jahn. Cutaway perspective rendering of the addition to the Chicago Board of Trade in relation to the original building, 1978. Printed Mylar, 127 x 101.5 cm. Lent by Murphy/Jahn Architects. (See plate 40.)

198. John Storrs. Maquette for the Ceres sculpture atop the Chicago Board of Trade

Building, 1928. Cast chrome steel, height 66 cm. Gift of John N. Stern, 1981. (See plate 38.)

199. Burnham Brothers. Perspective study of the Carbide and Carbon Building, 230 North Michigan Avenue, 1927-28. Pencil on tracing paper, 93.3 x 59.8 cm. Restricted gift of the Architecture Society and Friends of the Library, in honor of the Seventy-fifth Anniversary of the Burnham Library of Architecture, 1987.

200. Graham, Anderson, Probst and White. Perspective rendering of the Merchandise Mart, delineated by Hugh Ferriss, 1928. Charcoal and pencil on paper, approx. 51 x 71 cm. Lent by Merchandise Mart Properties, Inc.

201. Graham, Anderson, Probst and White. Model of the Merchandise Mart, 1929. Painted plaster, approx. 69.2 x 38.1 x 33 cm. Lent by Merchandise Mart Properties, Inc.

202. Graham, Anderson, Probst and White. Perspective rendering of the entrance to the Field Building, 135 South LaSalle Street, delineated by Henry Harringer, c. 1930-31. Charcoal and pencil on tracing paper, 40.6 x 31.9 cm. Gift of Olaf Harringer, 1982.

203. Vitzthum and Burns. Perspective rendering of the Steuben Club Building, 188 West Randolph Street, delineated by E. Tronnes, c. 1928. Watercolor on paper, 77 x 29.3 cm. Through prior gifts of Three Oaks Wrecking Company, 1990. (See plate 41.)

204. Thielbar and Fugard. Perspective rendering of the Trustee System Service Building (later the Corn Exchange), 201 North Wells Street, delineated by F. Holcomb, 1930. Pencil and watercolor, mounted on board, 42.5 x 32.5 cm. Gift of Fugard, Orth and Associates, 1982. (See plate 42.)

191   206

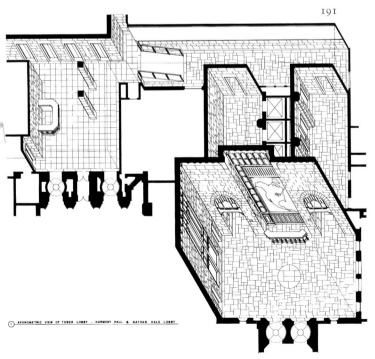

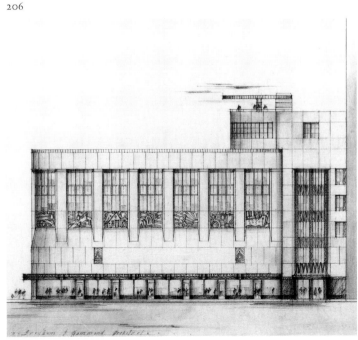

211

213

205. Huszagh and Hill. Perspective rendering of the proposed Pullman Building, c. 1930. Charcoal on paper, 51.6 x 33.2 cm. Lent by the Chicago Historical Society.

206. Burnham and Hammond. Elevation drawing of a proposed low-rise office building, 1937. Pencil and colored pencil on tracing paper, 64 x 78 cm. Restricted gift of the Friends of the Library and the Architecture Society in honor of the Seventy-fifth Anniversary of the Burnham Library of Architecture, 1987.

207. Skidmore, Owings and Merrill; Walter A. Netsch, Jr., designer. Preliminary model for the Inland Steel Building, 30 West Monroe Street, 1954. Plexiglas and enameled steel, 18.3 x 27.2 x 26 cm. Gift of Walter A. Netsch, Jr., 1981.

208. Skidmore, Owings and Merrill; Bruce J. Graham, designer. Five working drawings for the Inland Steel Building, 1955: second-floor plan, May 2, 1955; alternative exterior facing of service tower with granite on concrete block, delineated by Bruce J. Graham, November 1, 1955; alternative exterior facing of service tower with precast stone panels, delineated by F.E.W., November 1, 1955; exterior details of upper part of main building, showing section details of spandrel construction, delineated by F.W. and G.E., September 19, 1955; and south and west elevations, delineated by E.P., September 19, 1955. Pencil on tracing paper, each 68.5 x 101.5 cm. Lent by Skidmore, Owings and Merrill.

209. L. Morgan Yost and D. Coder Taylor. Perspective study of Yost and Taylor's offices, 500 Green Bay Road, Kenilworth, December 28, 1952. Pencil and colored pencil on tracing paper, 22 x 31 cm. Gift of L. Morgan Yost, 1978.

210. Yost and Taylor. Proposed addition to 444 Green Bay Road (Radium and Radon Corp.), Kenilworth, delineated by D. Coder Taylor, 1958. Pencil, pastel, and tempera on laid paper, 27.8 x 33.5 cm. Gift of D. Coder Taylor, 1981.

211. Yost and Taylor. Proposed office building for 510 Green Bay Road, Kenilworth, delineated by D. Coder Taylor, c. 1958. Pencil on paper, mounted on board, 25.3 x 39 cm. D. Coder Taylor, 1981.

212. Brenner Danforth Rockwell; Daniel Brenner, designer. Four design studies for the remodeling of the Chicago Stock Exchange Building by Adler and Sullivan, entrance arch on LaSalle and Washington streets, 1965. Pencil and colored pencil on tracing paper, each approx. 19 x 25 cm. Gifts of Danforth, Rockwell, Carrow, 1985.

213. Brenner Danforth Rockwell; Daniel Brenner, designer. Jackson Boulevard entrance study for the Monadnock Building by Burnham and Root, Jackson and Dearborn streets, c. 1965. Ink on photomontage, 36.5 x 50 cm, delineated by Daniel Brenner and John Vinci. Gift of George E. Danforth and H. P. Davis Rockwell, 1989.

222

214. Perkins and Will. Photograph of the U.S. Gypsum Building, 101 South Wacker Drive, 1964, signed by Philip Will, Jr., and Laurence B. Perkins. Photoprint on paper, 76 x 101.5 cm. Lent by Hedrich-Blessing, Photographers.

215. Perkins and Will; C. William Brubaker, designer. Seven sketches related to the development of the First National Bank of Chicago, Madison, Dearborn, and Clark streets, 1966. Ink on paper, each 30.7 x 23 cm. Gift of C. William Brubaker, 1982.

216. Powell/Kleinschmidt. Model of the remodeling of the executive dining facility on the 57th floor of the First National Bank of Chicago, 1989. Mixed media, 120.5 x 49.5 x 22.5 cm. Lent by Powell/Kleinschmidt, Inc.

217. Skidmore, Owings and Merrill. Photograph of the John Hancock Center, 875 North Michigan Avenue, 1969, signed by Bruce J. Graham. Photoprint on paper, 101 x 76 cm. Lent by Hedrich-Blessing, Photographers.

218. Skidmore, Owings and Merrill; Bruce J. Graham and Fazlur Khan, designers. Elevations labeled "Sky Lobby Scheme 1" for the John Hancock Center, 875 North Michigan Avenue, c. 1964-65. Ink on tracing paper, 101.3 x 76 cm. Lent by Skidmore, Owings and Merrill.

219. Skidmore, Owings and Merrill; Bruce J. Graham and Fazlur Khan, designers. Four working drawings for partial elevations and sections, building section, ramp structure elevations and details, and tower base plate and typical column details for the John Hancock Center, July 26, 1965. Pencil on linen, each approx. 82.5 x 122 cm. Lent by Skidmore, Owings and Merrill.

220. Harry Weese and Associates. Two perspective studies of the Time-Life Building, 541 North Fairbanks Court, delineated by Robert E. Bell, 1966. Graphite and green marker on yellow tracing paper, 30.2 x 19 cm and 30.1 x 18.4 cm. Gifts of Robert E. Bell, 1991. (See plate 44.)

221. Harry Weese and Associates. Photograph of the Time-Life Building, 1969-70, signed by Harry Weese. Photoprint on paper, 76 x 101.5 cm. Lent by Hedrich-Blessing, Photographers.

222. Minoru Yamasaki. Perspective study of the Montgomery Ward Tower, 535 West Chicago Avenue, delineated by Carlos Diniz, 1970. Ink and colored ink on board, 93.5 x 68 cm. Gift of the Dearborn Land Company, 1984.

223. Skidmore, Owings and Merrill. Meigs Field clearance surface study, in relation to construction of the Sears Tower, n. d. Ink and collaged Mylar, 116.4 x 86.5 cm. Lent by Skidmore, Owings and Merrill.

224. Skidmore, Owings and Merrill; Bruce J. Graham and Fazlur Khan, designers. Proposed fiberglass window wall elevations for the Sears Tower, 233 South Wacker Drive, delineated by G. D., May 14, 1971. Pencil and ink on printed Mylar, 116.5 x 86.5 cm. Lent by Skidmore, Owings, and Merrill. (See plate 50.)

225. Skidmore, Owings and Merrill; Bruce J. Graham and Fazlur Khan, designers. Elevator section for the Sears Tower, December 1, 1970. Ink and pencil on Mylar, 116.6 x 86.5 cm. Lent by Skidmore, Owings and Merrill.

226. Robert Vogele, Inc. *Heil Who?* a propaganda brochure for advertising, n.d. Ink on paper, 22.9 x 22.9 cm. Lent by Special Collections, The University Library, University of Illinois at Chicago.

227. Moore, Ruble and Yudell. Perspective rendering of a Late Entry to the Chicago Tribune Tower Competition, 1980. Colored pencil on tracing paper, 152.5 x 76.3 cm. Restricted gift of the Architecture Society Fellows, 1983. (See plate 68.)

228. Fred Koetter, assisted by John Halper, Waldo Maffei, and John Medler. "Variation on a Theme no. WG-23," a Late Entry to the Chicago Tribune Tower Competition, 1980. Ink and wash on paper, 152.5 x 76.3 cm. Restricted gift of the Architecture Society Fellows, 1985.

229. Robert A. M. Stern. Perspective rendering of a Late Entry to the Chicago Tribune Tower Competition, 1980. Airbrushed ink on illustration board, 152.4 x 76.2 cm. Restricted gifts of Mr. and Mrs. Thomas J. Eyerman; Mr. and Mrs. David Hilliard; Mrs. Irving F. Stein, Sr., in memory of B. Leo Steif; and Mr. and Mrs. Ben Weese, 1983.

230. Fujikawa, Conterato, Lohan and Associates. Four elevations of the Lodge, McDonald's Corporation Office Campus, Oak Brook, delineated by Gilbert Gorski, 1981. Pencil, colored pencil, and craypas on paper, 76.5 x 121 cm. Gift of Dirk Lohan, 1982.

231. Hammond, Beeby and Babka; Thomas H. Beeby, designer. Proposed (but unexecuted) mural for the Tri-State Center Office

229

Building, 2215 Sanders Road, Northbrook, delineated by Dennis Rupert, 1977-79. Ink on tracing paper, 78 x 76.5 cm. Gift of Helmut Jahn, 1981.

232. Hammond, Beeby and Babka. Elevation and plan of the Tri-State Center Office Building, Northbrook, 1977. Ink on Mylar, 76.2 x 106 and 76.3 x 106.6 cm. Lent by the Chicago Historical Society.

233. Shaw and Associates. Elevation studies for President's Plaza I, I-94 and Cumberland Avenue, c. 1978. Pencil on tracing paper, three sheets: 31.5 x 76, 35.5 x 76, 36 x 76 cm. Gift of Shaw and Associates, 1991.

234. Shaw and Associates. Partial elevation, plan, and section studies for the fenestration of President's Plaza I, c. 1978. Pencil on tracing paper, three sheets, each 46.5 x 76 cm. Gift of Shaw and Associates, 1991.

235. Shaw and Associates. Site plan for President's Plaza I, II, and III in relation to the Kennedy Expressway and CTA Cumberland Station, c. 1983. Sepia print with pencil and presstype, 76.3 x 106.5 cm. Gift of Shaw and Associates, 1991.

246

236. Shaw and Associates. Site plan for President's Plaza III, October 20, 1983, with later revisions. Ink and pencil with presstype on Mylar, 76.5 x 107 cm. Gift of Shaw and Associates, 1991.

237. Shaw and Associates. Site section through the easternmost building of President's Plaza III, October 20, 1983, with later revisions. Ink and pencil with presstype on Mylar, 77 x 106.7 cm. Gift of Shaw and Associates, 1991.

238. C. F. Murphy Associates; Helmut Jahn, designer. Perspective elevation of One South Wacker Drive Building, delineated by James Goettsch, 1981. Prismacolor and silver tape on paper, 165 x 118 cm. Gift of Helmut Jahn, 1982. (See plate 45.)

239. C.F. Murphy Associates; Helmut Jahn and Rainer Schildknecht, designers. Interior perspective section of the proposed renovation of the Santa Fe Building, 224 South Michigan Avenue (formerly the Railway Exchange Building), delineated by Helmut Jahn, assisted by Rick Wordell, 1981. Ink on Mylar, 95.5 x 91.9 cm. Gift of Helmut Jahn, 1982.

Commerce and Business 427

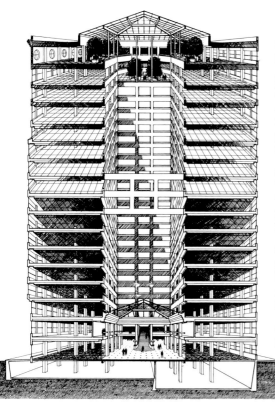

239

79 x 38 cm. Gift of Peggy Wolff, 1985. (See plate 47.)

246. Christopher Rudolph. Standard Oil Building, 200 East Randolph Street, Chicago Architectural Club "Tops" Competition, 1983. Ink, colored pencil, marking pen, and photoprint collage on paper, 71.5 x 33 cm. Gift of Christopher H. Rudolph, 1985.

247. Michael Janis with Tony Porto. Tribune Tower, Chicago Architectural Club "Tops" Competition, 1983. Pencil on paper, 75 x 33 cm. Gift of Michael Janis and Tony Porto, 1985.

248. Kohn Pedersen Fox Associates. Photograph of 333 West Wacker Drive, 1983, signed by William Pedersen. Photoprint on paper, 101.5 x 76 cm. Lent by Hedrich-Blessing, Photographers.

249. Kohn Pedersen Fox Associates. Site plan, elevation, plan, and perspective studies for 333 West Wacker Drive, delineated by William Pedersen, May 28, 1981. Colored pencil and pencil on notebook paper, 28 x 21.5 cm. Lent by Kohn Pedersen Fox Associates. (See plate 55.)

250. Kohn Pedersen Fox Associates. Elevation study for the base of 333 West Wacker Drive, c. 1982. Colored pencil on yellow tracing paper, approx. 30.5 x 79 cm. Lent by Kohn Pedersen Fox Associates.

251. Eva Maddox Associates. Plan and axonometric view of the law offices of Portes, Sharp, Herbst, and Kravets, 333 West Wacker Drive, 5th floor, 1988. Ink on paper, 71 x 91.5 cm. Lent by Eva L. Maddox, Eva Maddox Associates, Inc.

252. Pappageorge/Haymes. Elevation, plans, and construction sequence for alterations and additions to Washington Square, 651 West Washington Street, c. 1985. Printed paper, 76 x 101.5 cm. Lent by Pappageorge/Haymes, Ltd.

253. John Burgee with Philip Johnson, and Shaw and Associates, associate architects. Model of exterior, 190 South LaSalle Street, 1983-84. Mixed media, 149 x 58.3 x 45.5 cm. Gift of The John Buck Company, 1988.

254. John Burgee with Philip Johnson, and Shaw and Associates, associate architects. Cutaway model of the lobby of 190 South LaSalle Street, 1983-84. Mixed media, 129.5 x 66 x 46 cm. Gift of the John Buck Company, 1988. (See plate 62.)

255. John Burgee with Philip Johnson, and Shaw and Associates, associate architects. Preliminary sketch for the lobby of 190 South LaSalle Street, c. 1985. Pencil and colored pencil on paper, 76.2 x 50.8 cm. Lent by the John Buck Company.

256. John Burgee with Philip Johnson, and Shaw and Associates, associate architects. Renderings of the exterior of 190 South LaSalle Street, c. 1986. Pencil on paper, 76.5 x 51 cm. Lent by the John Buck Company.

257. John Burgee with Philip Johnson, and Shaw and Associates, associate architects. Elevation of 190 South LaSalle Street, c. 1986. Numbered print, 107.5 x 46 cm. Lent by the John Buck Company.

258. Powell/Kleinschmidt. Typical floor plan, conference floor plan, and typical elevator lobby for the law offices of Mayer, Brown and Platt, 190 South LaSalle Street, 1985-87. Printed Mylar, 127 x 101.5 cm. Lent by Powell/Kleinschmidt, Inc.

259. Kohn Pedersen Fox Associates. Exterior elevation of One O'Hare Center, 600 River Road, Rosemont, delineated by William C. Louie, 1984. Colored pencil on tracing paper on board, 42 x 66 cm. Lent by Kohn Pedersen Fox Associates.

260. Holabird and Root; Gerald Horn, designer. Elevation and details of a suburban office building for the John Buck Company, AT&T Plaza, 1111 West 22nd Street, Oak Brook, 1985-86. Colored and printed paper, 101.5 x 76 cm. Lent by Holabird and Root.

253

240. John Vinci. Key sheet and partial east elevation of the South Building of the Monadnock Building, showing terracotta replacement, Dearborn and Jackson streets, August 31, 1983. Ink on Mylar, two sheets (A-23 and A-16), each approx. 76.2 x 101.5 cm. Lent by the Office of John Vinci.

241. Hasbrouck, Peterson; Wilbert Hasbrouck, designer. Hand-colored composite of a section through the lobby and light-court, looking north, and a north-south section of the Rookery Building, 209 South LaSalle Street, showing proposed restoration, 1986. Colored pencil and ink on Mylar, 91.5 x 71.1 cm. Lent by Hasbrouck Peterson Zimoch Sirirattumrong.

242. Booth/Hansen and Associates; Laurence Booth, designer. Elevation study of 320 North Michigan Avenue, 1981. Pencil and colored pencil on tracing paper, 61 x 45.3 cm. Anonymous gift, 1981.

243. Holabird and Root; Gerald Horn, designer. Exploded axonometric view of Hollister, Inc., 2000 Hollister Drive, Libertyville, 1982. Colored printed paper, 76 x 101.5 cm. Lent by Holabird and Root.

244. Nagle, Hartray and Associates. Detail of the entrance elevation and a perspective view of the remodeling of 20 North Michigan Avenue, delineated by James L. Nagle, 1983. Ink and colored pencil on yellow tracing paper, mounted on foamcore, 127 x 101.5 cm. Gift of Nagle, Hartray and Associates, 1983. (See plates 57-58.)

245. Peggy Smolka Wolff. John Hancock Center, Chicago Architectural Club "Tops" Competition, 1983. Mixed media on Mylar,

261. Skidmore, Owings and Merrill; Adrian Smith, designer. Design study of the NBC Tower, 454 Columbus Drive, 1986. Colored pencil on paper, approx. 76 x 51 cm. Gift of Stanley Freehling, 1986. (See plate 71.)

262. Murphy/Jahn. Elevation of Oakbrook Terrace Tower, One Tower Lane, Oak Brook, 1986-88. Colored pencil on paper, 92.5 x 62 cm. Lent by Murphy/Jahn Architects.

263. Murphy/Jahn; Helmut Jahn, designer. Elevations and plan of Two Energy Center, Route I-88, Naperville, 1986. Photoprint on paper, approx. 66 x 101.5 cm. Lent by Murphy/Jahn Architects.

264. The Landahl Group. Plans, views, and a sail fragment from the office for Pannell Kerr Forster, 1984. Printed silk, approx. 163 x 122 cm. Lent by Gregory W. Landahl, FAIA, The Landahl Group, Inc.

265. Skidmore, Owings and Merrill; Adrian Smith, designer. Three elevation study models for the top of the AT&T Corporate Center, 227 West Monroe Street, c. 1985. Glued plastic and plexiglas, each approx. 80 x 21 x 10 cm. Lent by Skidmore, Owings and Merrill.

266. Skidmore, Owings and Merrill; Adrian Smith, designer. Partial elevations, plans, and views of the AT&T Corporate Center, 1989. Colored inks on computer printout paper, mounted on foamcore, 52.8 x 44.3 cm. Lent by Skidmore, Owings and Merrill.

276

267. Skidmore, Owings and Merrill; Joseph Gonzalez, designer. Computer-generated perspective rendering of One North Franklin Street, 1989. Ink and colored ink on printout paper, 82 x 44 cm. Lent by Skidmore, Owings and Merrill. (See plate 73.)

268. Perkins and Will; Ralph Johnson, design principal. Final model for the Morton International Building, 100 North Riverside Plaza, 1988-90. Mixed media, 44.5 x 24 x 54 cm. Lent by Perkins and Will.

269. Perkins and Will; Ralph Johnson, design principal. Study models for the Morton International Building, 1988. Mixed media, 117.5 x 32 x 47 cm. Lent by Perkins and Will.

270. Perkins and Will; Ralph Johnson, design principal. Preliminary study for the Morton International Building, 1987. Marker on tracing paper, 44.5 x 30.5 cm. Lent by Perkins and Will.

271. Perkins and Will; Ralph Johnson, design principal. Axonometric view from the south of the Morton International Building, 1989. Printed Mylar with color, 121.5 x 50.5 cm. Lent by Perkins and Will.

272. Perkins and Will; Ralph Johnson, design principal. Exploded axonometric view of the Morton International Building, 1988-89. Ink on Mylar, 71.7 x 45 cm. Lent by Perkins and Will.

273. Perkins and Will; Ralph Johnson, design principal. Perspective view of the lobby of the Morton International Building, 1988-89. Ink on Mylar, 36.5 x 63.6 cm. Lent by Perkins and Will. (See plate 70.)

274. Kenzo Tange, with Shaw and Associates, associate architects. Study models for the American Medical Association Building, 515 North State Street, 1988. Glued and painted plexiglas, various sizes. Lent by the John Buck Company.

275. Kenzo Tange, with Shaw and Associates, associate architects. Site plan and elevations of the American Medical Association Building, 1988-90. Ink on Mylar, 76.2 x 101.6 cm. Lent by Pat Shaw.

276. Loebl, Schlossman and Hackl; Steven Wright, designer. Model of the addition to the Prudential Building (1952-53), 1989. Mixed media, approx. 102 x 63.5 x 63.5 cm. Lent by Loebl, Schlossman and Hackl.

277. Murphy/Jahn. Northwest perspective view of proposed commercial buildings on Block 37 at State and Washington streets, initialed M.B., 1989. Ink and colored pencil on paper, 114 x 91.5 cm. Lent by Murphy/Jahn Architects.

278. Lohan Associates. Plan, section, and elevation of Safety-Kleen, Randall Road, Elgin, 1990. Ink, watercolor, and colored pencil on paper, 101.5 x 127 cm. Lent by Lohan Associates.

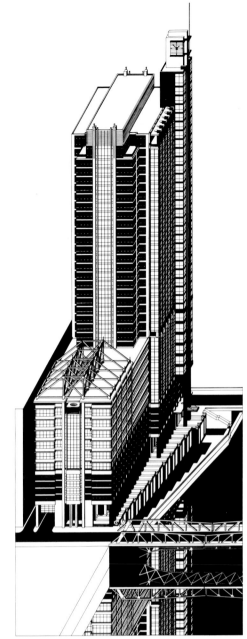

271

279. Kohn Pedersen Fox Associates. Elevations on Wacker Drive and Franklin Street for 225 West Wacker Drive, delineated by Gary Handel, c. 1989. Printed paper, 71 x 91.5 cm. Lent by Kohn Pedersen Fox Associates. (See plates 52-53.)

280. Kohn Pedersen Fox Associates. Elevation detail of the base of 311 South Wacker Drive, 1986. Ink on polyester film, 22.3 x 36 cm. Lent by Kohn Pedersen Fox Associates.

281. Kohn Pedersen Fox Associates. Two preliminary bird's-eye view studies for proposed top of 311 South Wacker Drive, delineated by Richard del Monte, March 18, 1986. Ink on yellow tracing paper, 30.5 x 31 and 30.7 x 48.3 cm. Lent by Kohn Pedersen Fox Associates.

282. Kohn Pedersen Fox Associates. Exterior elevation of the Chicago Title and Trust Center, delineated by Gilbert Gorski, August 1990. Colored pencil and watercolor on paper, 144.8 x 54 cm. Lent by The Linpro Company

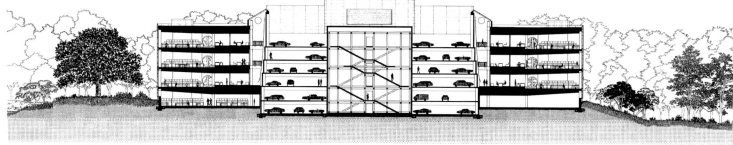

278

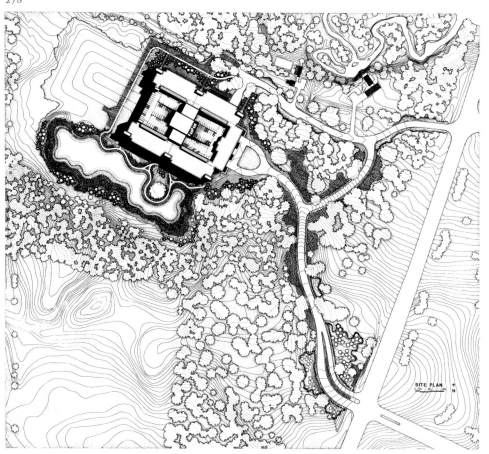

and subsidiaries of Shell Pension Fund Foundation (The Netherlands).

283. Murphy/Jahn; Helmut Jahn, designer. Perspective rendering of 120 North LaSalle Street, delineated by Rael D. Slutsky and Associates, 1990. Printed paper, 72 x 36 cm. Lent by Rael D. Slutsky and Associates.

284. Cesar Pelli. Conceptual sketches for 181 West Madison Street, c. 1986. Three sketches, colored pencil on paper, each 30.5 x 33 cm, with a letter from Cesar Pelli to J. Paul Beitler. Lent by Miglin-Beitler, Inc.

285. Cesar Pelli. Studies for the entrance, lobby, and building top for 181 West Madison Street, c. 1990. Six sketches, charcoal on toned paper, each approx. 43 x 28 cm. Lent by Miglin-Beitler, Inc. (See plate 67.)

286. The Landahl Group. Plan, concept studies, and views of the corporate office for Miglin-Beitler Development, 181 West Madison Street, 1990. Pencil on note paper, mixed media, 127 x 101.5 cm. Lent by Gregory W. Landahl, FAIA, The Landahl Group, Inc.

287. Cesar Pelli. Model for the proposed Miglin-Beitler Tower, 201 West Madison Street, c. 1990. Painted plastic, 44.5 x 33 cm. Lent by Miglin-Beitler, Inc.

288. Roche and Dinkeloo. Elevations of proposed skyscraper for One North Wacker Drive, signed by Kevin Roche, 1991. Printed paper, 93.5 x 68.3 cm. Gift of Harvey Walken, 1991.

289. Holabird and Root; Roy Solfisburg assisted by Michael Murphy. Axonometric view of the atrium with a bird's-eye view of the building for the Lumberman's Mutual Casualty Company, Kemper Group, One Kemper Drive, Long Grove, 1991. Colored printed paper, 101.5 x 76 cm. Lent by Holabird and Root. (See plate 60.)

290. Perkins and Will; David Hansen, design principal. Perspective view of the lobby of the Sears Merchandise Group Home Office, 3333 Beverly Road, Hoffman Estates, 1990. Ink on Mylar, 94 x 94 cm (framed). Lent by Perkins and Will. (See plate 51.)

291. Perkins and Will; David Hansen, design principal. Exterior elevation and section through the Fitness Center of Kraft General Foods, Three Lakes Drive, Northfield, 1990-92. Ink on Mylar, 71.1 x 91.5 cm. Lent by Perkins and Will.

292. Perkins and Will; David Hansen, design principal. Bird's-eye view through the lobby of Kraft General Foods, Northfield, 1990-92. Colored pencil on paper, 94 x 94 cm. Lent by Perkins and Will.

293. Skidmore, Owings and Merrill; Joseph Gonzalez, designer. Computer-generated bird's-eye view of the proposed Spiegel Corporate Headquarters, 3500 Lacey Road, Downers Grove, 1991. Ink and colored ink on computer printout paper, 65.5 x 114 cm. Lent by Skidmore, Owings and Merrill. (See plate 74.)

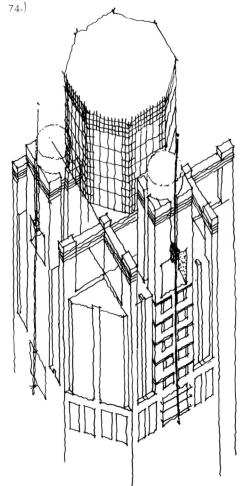

281

Industry

In the nineteenth century Chicago was a major industrial center, with manufacturing facilities for agricultural and railroad machinery, and meat-packing facilities adjoining its extensive stockyards. Related to the consolidation of the stockyards that had occurred at the end of the Civil War was the creation, in 1890, of a Central Manufacturing District (CMD) just north of the yards on the South Branch of the Chicago River. The CMD opened a large new park, the Pershing Trust, in 1915, and during World Wars I and II this enlarged district became a national clearinghouse for military supplies. Other districts comparable to this were soon developed for industrial use just outside the city limits, the most notable being the Clearing Industrial District, now in Bedford Park southwest of Midway Airport, with its buildings from the 1920s, 1930s, and later (pls. 78-79).

Chicago's position as the capital of a significant industrial region continues even today. Although this area of the Midwest has been labeled a part of the "Rust Belt" of decayed and deteriorated industrial facilities that have continued to close since the recession of the mid-1970s (for example, the recently closed South Works of U.S. Steel in Chicago), there are still major industrial complexes at work just outside the city limits, from Amoco's refineries in Whiting, Indiana, to Bethlehem Steel's casting facilities in Burns Harbor, Indiana. New plants have also been constructed for such companies as the Chicago Tribune and Motorola Electronics. In addition, new facilities, such as the Bradley Place Business Center, serve to revitalize light industry within the city. Thus, Chicago and its region continue to be an industrial locale. But of the region's industries, two related to architecture and construction deserve discussion here.

The Chicago Bridge and Iron Company was begun by Horace E. Horton, George H.

Pineapple theme water tank, Honolulu, Hawaii, 1927.

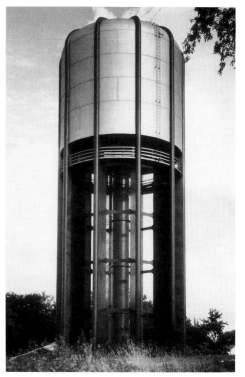

Eugene Voita. Prize-winning design for a water tower constructed in Towson, Maryland, 1932.

Wheelock, and William B. Wheelock in 1889 as an outgrowth of the Kansas City Bridge and Iron Company. The company specialized in building small county bridges throughout the Midwest. Horace's son, George T. Horton, diversified their construction interests by adding other types of projects to their repertory, namely elevated water towers and oil storage tanks. The company prospered with successful patents for both types of structure. Of particular note are the decorated theme water towers built for a variety of clients, the most famous being the 100,000-gallon pineapple-shaped tower of 1927 in Hawaii, as well as the company's sponsorship of an international design competition in 1931. The win-

ning tower design by Eugene Voita was constructed the next year near Baltimore. During World War II, the company established the Seneca Shipyard on the Illinois River, along with others, to build Landing Ship Tanks (LST) for invasions in the Pacific and Europe. After the war, Chicago Bridge and Iron continued to design and build structures related to oil and water storage and built other energy-related constructions, such as steel containment vessels for nuclear power plants in Morris, Illinois, and Marble Hill, Indiana. Their recent work, as CBI Industries, for defense industries includes supersonic wind tunnels at various aerospace plants.

Another local company whose work runs continuously from the early twentieth century to the present is the Great Lakes Dredge and Dock Company. Founded in 1890 and incorporated under its present name in 1905, they created Chicago's lakefront in the 1920s and 1930s, from 50th Street on the South Side to Grant Park, and constructed the shore protection jetties from North Avenue to Fullerton Avenue. The firm's history also relates to the city's bridges, their two most famous being the Michigan Avenue Bridge of 1918-20 and the Outer Drive Bridge of 1937 (see Zukowsky, fig. 9). During World War II, the company constructed the MacArthur Lock at Sault St. Marie, Michigan, and dredged for docks on the East Coast that were involved in the construction of battleships. The dredges used to create Chicago's lakefront and, from 1928 to 1931, to straighten portions of the Chicago River include the *New Jersey* (1927-28), *Mogul* (1926-27), and *Crest* (1926).

Amoco Refineries in Whiting, Indiana.

Skidmore, Owings and Merrill; Diane Legge, designer. Printing plant for the Chicago Tribune Company, the Chicago River near Chicago Avenue, 1986.

Although the Mogul is still in operation, the *New Jersey* served with the Navy in World War II and the *Crest* was destroyed in 1988. A new generation of dredges is now in operation, with the *Illinois* and others like it operating in various harbors from North America to the Middle East.

Recent problems have catalyzed questions about the city's infrastructure. In some ways, this relates to local industry as well. The Great Lakes Dredge and Dock Company found itself at the center of the controversy about the "Great Chicago Flood" of 1992. New pilings installed in the Chicago River near the Kinzie Street Bridge pierced the turn-of-the-century freight tunnel underneath, eventually permitting water to flood the entire tunnel system under Chicago's historic

Loop, deluging the basements of many buildings on April 13, 1992. The flood caused an estimated billion dollars in lost revenues and damages over almost a week. All the while, engineers sought to find a way to drain the water from that system into the so-called "Deep Tunnel" storm drains of the Metropolitan Water Reclamation District. Although litigation that followed the initial investigations continues in its attempts to ascertain whether the City of Chicago or the Great Lakes Dredge and Dock Company is accountable for those misplaced pilings, the incident has led many to question the safety of the city's aging infrastructure. This is particularly the case with the original steel sections of Chicago's Loop Elevated Railroad, which celebrated its centennial in 1992.

for a hanging lamp, c. 1920-30. Graphite on buff tracing paper, 31.3 x 22 cm. Lent by Decorators Supply Corporation.

299.   Decorators Supply Corporation. Sketch for a hanging lamp, c. 1920-30. Colored pencil and ink on buff tracing paper, 25.1 x 14.9 cm. Lent by Decorators Supply Corporation.

300.   Decorators Supply Corporation. Figure of a caryatid, c. 1980-85. Fiber over wood, 38.1 x 14.7 x 6.4 cm. Lent by Decorators Supply Corporation.

301.   Decorators Supply Corporation. Antefix, "Greek Acropolis," c. 1980-85. Composition over wood, 7.6. x 7.6 x 10.2 cm. Lent by Decorators Supply Corporation.

302.   Decorators Supply Corporation. Roman Corinthian capital, "Pantheon," c. 1980-85. Composition over wood, 12.7 x 12.7 x 12 cm. Lent by Decorators Supply Corporation.

303.   Working drawing showing the plan and elevation of the dredge "Mogul," June 1929. Blueprint, approx. 76.2 x 108.5 cm. Lent by Great Lakes Dredge and Dock Company.

304.   Working drawing for the repair of the dipper lip of the 12-yard rock dipper "Crest," November 10, 1938. Van Dyke print, approx. 59.8 x 93 cm. Lent by Great Lakes Dredge and Dock Company.

305.   Working drawing showing dipper lip details of the "Crest," October 29 and November 25, 1925. Van Dyke prints, approx. 58.5 x 90.5 cm. Lent by Great Lakes Dredge and Dock Company.

294.   Dubin and Eisenberg. Working drawings for the Kosher Star Manufacturing Company additions, 1006-10 Maxwell Street, 1923. Ink on linen, each approx. 77 x 107 cm. Gift of Dubin, Dubin and Moutoussamy, 1986.

295.   A. Epstein, Structural Engineer. North and south elevations and longitudinal section, and details of typical piers of the building for the Great Atlantic and Pacific Tea Company, 100-108 West 57th Place, delineated December 22, 1926, with revisions January 11 and 16, 1927. Pencil on tracing

paper with taped repairs, 62 x 128.3 cm. Lent by A. Epstein and Sons International, Inc.

296.   Decorators Supply Corporation. Specifications for a 3-inch Roman Corinthian capital, "Pantheon," c. 1900. Two-color hectograph on paper, 36.3 x 25.2 cm. Lent by Decorators Supply Corporation.

297.   Decorators Supply Corporation. Small bracket, "Roman Vatican," c. 1910. Composition over wood, 7 x 5.1 x 3.9 cm. Lent by Decorators Supply Corporation.

298.   Decorators Supply Corporation. Sketch

306.   Working drawing showing longitudinal section, plan of hold, and plan of main deck of the dredge "New Jersey," March 31, 1927. Blueline print, approx. 57.3 x 92.4 cm. Lent by Great Lakes Dredge and Dock Company.

307.   John Haynes, modelmaker. Model of the dredge "Illinois," 1990. Wood, aluminum, brass, and acrylic, 152.4 x 8 cm. Lent by Great Lakes Dredge and Dock Company.

308.   Field notebooks, showing blueprints of water tower designs from the 1920s through the 1970s built by the Chicago Bridge and Iron Company. Printed paper, 18 x 21.5 cm. Lent by Chicago Bridge and Iron Company. (See plate 89.)

309.   Artist's renderings of proposed theme water towers for Louisville Slugger Baseball Bats and Disneyworld, c. 1980. Photoprints, 30.5 x 42 and 35.5 x 28 cm. Lent by Chicago Bridge and Iron Company.

310.   Artist's rendering of a water tunnel designed for the U.S. Navy, 1990. Ink on paper, 32 x 42 cm. Lent by Chicago Bridge and Iron Company.

311.   Emory Stanford Hall with Bisbee and Rhenisch. Perspective rendering of a ware-

FRONT   ELEVATION
Scale ¼"=1'0"

house for Jackson Storage and Van Company, 1928. Gouache on paper, 95.8 x 49.3 cm. Lent by the Chicago Historical Society.

312. Paul Schweikher. Plan, front and side elevations, and perspective view of an armchair with webbing, a furniture study for Chicago Workshops, 1930. Pencil and colored pencil on buff paper, 27.9 x 21.6 cm. Gift of Dorothy and Paul Schweikher, 1984.

313. Abel Faidy. Side elevation of a tubular steel side chair, 1934. Black and blue pencil on notepaper, 26.5 x 20.4 cm. Gift of Diana Faidy, 1981.

314. Wolfgang Hoffman, designer; W. W. Howell and Company, manufacturer. Chromesteel "S" chair, c. 1935. Chromesteel, vinyl, upholstery, and cloth, 80 x 38 x 48 cm. Lent by the Decorative and Industrial Arts Collection, Chicago Historical Society.

315. L. Morgan Yost. Two perspective sketches for radios, 1935. Pencil on tracing paper, each 26.2 x 21.1 cm. Gift of L. Morgan Yost, 1978.

316. Holabird and Root. Model of the Chrysler Pavilion at the Century of Progress Exposition, 1933. Aluminum, frosted glass, and wood, 83.8 x 61 x 45.7 cm. Lent by the Chicago Historical Society.

317. Holabird and Root. Kellogg Cereal Display Building for the second year of the Century of Progress Exposition, 1934. Pencil on tracing paper, 58.8 x 67.3 cm. Lent by Chicago Historical Society.

318. Alfonso Ianelli. Maquette for the Radio Flyer Pavilion on the Enchanted Island of the Century of Progress Exposition, 1933. Polychromed plaster, 58.8 x 53.3 cm. Lent by Radio Flyer, Inc. (See plate 76.)

319. Albert Kahn. Site plan, plan, elevations, and details of the General Motors Building at the Century of Progress Exposition, April 14, 1932. Ink on linen, each 78.8 x 119.8 cm. Lent by Albert Kahn Associates, Inc.

320. Albert Kahn. Site plan and elevations of the Ford Motor Company Pavilion at the Century of Progress Exposition, February 10, 1934. Ink on linen, each 61 x 152.4 cm. Lent by Albert Kahn Associates, Inc.

321. Albert Kahn. First-floor plan and elevations for the Lady Esther Plant, 7171 West 65th Street, in the Clearing Industrial District, July 31, 1937 (facade now greatly altered). Ink on linen, each 106.7 x 109.2 cm. Lent by Albert Kahn Associates, Inc. (See plates 78-79.)

322. Childs and Smith and Frank D. Chase, associated architects. Preliminary rendering of the east facade of the Campana Sales Company Factory, Batavia, 1937. Pencil and colored pencil on tracing paper, 30 x 70 cm. Architecture Department purchase, 1984.

323. Schmidt, Garden and Erikson; Vale Faro, designer. Facade study for the Eastman Kodak Company, Route 31, 2712-18 South Prairie Avenue, 1940. Photoprint mounted on black paper, 21.5 x 27.5 cm. Lent by Schmidt, Garden and Erikson.

324. Albert Kahn. Elevations of the office building for the American Steel Foundries Cast Armor Plant, East Chicago, Indiana, December 16, 1941. Ink on linen, 73.7 x 106.7 cm. Lent by Albert Kahn Associates, Inc. (See plates 80-85.)

325. Albert Kahn. Plans and elevations of office building no. 2, Dodge Chicago Plant, between Cicero Avenue and Pulaski Road, July 8, 1942. Ink on linen drawings, 83.8 x 120.7 cm. Lent by Albert Kahn Associates, Inc. (See plates 80-85.)

326. Bertrand Goldberg Associates. Bird's-eye view of a proposed mobile delousing unit, 1942. Printed paper, 71 x 91.5 cm. Lent by Bertrand Goldberg Associates.

327. Bertrand Goldberg Associates. Model of a mobile penicillin laboratory, 1943. Mixed media. Lent by Bertrand Goldberg Associates.

328. John Reed Fugard. Perspective study of a rural cheese plant for the Kraft Cheese Company, constructed of stainless armorply, 1944. Pencil on linen, 62.8 x 99.1 cm. Lent by the Chicago Historical Society.

329. Motorola, Inc. Radio receiver and transmitter, "Handie-Talkie," 1945. Metal, 43.2 x 10.2 x 17.8 cm. Lent by The Motorola Museum of Electronics.

330. Motorola, Inc. Jewel box portable radio, 1951. Plastic and metal, 12.7 x 19.7 x 11.5 cm. Lent by The Motorola Museum of Electronics.

331. Motorola, Inc. AM portable radio, 1956. Metal, plastic, and fabric, 22.6 x 26 x 8.3 cm. Lent by The Motorola Museum of Electronics.

332. Daniel Brenner. Concert hall project, 1946. Papers, foil, and wood veneer on photographic enlargement, mounted on board, 36 x 74.2 cm. Gift of Rachael, Jon, and Ariel Brenner, 1981.

333. Yost and Taylor Architects. Perspective view of the Driscoll and Company additions, Troy Street and Grand Avenue, c. 1952-53. Pencil on tracing paper, 40.8 x 76.5 cm. Gift of L. Morgan Yost, 1978.

334. A. Epstein and Sons, Engineers. Elevations and site plan for the office and bakery building for the Kitchens of Sara Lee, 5337-39 North Elston Avenue, initialed by Thomas W. Roach and Ralph J. Epstein,

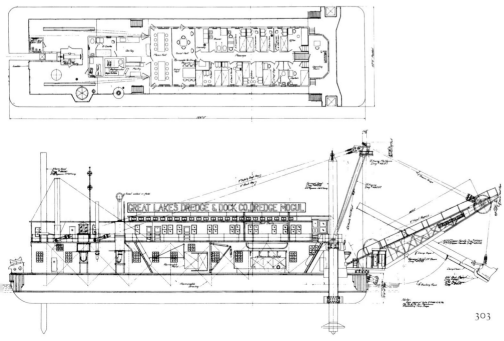

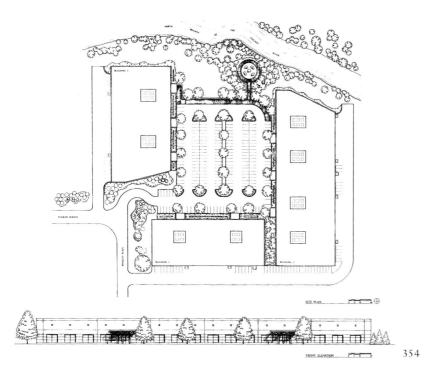

SITE PLAN

FRONT ELEVATION

354

August 19, 1957 (now demolished). Ink on linen, each 79 x 107 cm. Lent by A. Epstein and Sons International, Inc.

335. Keck and Keck. Perspective rendering of the addition to the Peerless Confection Company, 1254 West Schubert, c. 1963. Ink and watercolor on paper, 32 x 58.5 cm. Gift of the Peerless Confection Company, 1990.

336. John Massey, designer. Poster for the Container Corporation of America, 1950-60. Ink on paper, 101.6 x 68 cm. Lent by Special Collections, The University Library, University of Illinois at Chicago.

337. John Massey, designer. Great ideas poster for the Container Corporation of America, 1950-60. Ink on paper, 114.3 x 76.2 cm. Lent by Special Collections, The University Library, University of Illinois at Chicago.

338. Bruce Beck, designer. Designs for the Jewel and Osco logos, 1979-80. Ink on Mylar, 25.3 x 38.1, 31.8 x 22.2, and 22.2 x 26.7 cm. Lent by Special Collections, The University Library, University of Illinois at Chicago.

339. Unknown designer. Calendar box for the Container Corporation of America, 1977. Ink on cardboard, 20.3 x 16.2 x 5.1 cm. Lent by The University Library, University of Illinois at Chicago.

340. Holabird and Root; Gerald Horn, design principal. Elevation and details of the 4A Building for Illinois Bell Telephone Company, 2029 Walters Avenue, Northbrook, 1972. Colored printed paper, 76 x 101.5 cm. Lent by Holabird and Root.

341. Skidmore, Owings and Merrill; Myron Goldsmith, designer. Three working drawings of the Republic Newspaper Plant, 332 2nd Street, Columbus, Indiana, August 25, 1969. Elevations and sections drawn by J. K.; site and utility plan and details drawn by W. S. and G. R.; and exterior wall details drawn by R. Rivera. Pencil on linen, each 74 x 117 cm. Lent by Skidmore, Owings and Merrill.

342. Skidmore, Owings and Merrill; Myron Goldsmith, designer. Two working drawings for Baxter Travenol Laboratories, Baxter Parkway, Deerfield, March 9, 1973. Elevations of Building C and section of Building C. Pencil on linen, each 74 x 116.6 cm. Lent by Skidmore, Owings and Merrill. (See plate 91.)

343. Stanley Tigerman. "The Titanic," 1978. Photomontage, 28 x 35.7 cm. Gift of Stanley Tigerman, 1984.

344. Murphy/Jahn. Axonometric views of the Argonne Program Support Facility of the Argonne National Laboratories, 9700 South Cass Avenue, Argonne, 1978-82. Airbrushed colored ink, 183 x 103 cm. Lent by Murphy/Jahn Architects.

345. Skidmore, Owings and Merrill; James R. DeStefano, designer. Perspective view of the proposed Caterpillar Training Center, Peoria, delineated by David A. Hansen, 1981. Ink on yellow paper, 30.5 x 45.7 cm. Gift of Skidmore, Owings, and Merrill, Chicago, 1982.

346. Krueck and Sexton (formerly Krueck and Olsen). Elevation and section of Smith Kline Beecham (formerly Bio-Science Laboratories), 506 East State Parkway, Schaumburg, 1982-83. Colored inks on paper, 61.5 x 143.5 cm. Lent by Ronald Krueck, Krueck and Sexton Architects.

347. Skidmore, Owings and Merrill; Diane Legge, designer. Elevations of scheme A of the Chicago Tribune Printing Plant, 777 West Chicago Avenue, June 10, 1974. Sepia print, approx. 101.5 x 134 cm. Lent by Skidmore, Owings and Merrill.

348. Tigerman McCurry; Stanley Tigerman, designer. Dearborn Street elevation of the Commonwealth Edison Substation in relation to the former Chicago Historical Society Building by Henry Ives Cobb, southwest corner of Dearborn and Ontario Streets, 1986-89. Watercolor on paper, 77.5 x 112 cm. Lent by Tigerman McCurry Architects.

349. Meyer Glass Design. Patent sketch for a movable elephant, delineated by Dick Martino, 1987-88. Pencil on paper, 21.5 x 28 cm. Lent by Meyer Glass Design.

350. Meyer Glass Design. Patent sketch for a baby doll, delineated by Dick Martino,

357

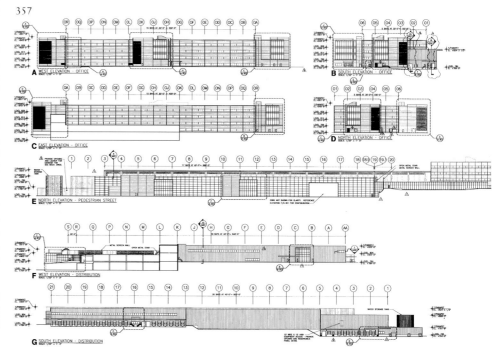

A WEST ELEVATION - OFFICE

B SOUTH ELEVATION - OFFICE

C EAST ELEVATION - OFFICE

D NORTH ELEVATION - OFFICE

E NORTH ELEVATION - PEDESTRIAN STREET

F WEST ELEVATION - DISTRIBUTION

G SOUTH ELEVATION - DISTRIBUTION

1988. Pen on paper, 21.5 x 28 cm. Lent by Meyer Glass Design.

351. Meyer Glass Design. Patent sketch for a soldier doll, delineated by Dick Martino, 1985. Pen on paper, 21.5 x 28 cm. Lent by Meyer Glass Design.

352. Marvin Glass Associates; B. C. Meyer, principal designer. Patent sheet for "Lite Brite," 1967. Ink on paper, 21.5 x 28 cm. Lent by Meyer Glass Design.

353. Holabird and Root; Gerald Horn, designer, assisted by James Baird. Site plan, elevation, and details of wall construction for a remote switching unit for Illinois Bell Telephone, Route 22, Lincolnshire, 1988. Colored printed paper, 76 x 101.5 cm. Lent by Holabird and Root.

354. Nagle, Hartray and Associates. Site plan and elevation for the Bradley Place Business Center, Talman Avenue on the Chicago River, 1987-89. Printed Mylar, 71 x 91.5 cm. Lent by Nagle, Hartray and Associates.

355. Arquitectonica Chicago; Dana Terp, designer. Plan, elevation, and section of the renovation of Tang Industries, 1965 Pratt Boulevard, Elk Grove Village, 1989. Printed Mylar, 101.5 x 76 cm. Lent by Arquitectonica Chicago, Inc.

356. Booth/Hansen and Associates. Cutaway model of the Motorola Museum of Electronics, 1297 East Algonquin Road, Schaumburg, 1988-91. Glued and painted foamcore and Strathmore board, 110.5 x 95.5 x 38 cm. Lent by Booth/Hansen and Associates, Ltd.

357. A. Epstein and Sons; Sheldon Schlegman, designer. Floor plan and perspective view of Motorola, Inc., 620 U.S. Highway 45,

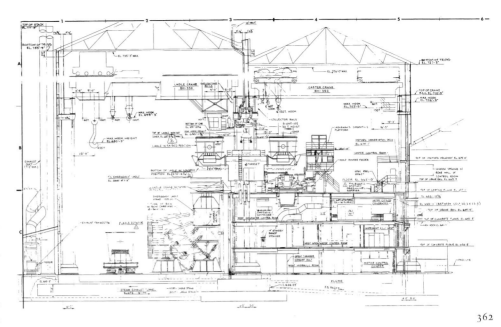

362

Libertyville, delineated by Gilbert Gorski, June 21, 1991. Lent by A. Epstein and Sons International, Inc.

358. Skidmore, Owings and Merrill; Adrian Smith, designer. Lake Street elevation of the proposed Commonwealth Edison Substation, 1 East Lake Street, 1991. Ink and colored ink on computer paper, 71 x 91.5 cm. Lent by Skidmore, Owings and Merrill.

359. Doyle and Associates; Deborah Doyle, designer, assisted by Eric Mullendore and Rachel Garbow. Proposed Lowden and Company Office Building, Dyer, Indiana, 1991. Mixed media collage, 76.2 x 76.2 cm. Lent by Deborah Doyle of Doyle and Associates Architects.

360. Eva Maddox Associates. Plans and views of the E. I. DuPont DeNemours Resource Center, Room 10-111 in the

Merchandise Mart, 1989, showing the evolution of the space through the present. Three sketches, colored pencil on toned paper, each approx. 39 x 56 cm. Lent by Eva L. Maddox, Eva Maddox Associates, Inc.

361. Eva Maddox Associates. View of the showroom for AGI Industries, Room 310 in the Merchandise Mart, 1991. Ink on paper, 76 x 101.5 cm. Lent by Eva L. Maddox, Eva Maddox Associates, Inc.

362. Bethlehem Steel. Number 2 slab caster, arrangement section AA: ladle and casting aisles, 1985. Lineprint on polyester film, 60.5 x 91.5 cm. Lent by Bethlehem Steel Corporation.

363. Bethlehem Steel. Present general plan for Bethlehem Steel, Burns Harbor, Indiana, 1991. Photoprint on Mylar, 60.5 x 91.5 cm. Lent by Bethlehem Steel Corporation.

Shopping

The Depression and World War II changed the nature of shopping in Chicago. Retail services had long been concentrated either in the Loop's large department stores like Marshall Field's, or throughout various residential neighborhoods in the city and adjacent suburbs. The postwar boom and construction of transportation systems, particularly highways, to connect the city with new suburban residential areas required that these new communities have expanded retail services for their residents. Such services were clustered in shopping malls, one of the first of which was built in Park Forest, south of Chicago, from 1947 to 1950. Mall followed mall within the new residential suburbs, many of them designed by the firm of Loebl, Schlossman, Bennett, and Dart. These new suburban malls featured large anchor stores, such as Fields, Carson, Pirie, Scott and Co., and Sears, Roebuck and Co. (pls. 95-96), as well as smaller

specialty shops. The malls created a new neighborhood of large and small services with plenty of parking lots, something that space restrictions prevented in the older urban neighborhoods.

To assist the suburban malls in drawing shoppers away from urban locations, some architects, especially SITE, created very clever marketing images for their suburban clients. The cities themselves counterattacked by bringing the suburban mall into the city. Although this was, in some ways, an idea that was in use before the Depression, its full potential was not realized until the construction of Water Tower Place on Michigan Avenue in 1976 (see Harris, figs. 19-22). The conversion of North Michigan Avenue into the "Magnificent Mile" was a real estate strategy promoted by developer Arthur Rubloff and others after World War II. The construction of Water Tower Place, a multi-

use building containing an urban mall, a hotel, and luxury apartments, was repeated in several other multi-use buildings from the early to late 1980s along this same avenue: One Magnificent Mile by Bruce J. Graham of Skidmore, Owings and Merrill in 1982; 900 North Michigan Avenue by Kohn Pedersen Fox of 1988 (see pls. 97-102); and Chicago Place of 1989 by Skidmore, Owings and Merrill, with apartments behind by Solomon Cordwell Buenz and Associates.

These malls, plus the further lining of Oak Street and Michigan Avenue with specialty boutiques (pls. 103-05), have created an image of these thoroughfares as the premier shopping streets of any midwestern city. Yet, increased traffic by residents, suburbanites, and tourists has strained the infrastructure of this area. Thus, the architectural solution of bringing the services of a suburban mall to an overbuilt and crowded city center has itself, when

John Eberson. Calumet National Bank (under construction), 91st Street and Commercial Avenue, May 2, 1927 (now demolished).

SITE. Best Store, Brown Deer Road, near Milwaukee, Wisconsin, 1985.

replicated too often, created some other unforeseen problems.

In order to compete with Michigan Avenue stores, the stores on State Street that survived the flight of shoppers to the suburbs began to restore and extensively renovate their own facilities. In 1979 Carson, Pirie, Scott and Co. undertook the renovation of its flagship store, originally designed by Louis Sullivan, featuring restoration of the exterior and corner rotunda lobby by the office of John Vinci. This was followed by a very clever creation of a circulation core within the empty space between the structures that constitute Marshall Field's State Street store, executed by the firm of HTI-Space Design International. The

Field's project was begun in 1987 and finished, along with the restoration of the grand spaces within D. H. Burnham's original stores, in 1992. Other disused stores on State Street have also been recently recycled. Wieboldt's, located between Carson's and Field's, was renovated in 1991 into offices, with smaller discount department stores occupying the ground and basement floors. Recently, the decline in retail sales during 1990 and 1991 has prompted a number of major American stores to file for reorganization under the bankruptcy laws. The strip malls and minimalls that revitalized some urban neighborhoods during the mid- to late 1980s have experienced similar financial setbacks.

364. Alfred S. Alschuler. Elevations and window details of the Cooper, Winston and Manierre Trust Building, 512-522 North State Street, March 3, 1925. Ink on linen, 71 x 92 cm. Gift of Friedman, Alschuler and Sincere, 1980.

365. John Eberson. Section and first-floor plan of the Calumet National Bank, 9051-53 South Commercial Avenue, 1926 (now demolished). Ink on linen, approx. 79 x 101 cm. By prior exchange of Three Oaks Wrecking Company, 1990.

366. Harringer-Jacobson-Colvin; Henry Harringer, designer and delineator. Perspective study of the Store for Tomorrow project, delineated for *Apparel Arts* 1, no. 2 (1932), p. 44. Pencil and gouache on illustration board, 19.8 x 32.5 cm. Gift of Olaf Harringer, 1982. (See plate 93.)

367. L. Morgan Yost. Plan and perspective sketch of a proposed building for Alten Mortuary, Wilmette, 1940. Pencil and colored pencil on tracing paper, 32.5 x 40 cm. Gift of L. Morgan Yost, 1978.

368. Yost and Taylor Architects; L. Morgan Yost, designer. Perspective view of a proposed Maxon Coiffure, 500 Green Bay Road, Kenilworth, c. 1955. Ink, colored pencil, and tempera on paper, mounted on board, 35.7 x 59.9 cm. Gift of L. Morgan Yost, 1978.

369. Loebl, Schlossman and Bennett; Richard Bennett, designer. Site plan and details of sunken garden, Old Orchard Shopping Center, Skokie, 1955-56. Ink on Mylar, 33.6 x 32.3, and graphite on tracing paper, 54 x 51.8 cm. Lent by the Chicago Historical Society.

370. Loebl, Schlossman and Bennett. Plan for the Crabapple Restaurant by Marshall Field and Company, Old Orchard Shopping Center, June 14, 1956, with subsequent revi-

365

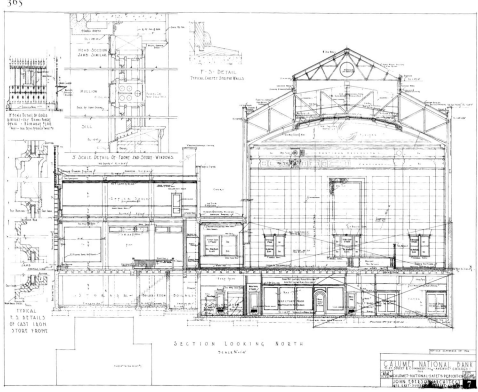

sions. Pencil on tracing paper, 61.5 x 91.5 cm. Lent by Loebl, Schlossman and Hackl.

371. Loebl, Schlossman and Bennett. Site plan of Old Orchard Shopping Center, November 16, 1962, with subsequent revisions 1963, 1965, 1966, and 1975. Pencil on Mylar, 91.5 x 140 cm. Lent by Loebl, Schlossman and Hackl.

372. Loebl, Schlossman and Bennett. Elevations of proposed Bonwit Teller Store, Old Orchard Shopping Center, December 4, [1969?]. Pencil on tracing paper, 73.5 x 92 cm. Lent by Loebl, Schlossman and Hackl.

373. Coder Taylor Associates; David Laughlin, delineator. Kroch's and Brentano's suburban store, Old Orchard Shopping Center, 1968. Oil on board, 30.8 x 53 cm. Gift of D. Coder Taylor, 1981.

374. Richard Yoshijiro Mine. Aerial perspective view of a proposal for Sears, Roebuck and Company Store, 1961. Pencil and colored pencil on tracing paper, 56 x 72.6 cm. Gift of Richard Yoshijiro Mine, 1979.

375. Coder Taylor Associates. Perspective view of Kroch's and Brentano's Party and Gift Center, 62 East Randolph Street, 1962. Colored print on board, 49.7 x 49.5 cm. Gift of D. Coder Taylor, 1981.

376. C.F. Murphy Associates in association with Loebl, Schlossman, Dart and Hackl; Gene Summers and Helmut Jahn, designers, with Warren Platner. Preliminary perspective study of Water Tower Place, 845 North Michigan Avenue, delineated by Wojciech Madeyski, 1970. Pencil and marker on paper, 115 x 83.5 cm. Gift of Wojciech Madeyski.

377. Loebl, Schlossman, Bennett and Dart; C.F. Murphy Associates, associated architects; Warren Platner, architectural consultant. Second-floor reflected ceiling plan (west half) of Water Tower Place, delineated by R. L., checked by G. G., and approved by D. H. (Donald Hackl), November 26, 1973, with subsequent revisions, 1975-76. Pencil, ink, and colored pencil on Mylar, 91.5 x 127 cm. Lent by Loebl, Schlossman and Hackl.

378. Loebl, Schlossman, Bennett and Dart; C.F. Murphy Associates, associated architects. Michigan Avenue entrance lobby elevations and sections for Water Tower Place, delineated by W. V., checked by G. G., and

approved by D. H. (Donald Hackl), November 26, 1973, with subsequent revisions, 1974. Pencil and ink on Mylar, 91 x 127 cm. Lent by Loebl, Schlossman and Hackl.

379. John Vinci. Interior elevations, plan, and details for the restoration of the rotunda for Louis Sullivan's Carson, Pirie, Scott Store, State and Madison streets, August 24, 1978. Three ink on Mylar sheets, each 76.2 x 106.8 cm. Lent by the Office of John Vinci.

380. HTI Space Design International; John Kuntz, modelmaker. Model of the atrium of Marshall Field's, State Street between Randolph and Washington streets, 1987. Acrylic plastic, 76.2 x 76.2 x 106.7 cm. Lent by Marshall Field's, the Department Store Division of Dayton Hudson Corporation.

381. Skidmore, Owings and Merrill; Bruce Graham, design partner (with Richard E. Lenke, Christopher Cedargreen, Peter G. Ellis, and Robert W. Siegle). Entrance elevation study of One Magnificent Mile, 920 North Michigan Avenue, delineated by David S. Froelich and William J. Schroeder, c. 1981. Ink and colored pencil on yellow tracing paper, 76.2 x 92 cm. Gift of Skidmore, Owings and Merrill, 1982.

382. Himmel Bonner. Plan and section of Stanley Korshak's, 920 North Michigan Avenue, delineated by Darcy R. Bonner, Jr.,

1981-82. Pencil and Prismacolor on collaged paper, four sheets, approx. 172.5 x 96.5 cm. Lent by Himmel Bonner Architects.

383. Kohn Pedersen Fox Associates. Contextual site plan and Michigan Avenue elevations of 900 North Michigan Avenue, delineated by Ilona Rider, 1986-88. Printed paper, 71 x 91.5 cm. Lent by Kohn Pedersen Fox Associates.

384. Kohn Pedersen Fox Associates. Window wall study for 900 North Michigan Avenue, delineated by Sudhir Jambhekar, c. 1986. Pencil and colored pencil on tracing paper, 60 x 46 cm. Lent by Kohn Pedersen Fox Associates.

385. Kohn Pedersen Fox Associates. Bird's-eye view study of the towers for 900 North Michigan Avenue, delineated by Yolanda Cole, c. 1986. Printed paper, 71 x 91.5 cm. Lent by Kohn Pedersen Fox Associates.

386. Kohn Pedersen Fox Associates. Proposed storefront for Gumps, 900 North Michigan Avenue, delineated by John Halper, c. 1986. Printed paper, 45.5 x 55.7 cm. Lent by Kohn Pedersen Fox Associates.

387. Kohn Pedersen Fox Associates. Model of the interior shopping atrium of 900 North Michigan Avenue, 1988. Mixed media, approx. 81 x 104 x 100 cm. Gift of JMB Realty, 1990.

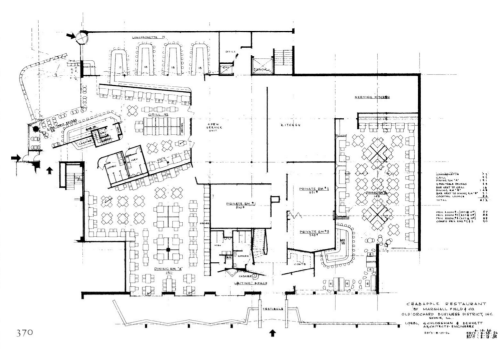

370

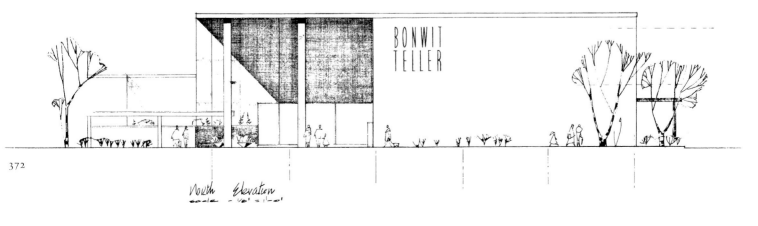

372

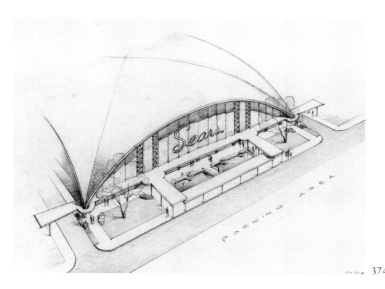

374

388. HTI/Space Design International; James Terrell, principal designer. Rendering of the ground floor of Bloomingdale's, 1987. Watercolor airbrushed on photographic paper, 20.4 x 25.4 cm. Lent by HTI Space Design International.

389. Florian-Wierzbowski. Facade model for Oilily, 900 North Michigan Avenue, 1988. Glued and painted plexiglas, approx. 52 x 56 cm, framed 73.7 x 68.5 cm. Lent by Florian-Wierzbowski Architecture P.C.

390. Florian-Wierzbowski. Eight design sketches for Oilily, April 20, 1988. Ink on tracing paper, each 30.5 x 22.5 cm. Lent by Florian-Wierzbowski Architecture P.C. (See plates 98-100.)

391. Himmel Bonner. Perspective rendering of Boogie's Diner and Store, 900 North Michigan Avenue, delineated by Rael Slutsky, 1988. Printed paper, approx. 58 x 101 cm. Lent by Darcy R. Bonner, Jr., Scott Himmel, James Stapleton, and David Piper. (See plate 101.)

392. Himmel Bonner. Views of Glasses, Ltd., 900 North Michigan Avenue, delineated by Scott Dimit, 1987. Photomontaged and collaged paper, mixed media, approx. 38 x 38 cm. Lent by Darcy R. Bonner, Jr., Scott Himmel, James Stapleton, and David Piper.

393. Tigerman McCurry; Stanley Tigerman, designer. Working drawings for Elephants, 900 North Michigan Avenue, February 3, 1989. Two sheets of printed Mylar, each 30.5 x 45.7 cm. Lent by Tigerman McCurry Architects.

394. Tigerman McCurry; Stanley Tigerman, designer. Rendered plan of improvements for Oak Street, 1987. Watercolor on paper, 65.5 x 146 cm. Lent by Tigerman McCurry Architects.

395. Tigerman McCurry; Stanley Tigerman, designer. Axonometric views of Sugar Magnolia, 34 East Oak Street, 1990. Ink on paper, mounted on foamcore, 66 x 95.8 cm. Lent by Tigerman McCurry Architects.

396. Solomon Cordwell Buenz and Associates. Elevation of the Mall (designed by Skidmore, Owings and Merrill) and Apartments (designed by Solomon Cordwell Buenz) at 700 North Michigan Avenue, 1988. Colored pencil on printed paper, approx. 150 x 68.5 cm. Lent by Solomon Cordwell Buenz and Associates.

397. Rael D. Slutsky and Associates. Study sketch of the escalator atrium for Chicago Place Mall, 1981. Marker and colored pencil on vellum, 40.6 x 50.8 cm. Lent by Rael D. Slutsky.

398. Rael D. Slutsky and Associates. Study sketch of a stained-glass window with escalator for Chicago Place Mall, 1981. Marker and colored pencil on vellum, 40.6 x 50.8 cm. Lent by Rael D. Slutsky.

399. Lubotsky Metter Worthington and Law; Jim Law, principal designer. Perspective drawing of the Fox Valley Village Green Mall, Route 34, Aurora, 1983. Graphite on yellow tracing paper, 76.2 x 101.6 cm. Lent by Jim Y. Law.

400. John Vinci. Site plan for the restoration of shops in Market Square, Lake Forest, 1985-89, originally designed by Howard Van Doren Shaw in 1913. Ink on Mylar, 76.2 x 106.8 cm. Lent by the Office of John Vinci.

401. John Vinci. Plan and elevation for Deerpath Arcade near Market Square, 1989. Ink and Mylar, 76.2 x 101.2 cm. Lent by the Office of John Vinci.

402. Loebl, Schlossman and Hackl. Three sketches for the renovation of the Ford City Shopping Center, originally the Dodge Chicago Plant (see pls. 80-81), delineated by Rene Steevensz, c. 1987. Ink and colored pencil on paper, each 28 x 43 cm. Lent by Loebl, Schlossman and Hackl.

403. Robert A. M. Stern. Site plan and elevations of the Wheaton Shopping Village, 2000 South Naperville Road, Wheaton, delineated by Andrew Zega, 1989-90. Three sheets, ink and watercolor on paper, each approx. 52.5 x 77 cm. Lent by Robert A. M. Stern Architects.

404. Pappageorge/Haymes. Plan and perspective views of the renovation and conversion of the Turtle Wax Factory, 1800 North Clybourn Avenue, 1989. Colored and printed Mylar, 76 x 101.5 cm. Lent by Pappageorge/Haymes Ltd.

405. Gelick Foran Associates. Elevations, section, and site plan of the North Avenue/Clybourn Avenue Shopping Center, the corner of Clybourn Avenue and Halsted Street,

375

1987-88. Printed paper with pastel, 101.5 x 76.5 cm. Lent by Gelick Foran Associates, Ltd.

406. Eva Maddox Associates. Views of the T. W. Best-Eastern News Stores in the Hotel Nikko and the Chicago and Northwestern Terminal Building atrium, 1988-89. Ink on paper, approx. 76 x 101.5 cm. Lent by Eva L. Maddox, Eva Maddox Associates, Inc. (See plate 106.)

407. Tigerman McCurry; Margaret McCurry, designer. Axonometric view of the Hayworth Showroom at the Merchandise Mart, 1991. Ink on tracing paper. Lent by Tigerman McCurry Architects.

408. Florian-Wierzbowski. Model of the Communicate Store, 808 West North Avenue, 1990. Painted foamcore, approx. 15 x 33 x 45.7 cm. Lent by Florian-Wierzbowski Architecture P.C.

409. Solomon Cordwell Buenz and Associates. Axonometric and cross section of the Crate and Barrel Store, 646 North Michigan Avenue, 1989-90. Printed Mylar, 71 x 91.5 cm. Lent by Solomon Cordwell Buenz and Associates.

410. Robert A. M. Stern. Three presentation drawings and two working drawings of the Banana Republic Store, 744 North Michigan Avenue, 1991. Presentation drawings: colored pencil on paper, each approx. 61 x 89 cm; working drawings: ink on Mylar, each 92.2 x 61.2 cm. Lent by Robert A. M. Stern Architects. (See plates 103-04.)

411. Loebl, Schlossman and Hackl. Two studies for the remodeling of the former Wieboldt's Store, 1 North State Street, into retail stores, 1990-91. Colored pencil on printed paper, mounted on foamcore, approx. 77.5 x 84 and 81 x 81 cm. Lent by Loebl, Schlossman and Hackl.

412. Loebl, Schlossman and Hackl. Perspective rendering of the interior of the entrance to stores at 1 North State Street, delineated by Timothy J. LeVaughn, 1990-91. Colored pencil on paper, 26.7 x 35.6 cm. Lent by Loebl, Schlossman and Hackl.

413. Booth/Hansen and Associates. Cutaway model of the First Oak Brook Bank, 1400 West 16th Street, Oak Brook, 1990-91. Glued and painted Strathmore and foamcore, 95 x 39.5 cm. Lent by Booth/Hansen and Associates, Ltd.

414. Cordogan, Clark and Associates. Composite exterior and interior elevations and floor plan of Park National Bank, 2100 North Elmhurst Road, Mount Prospect, 1991. Ink and watercolor on paper, 61 x 81.3 cm. Lent by Cordogan, Clark and Associates.

415. Cordogan, Clark and Associates. Composite exterior and interior elevations and floor plan of First American Bank, 5000 North Elston Avenue, 1991. Ink and watercolor on paper, 61 x 81.3 cm. Lent by Cordogan, Clark and Associates.

416. Decker and Kemp. Perspective rendering of the Tower Crossing Retail Center on Odgen Avenue and Naperville Road, Naperville, 1991. Printed Mylar copy of original ink drawing by Bruce Bondy, 45.7 x 56 cm. Lent by Decker and Kemp Architecture and Urban Design.

Houses and Housing

The 1920s in Chicago witnessed a continuation of established housing types, from the ubiquitous modest bungalow and the low-rise courtyard apartment, which was based on Boston prototypes, to luxury high-rises that could compete with any on New York's Fifth or Park avenues, best exemplified by 1500 Lake Shore Drive (1928) with its one apartment per floor. The production of homes and apartments slowed in the Depression and War years, the only real homes being done for selected wealthy owners or for subsidized housing projects (see essay by de Wit). Although Modern Movement houses were designed and occasionally built here in the 1920s and 1930s, it was the coming of Ludwig Mies van der Rohe that gave his elegant, minimal form of modernism greater acceptance through his contacts with students at the Illinois Institute of Technology. But the Wrightian ranch house was the form to reign supreme throughout the postwar American suburb, at least in a hybridized way (see pls. 107-12).

Housing for low- and middle-income groups spread as part of urban renewal in the decades following World War II, one of the most influential and controversial examples being Sandburg Village. This 1962 project of Solomon, Cordwell and Buenz with developer Arthur Rubloff demolished existing housing stock and replaced sixteen acres of neighborhood buildings on North Avenue and Clark, LaSalle, and Division streets with high-rise apartments and low-rise townhouses. With efforts to create new neighborhoods all over the city, citizens became more interested in preserving older neighborhoods and renovating humanly scaled older buildings, including lofts and factories. New townhouses and urban villas in the area and renovations, such as Cobbler Square (a renovated Dr. Scholl Factory), would not have been possible without the large-scale efforts of Sandburg Village — an urban renewal scheme that upgraded a large piece of somewhat deteriorated cityscape. Urban renewal supporters cite the success of projects like Sandburg Village, but

Solomon, Cordwell and Buenz. Sandburg Village, 1962.

Krueck and Olsen (now Krueck and Sexton). Steel and Glass House, 1949-1951 North Larrabee Street, 1981.

Schroeder, Murchie, Laya Associates. Cobbler Square, 1350 North Wells Street, 1983.

Tannys Langdon. Dining room interior of the Lopez House Remodeling, 1221 West Flournoy Street, 1989.

there has been an equal, if not greater, number of projects, such as Lake Meadows and Prairie Shores on the South Side of Chicago, whose impact on the broader neighborhood did not move much beyond their own property.

Today, architects, including many young designers, as varied as Daniel Wheeler, Tannys Langdon, Ronald Krueck, Darcy Bonner, and Garrett Eakin, provide a variety of creative design solutions for their clients within differing economic ranges. And such architects as Peter Landon, Weese Langley Weese, and Gelick Foran Associates are continuing to experiment with providing contextual, comfortable homes for low-income tenants. But, despite all these architectural efforts for better homes and housing, architects and developers have yet to provide, with either private or public funding, solutions to house the increasing numbers of homeless people in the 1990s or to supply quality housing for the millions of people in this country whose incomes are at or below the poverty level.

417. Dubin and Eisenberg. Perspective rendering of Boulevard Apartments, delineated by Charles Morgan, c. 1925. Pencil, chalk, and watercolor, mounted on board, approx. 73 x 91 cm. Gift of Dubin, Dubin and Moutoussamy, 1983.

418. Maurice L. Bein. Perspective rendering of Cornell Towers Apartment Building, 5346 South Cornell Avenue, delineated by Charles Morgan, c. 1925. Watercolor and crayon on tracing paper, mounted on board, 114.5 x 51 cm. Gift of William A. Bein, Joseph A. Bein, and Barbara Stone.

419. Tallmadge and Watson. East elevation and first-floor plan of the W. J. Clarkson House, 830 Franklin Avenue, River Forest, 1924. Black and brown ink on linen, each 37.5 x 53 cm. Gift of the Estate of Emma Watson, 1961.

420. Spencer S. Beman. North and south elevations of the F. H. McNabb House, Hill Road, Winnetka, c. 1924-29. Ink and colored ink on linen, approx. 85 x 92 cm. Gift of Suzanne Beman Dallmeyer and R. Ford Dallmeyer, 1990.

421. Rissman and Hirschfeld. Perspective rendering of 222 East Chestnut Street, delineated by J. R. Petter, 1928. Pencil, pastel, and watercolor on paper, mounted on board, 73.8 x 47.5 cm. Gift of Martin Reinheimer in honor of Leo Saul Hirschfeld, 1981.

422. McNally and Quinn. Perspective rendering of 1500 North Lake Shore Drive Apartment Building, delineated by B. C. Greengard, 1927-28. Photostatic copy of pencil or charcoal on paper, 53.7 x 33.7 cm. Gift of J. Edwin Quinn, 1980.

423. McNally and Quinn. Preliminary perspective sketch of the east elevation of penthouse, 1500 North Lake Shore Drive, c. 1928. Pencil on drawing paper, 48.5 x 61 cm. Gift of J. Edwin Quinn, 1980.

424. McNally and Quinn. Detail of urns at tea garden, patio, and 24th-floor balconies, 1500 North Lake Shore Drive, delineated by George A. Hossack, 1928. Pencil and graphite on tracing paper, 68 x 105.5 cm. Gift of J. Edwin Quinn, 1980.

425. McNally and Quinn. Lighting fixture no. 395039 for the driveway at 1500 North Lake Shore Drive, manufactured by C. G. Everson and Company, c. 1928. Pencil and tempera on paper, 36 x 23.3 cm. Gift of J. Edwin Quinn, 1980.

426. Klaber and Grunsfeld. First-floor plan and elevations of apartment houses for the Michigan Gardens Building Corporation, 50 East 47th Street, 1928. Blueprints, each 75.5 x 107 cm. Gift of Mr. and Mrs. Ernest A. Grunsfeld III, 1980.

427. Pond and Pond. Perspective study of apartments in the Back of the Yards area, c. 1930. Ink and colored pencil on tracing paper, 31.7 x 45.1 cm. Gift of the Irving Kane Pond Estate, 1939.

428. McNally and Quinn. Perspective view of the Hearthstone Hotel Apartment Building project, Chicago River and Michigan Avenue, 1931. Charcoal and pencil on board, 51.2 x 46 cm. Gift of J. Edwin Quinn, 1980.

429. Dubin and Eisenberg. Northwest elevation and first-floor plan of "Battle Deck House," Henry Dubin House, 441 Cedar Avenue, Highland Park, 1930. Ink on tracing paper, each approx. 23.5 x 36.1 cm. Gift of Arthur Dubin of Dubin, Dubin and Moutoussamy, 1980.

430. R. Buckminster Fuller. Elevation of a Minimum Dymaxion Home, 1931. Pencil on tracing paper, 61.3 x 72 cm. Through prior gift of Three Oaks Wrecking Company, 1990.

431. George Fred Keck. Perspective study of a small residence, exhibited at the Century of Progress Exposition, 1933. Watercolor on board, 33 x 39.5 cm. Gift of William Keck, 1983.

432. George Fred Keck. West elevation and section of the House of Tomorrow for the Century of Progress Exposition, 1933. Pencil on paper, approx. 36 x 50 cm. Lent by the State Historical Society of Wisconsin.

433. Leland Atwood, designer; W. W. Howell and Company, manufacturer. Chair for the House of Tomorrow at the Century of Progress Exposition, 1933. Chrome-plated tubular steel, 73.9 x 50.3 x 47 cm. Lent by the Elvehjem Museum of Art.

434. Leland Atwood, designer; W. W. Howell and Company, manufacturer. Gooseneck lamp from the House of Tomorrow at the Century of Progress Exposition, 1933. Chrome-plated tubular steel, height 184.2 cm. Lent by the Elvehjem Museum of Art.

435. George Fred Keck. Perspective rendering of the Crystal House for the Century of Progress Exposition, showing an airplane and Dymaxion Car, 1934. Ink and watercolor on board, approx. 36 x 50 cm. Lent by the State Historical Society of Wisconsin.

436. Ernest A. Grunsfeld, Jr. Exterior and interior elevations of the Lumber House, Century of Progress Exposition, delineated by W. Y., 1933. Pencil on tracing paper, 60 x 94 cm. Gift of Mr. and Mrs. Ernest Grunsfeld III, 1981.

437. L. Morgan Yost. Perspective sketches of chair designs, 1935. Pencil on tracing paper, mounted on cardboard, 18.2 x 26.2 and 21.2 x 26.5 cm. Gift of L. Morgan Yost, 1978.

438. Paul Schweikher. Thirteen sheets of furniture designs, c. 1930-35. Colored pencil on blackline prints, various sizes. Gift of Dorothy and Paul Schweikher, 1984.

439. Grunsfeld, Holabird, Armstrong, Jensen, Maher, Chatten, Merrill, Walcott, Huszagh, Hodgdon, associate architects for the West Side Housing Project. Site plan, typical floor plan, and elevations of the Jane Addams Housing Project addition, Roosevelt Road and Racine Street, 1936. Blueprints, each 77 x 107.5 cm. Gift of Mr. and Mrs. Ernest Grunsfeld III, 1980-81.

440. Diversey Housing Project Associated Architects; Robert S. DeGolyer, chief architect. Entrance details of the Julia C. Lathrop Homes, 1937. Ink on Mylar, 71.1 x 91.4 cm. Courtesy of the Chicago Housing Authority.

441. Diversey Housing Project Associated Architects; Robert S. DeGolyer, chief architect. Elevations of the Julia C. Lathrop

422

Homes, 2000 West Diversey, 1937. Ink on Mylar, 71.1 x 91.4 cm. Courtesy of the Chicago Housing Authority.

442. Philip B. Maher. Perspective rendering of 1350 North Astor Street Apartment Building, c. 1938-40. Pencil and white ink on drawing paper, 45.3 x 25 cm. Architecture Department purchase, 1990. (See plate 113.)

443. David Adler. Preliminary plans and elevation for the Louis B. Kuppenheimer House, southwest corner of Burr and Laurel avenues, Winnetka, 1937-38. Pencil on tracing paper sheets, 27 x 53.7, 27 x 53.8, and 27 x 59 cm. Gift of Bowen Blair, Executor of the Estate of William McCormick Blair, 1989.

444. Frank Lloyd Wright. Four elevations and rug layout plan for the First Jacobs House, 441 Toepfer Road, Madison, Wisconsin, 1937. Elevations: pencil and colored pencil on tracing paper, approx. 74.5 x 90.6; rug layout: graphite and colored pencil on lineprint on paper, 53 x 39 cm. Gift of Herbert and Katherine Jacobs to the Ryerson and Burnham Libraries, The Art Institute of Chicago, 1974.

445. Paul Schweikher. Plan and aerial perspective, Schweikher Home and Studio, 645 Meacham Road, Roselle (now Schaumburg), 1938. Pencil on tracing paper, mounted on board, 26.6 x 16.3 cm. Joint gift of Dorothy and Paul Schweikher.

446. J. Edwin Quinn. Perspective rendering of the Vincent J. Sheridan House, 9323 South Bell Avenue, delineated by George Hossack, 1940. Graphite and wax charcoal pencil on lightweight board, 28.6 x 37 cm. Gift of J. Edwin Quinn, 1980.

447. William F. Deknatel. Perspective rendering of the Lambert H. Ennis House, 200 Dempster Street, Evanston, 1941. Pencil on tracing paper, 34.5 x 71 cm. Gift of Diane Deknatel Pierson.

448. James Prestini, designer. Three bowls designed at the New Bauhaus, 1939. Various woods; largest bowl 35.6 cm diameter. Lent by George E. Danforth.

449. Ludwig Mies van der Rohe. Perspective studies for the interior of a courthouse, c. 1931-38. Ink on paper, 21.4 x 29.9 cm. Gift of A. James Speyer, 1981.

450. Angelo Testa, designer. Fabric designed at the Institute of Design, between 1943 and 1965. Woven fabric, 29.9 x 42.6 cm. Lent by Pauline A. Saliga through Penny McCue.

451. Ludwig Karl Hilberseimer. Site plan, plan of L-shaped house, plan of rectangular house, perspective view of L-shaped house (possibly rendered by Alfred Caldwell), settlement units, density studies, c. 1940. Ink on board, 50.9 x 76.5 cm. Gift of George E. Danforth, 1984.

452. Associated Housing Architects; Henry

417

K. Holsman, chairman. Elevations and building types for the low-rent housing project Frances Cabrini Homes, 418 West Oak Street, 1942. Ink on Mylar, 71.1 x 91.4 cm. Courtesy of the Chicago Housing Authority.

453. L. Morgan Yost. "Prefab Bathroom Unit," published in *Small Homes Guide* (Spring 1944). Ink on tracing paper, 13.5 x 13.5 cm. Gift of Lloyd Morgan Yost, 1985.

454. Bertrand Goldberg Associates. Prefabricated bathroom, 1946. Mixed media, approx. 76 x 214 x 107 cm. Lent by Bertrand Goldberg Associates.

455. L. Morgan Yost. Four elevations of the Norman C. Deno House, 1724 South Green Bay Road, Highland Park, 1944. Graphite, ink, and colored pencil on tracing paper, 48.5 x 35.8 cm. Gift of L. Morgan Yost, 1978.

456. L. Morgan Yost. Interior plan of the living room and elevations of the Norman C. Deno House, 1944. Ink, pencil, and colored pencil on tracing paper, 21.5 x 35.3 cm. Gift of L. Morgan Yost, 1978.

457. Frank Lloyd Wright. Perspective rendering of the Second Jacobs House, Old Sauk Road, Middleton, Wisconsin, 1944. Ink on paper, 58 x 73.5 cm. Gift of Herbert and Katherine Jacobs, 1979.

458. Frank Lloyd Wright. Furniture plan for the Second Jacobs House, 1944. Ink and colored pencil on tracing paper, 56.7 x 76.8 cm. Gift of Herbert and Katherine Jacobs, 1979.

459. R. Buckminster Fuller, architect; L. Don Royston, delineator. Plan, elevation, and section of the Airbarac-Beech Aircraft Company, Wichita House, March 29, 1945. Pencil on tracing paper, approx. 67.3 x 91.8 cm. Through prior gift of Carson, Pirie, Scott and Company and the Three Oaks Wrecking Company, 1991.

460. Frederick E. Sloan. Perspective rendering of prizewinning design, *Chicago Tribune* Chicagoland Prize Homes Competition, delineated by Charles Kemp, 1945. Watercolor

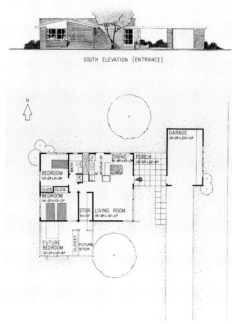

SOUTH ELEVATION (ENTRANCE)

468

on illustration board, 33.2 x 46.8 cm. Gift of D. Coder Taylor, 1981. A house based on alterations of this design was constructed at 2852 North Pratt Boulevard. (See plate 110.)

461. Raymond W. Garbe. Perspective rendering of prizewinning design, *Chicago Tribune* Chicagoland Prize Homes Competition, 1945. Pencil and gouache on illustration board, 33 x 50.7 cm. Gift of D. Coder Taylor, 1981. A house based on this design (now slightly altered) was constructed at 6820 North Francisco Avenue. (See plate 109.)

462. Lucille McKirahan. Perspective rendering of prizewinning design, *Chicago Tribune* Chicagoland Prize Homes Competition, delineated by Ted Kautzsky, 1945. Pencil and watercolor on illustration board, 31 x 48.5 cm. Gift of D. Coder Taylor, 1981.

463. D. Coder Taylor. Perspective rendering of prizewinning design, *Chicago Tribune* Chicagoland Prize Homes Competition, delineated by Ted Kautzsky, 1945. Watercolor

and pencil on paper, 26 x 47 cm. Gift of D. Coder Taylor, 1980. A house based on this design was constructed at 205 Barberry Road, Highland Park. (See plate 111.)

464. W. R. Burns, Jr. Perspective rendering of prizewinning design, *Chicago Tribune* Chicagoland Prize Homes Competition, delineated by I. Floyd Yewell, 1945. Watercolor on illustration board, 42 x 57 cm. Gift of D. Coder Taylor, 1981. A house based on alterations of this design was constructed at 6817 North Francisco Avenue. (See plate 112.)

465. Charles W. Schroeder. Perspective rendering of prizewinning design, *Chicago Tribune* Chicagoland Prize Homes Competition, 1945. Pencil and watercolor on illustration board, 31.5 x 38.8 cm. Gift of D. Coder Taylor, 1981.

466. Walter J. Thies. Perspective rendering of prizewinning design, *Chicago Tribune* Chicagoland Prize Homes Competition, delineated by I. Floyd Yewell, 1945. Watercolor on illustration board, 41.8 x 57 cm. Gift of D. Coder Taylor, 1981. A house based on alterations of this design was constructed at 2915 North Farwell Avenue. (See plate 108.)

467. Carl L. Cedarstrand. Perspective rendering of prizewinning design, *Chicago Tribune* Chicagoland Prize Homes Competition, 1945. Watercolor on illustration board, 41 x 56.8 cm. Gift of D. Coder Taylor, 1981. A house based on alterations of this design was constructed at 2909 North Farwell Avenue. (See plate 107.)

468. L. Morgan Yost. Plan and elevation for House No. IS-2 for Western Homes, Inc., planned for Highland Park, delineated by Walter A. Netsch, 1946. Ink, pencil, and colored pencil on paper, 51 x 38.3 cm. Gift of L. Morgan Yost, 1978.

469. Grunsfeld, Yerkes, Lichtmann and Koenig. Proposed neighborhood study in West Englewood, Community Planning for Southtown Planning Association, 63rd and Racine streets, 1946. Pencil and colored pencil on

472

474

lineprint, 63.3 x 96.5 cm. Gift of Mr. and Mrs. Ernest A. Grunsfeld III, 1980.

470. Grunsfeld, Yerkes, Lichtmann and Koenig. Proposed floor plan and elevations, Community Planning for Southtown Planning Association, 63rd and Racine streets, 1946. Elevations: pencil on tracing paper; plan: pencil and colored pencil on tracing paper, each 85.5 x 104 cm. Gift of Mr. and Mrs. Ernest A. Grunsfeld III, 1980.

471. Bruce Goff. Elevation, section, and plan drawings for the Ruth Ford House, 404 South Edgelawn, Aurora, 1947. Graphite on tracing paper, 44.4 x 86.2 cm. Gift of Shin én Kan, Inc., 1990.

472. Hugh M. G. Garden. Perspective rendering of a suburban house with a parabolic roof, 1947. Ink and colored pencil on acetate, 28 x 39.3 cm. Gift of the Struve Gallery, Chicago, 1987.

473. Hugh M. G. Garden. Perspective rendering of a modernist suburban home, 1947. Ink and colored pencil on acetate, 25.5 x 37.5 cm. Restricted gift of the Chicago Dock and Canal Trust, 1987.

474. Carter H. Manny, Jr. Perspective view of a court house, 1947. Pencil on illustration board, 76.2 x 101.6 cm. Gift of Carter H. Manny, Jr., 1990.

475. George Fred Keck and William Keck. Perspective rendering of the entrance facade of a proposed house for Mr. and Mrs. Mayer Stern, Flossmoor, c. 1947. Pencil, ink, and watercolor on illustration board, 38.2 x 50.8 cm. Gift of Mr. and Mrs. Mayer Stern, 1986.

476. Ludwig Mies van der Rohe. Perspective sketch for a high-rise apartment, possibly 860-880 North Lake Shore Drive, c. 1946-48. Pencil on paper, 15.4 x 21.5 cm. Restricted gifts of the Architecture Society and the Alexander C. and Tillie S. Speyer Foundation in honor of John Zukowsky; through prior gift of the Three Oaks Wrecking Company and Carson, Pirie, Scott and Company; Samuel P. Avery Endowment and Edward E. Ayer

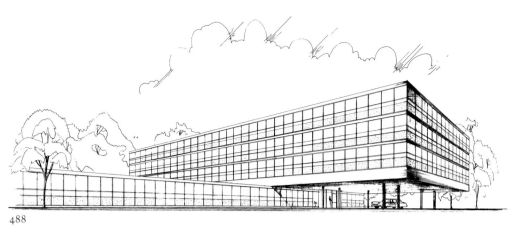
488

Endowment in memory of Charles L. Hutchinson. (See plate 115.)

477. Ludwig Mies van der Rohe with Pace Associates and Holsman, Holsman, Klekamp and Taylor. Plot plan, typical floor plan and elevations, and window details, 860-880 North Lake Shore Drive, 1949-50. Pencil on linen, 91.5 x 116.4 cm. Gift of Charles and Shirley Genther, 1986. (See plate 116.)

478. Harry Weese and Associates. Perspective study of a high-rise apartment building, possibly delineated by Brewster Adams, late 1940s/early 1950s. Graphite and colored pencil on yellow tracing paper, approx. 65.3 x 56 cm. Gift of Ben and Cynthia Weese, 1991.

479. Harry Weese and Associates. Perspective study for a low-rise apartment building, possibly delineated by Brewster Adams, late 1940s/early 1950s. Graphite and colored pencil on yellow tracing paper. 41.5 x 46.2 cm. Gift of Ben and Cynthia Weese, 1991.

480. Motorola, Inc. Music box AM portable radio, 1949. Plastic, 16.5 x 19 x 11.5 cm. Lent by the Motorola Museum of Electronics.

481. Motorola, Inc. Television table, Golden View, late 1940s/early 1950s. Wood, metal, and plastic, 24.7 x 41.9 x 40.7 cm. Lent by the Motorola Museum of Electronics.

482. Friedman, Alschuler and Sincere and Ernest A. Grunsfeld, Jr. Exterior elevation of a low-rent housing project, the Ida B. Wells extension, Browning and Rhodes streets, 1953.

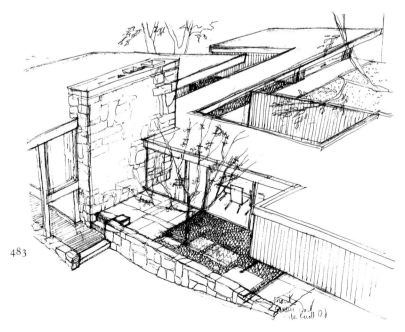
483

Ink on Mylar, 71.1 x 91.4 cm. Courtesy of the Chicago Housing Authority.

483. Edward Dupaquier Dart. Aerial perspective view of Edward Dart House, Oak Knoll Road, Barrington, 1951. Graphite and blue ink on tracing paper, 35. x 41.5 cm. Gift of Mr. and Mrs. John T. McCutcheon, 1991.

484. Belli and Belli. Plot plan and elevation of a house for St. Williams Parish, "The Miracle House," Armitage and Nordica streets, October 13, 1953. Ink on Mylar, 76.2 x 101.6 cm. Lent by Belli and Belli Architects and Engineers.

485. Milton M. Schwartz and Associates. Preliminary plan and elevation of 320 West Oakdale Avenue, November 1, 1952. Blueprint, 57.5 x 81.5 cm. Lent by Milton M. Schwartz.

486. Milton M. Schwartz and Associates. Five sheets of preliminary studies for the structure and building base of 320 West Oakdale Avenue, c. 1953. Blueprints, various sizes up to 34 x 29.5 cm. Lent by Milton M. Schwartz.

487. Milton M. Schwartz and Associates. Perspective rendering of 320 West Oakdale Avenue, c. 1953. Pencil on board, 80 x 54.5 cm. Lent by Milton M. Schwartz.

488. Milton M. Schwartz and Associates. Perspective view of the Sanjil Apartments, 510 Sheridan Road, Evanston, c. 1955. Pencil on tracing paper, 55 x 85.5 cm. Lent by Milton M. Schwartz.

489. Milton M. Schwartz and Associates. Rental plan of the Sanjil Apartments, c. 1955. Pencil on tracing paper, 56 x 36.5 cm. Lent by Milton M. Schwartz.

490. A. James Speyer, designer; George Danforth, associate architect. Presentation floor plan of the Ben Rose House (1952-54), Highland Park, delineated by George Danforth, 1957. Pencil on Strathmore board, 76.5 x 101.7 cm. Gift of George Edson Danforth, 1988.

491. David Haid and Associates. Site plan and exploded construction view of the pavilion for the Mr. and Mrs. Ben Rose House, 370 Beech Street, Highland Park, 1974. Two sheets of printed polyester film, each 71.2 x

492

501. Pace Associates. Elevation and section of a high-rise apartment project for low-rent housing, William Green Homes, Division Street and Ogden Avenue, 1961. Ink on Mylar, 71.1 x 91.4 cm. Courtesy Chicago Housing Authority.

502. Hausner and Macsai. East elevation of the Harbor House Apartments, 3200 North Lake Shore Drive, July 1, 1965, with later revisions. Ink and pencil on paper, 80 x 125 cm. Lent by John Macsai, principal of O'Donnell, Wicklund, Pigozzi, and Peterson.

503. Hausner and Macsai. Design diagram of sample apartments at Harbor House, 1965. Blackline print on Mylar, 97.3 x 86.8 cm. Lent by John Macsai, principal of O'Donnell, Wicklund, Pigozzi, and Peterson.

504. L. R. Solomon and J. D. Cordwell and Associates. Five working drawings for the early phases of Carl Sandburg Center, North, Clark, and LaSalle streets, 1962-63. Pencil, colored pencil, and ink on linen, each approx. 77 x 127 cm. Lent by Solomon Cordwell Buenz and Associates.

505. Harry Weese and Associates; Ben Weese, designer. Perspective view of Kenwood Gardens Townhouses, 55th Street between Kenwood and Kimbark avenues, 1965. Graphite on yellow tracing paper, approx. 33 x 71 cm. Gift of Ben and Cynthia Weese, 1991.

506. Dubin, Dubin and Black. Aerial perspective of the Lincoln Park Towers Apartment Building, Armitage Avenue at Clark

91.4 cm. Printed from a Hedrich-Blessing photograph, courtesy the Chicago Historical Society.

492. I. M. Pei. Bird's-eye view study of the University Apartments, 1400-50 East 55th Street, 1960. Chalk, charcoal, and pastel on paper, 40 x 41 cm. Lent by Pei Cobb Freed and Partners.

493. William F. Deknatel. Perspective rendering of the Maurice Rosenfield House, 55 Beach Road, Glencoe, 1956. Pencil on tracing paper, 44 x 61.9 cm. Gift of Diane Deknatel Pierson.

494. Milton M. Schwartz and Associates. Preliminary plan, elevation, and perspective studies of Wacker Plaza (later the Executive House), 73 East Wacker Drive, October 31, 1955. Pencil on tracing paper, 80.5 x 91.8 cm. Lent by Milton M. Schwartz.

495. Milton M. Schwartz and Associates. Front elevation of the Executive House, November 1, 1956. Pencil on tracing paper, 122.5 x 77 cm. Lent by Milton M. Schwartz.

496. Milton M. Schwartz and Associates. Typical floor plan (6th through 17th floors) of the Executive House, c. 1957. Ink on linen, 77 x 114 cm. Lent by Milton M. Schwartz.

497. Bertrand Goldberg Associates. Photo-blowup of Marina City, 300 North State Street, 1963, signed by Bertrand Goldberg. Photoprint on paper, 76 x 101.5 cm. Lent by Hedrich-Blessing, Photographers.

498. Bertrand Goldberg Associates. Idea-gram and typical floor plan with partial elevation of Marina City, 300 North State Street, 1959-64. Printed paper, 101.5 x 76 cm. Lent by Bertrand Goldberg Associates.

499. Bertrand Goldberg Associates. Working drawing for Marina City. Lent by Bertrand Goldberg Associates.

500. Bertrand Goldberg. Elevation and plan of Hilliard Homes (Raymond M. Hilliard Center), public housing for the CHA, Cermak and State streets, 1963. Elevation: pencil on paper; plan: pencil and pastel on paper, each 76 x 128 cm. Gift of Bertrand Goldberg, 1982.

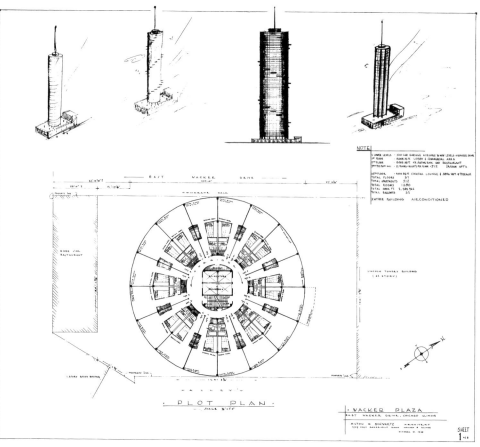

494

Street, delineated by H. Tan, 1965. Watercolor, tempera, and ink on illustration board, 100.4 x 73.7 cm. Gift of Dubin, Dubin and Moutoussamy, 1986.

507.   Marianne Willisch. Two perspective studies of the proposed living room of the Sigmund Edelstone apartment, c. 1965. Pencil, colored pencil, and collaged paper, each 45.5 x 60.5 cm. Gift of the Estate of Marianne Willisch, 1984.

508.   Solomon Cordwell Buenz. Site plan, tower elevation, and elevation of the lower floors of the Edgewater Beach Plaza Apartments, 5555 North Sheridan Road, 1971. Ink and pencil on Mylar, each 122 x 93.5 cm. Lent by Solomon Cordwell Buenz and Associates.

509.   Stanley Tigerman. Sketch of the Daisy House, 129th and Market streets, Porter, Indiana, prepared for the Venice Biennale, 1976. Mixed media on foamcore, 27 x 35.5 cm. Restricted gift of the Auxiliary Board, 1980.

510.   Stanley Tigerman. Two presentation drawings of the Daisy House, 1975-78. Pencil and ink on Mylar, each 77 x 77 cm. Gift of Margaret McCurry, 1989.

511.   Hammond, Beeby and Babka; Thomas Hall Beeby, designer. Four elevations of the proposed Theodore Seyfarth House, 170 Kimberley Road, North Barrington, 1977. Ink on tracing paper, colored markers on yellow tracing paper, each 46 x 51 cm. Anonymous gift, 1981.

512.   Weese Seegers Hickey Weese; Cynthia Weese, designer. Elevations of the Kuntz Residence, St. Charles, 1980. Ink on Mylar, 80 x 106 cm. Gift of Weese Seegers Hickey Weese, 1982.

513.   Kenneth Schroeder and Associates; David Haymes, assistant. Axonometric drawing of the Merganthaler Linotype Building renovation, 531 South Plymouth Court, 1980. Ink on Mylar, 61 x 81.4 cm. Gift of Kenneth Schroeder and Associates, 1982.

514.   Krueck and Olsen. Mural study of the Steel and Glass House, 1949-51 North Larrabee Street, 1981. Ink and hand-colored papers on Strathmore board, 76.6 x 192 cm. Gift of A. James Speyer, 1982.

515.   Krueck and Olsen. Plans and elevations of the Miles Kerrigan House remodeling, 1522 North Dearborn Parkway, 1981. Ink and colored pencil on polyester film, 123.6 x 78 cm. Gift of A. James Speyer, 1982.

516.   Cohen and Nereim. Plans and details, and sections and elevation of the Baron House addition, 2120 Sheridan Road, Highland Park, 1981. Watercolor on photocopy prints, each approx. 46 x 64.8 cm. Gift of Stuart Cohen and Anders Nereim, 1983.

517.   Booth/Hansen and Associates. Plans, section, and elevation sketches of the House

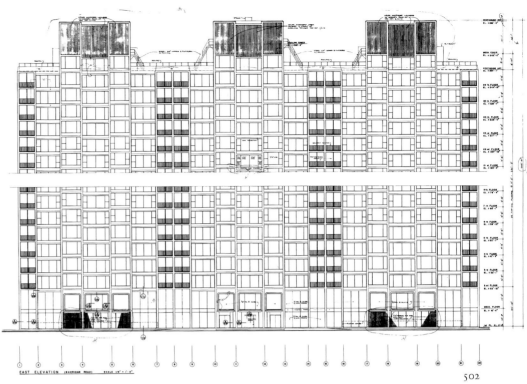

EAST ELEVATION (SHERIDAN ROAD)   SCALE 1/8" = 1'-0"

502

of Light, 1828 Orleans Street, 1981. Printed Mylar with colored pencil, 101.5 x 76 cm. Lent by Booth/Hansen and Associates, Ltd. (See plate 124.)

518.   Mastro and Skylar. Plans, elevation, and details of the 1925 North Howe Street additions, 1983. Pencil and watercolor on paper, 63.7 x 81.4 cm. Gift of James Mastro and Claudia Skylar, 1983.

519.   Mastro and Skylar. Sketch, first-floor plan, and west elevation, with details, of a residence, 1226 West Montana Street, 1991. Ink, pencil, and oil pastels on paper, 60.6 x 81.4 cm. Lent by Mastro and Skylar, Architects.

520.   Solomon Cordwell Buenz. Plans and elevations of 1418 North Lake Shore Drive, 1984. Printed Mylar, each 91.5 x 71

509

cm. Lent by Solomon Cordwell Buenz and Associates.

521. Pappageorge/Haymes. Elevation and first-floor plan of the Yadava House, Hunter Trails, Oak Brook, 1986-87. Colored print of Prismacolor on paper, each 61 x 71 cm. Lent by Pappageorge/Haymes Ltd.

522. Pappageorge/Haymes. Bird's-eye view rendering of the townhouses of City Commons, with the Willow Street elevation, delineated by Rael Slutsky, 1985. Printed paper, 76 x 101.5 cm. Lent by Pappageorge/Haymes Ltd.

523. Pappageorge/Haymes. Perspective rendering of the townhouses in Schubert Parkway, within the Embassy Club Development, bounded by Southport, Wrightwood, and Greenview, delineated by Rael Slutsky, 1988. Photoprint of ink and colored pencil on paper, approx. 76.5 x 102 cm. Lent by Pappageorge/Haymes Ltd.

524. Nagle, Hartray and Associates. Cutaway bird's-eye view and plans of the townhouses on the southwest corner of Schiller and LaSalle streets, 1986-88. Printed Mylar, 101.5 x 127 cm. Lent by Nagle, Hartray and Associates.

525. Schroeder Murchie Laya Associates; Ken Schroeder, principal designer. Residence, 610 West Belden Street, 1988. Watercolor on paper, 100.4 x 114.5 cm. Lent by Ken Schroeder, Schroeder Murchie Laya Associates.

526. Schroeder Murchie Laya Associates; Ken Schroeder, principal designer. Concept sketches for Cobbler Square, 1350 North Wells Street, 1985. Four sketches, colored

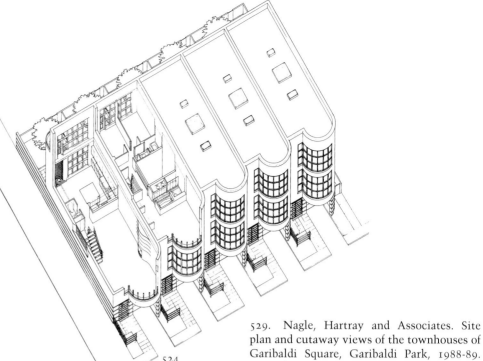

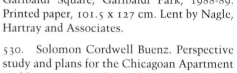

524

pencil and ink on paper, 64.7 x 64.2 cm. Lent by Ken Schroeder, Schroeder Murchie Laya Associates.

527. Nagle, Hartray and Associates. Axonometric view with floor plans of the Rosenberg House, Dean and Carey roads, Highland Park, 1985-87. Printed Mylar, 152.5 x 101.5 cm. Lent by Nagle, Hartray and Associates. (See plate 119.)

528. Tigerman McCurry; Stanley Tigerman, designer. Plan and bird's-eye view of the Pochis House on West Park Avenue, Highland Park, 1988-91. Printed Mylar, 71 x 91.5 cm. Lent by Tigerman McCurry Architects.

529. Nagle, Hartray and Associates. Site plan and cutaway views of the townhouses of Garibaldi Square, Garibaldi Park, 1988-89. Printed paper, 101.5 x 127 cm. Lent by Nagle, Hartray and Associates.

530. Solomon Cordwell Buenz. Perspective study and plans for the Chicagoan Apartment Building, 750 North Rush Street, 1988-90. Printed Mylar, 91.5 x 71 cm. Lent by Solomon Cordwell Buenz and Associates.

531. Jordan Mozer and Associates. Proposed entrance gate for the renovation of the Ludwig Drum Factory, 1750 North Damen Avenue, 1988. Ink and watercolor on paper, mounted on board, 33 x 33 cm. Lent by Jordan Mozer and Associates, Inc.

532. Florian-Wierzbowski. Four facade studies for the renovation of 1816 North Cleveland Avenue, 1986-88. Pencil and colored pencil on tracing paper, 30.5 x 35.5, 21.5 x 30.5, 27.5 x 21, and 30 x 30 cm. Lent by Florian-Wierzbowski Architecture P.C.

533. Krueck and Sexton. Plan and axonometric view of the Nadler Apartment, Chicago, 1988-89. Ink on paper, 76 x 101.5 cm. Lent by Ronald Krueck, Krueck and Sexton Architects. (See plate 122.)

534. Krueck and Sexton. Prototype side chair for the Nadler Apartment, manufactured by Tesko, 1989. Bent stainless steel with cardboard profiles and red crayon annotations, 42.5 x 46.5 x 87.5 cm. Lent by Ronald Krueck, Krueck and Sexton Architects. (See plate 120.)

535. Landon Architects. Site plan, plans, and elevations of the Douglas Patinkin House, 2307 North Janssen, 1989. Printed Mylar, 71 x 56 cm. Lent by Peter Landon Architects Ltd.

536. Banks/Eakin. Perspective view of a townhouse at 1910 North Dayton Street, 1988. Ink on Mylar, approx. 76 x 63.5 cm. Lent by Banks/Eakin Architects.

537. Banks/Eakin. Perspective view of a

538

townhouse at 1942 North Orchard Street, 1989. Ink on Mylar, approx. 76 x 63.5 cm. Lent by Banks/Eakin Architects.

538. Banks/Eakin. Perspective study of kitchen and plan for the kitchen and family room and arbor additions to the Power Residence, 344 West Wellington Street, 1991. Colored pencil on printed paper, approx. 71 x 56 cm. Lent by Banks/Eakin Architects.

539. Rudolph and Associates. Plans, sections, elevations, and perspective view of Haus Madison, 1038 Hillside Avenue, Madison, Wisconsin, 1989. Ink on Mylar, approx. 109 x 109 cm. Lent by Rudolph and Associates.

540. Tigerman McCurry; Stanley Tigerman, designer. Site plan, views, and details of Bluffsyde, Lake Bluff, delineated by Rene Stratton, 1989-91. Watercolor on paper, approx. 161 x 107 cm. Lent by Tigerman McCurry Architects.

541. John Syvertsen. Plans, elevation, and details for the renovation of the Lougee Residence (the former Ann Halstead Houses designed by Louis Sullivan), 1830 Lincoln Park West, 1989-91. Printed paper with colored pencil, 76 x 101.5 cm. Lent by John M. Syvertsen.

542. John Syvertsen. Sketches for the main staircase, main floor, of the renovation of the Lougee Residence, 1989. Four ink on tracing paper sheets, each approx. 30.5 x 35.5 cm. Lent by John M. Syvertsen.

543. Tannys Langdon. Four interior views of a Gothic Apartment, 20 East Cedar Street, 1989-92. Watercolor and pencil on yellow

551

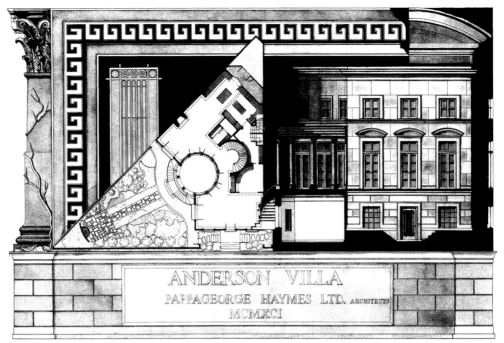

556

tracing paper, each 40 x 40 cm. Lent by Tannys Langdon. (See plates 126-27.)

544. Tannys Langdon. Audiovisual cabinet for a Gothic Apartment, 1989-92. Painted and carved wood, approx. 87.5 x 87.5 x 228.5 cm. Anonymous loan. (See plate 128.)

545. Tannys Langdon. Elevations, sections, and plans of the Lopez Residence remodeling, 1221 West Flournoy Street, 1989. Printed Mylar with mixed media, 71 x 91.5 cm. Lent by Tannys Langdon.

546. Tannys Langdon. South elevation and first-floor plan for the addition to, and remodeling of, the Engelbrecht Residence, Angus Farm, Henry, 1990. Ink and marker on paper, 101.5 x 76 cm. Lent by Tannys Langdon.

547. Quinn and Searl; Kathryn Quinn, project architect. Exterior elevation of an addition to, and renovation of, a townhouse, 2325 North Cleveland Street, 1988. Watercolor and pencil on paper, 61 x 86.4 cm. Lent by Kathryn Quinn Architects.

548. Landon Architects. Bird's-eye view and plan of the THI 3 Apartment Building, 62nd Street and Dorchester Avenue, 1990. Collage on ink on paper, 59 x 28.5 cm. Lent by Peter Landon Architects Ltd.

549. Landon Architects. Perspective studies of the lobby and a typical bedroom for an SRO residential development project, Division and Christiana streets, 1991. Ink and colored pencil on paper, each 28 x 35 cm. Lent by Peter Landon Architects Ltd.

550. Landon Architects. Exploded plan and axonometric view of a chair, 1991. Ink on Mylar, 61 x 46 cm. Lent by Peter Landon Architects Ltd.

551. Landon Architects. Side chair, 1991. Pegged and glued plywood, 78 x 43 x 48 cm. Lent by Peter Landon Architects Ltd.

552. Lohan Associates. Plan and street elevation of the Durchslag House, 1991. Ink and colored pencil on vellum, 91.5 x 71 cm. Lent by Lohan Associates.

553. Krueck and Sexton. Longitudinal section and stair-rail construction details for the Stainless Steel Apartment in 860 North Lake Shore Drive, 1991-92. Collage of pencil and Prismacolor drawings on printed paper, 76 x 101.5 cm. Lent by Ronald Krueck, Krueck and Sexton Architects.

554. Pappageorge/Haymes. Collaged views of loft townhomes at 1300 West Altgeld Street, 1991. Mixed media on paper, 76 x 101.5 cm. Lent by Pappageorge/Haymes Ltd.

555. Nagle, Hartray and Associates. West Side master plan for the Charles H. Shaw Company, Homan Avenue, 1991. Printed Mylar, 45.7 x 55.9 cm. Lent by Nagle, Hartray and Associates.

556. Pappageorge/Haymes. Plans and elevations of the Anderson House, 2030 North Magnolia Avenue, 1991. Watercolor on paper, 76 x 101.5 cm. Lent by Pappageorge/Haymes Ltd.

557. O'Donnell, Wicklund, Pigozzi and Peterson; John Macsai, principal designer. West elevation and section of congregate housing for the elderly, Fairfield Court, Old Glenview Road between Skokie Boulevard and Westmoreland Drive, Wilmette, 1989. Two sheets of colored pencil on printed paper; elevation: 61 x 113; section: 61 x 124.5 cm. Lent by John Macsai, principal of O'Donnell, Wicklund, Pigozzi and Peterson.

558. Frederick Phillips and Associates.

Elevations and plans of a three-flat house at 1518 North Mohawk Street, 1989. Prismacolor and ink on paper, 53.3 x 53.3 cm. Lent by Frederick Phillips and Associates. (See plate 129.)

559. Weese Langley Weese; Peter Landon, designer. Site model with plan and perspective view of the Bickerdike Redevelopment, scattered-site public housing near Humboldt Park (Leavitt and Evergreen streets, and various locales), 1989. Model: mixed media, approx. 37.5 x 53.5 x 17.5; plan and perspective: printed Mylar, 37.5 x 91.5 cm. Lent by Weese Langley Weese Architects, Ltd. (See plate 132.)

560. Landon Architects. Elevations and site plan of proposed community homes, 2013-31 West Crystal Street, Bickerdike Redevelopment, April 19, 1991. Pencil on tracing paper, 61 x 91.5 cm. Lent by Peter Landon Architects Ltd.

561. Solomon Cordwell Buenz. Plans and elevations of 440 North Wabash Avenue, 1990-91. Printed Mylar, 91.5 x 71 cm. Lent by Solomon Cordwell Buenz and Associates.

562. Triad Consortium. Floor plan and perspective of a proposed scattered-site housing project, 6817 South Dorchester Avenue, 1991. Ink and colored pencil on paper, 61 x 91.5 cm. Lent by Daniel Levin and the Habitat Co. as receiver for the CHA Scattered Site Program.

563. Bauhs and Dring. Floor plan and perspective of a scattered-site housing project, 1500-02 North Campbell Avenue, 1991. Ink and colored pencil on paper, 61 x 91.5 cm. Lent by Daniel Levin and the Habitat Co. as receiver for the CHA Scattered Site Program.

564. Roy H. Kruse and Associates. Floor plan and perspective of a prototype scattered-

site housing project, 2115-33 West 18th Place, 1991. Ink and colored pencil on paper, 61 x 91.5 cm. Lent by Roy H. Kruse and Associates.

565. Nagle, Hartray and Associates. Perspective rendering of 401 East Ontario Street, delineated by James Smith, 1990. Airbrushed ink on paper, 97 x 78 cm. Lent by Nagle, Hartray and Associates.

566. Nagle, Hartray and Associates. CHA scattered-site housing for the Habitat Company, 925 North California Avenue and 2933-37 West Walton Street, 1990-91. Printed paper, each 101.5 x 76 cm. Lent by Nagle, Hartray and Associates.

567. Gelick Foran Associates. Plans and elevations of scattered-site public housing for the Habitat Company at Hoyne, 18th Place, and 19th Street, 1991. Printed paper with pastel, 76.5 x 101.5 cm. Lent by Gelick Foran Associates, Ltd.

568. Decker and Kemp. East wing additions and restoration of "The Centaurs" estate by David Adler, 1115 East Illinois Street, Lake Forest, 1990. Site plan and garden front. Ink and wash on paper, 74.5 x 52.5 cm. Lent by Decker and Kemp Architecture and Urban Design.

569. Max Gordon with John Vinci, associate architects. Model of the house for Lewis and Susan Manilow, 1900 North Howe Street, 1990-91. Model by Richard Tickner, mixed media, approx. 81 x 107 x 33 cm. Lent by Lewis and Susan Manilow.

570. Tigerman McCurry; Stanley Tigerman, designer. Study model for the first phase of the Central Station Townhouses, 14th and 15th streets between Indiana Avenue and Central Station Drive, 1990-92. Glued foam-

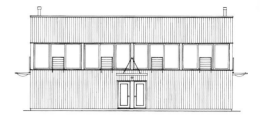

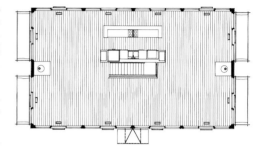

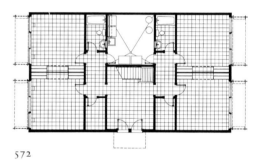

572

core, 12 x 35.4 cm. Lent by Stanley Tigerman of Tigerman McCurry Architects.

571. Booth/Hansen and Associates. Cutaway views and plans of the Fox House, 1 Rockland Place, Glencoe, built 1973 and remodeled 1991. Printed Mylar with colored pencil, 101.5 x 76.2 cm. Lent by Booth/Hansen and Associates, Ltd.

572. Wheeler Kearns; Daniel Wheeler, designer. Elevation and plans for the Lapoint House, Camp Madron, Buchanan Township, Michigan, 1990-91. Printed Mylar, 91.5 x 71 cm. Lent by Wheeler Kearns Architects.

573. Weese Langley Weese; Cynthia Weese, designer. Model for the addition to 1816 North Wells Street, 1990-91. Glued foamcore, mounted in a vitrine, 61 x 61 x 21 cm. Lent by Weese Langley Weese Architects, Ltd.

574. Himmel Bonner. Plans for the Presti Apartment in Lake Point Tower, 505 North Lake Shore Drive, delineated by Darcy Bonner, Jr., and James Stapleton, 1989-92. Collaged paper, approx. 61 x 61 cm. Lent by Darcy R. Bonner, Jr., Scott Himmel, James Stapleton, and David Piper.

575. Booth/Hansen and Associates. Floor plan, elevation, and collaged sketches of the Bendy House, Sheridan Road, Winnetka, 1992. Colored pencil and collaged paper, 61 x 88.9 cm. Lent by Booth/Hansen and Associates, Ltd.

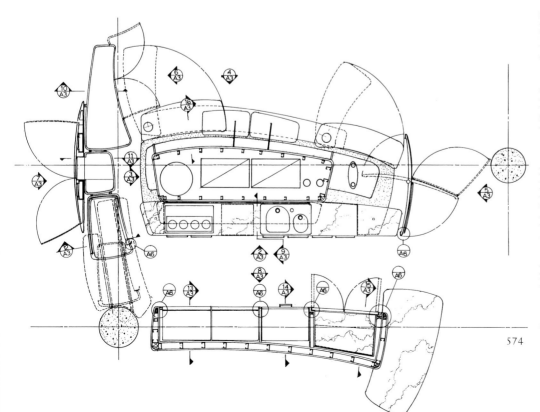

574

Recreation

The buildings encompassed by the broad category of recreation range from structures for amusement and entertainment – like Art Deco movie theaters or today's multi-plex cinemas (see pls. 135-37) – to those for sport and other athletic activities. Recreation also includes park design and landscape design that is enjoyed by a broad section of the public.

Of all the parks in Chicago and their architecture, Edward H. Bennett's Buckingham Fountain of 1927, with its seahorse sculptures by Marcel Loyau, is perhaps the most famous. In recent years the Chicago Park District has embarked on an active campaign to restore Lincoln Park and Grant Park. In many ways, their work in Lincoln Park will eventually have to connect with the expanding role of both the Chicago Historical Society and Lincoln Park Zoo as these institutions become increasingly involved in offering educational entertainment to the public. The Park District also plans to upgrade the lakefront beaches along the park, such as the shiplike North Avenue Beach House. In addition to those lakefront parks, which are doubtless the largest recreational facilities in this city, a number of other structures stand out for discussion.

Sports facilities are paramount in this group. Chicago's professional teams for baseball, football, basketball, and hockey have always had major stadiums, including several historic buildings: the landmark Wrigley Field, designed by Zachary Taylor Davis and home of the Chicago Cubs since 1914; Soldier Field by Holabird and Roche from 1922 to 1926, home of the Chicago Bears; the International Amphitheater of 1934 by A. Epstein, originally built for the Union Stockyards; and the Chicago Stadium by Hall, Lawrence and Ratcliffe, 1928-29, home of both the

Edward H. Bennett. Buckingham Fountain, 1927.

A. Epstein. Chicago Amphitheatre, 4220 South Halsted, 1934, and adjacent stockyards.

Zook and McCaughey, architects, with Alfonso Iannelli, interior designer. Interior of the Pickwick Theater, Park Ridge, 1931.

Hellmuth, Obata and Kassabaum. New Comiskey Park (at right), 1991, flanked by the old ballpark of 1910.

The Landahl Group. Exercise Playce, Oakbrook Terrace Tower,
1 Tower Lane, Oak Brook, 1986.

Kisho Kurokawa. Mountain-climbing Wall in the Sporting Club,
211 Stetson Drive, Illinois Center, 1990.

Chicago Bulls and Blackhawks. The city has not lacked its share of controversy surrounding sports arenas. These range from the lighting of historic Wrigley Field for night baseball games to the demolition of the original Comiskey Park of 1910 by Zachary Taylor Davis to make way for a new home for the Chicago White Sox, the new Comiskey Park of 1991 by Hellmuth, Obata and Kassabaum. In addition to renovating and creating those sports facilities, discussion is underway about building new stadiums for existing teams.

Beyond spectator sports, the concern for individual fitness has probably influenced the entire spectrum of society, from health clubs for upscale individuals to Camp Hoover, a summer camp for differently abled Boy Scouts, designed by Stanley Tigerman. The craze throughout America for healthy lifestyles has spawned a series of diverse designs for health clubs. In some ways these are much more than simply urban or suburban versions of country clubs. Exercise Playce by the Landahl Group, for example, is housed in the lower level of Oakbrook Terrace Tower, a Murphy/Jahn office building in the suburbs, and Landahl used the elevation of the building as the motif for designing the columns. Of the urban health clubs, the East Bank Club of the mid-1980s near the Merchandise Mart set the tone for Chicago's later clubs that combine the traditions of fine luncheon or dinner dining in restaurants and private clubs with the latest in athletic equipment. The Sporting Club of 1990 by Kisho Kurokawa tried to surpass the competition by incorporating in its design kinetic sculpture in addition to a spectacular mountain-climbing wall. The rivalry between these sports clubs continues today: Gelick Foran Associates has been engaged to expand the facilities of the East Bank Club to be more appealing to its members, old and new.

Finally, the desire for recreation affects architecture at two very different ends of the scale. Mies van der Rohe's famous Farnsworth House of 1950 (see Schulze, fig. 8) is one example from the immediate postwar era of the summer or weekend house. This architectural type has long existed, but an increasing number of vacation homes have been constructed in the past few years for moderate-income families as a retreat from urban pressures. At the other end of the scale are World's Fairs, which for a limited period of time offer large numbers of people a vast array of opportunities for entertainment, education, and leisure. The 1933-34 Century of Progress Exposition in Chicago was one of the most successful of World's Fairs in economic and social terms, acting as a boost to local industry during the Great Depression. The organizers of the proposed Age of Discovery World's Fair, planned for Chicago in 1992, hoped to invoke the success of that previous fair, but they were unsuccessful in 1985 in courting politicians and the voting public to obtain the necessary support for such a venture. Perhaps, as some have said, the need for World's Fairs has passed, because of increased international travel and telecommunications and the variety of activities that satisfy our need for personal, individual recreation. Or, perhaps the group experiences offered by fairs are now better handled, on a continuing basis, by theme parks, Disney extravaganzas, and Omnimax movies.

576. Robert Work. Elevations of the clubhouse of Shoreacres Country Club, Sheridan Road, Lake Bluff, c. 1920-21. Ink on linen, approx. 93.5 x 71.1 cm. Gift of Bowen Blair, Executor of the Estate of William McCormick Blair, 1989.

577. Booth/Hansen and Associates. Remodeling plans with front door elevation and molding profiles of the Shoreacres Country Club, c. 1983. Printed Mylar with colored pencil, approx. 76 x 101.5 cm. Lent by Booth/Hansen and Associates, Ltd.

578. John Eberson with A. C. Liska. Elevation and longitudinal section of the Capitol Theatre, Halsted Street near Emerald Avenue, 1923 (now demolished). Ink on linen, approx. 94 x 143 cm. By prior exhange with Three Oaks Wrecking Company, 1990.

579. Bennett, Parsons and Frost; Edward Bennett, designer. General plan of Grant Park, traced by J. F. B., December 1925. Ink on linen, 67 x 95 cm. Gift of the City of Chicago, Chicago Park District, 1982.

580. Bennett, Parsons and Frost, and J. H. Lambert, associate architect. Plan, section, and elevation details, Buckingham Memorial Fountain, 1925. Ink on linen, 67 x 95 cm. Gift of Edward H. Bennett, Jr., 1953.

581. Marcel Loyau. Two maquettes for the sea horses, Buckingham Fountain, 1927. Bronze mounted on a limestone base, each 25.5 x 56 x 13 cm. Lent by Mr. and Mrs. Edward H. Bennett, Jr.

582. McNally and Quinn. Elevations, sections, and plans of the John Bigane and Sons Coal Office, and probable speakeasy, 3596 South Archer Avenue at South Irving Avenue, delineated by E. Nowlen and J. Storey, 1927. Black and brown ink on linen, 73.7 x 72.5 cm. Gift of J. Edwin Quinn, 1980.

583. Burnham Brothers, with Nimmons, Carr and Wright. Proposed Chicago Yacht Club on the lakefront at Monroe Street, 1928. Color on photoprint, mounted on board, 46.3 x 91 cm. Gift of George F. Getz, 1972.

584. George Fred Keck. Perspective rendering of the Miralago Ballroom, Wilmette, 1929. Watercolor on paper, mounted on board, 37.5 x 47 cm. Lent by the State Historical Society of Wisconsin.

585. Winold Reiss. Interior designs for lobby and club murals of the Tavern Club, 333 North Michigan Avenue, c. 1928-29. Colored crayon and gouache on paper, approx. 36.9 x 52.4, and silver, gouache, and graphite on paper, 37.5 x 50.5 cm. Restricted gifts respec-

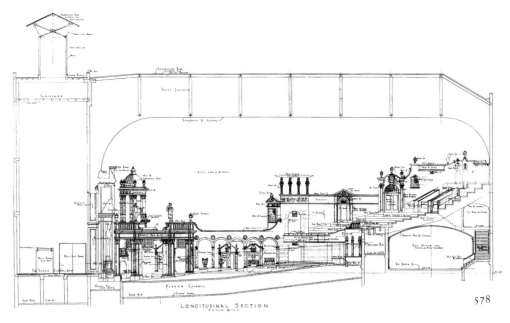

LONGITUDINAL SECTION

578

tively: by exchange, Carson, Pirie, Scott and Company, Urban Investment and Development Company, National Wrecking Company, and Luigi H. and Manly Mumford, 1989.

586. Voorhees, Gmelin and Walker. Preliminary design proposal, Tower of Water and Light, Century of Progress Exposition, delineated by Ralph Walker, c. 1929. Pencil on tracing paper, mounted on board, 61 x 58 cm. Restricted gift of Edward H. Bennett, Jr., Mrs. Michael Goodkin, Andrew McNally III, Mrs. C. Phillip Miller, Mrs. Roderick Webster, and James Wells in honor of Mrs. Eugene A. Davidson, 1980.

587. Voorhees, Gmelin and Walker; Ralph Walker, designer. Perspective rendering of the final design of the proposed Tower of Water and Light, Century of Progress Exposition, delineated by John Wenrich, 1930. Pencil and watercolor on illustration board, 66.5 x 44.6 cm. Gift of Haines Lundberg Waehler in honor of their Centennial, 1983. (See plate 133.)

588. Henry Harringer. Perspective rendering, proposed Ziegfield Fashion Theatre for the Century of Progress Exposition, 1930. Charcoal and pencil on tracing paper, 37.5 x 51.9 cm. Gift of Olaf Harringer, 1982.

589. Holabird and Root with Andrew Rebori. Preliminary elevation study of the entrance to the Streets of Paris at the Century of Progress Exposition, 1933. Graphite and crayon on tracing paper, 54 x 51.8 cm. Lent by the Chicago Historical Society.

590. Holabird and Root with Andrew Rebori. General plan of the Streets of Paris at the Century of Progress Exposition, 1933. Lineprint on paper, 55.9 x 86.4 cm. Lent by the Chicago Historical Society.

591. Paul Philippe Cret. Preliminary elevation study, Century of Progress Exposition, c. 1930. Pencil and colored pencil on tracing paper, 36 x 154 cm. Restricted gift of Benefactors of Architecture, John Buck and Stuart Nathan, 1987.

592. Paul Philippe Cret. Preliminary study of east and west elevations of the Hall of Science, Century of Progress Exposition, October 1, 1930. Pencil and colored pencil on tracing paper, 50 x 93.3 cm. Restricted gift of William B. Alter, Balcor Company, and Mr. and Mrs. David C. Hilliard, 1987.

593. Paul Philippe Cret. South elevation of the Hall of Science, Century of Progress Exposition, March 12, 1931. Pencil and colored pencil on tracing paper, 46 x 91.3 cm.

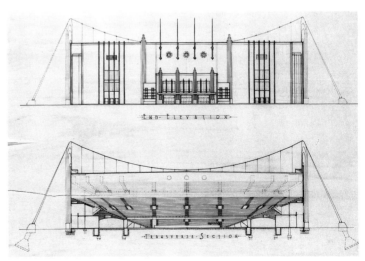

598   601

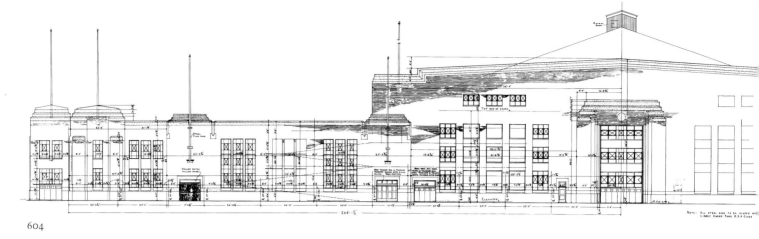

604

Restricted gift of Stuart Nathan, Richard Stein, and Mr. and Mrs. David Hilliard, 1987.

594.   Paul Philippe Cret. Axonometric drawing of the Hall of Science, Century of Progress Exposition, March 30, 1931. Pencil and colored pencil on tracing paper, 106.5 x 141 cm. Fellows of Architecture Society, 1987.

595.   Paul Philippe Cret. Elevation detail of southeast pavilion looking west; plan detail, Hall of Science, Century of Progress Exposition, March 2, 1931. Pencil and colored pencil on tracing paper, 64.5 x 125.5 cm. Restricted gift of the Architecture Society Fellows, 1987.

596.   Paul Philippe Cret. Section showing painted decoration for the Hall of Science, Century of Progress Exposition, March 2, 1931. Pencil and colored pencil on tracing paper, 74.4 x 104 cm. Through prior gift of Carson, Pirie, Scott and Company, and restricted gift of Miglin-Beitler Development, 1989.

597.   Paul Philippe Cret. Elevation of the interior of the Hall of Science, Century of Progress Exposition, January 27, 1932. Pencil and colored pencil on tracing paper, 35 x 39 cm. Restricted gift of Gordon Lee Pollack, 1990.

598.   Alfonso Iannelli. Elevation of the Magic Mountain Enchanted Island, Century of Progress Exposition, December 15, 1933.

Pencil and colored pencil on tracing paper, 41.3 x 60.4 cm. Through prior gift of the Three Oaks Wrecking Company, 1987.

599.   Schmidt, Garden and Martin. Bird's-eye view of the Italian Village for the Century of Progress Exposition, 1933. Lineprint on polyester film, 45.7 x 55.9 cm. Courtesy of Schmidt, Garden and Erikson.

600.   Mario de Renzi and Adalberto Libera, with Alex V. Capraro, associate architect. Working drawings for the Italian Pavilion, Century of Progress Exposition, 1932-33. Blueprints, 71.3 x 97.8 and 71.6 x 98.8 cm. Lent by the Chicago Historical Society.

601.   Klekamp and Whitmore. End elevation and transverse section of a hockey stadium for the Century of Progress Exposition, 1932. Black and brown ink on tracing paper, 65.4 x 100.6 cm. Lent by the Chicago Historical Society.

602.   Goes Lithograph Company; Sándor, designer. Poster for the Century of Progress Exposition, 1934. Lithograph, 101.6 x 66.9 cm. Lent by Special Collections, The University Library, University of Illinois at Chicago. (See plate 134.)

603.   Howells, Hood and Fouilhoux; Leo J. Weissenborn, associate architects; Ernest A. Grunsfeld, Jr., interior architect. Study for the auditorium and a longitudinal section through auditorium, WGN Studio addition, Chicago Tribune Tower, 1934. Pencil and col-

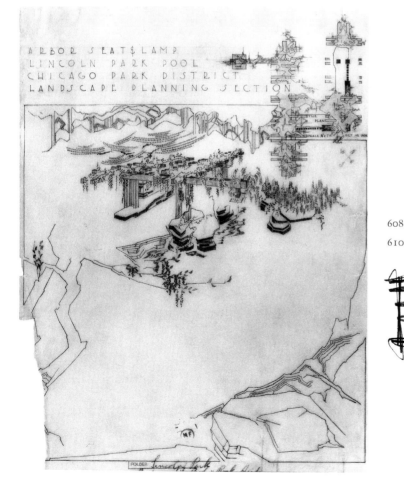

608

610

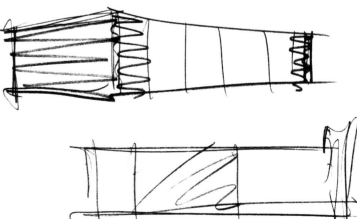

ored pencil on tracing paper, 38 x 58.3 and 37.8 x 63.5 cm. Gift of Mr. and Mrs. Ernest A. Grunsfeld III, 1980.

604. A. Epstein. Elevations on Halsted Street and Dexter Park, and spandrel sections of the International Amphitheatre for the Union Stockyard and Transit Company, September 8, 1934. Ink on linen, each 77 x 125 cm. Lent by A. Epstein and Sons International, Inc.

605. A. Epstein. Model showing the 200-foot span arches of the International Amphitheatre, destroyed by fire May 19, 1934. Soldered and welded metal, in a glass vitrine, 15 x 71 x 35 cm. Lent by A. Epstein and Sons International, Inc.

606. Rapp and Rapp. Elevations of the Will Rogers Theatre, Belmont and Parkside avenues, 1935 (now demolished). Pencil on tracing paper. Lent by the Chicago Historical Society.

607. Alfred Caldwell. Drawing for a gateway, Lincoln Park Lily Pool, April 20, 1937. Pencil and colored pencil on tracing paper, 30.5 x 61.4 cm. Lent by Chicago Park District Special Collections.

608. Alfred Caldwell. Arbor seat and lamp, Lincoln Park Lily Pool, October 10, 1936. Pencil and colored pencil on tracing paper, 30.3 x 43.2 cm. Lent by Chicago Park District Special Collections.

609. Alfred Caldwell. Chicago Park District central landscape study for Northerly Island, March 29, 1938. Ink and colored pencil on tracing paper, 33.8 x 127 cm. Lent by Chicago Park District Special Collections.

610. Ludwig Mies van der Rohe. Five sheets showing plans, elevations, and detail sketches of a weekend lodge on wooded terrain, 1941. Pencil on paper, each 15.2 x 21.1 cm. Through prior gift of Three Oaks Wrecking Company, 1990.

611. Ludwig Mies van der Rohe, assisted by Joseph Fujikawa. Study model of the Arts Club of Chicago, 109 East Ontario Street, c. 1949. Masonite, cardboard, wood, and plastic, 30 x 75.5 x 144 cm. Gift of the Arts Club of Chicago, 1987.

612. Art Paul, designer. Rabbit Head Design for Playboy Enterprises, Inc., 1953. Black and white glossy print, 20.3 x 25.4 cm. Lent by Playboy Enterprises, Inc.

613. Art Paul, designer. Cover of *Playboy Magazine*, April 1956. Ink on paper, 20.3 x 25.4 cm. Lent by Playboy Enterprises, Inc.

614. Robert L. Taege and Associates; Paul Magierek, principal designer. Exterior rendering of the Playboy Resort and Country Club, Lake Geneva, Wisconsin, 1969. Ink on Mylar, 35.6 x 45.7 cm. Courtesy of Playboy Enterprises, Inc.

614

616

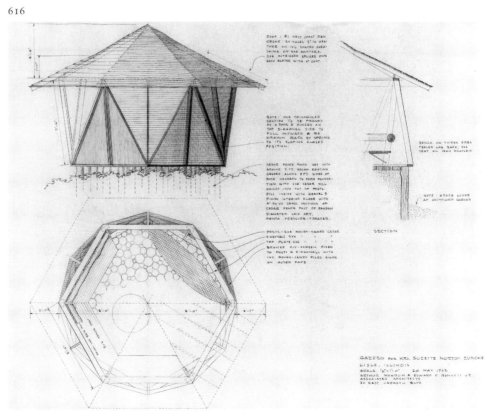

619

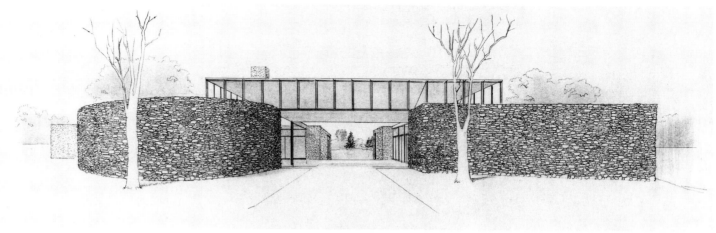

615. Himmel Bonner. Views of the Playboy Corporate Offices, 680 North Lake Shore Drive, 1988, delineated by Darcy R. Bonner, Jr., and James Stapleton, 1988. Four photomontaged and collaged prints on paper, mixed media, three 30.5 x 25.5, one 30.5 x 76.2 cm. Lent by Darcy R. Bonner, Jr., Scott Himmel, James Stapleton, and David Piper.

616. Brenner Danforth Rockwell. Perspective view of dining room for Horowitz Restaurants, c. 1965-66. Pencil on paper, 46.4 x 61.4 cm. Gift of H. P. Davis Rockwell and George Danforth, 1990.

617. David Haid and Associates. Site plan and elevation and exploded construction view of the Hickman Weekend House, Lakeshore Road, Lakeside, Michigan, 1965. Two sheets of polyester film, each 45.7 x 55.8 cm. Printed from a Hedrich-Blessing photograph, courtesy the Chicago Historical Society.

618. Arthur R. Myhrum and Edward H. Bennett, Jr. Plans, section, and elevations of a guest house for Mrs. Suzette Morton Zurcher, Lisle, 1964. Two sheets, pencil on tracing paper; elevations: 45.5 x 70.2; plans: 45.6 x 70.8 cm. Gifts of Charlotte W. Myhrum, 1991.

619. Arthur R. Myhrum and Edward H. Bennett, Jr. Plan, section, and elevation of the gazebo for the Mrs. Suzette Morton Zurcher House, Lisle, 1962. Pencil on tracing paper, 48.2 x 61 cm. Gift of Charlotte W. Myhrum, 1991.

620. Arthur R. Myhrum and Edward H. Bennett, Jr. Site plan and west elevation study of the Visitor Center, Morton Arboretum, Lisle, April 16, 1971. Pencil on tracing paper; plan: 61 x 91; elevation: 55.5 x 86 cm. Gifts of Charlotte W. Myhrum, 1991.

621. Brenner Danforth Rockwell. Sections of the Great Ape House, Lincoln Park Zoo, 2200 North Cannon Drive, 1973. Pencil and watercolor on tracing paper, each approx. 26.6 x 71.5 cm. Gift of Rachael, John and Ariel Brenner, 1985.

622. Garret Eakin and John Banks, Chicago Art and Architecture. Axonometric drawing of Johnny's Restaurant, 161 East Huron Street, delineated by James Smith, 1979 (now demolished). Ink on Mylar, 97.7 x 69 cm. Gift of Chicago Art and Architecture, 1981.

623. Skidmore, Owings and Merrill; Myron Goldsmith, partner-in-charge. Four sheets, Lincoln Park Zoo, Large Mammal Complex, delineated by David A. Hansen, c. 1980. Marker on tracing paper; timber wolf habitat plan, 46.4 x 69.8; elephant habitat plan, 45.7 x 86; polar bear pool plan, 47.9 x 54.6; and section through polar bear habitat, 60.3 x 104.1

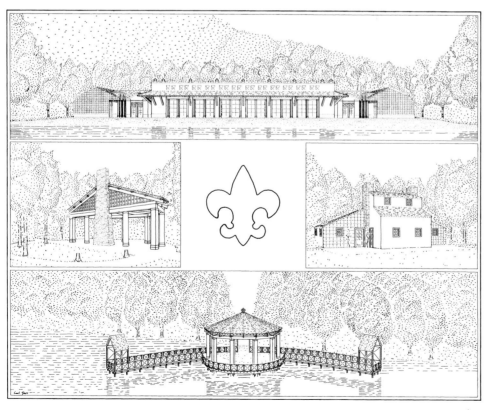

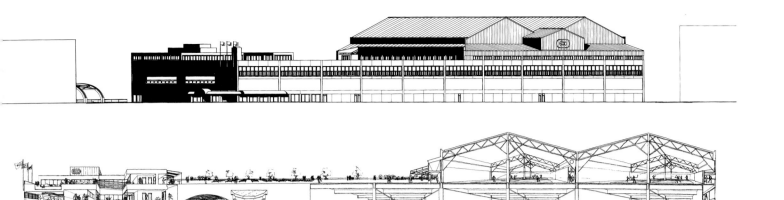

631

cm. Gift of Skidmore, Owings and Merrill, 1982.

624. Tigerman McCurry; Stanley Tigerman, designer. Ontario Street elevation of the Hard Rock Cafe (1984-86) shown in relation to the firm's Commonwealth Edison Substation (1986-89), 63 West Ontario Street, 1984-85. Watercolor on paper, 77.5 x 112 cm. Lent by Tigerman McCurry Architects.

625. The Landahl Group. Mock-up for column decoration in Exercise Playce, within the lower floor of Oakbrook Terrace Tower, 1986 (see cat. no. 262). Glass, cement, and wood, approx. 165.5 x 82 x 51 cm. Lent by Gregory W. Landahl, FAIA, the Landahl Group, Inc.

626. Holabird and Root; Roy Solfisburg, designer. Bird's-eye and cutaway views of the Lester and Dellora Norris Aquatics Center, Northwestern University, Evanston, 1987. Colored printed paper, 76 x 101.5 cm. Lent by Holabird and Root.

627. Tigerman McCurry; Stanley Tigerman, designer. Hoover Outdoor Education Center for Differently Abled Boy Scouts of the Boy Scouts of America, 11285A Fox Road, Yorkville, 1987-91. Perspective views of the fishing pavilion (lower center), winterized cabin (mid-right), swimming pool pavilion (top), activity shelter (left). Printed Mylar, 71 x 91.5 cm. Lent by Tigerman McCurry Architects.

628. Nagle, Hartray and Associates. Axonometric view and studio plan for the Fred Niles Film Studios, remodeled for Oprah Winfrey as Harpo Studios, 110 North Carpenter Street, 1989. Printed Mylar, 91.5 x 71 cm. Lent by Nagle, Hartray and Associates. (See plate 139.)

629. Jordan Mozer and Associates. Bird's-eye view of Cineplex Odeon Theatres, McCormick Road between Lincoln and Devon avenues, 1986-88. Watercolor on paper, 39 x 50.5 cm. Lent by Jordan Mozer and Associates, Ltd.

630. Gelick Foran Associates. Plans, facade

elevation, transverse section, and cutaway perspective for the remodeling of the Esquire Theater, 58 East Oak Street, 1990. Printed paper with pastel, 76.5 x 101.5 cm. Lent by Gelick Foran Associates, Ltd. (See plates 136-37.)

631. Gelick Foran Associates. Cutaway perspective section, site plan, floor plan, and elevation of the remodelings to the East Bank Club, originally designed by Ezra Gordon of Jack Levin and Associates, 500 North Kingsbury Street, 1987-91. Printed paper with pastel, 76.5 x 101.5 cm. Lent by Gelick Foran Associates.

632. Kisho Kurokawa with Fujikawa Johnson and Associates. Exterior and interior drawings of the Sporting Club, 211 North Stetson Avenue, 1988-90. Colored pencils on

bond papers, 59.5 x 84.1 and 62 x 89.3 cm. Lent by Kisho Kurokawa of Kisho Kurokawa Architect and Associates.

633. The Landahl Group. Four glass panels for the 1990 remodeling of the Ventana Restaurant atop the Hyatt Regency Hotel near O'Hare International Airport. Sandblasted glass mounted in a wooden frame, each 37 x 50.5 cm. Lent by Gregory W. Landahl, FAIA, the Landahl Group Inc.

634. Jordan Mozer and Associates. Perspective study of the vestibule of Vivere, in the Italian Village, 71 West Monroe Street, 1990. Watercolor on heavy paper, approx. 57 x 76 cm. Lent by Jordan Mozer and Associates, Ltd.

635. Jordan Mozer and Associates. Rendered

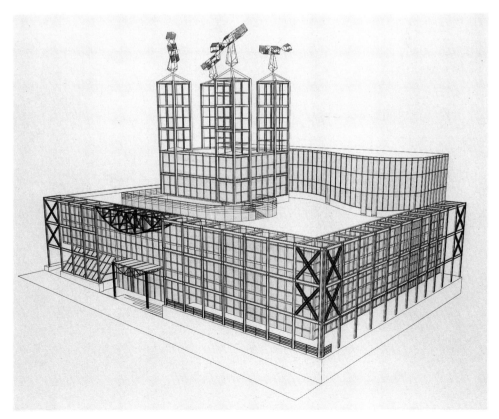

632

elevation of the entry corridor and seating area for Vivere, showing booths and wine-chest cabinet and coat closet, 1990. Cutout watercolor on board, 30.5 x 65.5 cm. Lent by Jordan Mozer and Associates, Ltd.

636. Jordan Mozer and Associates. Perspective study of a chair for Vivere, 1990. Watercolor on board, 34.3 x 65.5 cm. Lent by Jordan Mozer and Associates, Ltd.

637. Jordan Mozer and Associates. Pendant lamp for Vivere, 1990. Copper and slipped glass, diameter approx. 38 cm. Lent by Jordan Mozer and Associates, Ltd.

638. Jordan Mozer and Associates. Chair for Vivere, 1990. Wood and upholstery, 96.5 x 51 x 71.1 cm. Lent by Shelby Williams Industries. (See plate 142.)

639. Hellmuth, Obata and Kassabaum. Model of the old Comiskey Park. Mixed media, 35.5 x 110.5 x 110.5 cm. Lent by the Chicago White Sox.

640. Hellmuth, Obata and Kassabaum. Model of the New Comiskey Park, 1990-91. Mixed media, 40 x 106.7 x 110.5 cm. Lent by the Chicago White Sox.

641. Decker and Kemp. Two perspective

renderings for the Conway Farms Clubhouse, Lake Forest, delineated by Gilbert Gorski, 1991. Pencil and watercolor on heavy paper, each 30 x 38 cm. Lent by Decker and Kemp Architecture and Urban Design.

642. Decker and Kemp. Perspective studies for the ninth green and the practice putting area of the Conway Farms Golf Club, 2200 Conway Road, Lake Forest, delineated by Tuan Tran, 1991. Ink on paper, each approx. 19 x 25.5 cm. Lent by Decker and Kemp Architecture and Urban Design.

643. Booth/Hansen and Associates. Model for the Dunes Club, New Buffalo, Michigan, 1991. Glued Strathmore and foamcore, 41 x 41 x 41 cm. Lent by Booth/Hansen and Associates, Ltd.

644. Tigerman McCurry; Margaret McCurry and Stanley Tigerman, designers. Studies for their house, Lakeside, Michigan, by Stanley Tigerman, 1984. Ink on notepaper, 22 x 30.3 cm. Gift of Stanley Tigerman, 1984.

645. Tigerman McCurry; Margaret McCurry, designer. West elevation, longitudinal section, and floor plans for "Wit's End," Sawyer, Michigan, 1987. Two sheets of ink on heavy paper, each 73.7 x 58.5 cm. Lent by Tigerman McCurry Architects.

646. Schroeder Murchie Laya Associates; Ken Schroeder, principal designer. Elevation for the Boxcar House in Union Pier, Michigan, 1987. Ink on paper, 20.3 x 21.6 cm. Lent by Schroeder Murchie Laya Associates, Ltd.

647. Booth/Hansen and Associates; Lawrence Booth, designer. "Chicken Coop," a summer studio for the architect, Lake Bluff, 1988. Collaged sketches, 35.5 x 45.8 cm. Lent by Booth/Hansen and Associates, Ltd.

648. Landon Architects. Sketch plan and bird's-eye view of the Reilly-Lynch Weekend House, Lakeshore and Victor roads, Lakeside, Michigan, August 2, 1990. Pencil on tracing paper; plan: 30.5 x 43; bird's-eye view: 31 x 27.5 cm. Lent by Landon Architects Ltd.

649. Banks/Eakin. Plans, section, and elevation of additions to the Emig Summer Cottage, Grand Mere, Wisconsin, 1990-91. Colored pencil on printed paper, 71 x 91.5 cm. Lent by Banks/Eakin Architects.

650. Pappageorge/Haymes. Site plan, plans, and elevations of the Nemickas Weekend House, Grand Beach, Michigan, 1991. Ink on paper, 76.8 x 102 cm (framed). Lent by Pappageorge/Haymes Ltd.

651. Bertrand Goldberg Associates. Bird's-eye view of the Lakefront Recreational Center, Gary, Indiana, showing the phased development for the reuse of steel slag landfill to restore lakefront sand dunes, 1990. Printed and toned paper, 101.5 x 127 cm. Bertrand Goldberg Associates, Inc.

642

640

657 a

652. Cordogan, Clark and Associates. Night view of the Fox River Casino, north of Stolp Island, Aurora, 1991. Ink and watercolor on paper, 50.8 x 50.8 cm. Lent by Cordogan, Clark and Associates. (See plate 145.)

653. Schroeder Murchie Laya Associates; Ken Schroeder, principal designer. North Avenue Beach House, 1991. Two oil pastel drawings on paper, each 27.9 x 43.2 cm. Lent by Ken Schroeder, Schroeder Murchie Laya Associates, Ltd.

654. Wheeler Kearns; Lawrence Kearns, designer. Night rendering of a proposal for a prototype pool enclosure for the Chicago Park District, 1991. Ink on Mylar, 45.7 x 144.8 cm. Lent by Wheeler Kearns Architects.

655. Chicago Central Area Committee, University of Illinois at Chicago Design Charette Team "A," architects Darcy Bonner and Werner Seligmann with Linda Nelson and Chris Thomas. Detailed site plan of the Grant Park fairgrounds for the proposed 1992 Chicago World's Fair, 1983. Graphite and colored pencil on buff tracing paper, approx. 91 x 118 cm. Gift of the Chicago Central Area Committee, 1985.

656. Chicago Central Area Committee, University of Illinois at Chicago Design Charette Team "B," architects Peter Eisenmann, Helmut Jahn, and Ronald Krueck with Colby Lewis and Eugene Adaca. Aerial perspective sketch of fairground structures and

waterways for the proposed 1992 Chicago World's Fair, delineated by Helmut Jahn, 1983. Ink and craypas on yellow tracing paper, approx. 92 x 75 cm. Gift of the Chicago Central Area Committee, 1985.

657. Skidmore, Owings and Merrill, and William Brazley and Associates, in connection with Thomas Beeby, Charles W. Moore, Jacquelin T. Robertson, Robert A. M. Stern, and Stanley Tigerman. Perspective view of north lagoon and overall site plan for the proposed 1992 Chicago World's Fair, 1984. Ink and crayon on paper; lagoon: 99.1 x 145.2; plan: 104.5 x 254.3 cm. Gift of the Illinois State Archives, lent by the Chicago Historical Society.

657 b

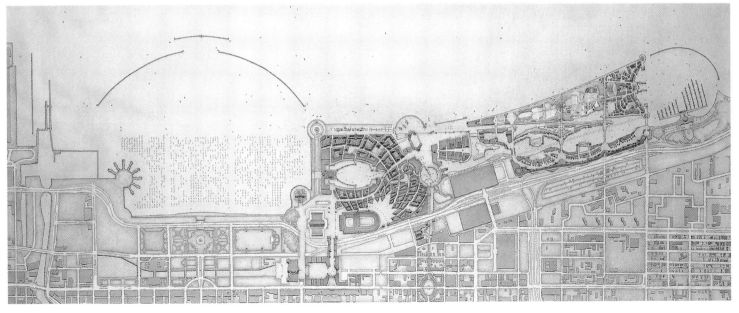

Biographical Glossary

Compiled by Maurice Blanks

David Adler

(1882-1949)

A native of Milwaukee, David Adler attended the Lawrenceville School before entering Princeton University in 1900 to study architecture. Upon graduation in 1904, he went to the Ecole des Beaux-Arts, Paris. He returned to Chicago in 1909 to take a job in the office of Howard Van Doren Shaw, and a year later, he formed a partnership with Henry C. Dangler that ended with Dangler's death in 1917. After a ten-year partnership with Robert Work, Adler established an independent practice as a residential architect in 1928 with a commission in Glencoe from his uncle, D. A. Stonehill. Over the next twenty years he designed elegant country houses, city homes, and apartments for Chicago's elite and gained a reputation for his classical designs and meticulous detailing in a variety of traditional architectural styles.

Alfred S. Alschuler

(1876-1940)

A native Chicagoan, Alfred S. Alschuler received his bachelor's and master's degrees in architecture from the Armour Institute of Technology (now the Illinois Institute of Technology), while occasionally attending classes at The School of The Art Institute of Chicago. In 1900, a year after graduating from the Armour Institute, he took a job in Dankmar Adler's office, where he worked for seven years before starting his own practice in Chicago. For much of his career, Alschuler specialized in the design of industrial architecture, but he also worked on a variety of other building types, including synagogues, theaters, apartments, and office buildings. Alfred Alschuler, Jr., continued his father's legacy with the industrial architecture firm of Friedman, Alschuler and Sincere, which merged with Metz Train Youngren in 1980.

Ira J. Bach

(1907-1985)

Ira Bach was a Chicago planner, public official, and author. Over his long career in public service he was executive director of the Chicago Land Clearance Commission, during the years in which Lake Meadows and Michael Reese Hospital were built; commissioner of city planning; executive director of the Chicago Dwellings Association; the first administrator of the Illinois-Indiana Bi-State Commission; director of city development; chairman of the Commission on Chicago Historical and Architectural Landmarks; and advisor to several successive mayors on planning, economic development, public works, landmarks, and aviation. He was the author of *Chicago on Foot*, which first appeared in 1973, a revised edition of *Chicago's Famous Buildings* (1980), *A Guide to Chicago's Historic Suburbs* (1981), and coauthor (with Mary Lackritz Gray) of *Chicago's Public Sculpture* (1983).

Banks/Eakin

John H. Banks (born 1948)
Garret Eakin (born 1947)

A native of Detroit, Michigan, John H. Banks earned his bachelor of architecture degree in 1972 from the University of Minnesota. He then came to Chicago to take a job with Skidmore, Owings and Merrill, where he worked as a senior designer. In 1968 he co-founded Banks/Eakin. Originally from Franklin, Pennsylvania, Garret Eakin earned his bachelor's degree in architecture from Oklahoma State University in 1971 and his master's from the University of Illinois in 1972. After a short time with Skidmore, Owings and Merrill's office in Chicago, Eakin worked for Perkins and Will from 1974 to 1978. Eakin has also been an associate professor at The School of The Art Institute of Chicago since 1981.

Bruce Beck

(born 1916)

Born in Harvard, Illinois, Bruce Beck attended Cornell College in Iowa and learned to set type with a jobbing printer. He came to Chicago in 1940 and took courses at the Institute of Design, part of the Illinois Institute of Technology, where László Moholy-Nagy was director, before going to work for a printer. After World War II, Beck became an art director at an advertising agency and then worked in the Whitaker-Guernsey studio before starting his own firm in 1954. His clients included Johnson Wax, Jewel, Rand McNally, and Abbott Laboratories. In the late 1960s he and designers in three other firms formed the Design Partnership. In 1985 he edited a book of essays in honor of R. Hunter Middleton, *RHM: Robert Hunter Middleton, The Man and His Letters*. Now retired, Beck prints various publications under his own imprint, The Turtle Press.

Belli and Belli

Edo J. Belli (born 1918)
Anthony Belli (born 1925)
James Belli (born 1947)
Allen Belli (born 1943)

Chicagoan Edo J. Belli received his bachelor's degree in architecture from the Armour Institute of Technology (now the Illinois Institute of Technology) in 1939 and founded the firm Belli and Belli with his brother Anthony in 1941. Edo Belli's sons, Allen J. and James J., joined the firm. Allen started with the firm in 1965, after earning a degree from the University of Illinois, and James joined in 1971, after studying at Notre Dame University and the University of Arizona, and working briefly with C. F. Murphy Associates. Allen and James became principals in the Illinois Belli and Belli company in 1978, and Anthony Belli retired a year later; Edo Belli remains active in the firm.

Alfred Benesch and Company

(founded 1946)

Alfred Benesch came to Chicago from Czechoslovakia, and was employed by structural engineers Lieberman and Hein. When these engineers went out of business during the Depression, Benesch went to work as engineer of grade separations for the Illinois Division of Highways in Springfield. During this period, he also helped initiate a research program in conjunction with the University of Illinois, which produced several seminal studies in bridge design. In 1946, after serving in the army during World War II, he formed the partnership Alfred Benesch and Company. Initially the firm specialized in structural engineering, but later it expanded into bridge design and construction management. The engineering firm played a substantial role in the development of O'Hare International Airport, participating in the initial design and expansion of the two-level roadway supported by unusually expressive splayed piers (1960-86), and the location, design, and construction engineering of the airport's Chicago Transit Authority rail station (1980s). Other recent major projects for which Alfred Benesch and Company has provided the structural engineers include Illinois Center (1970s), the Chicago Mercantile Exchange (1987), and 900 North Michigan Avenue, a mixed-use skyscraper (1988-89).

Edward H. Bennett
(1874-1954)

Born in England, Edward H. Bennett moved to San Francisco in the early 1890s, where he worked for a couple of years before returning to Europe in 1895 and enrolling in the Ecole des Beaux-Arts in Paris. In 1901 he earned his diploma, and in 1902 he returned to the United States to take a job in George B. Post's office in New York City. A year later Bennett moved to Chicago at the invitation of Daniel Burnham, with whom he collaborated on the plan for San Francisco in 1905 and coauthored the renowned *Plan of Chicago* in 1909. Following Burnham's death in 1912, Bennett worked independently until he took William E. Parsons as a partner in 1919, and in 1922 Harry T. Frost joined the pair to establish the firm Bennett Parsons Frost. Bennett was consulting architect to the Chicago Plan Commission until 1930 and was responsible for the general plan of the 1933-34 Century of Progress Exposition. Both independently and in association with others, Bennett was involved in the planning and zoning of more than a dozen American cities.

Booth/Hansen and Associates
Laurence Booth (born 1936)
Paul Hansen (born 1941)

Laurence Booth was born in Chicago and received his bachelor of arts degree from Stanford University in 1958. After attending Harvard University in 1958 and 1959, he went to the Massachusetts Institute of Technology, where in 1960 he received his bachelor of architecture degree. In 1966 he joined in a partnership with James Nagle, and in 1977, with John Hartray, they established the firm Booth, Nagle and Hartray. In 1979 Booth left the firm and, a year later, co-founded Booth/Hansen with Paul Hansen. Booth has been a visiting professor at Harvard University and the University of Illinois at Chicago. Paul Hansen, who was born in Le Mars, Iowa, received his bachelor's degree in architecture from Iowa State University in 1965 and went to work in the office of Harry Weese and Associates, where he later became vice-president and corporate director. While still with Harry Weese in 1976, he returned to school to earn a master of business administration degree from the University of Chicago. In 1980 he left Weese's office to join Laurence Booth in private practice.

Brenner Danforth Rockwell
Daniel Brenner (1917-1977)
George Edson Danforth (born 1916)
H. P. Davis Rockwell (born 1926)

Born in New York City, Daniel Brenner earned his bachelor's degree in architecture from Columbia University in 1939. After graduating, he took a job in the office of Alfred Easton Poor, but he soon moved to Chicago to work with Mies van der Rohe and attend the Illinois Institute of Technology. He took his master of architecture degree in 1949 and worked in Mies's office until 1958, when he began a partnership with Dorothy Turck. In 1961, with George Danforth and H. P. Davis Rockwell, he founded the firm Brenner Danforth Rockwell, where he was a partner until his death in 1977. Born in LaHarpe, Kansas, George Danforth began studying architecture in 1936 at the Armour Institute of Technology in Chicago, and also worked for the architecture firm Granger and Bollenbacher. In 1938 Mies van der Rohe was appointed director of the Department of Architecture at the Armour Institute (subsequently the Illinois Institute of Technology), and Danforth quickly landed a job as a draftsman in Mies's office. In 1940 he received his bachelor's degree but stayed on at IIT for three more years to pursue graduate studies and teach. After two years in the military, he returned to IIT in 1946 to resume teaching, and in 1953 he was hired to organize a new school of architecture for Case Western Reserve University in Cleveland. In 1959, a year after Mies's retirement, Danforth was asked to head the Department of Architecture at IIT, a position that he held until 1981. In 1961 he joined Daniel Brenner and H. P. Davis Rockwell in the firm Brenner Danforth Rockwell, which was succeeded in 1979 by Rockwell Carow Danforth. H. P. Davis Rockwell was born in Waterbury, Connecticut. He received a bachelor of science degree in 1949 from the Massachusetts Institute of Technology and a bachelor of architecture from IIT in 1957. He worked with Mies van der Rohe for three years before co-founding Brenner Danforth Rockwell.

Jacques C. Brownson
(born 1923)

Jacques Brownson received his bachelor of architecture degree in 1948 and his master's degree in 1954, both from the Illinois Institute of Technology. In 1957 he worked with Earl Bluestein, Alfred Caldwell, Ludwig Hilberseimer, and Reginald Malcolmson on a plan sponsored by the Southside Planning Board for the South Side of Chicago. In the 1960s Brownson worked on the Chicago Civic Center (1965) with C. F. Murphy and Associates, Loebl, Schlossman and Bennett, and Skidmore, Owings and Merrill. He also served as the managing architect for the City of Chicago Public Building Commission. Brownson, who retired in 1986, lives in Denver, Colorado.

Ernest Burgess (1886-1986)

Ernest Burgess was a University of Chicago sociologist who, with Robert Park, attempted to reveal regularities in the socio-spatial order that are similar to the ways that plant communities fill ecological niches in the natural world. Using Chicago both as a laboratory and as a model of the archetypal American city, Burgess and Park's "concentric ring" model depicts a city in which socioeconomic status ascends with each step outward from a strongly dominant central business district. Immigrant groups enter at the center and push outward, displacing those in the next outward ring through a process of "invasion and succession." The result is a classic picture of social patterning in the pre-automobile metropolis. Burgess came to the University of Chicago in 1916 and was active in civic affairs. He served as director of the Juvenile Protective Organization, the Chicago Crime Commission, and the Chicago Social Hygiene Council.

Ralph H. Burke
(1884-1956)

Born in Chicago, Ralph H. Burke graduated from the Massachusetts Institute of Technology in 1906 with a bachelor's degree in civil engineering. Burke began his engineering career in Chicago's Sanitation District, where he was employed as a construction supervisor from 1906 to 1920. In 1915 he was briefly chief engineer for the Illinois Waterway Commission. From 1920 to 1934 he worked in the private sector as chief engineer and general superintendent for the Forschner Contracting Company in Chicago. He returned to public service in 1934 as chief engineer for the Chicago Park District. He founded his own engineering firm, Ralph Burke and Associates, in 1946. The firm's major projects in the Chicago metropolitan area include Meigs Field (1948), O'Hare International Airport (1948-53), an award-winning North Lake Shore Drive improvement (c. 1944), the underground Grant Park Garage (1956), and the Pal-Waukee Airport (1978). Guided by Burke's protégé Larry Donoghue, who began working for the firm at its inception, the company has completed several important projects, including master planning for the Richmond International Airport in Virginia (1977), the Lexington Blue Grass Airport in Kentucky (1986), and Rapid City Regional Airport in South Dakota (1985).

Burnham and Root
D. H. Burnham and Company
Burnham Brothers
Burnham and Hammond
Daniel Hudson Burnham (1846-1912)
John Wellborn Root (1850-1891)
Hubert Burnham (1882-1968)
Daniel H. Burnham, Jr. (1886-1961)
C. Herrick Hammond (1882-1969)

Born in Henderson, New York, Daniel Hudson Burnham moved to Chicago with his family in 1854. He was rejected by both Harvard and Yale universities, and in 1867 he went to work for a year in William LeBaron Jenney's Chicago architecture firm, Loring and Jenney. He took a job at Carter, Drake and Wight in 1870, where he met John Wellborn Root, with whom he went into partnership in 1873. Root died prematurely in 1891, and the firm became D. H. Burnham and Company. In

1907 Burnham's son Hubert joined the firm, as did Daniel Burnham, Jr., who had studied at Harvard. Hubert studied at the Ecole des Beaux-Arts, Paris, in 1906-07, and returned to the Ecole in 1909-10. When Burnham died in 1912, his long-time employee Ernest R. Graham took over, changing the firm's name to Graham, Burnham and Company. In 1917 the firm split; Graham went into partnership with Anderson, Probst and White, and Burnham's sons revived the name D. H. Burnham and Company. In 1929 they again changed the name of the firm, this time to Burnham Brothers. In 1933 they joined C. Herrick Hammond of Chatten and Hammond, and until the firm was dissolved in the 1980s, it was known as Burnham and Hammond.

Dave Chapman (1909-1978)

Trained as an architect at the Armour Institute of Technology in Chicago (now the Illinois Institute of Technology) in the late 1920s, Dave Chapman began his career as a member of the design staff at the Century of Progress Exposition in Chicago in 1933. After the Exposition Chapman worked as an architect for Montgomery Ward, in the company's corporate design department, where he was appointed director of the product design division. After only a short time, Chapman left Montgomery Ward and started his own product design and consulting firm in 1935. Among the early employees at Dave Chapman were William Goldsmith and Kim Yamasaki, who both became partners in 1955, and the firm was renamed Dave Chapman, Goldsmith and Yamasaki. The firm grew to twenty-three full-time designers in the 1960s with such clients as Radio Corporation of America, Simoniz Corporation, and Outboard Marine Corporation. In 1970 Chapman returned to independent consulting, but the firm survives in Chicago as Goldsmith, Yamasaki, Specht.

Frank D. Chase (1877-1937)

Born in Riverside, Illinois, Frank D. Chase attended the Massachusetts Institute of Technology, and established his own firm, Frank D. Chase, Chicago engineers and architects, in 1913. Chase, who had also worked as an architect with the Western Electric Company, Illinois Central Railroad, and General Motors, specialized in industrial projects, such as railroads and newspaper plants.

Serge Chermayeff
(born 1900)

Serge Chermayeff emigrated to England in 1910 from his native Russia to attend Harrow School. From 1922 to 1925 he studied architecture in various schools across Europe, and in 1930 he went into private practice in London. While in England, he was active in MARS (Modern Architectural Research Society), the British equivalent of CIAM (International Congress of Modern Architects), and between 1933 and 1936 Chermayeff often collaborated with the architect Erich Mendelsohn. Chermayeff moved to New York to take a teaching position in the Department of Art at Brooklyn College, New York. In 1946 László Moholy-Nagy, the director of the Institute of Design in Chicago, died, and Chermayeff was appointed his successor. After he resigned in 1951, Chermayeff was a visiting critic at the Massachusetts Institute of Technology for one year, before taking a full professorship at Harvard University. In 1962, at the invitation of Paul Rudolph, he joined the faculty at Yale University, where he stayed until his retirement in 1971.

Chicago Plan Commission

Approved by the City Council, this advisory commission was established in conjunction with the Plan of Chicago in 1909. Relying on Daniel Burnham's and Edward Bennett's recommendations, the commission tried to plan for the future as engineers and architects completed various public works projects, such as Wacker Drive and bridges over the Chicago River, in anticipation of rapid urban growth. The Plan was commissioned by Chicago's leading businessmen, and one primary goal of the commission was to facilitate the efficient, convenient, and economical movements of commercial goods. Members of the commission included city department heads, park board officials, and officials from county, state, and federal agencies. Charles Wacker was chairman from 1909 to 1926, and James Simpson was chairman from 1926 to 1935.

Stuart Cohen (born 1942)

Born in Chicago, Stuart Cohen attended Cornell University, where he received his bachelor of architecture degree in 1965 and his master's degree in 1967. He then worked in New York in the offices of Richard Meier, Grunzen and Partners, and Philip Johnson before returning to Chicago in 1972 to start his own firm. From 1978 to 1981 he was associated with the firm Sisco/Lubotsky Associates and Stuart Cohen. In 1981 he formed a partnership with Anders J. Nereim, which lasted for seven years. Cohen then established his own firm, Stuart Cohen and Associates, and in 1991 he formed a partnership with Julie Hacker. Cohen, a member of the Chicago Seven, was a co-organizer of the 1976 "Chicago Architects" exhibition and currently serves as a professor at the University of Illinois at Chicago.

Carl W. Condit
(born 1914)

Professor Condit has been one of the most important chroniclers of the history of modern architecture in Chicago. Condit received a B.S. from Purdue University in 1936, an M.A. from the University of Cincinnati in 1939, and a Ph.D. from the University of Cincinnati in 1941. He began his long and varied career in Cincinnati, as an engineer for the New York Central Railroad and as a teacher of mathematics. He briefly taught English at Northwestern University and humanities at Carnegie Institute of Technology, before starting his tenure at Northwestern, which lasted from 1946 to 1982. At Northwestern he held appointments in English, history, art history, and urban affairs. Among his books were The Rise of the Skyscraper (1952), which led to his classic text The Chicago School of Architecture (1964); the two volumes of American Building Art, one on the nineteenth century, the other on the twentieth century; two volumes on Chicago in the twentieth century entitled Chicago, 1910-29 and Chicago, 1930-70; and The Port of New York: A History of the Rail and Terminal System from the Beginnings to Pennsylvania Station (1980). Forthcoming is The New York Skyscraper: Technological, Architectural, Urbanistic History, which Condit has written with Sarah Landau.

Oswald Cooper
(1879-1940)

Born in Mount Gilead, Ohio, Cooper studied lettering with Fredric Goudy at the Frank Holme School of Illustration in Chicago. In 1904 he formed Bertsch and Cooper with Fred Bertsch. The firm became a leader in providing typesetting, lettering, and layout services to Chicago's business community. Cooper was also a respected type designer. Among his best-known faces were Cooper Black, Cooper Hilite, Cooper Modern, and Cooper Oldstyle. Cooper was active in the Society of Typographic Arts and was one of the first members of 27 Chicago Designers.

Augustus Curtis
(1865-1931)

Born in Pennsylvania, Curtis attended The School of The Art Institute of Chicago. In 1890 he moved to Marinette, Wisconsin, to help found the M & M Box Company, where he served as secretary. He was also part-owner and business manager of the magazine Popular Mechanics. In 1900, along with Arthur Morgan and the inventor Everly L. Haines, he founded the National X-Ray Reflector Company in Chicago to manufacture the reflectors essential to indirect lighting, modern street lighting, and architectural illumination. X-Ray Reflectors were used on the first modern flood-lighted building, New York's Woolworth building, in 1913, and the firm's Lumitone system provided the remote control for the changing lighting display on Chicago's Buckingham Fountain. By 1924, the firm had changed its name to the Curtis Lighting Company and had offices in New York and Antwerp. The firm also had a building at the Century of Progress

Exposition in Chicago in 1933-34. Before Curtis's death, his son Kenneth assumed control of the firm. In the late 1950s, the firm began to undertake a series of mergers and changes of corporate identity, until finally, as the Alzack Division of Curtis Electro Corporation, it left Chicago in 1975.

Walter D'Arcy Ryan
(1870-1934)

Born in Nova Scotia, Walter D'Arcy Ryan was an illumination engineer (the neologism may first have been applied to him) who pioneered the use of lighting for architectural effect. Educated in Quebec and at the Massachusetts Institute of Technology, he went to work for the Thomas-Houston Company in Lynn, Massachusetts, in 1892, the same year the company merged with General Electric. When he began to specialize in illumination, he convinced GE to open an illumination engineering laboratory in Lynn; the laboratory moved to Schenectady, New York, in 1909. Ryan, a co-founder of the Illumination Engineering Society in 1906, did much to develop the profession as a science and as an art. He developed a photometer in 1901 and extensively researched lighting methods and illumination efficiency. Ryan engineered the floodlighting of the Singer Building in New York City in 1907; Niagara Falls for thirty nights in 1907, and permanently in 1925; the Hudson-Fulton celebration in New York in 1909; and the San Francisco Panama Pacific Exposition in 1915. With his "path of gold" streetlighting for Market Street in San Francisco in 1916, Ryan originated modern intensive street lighting, and he was the director of illumination for the Century of Progress Exposition in Chicago in 1933-34.

Decker and Kemp
Howard Decker (born 1949)
Kevin A. Kemp (born 1959)

A native of Evanston, Illinois, Howard Decker graduated from Northwestern University in 1972 with a bachelor of science degree. In 1978 he received his master's degree in architecture from the University of Illinois at Chicago. He started the firm of Decker and Kemp with Kevin Kemp in 1986, after working with Nagle Hartray and Associates, where he had become an associate partner. Decker was named Outstanding Young Architect of the Year in 1988 by the Chicago Chapter of the American Institute of Architects. He has served as a coeditor of *The Chicago Architectural Journal*, a contributing editor for *Inland Architect* magazine, and a founding board member of the Chicago Architectural Press. Born in Riverside, California, Kevin A. Kemp received his bachelor's degree in architecture from the University of Wisconsin at Milwaukee, where he also completed the master's program in 1982. He worked for the Chicago office of Skidmore, Owings and Merrill before co-founding Decker and Kemp.

Charles Dearing (1903-1972)

After graduating from George Washington University, Charles Dearing worked on the staff of the Brookings Institution in Washington, D.C., from 1929 to 1957. During the 1940s, Dearing advised the California legislature's Interim Committee on Highways and worked as a consultant to the United States Office of Defense Transportation, among many additional consulting positions related to national transportation policies. Dearing actively supported the toll-road movement, which allowed modern highways of advanced design to be constructed quickly in order to service the rapidly increasing numbers of motorists. Opened in 1940, the Pennsylvania Turnpike was the nation's first modern toll highway. Dearing had worked with Pace Associates to design an up-to-date system that eliminated the traffic hazards and highway design failures of earlier turnpikes. Dearing was the executive director of the Illinois State Toll Highway Commission from 1956 to 1962, and was director of research and planning from 1962 to 1964. As an economist, he coauthored, with Wilfred Owen, several studies about tollways and national transportation, including *National Transportation Policy* (1949) and *Toll Roads and the Problem of Highway Modernization* (1951).

William Ferguson Deknatel
(1907-1973)

Chicagoan William Ferguson Deknatel graduated from Princeton University in 1929 and left for Paris in 1930 to study at the Ecole des Beaux-Arts. That year he met and married Geraldine Eager, an interior design student at the Ecole, and the two returned to the United States in 1932 to study with Frank Lloyd Wright on the Taliesin Fellowship. After a brief return to Europe, where Deknatel worked in the office of André Lurcat, the couple settled in Chicago and opened an architectural and interior design firm specializing in suburban houses. Deknatel retired from practice in 1971.

Jay Doblin (1920-1989)

Jay Doblin began his industrial design career in 1939 as an office boy in Raymond Loewy's design firm in New York. After graduating from the Pratt Institute, he remained with Loewy, and eventually became an executive designer. In 1954 Doblin left Loewy and was appointed director of the Institute of Design at the Illinois Institute of Technology in Chicago. In 1964, while serving as the director of the Institute of Design and as the co-director of the School of Architecture at IIT with Mies van der Rohe, Doblin and several others started Unimark International, which grew into the largest graphic design firm in the world. Doblin resigned as director of the Institute of Design in 1969. For both his academic and professional achievements, Doblin received the Industrial Design Society of

America Personal Recognition Award. He was also a fellow of both the IDSA and the Royal Society of Arts.

Deborah Doyle
(born 1952)

A native of Chicago, Deborah Doyle received her bachelor of architecture degree from the Illinois Institute of Technology in 1975 and finished her graduate work at the Architectural Association in London in 1976. She then returned to Chicago to work in the office of Stanley Tigerman and Associates until 1980. She spent that year as an exchange professor at the Université de Paris, and in 1981 she returned to Chicago to open her own firm, Deborah Doyle and Associates. She has also served as an adjunct professor of architecture at the University of Illinois at Chicago.

Dubin, Dubin and Moutoussamy
Henry Dubin (1892-1963)
George Dubin (1890-1958)
Arthur Dubin (born 1923)
John T. Black (born 1917)
John Moutoussamy (born 1922)

A native Chicagoan, Henry Dubin received a degree in architecture from the University of Illinois in 1915 and won the Francis J. Plym Fellowship for European Study. Upon his return to Chicago, he went to work with his brother George in the firm Dubin and Eisenberg, which became Dubin and Dubin in 1932. Henry's sons, Arthur and Martin, later joined the firm. Arthur Dubin, who earned his bachelor's degree in architecture from the University of Michigan, has been a principal in the firm since 1950. Martin Dubin received his bachelor's degree in architecture from the University of Illinois and was named a principal in 1952. In 1965 John T. Black became a principal in the firm, which was renamed Dubin, Dubin and Black. Black, who received his bachelor of science degree in architectural engineering from the University of Oklahoma in 1942 and his master's in architecture from Harvard University in 1943, worked as an architect and planner for Michael Reese Hospital (1948-54) and Pace Associates (1954-64). In 1966 John W. Moutoussamy, who received his bachelor of science degree in architecture from the Illinois Institute of Technology, became a principal in the firm, which was renamed Dubin, Dubin, Black and Moutoussamy. In 1978 John Black retired and the firm became Dubin, Dubin and Moutoussamy. John Moutoussamy's son, Claude Louis, joined the firm in 1970 after receiving a degree in architecture from the University of Illinois at Chicago, and he has been a principal since 1990. Representing the third generation of Dubins, Peter Arthur Dubin earned a bachelor of fine arts in architecture at the Rhode Island School of Design in 1976 and a master's degree from the Massachusetts Institute of Technology in 1984, the year he joined his father's firm. He has been a principal since 1990.

Ray and Charles Eames
Charles Eames (1907-1978)
Ray Eames (1916-1988)

Born in St. Louis, Charles Eames graduated from the Washington University School of Architecture in 1926 and then worked for the St. Louis architecture firm of Trueblood and Graf until 1927. He established his own practice in St. Louis in 1930, and in 1937 he was appointed by Eliel Saarinen to head the Department of Experimental Design at Cranbrook Academy in Bloomfield Hills, Michigan. While working in Saarinen's office on furniture designs, he met Ray Kaiser, who was born in Sacramento, California, and studied painting with Hans Hoffmann from 1933 until 1939, when she began attending Cranbrook Academy. Eames and Kaiser, who were married in 1941, went on to establish one of the most famous design partnerships of the twentieth century. They opened their first workshop in Los Angeles, where Charles had been hired to design sets for the film studios of Metro-Goldwyn-Mayer. The Eameses began designing laminated and molded plywood furniture for the Evans Products Company of Detroit, and their workshop became the southern California headquarters for the firm. After a successful exhibition of the Eameses' work at the Museum of Modern Art in 1946, the Evans Company sold its interests in the Eameses' furniture to the Herman Miller Furniture Company, which put the now famous "Eames chairs" into mass production. Until Charles's death in 1978, the Eameses continued to collaborate on a wide variety of projects, ranging from filmmaking to architecture and industrial design.

A. Epstein and Sons
Abraham Epstein (1888-1958)

Born in Kiev, Ukraine, Abraham Epstein graduated from the Richelieu Gymnasium in Odessa in 1906. A year later he emigrated to the United States, where, in 1911, he graduated from the University of Illinois. In 1921 he opened his office, Abraham Epstein, in Chicago, and the firm grew to thirty employees by 1946, the year the office became A. Epstein and Sons. When their father died in 1958, Sidney and Raymond Epstein took control of the company, which continued growing steadily through the 1970s. At this time the firm opened offices in New York, Los Angeles, London, Paris, Tel Aviv, and Warsaw. The company, which is still based in Chicago, now employs approximately five hundred people and has expanded its services to include architecture, interior design, and construction management.

Abel Faidy (1894-1965)

Abel Faidy was born in Geneva, Switzerland, and studied briefly in England and Germany before returning to Switzerland in 1911 to attend the Académie des Beaux-Arts in Geneva. He then emigrated to the United States where he spent three years in San Francisco working for William Mooser and other architects. Faidy came to Chicago in 1918, after a year in Omaha, and began designing store fixtures. In the 1920s and 1930s he worked as a graphic and furniture designer, and he designed several buildings and interiors even though he was not a registered architect in Illinois. From 1953 until his death, he refused to accept commissions, dedicating his time instead to the independent study of architectural design.

Hugh Ferriss (1889-1962)

During his prodigious career as architectural delineator and design consultant from the 1920s to the 1950s, Hugh Ferriss produced renderings and visionary drawings that contributed as much to the development of the modern skyscraper as did any built work of the period. Born and educated in St. Louis, Ferriss received a degree in architecture from Washington University in 1911. After spending two years as a draftsman for a local firm, he left St. Louis to work for Cass Gilbert in New York City; by 1915 he had established himself as a free-lance architectural delineator. His pioneering series of "zoning envelope studies" (done in collaboration with Harvey W. Corbett), which depicted the form of the skyscraper prescribed by the setback restrictions of the 1916 New York City zoning law, established the powerful rendering style that would make Ferriss the preeminent architectural delineator of his time and an important force in interpreting the psychological power of the skyscraper in modern life. In his highly influential book *Metropolis of Tomorrow* of 1929, he presents his renderings of both existing buildings and "projected trends" and combines the two in his vision of an urban utopia.

Florian-Wierzbowski
Paul Florian (born 1950)
Stephen Wierzbowski (born 1953)

A native Chicagoan, Paul Florian studied art history at Johns Hopkins University before taking a bachelor of arts degree from Washington University, St. Louis, in 1973. He studied architecture at the Architectural Association in London, and received his degree in 1978. Florian worked as a project designer for two years with Sir Robert Matthew at Johnson Marshall and Partners in London, and for Welwyn Garden City. In Chicago Florian briefly worked for Holabird and Root, and in 1983 he received a master of architecture degree from the University of Illinois at Chicago. That year he formed a partnership with Stephen Wierzbowski. Florian has also served as an adjunct studio professor at the University of Illinois at Chicago. Born in Greensburg, Pennsylvania, Stephen Wierzbowski received his bachelor's degree in architecture in 1975 from Carnegie-Mellon University, Pittsburgh. He moved to Chicago in 1977 to take a job with Skidmore, Owings and Merrill, where he worked as a designer until 1981. He returned to school and took a master's degree in architecture in 1982 from the University of Illinois at Chicago. Since 1983 he has been in partnership with Paul Florian. Wierzbowski has also served as president of the Chicago Architectural Club and is a member of the adjunct faculty at the University of Illinois at Chicago.

Fujikawa Johnson and Associates
Joseph Fujikawa (born 1922)
Gerald L. Johnson (born 1936)

Joseph Fujikawa enrolled in architecture school at the University of California in 1940 but completed his undergraduate degree in 1944 at the Illinois Institute of Technology in Chicago, where he also received a master of architecture degree in 1953. In 1944 he joined the Office of Mies van der Rohe, and became a partner shortly before Mies's death in 1969. Seven years later the firm was renamed Fujikawa, Conterato, Lohan and Associates, and in 1982 Fujikawa left to start a firm with Gerald L. Johnson, who had joined Mies's office after graduating from IIT in 1960.

R. Buckminster Fuller
(1895-1983)

A native of Milton, Massachusetts, Richard Buckminster Fuller attended Harvard University from 1913 to 1915, but he never received a college degree. During World War I, Fuller spent two years in the United States Navy as a radio communications officer. After the war, he lived in Chicago and held a variety of industrial jobs while pursuing his own research in lightweight materials and highly efficient structures. He invented the Dymaxion House dwelling machine in 1927 and designed the Dymaxion car in 1932. Fuller began working on geodesic engineering in the 1940s and built the first geodesic domes in the 1950s. In 1959 he took a job as a research professor at Southern Illinois University in Carbondale, where he continued his explorations in design science and taught until 1972.

Gelick Foran Associates
Michael Gelick (born 1940)
Walter J. Foran (born 1940)

Born in Chicago, Michael Gelick received his bachelor's degree in architecture from the University of Minnesota and a master's degree from the Massachusetts Institute of Technology; he has also studied at The School of The Art Institute of Chicago, the University of Illinois at Chicago, and the University of Chicago. He worked for Fitch Larocca Carington Jones as director of design from 1966 to 1971, and in 1969 he established the firm Gelick Foran Associates with Walter J. Foran. Gelick, a former acting director of the School of Architecture, is a professor at

the University of Illinois at Chicago. Also born in Chicago, Walter J. Foran received his bachelor of architecture degree in 1963 from the Illinois Institute of Technology, and he received a master of business administration degree from De Paul University in 1976.

Charles Genther (1907-1987)

Lauded throughout his career as an architect, engineer, city planner, and teacher, Genther earned his B.S. degree in architectural engineering from the University of Oklahoma in 1939, and with the help of an Edward Langley scholarship from the American Institute of Architects, pursued graduate studies in 1939-40 and 1942-43 at the Armour Institute of Technology (later the Illinois Institute of Technology) under Mies van der Rohe and Ludwig Hilberseimer. After working with Skidmore, Owings and Merrill as a designer assigned to the Manhattan Project, Genther worked for one year with Holabird and Root, where he met Wilbur Binford. In February 1946 they founded Pace Associates, a firm offering comprehensive architectural and engineering services. As the firm's chief architect, Genther consulted as an architect-planner, developing town plans during the 1950s for mining companies in Minnesota and Michigan, and designing restaurant service areas and related facilities for the Illinois State Toll Highway Commission. From 1966, Genther taught architecture at the University of Illinois at Chicago, where his dedication to graduate students earned him an Illinois Council/AIA service award. As a student of Mies, Genther praised technology and modernism, and his firm designed buildings and transportation systems that were suited to modern industry and new engineering materials.

Paul Gerhardt, Jr. (1899-1966)

Born in Chicago, Paul Gerhardt, Jr., received his bachelor's degree in 1921 from Yale University. In 1926 he began an independent architectural practice that he maintained until 1952, when he helped found the firm Lundstrom, Blass, Gerhardt and Associates. He is principally known for the work he oversaw during his thirty-seven years as the architect for the City of Chicago, a position to which he was appointed in 1927. Gerhardt, who served on the City Planning Advisory Board for the City of Chicago, was the building commissioner for the city from 1942 to 1947.

Marvin Glass Associates
Marvin Glass (1914-1974)

Marvin Glass Associates was founded in 1942 as a manufacturer of paper, cardboard, and wooden toys. Under the creative direction of Marvin Glass, the firm became an international leader in toy design in the 1960s and 1970s with toys such as Rock'em Sock'em Robots (1954), Ants in the Pants (1969), and Phoney Baloney (1970). Although Glass died in the 1970s, his firm continued to prosper until it dissolved in the late 1980s, spawning a great number of smaller, independent toy design firms in Chicago.

Bruce Goff
(1904-1982)

Bruce Goff, born in Alton, Kansas, and raised in Tulsa, Oklahoma, became an apprentice at the age of twelve in the architecture firm of Rush, Endacott and Rush in Tulsa. In 1930, after having worked with the firm since 1916, he became a partner and the firm was renamed Endacott and Goff. Free of academic training of any kind, he found stimulation not only in the work of other architects, such as Frank Lloyd Wright and Antoni Gaudí, but also in that of painter Gustav Klimt and composer Claude Debussy. Goff left Tulsa during the Depression to work in Chicago for Alfonso Ianelli, a products design firm. After serving with the Seabees in World War II, he became chairman of the School of Architecture at the University of Oklahoma, Norman, where he remained until 1955. He went into private practice, moving from Oklahoma to Missouri and then to Texas, and continued to design primarily domestic architecture.

Bertrand Goldberg (born 1913)

A native of Chicago, Bertrand Goldberg attended Harvard University from 1930 to 1932, the Bauhaus in Berlin in 1932-33, and the Armour Institute of Technology (now the Illinois Institute of Technology) in 1933-34. He worked briefly in Mies van der Rohe's office while in school in Germany, and opened his own firm in 1937 in Chicago. In the 1950s Goldberg began experimenting with curving concrete forms for high-rise construction, and the circular apartment building would later become his signature. Bertrand Goldberg and Associates opened a branch office in Boston in 1964, but Goldberg continues to work in Chicago.

Morton Goldsholl

Morton Goldsholl studied at the Institute of Design under László Moholy-Nagy and Gyorgy Kepes. He founded a design firm in 1942 that specialized in corporate identity programs and package design. The firm designed the famous Motorola logo, the Good Design logo for the 1950s Merchandise Mart exhibitions of the same name, and many other logos and package designs in the 1960s and 1970s.

Gilbert Gorski
(born 1956)

Gilbert Gorski, who was born in Milwaukee, earned a bachelor's degree in architecture from the Illinois Institute of Technology in 1978. He was an associate principal with Lohan Associates until 1989, when he started his own practice specializing in architectural illustration. Gorski taught in the architecture department at IIT from 1985 to 1989, and in 1987 he was awarded the Burnham Prize by the Chicago Architectural Club and received a three-month fellowship at the American Academy in Rome. In 1990 he received the prestigious Hugh Ferriss Memorial Prize from the National Illustrator Society.

Graham, Anderson, Probst and White
Ernest Robert Graham (1886-1936)
Peirce Anderson (1870-1924)
Edward Probst (1870-1942)
Howard Judson White (1870-1936)

Born in Lowell, Massachusetts, Ernest Robert Graham was educated at Coe College in Cedar Rapids, Iowa, and at Notre Dame University. He began his career in 1888 as a draftsman in the office of Burnham and Root, where he was continually promoted to more important positions. After Burnham's death in 1912, Graham assumed control of the firm and renamed it Graham, Burnham and Company. Peirce Anderson, Edward Probst, and Howard Judson White, all longtime Burnham employees, joined Graham as full partners, establishing Graham, Anderson, Probst and White in 1917. It was purchased in 1970 by William Surman, who controls the firm today. Peirce Anderson was born in Oswego, New York, and graduated from Harvard University in 1892. At Daniel Burnham's suggestion, Anderson enrolled in the Ecole des Beaux-Arts, Paris, in 1894, and after four years of architectural study there, he returned to Chicago to take a job with Burnham as chief designer, a position he held until the establishment of Graham, Anderson, Probst and White. Before joining Daniel Burnham's firm in 1898, Chicagoan Edward Probst had worked for various architects, including Francis M. Whitehouse, Harry Wheelock, Simon Eisendradt, and William Brinkman. Probst's sons, Edward E. and Marvin G., followed in their father's footsteps and went to work for Graham, Anderson, Probst and White. Marvin Probst became president of the firm. Chicagoan Howard Judson White briefly studied architecture at the Manual Training School, then took a job as a junior draftsman at D. H. Burnham and Company, where he became a partner two years later. He was then a partner in Graham, Anderson, Probst and White until his death.

Jules Guérin
(1886-1946)

Jules Guérin's work included architectural renderings, murals, book illustrations, and theater set design. Born in St. Louis, Guérin studied at the Ecole des Beaux-Arts with the renowned painters J. B. Constant and J. P. Laurens. He began his career in Chicago, but after 1896 maintained his primary residence

and studio in New York City. Guérin's architectural renderings, most notable of which are those for the *Plan of Chicago*, are distinguished by the simple delineation of essential mass and detail, broad expanses of flat or subtly graded color, and unusual perspectives that combine oblique and extremely high or low vantage points. Guérin translated this technique to mural scale for the Civic Opera House and the Merchandise Mart, both in Chicago. His book illustrations included works for popular magazines, such as *Scribner's*, and for Robert Hichens's *Egypt and its Monuments* (New York, 1908) and Maria Lonsdale's *The Chateaux of Tourraine* (New York, 1906).

David Haid
(1928-1993)

Canadian David Haid came to Chicago to study under Mies van der Rohe at the Illinois Institute of Technology, also taking a job in Mies's office. After receiving his master of science in architecture in 1953, Haid continued working in Mies's office until 1960, when he moved to Texas and went into partnership with the Houston firm Cowell-Neuhaus. In 1963 he returned to Chicago to open his own firm, David Haid and Associates.

Hammond, Beeby and Babka
James Wright Hammond (1918-1976)
Thomas Hall Beeby (born 1941)
Bernard F. Babka (born 1933)

After studying architecture at the Illinois Institute of Technology, James Wright Hammond worked with Eliel and Eero Saarinen before founding his own firm in Chicago in 1961. Thomas Beeby joined Hammond in 1971 to form Hammond, Beeby and Associates. Thomas Beeby was born in Oak Park, Illinois. He attended Cornell University, where he studied under Colin Rowe and John Hejduk, and received his bachelor of science degree in 1964. A year later he received his master's degree from Yale University and then took a job with C. F. Murphy and Associates in Chicago, where he stayed until he went into partnership with James Hammond. Beeby has a long history as an educator, beginning in 1973, when he started teaching at the Illinois Institute of Technology. In 1980 he became director of the School of Architecture at the University of Illinois at Chicago, a position he held until 1985, when he was appointed dean of the School of Architecture at Yale University. In 1992 he left Yale and returned to his firm in Chicago. Bernard F. Babka received his bachelor of architecture from IIT in 1956 and took a job with Pace Associates. Babka joined Bertrand Goldberg Associates in 1961, then joined C. F. Murphy Associates as an associate partner in 1967. In 1977 Babka joined Hammond, Beeby and Associates as a partner and the firm was incorporated under its present name, Hammond, Beeby and Babka.

Henry T. Harringer (1892-1980)

Henry T. Harringer was born in Hamburg, Germany, where he attended the Academy of Applied Art. He later moved to Vienna to work for the Wiener Werkstätte and for the architecture and design firm Falkenstein. In 1918 he married a well-known fashion designer named Anke Berger, and the couple established the firm of Harringer Berger in Hamburg. In 1927 they emigrated to the United States, and Harringer went to work for the advertising agency Erwin Wasey as an art director. In 1929 Harringer co-founded Harringer Jacobson Colvin, a firm that specialized in advertising, packaging, industrial design, and store planning. From 1937 until 1945, when he took a job as art director at Encyclopedia Britannica, Harringer worked independently in Chicago as a packaging and industrial designer. Harringer left Encyclopedia Britannica in 1958 to pursue his interests in landscape and portrait painting, although he continued to work with various accounts that he had established earlier in his career.

Ludwig Karl Hilberseimer
(1885-1967)

Ludwig Karl Hilberseimer was born in Karlsruhe, Germany, where he studied architecture at the Technische Hochschule. After World War I he was a member of Novembergruppe, a revolutionary group of artists and architects, and was active in the Berlin Dada movement. In the 1920s he practiced architecture and was also active as a writer, curator, art and architecture critic, and city-planning theoretician. At this time he was a European correspondent for the *Chicago Tribune* and authored several important works on architecture. In 1928 he was appointed master of housing and city planning at the Bauhaus. When the school was closed in 1933, he went into private practice. He left Germany for the United States in 1938, and he was a professor at the Illinois Institute of Technology in Chicago until his death.

Himmel Bonner Associates
Scott Himmel (born 1954)
Darcy Bonner (born 1952)

Chicagoan Scott Himmel received his bachelor's degree in architecture from Tulane University in 1976, remaining in New Orleans to work for the architect Errol Barron. In 1979 he returned to Chicago with plans to attend graduate school, but instead started the firm Himmel Bonner Associates with former Tulane classmate Darcy Bonner. Born in Dallas, Bonner graduated from Tulane in 1976 and returned to Texas to work for the firm of Beran and Shelmire in Dallas. He then moved to Chicago to work with Booth, Nagle and Hartray and attend the University of Illinois at Chicago, where he received his master's degree in 1981.

Holabird and Roche
Holabird and Root
William Holabird (1854-1923)
Martin Roche (1855-1927)
John Augur Holabird (1886-1945)
John Wellborn Root, Jr. (1887-1963)

William Holabird and Martin Roche, who met while working in William Le Baron Jenney's office in Chicago, established the firm Holabird and Roche in 1882. In the 1920s two Holabird and Roche employees, John Augur Holabird, son of William Holabird, and John Wellborn Root, Jr., assumed control of the firm. John Holabird was born in Evanston, Illinois, and he graduated from the United States Military Academy at West Point in 1907. But two years later he resigned his commission and entered the Ecole des Beaux-Arts, Paris. While at the Ecole he met a fellow Chicagoan, John Wellborn Root, Jr., who was the son of the well-known architect and partner to Daniel Burnham. The younger Root received his bachelor's degree in architecture from Cornell University in 1909, then went to Paris to attend the Ecole des Beaux-Arts.

Holabird and Root received their diplomas in 1913, and they both returned to Chicago to work in the office of Holabird and Roche. Their careers were briefly interrupted by World War I, but in 1919 they returned to Holabird and Roche and began to take control of the firm, as William Holabird had become ill and Martin Roche was uninterested in running the office. With the deaths of William Holabird in 1923 and Martin Roche in 1927, the young Holabird and Root became the senior partners of the firm, which was renamed Holabird and Root. In 1948 Joseph Z. Burgee joined the firm, and it was briefly known as Holabird, Root and Burgee. Around this time both William Holabird II and, representing a third generation, John A. Holabird, Jr., joined the firm.

George T. Horton
(1873-1945)

George T. Horton was the son of Horace Ebenezer Horton, one of the founders of the Chicago Bridge and Iron Company. After graduating from Rensselaer Polytechnic Institute in 1893, George joined his father's company and became president when his father died in 1912. He invented a freezeproof water tank in 1912 for the Canadian transcontinental railroad, which was then under construction. He pioneered the development of theme tanks for advertising with the Milk Bottle Tank for the City Dairy of Ontario in 1915, and he helped invent, with E. G. Daniels, the Chibridge Spacer, a machine that made it economically feasible to fabricate steel plates for oil tanks. Horton's inventiveness helped the company remain in business during the Depression, and expand during World War II to a work force of over 20,000 people.

Homer Hoyt
(1895-1984)

A real estate economist and demographer with a long and varied career in business, academia, and government, Homer Hoyt was born in Missouri and received bachelor's and master's degrees from the University of Kansas and doctoral and law degrees from the University of Chicago. He taught at Beloit College, and the universities of North Carolina, Missouri, and Delaware. He was an economist with the War Trade Board (1918-19), a statistician for AT&T, a real estate broker in Chicago after 1925, the chief land economist for the Federal Housing Administration (1934-40), director of research for the Chicago Plan Commission (1941-43), and director of economic studies for the New York Regional Plan Association (1943-46). After the war he was founder and president of Homer Hoyt Associates, which was involved in the planning and market research for over two hundred shopping centers. He coauthored, with Arthur M. Weimer, *Principles of Real Estate*, long a standard text, but he is probably best known for his work before the war. In *One Hundred Years of Land Values in Chicago* (1933), he drew attention to the cyclical nature of land values in the city, and in *The Structure and Growth of Residential Neighborhoods in American Cities* (1939), he offered the "sector theory" of urban growth, the notion that land development patterns tend to follow radial transportation corridors.

Alfonso Iannelli
(1888-1965)

Born in Andretta, Italy, Alfonso Iannelli moved to the United States with his family at the age of ten. After several years as an apprentice in a jewelry factory in Newark, New Jersey, he moved to New York to attend art classes at the Art Students League. He took classes from Gutzon Borglum, who hired him as an assistant to work on the sculpture for the Cathedral of St. John the Divine. After five months working with Borglum, Iannelli established his own studio in New York. Then, in pursuit of a more stable career in the commercial arts, he moved to Cincinnati in 1908 to take a job as a designer with a lithograph company. In 1910 he moved to Los Angeles, where he met the architect John Lloyd Wright, who sparked Iannelli's interest in the Prairie School when Wright introduced him to the work of his father, Frank Lloyd Wright. Several years later, at the suggestion of John Lloyd Wright, Iannelli was hired by Frank Lloyd Wright to produce sculpture for the architect's project at Midway Gardens. After coming to Chicago, Iannelli occasionally worked with the architects Francis Barry Byrne and Bruce Goff and taught at The School of The Art Institute of Chicago. Perhaps one of his most famous works is the monumental relief sculpture of the Rock of Gibraltar on the Prudential Building of 1952.

Illinois State Toll Highway Commission (now the Illinois State Toll Highway Authority)

The Illinois legislature created the Illinois State Toll Highway Commission to design, construct, and operate a modern system of limited-access highways encircling and radiating from Chicago. The commission, part of a national postwar movement to build new turnpikes and toll roads, was assisted by administrative staff, consulting engineers and architects, and an advisory committee made up of senators, representatives, and citizens. The tollway is connected to the Chicago expressways, state highways, and the federal interstate highway system. The system has been financed by revenue bonds and toll collection to maintain and operate its more than 250 miles of divided concrete highways. The Illinois Tollway serves commercial and commuter traffic moving between the suburbs and the city, and provides a bypass route around the congested metropolitan area for regional commercial and commuter traffic traveling to other midwestern cities. Originally a 187-mile system, the tollway was constructed in only twenty-eight months, opening in August 1958. Additional revenues are provided from a share of the profits generated by the gasoline stations and fast-food chains that currently lease the Oasis restaurant and service areas.

Samuel Insull (1859-1937)

Born in London, Samuel Insull had his start in a long career in electric power as Thomas Edison's private secretary in 1881. Because of his administrative talents, he became manager of Edison's plant in Schenectady, New York, five years later. When Edison's company merged with others to form General Electric in 1892, Insull left for Chicago to become president of Chicago Edison, a small power company that merged with Commonwealth Electric in 1907 to become Commonwealth Edison, Chicago's major electricity supplier. Seven years later, Insull began to acquire and modernize with electricity interurban and urban rail lines. His troubles came well after the stockmarket crash of 1929, when in 1932 his creditors refused to extend their financial support, and he was eventually forced out of his electricity empire. He was prosecuted for mail fraud, embezzlement, and other charges related to the Bankruptcy Act, but was acquitted.

Albert Kahn
(1869-1942)

Born in Rhaunen, Germany, Albert Kahn's formal education ended at eleven when his parents left Germany for Detroit, Michigan. In 1884 he took a job as a draftsman in the office of Mason and Rice, where he would later become chief designer. He formed a partnership with George W. Nettleton and

Alexander B. Trowbridge in 1896, but only a few years later the firm dissolved when Nettleton died. In 1902 Kahn established his own office, and was joined by his brothers Julius and Moritz. The firm, which specialized in industrial buildings, eventually grew to over six hundred employees in the late 1930s and continued to attract prestigious national and international commissions until Kahn's death in 1942.

Keck and Keck
George Fred Keck (1895-1980)
William Keck (born 1908)

George Fred Keck was born in Watertown, Wisconsin, and studied engineering at the University of Wisconsin and architecture from 1915 to 1920 at the University of Illinois. Before starting an independent practice in 1926, he worked for D. H. Burnham and Company and for Schmidt, Garden and Martin, and he taught in 1923-24 at the University of Illinois. His brother William, who was also born in Watertown, graduated from the University of Illinois in 1931. After college the younger Keck joined his brother's architecture firm and became a partner in 1946. George Fred Keck, with László Moholy-Nagy and Gyorgy Kepes, founded the Institute of Design in 1938 in Chicago. Keck was head of its Department of Architecture until 1944.

Gertrude Lempp Kerbis (born 1926)

Gertrude Lempp Kerbis received her bachelor of science degree in architecture in 1948 from the University of Illinois and attended the Graduate School of Design at Harvard University in 1949-50. She received her master's degree from the Illinois Institute of Technology in 1954 and took a job in the Chicago office of Skidmore, Owings and Merrill. In 1959 she went to work for C. F. Murphy Associates, and in 1967 she established her own architecture practice. In 1970 she began teaching at the William Rainey Harper College in Palatine, Illinois, and in the same year was elected Fellow of the American Institute of Architects.

Klaber and Grunsfeld
Eugene Henry Klaber (1883-1971)
Ernest Alton Grunsfeld, Jr. (1897-1970)

New Yorker Eugene Klaber received his bachelor's degree in architecture from Columbia University in 1906, and served as Architecte Diplome par le Gouvernement in Paris in 1910. He established a partnership with Ernest Grunsfeld from 1924 to 1929. In 1942 he went into partnership with Victorine Homsey, and in 1944 he established an independent practice. Ernest Grunsfeld was born in Albuquerque, New Mexico, and received his bachelor of science degree in architecture from the Massachusetts Institute of Technology in 1918. He attended the Ecole des

Beaux-Arts, Paris, from 1920 to 1922 before co-founding Klaber and Grunsfeld in 1924. He worked independently from 1929 to 1939, then co-founded Grunsfeld, Yerkes and Koenig, a partnership that was dissolved in 1946 when Grunsfeld left to form Friedman, Alschuler, Sincere and Ernest A. Grunsfeld.

Kohn Pedersen Fox Associates
A. Eugene Kohn (born 1930)
William Pedersen (born 1938)
Sheldon Fox (born 1930)

A native of Philadelphia, A. Eugene Kohn attended the University of Pennsylvania, receiving his bachelor's degree in architecture in 1953 and his master's in 1957. He worked as a designer for Vincent G. Kling Associates from 1960 to 1965 and then took a job with Welton Becket Associates until 1967. Before forming Kohn Pedersen Fox in 1976, he was a president and partner with John Carl Warnecke and Associates. William Pedersen was born in St. Paul, Minnesota, and studied at the University of Minnesota, receiving his bachelor of architecture degree in 1961. He earned a master's degree at the Massachusetts Institute of Technology in 1963. After two years at the American Academy in Rome as the recipient of a Rome Prize, he worked as a designer with the architect Eduardo Catalano. In 1967 Pedersen joined I. M. Pei and Associates, where he was an associate until he joined John Carl Warnecke and Associates in 1971 as vice-president. New Yorker Sheldon Fox received his bachelor of architecture degree in 1953 from the University of Pennsylvania. He worked for Kahn Jacobs, then joined John Carl Warnecke and Associates in 1972, serving as senior vice-president.

Raymond A. Kroc (1902-1984)
A native Chicagoan, Raymond A. Kroc worked with the Lily Tulip Cup Company from 1923 to 1941 and then with the Mult-A-Mixer Company until 1955. He founded the McDonald's Corporation in 1955 and served as chairman until 1974, and then as senior chairman until 1984. He acquired the San Diego Padres baseball team in 1974 and served as the club's chairman, president, and treasurer until 1984. He wrote *Grinding it Out: The Making of McDonald's* in 1977.

Krueck and Sexton
Ronald Adrian Krueck (born 1946)
Mark P. Sexton (born 1956)

Born in Cincinnati, Ohio, Ronald Adrian Krueck received his bachelor's degree in architecture from the Illinois Institute of Technology in 1970 and went to work for C. F. Murphy Associates. A year later he took a job with Hammond, Beeby and Associates, and remained there until 1976. After two years studying painting at The School of The Art Institute of Chicago, he went into partnership

with Keith Rodney Olsen, a classmate of Krueck's from IIT. In 1991 Krueck joined Mark P. Sexton in establishing the office of Krueck and Sexton. Krueck, who served as an assistant professor at IIT from 1975 to 1983, has also taught at the Harvard Graduate School of Design and the University of Illinois at Chicago. Mark Sexton received his bachelor's degree in architecture from IIT in 1980, and while in school, he worked for Skidmore, Owings and Merrill and Danforth Rockwell Carow. In 1980 he joined Krueck and Olsen; he went into partnership with Ron Krueck in 1991.

Gregory W. Landahl
(born 1950)

Gregory Landahl received his bachelor's degree in 1972 from the University of Illinois. After a year studying in Paris at the Université Pedagogique d'Architecture, formerly the Ecole des Beaux-Arts, he took a job in the Chicago office of Skidmore, Owings and Merrill. In 1980 he founded the Landahl Group, which specializes in interior architecture. He has also taught at The School of The Art Institute of Chicago and the University of Illinois at Chicago, and was a recipient of the Young Architects Award of the Chicago Chapter of the American Institute of Architects in 1987. In 1991 he was named Designer of the Year by *Interiors* magazine.

Peter Landon
(born 1949)

Peter Landon, a native of Chicago, graduated from Kansas University in 1971. After college he worked in Chicago as a principal in the offices of Paolo Soleri, Harry Weese, and Weese Hickey Weese. He established his own firm, Landon Architects, in 1987. Landon was a co-founder of the Architecture Forum, a discussion group of young architects that was active in the early 1980s, and has served as a visiting critic at the University of Illinois at Chicago and at the Illinois Institute of Technology.

Landrum and Brown, Airport Consultants
(founded 1949)

Charles Brown, a civil engineer previously employed by the Army Corps of Engineers, met John Landrum while both were employed by the National Airport Terminal Corporation, a consortium of airlines operating Detroit Willow Run and Greater Cincinnati airports. With the demise of the corporation, Landrum and Brown established their own airport planning and design consulting firm, one of the first of its type in the country. After the founders retired, the firm exchanged hands several times; it is presently owned by Jeffrey N. Thomas and Stuart S. Holder. Almost since the founding of the firm, Landrum and Brown has played a continuous and crucial role in the development of

Chicago's airports. The firm's master planning projects include Lambert St. Louis International, Miami International (1974-79), the new Denver International master plan study (1986-89), and Detroit Metropolitan Wayne County (1988 to the present). Landrum and Brown have also provided financial and management services to the Dallas-Ft. Worth International Airport (1976) and the Federal Aviation Administration (1978).

Tannys Langdon
(born 1953)

Born in Winnipeg, Canada, Tannys Langdon received her bachelor's degree in interior design from the University of Manitoba in 1975 and her master's in architecture from the University of Illinois in 1978. She took a job in Chicago with Hammond, Beeby and Babka, where she became an associate in 1982 and a partner three years later. In 1987 Langdon opened an office with David Woodhouse, and in 1990 she established her own office. In 1984 she won the first Chicago Architectural Club Burnham Prize and received a three-month fellowship at the American Academy in Rome. Langdon has also taught at the University of Illinois at both the Chicago and the Champaign-Urbana campuses.

Richard Latham
(1920-1991)

Richard Latham's first job as a designer was in Montgomery Ward's Bureau of Design, where he experimented with the notion of product planning, under the direction of Ann Swainson. In 1944 Latham worked in Raymond Loewy's Chicago office under Fritz Wagner, designing for such clients as Greyhound, Armour, Frigidaire, and International Harvester. In the early 1950s Latham became director of design for Loewy's Chicago office, where he managed a team of 75 designers. Latham and two other Loewy designers — Robert Tyler and George Jensen — left the firm in 1955 to establish Latham, Tyler, Jensen, which eventually specialized in product planning. Latham became an advisor in product planning to Land's End, Bang and Olufsen, and Rosenthal China.

Loebl, Schlossman and Hackl
Jerrold Loebl (1899-1978)
Norman J. Schlossman (1901-1990)
Donald Hackl (born 1934)

Norman J. Schlossman was born in Chicago and received his bachelor's degree in architecture from the Armour Institute of Technology (now the Illinois Institute of Technology) in 1921. After a few years working in the Chicago office of Coolidge and Hodgdon, he founded Loebl Schlossman in 1925 with Jerrold Loebl, a former classmate at the Armour Institute. In 1946 Richard Marsh Bennett, who graduated from Harvard University with a master's degree in architecture

in 1931, became a partner in the firm, which was renamed Loebl, Schlossman and Bennett. Before joining the firm, Bennett worked for several architects, including Walter Darwin Teague and Edward Durrell Stone. He also formed Bennett and Hornbostel, which existed from 1938 to 1943. Bennett was with Loebl, Schlossman and Bennett until he joined the faculty at the Harvard University Graduate School of Design in 1975. In 1965 Edward Dart joined the firm, renamed Loebl, Schlossman, Bennett and Dart, and in 1975, with the retirement of Richard Bennett, Donald Hackl, an employee since 1962, was made a partner in the firm, which was renamed Loebl, Schlossman, Dart and Hackl; he is now its president. Hackl received a bachelor of architecture in 1957 and a master of architecture in 1958, both from the University of Illinois. After Edward Dart's death in 1976, the name of the firm was changed to the current Loebl, Schlossman, and Hackl.

Lohan Associates
Dirk Lohan (born 1938)

Born in Germany, Dirk Lohan came to Chicago in 1957 and enrolled in the architecture department at the Illinois Institute of Technology, where Mies van der Rohe, his grandfather, was director. He returned to Germany briefly to complete his degree at the Technische Hochschule in Munich in 1962, and upon his return to Chicago, Lohan took a job in Mies's office. Mies died in 1969, and Lohan, Bruno Conterato, and Joseph Fujikawa took over the Office of Mies van der Rohe, not officially changing the name to Fujikawa, Conterato, Lohan and Associates until seven years after Mies's death. In 1986, with Fujikawa's departure, the office was renamed Lohan Associates.

John Macsai
(born 1926)

John Macsai was born in Budapest, Hungary, where he studied architecture at the Polytechnical University. After winning a scholarship to continue his studies in the United States, he received his bachelor's degree in architecture from Miami University in Oxford, Ohio, in 1949. He worked in Chicago at Skidmore, Owings and Merrill and at Pace Associates, and he was a senior designer in architectural and product planning at the industrial design office of Raymond Loewy Associates. In 1955, with Robert O. Hausner, he co-founded the firm Hausner and Macsai, which existed until 1970, when he went into partnership with Wendell Campbell. In 1975 Macsai started his own firm, John Macsai and Associates, which in 1991 merged with O'Donnell, Wicklund, Pigozzi and Peterson, where Macsai is now a principal partner. Macsai, who has been a professor at the University of Illinois at Chicago since 1970, has worked on several books and published numerous articles on architecture.

Eva Maddox
(born 1943)

Eva Maddox, a native of McMinnville, Tennessee, graduated from the College of Architecture, Art and Planning at the University of Cincinnati. She worked in Cincinnati for several years before moving to Chicago and taking a job as a project director in the offices of RMM. In 1972 she went to work with Space Designs, serving as vice-president. She opened her own office, Eva Maddox Associates, in 1975. Maddox, who was a faculty member at the Harrington Institute of Design in Chicago, has served as an adjunct associate professor at the University of Illinois at Chicago since 1990.

Carter Hugh Manny, Jr.
(born 1918)

Carter Hugh Manny, Jr., who was born in Michigan City, Indiana, received his bachelor of arts degree from Harvard University in 1941 and his bachelor's degree in architecture from the Illinois Institute of Technology in 1948. He went to work for C. F. Murphy Associates, later Murphy/Jahn, where he became a partner in 1957. He was named senior vice-president of the firm in 1978 and retired in 1983. Since 1971 Manny has served as director of the Graham Foundation for Advanced Studies in the Fine Arts.

Samuel Abraham Marx
(1885-1964)

Born in Natchez, Mississippi, Samuel Abraham Marx received his bachelor's degree in 1907 from the Massachusetts Institute of Technology. He then attended the Ecole des Beaux-Arts, Paris, until 1909, working in the ateliers of Umberstock and Duquesne. He returned to the United States, where he began to attract national attention for his elegant hotel and residential interiors. Marx, who was a trustee and a member of the Board of Governors of The Art Institute of Chicago, also served on the advisory council for the Museum of Modern Art in New York.

Mastro and Skylar
James Mastro (born 1946)
Claudia Miller Skylar (born 1951)

Born in Tulsa, Oklahoma, where he lived only a short time before his parents moved to Chicago, James A. Mastro received his bachelor of architecture degree from the University of Illinois at Chicago in 1970. He worked for several firms, including Hammond and Roesch, Meister and Volpe, and Aubrey J. Greenberg and Associates, before establishing an architecture firm with his wife, Claudia Miller Skylar, in 1979. Born in 1951 in Shaker Heights, Ohio, Skylar received her bachelor of arts degree in art history from Wellesley College in 1972. She took her master's degree in architecture from the Massachusetts Institute of Technology in 1976 and worked

in Wisconsin for several years before moving to Chicago and establishing a firm with James Mastro. Since 1986 Skylar has been a professor in the Department of Interior Architecture at The School of The Art Institute of Chicago.

John Massey (born 1931)

Born in Chicago, Massey studied advertising design at the University of Illinois. He worked as an assistant to Herb Pinzke on the children's encyclopedia *Our Wonderful World* and then joined the University of Illinois Press as a book designer. In 1957 he went to the Container Corporation as an assistant to Ralph Eckerstrom and became director of design after Eckerstrom left in 1964. In 1967 Massey founded the Center for Advanced Research in Design (CARD) as a subsidiary of the Container Corporation that carried out projects for many corporate and civic clients, including Atlantic Richfield, the United States Department of Labor, and the City of Chicago. Massey started his own firm in 1983, and also became a professor of graphic design at the University of Illinois at Chicago, where he still teaches.

Merrill Church Meigs (1883-1968)

Meigs attended preparatory school at the Iowa Business College and later enrolled at the University of Chicago. After graduating, he began a career in the publishing and advertising industry. Meigs was advertising manager for the J. I. Case Threshing Machine Company from 1911 to 1914, director of advertising for the *Chicago Evening American* from 1918 to 1926, and vice-president of the *American Weekly* from 1933 to 1940. Beginning in about 1917, Meigs, a licensed pilot, became a leading proponent of the development of aviation activities and ground facilities in the Chicago metropolitan area. He was chairman of the Chicago Aero Commission, and during World War II he served as chief of the aircraft division of the War Production Board. After the conclusion of the war, when he returned to work in the publishing industry, he chaired a committee to select the site for what is now O'Hare International Airport. In 1950 the City of Chicago renamed the Northerly Island general aviation facility Meigs Field in his honor.

Ludwig Mies van der Rohe
(1886-1969)

Ludwig Mies (he later adopted his mother's name van der Rohe) was born in Aachen, Germany, where he attended the Domschule (1897-1900) and the Aachen Trade School (1900-02). Before moving to Berlin in 1905, he worked in his father's stonemason business and as a draftsman in a stucco decoration business. In Berlin he apprenticed with Bruno Paul, an architect and furniture designer,

from 1905 to 1907. After a year in private practice, he joined Peter Behrens's office, where he worked as an assistant from 1908 to 1911. Mies opened his own office in Berlin, and continued to practice independently after serving in the German Army during World War I. He became involved in the Deutscher Werkbund, for which he served as vice-president from 1926 to 1932, and was also involved in architectural education, as director of the Bauhaus in 1930. Three years later, when Hitler came to power, the school was closed. In 1938 Mies left Germany for the United States and was appointed director of the Illinois Institute of Technology. In 1940 he opened an office in Chicago; he resigned his position at IIT in 1953.

R. Hunter Middleton (1898-1985)

Born in Glasgow, Scotland, R. Hunter Middleton studied in the Department of Printing Arts at The School of The Art Institute of Chicago under Ernst Detterer. After completing his education, Middleton joined the Ludlow Typograph Company, where he spent his entire career, becoming director of typographic design in 1933. He designed a number of successful faces for Ludlow, such as Eusebius, Stellar, Record Gothic, Delphian, and Radiant, and maintained his own imprint, the Cherryburn Press, where he printed several books of Thomas Bewick's wood engravings. Middleton was influential in all Chicago's design organizations, including the Society of Typographic Arts and 27 Chicago Designers.

Richard Yoshijiro Mine (1894-1981)

A native of Japan, Richard Yoshijiro Mine received his bachelor's degree in architecture in 1919 from the University of Tokyo, and his master's degree from the University of Illinois in 1921. In 1922 his entry to the Chicago Tribune Tower Competition won one of the fifty honorable mentions. But Mine was unable to become a registered architect because of a United States immigration law that prevented Japanese people from becoming U.S. citizens, and instead of opening an independent practice, he took a job as an architect for General Motors in Flint, Michigan. In the 1940s and 1950s he worked for Holabird, Root and Burgee and for Schmidt, Garden and Erikson; he later became the chief architectural designer for Kraft Foods.

László Moholy-Nagy
(1895-1946)

Born in Bacsborsod, Hungary, László Moholy-Nagy began his career as a lawyer before becoming active as a painter, sculptor, photographer, designer, and educator. He worked as an artist in Berlin, then joined the Bauhaus faculty in 1923, where he directed one of the foundation courses, headed the metal workshop, and, with Walter Gropius, edited a series

of books. Moholy-Nagy left the Bauhaus in 1928 and worked as a free-lance designer in Berlin before emigrating to the Netherlands, then to England, and finally to Chicago, where he became the director of the New Bauhaus in 1937. He was director of the New Bauhaus, later renamed the Institute of Design, until his death in 1946. He wrote the important book *Vision in Motion*, which was published by Paul Theobald in 1947.

Jordan Mozer
(born 1950)

Born in Chicago, Jordan Mozer studied painting and drawing at The School of The Art Institute of Chicago and attended the University of Wisconsin, Madison, where he studied English literature and pre-engineering. He received his bachelor of arts in industrial design from the University of Illinois at Chicago, where he also earned his master's degree in architecture. In 1983-84 he worked in partnership with Paul Florian and Stephen Wierzbowski, and in 1986 he established Jordan Mozer and Associates, a firm specializing in the design of restaurant interiors.

Murphy/Jahn
(formerly C. F. Murphy Associates)
C. F. Murphy (1890-1985)
Helmut Jahn (born 1940)

Charles F. Murphy, Sr., was born in New Jersey and initially was trained as a stenographer. In 1911 he took a job in Daniel Burnham's office, where he became a personal assistant to Ernest R. Graham, who took over the firm, renamed Graham, Burnham and Company, after Burnham's death. When Graham left to found Graham, Anderson, Probst and White in 1917, Murphy joined him and stayed with the firm until Graham's death in 1936. At that time Murphy co-founded Shaw, Naess and Murphy with two other architects from Graham's firm. Alfred P. Shaw left the partnership in 1946, but Sigurd Naess and Murphy continued working together until 1959, when Naess retired and Murphy founded C. F. Murphy Associates. In 1967 Gene Summers, an Illinois Institute of Technology professor and alumnus, joined the firm as a designer, bringing with him a former student named Helmut Jahn. After Summers left the firm to move to California in 1973, Jahn inherited much of his responsibility and soon became the director of planning and design. In 1981 Jahn became a partner in the firm, renamed Murphy/Jahn, and was made president a year later. Born in Zindorf, Germany, Helmut Jahn graduated from the Technische Hochschule, Munich, in 1965. During college he worked as an intern for the Nuremberg architect Schlechtendau, and upon graduation he took a job in Munich with P. C. von Seidlein. In 1966 he received a scholarship that enabled him to come to the United States, and he enrolled at IIT in Chicago, studying under Myron Goldsmith, Fazlur Khan, and Gene Summers.

Nagle, Hartray and Associates
James Nagle (born 1937)
John F. Hartray (born 1930)

Born in Iowa City, James Nagle received his B.A. from Stanford University in 1959. After two years in the United States Navy, he attended the Massachusetts Institute of Technology, taking a bachelor's degree in architecture in 1962. Two years later he received a master's degree in architecture from the Graduate School of Design at Harvard University. Before forming a partnership with Laurence Booth in Chicago in 1966, Nagle worked for Benjamin Thompson at the Architecture Collaborative, Ashley Meyer and Associates, and Stanley Tigerman. John Hartray joined Booth and Nagle in 1977, and the firm was known as Booth, Nagle and Hartray until Booth left the partnership in 1979. John F. Hartray received his bachelor's degree in architecture from Cornell University in 1954. After two years in the Army Signal Corps in Korea, Hartray returned to Chicago, and worked with Skidmore, Owings and Merrill, Holabird and Root and Burgee, Naess and Murphy, and Harry Weese, before joining Booth, Nagle and Hartray.

Edward Henry O'Hare
(1914-1943)

Edward Henry O'Hare was born in St. Louis to a father, Edward J. O'Hare, who had connections to organized crime. The younger O'Hare attended Annapolis and became a naval aviator in 1940. He became the first American "Ace" in 1942 after he shot down five Japanese bombers and damaged a sixth in defense of his aircraft carrier, the USS Lexington. O'Hare was awarded the Congressional Medal of Honor, and ships and sites were named for him. His most notable namesake is Chicago's O'Hare International Airport, which was officially named thus by the City Council in 1949 after petitions demanding the new name were submitted by veterans' organizations and the public.

Pace Associates

Standing for planners, architects, and consulting engineers, Pace Associates was founded in January 1946 by Charles Genther and Wilbur Binford, along with John Kausal and William Cobb. Although Pace's early projects were collaborations with Mies van der Rohe, the firm sought commissions in town and site planning for industries, commerce, and residential areas; structural, electrical, industrial, and mechanical engineering; and construction supervision. By 1952, following rapid growth, the firm had added six associates and two hundred aides, including experts from the University of Chicago in economics and sociology, for example, those who helped shape residential developments. Well-known for its association with Mies in Chicago, the firm attracted national attention for the award-winning highway system it designed

for the Illinois State Toll Highway Commission. Contributing to the 1950s era of urban renewal, defined in part by goals to design buildings primarily for the public interest, Pace Associates won third prize in an influential competition, sponsored by Carson Pirie Scott, entitled "Redevelopment of the Central Area of Chicago." They proposed open urban pedestrian space for the downtown district based upon street and lot-line setbacks, and their ideas were incorporated into the city's 1957 Zoning Ordinance affecting public space planning for the Brunswick buildings and the Civic Center, among others. Pace also contributed to the city's plans to develop an underground network of pedestrian passages and arcades linking the subway system's major buildings in the Loop, a now completed project beneath several downtown retail stores near Marshall Field's.

The firm represented a belief held by many engineers that the architecture profession increasingly required the expertise of engineers trained to design with new structural materials, such as prestressed concrete. Lasting ten years, Pace's collaboration with Mies van der Rohe resulted in such landmarks as the Promontory Apartments, Algonquin Apartments, and 860-880 North Lake Shore Drive.

Pappageorge/Haymes
George Pappageorge (born 1954)
David A. Haymes (born 1954)

Chicagoan George Pappageorge received his bachelor's degree in architecture from the University of Illinois at Chicago in 1978. After a year working with Rudich Pappageorge and pursuing independent projects in Chicago, he went to work in the office of Kenneth A. Schroeder Associates. He established Pappageorge/Haymes with David Haymes in 1981. David A. Haymes, who was born in Colorado Springs, also received his bachelor of architecture degree from the University of Illinois at Chicago in 1978. He briefly worked as a staff designer with Roger Whitmer Associates before spending a year working independently in both Chicago and California. He then worked for Kenneth A. Schroeder Associates for two years before co-founding Pappageorge/Haymes. Both partners have taught at the University of Illinois at Chicago.

I. M. Pei (born 1917)
Born in Canton, China, I. M. Pei emigrated to the United States in 1935 and became a naturalized citizen in 1948. He received a bachelor of architecture in 1940 from the Massachusetts Institute of Technology and a master of architecture in 1946 from Harvard University's Graduate School of Design; he also taught at Harvard from 1945 to 1948. Pei was director of architecture at Webb and Knapp, New York, from 1948 to 1955, and since 1955 he has been a partner in I. M. Pei and Partners in New York.

Cesar Pelli (born 1926)
A native of Tucuman, Argentina, Cesar Pelli attended the National University of Buenos Aires, and, after coming to the United States in 1952, he attended the University of Illinois. In 1954 he went to work for Eero Saarinen, who at that time had offices in Bloomfield Hills, Michigan, and Hamden, Connecticut. In 1964 he moved to Los Angeles to work as director of design for Daniel, Mann, Johnson and Mendenhall. In 1968 Pelli went to work in the office of Gruen Associates, and in 1977 he was appointed dean of the School of Architecture at Yale University. He established the office of Cesar Pelli and Associates in New Haven. He resigned from Yale in 1984 and continues to work in New Haven.

Perkins and Will
Lawrence Bradford Perkins (born 1907)
Philip Will, Jr. (1906-1985)
C. William Brubaker (born 1926)
Ralph Johnson (born 1948)

A native of Evanston, Illinois, Lawrence Bradford Perkins attended the University of Wisconsin and received his bachelor of architecture degree in 1930 from Cornell University. In 1935 he formed a partnership with fellow Cornell graduate Philip Will. E. Todd Wheeler joined the firm, which was renamed Perkins, Wheeler and Will, as a partner from 1935 to 1941. Wheeler rejoined Perkins and Will in 1957 and directed the firm's health care planning and design projects until his retirement in 1972. Perkins also retired in 1972 and became an adjunct professor of architectural design at the University of Illinois at Chicago in 1974. Philip Will retired from the firm in 1971.

C. William Brubaker, who was born in South Bend, Indiana, graduated from the University of Texas in 1950. He moved to Chicago and took a job as a draftsman with Perkins and Will, becoming a design principal in 1958 and president in 1968. Since then he has served as executive vice-president for the firm's offices in Chicago, New York, and Washington, D. C. Chicagoan Ralph Johnson earned his bachelor's degree in architecture from the University of Illinois in 1971 and received his master's from the Graduate School of Design at Harvard University in 1973. Johnson spent two years in the office of architect Stanley Tigerman, and then worked independently for a short time before joining Perkins and Will in 1976. Johnson was named principal designer in 1979 and vice-president in 1983. David A. Hansen, also a design principal at Perkins and Will, received his bachelor of architecture in 1967 from the University of Illinois, where he pursued graduate studies in architecture in 1968. He joined Perkins and Will in 1986.

Frederick Phillips (born 1946)
Born in Evanston, Illinois, Frederick Phillips received his bachelor of arts from Lake Forest

College in 1969 and earned his master's degree in architecture from the University of Pennsylvania in 1973. He began working in Chicago in the office of Harry Weese and Associates in 1974, and established his own firm, Frederick Phillips and Associates, in 1976. He taught at the University of Illinois at Chicago in 1987 as an assistant professor.

Powell/Kleinschmidt
Donald D. Powell (born 1934)
Robert D. Kleinschmidt (born 1939)

Born in Minneapolis, Minnesota, Donald D. Powell received his bachelor's degree in architecture from the University of Minnesota in 1960. After studying in Europe on a Fulbright Traveling Fellowship, he worked for the Chicago office of Skidmore, Owings and Merrill. In 1976 he established Powell/Kleinschmidt in Chicago with Robert D. Kleinschmidt. A Chicagoan, Kleinschmidt received his bachelor of architecture degree in 1963 from the University of Illinois and took his master's degree in architecture from Columbia University in 1964. The same year, he was awarded a William Kenney Fellows Traveling Fellowship for Study in Europe.

James Prestini (born 1908)
Born in Waterford, Connecticut, James Prestini received a bachelor's degree in mechanical engineering in 1930 from Yale University. He also attended the Yale School of Education, the University of Stockholm, and the Institute of Design at the Illinois Institute of Technology in Chicago; in 1939 he studied under László Moholy-Nagy at the Institute of Design. In 1933 Prestini began teaching mathematics at Lake Forest Academy, where he first became interested in woodworking. His talent for creating fine wooden bowls began to attract national attention in the mid-1930s, and he taught from 1939 to 1946 at the Institute of Design. He then worked as a research engineer for the Armour Research Foundation at IIT, and in the 1950s Prestini moved to California to teach in the Department of Architecture at the University of California at Berkeley, where he was made a professor of design in 1962 and professor emeritus of design in 1975.

James Edwin Quinn
(1895-1986)

Born in Chicago, James Edwin Quinn attended evening courses in architecture at The School of The Art Institute of Chicago in 1914 and 1915. In 1920 he met Frank A. McNally, a structural engineer, when he took a job in the office of Eric E. Hall. In 1922 Quinn and McNally opened their own office, specializing in high-rise apartments. Their partnership dissolved in 1939. After World War II Quinn took a job with the Cook County Highway Department and worked on the design of prestressed concrete bridges for the new Chicago expressways.

Kathryn Quinn (born 1953)

Kathryn Quinn received her bachelor of architecture degree from the University of Illinois at Chicago in 1977. She also studied landscape architecture in London in 1973 and attended the Ecole des Beaux-Arts in 1976. In 1977 Quinn began working for both Harry Weese and Associates and Sisco/Lubotsky Associates; she was with Harry Weese for two years and Sisco/Lubotsky for four years. In 1981 she took a job with Hammond, Beeby and Babka, where she became an associate in 1984, remaining until 1985. She went into independent practice for one year in 1985, then formed the firm Quinn and Searle in 1986. She has headed her own firm since 1990. Quinn has been a visiting critic and lecturer at Notre Dame University, the University of Illinois at Chicago, Illinois Institute of Technology, and the University of Wisconsin at Milwaukee.

Rapp and Rapp
Cornelius Ward Rapp (1861-1927)
George Leslie Rapp (1878-1942)

The Rapp brothers were born in Carbondale, Illinois, Cornelius Ward (C. W.) Rapp in 1861 and George Leslie Rapp in 1878. After an apprenticeship with his father, a carpenter-architect, C.W. established his own practice around 1891. After graduating from the University of Illinois in 1899 with a degree in architecture, George took a job with the Chicago architect Edward Krause. In 1906 the brothers established the firm Rapp and Rapp, specializing in movie theater design. In 1917 the firm began designing for the Balaban and Katz chain, which merged with Paramount-Publix Theaters and expanded Rapp and Rapp's practice nationwide. The firm designed more than three hundred theaters before it was dissolved in 1965.

Andrew Nicholas Rebori
(1886-1966)

Andrew Nicholas Rebori went to work for the architect Charles Alling Gifford in his native New York City while he was still in high school. After briefly studying in the atelier of Henry Hornbostel, Rebori began attending the Massachusetts Institute of Technology in 1905, and in 1908 he went to Paris to study at the Ecole des Beaux-Arts on an MIT traveling fellowship. In 1909-10 Rebori worked with Cass Gilbert in New York, and after a brief stay at the American Academy in Rome, he came to Chicago to study at the Armour Institute of Technology (now the Illinois Institute of Technology), receiving his bachelor of science in architecture in 1911. Upon graduation he started working in the office of Jarvis Hunt, and he also taught at the Armour Institute. In 1921 he co-founded the firm of Rebori, Wentworth and Dewey, which became Rebori, Wentworth, Dewey and McCormick in 1923, and finally Rebori and Wentworth in 1930. After that partnership

dissolved in 1932, Rebori went into independent practice until World War II, when he worked as an engineering consultant for the United States Navy. He was a consulting architect for the Chicago office of DeLeuw, Cather and Co. from 1944 to 1955. He worked independently until he retired in 1961.

Arthur Rubloff (1902-1986)

Arthur Rubloff, for decades one of the major real estate figures in Chicago, started the business that bore his name, Arthur Rubloff and Company, in 1930. Among the major development projects with which he was associated were the Carl Sandburg Village apartment complex on the city's near North Side, Evergreen Plaza Shopping Center in southwest suburban Evergreen Park, and the Brunswick Building downtown. Rubloff's major role, however, was as deal maker and promoter. He coined the phrase "Magnificent Mile" for North Michigan Avenue in 1947, and commissioned the City Plan Proposal, a well-known study of the area, from John Root of Holabird and Root. In the late 1960s he turned the firm over to its employees and founded a new company, the Rubloff Development Company.

Christopher Rudolph (born 1952)

A native of Wilton, Connecticut, Christopher Rudolph received his bachelor of architecture degree in 1975 from the Illinois Institute of Technology. He worked briefly with Hammond and Beeby and Stanley Tigerman and Associates before taking a job in 1975 with Booth and Nagle. In 1981 he left the firm to work with Schmidt, Garden and Erikson. Then, after a brief affiliation with Cohen and Nereim in 1983, Rudolph opened his own office, which became Rudolph and Associates in 1988.

Harold Schiff (born 1927)

Born in New York, Harold Schiff attended Columbia University and graduated as a civil engineer in 1950. He worked as a manager of the London Sash and Door Company in Mt. Vernon, New York, and from 1953 to 1958 he ran Shildrake Realty Company and Schiff Construction Company in New York, which specialized in residential and commercial-industrial projects. From 1958 to 1975 he worked for the Diesel Construction Company, and after it merged with the Morse Company in 1970 and became Morse Diesel, he served as president and chief executive officer from 1967 to 1975. Some of the important buildings on which he worked as project manager are the Pan Am building in New York (1959) and the Tour Montparnasse in Paris (1975). He resigned from Morse Diesel in 1975 and joined Richard Halpern in the partnership of Schal Associates. With this company, he constructed the Chicago Board Options Exchange by Skidmore, Owings and

Merrill (1981), carried out the renovation of Orchestra Hall by the same firm (1985), and constucted 200 South Wacker Drive by Harry Weese and Associates (1981).

Schmidt, Garden and Erikson
Richard Ernest Schmidt (1865-1959)
Hugh M. G. Garden (1873-1961)
Carl A. Erikson (1888-1958?)

Bavarian-born Richard Ernest Schmidt moved to Chicago with his family just after the Civil War. He attended the Massachusetts Institute of Technology from 1883 to 1885 and then worked for several architecture firms in Chicago until he established his own practice in 1887. In 1895 he asked Hugh M. G. Garden to join the firm as an architectural designer, and in 1906 they formed Schmidt, Garden and Martin with Edgar Martin. Hugh M. G. Garden was born in Toronto in 1873 and came to Chicago around the time of the 1893 World's Fair. He worked with various architects, including Henry Ives Cobb, Howard Van Doren Shaw, and Frank Lloyd Wright, before joining Schmidt. In 1926, when Edgar Martin left the firm to become a partner in Pond, Pond, Martin and Lloyd, Carl A. Erikson, a longtime employee of Schmidt, Garden and Martin, became a partner in the firm, which was reorganized as Schmidt, Garden and Erikson. Erikson graduated from the University of Pennsylvania in 1910 and went to work for Schmidt, Garden and Martin in 1913. As Schmidt and Garden became less active in the firm, Erikson took control and shifted design responsibility to R. Vale Faro.

Kenneth A. Schroeder (born 1943)

Born in Chicago, Kenneth A. Schroeder received his bachelor's degree in architecture from the University of Illinois in 1967. He worked with the Chicago firm I. W. Colbourn, then returned to school and earned a master's degree in architecture from the University of Toronto in 1971. He was a partner at Hinds, Schroeder and Whitaker before co-founding Schroeder Murchie Laya Associates in 1976; he is senior principal of the firm. Schroeder is also an associate professor of architecture at the University of Illinois at Chicago.

Milton M. Schwartz and Associates
Milton M. Schwartz (born 1925)

Born in Chicago, Milton Meyer Schwartz attended the University of Illinois in 1947 and went into private practice in 1951, specializing in residential high-rise buildings. Five years later he established Milton M. Schwartz and Associates, which is still active today.

Paul Schweikher (born 1903)

Born in Denver, Colorado, Paul Schweikher attended the University of Colorado, Boulder

(1921-22), The School of The Art Institute of Chicago (1922-23), and the Illinois Institute of Technology (1924-26), receiving his bachelor of fine arts degree from Yale University in 1929. While he was in Chicago during the 1920s, Schweikher worked for several architects, including Granger and Bollenbacher, David Adler, and Russell Wolcott. After receiving his degree from Yale, he returned to Chicago and worked for Philip B. Maher as a chief designer (1931-33) and for General Houses as a designer and site planner (1933-34), subsequently establishing a partnership with Theodore Warren Lamb and Winston Elting in 1934. After Lamb left in 1946, the firm was renamed Schweikher and Elting. In 1953 Schweikher left Chicago to become chairman of the School of Architecture at Yale University, and he established Paul Schweikher Associates in New Haven. Four years later he relocated his firm to Pittsburgh when he was asked to head the Department of Architecture at Carnegie-Mellon University. In 1970 he resigned from Carnegie-Mellon and relocated to Sedona, Arizona.

Shaw and Associates

Alfred Shaw (1895-1970)
Patrick Shaw (born 1933)

Alfred Shaw was born in Dorchester, Massachusetts, and studied architecture at the Boston Architectural Club from 1911 to 1917. After working for various firms in Boston and New York, he took a job with Ernest Graham in Chicago in 1927. After serving as a junior partner in the firm from 1933 to 1937, Shaw left to establish Shaw, Naess and Murphy. In 1947 he formed Shaw, Metz and Dolio, which became Shaw, Metz and Associates in 1959, and later Alfred Shaw and Associates. His son Patrick Shaw was born in Chicago and received his B.A. degree in architecture from Harvard University, where he also attended the Graduate School of Design. He took a job with Holabird and Root in Chicago, then worked for Robert Woods Kennedy in Cambridge, Massachusetts, and later for Skidmore, Owings and Merrill in New York. He also worked briefly with John Carl Warnecke in San Francisco and Washington, D. C., before returning to Chicago to work in his father's firm, Shaw, Metz and Associates. In 1961 he joined the firm, which he inherited in 1972 and renamed Shaw and Associates.

James Simpson

(1874-1939)

As president and chairman of the board of Marshall Field and Company, chairman of the Chicago Plan Commission, and the head of the city's public utilities companies, James Simpson emerged as a powerful force in the shaping of Chicago's urbanism in the 1920s and 1930s. Simpson, born in Glasgow, Scotland, and brought to Chicago by his parents in 1880, rose in the Field organization from his first position in 1891 as clerk to become president and chairman of the board (1923-32) and chairman of the executive committee (1932-39). During his tenure, Simpson undertook the building of Field's Store for Men and the Merchandise Mart (1928-30), and shepherded the company through the difficult years of the Great Depression. He assumed control of Chicago's utilities companies in 1932, saving them from organizational collapse. As a member of the Commercial Club and one whose personal financial backing contributed to the Club's sponsorship of the *Plan of Chicago*, Simpson was appointed a charter member of the Chicago Plan Commission upon its establishment in 1909, and later served as its chairman (1926-35), succeeding Charles Wacker. Under Simpson's energetic leadership, projects such as the completion of Wacker Drive, the Outer Drive extensions, and the straightening of the Chicago River were carried out, and many more were developed.

Skidmore, Owings and Merrill

Louis Skidmore (1897-1962)
Nathaniel Owings (1903-1984)
John Merrill (1896-1975)
Walter Netsch (born 1920)
Bruce Graham (born 1925)
Myron Goldsmith (born 1918)
Fazlur Khan (1929-1982)
Adrian Smith (born 1944)
Diane Legge-Kemp (born 1949)
Joseph Gonzalez (born 1950)

In 1936 Louis Skidmore and Nathaniel Owings established the architecture firm Skidmore and Owings in Chicago; the firm became Skidmore, Owings and Merrill when John Merrill joined the partnership in 1939. Skidmore was born in Lawrenceburg, Indiana, and received his bachelor of architecture degree in 1924 from the Massachusetts Institute of Technology. After working for Maginnius and Walsh for two years, Skidmore was a visiting scholar at the American Academy in Rome in 1927. From 1929 to 1935, he served as assistant to the general manager at the Century of Progress Exposition in Chicago, where he worked with Nathaniel Owings. Skidmore retired from Skidmore, Owings and Merrill in 1955. Nathaniel Owings, who was born in Indianapolis, Indiana, attended the University of Illinois in 1921-22 and Cornell University in 1927. From 1948 to 1951 Owings served as chairman of the Chicago Plan Commission. John Ogden Merrill was born in St. Paul, Minnesota, and was educated at the University of Wisconsin, Madison, and at MIT, where he received his bachelor of architecture degree in 1921. He worked for the Chicago firm Granger and Bollenbacher and the United States Housing Administration before forming Skidmore, Owings and Merrill in 1939. Merrill retired in 1958.

Chicagoan Walter Andrew Netsch graduated from MIT in 1943. After three years in the United States Army Corps of Engineers, he took a job with the Chicago architect Lloyd Morgan Yost in 1946. He left only a year later to join Skidmore, Owings and Merrill. Netsch worked in SOM's offices in Oak Ridge, San Francisco, Tokyo, and Chicago before he was named a general partner in 1955. He retired in 1979.

Born while his parents were living in Bogotá, Colombia, Bruce Graham attended the University of Dayton, Ohio, and the Case School of Applied Sciences in Cleveland, and earned his bachelor's degree in architecture from the University of Pennsylvania in 1948. He worked in the office of Holabird, Root and Burgee between 1949 and 1951, and joined the Chicago office of Skidmore, Owings and Merrill as chief of design in 1951. He was chief design partner from 1960 to 1987, when he retired and established an independent practice with his wife in Hobe Sound, Florida.

Design partner Joseph Gonzalez joined Skidmore, Owings and Merrill in 1974 after graduating from Oklahoma State University with a bachelor's degree in architecture a year earlier. He won Harvard University's Loeb Fellowship in 1989.

A native of Chicago, Myron Goldsmith received his bachelor of science degree in 1939 from the Armour Institute of Technology (now the Illinois Institute of Technology). While pursuing graduate studies there, Goldsmith took a job as an architect and structural engineer in Mies van der Rohe's office in 1946. After receiving his master of science degree in architecture, Goldsmith won a Fulbright Fellowship and studied at the University of Rome under Pier Luigi Nervi from 1953 to 1955. He joined the San Francisco office of Skidmore, Owings and Merrill as chief structural engineer in 1955, and in 1958 became senior architectural designer and associate partner in the firm's Chicago office; he was made general partner in 1967. Beginning in 1961, Goldsmith also served as a professor of architecture at IIT.

Born in Dacca, India (now Bangladesh), Fazlur Khan received a bachelor's degree in engineering from the University of Dacca in 1950. He emigrated to the United States in 1952 and attended the University of Illinois, where he received his master's degree and his Ph.D. in structural engineering in 1952 and 1955, respectively. In 1955 he joined Skidmore, Owings and Merrill, and became a general partner in 1970.

Born in Chicago, Adrian Smith received his bachelor's degree in architecture from the University of Illinois in 1968. He took a job with the Chicago office of Skidmore, Owings and Merrill in 1967, designing large commercial structures.

Diane Legge-Kemp, who was born in Rochester, New York, received a bachelor of arts degree from Stanford University; she earned a master's degree in architecture from Princeton University. Before joining Decker and Kemp, she was a design partner at Skidmore, Owings and Merrill from 1977 to 1989. She received the Young Architect of the Year Award from the Chicago Chapter of the American Institute of Architects in 1984, and she now owns her own firm, Legge-Kemp Architecture and Landscape Consulting.

Rael D. Slutsky
(born 1949)

A native of Toronto, Rael Slutsky received his bachelor's degree in architecture from the University of Illinois in 1972. He spent a year in Pittsburgh working for Joseph Slutsky Architect and CMHK Architects before taking a job in the Chicago office of Skidmore, Owings and Merrill. In 1977 he established his own architectural practice, which offered both design and illustration services. Since 1980 the firm Rael D. Slutsky and Associates has been specializing exclusively in architectural illustration. Slutsky serves on the executive board of the American Society of Architectural Perspectivists, and has won eight ASAP awards since 1987. He also serves as vice-president on the executive board of the Newhouse Architecture Foundation, an organization that supports high school programs for students interested in architecture.

Solomon Cordwell Buenz
Louis R. Solomon (1905-1971)
J. D. Cordwell (born 1920)
John Buenz (born 1933)

A native Chicagoan, Louis R. Solomon worked briefly in the real estate division at the S. W. Strauss and Company Bank before studying architecture at the University of Illinois. He subsequently started his own firm, which specialized in office planning. In 1957 Solomon went into partnership with J. D. Cordwell. Cordwell, who had been educated in London at the Architectural Association and the School for Research and Regional Planning, had previously worked for Maxwell Fry and Jane Drew in London (1947-50) and Pace Associates in Chicago (1951-52). From 1952 to 1956 Cordwell served as director of planning for the Chicago Plan Commission. In 1963 John Buenz joined Solomon and Cordwell, and he was made a partner in 1968. A native of North Platt, Nebraska, Buenz received his bachelor's degree in architecture from Iowa State University and his master's from the Georgia Institute of Technology. Before joining the office of L. R. Solomon and J. D. Cordwell, Buenz worked with several architects, including Eero Saarinen (1958-60), Harry Weese (1960-61), and Keck and Keck (1962-63).

A. James Speyer
(1909-1986)

Born in Pittsburgh, Pennsylvania, A. James Speyer graduated from the Carnegie Institute of Technology, where he received his first architectural training. He also attended the Chelsea Polytechnic, London, and, from 1934 to 1937, the Sorbonne in Paris, before moving to Chicago in 1941 to study architecture at the Illinois Institute of Technology as Mies van der Rohe's first graduate student. World War II interrupted his career for five years, but in 1946 he returned to Chicago and established an independent architecture practice, specializing in residential work that reflected his Miesian training. Speyer also taught advanced architectural design at IIT and became a writer for *Artnews* magazine in 1955. His interest in art would eventually draw him out of architecture, and after a three-year visiting professorship at the University of Athens, Greece, he became curator of Twentieth-Century Painting and Sculpture at The Art Institute of Chicago in 1961.

Robert A. M. Stern (born 1939)

A native of New York City, Robert A. M. Stern earned his bachelor of arts degree in 1960 from Columbia University and his master's degree in architecture from Yale University in 1965. During the summer before his final year at Yale, he worked in the Washington, D. C., office of Perkins and Will, and after graduation in 1966 he worked briefly as a designer for the New York architect Richard Meier. Stern was a consultant to Philip Johnson on his "Eye on New York" television documentary, and then took a job as an urban designer and assistant for design policy at the Housing and Development Administration of the City of New York. In 1969 he went into partnership with John S. Hagman, and in 1977 he established his own firm, Robert A. M. Stern. In 1970 he began teaching at the Graduate School of Architecture, Planning and Preservation at Columbia University, where he is now a full professor. In 1984 he was appointed the first director of Columbia's Temple Hoyne Buell Center for the Study of American Architecture. Stern has also taught at the School of Architecture at Yale University and was president of the Architectural League of New York from 1973 to 1977. Stern has published numerous books and articles, and in 1986 he presented "Pride of Place," a television documentary on American architecture for the Public Broadcasting System.

Gene Summers (born 1928)

A native of San Antonio, Texas, Gene Summers earned his bachelor's degree in architecture in 1949 from Texas A & M University and his master's degree in 1951 from the Illinois Institute of Technology. Summers worked in the Office of Mies van der Rohe until 1967, when he became partner in charge of design at C. F. Murphy Associates. In 1973 Summers left C. F. Murphy to co-found, with Phyllis Lambert, Ridgway, an architecture firm in Newport Beach, California. In 1985 Summers left Ridgway and moved to France, where he sculpted furniture in bronze. In 1989 he moved to Chicago to become dean of the College of Architecture at IIT.

John Syvertsen (born 1950)

Born in Milwaukee, Wisconsin, John Syvertsen attended Georgetown University, where he majored in philosophy and earned a bachelor of arts degree in 1973. After receiving his master's degree in architecture from Princeton University in 1976, he took a job in Chicago in the office of Hinds, Schroeder and Whittaker. In 1977 he went to work for Hammond, Beeby and Babka and was named associate partner of that firm in 1980. Syvertsen established his own office in Chicago in 1987, which merged with O'Donnell, Wicklund, Pigozzi and Peterson in 1992. He has been an adjunct professor at the School of Architecture at the University of Illinois at Chicago since 1978.

Terp/Meyers
Lynn Betty Meyers (born 1952)
Dana George Terp (born 1953)

Born in Chicago, Lynn Meyers studied at the Royal Academy of Architecture in Copenhagen, Denmark, before receiving her bachelor of architecture degree in 1974 from Washington University, St. Louis, where she also took her master's degree in architecture in 1977. Meyers worked briefly with Holabird and Root in both 1973 and 1976, and in 1978 she took a job with the City of Chicago's Bureau of Architecture. She went into private practice in 1980, and in 1982 she founded the firm Terp/Meyers Architects, although her husband, Dana Terp, did not join it until 1984. A native Chicagoan, Terp received his bachelor's degree in architecture in 1974 from Washington University. He attended the Yale University School of Architecture in 1975 and 1976 and took a master's degree in 1977 in architecture from Washington University. He worked in the Chicago office of Skidmore, Owings and Merrill from 1978 to 1984. Since 1986 Terp has also been a principal in Arquitectonica, Chicago.

Angelo Testa
(1921-1984)

Angelo Testa was born in Springfield, Massachusetts. In 1940, when he was nineteen years old, his fabric designs were exhibited in the Museum of Modern Art in New York. Although Testa studied at the New York School of Fine and Applied Arts and the University of Chicago, he would later attribute the inspiration for his successful career to László Moholy-Nagy and the Bauhaus philosophy of the Institute of Design in Chicago, where, in 1945, he was the first student to graduate under Moholy-Nagy. In 1947 Testa designed the first collection of abstract fabric patterns to be mass-produced in the United States. He continued to draw inspiration from the aesthetic and design philosophies of the Bauhaus and produced nonobjective fabric designs and fiber patterns for most major furnishing companies, including Knoll Associates and Herman Miller. His work is now in the permanent collections of The Art Institute of Chicago, the Museum of Modern Art in New York, and the Walker Art Center in Minneapolis, and he has exhibited in over 240 museums and colleges.

Thielbar and Fugard

Frederick J. Thielbar (1866-1941)
John Reed Fugard (1886-1968)

A native of Peoria, Illinois, Frederick Thielbar studied at the University of Illinois. In 1925 Thielbar, a former partner with Holabird and Roche, joined John Fugard in founding Thielbar and Fugard. John Reed Fugard graduated from the College of Engineering at the University of Illinois in 1910, and later co-founded the firm Fugard and Knapp. During World War II, Fugard established the firm Fugard, Olson, Urbain and Neiler, which specialized in veteran's hospitals. The firm was reorganized several times over the next thirty years; in 1982 Fugard, Orth and Associates merged with Donahue and Hetherington.

Tigerman McCurry

Stanley Tigerman (born 1930)
Margaret McCurry (born 1942)

Born in Chicago, Stanley Tigerman began his study of architecture at the Massachusetts Institute of Technology in 1945 but left before taking a degree. He later received his undergraduate and graduate degrees in architecture from Yale University, both in 1961. Before going into partnership with Norman Koglin in 1964, Tigerman worked for a number of firms, including George Keck (1949-50), Milton M. Schwartz and Associates (1956-57), Skidmore, Owings and Merrill (1957-59), Paul Rudolph (1959-61), and Harry Weese (1961-62). In 1964 he started his own firm, Stanley Tigerman and Associates, which became Tigerman, Fugman and McCurry in 1980 when Robert Fugman and Margaret McCurry became partners; the firm has been Tigerman McCurry since 1988. Tigerman, who has been the director of the School of Architecture at the University of Illinois at Chicago since 1985, organized the Chicago Seven in the 1970s and was co-organizer of the 1976 "Chicago Architects" exhibition. He was a fellow at the American Academy in Rome and has written several books, including, most recently, *Architecture of Exile* (1988). Margaret McCurry was born in Chicago and received her bachelor of arts degree from Vassar College in 1964. After two years as a design coordinator with the Quaker Oats Company in Chicago, she went to work for Skidmore, Owings and Merrill, where she was a senior interior designer from 1966 to 1977. McCurry then established her own architectural practice in Chicago until the formation of Tigerman, Fugman and McCurry in 1980. She has taught at The School of The Art Institute of Chicago, the University of Illinois at Chicago, and Miami University at Oxford, Ohio.

John Vinci (born 1937)

Born in Chicago, John Vinci received his bachelor's degree in architecture from the Illinois Institute of Technology in 1960. He worked for a year in the Chicago office of Skidmore, Owings and Merrill, and in 1961 he joined the firm of Brenner Danforth Rockwell, where he worked on a number of restoration and remodeling projects. In 1970 he went into partnership with Lawrence G. Kenney, a fellow IIT classmate and Brenner Danforth Rockwell employee. In 1978 Vinci opened his own office, which has completed numerous historic restorations, exhibition designs, and residential projects. Vinci, who has written extensively on architecture, has been a graduate thesis advisor at IIT since 1972, and has taught at the University of Illinois at Chicago and Roosevelt University.

Kurt Voss
(born 1945)

Chicagoan Kurt Voss first began architectural rendering in 1963 when he took a job with Forest Studios in Park Ridge, Illinois. In 1968 he started working for Humen Tan and Associates; he was named partner in 1971 and the name of the firm was changed to Tan and Voss. With Humen Tan's departure for California, Voss took over the firm in 1979.

Charles H. Wacker
(1856-1929)

Charles H. Wacker, a native Chicagoan, was educated at Lake Forest Academy in Illinois and the University of Geneva in Switzerland; he also attended school in Stuttgart, Germany. In 1880 he became a partner in his father's malting firm, and was made president and treasurer of the company, Wacker and Birk Brewing and Malting, in 1884. Wacker was on the ways and means committee for the World's Columbian Exposition, 1893. He became president of the newly formed Chicago Plan Commission in 1909, and oversaw projects to improve the city. His most successful civic effort was his promotion of a double-deck boulevard along the southern side of the Chicago River, which was named Wacker Drive.

Ralph Walker
(1890-1973)

Born in Waterbury, Connecticut, Ralph Walker studied architecture at the Massachusetts Institute of Technology, and worked in Montreal, Canada. He returned to Boston and worked for three years in the office of James T. Ritchie. He won the Rotch Traveling Scholarship, but World War I prevented him from traveling abroad, and instead he went to New York. There he worked briefly in the office of Bertram Goodhue and then with York and Sawyer, before the United States entered the war and he was sent to France with the Army. In 1919 Walker returned to New York and found work with McKenzie, Voorhees and Gmelin, and soon became a junior partner. The year after he joined the firm, Walker took a four-month leave-of-absence to work at the American Academy in Rome. He was named senior partner in 1926 in the firm of Voorhees, Gmelin and Walker. The firm was subsequently known as Voorhees, Walker, Foley and Smith from 1939 to 1954, and finally as Voorhees, Walker, Smith and Smith.

Weese Langley Weese

Cynthia Weese (born 1940)
Benjamin Horace Weese (born 1929)
Dennis Langley (born 1947)

Born in Des Moines, Iowa, Cynthia Weese received her bachelor of science (1962) and bachelor of architecture (1965) degrees from Washington University in St. Louis. She worked independently until 1972, then joined the Chicago landscape architecture firm Joe Karr and Associates. A year later she went to work for Harry Weese and Associates, and in 1975 she started practicing independently again. In 1977 she was a founding principal in the new firm Weese Seegers Hickey Weese, which evolved into the current firm Weese Langley Weese. She was a founding member of the Chicago Architectural Club in 1979 and served as president in 1988 and 1989. Born in Evanston, Illinois, Benjamin Horace Weese earned both his bachelor and master of architecture degrees from Harvard University in 1951 and 1957, respectively, and he received a scholarship and certificate from the Ecole des Beaux-Arts in Paris in 1956. After completing his graduate studies, he returned to Chicago to work with his brother's firm, Harry Weese and Associates, becoming president and assistant head of design. In 1977 he joined his wife, Cynthia, in the firm Weese Seegers Hickey Weese. In 1966 he co-founded the Chicago Architecture Foundation and served as president of the Chicago Architectural Club in 1985 and 1986. A native of Terre Haute, Indiana, Dennis Langley received his bachelor of architecture degree in 1970 from the University of Illinois. After serving in the United States Army from 1971 to 1973, he joined the engineering firm Consoer Townsend and Associates. In 1978 he joined Weese Seegers Hickey Weese, which is now Weese Langley Weese.

Harry Weese
(born 1915)

Born in Evanston, Illinois, Harry Mohr Weese graduated from the Massachusetts Institute of Technology in 1938. He also attended Yale University and the Cranbrook Academy of Art in Bloomfield Hills, Michigan, where he studied city planning with Eliel Saarinen. During World War II, Weese served as an engineering officer in the United States Navy. He then worked at Skidmore, Owings and Merrill for a short time before going into partnership with Benjamin Baldwin in 1946. He opened his own firm, Harry Weese and Associates, just a year later. Weese, who is on the editorial board of *Inland Architect* magazine, has served on the Mayor's Advisory Council on Architecture since 1972.

Wheeler Kearns
Daniel Harding Wheeler (born 1957)
Lawrence Kearns (born 1962)

Born in Norwalk, Connecticut, Daniel Harding Wheeler earned a bachelor of fine arts in 1980 and a bachelor of architecture in 1981 from the Rhode Island School of Design. While in school he worked in the Boston office of Machado-Silvetti Architects, and after graduation he took a job as staff architect in the Chicago office of Skidmore, Owings and Merrill. In 1987 he opened his own firm, and in 1990 Lawrence Kearns, an architect in Wheeler's office since 1988, joined Wheeler as a full partner in Wheeler Kearns. Lawrence Kearns, who was born in Miami, Florida, received his bachelor's degree in architecture from the University of Miami in 1985. While in school Kearns worked in the office of Jan Hochstim, eventually becoming a partner and principal. After graduation Wheeler took a job as senior designer with the Chicago office of Skidmore, Owings and Merrill. He joined Daniel Wheeler in 1988.

Marianne Willisch (1897-1984)

While managing the shop of the Austrian Werkbund, Austria's semiofficial artists' guild, Marianne Willisch met American composer John Alden Carpenter and his wife. Mrs. Carpenter, a well-known Chicago interior decorator, subsequently arranged for the 1928 exhibition of Willisch's Friends of the Austrian Werkbund at the Arts Club of Chicago. Willisch moved to Chicago in 1930, where she helped to organize the Chicago Workshops, an artists' cooperative similar to the Austrian Werkbund. She opened a store in Diana Court at 540 North Michigan Avenue and sold furniture and crafts designed by the Chicago Workshops members, along with European imports. Willisch eventually designed her own line of furniture, overseeing its production for nearly fifty years with Italian cabinetmaker Alfred Mattaliano, and later with his son, Frank, at Wells Furniture Makers, their custom furniture shop in Chicago.

James Wines (born 1932)

Born in Oak Park, Illinois, James Wines received his bachelor of arts degree from Syracuse University in 1955. After college he received a Rome Prize for study at the American Academy in Rome. Upon his return to the United States, Wines worked as a sculptor in New York, and developed an interest in challenging the conventional relationship between public art and architecture. In 1969 he started the architecture firm SITE (Sculpture in the Environment), and took Emilio Sousa, Alison Sky, and Michelle Stone as partners in 1973. Wines has taught at colleges across the northeast, including the School of Visual Arts in New York, New York University, Cooper Union, and the New Jersey School of Architecture, where he became a professor in 1975.

Yost and Taylor
Lloyd Morgan Yost (1908-1992)
Darl Coder Taylor (born 1913)

Born in Ohio, Lloyd Morgan Yost attended Northwestern University and received a degree in architecture from Ohio State University in 1931. He came to Chicago to work with the architect Pierre Blouke, and in 1932 Yost opened his own office. During his twenty years in private practice, he also taught architecture at the University of Illinois and industrial design at The School of The Art Institute of Chicago. From 1952 to 1960 he was in a partnership with Darl Coder Taylor, and in 1967 he was named director of the Chicago School of Architecture Foundation, a position that he held until his retirement to Arkansas in 1970. Darl Coder Taylor was born in Fort Wayne, Indiana, and attended the Carnegie Institute of Technology and the University of Washington. In 1935 he took a job with the office of R. Harold Zook, becoming a partner four years later. After serving in the Civil Engineers Corps of the United States Navy during World War II, Taylor returned to Chicago to become a partner in the firm of Holsman, Holsman, Klekamp and Taylor. In 1952 he went into partnership with Lloyd Morgan Yost, and in 1960 he formed Coder Taylor Associates.

Hugh E. Young
(1886-1951)

After graduating with a degree in civil engineering from the University of Iowa in 1905, Hugh E. Young came to Chicago, where he was associated with the engineering departments of the Illinois Steel Company, the American Bridge Company, and several railroad companies. In 1914 he was appointed by the Civil Service Commission of Chicago as the engineer in charge of designing Chicago's bridges and highway structures. Working as the chief engineer for the Chicago Plan Commission, and frequently in consultation with the architect Edward H. Bennett, Young designed bridges over the Chicago River at Madison and Monroe streets, as well as several significant urban transportation improvements designed to ease automobile and commercial traffic circulation. Originating with the 1909 Chicago Plan, these projects included the construction of Wacker Drive, Outer Drive, and a lakefront airport, the straightening of the Chicago River, various street-widening projects, and a proposal for a series of raised superhighways running west of the city. He worked with the Chicago Plan Commission between 1920 and 1945, then joined Ralph H. Burke as chief engineer in planning for O'Hare International Airport; he retired in 1950. Young also served as a consultant to the commissioners of Lincoln Park and the South Parks. A member of the American Society of Planning Officials, the Western Society of Civil Engineers, and the American Society of Civil Engineers, Young published extensive planning reports and articles in professional journals, in which he described planning strategies for managing the automobile in the Loop. Among others, these strategies included his department's traffic control projects and major improvements based on the Chicago Plan, such as the Outer Drive improvement.

Harvey Zorbaugh
(1896-1965)

Born in Ohio and educated at Oberlin College, Vanderbilt University, and the University of Chicago, Zorbaugh was a Chicago school sociologist whose 1929 work, *The Gold Coast and the Slum*, still resonates as a depiction of the deep social and economic cleavages cutting through the metropolitan community. He later went to work for New York University and specialized in educational sociology and orthopsychiatry.

Index of Architects and Designers

Numbers in **bold type** refer to pages with illustrations.

Aalto, Alvar 273
Adler, Dankmar 322, 324
Adler, David 207, 311, 322, 458
Adler and Sullivan 24, 125
Agha, Dr. 295
Allen, Alfred P. 77, **77**
Allner, Walter 295
Alschuler, Alfred S. 63, **419**, 458
Anderson, Peirce 305, 308, 463
Armstrong, John **236**
Arquitectonica Chicago **375**
Atwood, Leland 207, **268**, 269
The Austin Company 84, **93**, 94, **372**
Averill, John 288
Axeman, James 293

B

B & D Design Associates 280
Babka, Bernard F. 464
Banks/Eakin 324, **446**, 458
Banks, John H. 458
Banse, Herbert G. **164**
Barr, Frank 293
Bauhs and Dring 325
Bayer, Herbert 293
Bec Var, Arthur 273
Beck, Bruce 290, 291, **293**, 294, 298, 458
Bedno, Ed 294, 299, 300
Bedno, Jane 299, 300
Beeby, Thomas H. 25, 306, 308, 311, 323, 324, **457**, 464
Behrens, Peter 271
Bel Geddes, Norman 65, 68
Belli, Allen 458
Belli, Anthony 458
Belli and Belli 24, **24**, **421**, 458
Belli, Edo J. 458
Belli, James 458
Bennett, Edward H. 15, 40, 54, **54**, 55, 56, 57, **57**, 58, 60, 64, 78, 99, 101, 102, **103**, 106-07, **221**, 251, 323, **449**, 459
Bennett, Edward H., Jr. **453**, **454**
Bennett, Parsons and Frost 40, **58**
Bertoia, Harry 273
Bertsch and Cooper 283, 288
Bertsch, Fred 283
Beyer Blinder Belle 116
Binder, Joseph 288, 289, 290
Black, Gilmer Vardiman 326
Black, John T. 461
Blake, Hayward 298
Blake and Weiss 298
de Blois, Natalie 326
Bofill, Ricardo 28, 48
Boller, Harri 298
Bonner, Darcy, Jr. **448**, 464
Booth/Hansen and Associates **396**, **397**, 459
Booth, Laurence 25, 26, 311, 323, **405**, 459
Booth and Nagle 324
Booth, Nagle and Hartray 323
Bourgeois, Louis **419**
Bowman Brothers 266, 324,
Boyington, W. W. 104, **105**

Brazeley, William, and Associates **457**
Brenner Danforth Rockwell 24, 325, **426**, **453**, 459
Brenner, Daniel 144, 275, 278, **278**, 311, **426**, 459
Brodovitch, Alexei 295
Brownson, Jacques 156, **246**, **254**, 306, 308, 325, 459
Brubaker, C. William **260**, 469
Buenz, John 472
Bunshaft, Gordon 22
Burgee, John 28, **360**
Burgee, John, with Philip Johnson 26, 28, **360**, **361**, **428**
Burke, David 300
Burke, Ralph H., Associates 75, 85-86, **85**, 87, 89, 459
Burnham Brothers 16, 43, 322, 459-60
Burnham and Co., D. H. 36, 125, **126**, **128**, **131**, **260**, 304, 322, 459-60
Burnham, Daniel H. 15, 18, 24, 40, 54, 55, 78, 99, 106-07, 128, 131, 180, 196, 248, 251, 304, 307, 308, 323, 325, 459-60
Burnham, Daniel H., Jr. 85, 459-60
Burnham and Hammond 82, **425**, 459-60
Burnham, Hubert 44, **221**, 237, **237**, 459-60
Burnham and Root 276, 307, **426**, 459-60
Burns, W. R., Jr. **389**
Burtin, Will 295
Burton, Robert 39

C

Caldwell, Alfred 325, 452
Capraro, Alexander V. 218, 224, **224**
Carpenter, Rue Winterbotham 265, 266
Carter, Drake and Wight 248, **248**
Cassandre, A. M. 292
Castro Buchel **414**
Cedarstrand, Carl **387**
Center for Advanced Research in Design (CARD) 298
Chapman, Dave 265, 266, 270, 275, 276, 277, 460
Charn, Victor L. **158**
Chase, Frank 460
Chatten, Melville 236, **236**
Chermayeff, Serge 19, 275, 460
Chirpe, Rodney 286, 288, 289, 290, 291
Christiansen, Roy 237, **237**
Coates, Ron 298
Coder Taylor Associates **438**
Cohen, Stuart 25, 323, 460
Coiner, Charles 292
Colburn, I. W. 323
Consoer and Morgan 80
Consoer, Townsend and Associates 93
Cooper, Oswald 283, 284, **284**, 286, 288, 291, 460

Corbett, Harvey Wiley 54, 59, **59**, 64, 224
Cordogan, Clark and Associates **408**
Cordwell, J. D. 472
Cret, Paul Philippe **223**, 224
Crosby, Bart 298

D

DaBoll, Ray 288, 289, 291, **292**
Dana, Eugene 293, 300
Danforth, George E. 459
Dart, Edward **443**
DeGolyer, Robert 237, **237**
De Renzi, Mario 218, 224, **224**
Decker, Howard 323, 461
Decker and Kemp **456**, 461
Deknatel, William F. **16**, 17, 210-11, **210**, **211**, 325, 461
Design Consultants Inc. 298
Design Partnership 298
Deskey, Donald 272
DeStefano, James 325, 326
Detterer, Ernst 284, 285, 286, 287
Dickens, Sid 275, 288, 289, 290, **290**, 291
Doblin, Jay 265, 275, 277, 280, 281, 297, 298, 299, 461
Doblin, Jay, and Associates 298
Dorfsman, Lou 295
Dotson and Darr 323
Doyle, Deborah 323, 324, 461
Dreyfuss, Henry 272
Dubin, Arthur 461
Dubin and Dubin **40**, **181**
Dubin, Dubin and Moutoussamy 461
Dubin and Eisenberg **432**, **441**
Dubin, George 461
Dubin, Henry 461
Dunning, N. Max 266
Dwiggins, W. A. 283

E

Eakin, Garret 458
Eames, Charles 273, 275, 462
Eames, Ray 273, 275, 462
Eberson, John **436**, **451**
Eckerstrom, Ralph 277, 278, 295, 296, **296**, 298
Elmes, Willard Frederic 285
Elting, Winston 323, 324, 326
Epstein, A., and Sons 41, 256, **257**, 324, **434**, **449**, **452**, 462
Epstein, Abraham 462
Erikson, Carl A. 470

F

Faidy, Abel 17, **17**, 265, 266, **267**, 273, 462
Faidy, Renor 273, **273**
Ferriss, Hugh 42, 59, **59**, 68, **100**, 108, **336**, **417**, 462
Fleming, William 291
Florian, Paul 324, 462
Florian-Wierzbowski 27, 325, **380**, 462

Foran, Walter J. 462-63
Fox, Sheldon 466
Freed, James Ingo 25
Frej, David 300
Frost and Granger 322
Fugard, John Reed 20, 243, 473
Fugard, Olsen, Urbain and Neiler **420**
Fugman Dakich and Associates 323
Fujikawa Johnson and Associates **421**, **455**, 462
Fujikawa, Joseph 462
Fuller, R. Buckminster 21, 65, 207, 214-15, **215**, 266, **268**, 336, 462
Fyfe, William Beye 207, 208

G

Garbe, Raymond W. **388**
Garden, Hugh M. G. 237, **237**, 324, **442**, 470
Garland, Chris **299**, 300
Gelick Foran Associates **403**, **455**, 462-63
Gelick, Michael 462-63
Genther, Charles 68, **69**, 324, 463
Gerhardt, Paul, Jr. **75**, 80, 82, **82**, 83, **83**, 463
Giammanco, Michael **282**
Giaver and Dinkelberg 43, **62**
Gillespie, Edwin 288
Gladych, Stanislaw 87, 156, 262, **304**, 305, 306, 308
Glaser, Milton 295
Glass, Henry P., Associates 280
Glass, Marvin, Associates 271, 279, **279**, 280, 463
Glass, Michael 300
Goettsch, James 325, 326, **353**
Goff, Bruce **213**, 214-16, **214**, 463
Goldberg, Bertrand 20, 21, 23, **23**, 25, **266**, **271**, 272, 326, **413**, 463
Golden, William 295
Goldsholl, Millie 290, 294
Goldsholl, Morton 290, 291, 294, 463
Goldsholl, Morton, Design Associates **289**, 298
Goldsmith, Myron **153**, 156, 258, 325, 471
Goldsmith, Yamasaki, Specht 280
Gonzalez, Joseph 27, 324, 471
Gordon, Ezra 326
Gordon, Max 28, **29**
Gorski, Gilbert 463
Goudy, Bertha 283
Goudy, Frederic 283, 286
Graham, Anderson, Probst and White 17, 22, 36, **36**, 38, 40, **41**, 42, **42**, 43, **98**, 99, **100**, 102, 106, **107**, 110, **110**, 111, **111**, **112**, **113**, 116, 127, **129**, **130**, 131, 132, **132**, **133**, 137, **154**, **167**, 186, 303, **303**, 304, 305, 308, 322, 323, **410**, 463
Graham, Bruce J. 22, 156, **157**, 258, 307, 308, 311, 324, 326, 471
Graham, Ernest R. 24, 107, 110, **234**, 303, 304, 305, 463
Greiner, John 298, 300

Griffin, Walter Burley   24, 324
Grillo, Maria   300
Gropius, Walter   271
Gruen, Victor   180, 183, **184**, 185, **188**, 189, 190, 196
Grunsfeld, Ernest A., Jr.   233, **234**, 236, **236**, 465-66

H

HTI/Space Design International   197
Hacker, Julie   323
Hackl, Donald   466-67
Haid, David   155, 156, **156**, 325, 464
Halprin, Lawrence   168, 185, 186
Hammond, Beeby and Babka   26, 323, 325, **344**, **345**, 464
Hammond, C. Herrick   459-60
Hammond, James W.   324, 325, 464
Hansen, Paul   459
Hanson, Oscar   285
Harringer, Henry T.   17, **41**, 42, 269, **269**, **376-77**, 464
Harringer-Jacobson-Colvin   **376-77**
Hartmann, William E.   24, 255-56
Hartray, John F.   468
Hasbrouck, Wilbert   24
Hausner and Macsai   **445**
Haymes, David A.   469
Heinrich, John   154, 156, 325
Hellmuth, Obata, and Kassabaum   **449**, **456**
Hickey, Thomas   325
Hilberseimer, Ludwig Karl   19, 464
Himmel Bonner Associates   325, **382**, **383**, **448**, 464
Himmel, Scott   464
Hinds, Schroeder and Whitaker   325
Hodgdon, Frederick   **236**
Hoffman, Wolfgang   272
Hofmann, Armin   296
Holabird, John A.   64, **221**, 236, **236**, 324, 464
Holabird and Roche   36, 37, 121, **121**, **122**, **125**, **181**, 308, 324, 464
Holabird and Root   **16**, 17, 22, 28, 36, 42, 43, 62, 104, 105, **106**, 107, **118**, **130**, **131**, 134-35, **135**, **165**, **182**, **183**, 225, **225**, **247**, 248, 324, **358**, **359**, **410**, **414**, **415**, 464
Holabird and Root and Burgee   24, 186, **244**, 311
Holabird, William   464
Holbert and Hollander   323
Holsman, Henry K.   235
Hood, Raymond   64, 107
Horn, Gerald   324
Horsley, S. Clements   **221**
Howells and Hood   **425**
Hudgins, Thompson, Ball and Associates   70, **70**
Hunt, Jarvis   322
Hurlburt, Allen   295
Huszagh and Hill   323
Huszagh, Ralph   236, **236**

I

IDEA   280
Iannelli, Alfonso   269, **368**, **449**, 465
Isozaki, Arata   279

J

Jacobson, Egbert   271, 286, 288, 289, 292, 293, 295
Jahn, Helmut   25, 27, **28**, **90**, 92, 116, **257**, **302**, 303, 306-08, **306**, 325, **340**, **341**, **415**, **422**, **428**, 468

Jardine, Hill and Murdock   62, **62**
Jenney, William Le Baron   146, **146**, 322, 325
Jensen, Elmer   236, **236**
Jickling, Lyman and Powell   **178**, **189**, 190
Johnson, Gerald L.   462
Johnson, M. Martin   291
Johnson, Philip   20, 28, 151, 192, 307
Johnson, Ralph   27, 324, **418**, **429**, 469
Jones, E. Willis   288
Jorgensen, J. B.   **162**
Juhl, Finn   275

K

KDA Industrial Design Consultants   280, **281**
Kahn, Albert   20, 21, 76, **83**, 144, **369**, **370**, **371**, 465
Kearney, Hall   299
Kearns, Lawrence   474
Keck, George Fred   **200**, 201, **203**, 204, 206, **206**, **207**, 208-10, **208**, **209**, 216, 241, 266, **268**, 324, 325, 465
Keck, William   **200**, 201, **203**, 204, 206, **206**, **207**, 208-10, **208**, **209**, 216, 241, 266, **268**, 324, 465
Keig, Susan Jackson   294
Kemp, Kevin A.   324, 461
Kepes, Gyorgy   19, 289, 290, 293
Kerbis, Gertrude L.   87, 88, 465
Ketchum, Gina and Sharp   **168**
Khan, Fazlur   156, **157**, 326, 471
Kittredge, Bill   286
Klaber, Eugene H.   465-66
Klaber and Grunsfeld   465-66
Kleihues, Josef Paul   28
Klein, Larry   300
Klein, William J.   **34**
Kleinschmidt, Robert D.   469
Klekamp and Whitmore   82
Kner, Albert   292, 293
Knight, Lester B., and Associates   **346**, **347**
Kohn, A. Eugene   466
Kohn Pedersen Fox Associates   28, **48**, **356**, **357**, **381**, **430**, **439**, 466
Koppe, Richard   293, 300
Kovach, Ron   298
Kramer, Ferdinand   271
Kroman, Lewis M.   63, **63**
Krueck and Olsen   325, **440**
Krueck, Ronald   325, 466
Krueck and Sexton   **395**, 466
Kula, Elsa   290, 291, 293, 294, **294**
Kurokawa, Kisho   28, **29**, **450**, **455**

L

LaGrange, Lucien, and Associates   68, **68**
Lamb, Ted   326
Landahl, Gregory W.   325, 466
The Landahl Group   **450**
Landon Architects   **447**
Landon, Peter   325, 466
Landrum and Brown   83, 87, 89, 90, 466
Langdon, Tannys   26, 311, 323, **398**, **440**, 466
Langley, Dennis   473
Latham, Richard   265, 270, 273, 275, 280, 466
Latham, Tyler, Jensen   298
Leavitt, Sarah   293

Leckie, Hubert   293
Legge-Kemp, Diane   324, 326, **432**, 471
Lesnikowski, Wojciech   324
Levin, Jack   326
Levy, Alexander L.   **34**
Libera, Adalberto   **218**, 224, **224**
Lienhart, Jim   298, 299, **299**
Linn, Lucy Blair   265
Lionni, Leo   295
Liska, A. C.   **451**
Little, Jack   266
Loebl, Jerrold   466-67
Loebl, Schlossman and Bennett   22, 168, 183, **184**, 185, **185**, 186, **186**, **187**, 189, 190, 240, **240**, 241, **246**, **253**, 255, **372**, **379**
Loebl, Schlossman, Bennett and Dart   190, 191, **191**, **192**, **193**, 194
Loebl, Schlossman and Hackl   27, 323, 324, **429**, 466-67
Loewenberg, Israel   **237**, 241
Loewenberg, Max   **237**, 241
Loewy Associates   273
Loewy, Raymond   277
Lohan Associates   **173**, **174**, **175**, **412**, **423**, **430**, 467
Lohan, Dirk   467
Long, Ann   294
Lubalin, Herb   295
Lynch, Edgar   272

M

Ma, Anthony   300
Mabrey/Kaiser   298
Macsai, John   467
Maddox, Eva   279, 325, **386**, 467
Magierek, Paul   **453**
Magnuson, Floyd   326
Maher, Philip B.   **236**, 265, **390**
Malcolmson, Reginald   311
Manny, Carter H., Jr.   24, 87, 90, 325, **442**, 467
Mao, Peter   **237**
Marshall and Fox   322
Marx, Flint, and Schonne   24
Marx, Samuel Abraham   322, 323, 467
Massey, John   296, **296**, 298, 300, 467
Mastro, James   296, **296**, 298, 300, 467
Mastro and Skylar   324, 467
Matter, Herbert   **293**, 295
Mayo, Earnest   **237**
McCurry, Margaret   324, 473
McMahon, Franklin   294
McNally and Quinn   17, **17**, 18, **18**, **441**
McNear, Everett   291, 294
McVicker, George   288, 290
Merrill, John   **236**, 325, 471
Metter, Andrew   324
Metz and Gunderson   **235**
Meyer Glass Design   280
Meyers, Lynn B.   472
Middleton, Robert Hunter   285, 286, 287, 288, 289, 291, 293, 295, 468
Mies van der Rohe, Ludwig   19, 20, 21, 22, 25, 69, 70, 140, 141-57, **141**, **142**, **143**, **145**, **147**, **148**, **149**, **150**, **151**, **152**, 207, 210, 241, 256, 257, **257**, 303, 305, 306, 307, 311, 323, 325, **343**, **391**, **392**, **393**, **420**, **421**, 452, 467-68
Mies van der Rohe, Office of   **410**
Mine, Richard Yoshijiro   17, **438**, 468

Mittelbusher and Tourtelot   24
Moholy-Nagy, László   19, 288, 290, 293, 468
Moore, Charles W.   **457**
Moore, John C. B.   **221**
Moore, Phoebe   294, **294**
Moore, Ruble, and Yudell   **363**, **427**
Moutoussamy, John   461
Mozer, Jordan   **406**, **407**, 468
van der Muelen, John   324, 325
Müller-Brockman, Josef   296
Muller-Munk, Peter   266
Mundie and Jensen   322
Murphy, C. F., Associates   23, 24, 28, 80, 86, **88**, 89, **89**, 90, 156, **246**, **253**, **254**, **257**, 258, **259**, **261**, 262, **302**, 303, **304**, 305-07, **305**, **306**, 323, 325, **428**, 468
Murphy, Charles F.   22-23, 24, 303-05, 308, 468
Murphy, Charles F., Jr.   305
Murphy/Jahn   28, **28**, 90, **90**, 92, 308, **309**, 325, 326, **334**, **335**, **340**, **341**, **346**, **347**, **350**, **353**, **415**, **422**, 468
Myhrum, Arthur   **453**, **454**

N

Naess and Murphy   23, 86, 107, **107**, 238, **239**, 255, 258, 303, **304**
Naess, Sigurd E.   86, **304**, 305, 308
Nagle, Hartray and Associates   **338**, **358**, **394**, **404**, **434**, **446**, 468
Nagle, James   25, 311, 468
Navigato, Rocco   **284**, 285
Nelson, George   277
Netsch, Walter   22, 23, **23**, 25, 305, 326, **442**, 471
Neufert, Ernst   21
Neumann, Hans   306
Nichols, Dale   288
Nimmons, Carr and Wright   **235**, **378**
Nimmons, George C.   121, 128, 265
Noorda, Bob   296
Novack, John M.   90, 306

O

O'Dell and Rowland   **203**
O'Donnell, Wicklund, Pigozzi and Peterson   324
O'Hare Associates   90, **92**, 93
Owings, Nathaniel   325, 471

P

Pace Associates   68-69, **69**, 325, 468-69
Palma, Joseph   265, 270, **270**
Palma Knapp Design   **275**
Pappageorge, George   469
Pappageorge/Haymes   325, 373, **447**, 469
Passonneau, Joseph   311, 324
Patterson, Rhodes   294
Paul, Arthur   295, **295**
Pedersen, William   **356**, 466
Pei, I. M.   89, 262, **339**, **444**, 469
Pelli, Cesar   27, **27**, **362**, 469
Pereira, Hal   265
Pereira, William C.   324, **403**
Perkins, Chatten and Hammond   **164**
Perkins, Lawrence B.   262, 276, 469
Perkins and Will   23, 27, 28, 93, **93**, 108, **169**, 170, **259**, **260**, **261**, 276, 324, **348**, **355**, **364**, **413**, **418**, **420**, **429**, 469

Perman, Norman   291, 294, 299, 300
Peterhans, Walter   19
Phillips, Frederick   325, **399**, 469
Phipps, Park   294
Pinzke, Herb   290, 293, 296
Platner, Warren   192, 194
Plunkard, James   323
Poore, Taylor   294
Porter, Allen   294
Potokar, Rich   324
Powell, Donald D.   469
Powell/Kleinschmidt   325, **361**, 469
Preiss, Fred   270
Prestini, James   469
Probst, Edward   463
Pursell, Werner   289

Q

Quinn, Everett   237, **237**
Quinn, James Edwin   **18**, **87**, **416**, 469
Quinn, Kathryn   470

R

RVI Corporation   298
Rajkovitch, Thomas   311, 323
Rand, Paul   295
Ransom, Will   286
Rapp, Cornelius W.   470
Rapp, George Leslie   470
Rapp and Rapp   **26**, 34, 470
Rapson, Ralph   324, 326
Ray, Bert   288, 291, **292**, 294
Reader, Henry, Associates   266
Rebori, Andrew N.   57, 62, **76**, 77, **77**, 78, **79**, **182**, 322, 323, 470
Rebori, Wentworth, Dewey and McCormick   **76**, 77, **77**, **118**
Regehr, Carl   294, **297**, 298, 300
Reid, Michael   300
Reinecke, Jean   265, 277
Ressinger, Paul   286, 288
Richardson, Henry Hobson   24, 109, **109**, 322
Robert, Francois   296, 298
Roberts, E. E.   **237**
Robertson, Jacquelin T.   **457**
Robertz, Henry   298
Roche and Dinkeloo   28
Roche, Martin   464
Rockwell, H. P. Davis   459
Root, John Wellborn   26, 248, 304, 307, 308, 459-60
Root, John Wellborn, Jr.   265, 324, 464
Roth, Randall   294, 300
Rudolph, Christopher   323, 325, 427, 470
Rudolph, Paul   275

S

SITE   29, **436**
Saarinen, Eero   24, 104, 273
Saarinen, Eliel   **58**, 59, 66, 276, **276**, **420**
Sackett, DeForest   290, **290**, 291
Sant'Elia, Antonio   108
Sasaki Associates   170
Schildknecht, Rainer   **428**
Schipporeit, George   **154**, 156, 325
Schipporeit-Heinrich Associates   **410**
Schleger, Hans   293
Schlegman, Sheldon   **434**
Schlossman, Norman J.   466-67

Schmidt, Garden and Erikson   22, **22**, 23, 24, **228**, 229, 230, 256, 257, 470
Schmidt, Garden, and Martin   324
Schmidt, Richard E.   22, 24, 324, 470
Schneider, Karl   270-71
Schroeder, Charles W.   211
Schroeder, Kenneth A.   470
Schroeder, Murchie, Laya Associates   325, 440
Schwartz, Milton M., and Associates   28, 324, **416**, **443**, **444**, 470
Schweikher, Paul   17, **204**, **205**, 206, **206**, 207-08, 216-17, 266, **267**, 323, 324, 326, 470-71
Sexton, Mark P.   466
Shaw, Alfred P.   22, 23, 111, 112, 113, **235**, **303**, 305, **412**, 471
Shaw and Associates   **195**, **360**, **361**, **424**, **428**, 471
Shaw, Howard Van Doren   311, 322
Shaw, Metz and Associates   23, **45**, **167**, **232**, **244**, **245**, **256**
Shaw, Metz and Dolio   **66**, 67, 324
Shaw, Naess and Murphy   **235**, 305
Shaw, Pat   471
Shepard, Otis   **287**, 288
Shepley, Rutan and Coolidge   322
Sisco/Lubotsky   323, 324
Skidmore, Louis   325, 471
Skidmore, Owings and Merrill   22, 23, **23**, 24, 27, **27**, 28, 67, **67**, 108, **108**, 115, 156, 170, **194**, **196**, 241, 242-43, **242**, **243**, 246, **253**, 255, **258**, **259**, 305, 324, 325, **329**, **338**, **354**, **355**, **365**, **366-67**, **374**, **421**, **432**, **457**, 471
Skylar, Claudia   467
Sloan, Frederick   388
Slutsky, Rael D.   382, 472
Smith, Adrian   27, **27**, 324, 471
Smith, Dan   294
Smith, H. B.   298
Solfisburg, Roy   324
Solomon Cordwell Buenz and Associates   **198**, **439**, 472
Solomon, Louis R.   472
Spadaro, Tony   298
Speyer, A. James   275, 472
Spuehler, Ernest   290
Stapleton, James   **448**
Starck, Otto   87, 258, **305**, 306, 308
Stern, Robert A. M.   **384**, **385**, **427**, **457**, 472
Steurmer, Ray   211
Stieringer, Luther   41
Storrs, John   **350**
Sullivan, Louis H.   24, 119, 155, 311, 322, 324, 325, 326
Summers, Gene   156, **257**, 303, 306-07, **306**, 307, 308, 323, 325, 472
Sutner, Ladislav   295
Swainson, Ann   270
Swan, David   324
Switzer, Robert   265, 266
Syvertsen, John   323, 472

T

Taege, Robert L., and Associates   **453**
Tague, Robert Bruce   324, 326
Takano, Ted   300
Takeuchi, Arthur   325
Tallmadge, Thomas E.   47, **47**, 237, **237**
Tallmadge and Watson   322
Tange, Kenzo   28
Taylor, D. Coder   211, 389, 474

Tempo   294
Terp, Dana G.   **375**, 472
Terp/Meyers   472
Testa, Angelo   472
Teubner, Peter   298
Thielbar, Frederick J.   473
Thielbar and Fugard   43, **62**, **235**, **351**, **420**, 473
Thies, Walter J.   387
Thirst   300
Thomas, Andrew J.   234, **234**
Tigerman, Fugman and McCurry   37, **37**, 323
Tigerman McCurry   325, **454**, 473
Tigerman, Stanley   25, **25**, 311, **418**, **445**, **454**, **457**, 473
Titel, Irving   293
Trowbridge and Livingston   **127**
Tschichold, Jan   287

U

Uhl, Earl   291, **291**
Unimark   265, 277, 278, 296, 298, 299

V

Valente, Antonio   **218**, 224, **224**
Valicenti, Rick   **282**, 300
Van Osdel, John M.   248, **248**
Vignelli, Massimo   277, 296, 298
Vinci, John   28, **29**, 325, **425**, 473
Vitzthum and Burns   **130**, **351**
Vogele, Robert   296, 298, 299
Voorhees, Gmelin and Walker   78, **79**, **342**, **401**

W

Wachsmann, Konrad   202, 211
Walcott, Chester Howe   236, **236**
Walcott, Russell   207
Walker, Ralph T.   44, 107, **401**, 473
Warner, Harry O.   266
Warren, Clinton J.   **249**
Watson, Vernon   237, **237**
Webb, Wayne   298
Weber, Bertram   237, **237**
Webster, Maurice   77, **77**
Weese, Benjamin H.   25, 325, 473
Weese, Cynthia   325, 473
Weese, Harry   23, 25, 273, 325, **412**, **422**, 473
Weese, Harry, Associates   24, 278, **352**, **412**
Weese Langley Weese   **400**, 473
Wheeler, Daniel H.   26, 27, **448**, 474
Wheeler Kearns   **26**, 324, **448**, 474
Whitaker-Guernsey   294
White, Charles   **237**
White, Howard Judson   463
Whitney, Patrick   280, 299
Wierzbowski, Stephen   462
Wight, Peter B.   248, **248**
Will, Philip, Jr.   469
Willisch, Marianne   266, **267**, 273, 474
Wilson, Fred   323
Wines, James   474
Wolff, Peggy Smolka   **354**
Wong, Y. C.   325
Wood, Richard C.   **221**
Wormley, Edward   275
Wright, Frank Lloyd   21, 26, 141, 155, 201, 202, 206, 207, 208, 211, 216, **216**, **217**, 311, 324, 325, 326, **349**

Wright, Russell   274, 275, 277
Wright, Steven   27, **429**

X Y Z

Xeno   300
Yamasaki, Minoru, and Associates   **344**, **426**
Yost, Lloyd Morgan   206, 211-12, **212**, 266, 273, 324, **442**, 474
Yost and Taylor   **426**, **433**, 474
Zeller, Herbert   277
Zook and Taylor   **418**, **449**

Photography Credits

Note. All photographs used as illustrations in the essays are in the collections of the The Art Institute of Chicago, except those indicated below, which were supplied by other institutions, agencies, or individual photographers. In the plate and catalogue sections, photographs of objects were supplied by lending institutions unless otherwise indicated below. Wherever possible, photographs have been credited to the original photographers, regardless of the source of the photograph.

Front cover: John Gronkowski
Frontispiece: John Gronkowski
Spine: John Zukowsky
Back cover: Hedrich-Blessing
Pages 12-13: Hedrich-Blessing

ESSAYS

Bouman
1. Hedrich-Blessing 939-C, courtesy of the Chicago Historical Society; 2. Courtesy of the Chicago Historical Society ICHi-23146; Kaufmann and Fabry, courtesy of the Chicago Historical Society ICHi-13712; 5. Courtesy of the Chicago Transit Authority 221-39; 9. Bruce Van Inwegen 138.04, courtesy of Tigerman McCurry; 11. Courtesy of the Chicago Historical Society ICHi-21631; 12. Walter Radebaugh, courtesy of the Chicago Historical Society ICHi-23635; 13. Courtesy of the Chicago Historical Society ICHi-23467; 14. Courtesy of Arthur Dubin; 15. Hedrich-Blessing 1660-B, courtesy of the Chicago Historical Society; 18. Hedrich-Blessing 1763-I, courtesy of the Chicago Historical Society; 21. Hedrich-Blessing 12633-L2, courtesy of Florsheim Shoe Company; 22. Copelin, courtesy of the Chicago Historical Society ICHi-23468; 23. Evanston Photographic Studios 512-46; 24. Gregory Murphey, courtesy of Kohn Pedersen Fox.

Brodherson
1. Hedrich-Blessing, courtesy of the Chicago Historical Society, ICHi-23506; 7. Courtesy of the Chicago Historical Society, Department of Architecture; 10, 19. Courtesy of United Airlines G63383; 12. Fred T. Richter, courtesy of the Chicago Historical Society ICHi-21742; 14. Courtesy of the Chicago Historical Society ICHi-18426; 15. Dave Chare Photography 81-6552, courtesy of Ralph Burke Associates; 16. Courtesy of Cook County Highway Department; 17. Geonex, Chicago Aerial Survey, Inc. 7508-014; 18. Hedrich-Blessing 25500-B2, courtesy of the Chicago Historical Society; 21. Courtesy of Murphy/Jahn; 23. Steinkamp/Ballogg, courtesy of Perkins and Will; 24. Courtesy of the Austin Company.

Bruegmann
1, 7, 14. Courtesy of Motorola Museum of Electronics; 2. Lawrence Okrent 101389-F05; 6. Courtesy of Mars, Inc., M & M Mars Division; 8. Edward Feeney, courtesy of the Chicago Historical Society ICHi-04693; 9. Courtesy of the Chicago Historical Society ICHi-23633; 10. Hedrich-Blessing 7039-B, courtesy of the Chicago Historical Society; 11. Courtesy of the Jewel Tea Company; 13. Brandt and Associates 119602; 16. Hedrich-Blessing 24470-G, courtesy of Perkins and Will; 17, 20. Lawrence Okrent 051189-H27, 100388-G06; 22. Courtesy of Lohan Associates; 23, 24. Hedrich-Blessing 50965-G, 50965-L, courtesy of Lohan Associates

Doordan
1. Kaufmann and Fabry Co.; 8, 10, 11, 13-15. Kaufmann and Fabry Co., courtesy of the University of Illinois at Chicago, The University Library, Century of Progress Records; 5. Courtesy of the Chicago Historical Society; 16. Courtesy of the Chicago Historical Society ICHi-23426; 17. The Mitchell Wolfson, Jr., Collection, courtesy of The Wolfsonian Foundation, Miami, Florida.

Harris
1, 18. Balthazar Korab 29361, 29358; 2. Courtesy of the Chicago Historical Society ICHi-17364; 3. Courtesy of the Chicago Historical Society ICHi-16786; 4, 5. Courtesy of Arthur Dubin; 6. Raymond Trowbridge, courtesy of the Chicago Historical Society ICHi-21560; 7. Hedrich-Blessing SN877-A, courtesy of the Chicago Historical Society; 8. Courtesy of the Historical Society of Oak Park and River Forest; 9. Courtesy of Loebl, Schlossman and Hackl; 10. Courtesy of Victor Gruen Associates; 11, 12. Hedrich-Blessing 20652-Q, 20652-A, courtesy of the Chicago Historical Society; 13. Ezra Stoller © ESTO 108X.31 WS 922328; 14, 15. Courtesy of Loebl, Schlossman and Hackl; 16, 17. Courtesy of Victor Gruen Associates; 19. Courtesy of Loebl, Schlossman and Hackl; 20-22. Courtesy of Warren Platner; 23. Hedrich-Blessing 50835-A, courtesy of Continental Bank; 25. Hedrich-Blessing 50329-A, courtesy of Skidmore, Owings and Merrill; 26. Courtesy of Marshall Field's; 27. Hedrich-Blessing 50247-F, courtesy of Crate and Barrel.

Margolin
1. Courtesy of Rick Valicenti/Thirst; 3, 7, 9-13, 15-17, 21. Courtesy of Special Collections, The University Library, University of Illinois at Chicago; 19. Courtesy of John Massey.

Miller, "City Hall"
1. Hedrich-Blessing 25252-H7; 2. Ross Miller; 3. Sigmund Osty, courtesy of the Chicago Historical Society ICHi-23027; 5. William T. Barnum, courtesy of the Chicago Historical Society ICHi-20186; 7. Ezra Stoller © ESTO 71CC3; 10. Courtesy of the Chicago Historical Society ICHi-20620; 14. Hedrich-Blessing, courtesy of the Chicago Historical Society ICHi-27043-O; 15. Hedrich-Blessing 36277-T; 16. Ezra Stoller © ESTO 28T-1; 17. Philip Turner, courtesy of Skidmore, Owings and Merrill; 18. Hedrich-Blessing 32821-W, courtesy of Murphy/Jahn; 19. Chicago Architectural Photographing Co., courtesy of David Phillips; 23. Hedrich-Blessing 32821-F2.

Miller, "Jahn"
1, 7, 9. Courtesy of Murphy/Jahn; 2. Chicago Architectural Photographing Company P.2455, courtesy of the Chicago Historical Society; 3. Orlando Cabanban 22572; 5. John Zukowsky; 6. Hedrich-Blessing 32241-A.

Robinson
1. Hedrich-Blessing 13711-K, courtesy of the Chicago Historical Society; 2. Kaufmann and Fabry Co.; 3. Courtesy of the Chicago Historical Society ICHi-23004; 4. Martin Schweig; 6, 7. Hedrich-Blessing 9276-Q, 9276-H; 9, 11. Hedrich-Blessing 13711-B, 13711-P, courtesy of the Chicago Historical Society; 10, 12. Courtesy of the State Historical Society of Wisconsin, Keck Archives Job # 387, 338; 13, 14. Hedrich-Blessing 10374-A, 10374-G, courtesy of the Chicago Historical Society; 15, 16. Hedrich-Blessing 9358-C, 9358-L; 19. Nowell Ward and Associates; 23. Courtesy of Buckminster Fuller Institute; 26. Ezra Stoller © ESTO 92L.6 WS 930550.

Rau
2. Michael Tropea; 3. Raymond Trowbridge, courtesy of the Chicago Historical Society; 7. Courtesy of the Merchandise Mart; 8, 18, 23, 24. Courtesy of the Merchandise Mart and Beyer Blinder Belle; 10. Courtesy of the Chicago Historical Society ICHi-14345; 11. J. Sherwin Murphy, courtesy of the Chicago Historical Society ICHi-23504; 12. Al Bloom, courtesy of the Chicago Historical Society ICHi-21102; 13. Ezra Stoller © ESTO 79CC.2; 15. Courtesy of the Chicago Historical Society DN-89286; 20. Courtesy of the Chicago Historical Society DN-91412; 25. Hedrich-Blessing 00915-K, courtesy of the Chicago Historical Society.

Saliga
1, 14. Courtesy of Motorola Museum of Electronics; 5. Hedrich-Blessing 1823-F, courtesy of the Chicago Historical Society; 6. Courtesy of the State Historical Society of Wisconsin, Keck Archives; 7. Hedrich-Blessing 061663-B, courtesy of the Chicago Historical Society; 9. Hedrich-Blessing 2781, courtesy of the Chicago Historical Society; 10, 17. Courtesy of Palma Knapp Design; 11. Courtesy of Life magazine © Time Warner Inc.; 12, 13. Courtesy of Zenith Radio Corporation; 15. Courtesy of the Chicago Historical Society Architectural Collection; 18. Hedrich-Blessing 6184-B, courtesy of the Chicago Historical Society; 19, 20. Michael Rougier, courtesy of Life magazine © Time Warner Inc. Set # 58108 (C2-15, C7-1); 21. Hedrich-Blessing, 22. Courtesy of Marvin Glass Associates; 23. Courtesy of KDA Industrial Design Consultants.

Schulze
3. Hedrich-Blessing 9970-G; 4. Hedrich-Blessing 47172-A; 5. Hedrich-Blessing 23907-G, courtesy of the Mies van der Rohe Archive, Museum of Modern Art, New York. Gift of Ludwig Mies van der Rohe; 6. Hedrich-Blessing 9767-A, courtesy of the Chicago Historical Society; 7. Hedrich-Blessing 09969-A, courtesy of the Chicago Historical Society; 9. Hedrich-Blessing 10199; 10. Hedrich-Blessing 15412-D, courtesy of the Chicago Historical Society; 13, 14, 17-21. Courtesy of the Mies van der Rohe Archive, Museum of Modern Art, New York. Gift of Ludwig Mies van der Rohe; 16. Hedrich-Blessing 12173-B; 22. Ezra Stoller © ESTO 67GG2; 23. Hedrich-Blessing 28204-W3, courtesy of the Chicago Historical Society; 24, 25. Hedrich-Blessing 38426-B, 38426-H; 26. Ezra Stoller © ESTO 7LL.26 WS 923022.

Sennott
1. Fred G. Korth, courtesy of the Chicago Historical Society ICHi-23466; 2. Courtesy of the Chicago Historical Society ICHi-04804; 4. Courtesy of the Chicago Historical Society ICHi-23634; 5. Courtesy of the Chicago Historical Society ICHi-04720; 7. Kaufmann and Fabry Co.; 12. Capes Photo; 15. Raymond Trowbridge, courtesy of the Chicago Historical Society ICHi-21560; 16. Chester Brummel; 17. Copelin, courtesy of the Chicago Historical Society ICHi-23469; 18. Courtesy of the Chicago Park District; 19. J. Sherwin Murphy, courtesy of the Chicago Historical Society ICHi-23470; 20. Hedrich-Blessing 47574-X, courtesy of Skidmore, Owings and Merrill; 22. Gregory Murphey, courtesy of Lucien LaGrange and Associates; 23, 25. Courtesy of the Illinois Toll Highway Authority; 24. Ray Jacoby Photography, Inc. 17463.

Tigerman
1. Lawrence Okrent, Okrent Associates.

Willis

2. Hedrich-Blessing 4529, courtesy of the Chicago Historical Society; 12. Irving Underhill, The American Art Publishing Co., New York; 13. The American Art Publishing Co., New York; 14. Raymond Trowbridge, courtesy of the Chicago Historical Society; 15, 22. Chicago Architectural Photographing Co., courtesy of David Phillips; 16. Holabird and Root Archives, courtesy of the Chicago Historical Society ICHi-19902; 18. Sheridan Gallagher; 23. Seidman Photo Service, New York; 25. Hedrich-Blessing 1325-J, courtesy of the Chicago Historical Society.

de Wit

1. Courtesy of the Chicago Historical Society ICHi-23505; 2. Mildred Mead, courtesy of the Chicago Historical Society ICHi-09273; 3. Fred G. Korth, courtesy of the Chicago Historical Society ICHi-18921; 4. Mildred Mead, courtesy of the Chicago Historical Society ICHi-23374; 5. Courtesy of the Chicago Historical Society ICHi-23379; 6. Courtesy of the Chicago Historical Society; 7, 9, 10, 15. Courtesy of the Chicago Housing Authority; 11. Mildred Mead, courtesy of the Chicago Historical Society ICHi-23373; 16. Michael J. Scilingo, courtesy of the Chicago Historical Society ICHi-23375; 14. Courtesy of Skidmore, Owings and Merrill; 17, 18. Clarence W. Hines, courtesy of the Chicago Historical Society; 19. Hedrich-Blessing 27549-E, courtesy of the Chicago Historical Society; 20. Hedrich-Blessing 23470, courtesy of the Chicago Historical Society.

Zukowsky

1. Courtesy of Landesbildstelle Berlin; 2. Chicago Architectural Photographing Co., courtesy of David Phillips; 10. Courtesy of Chicago Bridge and Iron Co.; 12. Courtesy of Schmidt, Garden and Erikson; 14. Steve Grubman, courtesy of Skidmore, Owings and Merrill; 15. Courtesy of Belli and Belli; 17. John Zukowsky; 18. William Kildow, courtesy of Wheeler Kearns; 19. Hedrich-Blessing 50214-O, courtesy of Skidmore, Owings and Merrill; 20. Courtesy of Miglin-Beitler Development; 21. Courtesy of Murphy/Jahn; 22, 23. Courtesy of the Office of John Vinci; 24. Courtesy of Kisho Kurokawa, Architect and Associates.

PLATES

2-5 Lawrence Okrent, Okrent Associates; 6. Kaufmann and Fabry Co., courtesy of I C Industries; 9, 19, 20, 31-34. Courtesy of Murphy/Jahn; 13, 17, 26, 44. John Zukowsky; 16, 138. Hedrich-Blessing, courtesy of Nagle, Hartray and Associates; 24. Hedrich-Blessing SN 799-K; 25. Hedrich-Blessing SN 799-P. 27, 30, 105, 140-41. Timothy Hursley, The Arkansas Office; 29. Judith Bromley; 35. Hedrich-Blessing, courtesy of Perkins and Will; 40. Hedrich-Blessing, courtesy of the Chicago Historical Society; 46, 48. Ezra Stoller © ESTO 4FF53, 4FF59, courtesy of Skidmore, Owings and Merrill; 50. Hedrich-Blessing 36150-F2, courtesy of Skidmore, Owings and Merrill; 54, 56. Gregory Murphey, courtesy of Kohn Pedersen Fox Associates; 60. Don DuBroff, Sadin Photo Group, courtesy of Holabird and Root; 61, 62. Courtesy of the John Buck Co.; 64. Hedrich-Blessing, courtesy of Powell/Kleinschmidt; 66. Hedrich-Blessing; 67. Courtesy of Miglin-Beitler Development; 69. Hedrich-Blessing, courtesy of Perkins and Will; 72. George Lambros, courtesy of Skidmore, Owings and Merrill; 75-77. Courtesy of Radio Flyer, Inc.; 78, 79. Chicago Architectural Photographing Co., courtesy of Albert Kahn Associates, Inc.; 80-85. Hedrich-Blessing, courtesy of Albert Kahn Associates, Inc.; 86, 87. Courtesy of McDonnell Douglas; 88. Courtesy of CBI Industries; 90. Hedrich-Blessing 47566-B, courtesy of Skidmore, Owings and Merrill; 92. Steinkamp/Ballogg; 94-96. Courtesy of Sears, Roebuck and Company Archives; 97, 131. Wayne Cable, Cable Studios; 100. Barbara Karant, courtesy of Kohn Pedersen Fox; 102. Courtesy of Himmel Bonner Associates; 106. Hedrich-Blessing, courtesy of Eva Maddox Associates; 114. Chicago Aerial Survey Co. 31082-D; 117. Hedrich-Blessing; 118. Howard N. Kaplan, courtesy of Nagle, Hartray and Associates; 120, 122. Hedrich-Blessing, courtesy of Krueck and Sexton; 124, 125. Paul Warchol, courtesy of Booth/Hansen and Associates; 128. Judith Bromley, courtesy of Tannys Langdon; 130. Courtesy of Frederick Phillips and Associates; 135. Orlando Cabanban, courtesy of Gelick Foran Associates; 142-44. David Clifton, courtesy of Jordan Mozer.

CATALOGUE

410 l. l., l. r. John Zukowsky; 413 top. John Zukowsky; 413 bottom. Hedrich-Blessing 13583-B, courtesy of Bertrand Goldberg Associates; 418 l. l. Howard N. Kaplan 2681-1, courtesy of Tigerman McCurry; 418 l. r. Hedrich-Blessing; 419. John Zukowsky; 420 l. l. Hedrich-Blessing SN799-I; 421 top. Hedrich-Blessing SN799-B2; 424 l. l. Hedrich-Blessing 46383F, courtesy of Miglin-Beitler Development; 424 l. r. Sadin Photo Group 83545-C, courtesy of Shaw and Associates; 431 top. Courtesy of CBI Industries; 431 bottom. Courtesy of Amoco; 432. Gregory Murphey 205-2, courtesy of Skidmore, Owings and Merrill; 436 top l. Kaufmann and Fabry Co.; 436 top r. John Zukowsky; 439. Howard Kaplan 7984-2, courtesy of Solomon, Cordwell and Buenz; 440 top. Hedrich-Blessing 44624-X; 440 middle. Sadin Photo Group 85676-B, courtesy of Schroeder, Murchie, Laya Associates; 440 bottom. Judith Bromley, courtesy of Tannys Langdon; 449 top. Chicago Architectural Photographing Co. R-6478, courtesy of David Phillips; 449 middle. Abernathy, courtesy of A. Epstein and Sons; 449 l. r. Courtesy of Hellmuth, Obata and Kassabaum; 450 top l. Hedrich-Blessing, courtesy of the Landahl Group; 450 top r. Courtesy of the Naiman Group.